WALKER & WALKER'S
ENGLISH
LEGAL SYSTEM

WALKER & WALKER'S ENGLISH LEGAL SYSTEM

SEVENTH EDITION

by

R J WALKER, LL B (Lond)
of Gray's Inn and the Inner Temple,
One of Her Majesty's Counsel,
and of the South-Eastern Circuit

and

RICHARD WARD, LL B
Solicitor,
Principal Lecturer in Law,
De Montfort University, Leicester

BUTTERWORTHS
LONDON, DUBLIN, EDINBURGH
1994

United Kingdom	Butterworth & Co (Publishers) Ltd, Halsbury House, 35 Chancery Lane, LONDON WC2A 1EL and 4 Hill Street, EDINBURGH EH2 3JZ
Australia	Butterworths, SYDNEY, MELBOURNE, BRISBANE, ADELAIDE, PERTH, CANBERRA and HOBART
Canada	Butterworths Canada Ltd, TORONTO and VANCOUVER
Ireland	Butterworth (Ireland) Ltd, DUBLIN
Malaysia	Malayan Law Journal Sdn Bhd, KUALA LUMPUR
New Zealand	Butterworths of New Zealand Ltd, WELLINGTON and AUCKLAND
Puerto Rico	Butterworth of Puerto Rico, Inc, SAN JUAN
Singapore	Butterworths Asia, SINGAPORE
South Africa	Butterworth Publishers (Pty) Ltd, DURBAN
USA	Butterworth Legal Publishers, CARLSBAD, California and SALEM, New Hampshire

A CIP Catalogue record for this book is available from the British Library.

Sixth edition 1985
Reprinted 1990, 1991, 1992

ISBN 0 406 50331 1

Typeset by Goodfellow & Egan Ltd, Cambridge
Printed and bound in Great Britain by Butler and Tanner Ltd, Frome and London

Preface

This long awaited new edition has been prepared within clear objectives, set for me at the outset. These were generally to revise and update the text within the style, approach and philosophy which provided the basis for the success of the sixth edition and its predecessors as a clear and comprehensive account of the main features of the courts, administration of justice and procedure. The fulfilment of those objectives has necessitated considerable rewriting, including two completely new chapters on the important areas of the European Community and the Police. Despite this, the extent to which it draws on the work of Ronald Walker in the preparation of previous editions will be apparent.

Inevitably, hard choices have had to be made as to which material has had to be deleted, and, with some regret, the decision was made to reduce the historical coverage. I believe that enough survives to provide the essential context for students. The new material covers considerable ground, but the pace of change is such that it has not proved possible to reflect as fully as I would wish the continued changes in the legal profession, further proposals for change in civil procedure and the significant changes proposed in the Criminal Justice and Public Order Bill, including the proposal to abolish committal proceedings.

The approach, objectives and style for this new edition were set by Ronald Walker, who also contributed to some of the textual revision. His contribution through the work undertaken for previous editions is also clearly evident, and gratefully acknowledged. However, the bulk of the detailed revision and rewriting has been undertaken by me. Gratitude is due to the various colleagues who have given advice from time to time, and to the helpful staff at Butterworths. More specifically, thanks are due to Professor Richard Card at De Montfort University, not only for his advice and encouragement, but also for reading part of the text in draft and commenting helpfully upon it. The responsibility for the text is, of course, that of the authors alone.

The text reflects the law as it was understood to be as at 1 January 1994. The inexhaustible patience of the publishers has, however, permitted the inclusion of a few later developments.

Richard Ward
Leicester
May 1994

Table of Contents

PART III—CIVIL PROCEDURE

PART IV—CRIMINAL PROCEEDINGS

PART V—EVIDENCE

Table of Statutes

References in this Table to *Statutes* are to Halsbury's
Statutes of England (Fourth Edition) showing the volume and
page at which the annotated text of an Act may be found.

Table of European Communities Legislation

List of Cases

Decisions of the European Court of Justice are listed both alphabetically and numerically. The numerical list follows the alphabetical.

PAGE

Decisions of the European Court of Justice are listed below numerically.
These decisions are also included in the preceding alphabetical List.

PART I

Sources of English Law

SUMMARY

CHAPTER 1

The Historical Sources

A INTRODUCTION

The legal system that exists today in England and Wales[1] is a product of evolution over many centuries. Of course, it is, in many respects, very different from that from which it has evolved. Modern problems and needs have led to widespread changes in the court system, in the organisation and functions of the legal profession, and in the procedures followed by the courts and those who work within them. New courts have been created.[2] A whole body of administrative justice has developed, leading to the resolution of many disputes between state and individual in tribunals and inquiries rather than in the courts themselves.[3] Old procedures have been developed and refined to meet modern needs: thus the old supervisory functions of the Crown have developed into the process of judicial review, which plays an important role in the scrutiny of executive bodies of the state.[4] Many other examples could be given.

Yet to concentrate exclusively upon these important modern developments is to acquire an incomplete picture, for many institutions, structures and procedures can only be understood in the light of an awareness of the historical background into which they fit. Though the modern courts may be different from their predecessors, both in terms of structure and jurisdiction,[5] the court system can be traced back to its quite ancient origins. Many rules of procedure owe their existence to the nature of the institutions in which they originally arose. For example, the modern criminal trial is still essentially oral in nature. This owes much to the old forms of trial of criminal offences, particularly trial by jury. Again the modern procedure of judicial review[6] already referred to can be traced back to the supervisory powers of the Crown, exercised from the twelfth century onwards through the prerogative writs used to control the actions of inferior bodies and courts. A further example are the modern principles of equity. These owe their origins to the development of concepts of equity

---

1 Scotland and Northern Ireland are separate jurisdictions with their own courts and laws. This book refers only to England and Wales.
2 See, eg, the Crown Court, created by the Courts Act 1971; p 155, post.
3 See p 175, post.
4 See p 121, post.
5 See further p 131, post.
6 See p 122, post.

originally by the King in Council, and, later, through the work of the old Court of Chancery.

Nor are the substantive rules of law themselves immune from this historical influence: the modern law of contract and tort can best be understood in the light of the historical development of those areas of the law, and in the light of the procedural advantages and limitations of the writ system through which they developed.[7]

Despite the fact that the detailed study of legal history has ceased to play a dominant role in the legal education of most students, some awareness of overall trends is therefore to be encouraged. Whilst, of course, many factors have contributed to the development of the modern legal system, two fundamental, but inter-related, issues dominate the development of our institutions and procedures. The first is the role of the monarch. The second is the development of the common law and equity.

1   The role of the monarch

Historically the sovereign is the fountain of justice in England. For this reason, the administration of justice is part of the prerogatives of the Crown, part of the residual common law powers that still exist and which are unique to the Crown.[8] The monarch is to be regarded as the head of the legal system. The superior courts[9] are "the Queen's courts". The senior judiciary is appointed by the Crown.[10] The Crown has a residual power, and duty, to ensure the maintenance of law and order,[11] and to ensure that justice is done. An example of this is the royal prerogative of mercy.[12] All these powers are exercisable by the monarch on the advice of her ministers, as of course is required by modern constitutional doctrine.

That the monarch has these powers at all demonstrates the crucial role the monarch has played historically. The development of the common law, which, as we shall see, is at the heart of the legal system, arose through the unifying influence and effect created by the actions of those administering justice on behalf of the monarch. In the eleventh and twelfth centuries, the King assumed control of the administration of justice throughout England through his judges and justices, thus creating, over a long period of time, a centralised system of courts, and which led to the decline (and eventual demise) of the local courts and jurisdictions.[13] This performance of legal functions by the King was originally through the King's Council, through his local representatives, the sheriffs,

---

7 See, for discussion: Maitland, *The Forms of Action at Common Law* (Cambridge University Press).
8 See p 121, *post.*
9 See p 141, *post.*
10 See p 181, *post.*
11 For a modern example, see *R v Secretary of State for the Home Department, ex parte Northumbria Police Authority* [1988] QB 26; [1988] 1 All ER 556.
12 See p 124, *post.*
13 See, generally: Baker, *An Introduction to English Legal History* (Butterworths, 3rd Edn, 1990). Certain local courts survived formally until 1973: the Bristol Tolzey and Pie Poudre Courts, the Liverpool Court of Passage, the Norwich Guildhall Court, all abolished by s 43 of the Courts Act 1971.

and, more importantly, through justices travelling the country on his behalf. The jurisdiction of the Kings's Council gradually gave rise to the emergence of the common law courts.[14] The old common law courts of Exchequer, Common Pleas and King's Bench developed, and each owed their existence to the practice of the King in Council issuing writs commanding that justice be done. Similarly with the Court of Chancery, which had as its principal function the administration of the principles and rules of equity.[15] These principles of equity developed as a response to the petitions that were made to the King complaining of the injustices caused by the provisions of, or gaps in, the common law. Over a period of time these petitions ceased to be dealt with by the King himself, but rather by the old Court of Chancery.[16]

Together these courts were the King's courts administering justice on behalf of the Crown. This power to provide and administer justice stemmed from the inherent power of the Crown itself, under what is now known as the Royal Prerogative. This historical basis remains important, even though the vast majority of courts now exist because of, and within the jurisdiction defined by, statute. The role of the monarch in ensuring that justice is done was historically performed through the issue of writs, royal commands that certain things should be done. The writ system was the mechanism through which developed the common law causes of action in contract and tort.[17] Equally importantly, royal writs were used to supervise the actions of inferior courts or bodies. As noted above, these prerogative writs today remain an important remedy to control the misuse of executive power, on judicial review.[18]

2 Common law and equity

Common law and equity are two of the three main historical sources of English law, the third being legislation. The term "common law" reflects the fact that the law as administered by the King's courts became the common law of England and Wales, gradually supplanting local custom, either by consolidation of customary local rules into rules of general application, or by the gradual erosion of local rules themselves. The law evolved from a mass of local custom (administered by local courts) into one system of law common throughout the country. The role of the monarch in this process was crucial: the development of administration of justice through the King himself, and through the King's representatives locally, whether the sheriff or itinerant justices acting on behalf of the King, ensured the development of common and consistent rules of law. These in turn led to the administration of these common rules by courts that evolved from the royal institutions into separate courts, administering justice independently from, but in the name of, the King. The three principal courts were the Court of Exchequer, the Court of Common Pleas, and the Court of King's Bench. Thus each owed its origin to the monarch's role as the fountain of justice, originally exercised by the King in Council. These

14 See p 131, *post.*
15 They are described in detail in the 6th edition of this work (1985), pp 47–55.
16 See p 138, *post.*
17 See: Milsom, *Historical Foundations of the Common Law* (Butterworths, 2nd Edn 1981).
18 See p 122, *post.*

courts, dispensing justice on behalf of the monarch, were abolished by the Judicature Acts 1873–75,[19] and their jurisdiction transferred to the High Court, principally, though not exclusively, to the Queen's Bench Division.

By contrast equity itself developed to remedy the deficiencies of the common law. As the common law, principally through the writ system, itself grew more rigid, those affected by that rigidity and who suffered injustice as a result would petition the King to exercise his prerogative in their favour. These petitions, at first dealt with by the King in Council and then delegated to the King's chief minister, the Chancellor, later became formalised and dealt with in the courts of equity, leading to the formal development of the Court of Chancery, which was the principal forum for the administration of the principles of equity until its abolition in 1875.[20]

B   THE HISTORICAL SOURCES

1   Common law

It will be clear from what has already been said that the common law is one of the most important of the historical sources of law. In civil matters the law developed through the procedures that existed. One basic principle underpinned its growth: that a common law right only existed if there was a procedure for enforcing it (*ubi remedium ibi ius*). For that reason substantive law became inextricably bound up with procedure, and, in particular, through the forms of action that developed in respect of various types of action, where *real* actions (involving land) or *personal* actions (involving claims) principally involved matters we would now categorise as contractual or tortious. The nature of the right sought to be enforced, and the nature of the procedure through which it could be enforced, would determine the court which would deal with such matters. Historically, such common law claims, enforced through what were known as the *forms of action*, became highly technical, with the nature of the form of action often determining the content of the law, and whether a particular claim could succeed. This rigid writ system was effectively abolished by the Common Law Procedure Acts 1852 and 1854, resulting in the categorisations of claims becoming far less important. The law now strives to concentrate upon substance rather than form. However, the dangers that rigid procedural distinctions can create have not totally disappeared since the abolition of the writ system as described above. As recently as 1991 HENRY J in *Doyle v Northumbria Probation Committee*[19] observed that the procedural requirements that now exist in respect of the challenge of public bodies was one area:

> ". . . where the forms of action abolished by the Common Law Procedure Act 1854 in the 19th Century appear to be in danger of returning to rule us from their graves."

In criminal matters the common law developed the forms of trial which, in nature if not in detail, still exist today. Ancient procedures such as Appeal

---

19 For the main courts prior to 1875, see pp 131–139, *post*.
20 Principles of equity are now administered and applied by all courts.
  1 [1991] 4 All ER 294; [1991] 1 WLR 1340.

of Felony, involving in many cases trial by battle, may have disappeared,[2] but trial on indictment, involving trial by jury,[3] is of ancient origin, and was undertaken in the old courts of Assize. With the Assize courts can be bracketed the courts of Quarter Session, where judges sat usually with justices of the peace, an office of some antiquity. Both courts existed until the creation of the Crown Court by the Courts Act 1971.[4] In addition to these two courts, the criminal law was also enforced summarily, through trial by justices of the peace[5] without a jury. Though procedures are much changed, these forms of trial are distinctly recognisable to modern eyes, and form the basis for the development of the common law rules of criminal law and evidence that still play a significant role.

2 Equity

The nature of equity, and the reasons for its development, have already been noted. The distinction between common law and equity caused significant problems. Frequently in conflict with the common law, equity both supplemented the common law and corrected its deficiencies. In so far as the former was concerned, it was not repugnant to common lawyers; by contrast, the correction of the deficiencies of the common law created direct conflict between two systems of law, ultimately resolved,[6] though not without continued conflict, in favour of equity. The fact remained that the existence of two separate systems of law, administered by separate courts was bound to cause not only conflict, but complex and inconvenient duality of jurisdiction, with differing procedures and remedies, and with different routes of appeal. Reform of a fundamental nature was under-taken by the Judicature Acts 1873–75. The purpose and immediate effect of this legislation was to create a unified system of courts and procedure. It did not, however, of itself merge the substantive rules themselves: it is still correct to talk, for example, about the principles of equity, or about equitable remedies.[7] However, the fact that the rules of common law and equity had not been administered and applied side by side led in reality to a merger not simply of procedures but of the rules themselves. Modern courts can apply equally rules of common law and equity, irrespective of their origins, and indeed it may not always be wholly clear to which side of historical development, common law or equity, a rule owes its parentage. Its effect upon substantive law is beyond doubt, principally in relation to matters affecting property and trusts, the law of contract, and through the development of important remedies, principally the injunction.

---

2 Trial by battle was not formally abolished until the decision in *Ashford v Thornton* (1818) 1 B & Ald 405 reminded Parliament that it still theoretically existed.
3 See p 197, *post.*
4 See p 155, *post.*
5 See pp 136, 162, *post.*
6 *Earl of Oxford*'s case (1615) 1 Rep Ch 1.
7 Injunctions are an important example. For remedies in civil proceedings, see p 289, *post.* For discussion generally of equity and equitable remedies, see Pettit, *Equity and The Law of Trusts* (Butterworths, 6th Edn, 1989).

3   Legislation

This is the third major historical source. Originally, scarcely distinguishable from common law, the growth of Parliament as the dominant force within the United Kingdom constitution[8] led to the growth of legislation as a major source of law in its importance transcending common law or equity. Its role today is unquestioned. Common law and equity essentially are concerned with the application and development of principles: whilst a modern lawyer would accept that even in such matters judges make law,[9] the courts usually consider themselves as not the appropriate forum for the development of wholly new principles of law, a task usually considered to be best left to Parliament.[10] Legislation can also amend or repeal existing statute. For these reasons legislation, and delegated legislation made thereunder, is the fundamental source of law, now to be considered also in the light of the legislation of the European Community.[11]

4   Custom

Custom is another, though now less important, source of law. The term has various meanings. In one sense, it merely identifies the very nature of the common law itself: the early common law was not an entirely new set of legal rules developed by judges on behalf of the King, but rather a unification and development of the many customs used and applied by the local courts. The early common law was not an entirely new set of rules but rather that body of rules resulting from the welding of the law and custom of England into one system of law, through the historical developments in the eleventh to the fourteenth centuries. In 1350 counsel declared that "common usage is common law".[12] These customs, such as monogamy, parental rights, the right to use the seashore for navigation and fishing[13] and most of the early criminal law, are no longer regarded as a separate source of law since they have either become part of the common law or been incorporated in statute.

A second use of the word "custom" is to describe conventional trade or business usage. This is really a misuse of the word since trade usage is usually relevant only to imply terms into contracts, so that the court can decide what terms the parties intended to apply. These are questions of fact rather than questions of law so that custom, in this context, is not a source of law at all. Trade customs need not be ancient[14] provided that they can be proved to be certain. However they must not be illegal or unreasonable and they may always be expressly excluded. Many trade

---

8 Through the development of the doctrine of the legislative supremacy of Parliament. Under this, no court can question the validity of an Act of Parliament. See *British Railways Board v Pickin* [1974] AC 765; [1974] 1 All ER 609.
9 See further, p 185, *post.*
10 See *Malone v Metropolitan Police Commissioner (No 2)* [1979] Ch 344; [1979] 2 All ER 620. *McLoughlin v O'Brian* [1983] 1 AC 410; [1982] 2 All ER 298.
11 See p 92, *post.*
12 10 YB 30 Edw 3, ff 25, 26.
13 Though not for bathing or beachcombing; see *Alfred F Beckett Ltd v Lyons* [1967] Ch 449; [1967] 1 All ER 833. For a modern example of reliance on customary fishing rights, see *Anderson v Alnwick District Council* [1993] 3 All ER 613.
14 See *Noble v Kennoway* (1780) 2 Doug KB 510 at 513, *per* LORD MANSFIELD.

customs were originally an elaborate method of granting discount to purchasers; hence the "baker's dozen" and the fact that 1,000 rabbits mean 1,200 rabbits to rabbit-dealers.[15] Ancient mercantile custom fulfilled a wider function than modern commercial usage since it was the basis of a set of rules of law collectively described as the law merchant. The law merchant, unlike trade usage, is a source of law and is considered below.

The third common use of the word "custom" is to describe local custom; rules of law which apply only in a definite locality. Custom, in this sense of the word, is a separate source of law. Local custom as a source of law, distinct from common law, has two elementary and unvarying characteristics; first, it must be an exception to the common law and, second, it must be confined in its application to a particular locality such as a county, borough or parish. It may be further limited to a class of persons within that locality, for example fishermen, but it cannot apply to a class of persons generally throughout the kingdom, for if it did it would be part of the common law and not an exception to it.

Many local customs have been abolished by statute. The type of local customary right still existing is in the nature of a right of way, or right to indulge in sports and pastimes on a village green[16] or a right to dry fishing-nets on land within the parish.[17] They only exist in law when formally recognised by judicial decision. Thus any person who alleges a customary right must plead it and prove its existence. This involves showing that the alleged custom satisfies certain tests. Blackstone's classification of these tests is the generally accepted arrangement and is as follows.

a Antiquity

Local custom must have existed from "time whereof the memory of man runneth not to the contrary" (time immemorial). This has been fixed by statute at 1189,[18] the first year of the reign of Richard I. In practice positive proof of existence in 1189 is rarely available so that the courts are willing to accept as proof evidence that the custom has existed for a long time. This is often done by calling the oldest available local inhabitant as a witness. The burden is then on the party denying the existence of the custom to prove that it did not exist in 1189 or that it could not have existed in 1189.

b Continuance

The right must have existed uninterrupted. Any interruption of the custom since 1189 defeats its existence. On the other hand mere non-use does not defeat the custom; a customary right, once acquired, can only be abolished or extinguished by Act of Parliament.[19]

---

15 *Smith v Wilson* (1832) 3 B & Ad 728.
16 *New Windsor Corporation v Mellor* [1975] Ch 380; [1975] 3 All ER 44.
17 *Mercer v Denne* [1905] 2 Ch 538.
18 Statute of Westminster I 1275.
19 *Hammerton v Honey* (1876) 24 WR 603; *New Windsor Corporation v Mellor* [1975] Ch 380; [1975] 3 All ER 44.

c   Peaceable enjoyment

A custom can only exist by common consent. It must not have been exercised by the use of force, nor secretly, nor under a revocable licence (since this would make the custom dependent upon the will of one individual rather than on public observance) (*nec per vim nec clam nec precario*). Thus, where the right to fish depended upon the grant of a licence by the owners of an oyster fishery, it was held that there was no customary right to fish since enjoyment had never been as of right, but only by licence.[20]

d   Obligatory force

Where the custom imposes a specific duty that duty must be obligatory. This is true of all rules of law. Indeed it is this which distinguishes a rule of law from a social convention or a moral obligation.

e   Certainty

The custom must be certain.

f   Consistency

Customs must be consistent with one another, since inconsistent local customs cannot stand together.

g   Reasonableness

The last and most important test that custom must satisfy is that of reasonableness. It is for the party refuting the custom to show that it is unreasonable. A custom which is repugnant to a fundamental principle of common law cannot be reasonable. For this reason the House of Lords rejected a custom which enabled a manorial lord to undermine his tenant's land without paying compensation for damage to buildings thereby caused.[1] Equally a customary right to commit a crime could not be reasonable.

Furthermore, if a custom must obviously have been unreasonable in 1189 (though not necessarily unreasonable at the present day) this will tend to show that the custom could not have existed in 1189 and it will be rejected on this ground rather than on the basis of it being unreasonable. In *Bryant v Foot*[2] the rector of a parish claimed thirteen shillings as a customary fee for the celebration of a marriage in the parish. It was held that, having regard to the value of money in 1189, the amount was totally unreasonable so that the custom could not have existed at that date.

5   Law merchant

The law of contract as administered in the common law courts in the thirteenth and fourteenth centuries was extremely rudimentary. Broadly speaking an action could only be brought within certain narrow circumstances. In addition the local courts had only a limited jurisdiction in

---

20 *Mills v Colchester Corporation* (1867) LR 2 CP 476; see also *Alfred F Beckett Ltd v Lyons* [1967] Ch 449; [1967] 1 All ER 833.
1 *Wolstanton Ltd and Duchy of Lancaster v Newcastle-under-Lyme Corporation* [1940] AC 860; [1940] 3 All ER 101.
2 (1868) LR 3 QB 497.

contract.[3] Thus the existing courts were ill-equipped to deal with the increasing volume of litigation arising from England's growth as a trading centre. The result was that a new set of courts sprang up to deal solely with disputes between merchants.[4] Since these courts were not common law courts they were not rigidly tied to the common law, and a new set of rules originating partly in custom and partly in international law evolved in these courts as a gloss on the common law. Since their decisions were subject to review by the Court of King's Bench by way of writ of error their rules and doctrines of necessity followed the fundamental tenets of the common law.

6 Canon law

The canon law, the law of the Western or Catholic Church, has influenced the growth of English law in two ways. First it was the basis of many concepts which were formulated in the lay courts and as such is a primary source of other sources of law. Examples of common law concepts which originated in the canon law are: the nature of criminal law and its close association with moral fault, imprisonment as a punishment for crime (the purpose of which the canonists conceived to be the possibility of repentance through solitary contemplation), and, of course, the nature of Christian marriage and family rights. In addition the old common law trial by ordeal relied for its efficacy on the participation of the clergy. Canon law also influenced the nature of equity, the strong moral content of which is attributable to the fact of the early Chancellors being clerics.

The second, and more important, way in which canon law became a source of English law was by its application in the ecclesiastical courts. In this context canon law was a system of law wholly independent of the common law since the ecclesiastical courts were, during the Middle Ages, completely outside the control of the King. Through a complex series of historical developments the jurisdiction of the ecclesiastical courts became clearly defined, and separate from the common law, except in areas of probate and matrimonial jurisdiction. Since 1857 the jurisdiction of the ecclesiastical courts has been confined to matters affecting members of the Church where this jurisdiction does not conflict with the jurisdiction of the ordinary courts.[5]

---

3 This was limited by the Statute of Gloucester 1278 to claims involving less than 40 shillings.

4 These included courts of fairs and boroughs, known as courts of "pie poudre". The name possibly derived from the Latin *pes pulvericatus* (dusty foot) or from the old French *pied pulderaux* (pedlar). Other such courts were staple courts, which sat in towns having the power to deal in certain commodities. The last of these courts, the Bristol Tolzey and Pie Poudre Courts, was abolished by s 43 of the Courts Act 1971. Some of the borough courts were abolished by the Municipal Corporations Act 1883, s 2 and the Justices of the Peace Act 1949, s 10 while as part of the reorganisation of local government whereby boroughs were abolished, 141 borough civil courts were abolished by the Local Government Act 1972, s 221 and Sch 28. Finally, the jurisdiction of most of the remaining local courts, including all courts of pie poudre, was formally abolished by the Administration of Justice Act 1977, s 23 and Sch 4. The High Court of Admiralty, which had existed since the fourteenth century had both civil and criminal jurisdiction over matters arising on the high seas; its jurisdiction was transferred to the Probate, Divorce and Admiralty Division of the High Court in 1875.

5 See p 172, *post*.

7   Roman law[6]

Roman law, the basis of most continental systems of law, is, surprisingly, of very minor importance as a source of English law. It is not a direct source at all in the sense that there was never a system of English courts applying solely Roman law. Any influence that Roman law has had on the growth of English law has been indirect. The source of law which owes most to Roman law is canon law. The reason is that the Chancellors and advocates in the ecclesiastical courts were indoctrinated with the civil law through their studies at Oxford and Cambridge. Thus the formal requirements of wills in many cases have their counterpart in Roman law as have many of the rules relating to parental authority. Roman law also undoubtedly influenced maritime and mercantile law since the Venetian and Genoese mercantile customs which these branches of the law utilised had a civilian basis.

The common law itself has from time to time borrowed from Roman law. The principal link between Roman law and common law is Bracton's treatise *De Legibus et Consuetudinibus Angliae* written in Latin in about the year 1250. Bracton was well versed in Roman law and the civilian principles he incorporated into his treatise owed much to the writings of the Roman jurist Justinian. Thus common law judges, faced with a case of first impression with little or no assistance to be gleaned from English precedents, have looked to Bracton for assistance and in doing so have adopted Romanist principles. The leading example is the judgment of HOLT C J in *Coggs v Bernard*[7] which classifies bailments in accordance with Bracton's classification, itself based on Roman law.

C   THE EUROPEAN SOURCES

The importance of the traditional sources of common law and equity has already been noted. Of equal importance to the modern legal system are the European sources. There are two such sources, of very different types.

The first is the European Community, which has a direct impact as a source of law, and the institutions of which fall to be regarded as integral parts of the law-making and law-enforcement machinery. The second is the European Convention on Human Rights, which is not a direct source of law, and the institutions of which cannot be regarded as integral to the English legal system.

1   The European Community

Since 1972 the United Kingdom has been a member of the European Community, a supra-national body with its own legal personality and capacity to make and enforce laws. By virtue of the European Communities Act 1972 (as amended) these laws of the European Community form part of English law. The importance of the Community cannot be underestimated, and is such as to warrant separate treatment as one of the

---

6 See Lee, *Elements of Roman Law.*
7 (1703) 2 Ld Raym 909.

sources of law.[8] It should not simply be regarded as a separate system of law, but rather as a fundamental and important source of English law.

2 European Convention on Human Rights

The United Kingdom is a signatory to the Convention for the Protection of Human Rights and Fundamental Freedoms (1950),[9] usually referred to as the European Convention on Human Rights. Conceived by the members of the Council of Europe as a mechanism for promoting European unity and for preventing abuse of human rights, it establishes both the European Commission of Human Rights and the European Court of Human Rights. Through this machinery the basic rights and freedoms recognised by the Convention are enforced. These include the right to life, the right not to be subjected to torture or inhuman or degrading treatment or punishment, the right not to be held in slavery or servitude, or to be required to perform forced or compulsory labour, the right to liberty and security of the person, the right to a fair trial, to respect for family life and home, to peaceful enjoyment of possessions, to education, to freedom of thought, conscience and religion, to freedom of expression, freedom of assembly, freedom of association and free elections.

These rights are not absolute. Limitations are usually permitted on the grounds stated in the Convention. Thus, the right of freedom of expression may be curtailed in the interests of national security, territorial integrity or public safety, for the prevention of disorder or crime, for the protection of health or morals, for the protection of the rights of others, for protection from the disclosure of information received in confidence, or to maintain the authority and impartiality of the judiciary.[10] The Court of Human Rights has therefore a broad function to perform, in determining the extent to which the aims of the Convention may be limited. In addition, most, though not all, of the rights may be limited by measures derogating from the obligations under the Convention in times of war or other public emergency. The United Kingdom has entered a derogation in respect of Article 5 following the decision of the Court of Human Rights in *Brogan v United Kingdom*[11] that the detention provisions of the Prevention of Terrorism (Temporary Provisions) Act 1984[12] were in breach of the Convention.

The Convention is enforced through the Commission and the Court. The Commission considers complaints of alleged breaches of the Convention from signatory states, and may also consider complaints made by individuals where the state complained against has recognised the right of individual petition. The United Kingdom recognised that individual right in 1966.[13] The applicant must show that all effective remedies in his own country have been exhausted, and the application must be lodged within six months of a final decision in his case by a national court or tribunal.[14]

---

8 See p 92, *post*.
9 Cmnd 8969. The United Kingdom is not a signatory to Protocols 4, 6 or 7.
10 Article 10(2).
11 (1988) 11 EHRR 117.
12 See, now, Prevention of Terrorism (Temporary Provisions) Act 1989.
13 Recognised by Declaration on 14 January 1966.
14 Article 25.

The admissibility of the complaint is determined by the Commission. If the complaint is admissible and not manifestly ill-founded the Commission may seek to achieve a friendly settlement. If it is unable to do so it has a choice of action open to it. It may report in respect of its findings to the Committee of Ministers of the Council of Europe.[15] Alternatively, it may refer a complaint to the European Court of Human Rights for decision.[16] Signatory states have undertaken to be bound by the decisions of the Court in any case to which they are parties, and, by Article 50, the Court can afford "just satisfaction" to the injured party, which may involve an order for the state to pay a sum of money by way of compensation and recompense for costs. Failure by a signatory state to comply with a judgment might, ultimately, lead to suspension of that state from the Council of Europe.

As a Treaty the European Convention does not form part of English law unless and until incorporated into law by an Act of Parliament.[17] No such incorporation has occurred, and thus the rights created are not directly enforceable in the courts. Despite this the Convention can act as an indirect source in influencing the interpretation of statute, or the development of the common law, and through being reflected in the decisions of the Court of Justice of the European Community.[18] The findings of the European Court of Human Rights may also provide the impetus for legislative action.[19]

The extent to which the Convention is in fact relied upon as an indirect aid varies greatly. The position was discussed by the House of Lords in *R v Secretary of State for Home Affairs, ex parte Brind*.[20] The House recognised that the Convention can be used for the resolution of ambiguity in primary or delegated legislation, and the presumption will be that Parliament intended to legislate in accordance with its international obligations.[1] This does not entitle the plain words of a statute to be distorted. Nor does the Convention limit how discretionary powers are to be exercised by Ministers, though it is a fact to which regard can be had.

In relation to the development of the common law, many examples can be found of the use of the Convention to justify a conclusion. In *R v Chief Metropolitan Stipendiary Magistrate, ex parte Choudhury*[2] it was held that Article 9 did not require the common law crime of blasphemy to be extended. Again, in *A-G v Guardian Newspapers Ltd*[3] LORD BRIDGE, in a dissenting speech, used the terms and likely application of the Convention

---

15 Article 26.

16 Article 48.

17 *Saloman v Customs and Excise Commissioners* [1967] 2 QB 116; [1966] 3 All ER 871. *R v Chief Immigration Officer, ex parte Bibi*; [1976] 3 All ER 843 [1976] 1 WLR 979.

18 See p 99, *post*.

19 Many examples exist. See, eg *Sunday Times v United Kingdom* (1979) 2 EHRR 245 (leading to Contempt of Court Act 1981); *Campbell and Cousens v United Kingdom* (1982) 4 EHRR 293 (leading to Education (No 2) Act 1986); *Malone v United Kingdom* (1984) 7 EHRR 14 (leading to Interception of Communications Act 1985).

20 [1991] 1 AC 696; [1991] 1 All ER 720. The approach taken in *Garland v British Rail Engineering Ltd* [1983] 2 AC 751 in the context of the European Community (see p 109, *post*) has no application in this context.

1 *Maclaine Watson & Co Ltd v Department of Trade and Industry* [1989] Ch 72; [1983] 3 All ER 257.

2 [1991] 1 QB 429, [1991] 1 All ER 306.

3 [1987] 3 All ER 316; [1987] 1 WLR 1248.

as a basis for concluding that interim relief to restrain publication of the book in question in that case should not be granted. It is noteworthy that LORD ACKNER, in the majority, used the tests required by the Convention under Article 10 as the starting point for reaching a completely opposite conclusion on the facts. In *R v Parole Board, ex parte Wilson*[4] the fact that Parliament had passed legislation to give effect to a ruling of the Court of Human Rights[5] was an important factor in persuading the Court of Appeal that a common law rule should be changed pending the coming into force of that statute.

In other cases the Convention may be noted, but has no discernible effect upon the application and development of the common law. Thus in *Malone v Metropolitan Police Commissioner (No 2)*[6] SIR ROBERT MEGARRY considered the legality of police interception of telephone calls. Even though not bound by authority on the substantive issue, and despite considering that the practice may well be in breach of Article 8 of the Convention,[7] he declined to develop the law in a way that would ensure compliance, ruling that that would be judicial legislation on a matter that should be dealt with by Parliament.[8]

D   THE ADMINISTRATION OF THE ENGLISH LEGAL SYSTEM

Historically there has not been a unified system for the administration of the English legal system, in the form of a "Ministry of Justice". That said, prime responsibility in many areas lies with the Lord Chancellor and the Lord Chancellor's Department.

By virtue of the Courts Act 1971[9] it is the responsibility of the Lord Chancellor to appoint such staff, and provide, equip and manage such buildings as is necessary for the purposes of carrying on the business of the Supreme Court[10] and county courts. Appointments of the judiciary are made by, or on the advice of, the Lord Chancellor, who also has responsibility for the appointment and training of justices of the peace.[11]

In performance of these functions the Lord Chancellor may draw on the advice of the Lord Chancellor's Advisory Committee on Legal Education and Conduct. Section 19 of the Courts and Legal Services Act 1990 imposes a duty on the Lord Chancellor to appoint such a committee, comprising representatives of the two branches of the profession, academic lawyers as well as independent members. This committee has the general duty[12] of assisting in the maintenance and development of standards in the education, training and conduct of those offering legal services. Whilst the

---

4 [1992] QB 740; [1991] 2 All ER 576.
5 Section 34 of the Criminal Justice Act 1991, giving effect to *Thynne, Wilson and Gunnell v United Kingdom* (1991) 13 EHRR 666.
6 [1979] Ch 344; [1979] 2 All ER 620.
7 In that it failed to be prescribed by law.
8 See now Interception of Communications Act 1985.
9 Sections 27–28.
10 For definition, see p 147, *post*.
11 See Justice of the Peace Act 1979, s 63. All magistrates receive training, overseen by the Judicial Studies Board.
12 *Ibid*, s 20.

recommendations of this committee may be addressed to any professional body or group,[13] it clearly will provide a basis for action by the Lord Chancellor in exercising his own powers both generally and under the 1990 Act. This action, often of importance, provides the basis for detailed change in the workings of the legal system.

Given the wide-ranging responsibilities and powers vested in the Lord Chancellor it is perhaps surprising that, until recently, there has been no direct accountability to the elected House of Commons. This gap was filled in 1991, when it was announced that a Minister was to answer in the House of Commons for the work of the Lord Chancellor, and that a department was to be appointed.[14]

It should not be overlooked that the Lord Chancellor does not have exclusive responsibility in respect of matters affecting the English legal system. In particular, the Home Secretary has responsibility for the exercise of the prerogative powers relating to the administration of justice, and responsibility for matters relating to criminal justice.

---

13 *Ibid*, Sch 2, para 5.
14 201 HC Official Report (6th series), col 250, 19 December, 1991.

CHAPTER 2

Legislation

A THE FUNCTIONS OF LEGISLATION

The broad function of all legislation is to create, alter or revoke law to give effect to the intention of the legislative body. Subordinate legislation fulfils various specific functions, scarcely capable of classification. The functions of Acts of Parliament, by far the most important form of legislation, may be classified as follows.

1 Revision of substantive rules of law

Although all statutes are concerned with law revision in the broadest sense, relatively few statutes are concerned with altering or revising substantive rules of law or "lawyers' law" as it is sometimes called. Such statutes are frequently passed when the law, through the restrictive operation of the doctrine of judicial precedent, has become stale and incapable of adaptation. The need for reform often manifests itself in a House of Lords decision.

Where a decision of the House of Lords is unpopular the law is usually altered by statute. There are many examples on the statute book of Acts passed with the apparent intention of overruling the effect of a House of Lords decision.[1] When a more general reform of the law is required the initiative frequently comes from lawyers. Until 1965 the machinery for generating law reform was conspicuously erratic in its operation, consisting mainly of the Law Revision Committee and, subsequently, the Law Reform Committee which considered, on their own initiative or at the invitation of the Lord Chancellor, branches of the law requiring reform and then published reports containing recommendations. The Committees consisted of practising lawyers who met from time to time, when pressure of other work permitted. Their recommendations often, but by no means always, were subsequently taken up by Parliament. Where the question was of wider public importance, heads of government departments might refer the question to a special committee for report or the Crown might set

---

1 Examples are: Parliamentary Papers Act 1840; Limitation Act 1963; Trade Disputes Act 1965; War Damage Act 1965; Criminal Evidence Act 1979. The apparent intention of these Acts is to reverse House of Lords decisions immediately preceding them though Acts of Parliament do not expressly name cases which they are obviously intended to overrule.

up a Royal Commission. A modern example of law reform based on the recommendations of a Royal Commission is the Courts Act 1971 which followed basically the recommendations of the so-called "Beeching Commission".[2] The controversial Courts and Legal Services Act 1990 was passed, in part, to implement recommendations of the Civil Justice Review Body.[3]

A major addition to the machinery of law reform was made by the Law Commissions Act 1965 which established the Law Commissions. Section 3(1) of the Act defines the duty of the Commissions (there is a separate Commission for Scotland) thus:

> ". . . it shall be the duty of each of the Commissions to take and keep under review all the law with which they are respectively concerned with a view to its systematic development and reform, including in particular the codification of such law, the elimination of anomalies, the repeal of obsolete and unnecessary enactments, the reduction of the number of separate enactments and generally the simplification and modernisation of the law."

The creation of the Law Commission was an important step forward in law reform. The Commissions, by reason of the appointment of full-time Commissioners of the highest calibre and of full-time administrative staff, have been able to produce a steady flow of reports, recommendations and draft Bills, most of which are implemented by Act of Parliament within a relatively short time.[4]

In consequence of the restrictive effect of the doctrine of judicial precedent the creation of new rights, and causes of action to enforce them, is virtually the prerogative of Parliament. Where a statute imposes a duty the question often arises whether or not breach of that duty gives rise to an action for damages (for the tort of breach of statutory duty). The question in each case is whether the legislature intended to confer on the plaintiff a private law cause of action, not whether the plaintiff belongs to a class which the statutory provision was intended to protect.

It might be thought that where a statute created rules but provided no criminal penalty for their breach, the intention of Parliament must have been to create a right of civil action to a person who suffers as a result of the breach:

> "for, if it were not so, the statute would be but a pious aspiration."[5]

This is not, however, invariably the case. Thus in *R v Deputy Governor of Parkhurst Prison, ex parte Hague*[6] the House of Lords held that the Prison Rules 1964 (made under the Prison Act 1952) conferred no right to sue for damages upon a convicted prisoner who had allegedly been restrained in a way not permitted by those Rules. The prisoner's remedies were to complain to the governor or board of visitors, and in the event of a complaint to the latter a report might be made to the Secretary of State

---

2 *Report of the Royal Commission on Assizes and Quarter Sessions*, Cmnd 4153 (1969).
3 *Report of the Review Body on Civil Justice*, Cmnd 394 (1988).
4 See, for example, Landlord and Tenant Act 1988, Law of Property (Miscellaneous Provisions) Act 1989, Children Act 1989.
5 *Cutler v Wandsworth Stadium Ltd* [1949] AC 398, at p 407; [1949] 1 All ER 544, at p 548 *per* LORD SIMONDS.
6 [1992] 1 AC 58; [1991] 3 All ER 733.

under the Act. He might also challenge any administrative decision of the Secretary of State or the governor by judicial review proceedings.

2 Consolidation of enactments

Where a branch of the law has evolved piecemeal, a consolidating statute may be passed, for the purpose of clarification, containing substantially the existing law in a consolidated form. There are three sorts of consolidating Acts: (1) "pure" consolidation (simple re-enactment); (2) consolidation under the Consolidation of Enactments (Procedure) Act 1949, which allows "corrections and minor improvements";[7] (3) consolidation with amendments recommended by the Law Commission, under a procedure adopted by Parliament since 1965. In practice most of the major consolidating legislation in recent years has incorporated Law Commission amendments in the light of the Commission's consideration of the relevant branch of the law.[8]

Consolidation Acts are not subject to parliamentary debate, but there are special procedures designed to ensure that the bill, when enacted, does not depart from the pre-existing statutory provisions which are to be consolidated.[9] The type of consolidation effected appears from the long title of the Act in question which will, in the case of pure consolidation, be in the form "an Act to consolidate . . ." while, in the case of consolidation with amendments under the 1949 procedure or with "Law Commission" amendments the long title will refer to the 1949 Act or to the Law Commission as the case may be.[10]

There are many who believe that the process of consolidation should be taken to the point of producing a consolidated statute book, similar to that which exists in many other countries, in which the whole of our statute law would be arranged under titles and kept up to date by textual amendment. However desirable this might be it is clear that it is not a reform which is likely to be implemented in the foreseeable future. In May 1973 the government set up a departmental committee (the Renton Committee) to review the form in which public Bills are drafted "with a view to achieving greater simplicity and clarity in statute law". The Committee reported in 1975[11] and concluded that "it would not be practicable to consolidate the whole statute book within a limited number of years, nor to do so on the principle of 'one Act, one subject'." Although the Committee made some 87 separate recommendations,

---

7 These are defined by s 2 of the 1949 Act as "amendments of which the effect is confined to resolving ambiguities, removing doubts, bringing obsolete provisions into conformity with modern practice or removing unnecessary provisions or anomalies which are not of substantial importance, and amendments designed to facilitate improvement in the form or manner in which the law is stated, and includes any transitional provisions which may be necessary in consequence of such amendments".

8 Examples are Water Industry Act 1991, Water Resources Act 1991, Social Security Contributions and Benefits Act 1992, Taxation of Chargeable Gains Act 1992.

9 For an explanation of this, and of the significance of the consolidating procedures in the context of construction of statutes, see the speech of LORD SIMON in *Farrell v Alexander*, [1977] AC 59, at pp 82–85; [1976] 2 All ER 721, at pp 733–736.

10 See, for examples, Employment Protection (Consolidation) Act 1978 (pure consolidation); Road Traffic Act 1988 (Law Commission amendments); Juries Act 1974 (1949 Act "corrections and improvements").

11 *The Preparation of Legislation*, Cmnd 6053 (1975).

notably that the preparation of a comprehensive new Interpretation Act should be put in hand, little if any radical change in the law was recommended and, although there was an Interpretation Act passed in 1978, this was only a consolidating Act, with Law Commission amendments, and it is difficult to envisage any sweeping reforms in the foreseeable future.

3 Codification

Codification differs from consolidation in that an Act may only be said to consolidate statute law, whereas it may codify both case law and statute law. Nevertheless codification is similar in function to consolidation in that in both cases the object of the statute is to simplify and clarify the existing law rather than to effect substantial alterations to it. Notable examples of major codifying statutes were the Bills of Exchange Act 1882, the Partnership Act 1890, the Sale of Goods Act 1893 and the Marine Insurance Act 1906. Since then there has been very little codification, and such as there has been, for example in the Criminal Law Act 1977, has been ancillary to law reform.

There is, in many areas of the law, a pressing need for codification. This is due to the manner in which Parliament approaches the task of amendment of statutes. Rather than produce a comprehensive re-enactment which would enable the relevant law on a topic to be clearly set out in a single statute, it is the practice simply to amend piecemeal by sections tucked away in a statute which may deal with a large number of different topics and amend an equally large number of earlier statutes. Subsequently the amending provision may itself be repealed or re-amended with the result that, in order to discover what the law is, it is necessary to pick one's way through a maze of separate statutory provisions.

This situation, in the field of industrial relations legislation, led to the following trenchant remarks by SIR JOHN DONALDSON MR in one case:[12]

> "My plea is that Parliament, when legislating in respect of circumstances which directly affect the 'man or woman in the street' or the 'man or woman on the shop floor', should give as high a priority to clarity and simplicity of expression as to refinements of policy. Where possible statutes, or complete parts of statutes, should not be amended but re-enacted in an amended form so that those concerned can read the rules in a single document. When formulating policy, ministers, of whatever political persuasion, should at all times be asking themselves and asking parliamentary counsel; 'Is this concept too refined to be capable of expression in basic English? if so, is there some way in which we can modify the policy so that it can be so expressed?' Having to ask such questions would no doubt be frustrating for ministers and the legislature generally, but in my judgment this is part of the price which has to be paid if the rule of law is to be maintained."

These remarks were expressly adopted by LORD DIPLOCK when the case reached the House of Lords[13] but they appear to have borne little fruit.

---

12 *Merkur Island Shipping Corporation v Laughton* [1983] 2 AC 570, at pp 594–595; [1983] 1 All ER 334, at p 351.
13 [1983] 2 AC, at p 612; [1983] 2 All ER 189, at pp 198–9.

4 Collection and disbursement of revenue

The annual Finance Act implementing the Budget proposals is concerned primarily with the collection of revenue by the Crown. Other Acts, notably the Income and Corporation Taxes Act 1988, fulfil the same function. Possibly on account of the considerable energies expended on the task of tax avoidance these statutes tend to promote rather more litigation than the average statute, including numerous "test cases" in which the Inland Revenue is concerned to discover whether the drafting of a measure has achieved the desired effect. Conversely, public expenditure is authorised by Parliament annually through Consolidated Fund Acts, which authorise payments out of the Consolidated Fund, and the Appropriation Act, which appropriates public expenditure to specific purposes.

5 Implementation of treaties

The United Kingdom, by entering into treaties, undertakes to implement the laws which form the subject matter of the treaty. For example directives and decisions of the Council and Commission of the EC usually require implementation either by statute or statutory instrument[14] while, arising out of its subscription to the European Convention on Human Rights, the United Kingdom has a duty to legislate so as to enforce decisions of the European Court of Human Rights.[15] With a view to standardising or harmonising branches of the law with an international element, the United Kingdom subscribes to specific treaties or conventions, following which they are implemented by domestic legislation. Examples of such legislation are the Civil Jurisdiction and Judgments Act 1982, the Taking of Hostages Act 1982, the Employment Act 1989, the Companies Act 1989 and the Civil Jurisdiction and Judgments Act 1991.

6 Social legislation

The law student, faced with a list of the Acts of Parliament passed in any single year, will probably feel that most of them do not concern him at all and will regard them as of secondary importance. These Acts are varied in their scope and functions but may be classified together as social legislation. Such Acts are concerned with regulating the day-to-day running of the social system rather than with creating criminal offences or rights and duties between individuals. There is an increasing tendency for Parliament to delegate to subordinate bodies the power to make regulations of this nature.

It is, of course, wrong to suppose that social legislation is of no interest to the lawyer. When legislation attempts to strike a balance between competing social priorities there is an inevitable tendency towards dispute and, as a result, litigation. An obvious modern example is legislation concerning landlord and tenant. Population increases and shortages of rented accommodation resulted in housing becoming a major social problem. Acts passed as a result, such as the Landlord and Tenant Acts

---

14 See p 25, *post.*
15 See p 13, *ante.*

and the Rent Acts, have become the subject of a huge volume of litigation over their interpretation.

B   FORMS OF LEGISLATION[16]

Early legislation in England took several different forms, such as charters,[17] provisions, ordinances and statutes. At the present day, however, there are only three different forms which United Kingdom legislation may take; Acts of Parliament, delegated legislation and autonomic legislation.

1   Acts of Parliament

Subject to compliance with the overriding legislation of the European Communities, Parliament is recognised as sovereign and as possessing unlimited legislative power. This has not always been so[18] but in modern times it had not been seriously contended that the courts have any power to override the intention of the legislature until in *British Railways Board v Pickin*[19] an attempt was made to impugn the validity of a private Act of Parliament, the British Railways Act 1968, on the ground that, in obtaining the enactment of part of the Act, the British Railways Board had fraudulently concealed certain matters from Parliament and thereby misled Parliament into an enactment which operated to deprive the plaintiff of his land or proprietary rights. If it was surprising that such a point should be pleaded it was, perhaps, more surprising that the Court of Appeal should have held that it raised a triable issue.[20] The House of Lords, however, allowed the Board's appeal and restored the judge's order that the pleading be struck out as being frivolous, vexatious and an abuse of the process of the court.[1] Accordingly, it is now clear that no court is entitled to go behind that which Parliament has enacted and that this rule is equally applicable to public and private Acts.

However where there is a potential conflict between a United Kingdom Act and legislation of the European Communities the courts have power to restrain enforcement of the former. This occurred in *R v Secretary of State for Transport, ex parte Factortame Ltd (No 2)*.[2] In that case the applicants, who were companies controlled by Spanish nationals, sought to challenge the validity of the Merchant Shipping Act 1988 on the basis that it contravened the provisions of the EC Treaty by depriving them of their Community law rights. Since determination of this issue by the European

---

16 This Chapter is confined to legislation within the United Kingdom. The important topic of legislation of the European Communities is dealt with elsewhere; see p 97, *ante*.

17 For a recent attempt to rely upon Magna Carta, see *R v Secretary of State for the Home Department, ex parte Wynne* [1992] QB 406; [1992] 2 All ER 301.

18 See, for example, dicta of COKE C J in *Bonham*'s case (1609), 8 Co Rep 113b and of HOLT C J in *City of London v Wood* (1701) 12 Mod Rep 669.

19 [1974] AC 765; [1974] 1 All ER 609.

20 The decision of the Court of Appeal is reported at [1973] QB 219; [1972] 3 All ER 923. For a further unsuccessful attempt to have an Act of Parliament declared *ultra vires*, in this case the Canada Act 1982 at the suit of 124 Canadian Indian Chiefs see *Manuel v A-G*, [1983] Ch 77; [1982] 3 All ER 822.

1 Under RSC, Ord 18, r 19; see p 338, *post* for details of this procedure.

2 [1991] 1 AC 603; [1991] 1 All ER 70.

Court was likely to take some time the applicants applied for an interim injunction to restrain the Secretary of State from enforcing the Act – in effect an order postponing the coming into force of the Act. The House of Lords' initial decision[3] was that the courts had no power to make any such order. However, they referred this issue to the European Court of Justice, which decided otherwise, in consequence of which the House of Lords, in the exercise of its discretion, did grant the applicants the interim relief sought. Such relief is not, however, automatic, but will be granted only where the facts of the individual case merit it. In deciding whether they do, the court does not seek to take a view on the meaning of the question of community law referred to the European court.[4]

The procedure for the passing of an Act of Parliament is, briefly, that a Bill is drafted by Parliamentary draftsmen under supervision, generally, of a Minister of the Crown. The Bill is then introduced in either the House of Commons or the House of Lords usually by a Minister. If it passes through all its stages within the Parliamentary session it receives the Royal Assent and becomes an Act of Parliament. The contents of the Act are set out in various publications, though references to present day Acts are to the Queen's Printer's Copy published by Her Majesty's Stationery Office and on sale there to the general public. The Stationery Office publishes these copies in annual volumes and also publishes annually an Index to the Statutes in Force, for reference purposes. In addition the Incorporated Council of Law Reporting publishes annually the texts of Acts taken from the Queen's Printer's Copies.

The mode of citation of statutes has undergone change. Early statutes were cited by the name of the place where Parliament met.[5] Subsequently statutes were cited by reference to their regnal year and chapter. Thus, for example, the Criminal Justice Act 1948 would be cited as 11 & 12 *Geo 6*, c 58 indicating that the Act was the fifty-eighth passed in the Parliamentary session extending over the eleventh and twelfth years of the reign of George VI. This exceedingly cumbersome method of citation was not abolished until 1962.[6] Although Acts still have chapter numbers (a legacy of the fiction that only one Act was passed in a Parliamentary session), reference is now to the calendar year rather than to the regnal year. In practice Acts are commonly cited by reference to their short title, and this is permissible by section 2 of the Short Titles Act 1896. Many Acts passed prior to 1896 have been endowed with short titles retrospectively and Acts passed since that date contain a section conferring upon themselves a short title.

2 Delegated legislation

"Delegated legislation" is the description given to the vast body of rules, orders, regulations and bye-laws created by subordinate bodies under specific powers delegated to those bodies by Parliament. The advantage of delegated legislation is that it enables regulations to be made and altered quickly without the need, usually, for placing them before Parliament. The

---

3 *Factortame Ltd v Secretary of State for Transport* [1990] 2 AC 85; [1989] 2 All ER 692.
4 *R v HM Treasury, ex parte British Telecommunications plc* (1993), *Times* 2 December.
5 Eg, Statute of Gloucester 1278; Provisions of Oxford 1258.
6 Acts of Parliament Numbering and Citation Act 1962 (10 & 11 Eliz 2, c 34).

vital feature which distinguishes Parliament from any other person or body having legislative power is that the latter is not sovereign. Delegated legislation is valid only if it is within the legislative powers conferred by Parliament (intra vires). If it is not it is said to be ultra vires and is, in that event, inoperative. Thus, for example, the Rules of the Supreme Court are delegated legislation, being passed by a Rule Committee under powers conferred by the Supreme Court Act 1981. The power conferred upon the Committee is limited to creating rules of procedure. Consequently, if any Rule of the Supreme Court has the characteristic of a rule of substantive law rather than a rule of procedure it is ineffective.[7] However, unless and until declared ultra vires by a final judgment in an action in the courts, a statutory instrument must be treated as part of the law and enforced accordingly.[8]

The fact that part of delegated legislation is ultra vires does not necessarily invalidate the whole of that legislation. The valid part may be textually severable, alternatively upheld if it is substantially severable so that what remains after severance is essentially unchanged in its legislative purpose, operation and effect.[9] Delegated legislation which is concerned solely with implementing the detail of a general policy contained in an Act of Parliament is useful and unexceptionable. However, the powers delegated are frequently defined in the widest terms with the effect of conferring a legislative function on some body almost equivalent to that of Parliament itself.[10] Sir John Donaldson MR in a recent case[11] drew attention to the Hallmarking Act 1973, which empowers the Secretary of State by statutory instrument to apply the Act to metals other than gold, silver and platinum and to include provisions "applying, extending, excluding or amending, or repealing or revoking, with or without savings, any provisions of this Act or an instrument under this Act." This power is always, of course, subject to control by Parliament but, where the legislative power is conferred upon a Minister of the Crown, this may not be an effective control.[12]

The highest form of delegated legislation is Order in Council[13] which is nominally an order of the Privy Council consisting of the Sovereign and Privy Councillors. Many Acts are brought into operation by Order in Council, the power to make the Order being contained in the Act itself.[14]

---

7 See *Re Grosvenor Hotel London (No 2)* [1965] Ch 1210; [1964] 3 All ER 354; *Ward v James* [1966] 1 QB 273; [1965] 1 All ER 563.

8 Cf *F Hoffman-La Roche & Co AG v Secretary of State for Trade and Industry* [1975] AC 295 at p 329; [1974] 2 All ER 1128.

9 For a full discussion of the principles, see *Director of Public Prosecutions v Hutchinson* [1990] 2 AC 783; [1990] 2 All ER 836.

10 The powers tend to be very widely defined in time of war. See, for example, the extraordinarily wide powers to make defence regulations conferred by the Supplies and Services (Transitional Powers) Act 1945 and the Supplies and Services (Extended Purposes) Act 1947, cited in *Law in the Making* by CK Allen (7th Edn), pp 540 *et seq.*

11 *Aden Refinery Co Ltd v Ugland Management Co* [1987] QB 650; [1986] 3 All ER 737.

12 For an example, see *Liversidge v Anderson* [1942] AC 206; [1941] 3 All ER 338; see also *Kruse v Johnson* [1898] 2 QB 91; *Buck v A-G* [1965] Ch 745; [1964] 2 All ER 663.

13 Note that Orders in Council can also amount to primary legislation pursuant to the Royal Prerogative: *Council of Civil Service Unions v Minister for the Civil Service* [1985] AC 374; [1984] 3 All ER 935.

14 An Act may be brought into force by Order in Council even though the power to make the order derives from the Act itself; Interpretation Act 1978, s 13.

In fact, though not in theory, an Order in Council is generally made by the government and merely sanctioned by the Privy Council. The effect, therefore, is to confer wide legislative power upon Government departments.[15]

Orders in Council and certain other regulations are published in statutory instruments[16] (formerly statutory rules and orders) by the Queen's Printer and available at Her Majesty's Stationery Office. They are cited by calendar year and number (for example; SI 1959 No 64) and, often, by a short title.

3 Autonomic legislation

This differs from delegated legislation in that an autonomous body has an independent power to legislate for its own members and, in some cases, for members of the general public. Though this power is usually conferred by Parliament this is not always so. The power is in all cases, however, sanctioned by Parliament. Examples of autonomous legislative bodies are public undertakings such as transport authorities, bodies created by Royal charter, such as universities, whose bye-laws may affect the public at large. The Church of England, the General Medical Council, The Law Society, trade unions and even limited companies are autonomous in the sense that they have power to control their own internal structure and to legislate for

---

15 In this context attention may be drawn to s 2(2) of the European Communities Act 1972 which provides that:

"subject to Schedule 2 to this Act, at any time after its passing Her Majesty may by Order in Council, and any designated Minister or department may by regulations, make provision –

(a) for the purpose of implementing any community obligation of the United Kingdom, or enabling any such obligation to be implemented, or of enabling any rights enjoyed or to be enjoyed by the United Kingdom under or by virtue of the Treaties to be exercised; or

(b) for the purpose of dealing with matters arising out of or related to any such obligation or rights or the coming into force, or the operation from time to time, of subsection (1) above;

and in the exercise of any statutory power of duty, including any power to give directions or to legislate by means of orders, rules, regulations or other subordinate instrument, the person entrusted with the power or duty may have regard to the objects of the Communities and to any such obligation or rights as aforesaid."

The above provision has been widely criticised on the ground that it confers legislative power which is so extensive that it ought properly to be exercised only by Parliament directly. Schedule 2 to the Act does, in fact, limit the powers somewhat in that it excludes power to make any provision imposing or increasing taxation, to make any retrospective provision or to create any new criminal offence punishable with imprisonment for more than two years or punishable on summary conviction with imprisonment for more than three months or with a fine.

16 Statutory Instruments Act 1946. Statutes conferring subordinate legislative powers frequently, though not always, provide that the statutory instrument made thereunder shall be laid before Parliament. In this event a copy of the instrument must be so laid before it comes into operation; Statutory Instruments Act 1946, s 4. The effect of laying the instrument before Parliament varies. In some cases the instrument does not take effect until expressly approved by resolution while in others it takes effect immediately subject to cancellation by negative resolution within forty "sitting" days.

It is permissible for "outside documents" to be referred to in the statutory instrument (but not laid before Parliament), provided the reference is to an existing document and there is no question of "sub-delegation"; see *R v Secretary of State for Social Services, ex parte Camden London Borough Council* [1987] 2 All ER 560; [1987] 1 WLR 819, where this practice was unsuccessfully challenged.

their members. It is arguable that such legislation does not affect the public but it does in a negative sense in that any individual who causes a breach of the regulations created by an autonomous body may commit a civil wrong.

In almost all cases autonomic legislation is confined in its extent by an Act of Parliament in which event it is subject to the doctrine of ultra vires. An important exception, however, is constituted by the prerogative jurisdiction of the Privy Council. This jurisdiction is principally concerned with legislating by Order in Council for Crown Colonies. The power is subject to the ordinary rules of English law though not to the doctrine of ultra vires.[17] It will thus be apparent that Orders in Council may be passed either under powers conferred by individual Acts or under a general prerogative power independent of statute. Both of these are subject to the law, although only the first is subject to the doctrine of ultra vires.[18]

4   Codes of Practice

Before leaving the topic of forms of legislation, it is necessary to refer to Codes of Practice, which are of increasing significance in certain legislative contexts. The most important of these, in practice, are the codes issued by the Home Secretary under section 66 of the Police and Criminal Evidence Act 1984[19] and those issued by by the Advisory, Conciliation and Arbitration Service ("ACAS") under section 6 of the Employment Protection Act 1975. ACAS may issue Codes of Practice containing "such practical guidance as the Service thinks fit for the purpose of promoting the improvement of industrial relations".[20] Provision for codes of this type was first made by the Industrial Relations Act 1971 and the first such code, the Code of Practice on Disciplinary Practice and Procedures in Employment, has been of immense importance, particularly in unfair dismissal cases, where the tribunals and courts have developed principles of "procedural unfairness", whereby a dismissal, although not substantially unfair, may be held unfair because of failure on the part of the employer to adopt a fair procedure, in accordance with the Code of Practice, prior to dismissal, for example by failure to carry out a proper investigation of allegations against an employee or failure to give an employee an opportunity to state his case.

Whether Codes of Practice promulgated pursuant to Acts of Parliament are classifiable as "legislation" is a moot point. In one sense they have the characteristic of delegated legislation in that the power to issue the code is conferred by statute upon a specified person or body and, presumably, a Code of Practice could be declared ultra vires. On the other hand a Code of Practice does not, by its very nature, have the force of law. That is not to say that it does not have legal effect. Codes issued under the 1975 Act are admissible in any proceedings before an industrial tribunal or the Central Arbitration Committee.[1] By section 67(11) of the Police and Criminal Evidence Act any code under the Act is admissible in evidence, and if appearing to be relevant to any question arising in the proceedings, "it shall be taken into account in determining that question."

---

17 *The Zamora* [1916] 2 AC 77, PC.
18 See *Buck v A-G* [1965] Ch 745; [1964] 2 All ER 663.
19 See p 258, *post*.
20 Employment Protection Act 1975, s 6(1).
 1 Employment Protection Act 1975, s 6(11); see p 176, *post*.

Codes of Practice approved or issued by the Health and Safety Commission under section 16 of the Health and Safety at Work etc Act 1974 have even greater force in that, in criminal proceedings under the Act, not only is the relevant Code admissible in evidence, but failure to comply with the Code amounts to *prima facie* proof of contravention of the provisions of the Act to which the Code relates.[2] Reference may also be made to the Highway Code, first issued pursuant to the Road Traffic Act 1930, failure to comply with the provisions of which is not, in itself, an offence but may be relied upon by any party in either civil or criminal proceedings.[3]

C   THE OPERATION OF STATUTES

In defining the scope of a statute it is necessary to advert both to its geographical area of operation and to the time during which it is operative.

1   Geographical operation

There is a presumption that an Act of Parliament is operative throughout the United Kingdom[4] but not elsewhere unless in either case a contrary intention appears in the Act itself. The contrary intention may either limit or extend the geographical operation of the Act. Thus Acts frequently contain a section restricting their operation to exclude Scotland or Northern Ireland. The Limitation Act 1963, for example, was in three parts; Part I applying to England and Wales, Part II to Scotland and Part III to Northern Ireland. A similar reduction in the geographical operation of legislation occurs in the case of Acts which are expressed to apply only to a limited locality; such Acts are described as "local Acts". An Act may be partly local and partly general. For example, sections 83 and 86 of the Fires Prevention (Metropolis) Act 1774 were held to be applicable throughout the United Kingdom although the operation of the Act as a whole was confined to the London area.

Conversely an Act may expressly or by necessary implication extend outside the United Kingdom, though there is a presumption against this.[5] For example, section 57 of the Offences Against the Person Act 1861 provides that the crime of bigamy is committed "whether the second marriage shall have taken place in England or Ireland, *or elsewhere.*" An Act which does have extraterritorial operation is, however, usually (but

---

2 Health and Safety at Work etc Act 1974, s 17(2).
3 Road Traffic Act 1988, s 38(6).
4 Since it lies within the prerogative power of the Crown to extend its sovereignty and jurisdiction to areas of land or sea over which it has not previously asserted sovereignty or jurisdiction, the words "United Kingdom" incorporate such area of land or sea as may from time to time be formally declared by the Crown to be subject to its sovereignty and jurisdiction as part of the United Kingdom; see *Post Office v Estuary Radio Ltd* [1968] 2 QB 740, at p 748; [1967] 3 All ER 663, at p 680, *per* DIPLOCK LJ.
5 The presumption is particularly strong in criminal cases; see *Cox v Army Council* [1963] AC 48; [1962] 1 All ER 880; *Air-India v Wiggins* [1980] 2 All ER 593; [1980] 1 WLR 815.

not always) limited to apply only to British subjects or persons owing allegiance to the Crown.[6]

2   Temporal operation

a When a statute begins to be operative

Until 1793[7] a statute came into force on the first day of the Parliamentary session in which it was passed. Consequently virtually all legislation was retrospective. The present law is that a statute comes into force on the day on which it receives the Royal Assent, unless some other date is specified in the Act itself. Frequently some future date will be specified to enable persons affected by the Act to prepare for its operation. Thus the Highways (Miscellaneous Provisions) Act 1961 came into operation on 3 August, 1964, the delay being for the purpose of enabling highway authorities, upon whom a new duty to maintain highways was imposed, to effect such repairs as were necessary to comply with the stringent provisions of the Act. Alternatively an Act may provide that it is to come into force on a "day to be appointed". The day is appointed by Order in Council unless the Act provides for appointment by a Minister. In either case the appointed day is published in a statutory instrument. The disadvantage of this practice is that it is slightly more difficult to determine when the Act is coming into force and it is necessary to consult the calendar of appointed days. Different parts of an Act or sections in an Act may be brought into force at different times. There are portions of Acts in existence which have never been brought into force.[8]

The effect of a statute coming into operation is that, if it is a Public Act, and every Act passed since 1850 is presumed to be a Public Act in the absence of a contrary provision, it immediately becomes effective and the courts take judicial notice of it.[9]

Delegated legislation generally comes into force when it is passed but section 3(2) of the Statutory Instruments Act 1946 provides that where a person is charged with contravening the provisions of a statutory instrument it shall be a defence to prove that the Instrument had not been issued by Her Majesty's Stationery Office at the date of the alleged contravention, unless it is proved that at that date reasonable steps had been taken for the purpose of bringing the purport of the instrument to the notice of the public, or of persons likely to be affected by it, or of the person charged.[10]

---

6 *Joyce v Director of Public Prosecutions* [1946] AC 347; [1946] 1 All ER 186; but cf Internationally Protected Persons Act 1978, under which attacks upon the person or property of "protected persons" (such as heads of state and their families) are offences justiciable in the United Kingdom, even though committed outside the United Kingdom by a person "whether a citizen of the United Kingdom and Colonies or not" (s 1); there are similar provisions in the Suppression of Terrorism Act 1978, s 4 in relation to certain offences specified in Sch 1 to that Act (eg murder, manslaughter, kidnapping and various offences under the Offences Against the Person Act 1861) when committed in countries who subscribed to the European Convention on the Suppression of Terrorism 1977, in the Taking of Hostages Act 1982, and in the War Crimes Act 1991.

7 Acts of Parliament (Commencement) Act.

8 Current Law Statutes Annotated incorporates a table "Legislation Not Yet in Force" to which reference may be made. See, *e.g.*, provisions in the Criminal Justice Act 1988 relating to criminal injuries.

9 Interpretation Act 1978, s 3.

10 See *R v Sheer Metalcraft Ltd* [1954] 1 QB 586; [1954] 1 All ER 542.

Retrospective operation — As a general rule a statute only affects factual situations which arise during the period of its operation. There is a presumption against the statute being retroactive although the courts have been keen to point out that it is in each case a question of ascertaining the intentions of Parliament. As STAUGHTON LJ stated in *Secretary of State for Social Security v Tunnicliffe:*[11]

> ". . . the true principle is that Parliament is presumed not to have intended to alter the law applicable to past events and transactions in a manner which is unfair to those concerned in them, unless a contrary intention appears. It is not simply a question of classifying an enactment as retrospective or non-retrospective. Rather it may well be a matter of degree – the greater the unfairness, the more it is expected that Parliament will make it clear if that is intended."

The presumption is particularly strong where the statute in question creates criminal penalties or tax obligations or would operate to deprive a person of a vested right in property.[12] However, Parliament is sovereign and statutes may be, and occasionally are, expressed to be retroactive even where this operates to deprive a person of a vested right in property. A modern illustration was the War Damage Act 1965 which operated to remove vested rights to compensation from the Crown and which was exceptional in that it was also expressed to apply to proceedings commenced before the Act came into force.[13] Also, statutes aimed at preventing tax avoidance, or recovering overpayments of state benefits paid in consequence of misrepresentation or failure to disclose a material fact, are sometimes expressed to be retroactive and there seems to be no presumption against retroactivity in the case of statutes of this type.[14] An Act of indemnity, the purpose of which is to validate or legalise *ex post facto* that which was initially invalid or illegal, must by its nature be retroactive.[15] A statute which alters rules of evidence or procedure rather than rules of substantive law is always retroactive, in the absence of a contrary intention, since the rules of evidence and procedure which a court is bound to observe are those in existence at the time of the hearing.[16]

---

11 [1991] 2 All ER 712, at 724, approved by the House of Lords in *L'Office Cherifien des Phosphates v Yamashita-Shinnihon Steamship Co Ltd* [1994] 1 All ER 20, [1994] 2 WLR 39.

12 *Yew Bon Tew v Kenderaan Bas Mara* [1983] 1 AC 553; [1982] 3 All ER 833. In *R v Fisher* [1969] 1 All ER 100; [1969] 1 WLR 8 the rule against retrospective operation operated, for once, against the accused in that he was convicted of an offence which had, at the time of his trial, been abolished by statute since the conduct in question had been, at the time of commission, an offence; see also *R v West London Stipendiary Magistrate, ex parte Simeon* [1983] 1 AC 234; sub nom *Metropolitan Police Commissioner v Simeon* [1982] 2 All ER 813. But a retrospective statute may affect a pending action; *Zainal bin Hashim v Government of Malaysia* [1980] AC 734; [1979] 3 All ER 241.

13 Section 1(2). The action affected was *Burmah Oil Co Ltd v Lord Advocate* [1965] AC 75; [1964] 2 All ER 348.

14 See, for example, Finance Act 1936, s 18; Social Security Act 1986, s 53 as construed in *Secretary of State for Social Security v Tunnicliffe* [1991] 2 All ER 712.

15 Examples of Acts of indemnity are: Indemnity Act 1920; Indian Divorces (Validity) Act 1921; Charitable Trusts (Validation) Act 1954.

16 See *Blyth v Blyth* [1966] AC 643; [1966] 1 All ER 524; *R v Cruttenden* [1991] 2 QB 66; [1991] 3 All ER 242 (evidence); cf *Yew Bon Tew v Kenderaan Bas Mara* [1983] 1 AC 553; [1982] 3 All ER 833 (limitation statute in Malaysia held not to revive statute-barred cause of action).

Even if the statutory provision itself does not take effect retrospectively, it may nevertheless be held to entitle a court to have regard to what has occurred prior to its passage. Thus in *L'Office Cherifien des Phosphates v Yamashita-Shinnihon Steamship Co Ltd*[17] the House of Lords held that "inordinate and inexcusable delay" which had occurred prior to section 13A of the Arbitration Act 1950 came into force entitled an arbitrator to dismiss a claim.[18]

b   *When a statute ceases to be operative*

No statute becomes obsolete by the passing of time. Nevertheless there are many ancient statutes more honoured in the breach than in the observance. At one time the approach of the legislature was to do nothing until the need for repeal manifested itself. Thus the plaintiff in a nineteenth century case was no doubt disturbed to discover that his opponent had a right to claim trial by battle;[19] two cases in modern times have involved statutes of 1351 and 1381 respectively[20] while resort to such provisions as the preamble to the Charitable Uses Act 1601, the Statute of Frauds 1677, s4 and the Bill of Rights 1688 is by no means uncommon.[1]

However, the present position is that the Law Commissions are expressly required to review "obsolete and unnecessary enactments" with a view to repeal.[2] In consequence there are now regular Statute Law (Repeals) Acts each of which repeals hundreds of obsolete enactments, following recommendations of the Law Commissions.

To the above rule that statutes do not become obsolete with the passing of time there is an exception. Certain statutes are expressed to be operative only for a limited period, usually because they are experimental or transitional though the best known statutes of this type, the Army Act and the Air Force Act, are re-enacted periodically so as to avoid the prohibition on keeping a standing army in time of peace.[3] Most of the provisions of the Prevention of Terrorism (Temporary Provisions) Act 1989 require annual renewal by order of the Home Secretary.[4]

Temporary statutes may acquire a new lease of life by the passing of an Expiring Laws Continuance Act which is effected solely for the purpose of renewing statutes which would otherwise expire. Thus Part I of the Commonwealth Immigrants Act 1962, an experimental measure expressed to last for only one year, was renewed annually until 1971 when the Immigration Act 1971 was passed to supersede it.

---

17 [1994] 1 All ER 20; [1994] 2 WLR 39.
18 Section 13A was incorporated into the 1950 Act by s 102 of Courts and Legal Services Act 1990. See p 282, *post*.
19 *Ashford v Thornton* (1818) 1 B & Ald 405.
20 *Hemmings v Stoke Poges Golf Club Ltd* [1920] 1 KB 720; *Joyce v Director of Public Prosecutions* [1946] AC 347; [1946] 1 All ER 186.
 1 See, for example, *Rost v Edwards* [1990] 2 QB 460; [1990] 2 All ER 641.
 2 Law Commissions Act 1965, s 3(1).
 3 Prior to 1955 this was done by means of annual Acts. However a new procedure was established by the Army Act 1955, s 226 and the Air Force Act 1955, s 224. Under this procedure the Acts are renewable annually by Order in Council, a new Act of Parliament being required only every five years.
 4 The 1989 Act was passed to replace the Prevention of Terrorism (Temporary Provisions) Act 1984, which in turn replaced a similar Act of 1976, each of which was renewable (and in fact renewed) annually.

Unless it is one of those which are expressed to be operative for a limited period a statute ceases to have effect only when repealed by another statute, since only Parliament is competent to repeal its own enactments.[5] Repeal may be express or implied. In modern times almost all repeal is express and it is common for a statute to include a schedule of repeals, expressly incorporated into the body of the Act, where there are several provisions repealed. Implied repeal is possible and occurs where two statutory provisions are inconsistent with one another. In this situation the later provision impliedly repeals the earlier to the extent of the inconsistency.[6] The courts, however, lean against implied repeal and will attempt to reconcile seemingly conflicting provisions wherever possible. In addition there is a rule that a public Act does not impliedly repeal a private or local Act (*generalia specialibus non derogant*).[7] Unless the contrary intention appears repeal does not have the effect of reviving any earlier repealed rule of law, statutory or otherwise.[8]

There is no reason why a statute should not create a power to revive the effect of a statutory provision that it elsewhere repeals. Indeed the Crown Proceedings (Armed Forces) Act 1987 did just this, section 2(1) conferring upon the Secretary of State a power to revive a provision repealed by section 1 of the same Act.[9]

D THE INTERPRETATION AND CONSTRUCTION OF STATUTES

1 The need for interpretation and construction

Where the words of a statute are clear and unambiguous persons affected by its provisions will regulate their conduct according to the terms of the statute and the need for judicial interpretation will not arise. However, if the meaning or extent of a statute is uncertain or ambiguous litigation is inevitable and the statute will fall to be interpreted. There is a technical distinction between interpretation and construction. "Interpretation" is simply the process whereby a meaning is assigned to the words in a statute. "Construction", on the other hand, is the process whereby uncertainties or ambiguities in a statute are resolved. It follows that every statute which comes before a court is interpreted whereas only uncertain or ambiguous provisions require construction. The processes are not usually distinguished by judges since, in the nature of things, litigation only arises around the wording of a statute where it is ambiguous or, at least,

---

5 Unless the enactment is impliedly repealed by legislation of the European Communities: *Amministrazione delle Finanze dello Stato v Simmenthal SpA* [1978] ECR 629; see p 107, *post*.
6 See, for example, *Smith v Benabo* [1937] 1 KB 518; [1937] 1 All ER 523; *Ellen Street Estates Ltd v Minister of Health* [1934] 1 KB 590; *Dryden v Dryden* [1973] Fam 217; [1973] 3 All ER 526.
7 Thus it was held in *Bishop of Gloucester v Cunnington* [1943] KB 101; [1943] 1 All ER 61, that the restrictions on the recovery of leasehold property imposed by the Rent and Mortgage Interest Restriction Acts 1920–39 did not affect the right of a bishop to recover possession of a parsonage under the Pluralities Act 1838.
8 Interpretation Act 1978, ss 15, 16(1).
9 The provision in question was Crown Proceedings Act 1947, s 10 (exclusions from liability in tort in cases involving the armed forces).

uncertain. However, LAWSON J clearly did distinguish the process of interpretation and construction in one case;[10]

> "I approach the answer to the question in two stages. Stage one is this; whether the meaning of the Cyprus Act 1960 in this respect is clear and unambiguous, and if so, what does it mean? at this stage I look at the words of the enactment as a whole, including the Schedule, and I use no further aids, no further extrinsic aids in order to reach a conclusion as to the clear and unambiguous meaning of the words . . . If I find that the answer on the first stage in my inquiry is that the meaning of the Act in this respect is ambiguous, then I have to go on to the second stage and consider two possible different meanings . . . Now if I get to this second stage, then in my judgment, and then only, am I entitled to look at extrinsic aids,[11] such as the long title, the heading, the side notes, other legislation; then only am I entitled to resort to maxims of construction . . ."

a   Ambiguity

Ambiguity arises, often through careless drafting, when words used in a statute are found to be capable of bearing two or more literal meanings. Language is an imprecise tool and even Parliamentary draftsmen, in using words intended to convey one meaning, occasionally contrive to give rise to an alternative meaning which neither they nor the legislature ever envisaged. Thus the Restriction of Offensive Weapons Act 1959 made it an offence to "offer for sale" certain offensive weapons including "flick knives". A shopkeeper who displayed weapons of this type in his window was held, by a divisional court, to be not guilty of an offence under the Act because, as every student of the law of contract knows, the exhibition of goods in a shop window does not constitute an offer.[12] Where the subject matter of a statute is a branch of the law which is intrinsically complex, such as landlord and tenant or income tax, it seems to be virtually impossible to choose language which is entirely free from ambiguity. Nevertheless the judiciary has on occasion been less than sympathetic to the draftsman's plight. Thus in *R v Royle*,[13] section 16 of the Theft Act 1968 was described as being so obscure as to have "created a judicial nightmare" while in *Central Asbestos Co Ltd v Dodd*[14] LORD REID said of

---

10 *Franklin v A-G*, [1974] QB 185, at p 199; [1973] 1 All ER 879, at p 886 (one of the cases arising out of the attempt by the plaintiff to proceed against the Crown by way of the ancient remedy of "petition of right").
11 The aids then referred to by LAWSON J are generally referred to as intrinsic (rather than extrinsic) aids since they appear in the text of the Queen's Printer's copy of the Act; see p 23, *post*.
12 *Fisher v Bell* [1961] 1 QB 394; [1960] 3 All ER 731; see also *Partridge v Crittenden* [1968] 2 All ER 421; [1968] 1 WLR 1204.
13 [1971] 3 All ER 1359, at p 1363; [1971] 1 WLR 1764, at p 1767, *per* EDMUND DAVIES LJ; cf *Director of Public Prosecutions v Turner* [1974] AC 357; [1973] 3 All ER 124 in which the House of Lords expressed its own dim view of the same section. The offending part of the section (s 16(2)(a)) was eventually repealed and replaced by the Theft Act 1978.
14 [1973] AC 518, at p 529; [1972] 2 All ER 1135, at p 1138; the Limitation Act 1975 (replacing that part of the 1963 Act) seemed to aim at similar distinction. The Acts concerned are now consolidated in the Limitation Act 1980.

the Limitation Act 1963 that it had "a strong claim to the distinction of being the worst drafted Act on the statute book".[15]

b Uncertainty

Uncertainty is far more common than ambiguity. Uncertainty occurs where the words of a statute are intended to apply to various factual situations and the courts are called upon to decide whether or not the set of facts before them amounts to a factual situation envisaged by the Act. For example the words "an accident arising out of and in the course of his employment" in the Workmen's Compensation Acts were the source of innumerable cases, not because they were in any way ambiguous but because their scope was uncertain, being adaptable to endless permutations of facts.[16] The use of general, and ostensibly clearly defined, words such as "road",[17] "park",[18] "premises",[19] and "board"[20] has created problems of construction which the legislature could not have envisaged, while, more recently, the courts have been called upon to resolve such conundrums as whether the cremation of humans is "the subjection of goods or materials to any process",[1] whether an orange squeezed by hand is a "manufactured beverage"[2] and whether video games constitute an "exhibition of moving pictures".[3] LORD DENNING once expressed the difficulty as follows:[4]

> "It must be remembered that it is not within human powers to foresee the manifold sets of facts which may arise, and, even if it were, it is not possible to provide for them in terms free from all ambiguity."

The primary difficulty in such cases is that the words themselves are almost the only guide which may be used to the meaning which Parliament intended. The view is often expressed, even by members of the judiciary themselves,[5] that the legislature should publish a statement of its aims in

---

15 See also *Great Western Rail Co v Bater* [1922] 2 AC 1, at p 11; *Barentz v Whiting* [1965] 1 All ER 685; [1965] 1 WLR 433; *London County Council v Lees* [1939] 1 All ER 191; *Davies v Warwick* [1943] KB 329; [1943] 1 All ER 309. For an enlightening insight into the draftsman's problems, and techniques for resolving them, see F Bennion, 'Legislative Technique', 129 New Law Journal, p 748.

16 The words continue to be used in social security legislation (currently the Social Security Contributions and Benefits Act 1992, s 94) where they continue to cause trouble; see *R v National Insurance Commissioner, ex parte Michael* [1977] 2 All ER 420; [1977] 1 WLR 109.

17 *Griffin v Squires* [1958] 3 All ER 468; [1958] 1 WLR 1106.

18 *Re Ripon (Highfield) Housing Confirmation Order 1938* [1939] 2 KB 838; [1939] 3 All ER 548.

19 *Whitley v Stumbles* [1930] AC 544; *Maunsell v Olins* [1975] AC 373; [1975] 1 All ER 16.

20 *Otter v Norman* [1989] AC 129; [1988] 2 All ER 897.

1 *Bourne (Inspector of Taxes) v Norwich Crematorium Ltd* [1967] 2 All ER 576; [1967] 1 WLR 691.

2 *Customs and Excise Commissioners v Savoy Hotel Ltd* [1966] 2 All ER 299; [1966] 1 WLR 948. For a delightfully sardonic exposition of the difficulty of ascertaining the "right" meaning of words, see the judgment of DIPLOCK LJ in *Slim v Daily Telegraph Ltd* [1968] 2 QB 157, at pp 171–172; [1968] 1 All ER 497, at p 504.

3 *British Amusement Catering Trades Association v Westminster City Council* [1989] AC 147; [1988] 1 All ER 740.

4 *Seaford Court Estates Ltd v Asher* [1949] 2 KB 481, at p 499; [1949] 2 All ER 155, at p 164 (affirmed [1951] AC 508; [1950] 1 All ER 1018).

5 See, for example, observations of LORD DU PARCQ in *Cutler v Wandsworth Stadium Ltd (in Liquidation)* [1949] AC 398, at p 410; [1949] 1 All ER 544, at p 549.

relation to any particular Act.[6] In fact such statements often are published but, in interpreting and construing the Act in question, the judiciary traditionally eschews them.[7]

2   Judicial approaches to interpretation

The basic task of the judge is to ascertain the intention of Parliament. Nevertheless there are alternative approaches to this task. These approaches, which differ radically, are commonly known as the "literal" approach and the "purposive" approach. It is never possible to know in advance which approach any particular court will favour. Certain decisions have been based on one of these approaches, others on the application of another.

Each of these approaches to interpretation must be considered individually.[8]

a   The literal approach

The basic approach to statutory interpretation, as already stated, is to ascertain the intention of the legislature. The literal rule of interpretation is that this intention must be found in the ordinary and natural meaning of the words used. If these words, interpreted literally, are capable of alternative meanings the literal rule clearly cannot be applied. Hence the approach breaks down in the face of an ambiguity. However, if the words are capable of only one literal meaning the literal rule is that this meaning must be applied even if it appears unlikely. The rule may be expressed as an irrebuttable presumption that Parliament intends the ordinary and natural meaning of the words it employs. The rule will, in most cases, produce a reasonable interpretation of the statute. Difficulty arises, however, where, in consequence of incompetent drafting, literal interpretation produces either an improbable result or, in extreme cases, a manifest absurdity. Where the literal interpretation merely produces a result which seems less plausible than one which Parliament might be supposed to have intended the literal rule ought nevertheless to be applied. Thus in *Inland Revenue Commissioners v Hinchy*[9] the House of Lords was called upon to construe section 25(3) of the Income Tax Act 1952 which provided that any person delivering an incorrect tax return should forfeit ". . . treble the tax which he ought to be charged under this Act". Although Parliament presumably intended[10] a penalty of treble the unpaid tax the House of Lords held that the literal meaning of the words of the subsection was that the respondent was liable to pay treble the whole amount of tax payable by him for the year. *Fisher v Bell*, cited earlier,[11] is a

---

6 The long title frequently does this, but generally too briefly to be of real assistance; see p 47, *post*.
7 See *London County Council v Central Land Board* [1959] Ch 386; [1958] 3 All ER 676.
8 As to the approach to the interpretation of legislation of the European Communities, see p 99, *post*.
9 [1960] AC 748; [1960] 1 All ER 505.
10 The law was in fact changed shortly after this decision by the Finance Act 1960, s 44.
11 [1961] 1 QB 394; [1960] 3 All ER 731; see p 32, *ante*. For further instances of the application of the literal rule, see *Magor and St Mellons Rural District Council v Newport*

further example of the application of the literal rule producing a result which appeared contrary to the intention of the legislature. On the other hand, where the application of the literal rule would produce a manifest absurdity it will not be applied. This is well illustrated by the unanimous decision of the House of Lords in *McMonagle v Westminster City Council*.[12] The appellant was charged with using premises as a "sex encounter establishment" without a licence. The statutory definition of those words was "premises at which performances *which are not unlawful* are given . . ., which wholly or mainly comprise the sexual stimulation of persons admitted to the premises . . ."

The appellant's defence was that the prosecution had failed to prove that the performances were not unlawful and that, if they were, according to the plain words of the statute a licence was not required. The House of Lords regarded this interpretation as manifestly absurd and rejected it. The reasoning was expressed by LORD BRIDGE as follows:[13]

> "I am satisfied that the main object of paragraph 3A(c) of Schedule 3 is to require any premises, not falling within the proviso, where live nude entertainment is provided to be licensed and that in order to avoid the substantial frustration of that object it is both necessary and legitimate that the words 'which are not unlawful' should be treated as surplusage and as having been introduced by incompetent draftsmanship for no other purpose than to emphasise . . . that a licence confers no immunity from the ordinary criminal law."

The difficulty, of course, lies in drawing the line between a literal interpretation which appears to the court to be improbable and one which produces a "manifest absurdity". Judges, from time to time, are inclined to resort to the doctrine of "manifest absurdity" so as to avoid an interpretation which appears to them to produce a result which they cannot believe to represent the legislative intention. LORD BRIDGE in another case[14] was highly critical of this inclination:

> "I would observe first that I believe there is a distinction to be drawn between what I would call a positive and a negative absurdity. It is one thing to abstain from giving to the language of a statute the full effect of its ordinary grammatical meaning in order to avoid some positively harmful or manifestly unjust consequence. This I would describe as a legitimate process of construction to avoid a positive absurdity. But it is quite another thing to read into a statute a meaning which the language used will not bear in order to remedy a supposed defect or shortcoming which, if not made good, will make the

---

Corporation [1952] AC 189; [1951] 2 All ER 839; *A-G v Prince Ernest of Hanover* [1957] AC 436; [1957] 1 All ER 49; *Barclays Bank Ltd v Cole* [1967] 2 QB 738; [1966] 3 All ER 948; *R v West Yorkshire Coroner, ex parte Smith* [1983] QB 335; [1982] 3 All ER 1098. The Law Commission report, *The Interpretation of Statutes* 1969 (Law Com No 21) recommended a statutory provision to the effect that "a construction which would promote the general legislative purpose underlying the provision in question is to be preferred to a construction which would not".

12 [1990] 2 AC 716; [1990] 1 All ER 993.
13 [1990] 2 AC at p 727; [1990] 1 All ER at p 998.
14 *R v Central Criminal Court, ex parte Francis & Francis* [1989] AC 346, at p 375; sub nom *Francis & Francis v Central Criminal Court* [1988] 3 All ER 775, at p 783. The speech of LORD BRIDGE was in fact a dissenting one; the majority found the relevant statutory provision to be ambiguous and therefore were able to adopt the interpretation which appeared to produce the more satisfactory result.

statutory machinery less effective than the court believes it ought to be in order to achieve its proper purpose. Even if the lacuna appears to the court as absurd, this is what I describe, inelegantly but in order to point the contrast, as a negative absurdity. I know of no legitimate principle of construction which permits such a negative absurdity to be remedied by implying words which the court thinks necessary to enhance the operation of the statutory machinery."

The diversity of judicial approach is well illustrated by the speeches of the House of Lords in *Kammins Ballrooms Co Ltd v Zenith Investments (Torquay) Ltd*.[15] The case turned on the interpretation of section 29(3) of the Landlord and Tenant Act 1954 which provides that "no application [for the grant of a new tenancy] shall be entertained unless it is made not less than two nor more than four months" after (*inter alia*) the tenant's request for a new tenancy. On the question of whether the court had power to consider an application made less than two months after the tenant's request, the House of Lords (VISCOUNT DILHORNE dissenting) held that the court did have such power, thereby appearing to disregard the clear words of the section for as VISCOUNT DILHORNE observed:[16]

> "the appellants' contention here is that the words 'no application . . . shall be entertained' must be interpreted as meaning that an application shall in certain circumstances be entertained notwithstanding that it is made too early or too late. That seems to me to involve implying something wholly inconsistent with the words expressly used. True it is that English is a flexible language but that does not mean that one can disregard the natural and ordinary meaning of the words used unless it is apparent that some other meaning was intended.
>
>   If language is clear and explicit, the court must give effect to it 'for in that case the words of the statute speak the intention of the legislature' (*Warburton v Loveland* (1832) 2 Dow & Cl 480, *per* TINDAL CJ at p 489) 'and in so doing it must bear in mind that its function is *jus dicere*, not *jus dare*; the words of a statute must not be overruled by the judges, but reform of the law must be left in the hands of Parliament' (*Maxwell on Interpretation of Statutes*, 12th edn (1969), p 1)."

VISCOUNT DILHORNE was, however, a lone voice in support of this traditional approach. LORD DIPLOCK, who was in the majority, expressed his reasoning as follows:[17]

> "Upon the literal approach, semantics and the rules of syntax alone could never justify the conclusion that the words 'No application . . . shall be entertained unless' meant that some applications should be entertained notwithstanding that neither of the conditions which follow the word 'unless' was fulfilled . . . It can be justified only upon the assumption that the draftsman of the Act omitted to state in any words used in the subsection an exception to the absolute prohibition to which Parliament must have intended it to be subject. A conclusion that an exception was intended by

---

15 [1971] AC 850; [1970] 2 All ER 871.
16 [1971] AC 850, at p 869; [1970] 2 All ER 871, at p 883.
17 [1971] AC 850, at p 880; [1970] 2 All ER 871, at p 892. This approach was enthusiastically adopted by LORD DENNING MR in *Nothman v London Borough of Barnet* [1978] 1 All ER 1243; [1978] 1 WLR 220 but, although the House of Lords upheld the decision in that case, LORD RUSSELL expressly disclaimed what he called the "sweeping comments" of the Master of the Rolls [1979] 1 All ER 142, at p 151; [1979] 1 WLR 67, at p 77.

Parliament, and what that exception was can only be reached by using the purposive approach."

It is, accordingly, rarely possible to predict with certainty which approach the court will adopt. In *Stock v Frank Jones (Tipton) Ltd*[18] (where the literal rule was applied by the House of Lords) LORD SIMON dealt with the rationale of the literal rule in considerabe depth and, while favouring the literal approach, acknowledged that where this produced an anomaly a court would be justified in departing from the plain words, but only were it satisfied that:

> "(1) there is clear and gross balance of anomaly; (2) Parliament, the legislative promoters and the draftsman could not have envisaged such anomaly and could not have been prepared to accept it in the interest of a supervening legislative objective; (3) the anomaly can be obviated without detriment to such legislative objective; (4) the language of the statute is susceptible of the modification required to obviate the anomaly."[19]

b   The purposive approach

The purposive approach to statutory interpretation, sometimes known as the "golden rule", is that words in a statute must be interpreted according to their natural, ordinary and grammatical meaning, so far as possible, but only to the extent that such an interpretation does not produce a manifestly absurd result. Perhaps the best known statement of the rule is to be found in the judgment of PARKE B in *Becke v Smith*:[20]

> "it is a very useful rule in the construction of a statute to adhere to the ordinary meaning of the words used, and to the grammatical construction, unless that is at variance with the intention of the legislature to be collected from the statute itself, or leads to any manifest absurdity or repugnance, in which case the language may be varied or modified so as to avoid such inconvenience, but no further."

Where the statute permits of two or more literal interpretations the court must adopt that interpretation which produces the least absurd or repugnant result. This application of the golden rule is not, of course, inconsistent with the literal rule since the latter cannot be applied in a case of ambiguity. This is the narrow aspect of the golden rule and has been adopted in several well-known cases. Thus, for example, section 57 of the Offences Against the Person Act 1861 provides that "whosoever, being married, shall *marry* any other person during the life of the former husband or wife" shall be guilty of bigamy. The word *marry* permits of alternative meanings. It may be construed to mean *contracts a valid marriage* or *goes through a ceremony of marriage*. Since the former meaning would produce an absurd result, the latter must be applied.[1]

---

18 [1978] 1 All ER 948; [1978] 1 WLR 231; the whole of this speech repays study.
19 At pp 952–954, pp 235–237.
20 (1836) 2 M & W 191 at p 195. The statement of LORD WENSLEYDALE in *Grey v Pearson* (1857) 6 HL Cas 61, at p 106, expressed in very similar terms, is also frequently cited as stating the rule; see, for example, *Lord Advocate v de Rosa* [1974] 2 All ER 849; [1974] 1 WLR 946. See, also, *Vacher & Sons Ltd v The London Society of Compositors* [1913] AC 107.
1 *R v Allen* (1872) LR 1 CCR 367; see also *Young v Clarey* [1948] Ch 191; [1948] 1 All ER 197; *Mills v Cooper* [1967] 2 QB 459; [1967] 2 All ER 100.

However, where the statute is capable of only one literal meaning and the court rejects that meaning in favour of a construction which is obviously more rational the golden rule is, in effect, being applied in preference to the literal rule. It has been noted above that this approach will be readily adopted in order to avoid "manifest absurdity". There is also a residual category of cases in which public policy requires the rejection of a literal interpretation of the statute. Thus in *Re Sigsworth*[2] the golden rule was applied to prevent a murderer from taking on the intestacy of his victim although he was, as her son, the sole "issue" on a literal interpretation of the Administration of Estates Act 1925.

A similar approach was recently adopted by the Court of Appeal in *R v Registrar General, ex parte Smith*.[3] The appellant, a double killer with psychotic illness involving extreme hatred for his adoptive parents, applied under section 51 of the Adoption Act 1976 for a copy of his birth certificate (to which he had a right under that Act). The Registrar General refused that request, apprehending that the appellant might use the information on the certificate to commit a serious crime against his natural mother. The appellant applied for judicial review of this decision, contending that the statute conferred no discretion to refuse his application. The Court of Appeal, on the ground of public policy, upheld the refusal of his application. It might be supposed that in cases such as these the court is refusing to give effect to a statute, which it is axiomatic that no court has power to do,[4] but this is not so. The court is simply interpreting the statute in accordance with the presumed intention of Parliament, the presumption being that Parliament did not intend to procure a consequence which would involve a person benefiting from his crime, or would facilitate the commission of a crime. The cases could, in fact, be regarded as specific instances of the "manifest absurdity" principle.

A major criticism of the wide application of the golden rule in preference to the literal rule is that it is inherently subjective. The judge who decides that a literal interpretation is contrary to the intention of the legislature is, *ipso facto*, ascertaining the intention of the legislature from some source or sources other than the statute itself, and this is, strictly, beyond his judicial function. Moreover he may expose himself to the criticism that he is giving effect to his own views as to what the policy of Parliament ought to be.[5]

Rejection of a literal interpretation on the ground of absurdity is, however, only possible where there is available a more rational interpretation of the provision under consideration. Thus if there is no other possible interpretation or only an alternative which is equally, or even more, absurd than the literal interpretation, the court has to adopt the latter.[6]

---

2 [1935] Ch 89.
3 [1991] 2 QB 393; [1991] 2 All ER 88.
4 See p 22, *ante*.
5 See *Duport Steels Ltd v Sirs* [1980] 1 All ER 529; [1980] 1 WLR 142; *Shah v Barnet London Borough Council* [1983] 2 AC 309; [1983] 1 All ER 226, in both of which cases the House of Lords warned the judiciary against this pitfall; see p 183, post.
6 The House of Lords found itself in this unenviable position in *Metropolitan Police Commissioner v Curran* [1976] 1 All ER 162; [1976] 1 WLR 87 and had to content itself with a unanimous and scathing attack on the draftsmanship of the provisions in question (s 9(3) of and Sch 4 to the Road Traffic Act 1972 – repealed by the Road Traffic Act 1988).

Supplying omissions — An interesting problem of construction arises when the court is faced with a factual situation for which the statute has not provided. Such a situation is termed a *casus omissus*. It can only be remedied by attributing to Parliament an intention which Parliament never had. This amounts to a legislative act on the part of the judiciary and is a function which the more conservative judges are slow to adopt. Thus DENNING LJ, in the Court of Appeal, expressed his personal view of the judicial function in respect of omissions as follows:[7]

> "We sit here to find out the intention of Parliament and of Ministers and carry it out, and we do this better by filling in the gaps and making sense of the enactment than by opening it up to destructive analysis."

On appeal LORD SIMONDS roundly condemned this approach and, in a now famous dictum, described it as a "naked usurpation of the legislative function under the thin disguise of interpretation".[8] "If a gap is disclosed," LORD SIMONDS explained, "the remedy lies in an amending Act."

Nonetheless it is a truism that hard cases make bad law and the courts have, from time to time, been prepared to assume the authority to supply omissions left by the legislature. An illustration of this is to be found in the majority decision of the House of Lords in *Edwards v Porter*[9] where it was held that, although a husband "need not be joined" in an action against his wife, he could be joined if the plaintiff so wished. The Married Women's Property Act 1882, the Act in question, was silent on this point.[10]

Whichever approach to interpretation is adopted, the court is still bound to interpret the words of the Act before it. If interpretation discloses an uncertainty or ambiguity the court will then be bound to construe the statute. The judges themselves have formulated a large body of rules for the interpretation and construction of statutes. These rules, which equate to the rules for the construction of documents generally, are exceedingly complex and only those most commonly encountered are discussed below, by way of example.

---

7 *Magor and St Mellons Rural District Council v Newport Corporation* [1950] 2 All ER 1226 at p 1236.
8 [1952] AC 189, at p 191; [1951] 2 All ER 839, at p 841. In *James Buchanan & Co Ltd v Babco Forwarding and Shipping (UK) Ltd* [1977] QB 208; [1977] 1 All ER 518, LORD DENNING reiterated what he had said in *Magor and St Mellons* in relation to a statute enacting an international convention (as to which, see p 52, *post*) on the basis of the more liberal approach to statutory interpretation adopted by the European Court (see p 56, *post*), but the House of Lords, once again, did not support his view (1978] AC 141; [1977] 3 All ER 1048); see also, in this context, the observations of LORD BRIDGE in *R v Central Criminal Court, ex parte Francis & Francis* [1989] AC 346; sub nom *Francis & Francis v Central Criminal Court* [1988] 3 All ER 775 (quoted on p 35, ante).
9 [1925] AC 1.
10 See also *Astor v Perry* [1935] AC 398; *Re Radio Communications in Canada Regulation and Control* [1932] AC 304; *Chandris v Isbrandtsen-Moller Co Inc* [1951] 1 KB 240; [1950] 1 All ER 768; *Wagg v The Law Society* [1957] Ch 405; [1957] 2 All ER 274; *Williams v Williams* [1971] P 271; [1971] 2 All ER 764.

3   Rules of interpretation and construction

a   The statute must be read as a whole

Words in isolation may import meanings different from that which they bear in conjunction.[11] A statute must be read as a whole. Every section must be read in the light of every other section,[12] especially in the light of an interpretation section, and Schedules, if incorporated into the body of the Act, must be read with the Act.

An interesting illustration of this, and other rules of interpretation, is afforded by the decision of the House of Lords in the leading case of *Beswick v Beswick*.[13] The case raised the question of whether Parliament had by section 56 of the Law of Property Act 1925 inadvertently abrogated the common law rule that a person cannot sue on a contract to which he is not a party. Section 56(1) provides that "a person may take an . . . interest in land or other property, or the benefit of any condition, right of entry, covenant or agreement over or respecting land or other property, although he may not be named as a party to the conveyance or other instrument . . .". Section 205(1) of the 1925 Act, the interpretation section, provides that "in this Act unless the context otherwise requires 'property' includes any thing in action . . .". It was argued that the combined effect of these provisions was to enable a stranger to a contract to enforce the contract. This argument prevailed in the Court of Appeal[14] but was rejected by the House of Lords. Their Lordships pointed out that section 56 is one of 25 sections in the Act grouped under the heading "conveyances and other instruments" and in those circumstances held that the context did require the word property to be limited in its effect to real property.

The long title and the short title, being part of the enactment, must, strictly, be consulted in interpreting any part of the Act though, in practice, the courts will only refer to the long title to resolve an ambiguity and do not regard the short title as an aid to interpretation at all. Headings, marginal notes, punctuation and Schedules which are not expressly incorporated into the text are not part of the enactment and are, accordingly, not aids to interpretation.

b   The mischief rule

The "mischief rule", or rule in *Heydon*'s case, is that where a statute was passed to remedy a mischief the court will, if possible, adopt the

---

11 See observations on the words "unfair competition" in *Lee v Showmen's Guild of Great Britain* [1952] 2 QB 329, at p 338; [1952] 1 All ER 1175, at p 1178.

12 See, for example, *Owens Bank Ltd v Cauche* [1989] 1 WLR 559 where the statute under consideration had inconsistent provisions, so that one had to prevail over the literal meaning of the other.

13 [1968] AC 58; [1967] 2 All ER 1197; see also *Crook v Edmondson* [1966] 2 QB 81; [1966] 1 All ER 833.

14 [1966] Ch 538; [1966] 3 All ER 1. The Court of Appeal appears to have overlooked the vital words "unless the context otherwise requires" in s 205(1). In the event the House of Lords was able to uphold the decision of the Court of Appeal by an ingenious use of the remedy of specific performance.

interpretation of the statute which will have the effect of correcting the mischief in question. In *Heydon*'s case[15] itself, the rule was defined thus:

". . . four things are to be discussed and considered; (1) what was the common law before the making of the Act; (2) what was the mischief and defect for which the common law did not provide; (3) what remedy the Parliament hath resolved and appointed to cure the disease of the commonwealth; and (4) the true reason of the remedy."

A more modern formulation is that of LORD DIPLOCK in *Jones v Wrotham Park Settled Estates*, where he specified three conditions which must be satisfied before the rule can be applied:[16]

(1) it must be possible to determine from consideration of the Act as a whole[17] precisely the mischief that it was the purpose of the Act to remedy;

(2) it must be apparent that the draftsman and Parliament had inadvertently overlooked, and so omitted to deal with, the mischief;

(3) it must be possible to state "with certainty"[18] what were the additional words that would have been inserted by the draftsman and approved by Parliament had the omission been drawn to their attention.

The rule is often used to resolve ambiguities in cases in which the literal rule cannot be applied. For example, a "single woman" for the purposes of affiliation proceedings is a woman with no husband to support her, not necessarily an unmarried woman, since the mischief which the Acts were passed to remedy is the possibility of a woman having an illegitimate child with no means of supporting it.[19]

In order to ascertain the mischief which the statute was passed to correct the judge may legitimately have regard to the preamble of the statute, the long title,[20] headings[1] and to extrinsic sources such as reports of Royal Commissions or Law Reform Committees which may indicate the state of the law before the passing of the Act.[2]

c   The eiusdem generis rule

This rule is but a particular aspect of the wider rule that the statute must be read as a whole. The rule is that general words which follow two or more particular words in an Act must be confined to a meaning of the same kind (*eiusdem generis*) as the particular words. It is common drafting practice, when the intention is to cover a wide range of similar circumstances, to use two or three particular examples to create a genus followed by a general

---

15 (1584) 3 Co Rep 7a.
16 [1980] AC 74, at 105; [1979] 1 All ER 286, at 289.
17 In fact, in a case of ambiguity the court may look to extrinsic aids (*infra*).
18 This cannot mean that the precise words that would have been used can be ascertained with total confidence, as the Court of Appeal pointed out in *Inland Revenue Commissioners v Trustees of Sir John Aird's Settlement* [1982] 2 All ER 929; [1982] 1 WLR 270.
19 *Kruhlak v Kruhlak* [1958] 2 QB 32; [1958] 1 All ER 154.
20 *Suffolk County Council v Mason* [1979] AC 705; [1979] 2 All ER 369; see p 47, *post*.
 1 *Qualter Hall & Co Ltd v Board of Trade* [1962] Ch 273; [1961] 3 All ER 389.
 2 See, generally, the full discussion of this topic by the House of Lords in *Black-Clawson International Ltd v Papierwerke Waldhof-Aschaffenburgh AG* [1975] AC 591; [1975] 1 All ER 810.

expression, such as "or other place", which has the effect of extending the operation of the enactment to all particular circumstances which are within the genus created.

The operation of the rule can best be illustrated by two examples. Section 1 of the Betting Act 1853 prohibited the keeping of a "house, office, room or other place" for betting with persons resorting thereto. In *Powell v Kempton Park Racecourse Co*[3] the point at issue was whether Tattersalls' ring at a racecourse was an "other place" within the meaning of the Act. The House of Lords held that it was not since the words "house, office, room" created a *genus* of indoor places within which a racecourse, being outdoor, did not fall. Similarly in *Brownsea Haven Properties Ltd v Poole Corporation*[4] it was held that regulations enabling a local authority to make orders for the direction of traffic "in all times of public processions, rejoicings, or illuminations, and in any case when the streets are thronged or liable to be obstructed" did not confer power to create a one-way traffic system for the six months of the summer holiday season.

It should be noted that there must be at least two specific words to create a genus. Thus where an Act referred to "theatres and other places of amusement" it was held that a funfair was within the Act even though not eiusdem generis with the word "theatres".[5]

d   *Penal provisions are construed narrowly*

Where a statute imposes criminal liability or tax obligations (which are treated as penal) and the statute is ambiguous or uncertain, it should be construed in favour of the individual.[6] Thus it has been held that the offence of "knowingly possessing an explosive" requires knowledge on the part of the accused that the substance possessed is explosive, not merely that he possesses the substance.[7] One aspect of this general rule is the presumption against the imposition of liability without fault.

However, this rule of interpretation is not strong enough to displace the literal rule. Consequently, where a statute unambiguously creates a criminal offence or a tax the court is bound to give effect to it, and the provision will be regarded as unambiguous if, in the judgment of the court, the intention of Parliament is clear, notwithstanding that the words are as a matter of semantics capable of bearing more than one meaning.[8]

---

3 [1899] AC 143; cf *Culley v Harrison* [1956] 2 QB 71; [1956] 2 All ER 254.
4 [1958] Ch 574; [1958] 1 All ER 205; see also *Director of Public Prosecutions v Jordan* [1977] AC 699; [1976] 3 All ER 775 (obscene publication justified "as being for the public good on the ground that it is in the interests of science, literature, art or learning, or of other objects of general concern" (Obscene Publications Act 1959, s 4(1)); the House of Lords held that "other objects of general concern", having regard to the preceding generic words, did not include the psychotherapeutic value of pornography to sexual deviants.
5 *Allen v Emmerson* [1944] 1 KB 362; [1944] 1 All ER 344. For a striking illustration of the operation of the rule see *Customs and Excise Commissioners v Savoy Hotel Ltd* [1966] 2 All ER 299; [1966] 1 WLR 948.
6 *Kingston-upon-Hull Dock Co v Browne* (1831) 2 B & Ad 43; *D'Avigdor-Goldsmid v Inland Revenue Commissioners* [1953] AC 347; [1953] 1 All ER 403.
7 *R v Hallam* [1957] 1 QB 569; [1957] 1 All ER 665.
8 See, for examples, *Director of Public Prosecutions v Ottewell* [1970] AC 642; [1968] 3 All ER 153; *Attorney-General's Reference (No 1 of 1988)* [1989] AC 971; [1989] 2 All ER 1; *Inland Revenue Commissioners v Hinchy* [1960] AC 748; [1960] 1 All ER 505, see p 34, *ante*.

e   Interpretation Act 1978

This Act, which consolidated with amendments the Interpretation Act 1889, prescribes definitions of certain words and phrases which are commonly encountered in Acts of Parliament. Thus:

> ". . . unless the contrary intention appears (a) words importing the masculine gender include the feminine; (b) words importing the feminine gender include the masculine; (c) words in the singular include the plural and words in the plural include the singular."[9]
>
> ". . . 'month' means calendar month".[10]

However these, and other, definitions are only presumptive and yield to a contrary intention, express or implied, in the Act being interpreted. Thus, although the word "person" is defined in Schedule 1 to the Interpretation Act to include a body corporate, it was held in one case that a corporation which undertook legal work was not guilty of the offence of acting as an unqualified "person" since the enactment in question could only apply to persons who could qualify as solicitors.[11]

4   Presumptions in construction

It is possible to express almost any rule of statutory interpretation in the form of a presumption. The rules against retrospective operation and against extraterritorial operation are often expressed as presumptions. The reasons for rules of statutory interpretation being described as presumptions is that their operation is rebutted by an express provision to the contrary in the Act itself. They thus have the quality of evidentiary presumptions. Nevertheless, although it is probably a mere matter of terminology, the following are always described as presumptions rather than as rules. However, care should be taken in their application: they are just a means to assist a court in finding the intention of Parliament.[12]

a   Presumption against alteration of the law

Parliament, like the judiciary, is presumed to know the law. Consequently if an Act does not expressly alter the law it will be presumed that Parliament did not intend it to have that effect. In the words of DEVLIN J:[13]

> "a statute is not to be taken as effecting a fundamental alteration in the general law unless it uses words which point unmistakably to that conclusion."

The decision of the House of Lords in *Beswick v Beswick*[14] is a paradigm of this presumption. Nevertheless it is important to remember that

---

9 Section 6. For an illustration of the application of this rule, see *Floor v Davis* [1980] AC 695; [1979] 2 All ER 677.

10 Section 5 and Sch 1.

11 *Law Society v United Service Bureau Ltd* [1934] 1 KB 343. This *lacuna* was filled by the Solicitors Act 1957 (now Solicitors Act 1974, s 20); see also *Penn-Texas Corporation v Murat-Anstalt (No 2)* [1964] 2 QB 647; [1964] 2 All ER 594.

12 *L'Office Cherifien des Phosphates v Yamashita-Shinnihon Steamship Co Ltd* [1994] 1 All ER 20; [1994] 2 WLR 39.

13 *National Assistance Board v Wilkinson* [1952] 2 QB 648, at p 661; [1952] 2 All ER 255, at p 260.

14 [1968] AC 58; [1967] 2 All ER 1197 (p 40, *ante*); see also *Black-Clawson International Ltd v Papierwerke Waldhof-Aschaffenburg AG* [1975] AC 591; [1975] 1 All ER 810.

Parliament can and does make fundamental alterations to the common law and, if such a change appears from a literal interpretation of the words used, the use of any presumption to the contrary is out of place. The presumption against fundamental change also applies in relation to statute law, one aspect being the presumption that a consolidating statute does not, simply by verbal alteration in the provision re-enacted, thereby introduce a fundamental change of meaning.[15] Conversely the mere fact that a statutory provision is re-enacted (whether by way of consolidation or otherwise) does not necessarily mean that Parliament is intending to give statutory force to judicial interpretations of the earlier enactment. The court must interpret the enactment as it stands though, if the scales were equally balanced, the fact that Parliament had re-enacted a provision which had been the subject of judicial interpretation might tip the balance in favour of that interpretation.[16]

b   Presumption against the imposition of liability without fault

This may be regarded as an aspect of the general presumption against fundamental change in the common law by mere implication. At common law *mens rea* is an element in all crimes,[17] though not in all torts. Although the legislature can, and frequently does, create offences of strict or absolute liability the intention so to do must be clear and unambiguous. LORD REID, in the leading case of *Sweet v Parsley*, explained the judicial approach as follows:[18]

> ". . . our first duty is to consider the words of the Act; if they show a clear intention to create an absolute offence, that is an end of the matter. But such cases are very rare. Sometimes the words of the section which creates a particular offence make it clear that *mens rea* is required in one form or another. Such cases are quite frequent. But in a very large number of cases there is no clear indication either way. In such cases there has for centuries been a presumption that Parliament did not intend to make criminals of persons who were in no way blameworthy in what they did. That means that, whenever a section is silent as to *mens rea*, there is a presumption that, in order to give effect to the will of Parliament, we must read in words appropriate to require *mens rea*."

An analogous presumption is that Parliament does not intend to create new criminal offences. This is of very limited application since, in the nature of things, when Parliament does intend to create a new criminal offence it will make that fact clear, in particular by specifying penalties for the offence. However, there is an ancient doctrine of "contempt of statute" under which breach of a statutory prohibition was an indictable misdemeanour. An unsuccessful attempt to invoke this doctrine was made in *R v Horseferry Road Justices, ex parte Independent Broadcasting Authority*,[19] the Queen's Bench divisional court holding that, while the offence

---

15 See *Beswick v Beswick* (*supra*); *Woolley v Woolley* [1968] P 29; [1966] 3 All ER 855.
16 See p 55, *post*.
17 See *R v Tolson* (1889) 23 QBD 168, at p 181; *Younghusband v Luftig* [1949] 2 KB 354; [1949] 2 All ER 72.
18 [1970] AC 132, at p 148; [1969] 1 All ER 347, at p 349; see also *R v Gould* [1968] 2 QB 65; [1968] 1 All ER 849.
19 [1987] QB 54; [1986] 2 All ER 666; the application of the IBA was to quash a summons issued on behalf of Mr Norris McWhirter, who alleged that transmission of images of him

might still exist, the inference that Parliament did not intend to create an offence in the absence of an express provision to that effect is, nowadays, "almost irresistible".

c Presumption against depriving a person of a vested right

In the absence of express provision the courts will not construe a statute as having the effect of depriving a person of a right vested in him before the statute came into operation. This is linked with the presumption against retrospective operation though it is more than an illustration of the latter presumption. For example, every person has a right to the use and enjoyment of his own land. The remedy for infringement of this right is an action in trespass or nuisance, depending on the character of the interference. Consequently where a statute authorises the performance of an act, which constitutes a nuisance to the plaintiff, the statute will not be construed as having the effect of removing the plaintiff's right unless it is clearly intended to have that effect.[20] Even stronger is the presumption against removing a right to compensation.[1] Nevertheless, this can be done expressly as evidenced by the War Damage Act 1965 which removed a right to compensation from the Crown in respect of damage to or destruction of property caused by the Crown in time of war, or in contemplation of the outbreak of war.[2]

d Presumption against ousting the jurisdiction of the courts

Individuals cannot, by contract, exclude the jurisdiction of the courts. Although Parliament may exclude an individual's recourse to the courts, the provision purporting so to do must be absolutely clear and unambiguous since the courts are extremely wary about permitting legislative or executive interference with their jurisdiction. The principle was stated by VISCOUNT SIMONDS as follows in *Pyx Granite Ltd v Ministry of Housing and Local Government*:[3]

> ". . . it is a principle not by any means to be whittled down that the subject's recourse to Her Majesty's courts for the determination of his rights is not to be excluded except by clear words. That is, as McNAIR J called it in *Francis v Yiewsley and West Drayton Urban District Council*[4] a

---

in the television programme "Spitting Image" infringed section 4(3) of the Broadcasting Act 1981, whereby the IBA was in contempt of statute.

20 *Metropolitan Asylum District Managers v Hill* (1881) 6 App Cas 193.

1 *Minister of Health v Stafford Corporation* [1952] Ch 730; [1952] 2 All ER 386. It was on this basis that the Court of Appeal held in *Allen v Thorn Electrical Industries Ltd* [1967] 1 QB 487; [1967] 2 All ER 1137 that the prohibition on pay increases introduced by the Prices and Incomes Act 1966 did not deprive the plaintiff of his right to an increase which had been agreed upon before the prohibition came into effect.

2 The right had been held to exist in *Burmah Oil Co Ltd v Lord Advocate* [1965] AC 75; [1964] 2 All ER 348.

3 [1960] AC 260, at p 286; [1959] 3 All ER 1, at p 6, cited with approval by LORD DONOVAN in *Ealing London Borough v Race Relations Board* [1972] AC 342, at p 353; [1972] 1 All ER 105, at p 108; the decision illustrates the application of the presumption in that the House of Lords held that the machinery established under the Race Relations Act 1968 for referring disputes to certain nominated county courts did not exclude the inherent jurisdiction of the High Court to make a declaration as to rights under the Act.

4 [1957] 2 QB 136, at p 148; the passage referred to does not appear in the report of the case in [1957] 1 All ER 825.

'fundamental rule' from which I would not for my part sanction any departure."

One application of this rule is the principle that a provision which expressly states that the decision of an inferior court, tribunal or administrative body shall be "final" does not exclude the prerogative jurisdiction of the High Court to review the decision:

". . . if a tribunal goes wrong in law and the error appears on the face of the record, the High Court will interfere by certiorari to quash the decision. It is not to be deterred by the enactment that the decision is 'final'. The decision may be final on the facts but it is not final on the law."[5]

e   Presumption that a statute does not bind the Crown

One of the few relics of the prerogative of the Crown is the rule that the Crown is not bound by a statute unless expressly named in it. The rule extends to the Crown and to its servants and agents though not to nationalised industries.[6] The Crown Proceedings Act 1947 placed the Crown, with certain exceptions, in the same position as a private person in the law of torts. Consequently, statutes which affect common law rights and duties are usually expressed to bind the Crown. Examples are the Limitation Act 1980 and the Occupiers' Liability Act 1957. In practice the general trend of modern legislation is towards the removal of the Crown's privileges and immunities.[7]

5   Material aids to construction

The distinction between interpretation and construction has already been noted. All statutes require interpretation but only statutes whose provisions are ambiguous or uncertain in extent require construction, though the processes of interpretation and construction are inextricably interrelated.

Judges frequently make no attempt to distinguish the processes of interpretation and construction. The distinction is, however, material since not all aids to construction are legitimate aids to interpretation. Thus the aids to construction which do not form part of the enactment may only be consulted where the process of interpretation has disclosed an uncertainty or an ambiguity.

There are two classes of aids to construction; internal aids and external aids.

a   Internal aids

An internal (or intrinsic) aid is an aid which is to be found within the Queen's Printer's copy of the statute itself. Those parts of the statute which form part of the enactment must, of course, be consulted as part of the general process

---

5 *Tehrani v Rostron* [1972] 1 QB 182, at p 187; [1971] 3 All ER 790, at p 793, *per* LORD DENNING MR; see also *R v Medical Appeal Tribunal, ex parte Gilmore* [1957] 1 QB 574; sub nom *Re Gilmore's Application* [1957] 1 All ER 796, where the earlier authorities are reviewed; *Sagnata Investments Ltd v Norwich Corporation* [1971] 2 QB 614; [1971] 2 All ER 1441. See also p 125, *post*.

6 *Tamlin v Hannaford* [1950] 1 KB 18; [1949] 2 All ER 327; for an account of the history of this presumption, and a recent illustration of its operation, see *Lord Advocate v Dumbarton District Council* [1990] 2 AC 580; [1990] 1 All ER 1.

7 See *Madras Electric Supply Corporation (in liquidation) v Boarland (Inspector of Taxes)* [1955] AC 667; [1955] 1 All ER 753.

of interpretation in applying the general rule that the statute must be read as a whole. Other parts of the Queen's Printer's copy are not aids to interpretation though some, but not all, are aids to construction. There has not, however, been a universal judicial adherence to these basic principles and the modern tendency is to regard those parts of the statute which are not strictly part of the enactment, that is to say punctuation, headings and marginal notes, as aids to construction in cases of ambiguity. Thus in *Director of Public Prosecutions v Schildkamp* LORD REID stated:[8]

". . . it may be more realistic to accept the Act as printed as being the product of the whole legislative process, and to give due weight to everything found in the printed Act. I say more realistic because in very many cases the provision before the court was never even mentioned in debate in either House, and it may be that its wording was never closely scrutinised by any member of either House. In such a case it is not very meaningful to say that the words of the Act represent the intention of Parliament but that punctuation, cross-headings and sidenotes do not.

So if the authorities are equivocal and one is free to deal with the whole matter I would not object to taking all these matters into account provided that we realise that they cannot have equal weight with the words of the Act. Punctuation can be of some assistance in construction. A cross-heading ought to indicate the scope of the sections which follow it. But a sidenote is a poor guide to the scope of the section for it can do no more than indicate the main subject with which the section deals."

It is necessary to identify and distinguish the constituent parts of a statute.

Long title — The long title of an Act begins with the words "an Act" and goes on to describe the general effect of the Act. Thus the Act whose short title is the "Law of Property Act 1925" has the long title; "An Act to consolidate the enactments relating to Conveyancing and the Law of Property in England and Wales". It might be supposed that the insertion of a long title would afford Parliament the opportunity of stating its general intention in passing the Act, but in fact long titles tend to be succinct rather than explanatory and generally do little more than identify the subject matter of the Act. Their insertion would appear to rest rather on tradition than on utility.

Until the nineteenth century the long title was not part of the Act itself and was therefore not regarded as a legitimate aid to interpretation. The modern long title, however, is part of the enactment and may be the subject of debate and amendment in Parliament. Consequently, it may be regarded as a legitimate aid both to interpretation and construction. A Master of the Rolls observed in 1899:[9]

"I read the title advisedly because now and for some years past the title of an Act of Parliament has been part of the Act. In the old days it used not to be so, and in the old books we are told not to regard it, but now the title is an important part of the Act and is so treated by both Houses of Parliament."

Although the long title is part of the Act, it is a minor aid to construction. There have been conspicuously few cases in which it has been consulted and it certainly cannot prevail over an express provision in the body of the Act.

---

8 [1971] AC 1, at p 10; [1969] 3 All ER 1640, at p 1641; see also *Limb & Co (Stevedores) v British Transport Docks Board* [1971] 1 All ER 828; [1971] 1 WLR 311.
9 LINDLEY MR in *Fielding v Morley Corporation* [1899] 1 Ch 1. at p 3; see also *Vacher & Sons Ltd v London Society of Compositors* [1913] AC 107; *R v Delmayne* [1970] 2 QB 170; [1969] 2 All ER 980.

Thus "an Act to amend the law with respect to wills of personal estate made by British subjects" (Wills Act 1861) was held to apply to the will of an alien.[10] The long title should not be confused with the preamble though, now that preambles are rarely encountered, judges do occasionally describe the long title as the preamble.[11]

Short title — This is the title by which Acts are commonly, and properly, cited. In theory the short title is a valid aid both to interpretation and to construction, but there appears to be no reported case in which the short title has been used to determine a point of construction, though reference has sometimes been made to it. The short title could certainly not be used to introduce ambiguity into the body of the Act and, indeed, the short titles of certain Acts do not reflect the content of the Act accurately. The Criminal Procedure Act 1865, for example, applies to both civil and criminal proceedings.

Preamble — The preamble is that part of the statute which precedes the enacting words and sets out the reason for the statute being passed, for example the mischief which the statute is passed to remedy. In old cases great weight was attached to the preamble as an aid to construction.[12] Important Acts such as the Statute of Uses 1535, the Statute of Frauds 1677 and the Parliament Act 1911 have long and instructive preambles. Probably the best known preamble is that of the Charitable Uses Act 1601 which is still regarded as containing the criteria to be adopted when considering whether a particular object is a "charitable" one.[13] Where a statute has a preamble, it traditionally begins with the word "whereas". Modern statutes, however, rarely contain a preamble and where one is included it is generally too brief to be of assistance.[14] Consequently the preamble is of little importance as an aid to construction. Although the preamble is part of the enactment, like the long title, it cannot be introduced to create an ambiguity in the body of the Act.

Headings — A section or group of sections in an Act may be preceded by a heading. Such headings are not part of the enactment and for that reason logic would suggest their exclusion. Notwithstanding, headings are often consulted as an aid to construction where the enactment is uncertain or ambiguous.[15] The modern judicial tendency appears to be to treat a heading as if it were a preamble.[16] In *Director of Public Prosecutions v Schildkamp*[17] LORD UPJOHN was in favour of according

---

10 *Re Groos* [1904] P 269; see also *R v Bates* [1952] 2 All ER 842; on appeal sub nom *R v Russell* [1953] 1 WLR 77; *R v Galvin* [1987] QB 862; [1987] 2 All ER 851.

11 Eg WINN LJ in *Crook v Edmondson* [1966] 2 QB 81, at p 89; [1966] 1 All ER 833, at p 835; BAKER J in *Limb & Co (Stevedores) v British Transport Docks Board (supra)*.

12 *Belasco v Hannant* (1862) 3 B & S 13; *Sussex Peerage Case* (1844) 11 Cl & Fin 85.

13 See, for example, *Incorporated Council of Law Reporting for England and Wales v A-G* [1971] Ch 626; [1971] 1 All ER 436; *McGovern v A-G* [1982] Ch 321; [1981] 3 All ER 493.

14 Compare secondary legislation of the European Communities which invariably has a long preamble; for the reasons for this, see p 56, *post*.

15 For an instructive case see *Crook v Edmondson* [1966] 2 QB 81; [1966] 1 All ER 833 in which the words "immoral purposes" were construed in the light of the group of sections of the Sexual Offences Act 1956 in which those words occurred; see also *Beswick v Beswick* [1968] AC 58; [1967] 2 All ER 1197 (p 43, *ante*).

16 *Martins v Fowler* [1926] AC 746; *Re Carlton* [1945] Ch 372; [1945] 2 All ER 370n, CA; *Qualter, Hall & Co Ltd v Board of Trade* [1962] Ch 273; [1961] 3 All ER 389.

17 [1971] AC 1; [1969] 3 All ER 1640.

greater weight to headings than were the other law lords, and accordingly observed:[18]

> "In my opinion, it is wrong to confine their role to the resolution of ambiguities in the body of the Act. When the court construing the Act is reading it through to understand it, it must read the cross-headings as well as the body of the Act and that will always be a useful pointer as to the intention of Parliament in enacting the immediately following sections. Whether the cross-heading is no more than a pointer or label or is helpful in assisting to construe or even in some cases to control the meaning or ambit of those sections must necessarily depend on the circumstances of each case."

Marginal notes — Marginal notes are not part of an Act and are inserted by the draftsman purely for facility of reference. It has happened that a marginal note has borne no relation to the content of a section which had been considerably altered during the passage of the Bill.[19] For this reason the old rule was that marginal notes were not regarded as a legitimate aid to construction, even in the event of ambiguity.[20] Nevertheless there have been cases in which the court has clearly adverted to the marginal note in construing a section.[1] Thus UPJOHN LJ observed in one case:[2]

> "While the marginal note to a section cannot control the language used in the section, it is at least permissible to approach a consideration of its general purpose and the mischief at which it is aimed with the note in mind."

In the light of the speeches of the House of Lords in *Director of Public Prosecutions v Schildkamp (supra)*, it would seem that the court is entitled to look at marginal notes in cases of ambiguity, though they clearly carry little weight and certainly cannot displace a meaning which appears from the enactment proper.[3]

Punctuation — Before 1850 Acts of Parliament were not punctuated; even after that punctuation was left to the draftsman and not scrutinised by Parliament. Accordingly there was some old authority for the proposition that punctuation could not be taken into account as an aid to construction. However the courts now adopt a far more realistic attitude and, following the observations of LORD REID in *Director of Public Prosecutions v Schildkamp (supra)*, the House of Lords has held[4] that punctuation can and should be taken into account by judges in interpreting statutes.

Interpretation sections — It is a relatively modern drafting technique to include an interpretation section in an Act, and nowadays most Acts include at least one such section. Although an interpretation section is as much a part of the Act as any other section, the interpretation of a word

---

18 [1971] AC at 28; [1969] 3 All ER at 1656.
19 Married Women (Maintenance in Case of Desertion) Act 1886, s 1(2).
20 See *R v Bates* [1952] 2 All ER 842; on appeal sub nom *R v Russell* [1953] 1 WLR 77; *Chandler v Director of Public Prosecutions* [1964] AC 763; [1962] 3 All ER 142.
 1 Eg, *Pride of Derby and Derbyshire Angling Association Ltd v British Celanese Ltd* [1953] Ch 149; [1952] 1 All ER 179; *R v Vickers* [1957] 2 QB 664; [1957] 2 All ER 741; *Tudor Grange Holdings Ltd v Citibank NA* [1992] Ch 53; [1991] 4 All ER 1.
 2 *Stephens v Cuckfield Rural District Council* [1960] 2 QB 373, at p 383; *Limb & Co (Stevedores) v British Transport Docks Board* [1971] 1 All ER 828; [1971] 1 WLR 311 (*supra*).
 3 See *R v Kelt* [1977] 3 All ER 1099; [1977] 1 WLR 1365.
 4 *Hanlon v The Law Society* [1981] AC 124; [1980] 2 All ER 199; see also *Bodden v Commissioner of Police of the Metropolis* [1990] 2 QB 397; [1989] 3 All ER 833.

depends rather on its context than on the interpretation section, and, in any event, if there is an inconsistency between an interpretation section and the body of an Act the latter prevails.

This is especially so when the interpretation section uses the word "includes". In this case the interpretation section will be regarded as extending rather than restricting the normal meaning of the words in question. Thus where an interpretation section defined "street" by stating that it "should apply to and include any highway, not being a turnpike road", the Court of Appeal held that the word "street" could include a turnpike road since the interpretation section extended rather than restricted the ordinary and natural meaning of the word.[5]

Schedules — Schedules are part of the enactment if expressly incorporated by a section in the Act itself. They are used (*inter alia*) for prescribing forms, furnishing illustrations, listing repeals effected by the Act and setting out transitional provisions. They cannot be regarded as altering or enlarging the ordinary meaning of words used in the Act. In *Ellerman Lines Ltd v Murray*[6] the House of Lords, in interpreting an Act passed to give effect to an international convention, steadfastly refused to look at a Schedule to the Act in which was set out the text of the convention because the words of the Act were unambiguous. It is to be presumed that the House would have considered the Schedule, had the Act been uncertain or ambiguous, in order to apply the mischief rule.[7] If the situation which arose in *Ellerman Lines Ltd v Murray* were to arise at the present day the contrary approach would be adopted, and indeed, the case itself was disapproved by the House of Lords in *James Buchanan & Co Ltd v Babco Forwarding and Shipping (UK) Ltd.*[8] With the increasing number of statutes which are passed to implement international conventions a new difficulty has arisen; that is that the convention (which is part of the enactment) is sometimes in a foreign language and, indeed, is sometimes set out in more than one language. The House of Lords grappled with this difficulty, in construing the French and English texts of the Warsaw Convention contained in Schedule 1 to the Carriage by Air Act 1961, in *Fothergill v Monarch Airlines Ltd.*[9] Reversing the decision of the Court of Appeal, it held that a loss of articles from a suitcase constituted "damage" to baggage. This conclusion was reached by not applying a literal interpretation of the word "damage" but rather a purposive one and by looking at extrinsic sources so as to ascertain that the word "avarie" (used in the French text) is capable of meaning "loss" as well as "damage".

---

5 *Nutter v Accrington Local Board of Health* (1878) 4 QBD 375.
6 [1931] AC 126.
7 See *Salomon v Customs and Excise Commissioners* [1967] 2 QB 116; [1966] 3 All ER 871. In *Corocraft Ltd v Pan American Airways Inc* [1969] 1 QB 616; [1969] 1 All ER 82 there was no ambiguity or uncertainty in the English Act but the Court of Appeal nevertheless adopted the text of the Convention (the meaning of which differed from that of the Act, the Carriage by Air Act 1932), distinguishing *Ellerman Lines Ltd v Murray* on the basis that in that case the intention of Parliament had been to give effect to the English text of the Convention whereas in the present case the intention was to give effect to the original Convention. There is a presumption that Parliament intends to fulfil, rather than break, its international obligations; cf *The Andrea Ursula* [1973] QB 265; [1971] 1 All ER 821.
8 [1978] AC 141; [1977] 3 All ER 1048.
9 [1981] AC 251; [1980] 2 All ER 696. The 1961 Act, s 1(2) expressly provides that in the event of inconsistency between the English and French texts, the latter is to prevail.

The Consumer Credit Act 1974 utilised a novel concept in Parliamentary drafting – the use of examples. Section 188(1) provides that "Schedule 2 shall have effect for illustrating the use of terminology employed in this Act" and that Schedule contains 24 examples, each expressed in the form of a set of facts and an analysis of the application of the new terminology to those facts. The examples are expressed not to be exhaustive and section 188(3) provides that in the case of conflict between Schedule 2 and any other provision of the Act, the latter shall prevail.

b External aids

An external (or extrinsic) aid to construction is an aid which is not to be found in the Queen's Printer's copy of the Act. Since the function of the courts is to ascertain the intention of the legislature, it might be thought that they would readily refer to statements made in Parliament as to the intention of the member or party introducing the Bill. In fact the reverse was until recently the case. The reports of debates on the Bill in its passage through Parliament were, until recently, rigidly excluded[10] as explanatory memoranda upon the effects of the Act, where these are issued, still are.[11] However, in 1993 the House of Lords in *Pepper v Hart*[12] reconsidered the position, and held (LORD MACKAY L C dissenting) that in certain circumstances a court should be entitled to refer to parliamentary materials. The pre-conditions for the exercise of this power were stated as follows by LORD BROWNE-WILKINSON:

> ". . . the exclusionary rule should be relaxed so as to permit reference to parliamentary materials where: (a) legislation is ambiguous or obscure, or leads to an absurdity; (b) the material relied upon consists of one or more statements by a minister or other promoter of the Bill together if necessary

---

10 *Assam Railways and Trading Co Ltd v Inland Revenue Commissioners* [1935] AC 445; In *Beswick v Beswick* [1968] AC 58, at p 74; [1967] 2 All ER 1197, at p 1202 reasons advanced for the rule were that it would add to the time and expense of preparing cases if counsel had to read all the debates in Hansard and that reports of debates in select committees are not available to the public. In *Davis v Johnson* [1979] AC 264; [1978] 1 All ER 1132, the House of Lords unanimously reaffirmed the rule that Hansard can never be relied upon by counsel in any court and can never be relied upon by the court in construing a statute or for any other purpose. However, in *Pickstone v Freemans plc* [1989] AC 66; [1988] 2 All ER 803 the House of Lords, in construing regulations made under s 2(2) of the European Communities Act 1972 for the purpose of implementing a Community obligation of the United Kingdom (as to which see p 102, *post*), in circumstances where the regulations had not been subject to any process of amendment by Parliament, was prepared to consider the explanations of the government and the criticisms voiced by members of Parliament (by reference to Hansard) as providing some indication of the intentions of Parliament.

11 *London County Council v Central Land Board* [1959] Ch 386; [1958] 1 All ER 806. However, in *Sagnata Investments Ltd v Norwich Corporation* [1971] 2 QB 614; [1971] 2 All ER 1441, LORD DENNING MR did refer to Hansard, Parliamentary Debates when considering the mischief intended to be remedied by the Betting, Gaming and Lotteries Act 1963, Sch 6 and did so again in *R v Greater London Council, ex parte Blackburn* [1976] 3 All ER 184; [1976] 1 WLR 550 (albeit having first said "I know that we are not supposed to do this"). In *Pickstone v Freemans plc (supra)* LORD OLIVER said that, though an explanatory note attached to the regulations was not part of the regulations, it was "of use in identifying the mischief which the regulations were attempting to remedy".

12 [1993] AC 593; [1993] 1 All ER 42.

with such other parliamentary material as is necessary to understand such statements, and their effect; (c) the statements relied upon are clear."

The objection that by so referring to parliamentary materials the courts would be in breach of Article 9 of the Bill of Rights 1688 was rejected. This provision, which prohibits the calling into question of anything said in proceedings in Parliament, did not prevent the courts using such materials as an aid to construction, and it was not upon this point that LORD MACKAY dissented. His dissenting speech highlighted his concerns about the effect the change proposed by the majority of the House would have on the costs of litigation, and feared that these would be immensely increased by the onerous task of researching the record of parliamentary proceedings in Hansard. The number of reported decisions using parliamentary materials as an aid to construction gives some support to LORD MACKAY's concerns.[13]

Perhaps the most striking example of the rule excluding the use of extrinsic aids to construction is the case of *Ellerman Lines Ltd v Murray*, noted above, where the House of Lords refused to look at the text of an international convention when interpreting a statute passed to give effect to that convention. However, in the event of ambiguity, it is now clearly established that, when construing a statute passed to give effect to a treaty obligation or to enact matters agreed at an international convention, the court is entitled to look at the convention to ascertain what Parliament must have intended.[14] Thus it probably makes no difference whether the text of the convention is scheduled to the Act or not. Where the convention is printed in more than one language (as will usually be the case) it is permissible to look at foreign texts as well as the English text, although the majority of the House of Lords in *James Buchanan & Co Ltd v Babco Forwarding and Shipping (UK) Ltd*[15] expressed the view that this was only permissible if the English text was ambiguous. This principle and the presumption that Parliament intends to fulfil its international obligations is of considerable practical importance now that the courts are so often called upon to construe legislation passed to implement the instruments of the European Community Institutions.

It may be observed that most continental countries adopt the opposite approach and encourage consultation of the parliamentary and political history of the statute. These materials are known as *travaux préparatoires* and are an invaluable aid to the task of discovering the intention of continental legislatures. In *Gatoil International Inc v Arkwright-Boston*

---

13 See, *eg, Warwickshire County Council v Johnson* [1993] 1 All ER 299 (reference made to Minister's speech in debate on a proposed amendment to s 20 Consumer Protection Act 1987); *Stubbings v Webb* [1993] 1 All ER 322 (reference made to the speech of the chairman of the Committee upon whose report the Limitation Act 1980, s 11 was based).

14 *The Banco* [1971] P 137; [1971] 1 All ER 524; cf the cases cited in fn 7, p 50, *ante*.

15 [1978] AC 141; [1977] 3 All ER 1048; LORD WILBERFORCE was in favour of consulting the foreign text for assistance, "if assistance is needed" without first discovering ambiguity in the English text, but if there were no ambiguity (or, at least, uncertainty) in the English text, it is difficult to see why assistance would be needed; cf *Fothergill v Monarch Airlines Ltd* [1981] AC 251; [1980] 2 All ER 696 (see p 50, *ante*) where some members of the House appear to have regarded the word "damage" as ambiguous in its context; but since the French text was the primary text, it could clearly have been relied upon by the parties whether the English text was ambiguous or not and the court would be bound to give effect to the French text. This is an important distinction between the two cases.

Manufacturers Mutual Insurance Co[16] the House of Lords decided that in construing an Act passed to implement an international convention, it was appropriate to consider *travaux préparatoires* relating to the convention for the purpose of resolving any ambiguity in the Act. In *Greenwich London Borough Council v Powell*[17] the House of Lords, in considering whether a caravan site provided by a local authority for the accommodation of gipsies was a "protected site" within section 5(1) of the Mobile Homes Act 1983 (thereby entitling the occupants to security of tenure), considered a Department of Environment circular as indicative of the policy underlying the legislation. However, although the general rule in relation to external aids is one of exclusion,[18] there are certain legitimate external aids to construction and these are set out below.

Dictionaries — Words in statutes are presumed to bear their ordinary and natural meaning and it is legitimate to consult a dictionary to ascertain the meaning of words which have no particular legal meaning. Thus in *Re Rippon (Highfield) Housing Confirmation Order 1938*[19] the court adopted the Oxford English Dictionary definition of the word "park". Nevertheless dictionaries bear only slight weight and, in context, the dictionary meaning may not be the one which Parliament presumably intended. Thus in *Mills v Cooper*[20] a divisional court rejected the Shorter Oxford English Dictionary definition of a "gypsy" while in *Thornton v Fisher & Ludlow Ltd*[1] the same dictionary's definition of a "passage" was not adopted. Words and phrases which have a particular legal meaning are described as "terms of art" and do not necessarily bear the meaning which laymen would attribute to them.[2] In interpreting a foreign text of a convention, the court is entitled to consult foreign dictionaries, textbooks and articles and, indeed, to receive expert evidence.[3]

Reports of committees — Reports of the Law Commissions, Law Reform

---

16 [1985] AC 255; [1985] 1 All ER 129. Note also s 3(3) of the Civil Jurisdiction and Judgments Act 1982 which expressly provides that in interpreting the conventions implemented by that Act, the court may consider certain reports by named individuals (which are reproduced in the Official Journal of the Communities).

17 [1989] AC 995; [1989] 1 All ER 65.

18 The Law Commission report, *The Interpretation of Statutes* (1969, Law Com No 21) recommended the admission of extrinsic material, other than reports of Parliamentary proceedings. LORD SIMON more than once advocated reference to parliamentary proceedings and other preparatory material as an aid to judicial interpretation of statutes (cf *McMillan v Crouch* [1972] 3 All ER 61, at p 76; [1972] 1 WLR 1102, at p 1119; *Charter v Race Relations Board* [1973] AC 868, at p 900; [1973] 1 All ER 512, at p 527) but his views on this topic attracted little support.

19 [1939] 2 KB 838; [1939] 3 All ER 548.

20 [1967] 2 QB 459; [1967] 2 All ER 100.

1 [1968] 2 All ER 241; [1968] 1 WLR 655; see also *A-G's Reference (No 1 of 1988)* [1989] AC 971; [1989] 2 All ER 1, where the Oxford English Dictionary's first meaning of the word "obtained" was rejected by the House of Lords, with the result that the appellant was guilty of insider dealing even if the confidential information came to him without any positive action on his part.

2 See *Sydall v Castings Ltd* [1967] 1 QB 302; [1966] 3 All ER 770, on the construction of the word "descendants" as a term of art; see also *Barclays Bank Ltd v Cole* [1967] 2 QB 738; [1966] 3 All ER 948, on the meaning of the word "fraud" and compare *Lloyds Bank Ltd v Marcan* [1973] 2 All ER 359; [1973] 1 WLR 339 where PENNYCUICK V-C gave a much wider meaning to the word "defraud" in s 172(1) of the Law of Property Act 1925 on the basis that the section was replacing a provision in an Act of 1571 in which the words "hinder, delay or defraud" were used.

3 *Fothergill v Monarch Airlines Ltd (supra)*.

Committees and similar bodies are legitimate aids to discovering the state of the pre-existing law and the mischief which the statute was passed to remedy.[4] Once again, however, if the words of a statute are unambiguous, it is not legitimate to interpret them otherwise in order to accord with the recommendations of a Committee which preceded its passing.[5] Thus in *Letang v Cooper*[6] the Court of Appeal held that the words "negligence, nuisance or breach of duty" in the Law Reform (Limitation of Actions, &c) Act 1954 were wide enough to embrace the tort of trespass to the person even though the Tucker Committee report,[7] which preceded the 1954 Act, expressed an intention to exclude this form of action from the shorter limitation period recommended in that report.

Other statutes — Where the words of one statute are ambiguous or uncertain, assistance as to their meaning may sometimes be gained from consideration of the way in which similar words have been used in other statutes, provided that they are *in pari materia* with the provision under consideration. Thus in *R v Wheatley*[8] the question before the Court of Appeal, Criminal Division, was whether a metal pipe bomb filled with fire-dampened sodium chlorate mixed with sugar was an "explosive" substance within the meaning of section 4 of the Explosive Substances Act 1883. The defendant's expert evidence was to the effect that the materials would produce only a pyrotechnic effect, and not an explosive one. The trial judge directed the jury that this was no defence, having regard to the definition of "explosive" in section 3(1) of the Explosives Act 1875, which included a substance used with a view to producing a "pyrotechnic effect". It was held that this direction was correct since, having regard to the long title of the 1883 Act ("An Act to amend the Law relating to Explosive Substances"), that Act was intended to amend, *inter alia*, the 1875 Act and both Acts were *in pari materia*. It followed that what was an explosive substance within section 4 of the 1883 Act was to be determined by applying the definition of "explosive" in section 3(1) of the 1875 Act.

c   Judicial precedents

The application of the doctrine of judicial precedent to the interpretation of statutes was explained as follows by LORD UPJOHN:[9]

> "It is quite clear that judicial statements as to the construction and intention of an Act must never be allowed to supplant or supersede its proper construction and courts must beware of falling into the error of treating the law to be that

---

4 See, for example, *Rookes v Barnard* [1964] AC 1129; [1964] 1 All ER 367; *National Provincial Bank Ltd v Ainsworth* [1965] AC 1175; [1965] 2 All ER 472; *Black-Clawson International Ltd v Papierwerke Waldhof-Aschaffenburg AG* [1975] AC 591; [1975] 1 All ER 810. In *A-G's Reference (No 1 of 1988)* (p 53, *ante*) the House of Lords considered two White Papers for the purpose of ascertaining the mischief at which the Company Securities (Insider Dealing) Act 1985 was aimed.
5 *Black-Clawson International Ltd v Papierwerke Waldhof-Aschaffenburg AG (supra)*.
6 [1965] 1 QB 232; [1964] 2 All ER 929.
7 Cmd 7740. In *Sagnata Investments Ltd v Norwich Corporation* (p 51, *ante*) LORD DENNING MR in considering the legislative history of the Betting, Gaming and Lotteries Act 1963, took into account the recommendations of the Royal Commission on Betting, Lotteries and Gaming (Cmd 8190 of 1951).
8 [1979] 1 All ER 954; [1979] 1 WLR 144.
9 *Ogden Industries Pty Ltd v Lucas* [1970] AC 113, at p 127; [1969] 1 All ER 121, at p 126.

laid down by the judge in construing the Act rather than found in the Act itself. No doubt a decision on particular words binds inferior courts on the construction of those words on similar facts, but beyond that the observations of judges on the construction of statutes may be of the greatest help and guidance but are entitled to no more than respect and cannot absolve the court from its duty in exercising an independent judgment."

Thus where a superior court has interpreted the words of an Act, an inferior court in the hierarchy is bound to adopt that interpretation if faced with the same words in the same Act. Similarly the Court of Appeal is bound to follow its own previous decision upon the interpretation of a statute to the same extent as it is bound to follow any other of its previous decisions. The position is less clear if the later court is called upon to interpret the same or similar words in another part of the same Act or in another Act. In this event the earlier decision may be referred to if the two provisions in the Acts in question are *in pari materia* (deal with the same subject matter). This occurs most commonly when the later Act is a consolidating statute and the earlier Act is one of those repealed and consolidated. However, even in the case of consolidation Acts, the court is not bound by a precedent based upon an earlier Act consolidated by the Act under construction. The correct approach is for the court to interpret the Act in accordance with the usual principles of statutory interpretation. Only where there is a real or substantial difficulty or ambiguity should the court refer to the legislation which has been repealed or precedents based upon that legislation.[10]

Similarly, if the later Act employs words or phrases which have been the subject of judicial interpretation in an earlier Act dealing with the same subject matter it may be inferred that they are intended to bear the same meaning, on the basis that Parliament is presumed to know the law.[11] For example, the House of Lords, in assigning a meaning to the word "wreck" in the Merchant Shipping Act 1925, adopted the interpretation of that word which had been given in a case decided on the wording of the Merchant Shipping Act 1894.[12] It is, however, no more than a possible inference and it must not be supposed that by re-enacting a statutory provision which has been the subject of judicial interpretation Parliament is thereby, in effect, giving statutory force to that interpretation. If it is a wrong interpretation then (provided it is not binding on the court in accordance with the doctrine of precedent) a court is perfectly free to disregard it.[13] Moreover, where the earlier decision is upon similar words in a statute which is not *in pari materia* with the statute requiring

---

10 *Farrell v Alexander* [1977] AC 59; [1976] 2 All ER 721; *R v Heron* [1982] 1 All ER 993; [1982] 1 WLR 451.
11 Cf *Maxwell on Interpretation of Statutes* (11th Edn, 1962) p 303, cited with approval in *R v Freeman* [1970] 2 All ER 413; [1970] 1 WLR 788 in which the Court of Appeal held that, since there was no relevant distinction between the definition of "firearm" in s 57(1) of the Firearms Act 1968 and the definitions in earlier Firearms Acts, Parliament must be taken to have adopted in the 1968 Act the interpretation which had been placed on the definition in the Firearms Act 1920.
12 *The Olympic* [1913] P 92; *Barras v Aberdeen Steam Trawling and Fishing Co Ltd* [1933] AC 402.
13 See *Dun v Dun* [1959] AC 272; [1959] 2 All ER 134; *Farrell v Alexander (supra)*; *R v Chard* [1984] AC 279; [1983] 3 All ER 637 (in which the House of Lords expressly

interpretation, or where the words are used in a different context, that decision is of little, if any, value.[14]

6   Interpretation of European Community legislation

The rules, refinements, technicalities and artifices which English courts have developed over the centuries in their approach to the interpretation of statutes have been described above. They have led to, and sprung from, the meticulous care which is exercised in the drafting of our legislation. Community legislation is not drafted in the same mould. It is expressed (as the domestic legislation of the other Community countries tends to be drafted) in terms of broad principle, leaving the courts to supply the detail by giving effect, in particular cases, to the general intention of the institution that has enacted the instrument in question. Thus regulations, Directives and Decisions of the Council and of the Commission have to state the reasons on which they have been based and have to refer to any proposals or opinions which were required to be obtained pursuant to the Treaties.[15] These reasons are normally set out in the preamble to the instrument in question.

Accordingly, in terms of the traditional approaches to interpretation which have been adopted in this country, the "literal rule" plays little or no part in the Community legislation, the purposive approach being the appropriate one. English judges are required to apply a European approach in the interpretation of Community law, making references of points of law to the Court of Justice when necessary or required.[16] In addition, the requirements of Community law may require a United Kingdom statute to be construed in a particular way. Both these matters are returned to later.[17]

---

disapproved *dicta* to the contrary in *Barras v Aberdeen Steam Trawling and Fishing Co Ltd* (*supra*)).
14 *London Corporation v Cusack-Smith* [1955] AC 337; [1955] 1 All ER 302; *Goodrich v Paisner* [1957] AC 65; [1956] 2 All ER 176.
15 EC Treaty, Art 190.
16 See p 113, *post*.
17 See p 109, *post*.

CHAPTER 3

Law Reports and Precedents

A THE RELATIONSHIP BETWEEN LAW REPORTS AND THE DOCTRINE OF PRECEDENT

The operation of the doctrine of precedent is inextricably bound up with law reporting. The rule is that any decision may be cited to a court provided that it is vouched for by a barrister, solicitor or person with a Supreme Court qualification[1] who was present when judgment was delivered. In addition, since judges take judicial notice of the whole of English law, an individual judge may rely upon a precedent of which he is aware even though the decision is unreported. There is, thus, no rule that a case may only be cited or relied upon as a precedent if it is reported. Nevertheless personal recollection is so impermanent and haphazard that it could not possibly form the basis of a workable system.

Hence precedents are almost always contained in law reports. The close nexus between law reporting and the doctrine of judicial precedent is evidenced by the fact that the modern doctrine of binding precedent was formulated only when an integrated system of law reporting evolved in the nineteenth century.

In the face of the undoubted principle that reported and unreported cases are of equal authority some observations of LORD DIPLOCK (with which all the other members of the House concurred) in *Roberts Petroleum Ltd v Bernard Kenny Ltd*[2] caused considerable consternation among some sections of the profession. After referring to a growing practice of citing unreported decisions of the Court of Appeal,[3] LORD DIPLOCK went on:

> "My Lords, in my opinion, the time has come when your Lordships should adopt the practice of declining to allow transcipts of unreported judgments of the Civil Division of the Court of Appeal to be cited on the hearing of appeals to this House unless leave is given to do so, and that such leave should only be granted on counsel's giving an assurance that the transcript contains a statement of some principle of law, relevant to an issue in the appeal to this House, that is binding on the Court of Appeal and of which

---

1 Courts and Legal Services Act 1990, s 115. See pp 209–211, *post*.
2 [1983] 2 AC 192, at pp 200–202; [1983] 1 All ER 564, at pp 566–568.
3 Transcripts of judgments of the Court of Appeal and House of Lords are filed in the Supreme Court Library in London.

the substance, as distinct from the mere choice, of phraseology, is not to be found in one of the generalised or specialised series of reports."

It is important to distinguish a law report from a court record. The court record contains, basically, the names of the parties, the pleadings and the decision or order of the court. A law report contains most of these and, in addition, the judgment of the court containing the reasoning upon which the decision has been based. It is this reasoning which is the important element in the decision for the purposes of the doctrine of precedent. For this reason court records, such as the Plea Rolls, copies of which dating from the twelfth century are preserved in the Public Record Office, are of little value as precedents.

One might suppose that, because law reports are fundamental to the doctrine of precedent which is the cornerstone of the English legal system, the courts would have created a methodical system of producing law reports. It is an extraordinary anomaly that this has never been done. Law reporting has been left entirely to private enterprise so that, even at the present day, there is an element of chance and individual preference in the matter of whether or not a case is reported.

The historical evolution of the modern system of law reporting is considered below, but first the operation of the precedent system requires detailed examination.

B   THE OPERATION OF THE DOCTRINE OF PRECEDENT

1   The doctrine of binding precedent

The traditional view of the function of an English judge is that it is not to make law but to decide cases in accordance with existing legal rules. This gives rise to the doctrine of binding precedent whereby the judge is not merely referred to earlier decisions for guidance; he is bound to apply the rules of law contained in those decisions. The operation of the doctrine depends upon the hierarchy of the courts. All courts stand in a definite relationship to one another. A court is bound by decisions of a court above itself in the hierarchy and, usually, by a court of equivalent standing. Given that the doctrine of precedent has binding force within this framework, the question naturally arises of how the law may develop if cases are always to be determined according to ageless principles. In practice there are several ways in which the doctrine retains its flexibility. These are dealt with in detail below[4] but it is sufficient to note at this juncture two basic principles; first, that superior courts have power to overrule decisions of inferior courts and, in certain cases, to overrule their own earlier decisions, and, secondly, that any rule of law may be changed by statute. Consequently every rule of law is subject to change, either by the judges themselves or by Parliament. However, the disadvantage of legislation as a source of law is that statutes require interpretation by judges, and these interpretations are in themselves judicial precedents. Therefore it is an oversimplification to regard legislation as superior to precedent as a source of law.

The advantages of the precedent system are said to be certainty,

---

4 See p 67, *post.*

precision and flexibility.[5] Legal certainty is achieved, in theory at least, in that, if the legal problem raised has been solved before, the judge is bound to adopt that solution. Precision is achieved by the sheer volume of reported cases containing solutions to innumerable factual situations arising in any particular branch of the law. No code or statute, no matter how carefully drafted, could anticipate the legal problems which these variations of fact may promote. Consequently, the judge in a continental legal system must generally decide cases on the basis of broad principles. Finally, flexibility is achieved by the possibility of decisions being overruled and by the possibility of distinguishing and confining the operation of decisions which appear unsound, the latter process being of particular importance.

The obvious disadvantages of the system are its inherent rigidity, which may occasionally cause hardship, and the vast and ever-increasing bulk of reported cases to which the court must advert to determine what is the law, since an excess of case law tends to obscure basic principles.[6]

Finally, it is self-evident that there cannot be an infinite regression. Every rule of law must have its origin. If it was not created by statute, then it must have been created by a court. Thus where there is no precedent the doctrine breaks down and the judge is bound to reach a decision in accordance with general principles. Even in modern times cases arise for which there is no precedent. These cases are described as cases of first impression and require the judge to make law rather than to apply it.[7] This he will do by reference to analogous principles but even legal principles must have their origin so that the declaratory theory of the common law is not of universal application.[8]

Before considering in detail the doctrine of binding precedent (or *stare decisis*) it is necessary to express a possible reservation as to its universal applicability in the English courts, which arises from the judgments of the majority of the Court of Appeal in *Trendtex Trading Corporation Ltd v Central Bank of Nigeria*.[9] The question at issue was whether the defendant bank could claim sovereign immunity from action, on the basis that it was a department or organ of the state of Nigeria. The Court of Appeal held that

---

5 See observations of RUSSELL LJ in *Gallie v Lee* [1969] 2 Ch 17, at p 41; [1969] 1 All ER 1062, at p 1076 (affirmed sub nom *Saunders v Anglia Building Society* [1971] AC 1004; [1970] 3 All ER 961) and of LORD HAILSHAM in *Cassell & Co Ltd v Broome* [1972] AC 1027, at p 1054; [1972] 1 All ER 801, at p 809 ("in legal matters, some degree of certainty is at least as valuable a part of justice as perfection").

6 The current attitude of appellate courts, faced with ever-increasing demands upon court time, is to discourage extensive citation of authorities, particularly where they are merely illustrative of general principles which are adequately set out in a leading case; see observations of LORD DIPLOCK in *Lexmead (Basingstoke) Ltd v Lewis* [1982] AC 225; sub nom *Lambert v Lewis* [1981] 1 All ER 1185.

7 Eg *Philips v Brooks Ltd* [1919] 2 KB 243; *Noble v Harrison* [1926] 2 KB 332; *Lancashire Loans Ltd v Black* [1934] 1 KB 380; *British Transport Commission v Gourley* [1956] AC 185; [1955] 3 All ER 796; *Malone v Metropolitan Police Commissioner (No 2)* [1979] Ch 344; [1979] 2 All ER 620; *Midland Bank Trust Co Ltd v Green (No 3)* [1982] Ch 529; [1981] 3 All ER 744; *Parker v British Airways Board* [1982] QB 1004; [1982] 1 All ER 834.

8 See LORD SIMON's observations upon the declaratory theory of the common law in *Jones v Secretary of State for Social Services* [1972] AC 944, at p 1026; [1972] 1 All ER 145, at p 198, quoted at p 187, *post*.

9 [1977] QB 529; [1977] 1 All ER 881. The question at issue in the case has now been resolved by the State Immunity Act 1978, s 3(1); see p 297, *post*.

it could not; firstly, because it had not established that it was a department of the state (a ground upon which the court was unanimous) and secondly (STEPHENSON LJ dissenting) on the ground that there was a rule of international law that the doctrine of sovereign immunity was not applicable to the ordinary commercial transactions, as distinct from the governmental acts, of a sovereign state, which rule was part of English law. The difficulty in the path of the second ground was that there was authority of the Court of Appeal against it which, according to the ordinary rules,[10] would bind the court in the instant case. However, LORD DENNING MR, with whom SHAW LJ agreed, overcame this difficulty by stating, as a principle, that the rule of *stare decisis* had no application to the rules of international law and, therefore, no application to that part of English law which embodies current international law. The point does not appear to have been judicially considered since that case. Being a decision of the Court of Appeal it must, for the time being, be taken as an accurate statement of the law and to constitute an important, albeit limited, exception to the doctrine of binding precedent.

2   The binding element in precedents

a   The ratio decidendi

It is a misstatement to speak of a "decision" as being binding, just as it is not technically correct to regard a "decision" as overruled. It is not the decision which binds, any more than it is the decision which is overruled; it is the rule of law contained in the decision. This element in a decision is termed the *ratio decidendi* of the case. Not every statement of law made by a judge in the course of his judgment is part of the *ratio*. For this reason it is important to be able to analyse a decision and isolate from it the *ratio decidendi*.

Every decision contains the following basic ingredients:

(1)   findings of material facts, direct and inferential. An inferential finding of fact is the inference which the judge (or jury if there is one) draws from the direct, or perceptible, facts. For example, from the direct facts of the speed of a vehicle, the length of skid marks and the state of the road the judge or jury may infer negligence. Negligence is an inferential finding of fact. Similarly, unreasonable behaviour, in matrimonial proceedings, is an inference of fact which may or may not be drawn from the direct facts of the respondent spouse's treatment of the other spouse during the marriage;

(2)   statements of the principles of law applicable to the legal problems disclosed by the facts; and

(3)   judgment based on the combined effect of (1) and (2).

For the purposes of the parties themselves and their privies, (3) is the material element in the decision for it determines finally their rights and liabilities in relation to the subject matter of the action. However, for the purpose of the doctrine of precedent, (2) is the vital element in the decision. This is, indeed, the *ratio decidendi*. Thus the *ratio decidendi* may

---

10 As to which, see p 72, *post*.

be defined as the statement of law applied to the legal problems raised by the facts as found upon which the decision is based. The two other elements in the decision are not precedents. The judgment is not binding (except directly on the parties themselves); nor are the findings of fact. This means that, even where the direct facts of an earlier case appear to be identical to those of the case before the court, the judge or jury is not bound to draw the same inference as that drawn in the earlier case. *Qualcast (Wolverhampton) Ltd v Haynes*[11] is a good example of this point. In that case an employee sued his employers for damages for negligence in failing to provide a safe system of work. The county court judge, at first instance, held himself bound to find the defendant liable by earlier cases in which employers, having taken similar precautions to those taken by the defendant in the instant case, had been held liable. This was wrong for, as the House of Lords explained, these cases, even though decided by a judge sitting alone rather than with a jury, were decisions based upon inferences of fact which were not to be regarded as binding. Otherwise, as LORD SOMERVELL observed:[12] "the precedent system will die from a surfeit of authorities".

Moreover, not every statement of law in a judgment is binding. Only those statements which are based upon the facts as found and upon which the decision is based are binding. Any other statement of law is, strictly, superfluous and is described as an *obiter dictum* (something said "by the way").

b Obiter dicta

There are two types of *obiter dicta*. First, a statement of law is regarded as *obiter* if it is based upon facts which either were not found to exist or, if found, were not found to be material. For example, the famous statement of equitable estoppel contained in the judgment of DENNING J in *Central London Property Trust Ltd v High Trees House Ltd*[13] is clearly *obiter* since it applied to a set of facts which were not found to be present in the case. Similarly, in *Rondel v Worsley*[14] the House of Lords expressed opinions to the effect that a barrister might be held liable in tort when acting outside the province of litigation and that a solicitor, when acting as advocate, might enjoy immunity from action. Since the case concerned only the liability of a barrister when acting as advocate, the opinions in question were necessarily *obiter*.

A second type of *obiter dictum* is a statement of law which, although based on the facts as found, does not form the basis of the decision. An obvious example is a statement of law in support of a dissenting judgment. Similarly, where a court makes statements of law leading to one conclusion and then adopts a contrary decision on the facts for a different reason, those statements are necessarily *obiter* since they do not support the decision. This is illustrated by the seminal case of *Hedley Byrne & Co Ltd v Heller & Partners Ltd*.[15] The proposition of law in that case, that the maker of a statement

---

11 [1959] AC 743; [1959] 2 All ER 38.
12 [1959] AC at p 758; [1959] 2 All ER at p 43. It should be remembered that, in the tort of negligence, only the existence of a duty of care is a question of law; whether or not the defendant has broken his duty is a question of fact.
13 [1947] KB 130; [1956] 1 All ER 256n.
14 [1969] 1 AC 191; [1967] 3 All ER 993; see p 228, *post*.
15 [1964] AC 465; [1963] 2 All ER 575.

owes a duty of care, in certain circumstances, to persons whom he may expect to rely upon that statement, is, strictly, *obiter* since the bank which gave the advice was protected by its disclaimer of responsibility. That being so, the further statement as to what rule of law would have been applied but for the disclaimer cannot be regarded as essential to the decision. Nevertheless, *Hedley Byrne* does illustrate that the strict rules for isolating the *ratio decidendi* of a case are sometimes of limited value since, the reasoning of the House of Lords, having been expressly applied in the Court of Appeal and approved in the House of Lords,[16] undoubtedly represents the present state of the law. It seems that where the House of Lords states a rule of law and expressly overrules earlier contrary decisions, that statement will be treated as binding even though not strictly essential to the decision.

It is sometimes difficult to isolate the *ratio decidendi* of a case which is argued on more than one ground. If the court is willing to decide the case on one ground it will usually refrain from expressing an opinion on any other point of law raised. Such a point is then said to be "left open". However the court sometimes feels constrained to deal with every point of law raised and then to give its decision. Which of these statements of law is the *ratio decidendi* of the case? The problem often arises when considering the decisions of appellate courts where different members of the court have arrived at the same conclusion, but for different reasons. A reason adopted by a majority of the court is, *prima facie*, *ratio* whereas a reason adopted only by a minority is usually regarded as inessential to the decision and, therefore, not binding. The position is even more complicated where no one reason is favoured by a majority. Clearly every case must have a *ratio decidendi* and the answer seems to be that it depends upon which of the alternative reasons subsequent courts are prepared to accept as *rationes*.

It is certainly possible for a case to have two or more *rationes decidendi*. The case of *Fairman v Perpetual Investment Building Society*[17] is an example. The House of Lords in that case gave two reasons for its decision, both of which were accepted as binding by the House itself in *Jacobs v London County Council*.[18] On the other hand, in *Read v J Lyons & Co Ltd*[19] the House of Lords advanced two reasons for its decision that the defendants were not liable under the rule in *Rylands v Fletcher*:[20] (1) that the rule did not apply in the absence of an escape of the dangerous substance from the defendant's occupation or control; and (2) that the rule did not apply unless the plaintiff had an interest in land affected by the escape. The second reason, which is principally contained in the speech of LORD MACMILLAN, was, in a later case,[1] treated by the Court of Appeal as *obiter*, on the basis that it was not essential to the decision. The position is complicated in that the statement to this effect in the Court of Appeal case was, itself, *obiter* because the plaintiff's action failed for another reason.

---

16 *Arenson v Casson, Beckman, Rutley & Co* [1977] AC 405; [1975] 3 All ER 901.
17 [1923] AC 74.
18 [1950] AC 361; [1950] 1 All ER 737. The case is particularly notable in that one of the two reasons given in *Fairman's* case was clearly not essential to the decision.
19 [1947] AC 156; [1946] 2 All ER 471.
20 (1868) LR 3 HL 330.
 1 *Perry v Kendricks Transport Ltd* [1956] 1 All ER 154; [1956] 1 WLR 85.

Consequently it remains undecided whether the second reason in *Read v J Lyons & Co Ltd* is *ratio* or *obiter*.[2]

A variation of the difficulty described above arises where the majority of a court favour a reason which does not support the decision which the court in the event gives. That reason cannot, by definition, be a *ratio decidendi* because it does not support the decision; on the other hand to treat the contrary reasoning of the minority as *ratio*, although theoretically defensible, is logically odd. The occasions on which such a dilemma will arise are likely to be very rare, but the hearing by the House of Lords of the appeal in *Central Asbestos Co Ltd v Dodd*[3] was such an occasion. The question before the House turned on the construction of the ill-drafted provisions of section 7(3) of the Limitation Act 1963. LORDS REID and MORRIS took one view of the law, LORDS SIMON and SALMON a different view. The fifth member of the court, LORD PEARSON, was in favour of deciding the appeal in the same way as LORDS REID and MORRIS, but for a different reason, his view on the point of law substantially supporting that of LORDS SIMON and SALMON.

It was not long before the Court of Appeal was called upon to decide the point of law which had arisen in *Dodd*'s case (which was, put simply, whether time ran against a plaintiff who knew the facts upon which his action was based but did not know that these facts gave him a cause of action). The Court of Appeal held[4] that, since *Dodd*'s case had no discernible *ratio decidendi*, the Court of Appeal would go back to the law as contained in the earlier cases.

It would be erroneous to suppose that *obiter dicta* are of no authority. Strictly, they are not of binding authority but have only persuasive authority. Nevertheless, where the statement in question has come from a court of high authority and is a deliberate statement of law as opposed to a casual expression of opinion it will usually be followed in the absence of binding authority to the contrary. By way of example may be cited the case of *Adams v Naylor*[5] in which the House of Lords disapproved the practice of government departments setting up a nominal defendant to avoid the Crown's immunity from actions in tort. Although this disapproval was *obiter*, the Court of Appeal in *Royster v Cavey*[6] adopted it and refused to sanction this long-standing practice. There could be no more striking example, finally, than the "neighbour principle" propounded by LORD ATKIN in *M'Alister (or Donoghue) v Stevenson*.[7] This statement of law,

---

2 The Court of Appeal in *Dunne v North-Western Gas Board* [1964] 2 QB 806; [1963] 3 All ER 916, expressly left the point open.

3 [1973] AC 518; [1972] 2 All ER 1135.

4 *Harper v National Coal Board* [1974] QB 614; [1974] 2 All ER 441. The cases are of no more than academic interest, so far as the limitation point is concerned, since Parliament intervened by passing the Limitation Act 1975 (now the Limitation Act 1980), which supports the view that the interpretation of the law intended by Parliament was that favoured by the minority in *Dodd*'s case. In *Miliangos v George Frank (Textiles) Ltd* [1976] AC 443, at p 479; [1975] 3 All ER 801, at p 822 LORD SIMON was critical of the Court of Appeal in *Harper* for not following the minority reasoning in *Dodd* but, since that reasoning did not support the decision, it is difficult to support LORD SIMON's criticism and, indeed, difficult to see what other course was open to the Court of Appeal.

5 [1946] AC 543; [1946] 2 All ER 241.

6 [1947] KB 204; [1946] 2 All ER 642. This decision precipitated the passing of the Crown Proceedings Act 1947 which enabled the Crown to be sued in tort.

7 [1932] AC 562.

though far wider than the decision required, has become the basis of the modern tort of negligence and has been cited and applied on occasions too numerous to mention.

3   Precedents which are not binding

a   *Persuasive authorities*

Only the *ratio decidendi* of a decision is binding. *Obiter dicta* are of persuasive authority. It has already been noted that the *dicta* of an appellate court may carry great weight. However, *dicta*, of whatever weight, may be rejected if a later court wishes to adopt a contrary solution. Other persuasive authorities are decisions of courts inferior in the hierarchy to the court which is invited to follow their decisions. Thus, for example, Court of Appeal decisions are of persuasive authority in the House of Lords.

A third class of persuasive authorities consists of the decisions of Scottish, Irish, Commonwealth and foreign courts. There is an increasing tendency on the part of English judges to draw analogies from other legal systems but these authorities are accepted as being of persuasive authority only. Special mention must be made of "decisions" of the Judicial Committee of the Privy Council. The advice of the Privy Council to Her Majesty is not strictly binding on any English judge. Thus, in theory, even a first instance judge may legitimately decline to follow a decision of the Privy Council.[8] However, Privy Council decisions are of very great persuasive authority for the obvious reason that the Council is in practice composed, for judicial sittings, of those persons who usually sit in the House of Lords.

Nevertheless, despite the similarity in composition between the Privy Council and the House of Lords, there had not been any suggestion that Privy Council authorities were of equivalent weight to House of Lords cases until the Court of Appeal in *Doughty v Turner Manufacturing Co Ltd*[9] expressed the view (albeit *obiter*) that the Court of Appeal's own decision in *Re Polemis*[10] was no longer good law in the light of the subsequent Privy Council decision in *The Wagon Mound*.[11] Subsequently, in *Worcester Works Finance Ltd v Cooden Engineering Co Ltd*[12] the Court of Appeal, faced with a conflict of authority between previous decisions of the Court of Appeal and a later decision of the Privy Council, had no hesitation in preferring the latter, LORD DENNING MR expounding the principle that when the Privy Council disapproves of a previous decision of the Court of Appeal, the latter is at liberty to depart from its previous decision. The Privy Council itself has stated that, where the applicable law is English, the Judicial Committee will follow a House of Lords decision which covers the point at issue, since it is the House of Lords and not the

---

8 DIPLOCK J did so in *Port Line Ltd v Ben Line Steamers Ltd* [1958] 2 QB 146; [1958] 1 All ER 787; see also *Dulieu v White* [1901] 2 KB 669.
9 [1964] 1 QB 518; [1964] 1 All ER 98.
10 [1921] 3 KB 560.
11 *Overseas Tankship (UK) Ltd v Morts Dock and Engineering Co Ltd* [1961] AC 388; [1961] 1 All ER 404.
12 [1972] 1 QB 210; [1971] 3 All ER 708.

Judicial Committee of the Privy Council which is the final judicial authority for the determination of English law.[13]

b Precedents which have been overruled

A precedent does not lose its authority with the passing of time. Indeed the strength of a precedent increases with age in that courts tend to be reluctant to overrule long-standing authorities, unless they are clearly wrong. Apart from the desirability of attaining certainty, the main reason for the reluctance of judges to overrule old decisions is the fact that, since overruling operates retrospectively, it might have the effect of disturbing financial arrangements, depriving persons of vested proprietary rights and even imposing criminal liability. Thus in *Re Compton*[14] the Court of Appeal would not overrule a long line of old authorities concerning charitable trusts although it considered these cases anomalous. Similarly the rule in *Pinnel's* case,[15] though plainly anomalous, has never been overruled. In *Foakes v Beer*[16] the House of Lords would not overrule *Pinnel's* case; LORD FITZGERALD, though doubting that the rule was a good one, did not feel that the House would be justified in overruling it having regard simply to its longevity.[17] On the other hand there is little hesitation felt in overruling decisions which the court considers to be clearly wrong. Thus in *Bourne v Keane*[18] the House, considering an aspect of the law of trusts, overruled by a majority a series of long-standing decisions even though this had the effect of disturbing many existing trusts and settlements. More recently in *Button v Director of Public Prosecutions*[19] the House of Lords, in holding that the common law offence of affray could be committed in a private place, overruled a line of authority to the effect that an affray could take place only in a public place, while in the leading case of *Miliangos v George Frank (Textiles) Ltd*[20] the House of Lords overruled[1] its own decision in *Re United Railways of the Havana and Regla Warehouses Ltd*[2] which embodied one of the clearest and most firmly entrenched rules of English law, namely that judgment must be given in sterling.

The process of overruling must be carefully distinguished from the process of reversing a decision. A decision altered on appeal is said to be "reversed". Reversing differs from overruling in that the former affects the

---

13 *Tai Hing Cotton Mill Ltd v Liu Chong Hing Bank Ltd* [1986] AC 80; [1985] 2 All ER 947.
14 [1945] Ch 123; [1945] 1 All ER 198.
15 (1602), 5 Co Rep 117a.
16 (1884) 9 App Cas 605.
17 *Ibid* at p 630. The rule has, of course, been undermined by the doctrine of equitable estoppel; see *D & C Builders Ltd v Rees* [1966] 2 QB 617; [1965] 3 All ER 837.
18 [1919] AC 815. On the other hand, in *Prudential Assurance Co Ltd v London Residuary Body* [1992] 2 AC 386; [1992] 3 All ER 504, the House of Lords felt unable to overrule ancient authorities which embodied the rule requiring the maximum duration of a term of years to be determinable at the outset, on the ground that to do so might upset long-established titles, notwithstanding that this led to a "bizarre outcome" in the instant case.
19 [1966] AC 591; [1965] 3 All ER 587.
20 [1976] AC 443; [1975] 3 All ER 801.
1 Although the majority of the House stated that it was "departing from" the decision in the *Havana* case, it amounted in effect to overruling that case.
2 [1961] AC 1007; [1960] 2 All ER 332.

decision in the case whereas the latter only affects the rule of law upon which the decision is based. Semantically, it is not correct to speak of a decision as "overruled" since it is only the rule of law contained in the decision which is affected, not the decision itself.

A decision may be overruled either by statute or by a higher court. If it is overruled by a higher court the earlier decision is deemed to have been based on a misunderstanding of the law. The earlier rule of law is deemed never to have existed. This is the declaratory theory of the common law. The common law is never changed; it is merely restated correctly. Consequently all judicial overruling operates retrospectively. It is this which distinguishes judicial overruling from overruling by statute, since the latter (in the absence of an express provision to the contrary) operates only when the statute becomes operative. Another difference between judicial overruling and overruling by statute is that statutes, unlike judges, do not expressly name the decisions which they overrule. Nevertheless it is not usually difficult to identify the cases which are overruled by a statute, particularly where the statute follows closely upon an unpopular decision of a superior court, often the House of Lords.

It appears that in the Supreme Court of the United States there is power to overrule decisions prospectively, that is to apply the earlier decision to the facts of the instant case but to overrule it in so far as it may affect future cases.[3] In the United States Supreme Court the power is held to be based on the common law, though it has never been recognised in this country. However, in *Jones v Secretary of State for Social Services*[4] a case in which the House of Lords declined to overrule one of its own previous decisions although a majority were of the opinion that the *ratio* of the earlier decision was wrong, LORD SIMON advanced the opinion that the most satisfactory method of dealing with the appeal would have been to allow it on the basis that it was covered by the earlier decision but to have overruled the earlier decision prospectively. In the event, however, he simply concurred in allowing the appeal and went on to say that, although an extension of judicial power to include prospective overruling should be considered (a suggestion with which LORD DIPLOCK agreed), it would preferably be the subject of Parliamentary enactment, adding:[5]

> "In the first place, informed professional opinion is probably to the effect that your Lordships have no power to overrule decisions with prospective effect only; such opinion is itself a source of law; and your Lordships, sitting judicially, are bound by any rule of law arising extra-judicially. Secondly, to proceed by Act of Parliament would obviate any suspicion of endeavouring to upset one-sidedly the constitutional balance between executive, legislature and judiciary. Thirdly, concomitant problems could receive consideration – for example whether other courts supreme within their own jurisdictions should have similar powers as regards the rule of precedent; whether machinery could and should be devised to apprise the courts of the potential repercussions of any particular decision; and whether any court (including the appellate

---

3 *Linkletter v Walker* 381 US 618 (1965), cited in *Jones v Secretary of State for Social Services* (*infra*).
4 [1972] AC 944; [1972] 1 All ER 145; see p 187, *post*.
5 [1972] AC, at pp 1026–1027; [1972] 1 All ER, at p 198; LORD SIMON advanced substantially similar suggestions in *Miliangos v George Frank (Textiles) Ltd* [1976] AC 443, at p 490; [1975] 3 All ER 801, at p 832.

committee of your Lordships' House) should sit in banc when invited to review a previous decision."

The passage above illustrates clearly the reasons why it is preferable for major changes in the law to be made by Parliament, rather than by the judiciary.

c   Precedents which can be distinguished

The process of "distinguishing" is probably the major factor in enabling the doctrine of precedent to remain flexible and adaptable. Cases are distinguished on their facts. The *ratio decidendi* of a case is, by definition, based upon the material facts of that case. Consequently if the court is willing to regard as material any fact not common to the case before it and the precedent cited, the two cases can be distinguished. The law reports are full of strained distinctions where the court was evidently anxious not to follow an apparently binding precedent. In theory it is possible to distinguish virtually any precedent since factual situations will almost never precisely duplicate themselves. Nevertheless there are practical limits beyond which the court will be unlikely to go. Cases which are indistinguishable are described as being "on all fours" with one another. To illustrate how fine a distinction may be drawn between ostensibly parallel factual situations reference may be made to two well-known cases concerning the tort of conversion. In *England v Cowley*[6] the defendant refused to allow the plaintiff to remove goods from his, the defendant's, premises. This was held not to be conversion since there was no absolute denial of title. This case was distinguished by the Court of Appeal in *Oakley v Lyster*[7] in which the defendant refused to allow the plaintiff to remove material from his, the defendant's, land and, in addition, asserted his own title to the material. This was held to be an act of conversion, the assertion of title apparently making the denial of title absolute.

d   Statements of law made per incuriam

The Court of Appeal in the leading case of *Young v Bristol Aeroplane Co Ltd*[8] established the principle that the Court of Appeal was not bound to follow its own earlier decision if satisfied that the decision in question was reached *per incuriam* (through lack of care). This almost always means that some relevant statutory provision or precedent, which would have affected the decision, was not brought to the attention of the court, although the principle is not necesssarily confined to such cases. Where it is argued that a decision was reached *per incuriam* on the ground that relevant material was overlooked by the court, it is not sufficient that the material in question *might* have led the court to a different conclusion; the criterion is that it *must* have done so.[9] Although the principle in *Young*'s case was expressed to apply only to the Court of Appeal, it has been applied in other

6 (1873) LR 8 Exch 126.
7 [1931] 1 KB 148.
8 [1944] KB 718; [1944] 2 All ER 293 (affirmed [1946] AC 163; [1946] 1 All ER 98); see p 72, *post.*
9 *Duke v Reliance Systems Ltd* [1988] QB 108; [1987] 2 All ER 858, affirmed [1988] AC 618; [1988] 1 All ER 626.

courts. Thus in *R v Northumberland Compensation Appeal Tribunal, ex parte Shaw*[10] a divisional court of the King's Bench Division declined to follow a Court of Appeal decision on the ground that the latter had been reached *per incuriam*, a relevant House of Lords decision not having been cited to the Court of Appeal. However, in *Cassell & Co Ltd v Broome*[11] the House of Lords rejected in condemnatory terms the Court of Appeal's decision to the effect that the decision of the House of Lords in *Rookes v Barnard*[12] on the issue of exemplary damages had been reached *per incuriam* because of two previous decisions of the House. Lord Hailsham LC, in the course of the leading speech for the majority, asserted that:[13]

> ". . . it is not open to the Court of Appeal to give gratuitous advice to judges of first instance to ignore decisions of the House of Lords in this way . . . The course taken would have put judges of first instance in an embarrassing position, as driving them to take sides in an unedifying dispute between the Court of Appeal . . . and the House of Lords."

while Lord Reid[14] took the view that it was "obvious that the Court of Appeal failed to understand Lord Devlin's speech". The words of Lord Hailsham proved to be prophetic because in *Miliangos v George Frank (Textiles) Ltd*[15] Bristow J (as he expressly acknowledged) found himself in the position of embarrassment foreseen by Lord Hailsham. That the learned judge found himself in such a position was due to the fact that in *Schorsch Meier GmbH v Hennin*[16] the Court of Appeal had held that the rule of law whereby money judgments could only be expressed in sterling had ceased to exist, notwithstanding clear House of Lords authority for the existence of the rule. Bristow J preferred to follow the House of Lords authority; the Court of Appeal (perhaps not surprisingly) stated that he was wrong in so doing because *Schorsch Meier* was binding upon him. On appeal[17] the House of Lords decision in question[18] was overruled, although not on any of the grounds on which the Court of Appeal had cited either in the instant case or in *Schorsch Meier*.

The *per incuriam* principle is of limited application. Very few decisions

---

10 [1951] 1 KB 711; [1951] 1 All ER 268.
11 [1972] AC 1027; [1972] 1 All ER 801.
12 [1964] AC 1129; [1964] 1 All ER 367. This decision had already been subjected to devastating criticism in the courts of the Commonwealth and had been repudiated by the Privy Council; see *Australian Consolidated Press Ltd v Uren* [1969] 1 AC 590; [1967] 3 All ER 523. No less devastating was the criticism of Lord Denning MR, culminating in the description of the doctrine laid down by Lord Devlin in *Rookes v Barnard* as "hopelessly illogical and inconsistent": *Broome v Cassell & Co Ltd* [1971] 2 QB 354, at p 381; [1971] 2 All ER 187, at p 199, an approach which attracted vehement criticism from the majority of the House of Lords.
13 [1972] AC 1027, at p 1054; [1972] 1 All ER 801, at p 809.
14 [1972] AC at p 1084; [1972] 1 All ER at p 835.
15 [1975] QB 487; [1975] 1 All ER 1076.
16 [1975] QB 416; [1975] 1 All ER 152; [1975] 1 CMLR 20.
17 [1976] AC 443; [1975] 3 All ER 801.
18 *Tomkinson v First Pennsylvania Banking and Trust Co* [1961] AC 1007, sub nom *Re United Railways of the Havana and Ragla Warehouses Ltd* [1960] 2 All ER 332 (a decision to which Lord Denning himself had been a party).

have subsequently been regarded as having been reached *per incuriam* and in *Morelle Ltd v Wakeling*[19] SIR RAYMOND EVERSHED MR reaffirmed that:

> "As a general rule the only cases in which decisions should be held to have been given per incuriam are those of decisions given in ignorance or forgetfulness of some inconsistent statutory provision or of some authority binding on the court concerned; so that in such cases some part of the decision or some step in the reasoning on which it is based is found, on that account, to be demonstrably wrong. This definition is not necessarily exhaustive, but cases not strictly within it which can properly be held to have been decided *per incuriam* must, in our judgment, consistently with the *stare decisis* rule which is an essential feature of our law, be, in the language of LORD GREENE MR of the rarest occurrence."

Thus the doctrine will not be extended to cases which were merely not fully or expertly argued,[20] or were argued on one side only (as *Schorsch Meier* was), or were cases in which the court appeared to misunderstand the law or was not aware of considerations of policy underlying a statute[1] or adopted a statutory interpretation which appears to be wrong. However, if it appeared to a court that a previous court's interpretation of a statute was an impossible interpretation (as opposed merely to an incorrect one) then it would seem that the duty of the later court is to apply a correct interpretation;[2] whether this would be an example of the *per incuriam* doctrine or simply an illustration of the general rules relating to the interpretation of statutes, and the obligations of judges in relation thereto, is problematical.

4 The hierarchy of the courts

It has already been noted that the doctrine of binding precedent depends for its operation upon the underlying principle that the courts form a hierarchy with each court standing in a definite position in relation to every other court. The structure of this hierarchy must now be considered for the purposes of the doctrine of precedent.

a European Court[3]

In matters concerning: (1) the interpretation of the Treaties; (2) the validity and interpretation of acts of the Community institutions; and (3) the interpretation of the statutes of bodies established by an act of the Council,

---

19 [1955] 2 QB 379, at p 406; [1955] 1 All ER 708, at p 718; see also *Miliangos v George Frank (Textiles) Ltd* [1976] AC 443, at p 477; [1975] 3 All ER 801, at p 821, *per* LORD SIMON.

20 *Joscelyne v Nissen* [1970] 2 QB 86; [1970] 1 All ER 1213; *Morelle Ltd v Wakeling (supra)*.

1 *Farrell v Alexander* [1976] QB 345; [1976] 1 All ER 129 (decision reversed [1977] AC 59; [1976] 2 All ER 721); but see *Industrial Properties (Barton Hil) Ltd v Associated Electrical Industries Ltd* [1977] QB 580; [1977] 2 All ER 293 in which the Court of Appeal declared one of its previous decisions *per incuriam* where the court had misunderstood an earlier case because of deficiencies in the law report of that case to which it had been referred, and *Dixon v British Broadcasting Corporation* [1979] QB 546; [1979] 2 All ER 112 in which one *ratio* of an earlier case was treated as *per incuriam* on the ground that the statutory provision under construction had apparently been considered in isolation rather than in context; for an illustration of the *per incuriam* principle in the Court of Appeal, Criminal Division, see *R v Martindale* [1986] 3 All ER 25; [1986] 1 WLR 1042.

2 *Ibid*.

3 See Hartley, *Foundation of European Community Law* (2nd edn) pp 75–76.

the Court of Justice of the European Communities is the supreme tribunal. Accordingly its decisions, in these areas of jurisdiction, will be binding on all English courts. Indeed section 3(1) of the European Communities Act 1972 expressly provides that:

> "for the purpose of all legal proceedings any question as to the meaning or effect of any of the Treaties, or as to the validity, meaning or effect of any Community instrument, shall be treated as a question of law (and, if not referred to the European Court, be for determination as such in accordance with the principles laid down by and any relevant decision of the European Court)."

The European Court appears not to observe a doctrine of binding precedent and does not regard itself as bound by its previous decisions.[4]

b   House of Lords

The House of Lords stands at the summit of the English hierarchy of courts. Decisions of the House of Lords are binding upon all other courts trying civil or criminal cases, whether or not appeal lies to the House from those courts.

Formerly the House of Lords regarded itself as strictly bound by its own earlier decisions, which were thus immutable except by legislation.[5] However in 1966 LORD GARDINER LC, on behalf of himself and the Lords of Appeal in Ordinary, made a statement to the effect that their Lordships proposed in future to depart from their own earlier decisions "when it appears right to do so".[6] They would, however, bear in mind the danger of disturbing retrospectively financial arrangements and rights in property and the especial need for certainty as to the criminal law. The Lord Chancellor made it clear, moreover, that this statement was not intended to apply elsewhere than in the House of Lords.

Although this statement was not made in the context of an actual decision it has the force of law, and the House does depart from its own earlier decisions, albeit rarely. The practical consequences of this change in the law were, at first, slight. In the five years following LORD GARDINER's statement the House of Lords did not overrule any of its previous decisions. Their reticence is aptly demonstrated by *Jones v Secretary of State for Social Services*.[7] In this important case, involving the construction of the National Insurance (Industrial Injuries) Act 1946, a majority of the House (consisting of seven members) declined to overrule a previous decision of the House[8] although a majority of their Lordships were of opinion that the *ratio* of the earlier decision was wrong. Since there was no suggestion that the earlier authority could be distinguished it might appear that, a majority of the House being of the opinion that the decision was wrong, there would be no alternative but to overrule it. Three of the majority of four who believed the earlier authority to be wrong were in

---

4 Case 28–30/62; *Da Costa en Schaake NV v Nederlandse Belastingadministratie* [1963] CMLR 224, cited in *HP Bulmer Ltd v J Bollinger SA* [1974] Ch 401; [1974] 2 All ER 1226.
5 This principle was established in *London Street Tramways Co v London County Council* [1898] AC 375.
6 Reported at [1966] 3 All ER 77; [1966] 1 WLR 1234.
7 [1972] AC 944; [1972] 1 All ER 145.
8 *Minister of Social Security v Amalgamated Engineering Union* [1967] 1 AC 725; [1967] 1 All ER 210.

favour of overruling it and had the fourth, Lord Simon, agreed, the House would undoubtedly have overruled its own earlier decision. However Lord Simon gave several reasons why, in his opinion, it would be wrong to depart from *Dowling*'s case, notably that the power to depart from a previous decision "is one to be most sparingly exercised", and that a variation of view on a matter of statutory construction would rarely provide a suitable occasion.

However, the wait for a suitable occasion was not a long one and in *British Railways Board v Herrington*[9] the House, on the question of the extent of the duty of care owed by an occupier of land to trespassers, restated the law and refused to follow the statement of the law, which had stood for over 40 years, laid down in *Robert Addie & Sons (Collieries) Ltd v Dumbreck*.[10]

As indicated above, the power is exercised sparingly. As Lord Reid observed in one case:[11]

> ". . . our change of practice in no longer regarding previous decisions of this House as absolutely binding does not mean that whenever we think a previous decision was wrong we should reverse it. In the general interest of certainty in the law we must be sure that there is some very good reason before we so act."

Notwithstanding the "especial need for certainty as to the criminal law", in *R v Shivpuri*[12] the House, dealing with the law relating to criminal attempts, departed from its own earlier decision.[13] The latter had been reached less than a year earlier but had meanwhile been the subject of devastating academic criticism. Lord Bridge (who had been a party to the earlier decision) gave the following reasons:[14]

> "Firstly, I am undeterred by the consideration that the decision in *Anderton v Ryan* was so recent. The 1966 Practice Statement is an effective abandonment of our pretention to infallibility. If a serious error embodied in a decision of this House had distorted the law, the sooner it is corrected the better. Secondly, I cannot see how, in the very nature of the case, anyone could have acted in reliance on the law as propounded in *Anderton v Ryan* in the belief that he was acting innocently and now find that, after all, he is to be held to have committed a criminal offence."

Apart from the possibility of the House of Lords being prepared to depart from its own earlier decisions there are three basic means by which a House of Lords decision may lose its authority. Firstly, and most obviously, it may be overruled by statute or a decision of the European Court. Secondly, it may be distinguished. The process of distinguishing applies in the House of Lords as in other courts. Indeed, before the 1966 Practice Statement it was applied with more force in the House of Lords than elsewhere because there was no other judicial means of avoiding a

---

9 [1972] AC 877; [1972] 1 All ER 749.

10 [1929] AC 358; see also *The Johanna Oldendorff* [1974] AC 479; [1973] 3 All ER 148; *Vestey v Inland Revenue Commissioners* [1980] AC 1148; [1979] 3 All ER 976; *Murphy v Brentwood District Council* [1991] 1 AC 398; [1990] 2 All ER 908.

11 *Knuller (Publishing, Printing and Promotions) Ltd v Director of Public Prosecutions* [1973] AC 435, at p 455; [1972] 2 All ER 898, at p 903; see also, to similar effect, *Fitzleet Estates Ltd v Cherry* [1977] 3 All ER 996; [1977] 1 WLR 1345.

12 [1987] AC 1; [1986] 2 All ER 334.

13 In *Anderton v Ryan* [1985] AC 560; [1985] 2 All ER 355.

14 [1987] AC, at p 23 ; [1986] 2 All ER, at p 345.

precedent which the House felt to be wrong, although this has not been the case since then.

Finally, it is possible for a House of Lords decision to be rejected if given *per incuriam*, although in modern conditions it would be virtually inconceivable that a case could progress through the House of Lords with a crucial authority being overlooked.

Although the House of Lords may reject its own earlier decisions as being given *per incuriam* it is clear that no other court can legitimately do so. As noted earlier, the Court of Appeal in *Broome v Cassell & Co Ltd*[15] regarded a House of Lords decision as being given *per incuriam* on the basis that two House of Lords authorities were not cited to the House. Reference has already been made to the manner in which the House of Lords disapproved the Court of Appeal's application of the *per incuriam* doctrine. LORD DIPLOCK was alone, however, in going so far as to state that the Court of Appeal had no power to treat a decision of the House of Lords in this way:[16]

> "The Court of Appeal found themselves able to disregard the decision of this House in *Rookes v Barnard* by applying to it the label *per incuriam*. That label is relevant only to the right of an appellate court to decline to follow one of its own previous decisions, not to its right to disregard a decision of a higher appellate court or to the right of a judge of the High Court to disregard a decision of the Court of Appeal."

However, this *dictum* has been approved[17] and may be treated as authoritative. By contrast, where two House of Lords decisions conflict, a court is entitled and bound to follow the later decision.[18]

c   Court of Appeal

Civil division — Decisions of the Court of Appeal are binding on all inferior courts trying civil or criminal cases, including divisional courts.[19] The Court of Appeal is bound by decisions of the European Court, the House of Lords, and by its own earlier decisions.[20] The latter principle was affirmatively established in the leading case of *Young v Bristol Aeroplane Co Ltd*[1] LORD GREENE MR, who delivered the judgment of the court, cited three exceptional circumstances in which an earlier decision of the Court of Appeal would not be regarded as binding.

(1) Where there are two conflicting decisions, the court may choose which it will follow, the decision not followed being deemed to be overruled. Thus, in *Fisher v Ruislip-Northwood Urban District*

---

15 [1971] 2 QB 354; [1971] 2 All ER 187; see p 68, *ante*.
16 *Cassell & Co Ltd v Broome* [1972] AC 1027, at p 1131; [1972] 1 All ER 801, at p 874.
17 See *Baker v R* [1975] AC 774; [1975] 3 All ER 55; *Miliangos v George Frank (Textiles) Ltd* [1976] AC, at p 479; [1975] 3 All ER, at pp 822–823, *per* LORD SIMON.
18 *Moodie v Inland Revenue Commissioners* [1993] 2 All ER 49; [1993] 1 WLR 266.
19 *Brownsea Haven Properties Ltd v Poole Corporation* [1958] Ch 574; [1958] 1 All ER 205.
20 *Sed quaere*; is it bound by a decision of the Judicial Committee of the Privy Council? see p 64, *ante*. The Court of Appeal is also bound by decisions of courts which exercised equivalent jurisdiction prior to 1875: the Court of Exchequer Chamber and the Chancery Court of Appeal; see *Ex parte M'George* (1882) 20 Ch D 697.
1 [1944] KB 718; [1944] 2 All ER 293 (affirmed [1946] AC 163; [1946] 1 All ER 98).

Council[2] the court, of which LORD GREENE was again a member, was required to choose between conflicting lines of authorities concerning the liability of local authorities to motorists who collided with unlit air-raid shelters while in *Tiverton Estates Ltd v Wearwell Ltd*[3] the Court of Appeal was able to avoid following its own recent decision in the controversial case of *Law v Jones*[4] (to the effect that it was unnecessary for a memorandum under section 40 of the Law of Property Act 1925 to acknowledge the existence of a contract) because it was in conflict with earlier decisions of the court.

(2) The court is bound to refuse to follow a decision of its own which, though not expressly overruled, cannot stand with a later House of Lords decision.[5]

(3) The court is not bound to follow a decision of its own if that decision was given *per incuriam*.

This principle, explained earlier, is not confined to the Court of Appeal. The *per incuriam* principle usually involves there having been overlooked by the previous court a relevant statutory provision or an authority binding on the court. There is, however, a residual undefined category of other cases in which the principle may be invoked, as LORD GREENE had acknowledged in *Young*. During his tenure of the office of Master of the Rolls LORD DONALDSON occasionally tapped this slender stream. Thus in *Williams v Fawcett*[6] the Court of Appeal regarded a number of earlier authorities on a point as having been reached *per incuriam* on the ground that there had been a "manifest slip or error" in an area in which the liberty of the subject was involved (committal for contempt of court) and in which cases were most unlikely ever to reach the House of Lords. Again, in *Rickards v Rickards*[7] the court, again presided over by LORD DONALDSON, applied the "manifest slip or error" test when refusing to follow an earlier decision which involved a wrongful rejection of jurisdiction by the court in circumstances in which there was no possibility of an appeal to the House of Lords.

While he was Master of the Rolls, LORD DENNING engaged in a tireless, but ultimately unsuccessful, campaign to gain for the Court of Appeal the

---

2 [1945] KB 584; [1945] 2 All ER 458.

3 [1975] Ch 146; [1974] 1 All ER 209.

4 [1974] Ch 112; [1973] 2 All ER 437; see also *Starr v National Coal Board* [1977] 1 All ER 243; [1977] 1 WLR 63; *WA Sherratt Ltd v John Bromley (Church Stretton) Ltd* [1985] QB 1038; [1985] 1 All ER 216.

5 This exception, it will be observed, does not apply to cases in which a decision of the Court of Appeal is inconsistent with an earlier House of Lords decision. It may be that LORD GREENE did not entertain this as a possibility and indeed it is clearly a situation which should not arise since the Court of Appeal, unless it was not referred to the earlier House of Lords decision (in which event its own decision would be *per incuriam*) should not reach decisions which are inconsistent with existing authority of the House of Lords. When however that situation does arise, probably the better view is that the Court of Appeal should follow its own decision and give leave to appeal to the House of Lords; cf *Miliangos v George Frank (Textiles) Ltd* [1976] AC, at p 479; [1975] 3 All ER, at p 823, per LORD SIMON. But see *Turton v Turton* [1988] Ch 542; [1987] 2 All ER 641, where the Court of Appeal disapproved its own earlier decision in *Hall v Hall* (1981) 3 FLR 379 on the ground that it was inconsistent with the House of Lords case of *Gissing v Gissing* [1971] AC 886; [1970] 2 All ER 780.

6 [1986] QB 604; [1985] 1 All ER 787.

7 [1990] Fam 194; [1989] 3 All ER 193.

freedom that the House of Lords has to depart from its own previous decisions at will. In *Gallie v Lee*[8] LORD DENNING evinced a desire to depart from the rule in *Young's* case in the following words:

> "We are, of course, bound by the decisions of the House [of Lords], but I do not think we are bound by prior decisions of our own, or at any rate, not absolutely bound. We are not fettered as it was once thought. It was a self-imposed limitation; and we who imposed it can also remove it. The House of Lords have done it. So why should not we do likewise?"

This was, however, a minority opinion RUSSELL LJ saw the position of the House of Lords in quite a different light, saying of the Master of the Rolls:[9]

> "I think that in one respect he has sought to wield a broom labelled 'for the use of the House of Lords only' . . . I do not support the suggestion that this court is free to override its own decisions . . . the availability of the House of Lords to correct error in the Court of Appeal makes it in my view unnecessary for this court to depart from its existing discipline."

Again in *Barrington v Lee*, a case concerned with liability as between vendor and purchaser in respect of an estate agent's default over a deposit, LORD DENNING, dealing with the effect of an earlier decision on similar facts, boldly asserted:[10]

> "We are not absolutely bound by *Burt's* case. We no longer look to see if the case can be brought within the exceptions stated in *Young v Bristol Aeroplane Co Ltd*.

Once again, however, LORD DENNING was expressing a minority view for EDMUND DAVIES and STEPHENSON LJJ, though concurring in the result of the appeal by distinguishing *Burt's* case, both reaffirmed the principles of *Young's* case and disagreed with the view of LORD DENNING quoted above. STEPHENSON LJ's judgment epitomises the traditional approach:[11]

> ". . . what may be thought timorous subservience to judicial precedent is, in my judgment, preferable to the uncertainty which will be introduced into the law in fields not easy to delimit by the bolder work of demolition and restoration proposed by LORD DENNING MR in this case . . . We must take care lest in struggling to straighten out the law we bend it until it breaks."

Faced with such opposition to his views LORD DENNING was constrained to resile from the statements he had made in *Gallie v Lee* and *Barrington v Lee*; indeed in *Miliangos v George Frank (Textiles) Ltd*[12] the Master of the Rolls expressly applied the principles in *Young v Bristol Aeroplane Co Ltd*. Nevertheless in *Davis v Johnson*, a controversial case dealing with the

---

8 [1969] 2 Ch 17, at p 37; [1969] 1 All ER 1062, at p 1072 (affirmed sub nom *Saunders v Anglia Building Society* [1971] AC 1004; [1970] 3 All ER 961).

9 [1969] 2 Ch, at p 41; [1969] 1 All ER, at p 1082; the third member of the court, SALMON LJ, took a middle view and stated that a change in policy, though possibly desirable, would require a pronouncement of the whole Court of Appeal. Nevertheless, in *Davis v Johnson* [1979] AC 264; [1978] 1 All ER 1132, LORD SALMON, in common with the other members of the House of Lords, expressly reaffirmed *Young's* case.

10 [1972] 1 QB 326, at p 338; [1971] 3 All ER 1231, at p 1238; see also *Hanning v Maitland (No 2)* [1970] 1 QB 580, at p 587; [1970] 1 All ER 812, at p 815.

11 [1972] 1 QB, at p 345; [1971] 3 All ER, at p 1245. The law was, eventually, clarified by the House of Lords in *Sorrell v Finch* [1977] AC 728; [1976] 2 All ER 371. See also *Tiverton Estates Ltd v Wearwell Ltd* [1975] Ch 146; [1974] 1 All ER 209.

12 [1975] QB 487; [1975] 1 All ER 1076.

power of the courts to protect "battered wives", LORD DENNING led the full Court of Appeal in yet another attack on *Young*'s case, which attack was, again, repulsed when the case reached the House of Lords,[13] where the rule in *Young* was, in LORD DIPLOCK's words, "expressly, unequivocally and unanimously" reaffirmed. It is not now to be anticipated that any further attempt will be made by the Court of Appeal to suggest that it is not bound by its own previous decisions (subject to the recognised exceptional cases referred to in *Young*).

The civil division of the Court of Appeal is certainly not bound by decisions of the now defunct Court of Criminal Appeal. It is uncertain whether the civil division will regard itself as bound by decisions of the criminal division of the Court of Appeal, which now exercises that jurisdiction formerly exercised by the Court of Criminal Appeal. The better view appears to be that the civil division will regard itself as bound by decisions of the criminal division so that an unedifying conflict such as has, in the past, existed between the civil and criminal appeal courts[14] is now unlikely to recur.

It may be noted finally that a "full court" of five or more judges of the civil division is sometimes convened to hear cases involving particularly important or difficult points of law. The full court of the civil division has, however, no greater authority than the normal court and its decisions carry no more weight as precedents.[15]

Criminal division — Decisions of the criminal division of the Court of Appeal bind inferior courts trying criminal cases, including the divisional court of the Queen's Bench Division, and will probably be regarded as binding upon inferior courts trying civil cases. The division regards itself as bound by decisions of its predecessor, the Court of Criminal Appeal, and by decisions of the civil division of the Court of Appeal subject to the exceptions contained in *Young v Bristol Aeroplane Co Ltd*.[16] Thus in *R v Merriman*[17] the criminal division allowed an appeal, totally lacking in merit, "with the utmost reluctance" because of the existence of a direct authority of the Court of Criminal Appeal in favour of the appellant. However, the court certified a point of law of general public importance and granted leave to appeal to the House of Lords where the appeal was allowed and the earlier authority overruled.[18]

The Court of Criminal Appeal formulated the principle that it would not be bound by its own previous decision where this would cause injustice to

---

13 [1979] AC 264; [1978] 1 All ER 1132.
14 The historic conflict occurred in the cases of *R v Denyer* [1926] 2 KB 258, CCA and *Hardie and Lane v Chiltern* [1928] 1 KB 663, CA in which the Court of Appeal, on the subject of the legality of trade stop-lists, declined to follow the earlier decision of the Court of Criminal Appeal and expressly disapproved it. The conflict on this point could thus be solved only by the House of Lords and this was done in *Thorne v Motor Trade Association* [1937] AC 797; [1937] 3 All ER 157.
15 This was established in *Young v Bristol Aeroplane Co Ltd* [1944] KB 718; [1944] 2 All ER 293. Likewise the authority of a two-judge court is no less than that of a three-judge court: *Langley v North West Water Authority* [1991] 3 All ER 610; [1991] 1 WLR 697.
16 For an example of the criminal division treating an earlier decision of the Court as *per incuriam*, see *R v Martindale* [1986] 3 All ER 25; [1986] 1 WLR 1042.
17 [1971] 2 QB 310; [1971] 2 All ER 1424.
18 [1973] AC 584; [1972] 3 All ER 42; for the point in the case, see p xxx, *post*. A similar course was followed in *Director of Public Prosecutions v Kilbourne* [1973] AC 729; [1973] 1 All ER 440; see p 570, *post* for a discussion of this case.

an appellant, the rationale of this principle being that the desire for attaining justice transcends the desirability of certainty. The rule was stated by Lord Goddard CJ in *R v Taylor*[19] in the following terms:

> "This court, however, has to deal with questions involving the liberty of the subject, and if it finds, on reconsideration, that, in the opinion of a full court assembled for that purpose, the law has been either misapplied or misunderstood in a decision which it has previously given, and that, on the strength of that decision, an accused person has been sentenced and imprisoned, it is the bounden duty of the court to reconsider the earlier decision with a view to seeing whether that person had been properly convicted. The exceptions which apply in civil cases ought not to be the only ones applied in such a case as the present."

This rule was adopted by the criminal division of the Court of Appeal in *R v Gould*.[20]

In the past, decisions of the Court of Criminal Appeal have been somewhat less reliable as precedents than the decisions of other appellate courts. This is accounted for by the fact that the court rarely reserved judgment, that only one judgment was usually given and that dissents were not recorded. Although the Supreme Court Act 1981, s 59 expressly provides that separate judgments may be pronounced on a question of law, precedents of the criminal division of the Court of Appeal are still regarded with more circumspection than decisions of the civil division.

d   High Court

Divisional courts — In civil matters divisional courts are bound by decisions of the House of Lords and Court of Appeal (including, probably, the criminal division), subject to the exceptions set out in *Young v Bristol Aeroplane Co Ltd*,[1] and also by their own earlier decisions. Divisional court decisions in civil cases are binding on judges of the same division of the High Court sitting alone, and, possibly, on judges of other divisions.[2]

---

19 [1950] 2 KB 368; [1950] 2 All ER 170; see also observations of Lord Diplock in *Director of Public Prosecutions v Merriman* [1973] AC 584, at 605; [1972] 3 All ER 42, at 58; *R v Howe* [1986] QB 626; [1986] 1 All ER 833 (affirmed [1987] AC 417; [1987] 1 All ER 771); but cf *R v Charles* [1976] 1 All ER 659; [1976] 1 WLR 248 (affirmed sub nom *Metropolitan Police Commissioner v Charles* [1977] AC 177; [1976] 3 All ER 112).

20 [1968] 2 QB 65; [1968] 1 All ER 849; the necessity for a "full court" of five or more judges seems to have been tacitly abolished; cf *R v Newsome* [1970] 2 QB 711; [1970] 3 All ER 455 which appears to assert greater power for a court of five to depart from the earlier decision of a court of three than a court of three would possess. In *R v Jackson* [1974] QB 802; [1974] 1 All ER 640, a case in which the court had to choose between conflicting decisions on an important question of sentencing principle, a full court was convened; on occasions when the need to choose between conflicting decisions arises, this practice is sometimes adopted: see, generally, G Zellick, 'Precedent in the Court of Appeal, Criminal Division' [1974] Crim LR 222.

1 See p 72, *ante*; *R v Northumberland Compensation Tribunal, ex parte Shaw* [1952] 1 KB 338; [1952] 1 All ER 122; *Huddersfield Police Authority v Watson* [1947] KB 842; [1947] 2 All ER 193.

2 *Bretherton v United Kingdom Totalisator Co Ltd* [1945] KB 555; [1945] 2 All ER 202; *Re Seaford, Seaford v Seifert* [1967] p 325; [1967] 2 All ER 458 (reversed [1968] p 53; [1968] 1 All ER 482) in which a judge of the Probate, Divorce and Admiralty Division regarded himself as bound by a decision of the divisional court of the Queen's Bench Division; cf *Elderton v United Kingdom Totalisator Co Ltd* (1945) 61 TLR 529 (affirmed [1946] Ch 57; [1945] 2 All ER 624).

In criminal cases the position of the divisional court of the Queen's Bench Division is closely analogous to that of the criminal division of the Court of Appeal. Thus it is free to depart from its own decisions in the same circumstances as in that court. When exercising its supervisory jurisdiction, a divisional court is in the same position as a High Court judge sitting alone; thus it may depart from its own previous decision when convinced that such decision is wrong. The above principles appear from the judgment of the Queen's Bench divisional court, delivered by GOFF LJ in *R v Greater Manchester Coroner, ex parte Tal*.[3]

Judges at first instance — Decisions of High Court judges sitting alone at first instance are binding on inferior courts but are not binding on other High Court judges. For this reason it is a dangerous practice to rely upon principles of law which are contained only in first instance decisions, since they are not binding in any High Court action. Naturally, they are of persuasive authority and a High Court judge will hesitate before "not following" the decision of one of his brethren, if only for reasons of comity. Nevertheless, where a first instance judge is clearly convinced that an earlier decision at first instance is wrong, he will be free to refuse to follow that decision. There have been several direct clashes between decisions of first instance judges, a notable modern example occurring in relation to the question of whether failure on the part of a driver or passenger in a motor vehicle to wear a seat belt amounted to contributory negligence in the event that injury suffered in an accident was aggravated by such failure. This question virtually divided the judges of the Queen's Bench Division in some fourteen reported cases on the topic between 1970 and 1975 until the Court of Appeal resolved the conflict in *Froom v Butcher*[4] where it was held that failure to wear a seat belt did, in the ordinary way, amount to contributory negligence.[5]

It is sometimes said that judges of the Chancery Division are less willing to depart from decisions of their brethren than are judges of other divisions. This is only true insofar as to depart from any earlier authority might have the effect of disturbing financial arrangements or depriving a person of a vested proprietary right.

High Court judges are bound by decisions of the Court of Appeal and House of Lords. Where there appears to be a conflict between previous decisions of the Court of Appeal and House of Lords, the High Court judge should give effect to the decision of the immediately higher court, viz the Court of Appeal. The reasoning behind this is that the conflict could only arise if the Court of Appeal had been able to distinguish or otherwise avoid following a House of Lords decision; in those circumstances the High

---

3 [1985] QB 67; [1984] 3 All ER 240. A "full" divisional court of five or more judges has no greater authority than the normal court of two or three: *Younghusband v Luftig* [1949] 2 KB 354; [1949] 2 All ER 72.

4 [1976] QB 286; [1975] 3 All ER 520; all of the reported cases on the subject are reviewed in the judgment of LORD DENNING, MR in this case.

5 For other illustrations of clashes between judges at first instance, see *Esso Petroleum Co Ltd v Harper's Garage (Stourport) Ltd* [1966] 2 QB 514; [1965] 2 All ER 933 and *Petrofina Ltd v Martin* [1965] Ch 1073; [1965] 2 All ER 176; *Metropolitan Police District Receiver v Croydon Corporation* [1956] 2 All ER 785; [1956] 1 WLR 1113 and *Monmouthshire County Council v Smith* [1956] 2 All ER 800; [1956] 1 WLR 1132; *Wood v Luscombe*, [1966] 1 QB 169; [1964] 3 All ER 972; *Wall v Radford* [1991] 2 All ER 741 and *Randolph v Tuck* [1962] 1 QB 175; [1961] 1 All ER 814.

Court judge should assume that the Court of Appeal had correctly distinguished or otherwise avoided such decision.[6]

e   Inferior and other courts

Magistrates' courts, county courts and other inferior tribunals are bound by the decisions of all superior courts, not excluding first instance decisions of the High Court. The position of the Crown Court in the hierarchy, in relation to the doctrine of precedent, has not been authoritatively determined. When a High Court judge presides the court is, presumably, equivalent to a judge of the High Court sitting at first instance. However, when a circuit judge or Recorder presides it would seem reasonable to regard the court as inferior in status to a judge of the High Court and, therefore, bound by decisions of the High Court.[7] The decisions of one inferior court are not binding upon any other inferior court, chiefly because the decisions of inferior courts are not reported. The Employment Appeal Tribunal is bound by decisions of the Court of Appeal and House of Lords but does not regard itself as bound by decisions of the High Court (nor, presumably by its own decisions) or of the Tribunal's predecessor, the National Industrial Relations Court.[8]

In conclusion it would probably be optimistic to state categorically that the doctrine of binding precedent as applied in English courts achieves certainty while retaining flexibility. Its operation depends, as with the interpretation of statutes, on the conception of the particular judge or court trying a case of the judicial function. The rules for determining the *ratio decidendi* of a case and the hierarchy of the courts are sufficiently well defined to achieve legal certainty. On the other hand, the *per incuriam* doctrine, the process of distinguishing, the capacity of superior courts to overrule decisions and the absolute power of Parliament to change the law all serve to keep the doctrine flexible. In the last analysis the doctrine of precedent is usually seen to operate fairly, though how far this is attributable to the inherent qualities of the doctrine and how far to the good sense of English judges is a matter of debate.

C   THE HISTORICAL DEVELOPMENT OF LAW REPORTING

As stated at the beginning of this chapter, the doctrine of binding precedent became a part of English law only when the system of law reporting had become comprehensive. The doctrine of precedent, as such, is of far greater antiquity but it was only in the nineteenth century that precedents became binding rather than merely persuasive. As late

---

6 This was the analysis of Lord Simon in *Miliangos v George Frank (Textiles) Ltd* [1976] AC 443; [1975] 3 All ER 801; see p 74, *ante*.
7 In *R v Colyer* [1974] Crim LR 243 a circuit judge presiding over the Crown Court at Ipswich took the bold course of refusing to follow a decision of the divisional court of the Queen's Bench Division on the ground that it was not binding on him. This must surely have been incorrect. Since the divisional court is bound by its own previous decisions (*supra*) it would be bizarre if a circuit judge were not bound by them.
8 *Portec (UK) Ltd v Mogenson* [1976] 3 All ER 565.

as 1762 Lord Mansfield, a bitter opponent of mulish adherence to precedent, could state:[9]

"the reason and spirit of cases make law, not the letter of particular precedents."

Nevertheless the growth of a comprehensive system of law reporting brought with it the modern doctrine of binding precedent. If it were possible to mark the turning point, the decision of Parke B in *Mirehouse v Rennell* in 1833[10] would appear to herald the evolution of the modern system.

It is, therefore, instructive to trace the evolution of law reporting and, incidentally, to note the methods of citation and reference.

The history of law reporting can be roughly divided into three periods; first, the period of the Year Books extending approximately from 1272 to 1535; secondly, the period of the private named reporters extending from 1535 to 1865 and, thirdly, the modern semi-official system of reporting which began in 1865.

1 The Year Books

The Year Books are the first available law reports. They were first compiled during the reign of Edward I. Exactly what function they were intended to and did fulfil at that time is uncertain. They were certainly not intended for use by the judges as precedents, and were probably simply notes compiled by students and junior advocates for use, by advocates, as guides to pleading and procedure. While they contain legal argument of counsel and notes of exchanges between bench and bar they are very far from being law reports in the modern sense. Since most litigation in the thirteenth and fourteenth centuries took the form of disputes over title to land it is natural to find that most Year Book cases are land law cases, generally being decisions of the Court of Common Pleas.

Although Year Book reports were in no sense official and were not, apparently, intended for use by the judges, there are indications that they may have been used by some judges as a direct source of precedent. Thus in 1310 Stanton J referred to a case decided at least ten years earlier[11] while Bereford CJ in 1312 cited a decision some twenty-five years old.[12] Even allowing for the longevity of judicial recollection of case law, it seems likely that these judges were basing their knowledge upon some written record of the cases in question. By the fifteenth century there are many examples of Year Book cases in which the judge is reported as having relied upon a number of very old authorities. This is the origin of the doctrine of precedent in English law and there is ample evidence[13] that the judges were conscious that their decisions were being recorded for use as precedents.

---

9 *Fisher v Prince* (1762) 3 Burr 1363. This theme runs through many of Lord Mansfield's judgments. See, for example: *Jones v Randall* (1774) 1 Cowp 37; *R v Bembridge* (1783) 3 Doug KB 327.
10 (1833) 1 Cl & Fin 527.
11 *Kembeare v K* YB 4 Ed 2 (SS iv), 153. Note the method of citation by regnal year.
12 *Anon* YB 6 Ed 2 (SS xiii), 43.
13 For examples see Allen, *Law in the Making* (7th Edn), pp 190 *et seq.*

With the introduction of printing in the fifteenth century many Year Book manuscripts were printed in the so-called "Black Letter" editions. The most widely used modern printed editions of the Year Books are the Rolls Series (RS) and the Selden Society Series (SS). Both series date from early in the present century and contain the original text of the Year Book manuscripts, which are in "law French", a peculiar combination of Norman French, English and Latin, together with an English translation. The Selden Society continue to edit and produce collections of Year Book reports. Citation of Year Book cases is usually by reference to one of these two editions.

Abridgements

The excellence of the printed editions of the original Year Books which are available has rather lessened the value of the Abridgements. These are merely collections of Year Book cases according to their subject matter in chronological order compiled by judges and lawyers, generally for their own use. Some of these Abridgements were published and may be compared to modern case books. The best known Abridgements are those of Fitzherbert and Brooke, published in 1516 and 1568 respectively.

2   The private reports

Compilation of printed Year Books ceased in about 1535.[14] Almost immediately private sets of reports began to be produced, printed and published under the name of the law reporter. At first the private reports were scarcely fuller than the Year Book reports had been. Very soon, however, many sets of private reports became far more detailed, reproducing much of counsel's argument and virtually the whole of the judgment. The private reporters generally attached themselves to one court, probably the court in which they intended to practise, and took notes of the proceedings. These notes would later be revised and published as reports. The citation of precedents became progressively more common as the private reports became more comprehensive.

The private reporters proliferated in the period 1535 to 1865. The standard of reporting varied greatly. At one end of the scale were the reporters whose reports contain what are still regarded today as classic expositions of the common law. These reporters did not, until the end of the eighteenth century, produce their reports contemporaneously with the decisions they were reporting. Consequently the reporter's invention and personality played no little part in the compilation of the reports. This is particularly true of Coke, possibly the greatest of all law reporters. Coke's Reports (Co Rep) are so well known as to be citable merely as "reports" (Rep). They contain comprehensive expositions of virtually every aspect of the common law supported by a wealth of authority assiduously gleaned from the Year Books and even the ancient Plea Rolls, which Coke had copied for his own use. Coke's great industry and scholarship have made his Reports and textbooks a primary literary source of the common law. Nowadays there is rarely any need to look beyond Coke to trace the origin

14 Although manuscript Year Books continued to be produced into the seventeenth century.

of any old common law rule. His Reports, published between 1600 and 1658, contain many of the great constitutional cases of the seventeenth century, such as *Prohibitions del Roy*,[15] *Proclamations*,[16] and *Magdalen College*.[17]

It will be observed that Coke was a judge as well as a law reporter. This is true of many of the great reporters, notably Dyer, who was Chief Justice of the Common Pleas, and Saunders, Chief Justice of the King's Bench. To the great names of Coke, Dyer and Saunders may be added those of Plowden and, later, Burrow. Burrow's Reports are of cases in the Court of King's Bench between 1751 and 1772 and thus include many of Lord Mansfield's famous judgments. They are widely regarded as the first set of law reports produced in the modern pattern. They contain headnotes and the argument of counsel is carefully separated from the judgment. Nevertheless they were not contemporaneous reports. The first reports which attempted to be contemporaneous were the Term Reports which are of cases in the King's Bench in the period 1785–1800.

It must not be thought that every one of the private law reporters was a Plowden or a Coke. At the other end of the scale were reporters such as Barnardiston, Atkyns and Espinasse whose reports became virtually uncitable, so low were they held in judicial esteem.[18] Lord Mansfield, in particular, would not permit certain series of reports to be cited to him, while HOLT CJ observed feelingly that "these scambling reports . . . will make us appear to posterity for a parcel of blockheads".[19]

Citation of private reports

The private reports are cited by the name of the reporter (usually abbreviated) and a volume and page number. The date of the report is not part of the reference but is usually inserted in ordinary round (not square) brackets. Thus the reference to the case of *Ashford v Thornton* is (1818), 1 B & Ald 405 which indicates that the case is reported in volume 1 of Barnewall and Alderson's Reports at page 405. The reference to *Pillans v Van Mierop* (1765), 3 Burr 1664 indicates that the case can be found in the third volume of Burrow's Reports at page 1663.

In practice most law libraries have the reports of the private reporters in the reprinted edition known as "the English Reports" (ER or Eng Rep). The English Reports are published in 176 volumes and contain all the available reports of the private reporters. With the English Reports is published a reference chart showing in which volume the reports of any individual reporter are contained.

---

15 (1607) 12 Co Rep 63.
16 (1610) 12 Co Rep 74.
17 (1615) 11 Co Rep 66b.
18 For an assessment of the relative merits of the private reporters see Allen, *Law in the Making* (7th Edn), pp 221 *et seq*.
19 *Slater v May* (1704) 2 Ld Raym 1071.

3   The present system of law reporting

a   The Law Reports

In 1865 the system of private reporting gave way to the system which still exists at the present day. A Council was established to publish, as cheaply as possible, reports of decisions of superior courts. The Council was, from its inception, under professional control and contained representatives of the Inns of Court and The Law Society. The Council was incorporated in 1870 as the Incorporated Council of Law Reporting for England and Wales.[20] The Council produces the Law Reports, the Weekly Law Reports (WLR), the Industrial Cases Reports (ICR) and the Law Reports Statutes. The Law Reports are not an official publication but, by convention, they are the series of reports to which counsel should refer when citing a case which is reported in the Law Reports.[1] In addition the judges are given the opportunity of revising reports of their own judgments. The reporters, in order for the report to be receivable, must be present in court when judgment is delivered and must be barristers, solicitors or have a Supreme Court qualification.[2]

b   The Weekly Law Reports

Up to and including 1952 the Incorporated Council of Law Reporting published "Weekly Notes" (WN). These reports were in the form of a current precis and did not enjoy the authority of the Law Reports. They were, indeed, not strictly citable as reports.[3]

Weekly Notes were replaced in 1953 by the Weekly Law Reports. The Weekly Law Reports include a report of every decision which will ultimately appear in the Law Reports proper. The cases are reported in full, except that legal argument is omitted because of the restriction on space. In addition many cases are published in the Weekly Law Reports which it is not intended to include subsequently in the Law Reports. These cases are published in Volume 1 of the Weekly Law Reports whereas cases which are destined to reach the Law Reports are published in Volumes 2 and 3.

c   Citation of the Law Reports and the Weekly Law Reports

The citation of the Law Reports prior to 1891 was somewhat complex. Before 1875 a case was cited by reference to the court in which it was decided and a serial number dating from 1865, prefixed by the letters LR.

---

20 The Council is a charity: *Incorporated Council of Law Reporting for England and Wales v A-G* [1972] Ch 73; [1971] 3 All ER 1029.

 1 *Practice Note* [1991] 1 All ER 352. The House of Lords has stated that counsel may refer to a report in Tax Cases, rather than the Law Reports, if they think it convenient to do so: *Bray v Best* [1989] 1 All ER 969; [1989] 1 WLR 167. An advantage of the Law Reports over other series is that legal argument, as well as the judgments, is published. Where the court has adjourned to take time to consider its decision judgment is said to be "reserved". This fact is indicated in reports by the insertion of the words *curia advisari vult, cur ad vult* or *cav*, before the judgment. Reserved judgments are generally accorded greater weight than *ex tempore* judgments.

 2 Defined by the Courts and Legal Services Act 1990, s 115.

 3 See *Re Loveridge* [1902] 2 Ch 859, at p 865, *per* BUCKLEY J.

The date, not being part of the reference, was inserted in ordinary round brackets. Thus *Irving v Askew* (1870), LR 5 QB 208 was reported in the fifth volume of Reports of cases in the Court of Queen's Bench at page 208.

Between 1875 and 1890 citation was by an abbreviation of the appropriate division of the High Court (Ch D; QBD; PD; CPD; Ex D[4]) or App Cas for an appeal case. The date was still not part of the reference and the serial number dated from 1875. The prefix LR was dropped. An example of citation during this period is *Symons v Rees* (1876), 1 Ex D 416.

In 1891 the date was, for the first time, made part of the reference in place of a serial number and the letter D (for Division) was dropped. The fact that the date is part of the reference is signified by its inclusion in square brackets. There is a separate volume of Reports for each division of the High Court (QB; Ch; Fam)[5] and a separate volume for House of Lords and Privy Council cases (AC).[6] Court of Appeal decisions are reported in the volume for the division of the High Court from which the appeal came. County court appeals and appeals to the criminal division of the Court of Appeal are usually reported in the volume for the Queen's Bench Division. There is thus nothing in the reference to distinguish a Court of Appeal decision from a decision at first instance. This is the modern method of citation.

In the case of the Weekly Law Reports the year is, as with the Law Reports, part of the reference and appears in square brackets. There is, however, no attempt to classify cases by the court in which they were decided. All cases appear in 1 WLR, 2 WLR or 3 WLR irrespective of whether they are House of Lords or first instance decisions.

d Other series of reports

A case which is reported in the Law Reports should be cited by its Law Report reference in preference to any other reference, though only as a matter of practice. In addition to the Law Reports (and other reports published by the Council) there are series of reports published under government authority; these include Reports of Tax Cases, Reports of Patent, Design and Trade Mark Cases, Immigration Appeal Reports, Industrial Tribunal Reports and Value Added Tax Tribunal Reports.

There are also many series of reports published commercially. The most highly regarded of these are the All England Law Reports. These are

---

4 The last two were abolished in 1880 with the fusion of the Common Pleas Division and the Exchequer Division into the Queen's Bench Division; see p 5, *ante*.

5 When the Family Division was named the Probate, Divorce and Admiralty Division, this volume of Reports was cited by the letter P.

6 It may be noted that, prior to 1974, when a case reached the House of Lords (or Privy Council or divisional court on appeal) the appellant's name used to be cited first. Thus, for example, the case known in the Court of Appeal as *Lever Brothers Ltd v Bell* [1931] 1 KB 557 became *Bell v Lever Brothers Ltd* [1932] AC 161 in the House of Lords because the defendant, Bell, was the appellant in the House of Lords. However this practice was altered, in relation to House of Lords cases, by a *Procedure Direction* (reported at [1974] 1 All ER 752; sub nom *Practice Direction* [1974] 1 WLR 305) whereby petitions for leave to appeal and appeals to the House of Lords carry the same title as that which obtained in the court of first instance. In criminal cases this has the effect of terminating the practice (which appears to have dated from *Director of Public Prosecutions v Beard* [1920] AC 479) whereby the *Director of Public Prosecutions* was substituted for *Rex* (or *Regina*). The All England Law Reports, since 1979, have adopted this method of citation.

published weekly and their virtue lies principally in the speed with which they follow the decision. In addition many cases are reported in the All England Law Reports which do not find their way into the Law Reports. The All England Law Reports are cited by the year in square brackets followed by the abbreviation All ER and a page number. There are usually three or four volumes of All England Law Reports published each year though, unlike the Weekly Law Reports, there is no significance in the volume number.

The Law Journal Reports (LJ) and Law Times Reports (LT) have been incorporated in the All England Law Reports. The Times Law Reports (TLR) have also ceased to function independently. However, the Criminal Appeal Reports (CAR or Cr App Rep), first published shortly after the creation of the Court of Criminal Appeal, are still produced and report a number of criminal cases not reported elsewhere. Similarly Lloyd's List Law Reports (Lloyd's Rep) contain a number of commercial cases not reported elsewhere while the Road Traffic Reports (RTR) contain, as the title would suggest, reports of road traffic cases. Other specialist series in general use are Local Government Reports (LGR), Building Law Reports (BLR), Simon's Tax Cases (STC), Ryde's Rating Cases (RRC), Property and Compensation Reports (PCR), Industrial Relations Law Reports (IRLR), Housing Law Reports (HLR) and Fleet Street Patent Law Reports (FSR). European Community law decisions are to be found principally in the Common Market Law Reports (CMLR) and European Court Reports (ECR). Periodicals such as the *Solicitors Journal, Justice of the Peace, Estate Gazette, Criminal Law Review, New Law Journal* and *Current Law* include notes of cases to which reference may be made in the absence of a full report in a recognised series. Among newspapers only the reports of The Times are commonly cited (not to be confused with the Times Law Reports).

The chief criticism which may be advanced of the present system of law reporting in England is its informality. The selection of cases for reporting is entirely at the discretion of the law reporters. The Court of Appeal, for example, decides about 3,000 cases every year, of which only a small proportion are reported. Although there cannot be many cases of importance which escape the elaborate net of the law reporters there are undoubtedly some. The citation of unreported cases in court is still by no means unknown while the citation of cases reported only in series of reports other than the Law Reports is quite common.[7] With the advent of computerised data bases, such as LEXIS, unreported decisions, together with decisions of overseas courts, have become much more accessible to practitioners. It was this phenomenon, and the spectre of protraction of legal argument that it spawned, which led LORD DIPLOCK to make the controversial statement which he did in *Roberts Petroleum Ltd v Bernard*

---

7 For examples see Allen, *Law in the Making* (7th Edn), pp 367 *et seq*; see also *Barrington v Lee* [1972] 1 QB 326; [1971] 3 All ER 1231 from which it appears that the Court of Appeal in *Ryan v Pilkington* [1959] 1 All ER 689; [1959] 1 WLR 403 may have gone wrong because two important unreported authorities were not before the court. These cases, decided in 1948 and 1958, have since been reported (in [1971] 2 QB 439, 443; [1971] 2 All ER 628, 631).

Kenny Ltd,[8] restricting counsel's right to cite unreported transcripts of the Court of Appeal in either the Court of Appeal or the House of Lords.

A second criticism of the system is the unnecessary duplication of effort. Many cases are reported more or less fully in three or four different series of reports and noted in many periodicals.

On the initiative of the then Lord Chancellor a Committee was set up to report on the state of law reporting. Its report, published in 1940, was somewhat negative in character. It rejected the proposal to grant a monopoly to the Incorporated Council of Law Reporting, being content to state that the Law Reports should be cited in preference to any other series. The Committee also rejected, in the interest of publicity of judicial proceedings, a proposal to grant licences to reporters without which they would be incompetent to report. Most of the positive recommendations in the 1940 Report were contained in the minority report of Professor Goodhart. Professor Goodhart's main suggestion was that each court, through an official shorthand writer and the judge, should produce an authenticated transcript which would be filed with the court records. Copies of these transcripts would be available for sale to law reporters and other interested persons. This would amount to making law reports official. The majority of the Committee rejected Professor Goodhart's proposal as expensive and inconvenient. At the present day the main objection to Professor Goodhart's proposal would be the additional strain it would impose upon an already overworked judiciary.

---

8 [1983] 2 AC 192, at 200–202; [1983] 1 All ER 564, at 566–568 (see p 57, ante).

CHAPTER 4

Textbooks

A textbook differs from a statute or a law report in that it is not an original literary source of law. Textbooks, even if of the highest authority, contain only opinions as to the state of the law. In short they are descriptive rather than creative. Nevertheless it would be unrealistic in any consideration of the literary sources of English law to ignore textbooks for they are, in some cases, the earliest authority for the existence of a common law rule. The importance of textbooks as a source of law is, historically, in inverse proportion to the availability of law reports. Thus, in modern times textbooks are of comparatively little value since direct authority can almost always be found in a law report. Conversely, in the infancy of law reporting when such reports as existed were of a highly personalised nature the textbooks were, and are, the main source of authority. Indeed the line between a law report and a textbook opinion is often a narrow one, particularly in the case of Coke whose *Institutes* (*Inst*) are cited quite as often as his Reports and are generally accorded equivalent authority.

It will thus be apparent that there are two types of legal textbook. The first is the ancient textbook which is commonly used as an original source of common law. This type of book is a book of authority. The second type of textbook is the modern textbook which, however well respected and frequently cited, is not a book of authority. That is to say it is not a source of law and is only of use in that it indicates where a direct source, such as a statute or a law report, may be found. The dividing line between books of authority and modern textbooks is purely historical and depends, as stated above, on the availability of direct literary sources. Blackstone's *Commentaries on the Laws of England*, published in 1765, is probably the watershed in that, although it is often cited as a book of authority, it was also the forerunner of the modern textbook.

A   SOME BOOKS OF AUTHORITY

Textbooks of English law have not become books of authority merely by reason of their antiquity. Of the many works produced as legal textbooks, only about a dozen are universally accepted by the legal profession and the judiciary alike as books of authority. It is no accident that almost all the authors of these works were judges. The academic lawyer in the modern sense did not appear until Blackstone, in the eighteenth century, and Blackstone himself was also a judge. The following are some of the major textbook writers whose works may be said to be sources of English law.

1   Glanvill and Bracton

Glanvill's treatise *De Legibus et Consuetudinibus Angliae* (concerning the laws and customs of England), written in about 1187, is the first major commentary on the common law in existence. Written in Latin, the manuscripts merely indicate that the treatise was written in the time of Glanvill who was Henry II's chief justiciar,[1] so that it is doubtful whether Glanvill was personally responsible for its composition. The subject matter of the treatise principally concerns land law, the basis of the common law. The form of the treatise set the pattern for legal writing for centuries to come in that it approached the common law from the standpoint of procedure, setting out the existing forms of action with a commentary on the scope of each. Glanvill is still cited as a book of authority[2] though not as frequently as the larger and more comprehensive treatise of Bracton.

Bracton's treatise, written in about 1250, was, like Glanvill's treatise, written in Latin and entitled *De Legibus et Consuetudinibus Angliae*. Although uncompleted it is a far more ambitious and comprehensive survey of English law than Glanvill's work. It adopted Glanvill's pattern of a summary of the forms of action glossed with a commentary but went further in that it illustrated the commentaries with case law. The cases in Bracton's treatise are set out very fully, generally including as much detail as the Year Books. In addition the treatise contains a long exposition of English law by way of introduction. Bracton appears to have been thoroughly grounded in Roman law and his treatise draws many Roman law analogies. Virtually all the principles of Roman law which have found their way into English law have done so *via* Bracton.[3] Perhaps the best known case in which Bracton's civilian analogies have been adopted into English law is *Coggs v Bernard*[4] in which HOLT CJ developed the law of bailments in accordance with Roman law concepts gleaned from Bracton. The development of the law of easements also owes much to Bracton's exposition of Roman law.[5] Nevertheless, Bracton is first and foremost a chronicler of the common law and his treatise stands as the major academic work on the common law prior to Coke's *Institutes*.

2   Littleton

After Bracton there is no book of authority until the late fifteenth century when Littleton's treatise *Of Tenures* was published. This important work was the first comprehensive study of English land law which was, at the time, exceedingly complex. The work differs from that of Bracton in that it approaches the subject from the standpoint of substantive law rather than

---

1 The justiciar was the forerunner of the Chancellor.
2 See, for example: *Ashford v Thornton* (1818) 1 B & Ald 405; *Warner v Sampson* [1959] 1 QB 297; [1959] 1 All ER 120.
3 See p 12, *ante*.
4 (1703) 2 Ld Raym 909.
5 *Dalton v Angus* (1881) 6 App Cas 740.

of procedure. Also it appears that the work was intended for use as a textbook and it was, in fact, used for this purpose for centuries after its composition. Coke's praise of Littleton was fulsome and he described the work as being of absolute perfection, "the ornament of the common law, and the most perfect and absolute work that ever was written in any human science". Indeed, the first of Coke's *Institutes* is a commentary on Littleton's *Of Tenures*.

The work is also notable as being the first major legal work to be printed, rather than written.

3   Coke

Probably the greatest of textbook writers was Coke himself. This may be added to his other accomplishments as a judge, parliamentarian and law reporter. Coke's great contribution to academic literature, apart from the Reports, which undoubtedly contain much subjective exposition, are his *Institutes of the Laws of England*. Coke's *Institutes* were composed chiefly towards the end of his life after he had ceased to hold judicial office. They are so well known as to be citable merely as *Inst* without reference to the author.

There are four *Institutes*. The first, published in 1628, is a treatise on Littleton's *Of Tenures* and is commonly cited as *Co Litt*. The second, and perhaps least valuable, *Institute* is a summary of the principal medieval statutes. The third is concerned with criminal law, defining and describing all the Pleas of the Crown, and the fourth *Institute* deals with the jurisdiction of the courts. The reason for the exalted position of the *Institutes* as a direct source of the common law is Coke's acquaintance with the Year Books. Coke's mastery of the Year Books has probably never been equalled and his recollection in the *Institutes* is so accurate that, even shortly after his death, virtually no one would look beyond Coke as a direct source. For this reason the Year Books are cited comparatively infrequently while the *Institutes* have been cited to English courts probably more frequently than any other book of authority.

A modern instance of reliance upon Coke as a work of authority is to be found in the decision of the Court of Appeal in *Reid v Metropolitan Police Commissioner*.[6] The case was concerned with the meaning of the words "market overt" in section 22(1) of the Sale of Goods Act 1893 and, in particular, whether the operation of that section was confined to sales between sunrise and sunset:

> "to solve this question we have to go back to the works of Sir Edward Coke. In 1596 there was an important case about market overt;[7] Coke reported it. He afterwards expounded the law of market overt in his Institutes[8] . . . I think we should follow the words of Sir Edward Coke rather than those of Sir William Blackstone."[9]

The words that the Court of Appeal followed began:

> "the sale must not be in the night, but between the rising of the sun, and the going downe of the same"[10]

so that a purchaser who bought the plaintiff's goods some one hour before sunrise at the New Caledonian Market in Southwark was held not to have acquired a good title to them under the Sale of Goods Act.

---

6 [1973] QB 551; [1973] 2 All ER 97.
7 *Market-Overt case* (1596) 5 Co Rep 83b.
8 (1642) vol 2, pp 713, 714.
9 [1973] QB 551, at 559; [1973] 2 All ER 97, at 99, *per* LORD DENNING MR.
10 *Market-Overt case* (1596) 5 Co Rep 83b.

The only weakness in Coke's work is his total devotion to the common law to the exclusion of every other branch of English law. His total abhorrence of equity and admiralty undoubtedly did much to maintain the separate administration of these branches of the law for so long.

4 Blackstone

After Coke a large number of legal textbooks were produced. A few of these, such as the works of Hale, Hawkins and Foster are citable as books of authority particularly in relation to the criminal law.[11] Due to the poverty of early reports of criminal cases judges, when faced with a question of basic principles of criminal law, usually look no further than the early textbooks, particularly those of Coke, Hale, Hawkins, Foster and Blackstone. In the leading case of *Joyce v Director of Public Prosecutions*[12] the House of Lords, in deciding that a foreigner who enjoyed the protection of the Crown could be guilty of treason under the Treason Act 1351, relied almost entirely on Foster's *Crown Cases*, Hale's *Pleas of the Crown*, Hawkins' *Pleas of the Crown*, East's *Pleas of the Crown* and Coke's *Institutes*. More recently, in defining the common law offence of affray in the House of Lords, LORD GARDINER LC referred (*inter alia*) to Fitzherbert, Coke, Hale, Hawkins and Blackstone.[13]

Blackstone's *Commentaries on the Laws of England*, published in 1765, is probably the last book of authority to be written. It differs from works such as those of Hale and Hawkins in that it covers a far wider field. The four books comprising the *Commentaries* deal with constitutional law, family law, the law of real and personal property, succession, contract and tort, criminal law and civil and criminal procedure. It is, however, in the fields of tort and criminal law that Blackstone's authority is greatest. The authority of the *Commentaries* is rather less weighty than the authority of the earlier works cited in this section.[14] There are two reasons for this. First, the scope of the work is so wide that it cannot do more than state principles where works of narrower range can probe detail. Secondly, the *Commentaries* are later in point of time than Coke, Hale, Foster and the others so that in the event of an inconsistency between them the earlier work is almost bound to prevail. This is well illustrated by the case of *Button v Director of Public Prosecutions*[15] in which a statement of Blackstone[16] to the effect that a common law affray could take place only in a public place was rejected by the House of Lords as inconsistent with earlier statements in the works of Hale and Hawkins.

---

11 See *Ashford v Thornton* (1818) 1 B & Ald 405; *R v Casement* [1917] 1 KB 98; *Joyce v Director of Public Prosecutions* [1946] AC 347; [1946] 1 All ER 186.
12 [1946] AC 347; [1946] 1 All ER 186.
13 *Button v Director of Public Prosecutions* [1966] AC 591; [1965] 3 All ER 587.
14 Cf *Reid v Metropolitan Police Commissioner* (*supra*) in which Blackstone's definition of market overt was rejected in favour of that of Coke.
15 *Supra.*
16 4 Comm 145.

B   MODERN TEXTBOOKS

The growth of law reporting after Blackstone's era and the fact that the basic principles of the common law were well established and chronicled by that time have made it unnecessary to look at any more recent textbook as a direct source of a common law rule. Nineteenth-century works such as Stephen's *Commentaries on the Laws of England* are sometimes consulted, but only as guides, not as sources. They are not books of authority.

There are, however, many standard textbooks widely used by the legal profession, and even by judges, which are of the highest persuasive authority. Virtually every branch of the law has its standard work and the judge will think twice before gainsaying a statement of law appearing in such a work. Nevertheless judges never lose sight of the fact that these works are not books of authority and, in the event of a statement in a standard textbook being inconsistent with a principle contained in a precedent or a statute, the latter will always prevail. For example, in *Watson v Thomas S Whitney & Co Ltd*[17] the Court of Appeal, in deciding that an appeal from the registrar of the (now defunct) Liverpool Court of Passage lay to the Court of Appeal, declined to adopt clear statements in *Halsbury's Laws of England* and the *Annual Practice 1966*, to the effect that the appeal lay to the divisional court of the Queen's Bench Division. Similarly, in *Button v Director of Public Prosecutions*[18] the House of Lords drew attention to errors in *Archbold's Pleading, Evidence & Practice in Criminal Cases* and *Russell on Crimes and Misdemeanours*, both standard works on the criminal law. In *Shenton v Tyler*[19] the then Master of the Rolls, in considering the scope of marital privilege, referred to some dozen textbooks on evidence, including those of Best, Cockle, Phipson and Stephen, before deciding that all were wrong.

The above, however, are exceptional occurrences. On the whole the persuasive authority of a standard textbook is of considerable weight. There have been several cases in which a court has been willing to accept almost verbatim the view of a distinguished academician upon the law. Thus the description of easements contained in *Cheshire's Modern Real Property* was adopted by the Court of Appeal in *Re Ellenborough Park*[20] while the House of Lords in *A-G v De Keyser's Royal Hotel Ltd*[1] expressly accepted Dicey's definition of the royal prerogative. To go one step further, counsel for the respondents in *Rookes v Barnard*[2] postulated the rather startling proposition that the tort of intimidation had been created by Sir John Salmond in his leading work on the law of torts.

There was formerly a rule of practice that a textbook could not be cited in court during the lifetime of its author. The rule, which appears to have rested on no very logical foundation, has now been discounted and several textbook writers, and even the authors of articles in legal periodicals, have had the satisfaction of seeing their opinions judicially endorsed during their

---

17 [1966] 1 All ER 122; [1966] 1 WLR 57.
18 [1966] AC 591; [1965] 3 All ER 587 (*supra*).
19 [1939] Ch 620; [1939] 1 All ER 827.
20 [1956] Ch 131; [1955] 3 All ER 667.
 1 [1920] AC 508.
 2 [1964] AC 1129; [1964] All ER 367.

own lifetimes.[3] In *R v Shivpuri*, in which the House of Lords overruled its own previous decision of less than a year before in the face of considerable academic criticism, LORD BRIDGE (who had also been a party to the earlier decision) graciously ended his speech with the following tribute:[4]

> "I cannot conclude this opinion without disclosing that I have had the advantage, since the conclusion of the argument in this appeal, of reading an article by Professor Glanville Williams entitled 'The Lords and Impossible Attempts, or Quis Custodet Ipsos Custodies?'[1986] CLJ 33. The language in which he criticises the decision in *Anderton v Ryan* is not conspicuous for its moderation, but it would be foolish, on that account, not to recognise the force of the criticism and churlish not to acknowledge the assistance I have derived from it."

---

3 See, for example, *Performing Right Society Ltd v Mitchell and Booker* (*Palais de Danse*), *Ltd* [1924] 1 KB 762; *Read v J Lyons & Co Ltd* [1945] KB 216; [1945] 1 All ER 106 (affirmed [1947] AC 156; [1946] 2 All ER 471); *Director of Public Prosecutions v Humphrys* [1977] AC 1; [1976] 2 All ER 497.
4 [1987] AC 1, at 23; [1986] 2 All ER 334, at 345.

CHAPTER 5

The European Community

A INTRODUCTION

The United Kingdom has, since 1 January 1973 (the date specified in the Treaty of Accession), been a member state of the European Communities. Of three Communities that exist, the most important is that now known as the European Community.[1] Created in 1957 by the Treaty of Rome, and known as the European Economic Community, initially it comprised six members, but has expanded in size to twelve member states.[2] The Treaty reflected a post-war desire to achieve stability through European unity, and its Preamble stated an aim of "ever closer union" amongst the peoples of Europe. This was to be achieved in areas of economic activity. Article 2 speaks of the promotion throughout the Community of:

> "a harmonious development of economic activities, a continuous expansion, an increase in stability, an accelerated raising of the standard of living and closer relations between the states belonging to it."

Article 3 identifies a wide range of activities permissible in order to achieve the economic and social goals of the Community. These include common policies in respect of agriculture and transport, regulation of competition policy, free movement for workers, goods and services, and the elimination of trade barriers. In addition to the specific provisions of the Treaty, Article 100 provides for:

> "the approximation of such provisions laid down by law, regulation and administrative action in member states as directly affect the establishment or functioning of the common market."

A framework was thus created for common action in the economic field, not simply as joint and co-ordinated action by member states, but through the Community as a distinct legal entity. The Community was to have its own institutions and laws, that could regulate the powers and obligations of member states in the economic field.

The Community has developed far beyond the original aims set by the

---

1 The other Communities are the European Coal and Steel Community (ECSC) and the European Atomic Energy Community (Euratom). References in the text are to the Economic Community and to the Treaty of Rome (1957) unless otherwise stated.

2 Belgium, Denmark, France, Germany, Greece, Italy, Luxembourg, Netherlands, Portugal, Republic of Ireland, Spain and the United Kingdom. Four more countries are currently applicants to join.

Treaty of Rome. Not only has its membership increased, its role has expanded beyond the economic into social, financial and political areas of competence. In 1987 the Single European Act[3] was adopted. In addition to strengthening the institutional position of the Parliament, it set as an objective the "making of concrete progress towards European unity", and in various areas sought to achieve this by amendment of the Treaty of Rome. This process has been continued by the Treaty on European Union (1992), more commonly known as the Maastricht Treaty. This Treaty was, after considerable political controversy, ratified by the United Kingdom in 1993,[4] and given effect in law (as from 1 November 1993) by the European Communities (Amendment) Act 1993. The Treaty not only formally changes the name to the European Community, but also radically amends the Treaty of Rome in order to achieve its aims. These are stated in its Preamble to be a continuation of the process of "ever closer union", economic and monetary union, including the development of a single currency, common citizenship, common foreign and defence policies, and the enhancement of the democratic functions of Community institutions.

This movement towards political union, and the extension of Community competence, is controversial. In particular, the United Kingdom has reserved its position in respect of the later stages of economic and monetary union, which leads to detailed modification to the operation of certain Treaty provisions in the United Kingdom. Despite this, significant change is made. A European Union is established, the development of which is entrusted to a European Council[5] which will develop the political guidelines for the development of that Union. The area of legal competence of the Community is extended, building upon the changes made by the Single European Act. This now extends to common citizenship of the European Union, with expanded rights of movement and voting, greater co-ordination of general economic policy with the establishment of a Central Bank, increased rights for workers, the development of culture and heritage, public health and the environment. The new European Union will develop a common foreign and security policy in line with Title V of the Maastricht Treaty.

B THE SCOPE OF EUROPEAN LAW

It would be a mistake to regard English and European law as two separate systems of law. The latter has now reached the stage of being a significant source of English law. In *HP Bulmer Ltd v J Bollinger SA*[6] LORD DENNING MR stated:

> "The first and fundamental point is that the treaty concerns only those matters which have a European element, that is to say matters which affect people or property in the . . . countries of the Common Market besides ourselves. The

---

3 A Treaty between the signatory states, not to be confused with an Act of the United Kingdom Parliament.

4 For unsuccessful challenge to the incorporation of the Treaty, see *R v Secretary of State for Foreign Affairs, ex parte Lord Rees-Mogg* [1993] 3 CMLR 101.

5 Formerly the Council of the European Community: see OJ Nov 1993.

6 [1974] Ch 401, at 418; [1974] 2 All ER 1226, at 1231; for the points arising from this case, see p 116, *post*.

treaty does not touch any of the matters which concern solely the mainland of England and the people in it. These are still governed by English law. They are not affected by the treaty. But when we come to matters with a European element, the treaty is like an incoming tide. It flows into the estuaries and up the rivers. It cannot be held back . . . In future, in transactions which cross the frontiers we must no longer speak or think of English law as something on its own. We must speak or think of Community law, of Community rights and obligations, and we must give effect to them . . ."

This statement underestimated the extent of involvement of Community law beyond matters that "cross frontiers". Transactions which concern "solely the mainland of England and the people in it" may nonetheless be affected by Community provisions. Some of the provisions of the Treaty, and of the legislation of the community, concern and enforce obligations of an economic character imposed on the member states rather than individuals within states. However, others are directly effective,[7] and may therefore be taken to create individually enforceable rights even within litigation that appears on its face to have no European context. Thus Article 119 regulates equality of treatment of men and women employees. Article 30 affects the legality of Sunday trading in England and Wales. Article 130r provides for the regulation of environmental matters. Article 118a deals with health and safety matters. Even where implementation of Community obligations is achieved by domestic legislation the influence of European law is clear, and in no way limited to disputes with a distinct European context. The role of Directives, which require implementation, is an illustration: they can still be decisive of litigation despite the need for further action by way of implementation, either because they are directly effective or because of their impact on the interpretation of the implementing provision.

The scope of provision by the Community is subject only to the limits imposed by the Treaty and other fundamental sources, though the terms of the Treaty are sometimes broad enough to give scope for creative expansion of the Community role. For example, Article 235 grants power to take action necessary to attain any of the objectives of the Treaty.[8] This has been a powerful tool in developing Community policy in areas such as environmental protection, not, until 1987, specifically within its area of competence. Article 3b of the Treaty (as amended) attempts to define the relationship between Community institutions and member states through the principle of subsidiarity. It states as follows:

"The Community shall act within the limits of the powers conferred on it by this Treaty and of the objectives assigned to it therein. In areas which do not fall within its exclusive competence, the Community shall take action, in accordance with the principle of subsidiarity, only and in so far as the objectives of the proposed action cannot be sufficiently achieved by the member states and can therefore, by reason of the scale or effects of the proposed action, be better achieved by the Community.

---

7 For the doctrine of direct effects, see p 101, *post*.
8 Article 235 ought only to be relied upon as the basis for legislative action not specifically authorised by other provisions: see *EC Commission v EC Council* Case 45/86 [1987] ECR 1493; [1988] 2 CMLR 131.

Any action by the Community shall not go beyond what is necessary to achieve the objectives of this Treaty."

The meaning of this provision is unclear, and the application of the principle will no doubt be the subject of challenge in the Court of Justice.

It may be that a member state, or individual, considers that an institution of the Community has exceeded the powers granted to it. Challenges to the legal competence to act in a particular area, or in a particular way, can be made by the Commission or by member states under Article 173, to the Court of Justice, which can rule as to the legality of the challenged act; the courts of member states have no power to declare invalid the actions of Community institutions.[9] The capacity of individuals to challenge under Article 173 is limited both by its terms,[10] and by restrictive interpretations of the requirements of standing (*locus standi*) to bring such an action.[11]

C THE INSTITUTIONS[12]

The institutions of the three Communities are largely common, each operating through the Council, Commission, Court of Justice and the European Parliament.

1 The Council

This is the legislative body of the Communities. Under Article 145 it is responsible for the general co-ordination of the economic policies of the member states, has power to take decisions and legislate for the Communities, and has power to confer authority to act upon the Commission. It comprises twelve members. Each member state holds the office of President of the Commission for rotating periods of six months.[13] Its membership is not fixed in terms of personnel: attendance will be by the appropriate Minister or Head of State for the matters under consideration. For continuity a permanent committee of officials (COREPAR) conducts much of the routine work of the Council, for later ratification.

Sometimes unanimity is required by the Treaty. More usually it acts by a majority of its members, although Article 148 also provides for a qualified voting procedure to apply where specified in the Treaty. This weights the votes of the various member states.[14] A qualified majority means that 54

---

9 *Firma Foto-Frost v Hauptzollamt Lübeck-Ost* Case 314/85 [1987] ECR 4199; [1988] 3 CMLR 57.
10 Article 173 allows individual challenge in respect of Decisions addressed to themselves or against a Decision which, though in the form of a Regulation or Decision addressed to another person, is of direct and individual concern. For the meaning of "Decision", see *Cimenteries CBR Cementbedrijven NV SA v EEC Commission* Cases 8–11/66 [1967] ECR 75 sub nom *Re Noordwijks Cement Accord* [1967] CMLR 77; *Plaumann & Co v EEC Commission* Case 25/62 [1963] ECR 95.
11 *Plaumann v Commission, supra.*
12 See generally Hartley, *The Foundations of European Community Law* (2nd edn 1988, Clarendon Press).
13 Article 2 of the Merger Treaty, replacing Article 146 of the Treaty of Rome.
14 Germany, France, Italy, United Kingdom: 10 votes each; Spain: 8 votes; Belgium, Greece, Netherlands, Portugal: 5 votes each; Denmark, Ireland: 3 votes each; Luxembourg: 2 votes. The figures quoted in the text will change in due course: see Times, 28 March 1994.

votes should be obtained, or, if acting other than on a proposal from the Commission, 54 votes cast by at least 8 member states. The purpose of these provisions is to prevent domination of the decision-making process by the largest and most dominant member states. The fact remains that occasionally the interests of the Community as a supra-national body and those of individual member states may not coincide.

Such conflicts are often resolved by political agreement and compromise. If a member state considers that a Community Act adopted by the Council is not valid, it may challenge that act in the Court of Justice, under Article 173. Conversely, if it is considered that a member state is not fulfilling obligations under the Treaty, an action can be brought by the Commission under Article 169, or by another member state under Article 170. A continued failure by a member state to fulfil its Treaty obligations will be resolvable only by political, not legal, means.

2   The Commission

The Commission acts as the proposer and implementer of Community policy: by Article 155 it is under a duty to ensure the provisions of the Treaty are applied, to formulate recommendations or deliver opinions on matters under the Treaty, and has the power of decision-making conferred upon it by the Treaty, or by the Council.[15] It comprises 17 members, drawn from member states but independent of them.[16] Each state provides at least one, but not more than two, Commissioners, who hold office for renewable terms of five years.

3   The Parliament

The role of the Parliament was originally stated in Article 137 to be "advisory and supervisory", but now has a greater role in the legislative process, in the approval of the Community budget and in the scrutiny of the actions of the other Community institutions. Although originally comprising members nominated by member states, since 1979 it has been directly elected,[17] although the aim of a uniform procedure of direct universal suffrage, stated in Article 138(3), has yet to be achieved. The Parliament can censure the Commission and remove it if such a motion of censure is passed by a two-thirds majority of the votes cast.[18] This drastic power makes it a more theoretical than real sanction. It can ask questions of the Commission and Council, and has elements of budgetary control. The Treaty contains complex provisions relating to the passage of legislation.[19] In some circumstances a co-operation procedure applies, which involves the Parliament in the legislative process.[20] Which legislative process specified by the Treaty applies will depend upon the terms of the enabling provision of the Treaty, but care has to be taken in the choice of procedure by the Council. In *EC Commission v EC*

---

15 Article 155 of the Treaty of Rome.
16 Article 10 of the Merger Treaty, replacing Article 157 of the Treaty of Rome.
17 Implemented in the United Kingdom by European Assembly Elections Act 1978, s 1.
18 Article 144 of the Treaty of Rome.
19 Article 148 of the Treaty of Rome.
20 Article 7 of the Single European Act, replacing Article 149 of the Treaty of Rome.

Council[1] a successful challenge was made by the Commission to a directive which had been made by the Council under Article 130s of the Treaty of Rome. The use of this provision avoided the use of the co-operation procedure which would have given a power of amendment to the Parliament. The Court of Justice decided that this choice of enabling power was contrary to Community law because the purported reliance upon Article 130s, rather than on other provisions which would have required the use of the co-operation procedure, weakened the participatory role of the Parliament.

4 The Court of Justice

Its role is fundamental in ensuring legal enforcement of Community obligations, and in ensuring uniform interpretations of European law throughout the Community. Cases reach the court either through direct actions, most usually available to the Commission or other Member States, or through references of points of Community law by national courts, under Article 177. European law has been incorporated into English law by virtue of the European Communities Act 1972. By virtue of European law an obligation is imposed to apply the principles of European law.[2] The fulfilment of this requirement is specifically achieved through section 3 of the 1972 Act. Questions of European law should be treated as questions of law and ". . . if not referred to the European Court be for determination as such in accordance with the principles laid down by and any relevant decision of the European Court or any court attached thereto."

D   THE SOURCES OF COMMUNITY LAW

1   Legislation

The Treaties[3] are the primary source, creating a framework of powers, duties and, sometimes, individual rights. The Treaty provisions are framed in broad terms, requiring further legislative action, and subsequent interpretation by the Court of Justice. By Article 189 the Council and Commission are empowered to make Regulations, issue Directives, make Recommendations and deliver Opinions. These are the instruments through which the policies inherent in the Treaties, and those adopted by the Council in fulfilment of the Treaties, are achieved. Regulations, Directives and Decisions may be classed as Community legislation: since

---

1 The *Titanium Dioxide* case, Case C-300/89, [1993] 3 CMLR 359.
2 *Van Gend en Loos v Nederlandse Administratie de Belastingen* Case 26/62 [1963] ECR 1; [1963] CMLR 105; *R v Secretary of State for Transport, ex parte Factortame (No 2)* [1990] 3 CMLR 1.
3 The original, and main, treaties comprise the Treaty of Paris which established the European Coal and Steel Community (the "ECSC" Treaty) the Treaty of Rome, which established the European Economic Community (the "EEC" Treaty), the Single European Act and Maastricht Treaties, both of which significantly amended the Treaty of Rome, a second Treaty of Rome, which established the European Atomic Energy Community (the "EURATOM" Treaty), and further Treaties of Brussels and Luxembourg which merged the main institutions of the Communities. In addition, there are numerous ancillary treaties in the form of international agreements, protocols and annexes, declared to be treaties by Order in Council by s 1(3) of the European Communities Act 1972.

they are made under the authority of the Treaty they are to be regarded as delegated legislation. Their legality may be challenged in the Court of Justice, but not directly in national courts, which have no power to declare Community measures invalid.[4] The legality of such measures may arise during other proceedings: in that situation it will be the duty of the national court to make a reference under Article 177, to the Court of Justice.

It is, generally, the Council in which the power to make such instruments lies. On a proposal by the Commission, and after consultation with the European Parliament, the Council may promulgate the instrument. We have already seen that in some cases a complex "co-operation procedure" gives a greater role to the Parliament, allowing its rejection of proposals to be overridden only by a unanimous vote of the Council. In addition, there is an Economic and Social Committee,[5] which comprises 189 members representative of professions, occupations and other interest groups, and which has a consultative role in the legislative process.

The differences between the various types of measure are identified by Article 189:

> "A Regulation shall have general application. It shall be binding in its entirety and directly applicable in all member states.
>
> A Directive shall be binding, as to the result to be achieved, upon each member state to which it is addressed, but shall leave to the national authorities the choice of form and methods.
>
> A Decision shall be binding in its entirety upon those to whom it is addressed.
>
> Recommendations and Opinions shall have no binding force."

A distinction thus exists between Regulations and Decisions on the one hand and Directives, Recommendations and Opinions on the other. Only the former are immediately binding, although the doctrine of direct effects may confer on Directives a similar status in practice. Those measures that do not attract immediate binding force may, and sometimes must, be implemented by member states themselves. The nature of the measure may have other legal consequences: the rights of an individual to challenge are limited to a Decision addressed to that person, or to a Decision which, although in the form of a Regulation or Decision addressed to another, individual, is of direct and individual concern to that individual.[6] In applying this provision, the Court of Justice has regard to the realities not the form: if a provision is not of general application it will be treated as a Decision even if it bears the name "Regulation".[7]

Regulations are published in the Official Journal. There is no requirement to publish Directives and Decisions, which are notified to those to whom they are addressed. All three types of measure shall state the reasons upon which they are based, including a statement of the facts and law which led the institution in question to adopt them.[8] This is required to facilitate the task of the Court of Justice on review, and so that

---

4 *Firma Foto-Frost*, p 95, n 9, *ante*.
5 Articles 193–198.
6 Article 173.
7 *Confédération Nationale des Producteurs de Fruits et Légumes v Commission* Case 16–17/62, [1962] ECR 471.
8 Article 190. See also *Germany v EEC Commission* Case 24/62, [1963] ECR 63.

member states and others affected may judge the legality of the Community measure.

2   Case law

Besides Community legislation, the case law of the Court of Justice is an important source. The doctrines that establish the supremacy of community law over national law, and of direct effects, both owe their origin to the judicial creativity of the court. In addition, the Treaty is framed in broad terms: it is the duty of the court to interpret and apply it, and Community legislation, in ways that fulfil the spirit and policy of the Treaties.

Besides this interpretative role, the court has developed general principles of Community law. These can be identified as follows:

(a) *Legal certainty*. This principle applies in various ways. A measure may not be altered once it has been adopted. It will be presumed that provisions are not retrospective in their operation. In *Officier van Justitie v Kolpinghuis Nigmegen*[9] Dutch authorities sought to rely in criminal proceedings upon the direct effectiveness of a Directive that had not been implemented. The Court of Justice held that criminal liability could not be imposed in this way. The legitimate expectations of individuals who are affected by Community measures will also be protected.[10]

(b) *Natural justice*. Community bodies will be required to give reasons for their actions, and not to act arbitrarily.[11]

(c) *Equality of treatment in comparable situations*.[12]

(d) *Proportionality*. Obligations may not be imposed on an individual except to the extent necessary to achieve the purpose of the measure.[13] The concept will apply not only to Community measures, but also in determining the legality of action by member states in the light of the Treaty. Thus HOFFMAN J in *Stoke-on-Trent City Council v B & Q plc*[14] had to determine whether the restrictions on Sunday trading in the Shops Act 1950 were proportionate to the restrictions permitted by Article 36, a question ultimately decided in the affirmative by the House of Lords. The concept of proportionality may apply equally to the remedy the court is being asked to grant. In *Taittinger v Allbev*[15] the court granted an injunction to restrain the use of the expression "Elderflower Champagne", prohibited by Community Directive. the court of appeal rejected a submission that the grant of such a remedy was disproportionate to the infringement of the directive found to exist.

(e) *Fundamental rights*. The Community attaches importance to the

---

9 Case 80/86, [1987] ECR 3969.
10 The phrase is borrowed from English law. See Usher "The Influence of National Concepts on Decisions of the European Court" [1976] 1 ELRev 359. For an example, see *EC Commission v EC Council* Case 81/72 [1973] ECR 575.
11 *Transocean Marine Paint Association v EC Commission* Case 17/74, [1974] ECR 1063.
12 *Sabbatini v European Parliament*, Case 20/71, [1972] ECR 345.
13 *Internationale Handelsgessellschaft mbH v Einfuhr- und Vorratsstelle für Getreide* Case 11/70 [1970] ECR 1125; [1972] CMLR 255; *Johnston v Chief Constable of the RUC* Case 222/84, [1987] QB 129; [1986] 3 All ER 135.
14 [1991] 4 All ER 221.
15 [1993] 2 CMLR 741.

protection of fundamental rights. In a Joint Declaration in 1977[16] the role of the European Convention on Human Rights was stressed, as were the rights protected by the constitutions of member states. The Court of Justice held in *Nold v Commission*[17] that these can supply guidelines which should be followed. It should also be noted that the Treaties themselves may confer rights. Article 7 states that:

> "within the scope of application of this Treaty, and without any special provisions contained therein, any discrimination on grounds of nationality shall be prohibited."

This provision has been used to protect rights which would otherwise not fall within Community law.[18] It may also be noted that the trend is towards further Community protection of individual rights. The Social Charter,[19] to which the United Kingdom is not, at the present time, a signatory, creates a wide range of individual rights for workers.

E   THE RELATIONSHIP BETWEEN COMMUNITY AND NATIONAL LAW

1   General approach of the Court of Justice

In a series of important rulings the Court of Justice has developed the doctrine of supremacy of Community over national law. In *Van den en Loos v Nederlandse Administratie der Bertastingen*[20] the Court of Justice stated that member states had:

> "limited their sovereign rights, albeit within limited fields."

In *Costa v ENEL*[1] it stated:

> "The transfer by the states from their domestic legal system to the Community legal system of the rights and obligations arising under the Treaty carries with it a permanent limitation of their sovereign rights, against which a subsequent unilateral act incompatible with the concept of the Community cannot prevail."

The concept of supremacy of Community law has been held to extend to the enforcement of Community rights even if national courts are required to override national legislation. In *Amministrazione delle Finanze dello Stato v Simmenthal*[2] the court ruled that the Treaty and directly applicable measures made thereunder:

> ". . . not only by their entry into force render automatically inapplicable any conflicting provision of current national law, but . . . also preclude the valid

16 Joint Declaration by the European Parliament, Council and Commission (OJ, 1977, C103/1). The Community Charter of Fundamental Social Rights of Workers made in 1989 has not been adopted by the United Kingdom.
17 Case 4/73 [1974] ECR 491. For discussion of the effect of this, see Drzemczewski "The Domestic Application of the European Human Rights Convention as European Community Law" (1981) 30 ICLQ 118.
18 See *Forcheri v Belgian State* Case 152/82, [1983] ECR 2323; [1984] 1 CMLR 334.
19 See n 17, *ante*.
20 Case 26/62, [1963] ECR 1.
 1 Case 6/64, [1964] ECR 585.
 2 Case 106/77, [1978] ECR 629.

adoption of new national legislative measures to the extent to which they would be incompatible with Community provisions."

The national court must if necessary refuse to apply any conflicting national measure, without waiting for it to be set aside by legislative or other constitutional means. A similar approach is taken even in the case of inconsistent national constitutional provisions.[3]

Directly applicable Community law therefore prevails in any situation of conflict. In addition, member states are under a duty to take action necessary to implement Community law. Article 5 states:

> "Member States shall take all appropriate measures, whether general or particular, to ensure fulfilment of the obligations arising out of this Treaty or resulting from actions taken by the Institutions of the Community. They shall facilitate the achievement of the Community's tasks.
>
> They shall abstain from any measure which could jeopardise the attainment of the objectives of this Treaty."

The effect of this has been held by the Court of Justice in *R v Secretary of State for Transport, ex parte Factortame*[4] to require national courts to ensure the legal protection of the rights which persons derive from directly applicable Community law ie those arising from the Treaty, Regulations, or pursuant to rulings of the Court of Justice. Where rules of national law prevent this, they must be set aside.

2 Direct applicability

Those provisions of European law which are incorporated automatically into law are said to be "directly applicable" or "self-executing", and may be relied upon in the domestic courts. Direct applicability is achieved in the United Kingdom by virtue of section 2(1) of the European Communities Act 1972, which states:

> "All such rights, powers, liabilities, obligations and restrictions from time to time created or arising by or under the Treaties, and all such remedies and procedures from time to time provided for by or under the Treaties, as in accordance with the Treaties are without further enactment to be given legal effect or used in the United Kingdom shall be recognised and available in law, and shall be enforced, allowed and followed accordingly; and the expression 'enforceable Community right' and similar expressions shall be read as referring to one to which this subsection applies."

3 Direct effects

If a provision is not directly applicable then although it imposes obligations upon the United Kingdom government under Article 5, which may be enforced by the Court of Justice, it does not directly affect the rights and duties of individuals within the domestic system. In this context the phrase "direct effects" is sometimes used to denote whether a specific provision creates rights upon which an individual may rely upon in the courts. A

---

3 *Internationale Handelsgesellschaft v Einfuhr- und Vorratsstelle für Gestreide* Case 11/70, [1970] ECR 1125, [1972] CMLR 255.
4 Case C-213/89, [1990] ECR I–2433; [1990] 3 CMLR 1.

distinction of academic creation,[5] widely used for the purposes of analysis, the courts (whether European or those in the United Kingdom) have tended to use the phrases interchangeably, and without full consideration as to possible differences in meaning.[6] "Direct applicability" can usefully describe whether a provision needs further action by way of implementation. Thus, Directives and Decisions of the Council and Commission usually require implementation by specific member state action. In the United Kingdom power to implement such provisions by statutory instrument is contained in section 2(2) of the 1972 Act. Not all implementation can be by these means: some obligations can be implemented only through Act of Parliament or statutory instrument made under an enabling power other than the 1972 Act itself. This requirement arises out of section 2(1) of and Schedule 2 to the 1972 Act, since it is expressly provided in that Schedule that the power to implement Community obligations by statutory instrument does not include power:

> ". . . (a) to make any provision imposing or increasing taxation; or
> (b) to make any provision taking effect from a date earlier than that of the making of the instrument containing the provision; or
> (c) to confer any powers to legislate by means of orders, rules, regulations or other subordinate instrument, other than rules of procedure for any court or tribunal; or
> (d) to create any new criminal offence punishable with imprisonment for more than two years or punishable on summary conviction with imprisonment for more than three months or with a fine . . .."

A Community provision has direct effect if it may be relied upon by an individual because it creates legally enforceable rights upon which that individual may rely. Not all Treaty provisions or regulations are directly effective: much depends upon the interpretation of the provision itself. The matter will primarily be one for the court before which the issue arises, though there is a power, and sometimes a duty, to refer the question as to individual rights to the Court of Justice under Article 177. A finding of direct effectiveness not only opens the way to individual enforceability, but also has important consequences as to how conflicting domestic legislation should be construed. It will later be apparent that this distinction between direct applicability and direct effects may be theoretical rather than real, and have little significance. The crucial question in any case is simply: can the provision be relied upon in the national court?

a   The Treaties

Treaty provisions are directly applicable, and therefore require no further implementation. Not all Treaty provisions create direct effects: a Treaty provision only creates individually enforceable rights where various conditions are satisfied:

(a) it must not relate to inter-state relations alone;
(b) it must be clear and precise;
(c) no further action by the State for implementation must be necessary;

---

5 See, in particular, Winter "Direct Applicability and Direct Effects" (1972) 9 CMLRev 425. The phrase is not that of the Court of Justice itself.
6 See, for example, *Johnston v Chief Constable of the RUC* Case 222/84, [1987] QB 129; *Van Duyn v Home Office (No 2)* Case 41/74, [1975] Ch 358; [1975] 3 All ER 190.

(d) it must not be conditional at the time of enforcement.[7]

These criteria can be satisfied even where, as in *Van Gend en Loos*, the Article of the Treaty in question was addressed on its face only to member states. Whether a particular provision fulfils these criteria is a question of interpretation, to be determined as a question of European law, and where appropriate by the Court of Justice.

A number of Articles of the Treaty of Rome have been held by the Court of Justice to be directly effective, and may therefore, be taken to create rights and obligations within English law. These include Article 12, which prohibits the introduction of new customs duties, and held in the *Van Gend en Loos* case to be enforceable at the instance of an individual despite being addressed to the State. Other Treaty provisions found to be capable of conferring direct effects include Article 53[8] (which prohibits the introduction by member states of new restrictions on the establishment in their territories of nationals of other member states), Article 95[9] (which prohibits the imposition by a member state of internal charges on the products of other member states in excess of those applied to similar domestic products), Article 119[10] (which states that men and women should receive equal pay for equal work) and Article 48[11] (which requires the abolition of discrimination based on nationality between workers of the member states and the taking of steps to ensure the free movement of workers within the Community).

b Regulations

These have general application, are binding in their entirety and are directly applicable. In the United Kingdom there is no need for further legislation for implementation purposes. By their very nature Regulations are likely to have the characteristics set out above as essentials for direct effect, though exceptional cases may arise when further implementation by the member state is required.

c Directives

Unlike Regulations, Directives do not necessarily have immediate binding force. They are addressed to member states but it is left to the individual national authority to implement them. In the United Kingdom this may be done by Order in Council or statutory instrument made pursuant to section 2(2), or by means of specific legislative provision or subordinate legislation under another enabling Act.

Nevertheless, although Article 189 of the Treaty of Rome distinguishes between Regulations, which are not only binding but also directly applicable in the member states, and Directives which, whilst binding on member states as to the result to be achieved, have in principle no direct applicability, the Court of Justice has been prepared to develop legal

---

7 *Van Gend en Loos v Nederlandse Administratie der Belastingen* Case 26/62, [1963] ECR 1.
8 *Costa v ENEL, supra*, n 1, p 100.
9 *Alfons Lütticke GmbH v Hauptzollampt Saarelouis* Case 57/65, [1966] ECR 205; [1971] CMLR 674.
10 *Defrenne v Sabena* Case 43/75, [1976] ECR 455; [1976] 2 CMLR 98.
11 *Van Duyn v Home Office (No 2)* Case 41/74, [1975] Ch 358; [1975] 3 All ER 190.

doctrines in such a way as to confer, in appropriate circumstances, significant legal impact. This has occurred in two distinct ways; first, through the doctrine of direct effects, and secondly through their potential operation upon the process of statutory interpretation.

At first sight Directives would not seem capable of direct effects, because they require implementation and are not directly applicable. Despite this in *Grad v Finanzampt Traunstein*[12] the Court of Justice ruled that a Directive, in conjunction with a Decision which was likewise in issue, could give rights enforceable by an individual. Not to recognise such rights would be to weaken the effect of such measures. This ruling was developed in *SACE v Italian Ministry of Finance*,[13] where direct effects were accorded to a Directive imposing a date for implementation of a Community obligation, and put beyond doubt by the Court in *Van Duyn v Home Office*,[14] where the argument that a Directive should be treated differently from a Regulation was rejected. The philosophy of this judicial creativity is to ensure that the fulfilment of the Community objectives and policies is not weakened by non-implementation by member states: in the absence of direct effects for Directives the sole remedy would be through the Court of Justice, with the delays that would entail. Nor has the fact that Directives are not required to be published provided a basis for refusing direct effects to Directives against the State, since the State will be aware of the obligation of which it is in breach. Different considerations apply to proposed enforcement against other individuals. Various limits to the operation of the doctrine exist.

(i) The conditions for direct effect must be fulfilled. That therefore requires that the time-limit for implementation must have expired. In *Pubblico Ministero v Ratti*,[15] the Court of Justice held that whilst one Directive could be directly effective, and prevent the Italian court from relying on domestic laws relating to solvents, another, dealing with other products containing dangerous substances, could not be relied upon by the individual because the date for implementation had not yet passed.

(ii) Directives only attract direct effects against the State. In *Becker v Finanzamt Münster-Innenstadt*[16] the Court of Justice appeared to accept that the state could not rely on national powers kept alive by its own failure to adopt a Community Directive which would have conferred rights on the litigant. In *Marshall v Southampton and South West Hampshire Area Health Authority*,[17] Advocate-General Slynn repeated his statement in *Becker* that a Directive could not impose obligations on another individual – known as "horizontal" direct effects. These could be imposed only against the State – "vertically". This submission was accepted by the Court of Justice. *Marshall* was a case where the Directive achieved vertical direct effects, the Health Authority being a

---

12 Case 9/70, [1970] ECR 825; [1971] CMLR 1.
13 Case 33/70, [1970] ECR 1213; [1971] CMLR 123.
14 See n 11, *supra*.
15 Case 148/78, [1979] ECR 1629; [1980] 1 CMLR 96.
16 Case 8/81, [1982] ECR 53; [1982] CMLR 499.
17 Case 152/84, [1986] QB 401; [1986] 2 All ER 584. For the subsequent United Kingdom litigation, see *Marshall v Southampton, Hampshire and South West Area Health Authority (No 2)* [1991] ICR 136.

State body. in *Foster v British Gas*[18] a group of female employees complained that their compulsory retirement at age 60 infringed a Community Directive. On a reference under Article 177 the Court of Justice ruled that a Directive could be relied upon in a claim for damages against a body which, whatever its legal form, had been made responsible, pursuant to a measure adopted by the State, for providing a public service under the control of the State, and which exercised special powers for that purpose beyond those which resulted from the normal rules applicable in relations between individuals. In applying this the House of Lords[19] held that British Gas (at a time when it was a public corporation) was provided by statute with the duty of performing a public service, under the control of the State, which could dictate its policies and reclaim revenue. It had a monopoly power, and thus the Directive created direct effects.[20]

This distinction between vertical and horizontal direct effects causes difficulties, not only in determining what is a body under the control of the State, but also by applying rules unevenly. For example, rights in employment law may depend upon whether the employer is within the public or private sector. In the light of other rulings of the Court of Justice, though, the distinction may prove less important.

The Court of Justice in *von Colson v Land Nordrhein-Westfalen*[1] stated:

> ". . . The member states' obligation arising from a Directive to achieve the result envisaged by the Directive and their duty under Article 5 of the treaty to take all appropriate measures, whether general or particular, to ensure the fulfilment of that obligation, is binding on all the authorities of member states including, for matters within their jurisdiction, the Courts. It follows that, in applying the national law and in particular the provisions of a national law specifically introduced in order to implement [the Directive], national courts are required to interpret their national laws in the light of the wording and the purpose of the Directive in order to achieve the result referred to in the third paragraph of Article 189 . . . It is for the national court to interpret and apply the legislation adopted for the implementation of the Directive in conformity with the requirements of Community law, *so far as it is given discretion to under national law*." [Emphasis added].

This requirement to construe implementing provisions consistent with the Directive being implemented may have been further strengthened by the Court in *Marleasing SA v La Comercial Internacional de Alimentatión SA*[2] where the Court ruled that where there is a national provision falling within the scope of a Directive, then the national court must apply national law in accordance with the Directive, irrespective of whether the Directive pre-dates or post-dates the legislation. In terms of Community law, therefore, it is the duty of national courts to interpret legislation consistent with provisions of Directives if allowed to do so by national law. Such provisions which might hinder this would run counter to Article 5. In

---

18 Case C-188/89 [1991] 1 QB 405; [1990] 3 All ER 897.
19 [1991] 2 AC 306; [1991] 2 All ER 705.
20 In *Doughty v Rolls-Royce plc* [1992] 1 CMLR 1045 the court left open the question as to whether the *Foster* test was appropriate in all circumstances. Despite the government being the controlling shareholder, this did not have the consequence of making the company a public body for the purposes of direct effects.
1 Case 14/83, [1984] ECR 1891; [1986] 2 CMLR 430.
2 Case 106/89 [1990] ECR I-4135; [1992] 1 CMLR 305.

developing in this way European law is significantly reducing the importance of the distinction between directly and non-directly effective Directives: through an approach to interpretation the Court of Justice may therefore have rendered the doctrine of direct effects unimportant. It is by no means clear how far English courts will apply the *von Colson* and *Marleasing* principles in their interpretations of statutory provisions, but authority suggests that English courts do not regard themselves as having discretion in these circumstances to do other than apply the clear and plain words of the statute.[3]

(iii) In some circumstances the failure of the member state to implement a Directive may give rise in Community law to an action for damages. In *Francovich v Italian State*[4] the Court of Justice held that an individual had a claim for financial loss suffered as a result of the non-implementation of a non-directly effective Directive, given that the amount of the claim was quantifiable from that Directive. Though the right to seek damages for breach of Community obligations has not been generally accepted by English law,[5] the decision in *R v Secretary of State for Transport, ex parte Factortame (No 2)*[6] may have the effect of requiring the national court to confer effective protection upon Community rights. This has been developed more recently in dicta in the speeches in the House of Lords in *Kirklees Metropolitan Borough Council v Wickes Building Supplies*.[7] The House had to consider whether an undertaking in damages was required of a local authority seeking an interim injunction to prevent breach of the Sunday trading legislation. In concluding that it was not, LORD GOFF indicated that damages might be available to the respondent company if the Sunday trading laws were found to be in breach of Community law. He left open for future reconsideration the correctness of the majority ruling in *Bourgoin SA v Minister of Agriculture, Fisheries and Food.*[8]

4   Decisions

These may be made by the Council and Commission as a formal method of enunciating policies or initiating actions. They are binding upon those to whom they are addressed. Like Directives, they can have direct effect.

---

3 *Duke v GEC Reliance Ltd* [1988] AC 618; [1988] 1 All ER 626. See also *Webb v EMO Air Cargo* p 110, *post.*
4 Case 6–9/90, [1992] IRLR 84. Note that in *Emmott v Minister for Social Welfare* Case C-208/90 [1993] ICR 8 the Court of Justice ruled that where a State fails to implement a Directive properly the individual may sue the State in reliance on that directive)if directly effective) until proper implementation occurs.
5 *Bourgoin SA v Ministry of Agriculture Fisheries & Food* [1986] QB 716 [1985] 3 All ER 585. The earlier decision in *Garden Cottage Foods v Milk Marketing Board* [1983] 2 All ER 770 was distinguished on the basis that that case involved the award of damages for the infringement of Community rights by one individual against another.
6 Case C-213/89, [1990] ECR I-2433; [1990] 3 CMLR 1.
7 [1993] AC 227; [1992] 3 All ER 717.
8 See n 5, *supra.*

F IMPACT UPON ENGLISH COURTS[9]

The insistence of Community law that it shall prevail over conflicting national law may be necessary if Community law is to develop as a coherent whole throughout Member States, but presents distinct challenges to constitutional orthodoxy in the United Kingdom. It was this potential conflict that led to the unsuccessful attempt in *Blackburn v AG*[10] to challenge Accession to the Treaty of Rome and the passage of the 1972 Act, the Court of Appeal ruling that the treaty-making power of the Crown was beyond challenge. The court also confirmed the traditional view that Parliament could in theory legislate in any way it chose, including repeal of the Act itself.

Implementation of the Treaty in English law was achieved by the passage of section 2(1) of the Act. In addition section 2(4) states that:

> ". . . any enactment passed or to be passed, other than one contained in this part of this Act, shall be construed and have effect subject to the foregoing provisions of this section . . ."

Therefore, in cases of community obligations which are directly applicable by virtue of section 2(1) they take precedence over conflicting national provisions. By these means Parliament has ensured that most conflicts between English law, whether statute or case law, and European law are resolved in favour of the latter. The constitutional challenge can be avoided by relying on the will of Parliament itself. In *Macarthys Ltd v Smith*,[11] the majority of the court took the view that the individual rights arising under Article 119 should prevail over what were considered the clear and unambiguous words of the Equal Pay Act 1970. By contrast LORD DENNING used Article 119 as an aid to construction, concluding as a result that the terms of the 1970 Act were capable of bearing a meaning that would allow compliance with Community obligations. Alternatively he considered that if Parliament had intended to derogate from its obligations under the Treaty it would, and could, do so by express words, but in their absence an intention to comply with Treaty obligations would be presumed.

The authority conferred by the 1972 Act to apply European law has enabled courts both to quash executive actions and to declare invalid delegated legislation. More fundamentally, the courts have now accepted that this principle extends to declaring provisions of an Act of Parliament inoperative. In *Factortame v Secretary of State for Transport*[12] the question was the extent of interim relief available to the plaintiff company, a group of Spanish fishermen alleging that their rights in Community law to fish in United Kingdom waters were being infringed by the Merchant Shipping Act 1988. The Divisional Court had made a reference under Article 177 on the substantive issues to the Court of Justice, and the question remained as to whether an interim injunction could be issued by English courts as interim relief pending resolution of the substantive issues. The House of

---

9 See generally, Collins, *European Community Law in the United Kingdom* (3rd Edn, 1991, Butterworths).
10 [1971] 2 All ER 1380; [1971] 1 WLR 1037.
11 Case 129/79 [1979] 3 All ER 325; [1979] 1 WLR 1189.
12 [1990] 2 AC 85; [1989] 2 All ER 692.

Lords ruled that English common law did not permit such interim injunctions to be granted. The court then referred to the Court of Justice the question as to whether Community law required such interim relief to be available. In *R v Secretary of State for Transport, ex parte Factortame*[13] the Court of Justice ruled that national courts were under a duty to give effective remedies for the protection of under Community law. As a result the House of Lords granted an interim injunction to suspend the operation of the Merchant Shipping Act 1988 pending a ruling of the substantive issues.[14] LORD BRIDGE stated:

> ". . . Whatever limitation of its sovereignty Parliament accepted when it enacted the European Community Act 1972 was entirely voluntary. Under the terms of the 1972 Act it has always been clear that it was the duty of a United Kingdom court, when delivering final judgment, to override any rule of national law found to be in conflict with any directly enforceable rule of Community law. Similarly, when decisions of the Court of Justice have exposed areas of United Kingdom statute law which failed to implement Council directives Parliament has always legally accepted the obligation to make appropriate and prompt amendments. Thus there is nothing in any way novel in according supremacy to rules of Community law in those areas to which they apply, and to insist that, in the protection of rights under Community law, national courts must not be inhibited by rules of national law from granting interim relief in appropriate cases is no more than a logical recognition of that supremacy . . . ."

Whether such an injunction will be granted depends upon the merits of the particular case, and is not automatic.[15] The relevant principles to be applied in the exercise of such discretion were identified by the House of Lords in the *Factortame* case, and developed further in *R v Secretary of State for the National Heritage, ex parte Continental Television BV.*[16] A significant factor will be the degree of likelihood of the Court of Justice giving a ruling which favours one or other party. If a trial judge considers that such a likelihood is evenly balanced, he is entitled to decide that the applicant's interest in having an Act of Parliament struck down is outweighed by the public interest in the application of that Act of Parliament in the interim. However, it is not for the court of trial to consider the disputed point of law in depth.[17]

The supremacy of Community law has thus been achieved. Under section 3 of the 1972 Act this will extend to the application of principles of European law developed by the Court of Justice. In *Stoke-on-Trent City Council v B & Q*[18] challenge was made to statutory prohibitions under the Shops Act 1950, on the basis of proportionality, a claim that was ultimately unsuccessful on its merits.[19] Further, the courts will, on judicial review, be able to issue a declaration to the effect that the United Kingdom is in breach of community obligations. The courts will be prepared to disapply

---

13 See n 6, *ante*.
14 [1991] 1 All ER 70.
15 *R v HM Treasury, ex parte British Telecommunications plc* (1993) Times, 2 December.
16 [1993] 3 CMLR 387.
17 See *Ex parte British Telecommunications plc, supra*, n 13.
18 [1990] 3 CMLR 31. For proportionality as a doctrine of European law, see p 99. For its different meaning in domestic law, and the problems it raises, see *R v Secretary of State for the Home Department, ex parte Brind* [1991] 1 AC 696; [1991] 1 All ER 720.
19 *Stoke-on-Trent City Council v B & Q plc* [1993] 2 CMLR 509.

an Act of Parliament to the extent necessary to give effect to a directly effective Community provision, or may make a declaration. Thus in *Equal Opportunities Commission v Secretary of State for Employment*[20] the court issued a declaration that the United Kingdom was in breach of article 119 and the Equal Pay Directive 57/117.

Direct conflicts with statutory provisions can often be avoided. The approach of LORD DENNING in *Macarthys Ltd v Smith*[1] was to use European law as an aid to construction to achieve a result in conformity with Community obligations. It is this interpretive approach that has generally found favour in English courts, avoiding as it does the problems raised by the disregard of words perceived to be clear and unambiguous. In *Garland v British Rail Engineering*[2] LORD DIPLOCK stated:

> "The instant appeal does not present an appropriate occasion to consider whether, having regard to the express direction as to the construction of enactments 'to be passed' which is contained in section 2(4), anything short of an express positive statement in an Act of Parliament passed after January 1, 1973, that a particular provision is intended to be made in breach of an obligation assumed by the United Kingdom under a Community treaty, would justify an English court in construing that provision in a manner inconsistent with a Community treaty obligation of the United Kingdom, however wide a departure from the prima facie meaning of the language of the provision might be needed in order to achieve consistency. For, in the instant case the words of section 6(4) of the Sex Discrimination Act 1975 that fall to be construed, 'provision in relation to . . . retirement', without any undue straining of the ordinary meaning of the language used, are capable of bearing either the narrow meaning accepted by the Employment Appeal Tribunal or the wider meaning preferred by the Court of Appeal but acknowledged by that court to be largely a matter of first impression. Had the attention of the court been drawn to Article 119 of the EEC Treaty and the judgment of the European Court of Justice in *Defrenne v Sabena* I have no doubt that, consistently with statements made by Lord Denning MR in previous cases, they would have construed section 6(4) so as not to make it inconsistent with article 119."

This approach was adopted in *Pickstone v Freeman's plc*[3] where the House of Lords considered that a provision of the Equal Pay Act 1970 (inserted into the Act by regulations made in 1983 to give effect to obligations arising from a Court of Justice ruling[4]) was capable of being so construed. Although on a literal reading the regulation did not give effect to the position under European law, the House of Lords was able to read words into the regulations to give effect to the clear intention of Parliament. In ascertaining what was the intention of Parliament in approving draft regulations it was entirely legitimate to refer to Hansard[5] in order to consider the terms in which the draft regulations were presented to Parliament. This purposive approach can be contrasted with that of the Court of Appeal in the same case which found the words of the 1970 Act

---

20 [1994] 1 All ER 910.
1 See n 11, *supra*.
2 Case 12/81 [1983] 2 AC 751; [1982] 2 All ER 402.
3 [1989] AC 66; [1989] 1 All ER 1134.
4 *Marshall v Southampton and South West Hampshire Area Health Authority* Case 152/84 [1986] QB 401; [1986] 2 All ER 584.
5 For the current position regarding the use of Hansard, see *Pepper v Hart* [1993] 1 All ER 42, and generally p 51.

(as amended) clear and unambiguous, but over which the obligations of Community law prevailed, and has again been followed by the House of Lords. In *Litster v Forth Dry Dock and Engineering Co Ltd*[6] regulations were made to give effect to a Directive. The plaintiff employee could not rely on the Directive itself, because the defendant company was not an organ of the State, and thus no direct effects could arise. in these circumstances it was successfully argued that it was the duty of the court to give a meaning to the regulation which accorded with the rulings of the Court of Justice on equivalent words in the Directive, a clear illustration of an application by the House of Lords of the *von Colson* principle.

This purposive approach, giving effect to Community obligations through broad interpretation, was not adopted in *Duke v GEC Reliance Ltd*.[7] In that case the court was considering the effect of a non-directly effective Directive upon legislation not passed to give effect to the Directive. The House of Lords held that section 2(4) of the 1972 Act only entitled a court to distort the meaning of a statute to give effect to a Community provision where it was directly enforceable. The Directive in this case did not have direct effects, and therefore the court was required by English law to give the clear words of a statute their ordinary and natural meaning. This restrictive ruling maintains the approach that the ordinary and natural meaning must be given to the words of a statute in conflict with a Directive sought to be enforced horizontally, where the statutory provision was not intended to implement the Directive. The *von Colson* ruling was not applicable because the court had no discretion as to the approach to interpretation. The extent to which this decision can be supported is debatable, since the duty to apply principles of European law arguably extends to a duty to apply the *von Colson* approach to interpretation: it is the House of Lords in its decision that is depriving itself of the power to interpret such legislation consistently with European Directives. Despite this, and despite the decision in the *Marleasing* case[8] which extends the principle, English courts have shown a willingness to follow *Duke v GEC Reliance*. In *Webb v Emo Air Cargo (UK) Ltd*[9] it was held by the Court of Appeal that in these situations the English court was not permitted to apply anything other than the ordinary and natural meaning. The House of Lords,[10] in making a reference to the Court of Justice under Article 177 observed that the duty imposed by the *Marleasing* case was to construe a domestic law to accord with the terms of a Directive in the same field only if it is possible to do so. It is, of course, not open to a court to do so if it is bound by the doctrine of precedent to an interpretation which runs counter to Community law.[11]

---

6 [1990] 1 AC 546; [1989] 1 All ER 1134.
7 [1988] AC 618; [1988] 1 All ER 626.
8 See p 105, *ante*.
9 [1992] 2 All ER 43.
10 [1992] 4 All ER 929; [1993] 1 WLR 49.
11 See p 71, *ante*.

G   THE EUROPEAN COURT

1   Composition and procedure

The Court comprises thirteen judges,[12] and is assisted by six Advocates-General whose duties are to present publicly, with complete impartiality and independence, reasoned conclusions on cases submitted to the court with a view to assisting the latter in the performance of its duties.[13] The role of Advocate-General has no direct parallel within the English legal system; comparisons with counsel acting as *amicus curiae* are inexact, because the latter act as advocates. By contrast the Advocate-General gives a reasoned opinion following the submissions, both written and oral, by the parties and others entitled to be heard. A more apt comparison is that of a judgment at first instance being considered by an appellate court. The opinion of the Advocate-General is not binding on the Court, but will be treated as of persuasive value. It is reported with the judgment of the Court, and such opinions can be instrumental in assisting in the development of legal doctrine by the Court.[14]

Judges and Advocates-General are chosen "from amongst persons of indisputable independence who fulfil the conditions required for the holding of the highest judicial office in their respective countries or who are jurists of recognised competence".[15] They are appointed for a term of six years by the governments of member states acting in common agreement. They retire in rota and are eligible for re-appointment; the President of the Court is appointed, for a term of three years, by the judges from among their number. The Court appoints its own registrar and lays down rules governing his service.[16]

The Court has the power to adopt its own rules of procedure, which must be submitted to the Council for unanimous approval. The Court must sit in plenary session save that it may set up chambers, comprised of three or five judges,[17] to deal with certain categories of case. It must always sit in plenary session to hear cases submitted to it by a member state or by one of the institutions of the Community, and where in such circumstances it is requested to do so. In addition to the Court of Justice itself, a Court of First Instance was created in 1988.[18] It comprises 12 members, who sit in chambers of three or five judges, though having the power in some circumstances to sit in plenary session. It exercises the jurisdiction of the Court of Justice in relation to (a) disputes between the Communities and their servants; and (b) actions brought by natural or other legal persons against the Community under Article 173. It does not have jurisdiction to deal with Article 177 references. There is a right of appeal to the Court of Justice on a point of law. The Court is of importance, and likely to be increasingly so. Its rulings can be of far-reaching effect: in *BASF AG v*

---

12 Article 165.
13 Article 166.
14 See p 104, *ante*, for the contribution of the Advocates-General in the development of the doctrine of direct effects.
15 The position generally is governed by Article 167.
16 Article 168.
17 Article 165.
18 See generally Article 168a.

EC Commission[19] decisions of the Commission were struck down for failure to comply with formal procedures required by Community law. The purpose in the creation of the Court was to lessen the workload of the Court of Justice itself, thus facilitating more speedy resolution of cases. Whether it achieves this aim remains to be seen: initial evidence suggests that no reduction in the length of time cases take to be dealt with by the Court of Justice has occurred.[20] The Council has the power to extend the jurisdiction of this new court.

2 Jurisdiction

The main jurisdiction is as follows:

(a) Judicial review of the actions of the Community institutions. Under Article 173, the Court can review the legality of acts of the Council and the Commission, other than Recommendations or Opinions. Similar powers are granted in respect of failures to act.[1] Such actions may be brought by a member state, the Council or the Commission, on the ground of lack of competence, infringement of an essential procedural requirement, infringement of a provision of the Treaty or of any rule of Community law. The capacity of an individual to bring such an action is limited: only those to whom a decision has been addressed, or to whom a decision addressed to another person is of direct or individual concern, may do so, and these terms have been restrictively interpreted. Matters are not of direct concern to an individual if there is a discretion as to their implementation. In *Alcan v EC Commission*[2] a refusal by the Commission to allocate a quota for the importation into Belgium of types of aluminium was held not to be of direct concern to the applicant because whether the quota was used depended upon the actions of the Belgium government. Where no real discretion exists,[3] or where implementation is automatic,[4] then the "direct concern" test is satisfied. The second limb of the test for *locus standi* is individual concern. In *Plaumann & Co v EEC Commission*[5] the Court of Justice stated:

> "Persons other than those to whom a decision is addressed may only claim to be individually concerned if that decision affects them by reason of certain attributes which are peculiar to them or by reason of circumstances in which they are differentiated from all other persons and by virtue of these factors distinguishes them individually just as in the case of the person addressed."

Thus, even though the applicant was a German importer of clementines, which were subject to customs duty, the applicant did not have locus standi, since any person might import clementines. The ruling has been followed in subsequent cases.[6] The proper remedy of aggrieved individuals

---

19 [1992] ECR II–1591, CFI.
20 See [1992] 17 CMLR 897.
 1 Article 175.
 2 Case 69/69, [1970] ECR 385.
 3 *International Fruit Co v NV Commission* Case 41–44/70, [1971] ECR 411.
 4 *Piraike-Patraiki v EC Commission* Case 11/82, [1985] ECR 207. *NTN Toyo Bearing Co v EC Council* Case 113/77, [1979] ECR 1185.
 5 Case 25/62, [1963] ECR 95
 6 See eg *Calpak SpA v EC Commission* Case 789–790/79, [1980] ECR 1949.

is through the Commission or the individual member states. Actions which an individual is entitled to bring are dealt with by the Court of First Instance.

(b) Actions brought by the Commission under Article 169. This states:

> "If the Commission considers that a member state has failed to fulfil an obligation under this Treaty, it shall deliver a reasoned opinion on the matter after giving the State concerned the opportunity to submit its observations.
>
> If the State concerned does not comply with the opinion within the period laid down by the Commission, the latter may bring the matter before the Court of Justice."

This basis of challenge is the single largest source of the work of the Court.

(c) Action brought by member states under Article 170. This has been little used.[7]

(d) The Court has power to deal with certain cases concerning disputes to which ordinary individuals (as opposed to member states or Community institutions) may be parties. Thus it has jurisdiction in disputes relating to compensation for damage caused by the institutions of the Communities or by their servants in the performance of their duties and in disputes between the Community and their servants within the limits and under the conditions laid down in staff regulations or the conditions of employment. This jurisdiction is exercised by the Court of First Instance.

(e) References under Article 177. This is a major source of work for the Court, and has important consequences for the courts of member states.

3   References under Article 177[8]

Article 177 creates a power, and in some circumstances imposes a duty, to refer questions concerning the interpretation of European law to the Court of Justice. It plays a key role in ensuring the preservation of the Community character of the law established by the Treaty, and has the object of ensuring that in all circumstances this law is the same in all states of the Community. Article 177 states:

> "(1) The Court of Justice shall have jurisdiction to give preliminary rulings concerning:
>
> (a) the interpretation of this Treaty;
> (b) the validity and interpretation of acts of the institutions of the Community;
> (c) the interpretation of the statutes of bodies established by an act of the Council, where those statutes so provide.
>
> (2) Where such a question is raised before any court or tribunal of a member state, that court or tribunal may, if it considers that a decision on the question is necessary to enable it to give judgment, request the Court of Justice to give a ruling thereon.

---

7 For an example see *France v United Kingdom* Case 141/78, [1979] ECR 2923.
8 See, generally Hartley, *op cit*, pp 246–319.

(3)   Where any such question is raised in a case pending before a court or tribunal of a Member State, against whose decisions there is no judicial remedy under national law, that court or tribunal shall bring the matter before the Court of Justice."

a   The power to refer

This is conferred upon courts or tribunals. This will include organs of the state exercising judicial functions.[9] An arbitrator conducting an arbitration under a private contract is not within the Article 177.[10] This will be something to borne in mind by a court in deciding whether or not to grant to grant leave to appeal against that arbitration.

b   The mandatory reference requirement

Save in cases to which subsection (3) above applies the court or tribunal has a discretion as to whether or not to refer a case to the European Court. Where subsection (3) does apply, no such discretion exists and there must be a reference. This clearly applies to the House of Lords but it is an open question whether it would apply to courts below the House of Lords even where the decision of the court was not one from which an appeal would lies in the particular case in question. The proper construction of Article 177(3) makes the supremacy of the court in the judicial hierarchy rather than the finality of a particular decision the governing factor. This approach found some support from LORD DENNING in *HP Bulmer Ltd v J Bollinger SA*.[11] However, Community law suggests a contrary approach.[12] Whether a court is one which falls within the mandatory reference requirements of Article 177(3) will itself raise questions of European law that may entitle, or require, a reference. It should also be noted that Article 177(3) applies only where there is an absence of judicial remedy: since inferior courts and tribunals are under the supervisory jurisdiction of the High Court it can be argued that such bodies will never be caught by the mandatory reference requirement, even if no right of appeal exists.[13] In order for there to be a duty to refer the question must be "necessary". This is so irrespective of whether a reference is mandatory or merely discretionary, for necessity is a pre-condition to the exercise of discretion. In *HP Bulmer Ltd v J Bollinger SA* LORD DENNING stated that, for reference to be necessary, the point of law must be conclusive of the case. This goes too far, and appears inconsistent with attitudes of European law. In the *CILFIT*[14] case the Court of Justice held there was no need to refer a question if it was not relevant, if the answer to the question "regardless of what it might be can in no way affect the outcome of the case." Other English courts have interpreted the phrase more liberally, as meaning "reasonably necessary" or as "substantially determinative" of the litigation.[15]

---

9 *Vaassen* case, Case 61/65; [1966] ECR 261.
10 *Broakmeulen* case, Case 246/80, [1981] ECR 2311; [1982] 1 CMLR 91.
11 [1974] Ch 401; [1974] 2 All ER 1226.
12 *Costa v ENEL* Case 6/64, [1964] ECR 585.
13 In *Re a Holiday in Italy* [1975] 1 CMLR 184 judicial review was considered by a National Insurance Commissioner to be a "judicial remedy". It should be noted that leave to apply is required.
14 *CILFIT Srl v Ministro della Sanita* Case 283/81 [1982] ECR 3415; [1983] 1 CMLR 472.
15 *Customs and Excise Commissioners v Aps Samex* [1983] 1 All ER 1042.

LORD DENNING in *HP Bulmer Ltd v J Bollinger SA* also stressed that a decision was not necessary if the same point, or substantially the same point, had already been decided by the Court of Justice. Moreover, it was not necessary when the point is "reasonably free from doubt". This mirrors the doctrine in European law of *acte clair*. In *CILFIT* the Court of Justice stated:

> "Finally the correct application of Community law may be so obvious as to leave no scope for any reasonable doubt as to the manner in which the question raised is to be resolved. Before it comes to the conclusion that such is the case, the national court or tribunal must be convinced that the matter was equally obvious to the courts of the other member states and to the Court of Justice."

In determining whether a point was *acte clair* regard should be had to the fact that Community law is drafted in several languages which may require comparison, that Community concepts may bear different meanings from similar concepts in domestic law, and that such points need to be considered in the context of Community law as a whole. The doctrine of *acte clair* applies equally to matters that fall within the mandatory and discretionary limbs of Article 177, though, it should be noted that since a national court has no power to declare actions of the Community invalid,[16] it will in such cases be necessary to make a reference even where the matter is clear.

The attitude of English courts in applying the *acte clair* doctrine has been uncertain. KERR LJ in *R v Pharmaceutical Society of Great Britain, ex parte the Association of Pharmaceutical Importers*[17] observed that an English court should "hesitate long" before reaching a conclusion that a point of European law was so obvious as to leave no room for reasonable doubt. Indeed, in *R v International Stock Exchange of the United Kingdom and Republic of Ireland Ltd, ex parte Else (1982) Ltd*[18] SIR THOMAS BINGHAM MR observed that the appropriate course is ordinarily to refer the issue to the Court of Justice unless the national court can with complete confidence resolve the issue itself. If it has any real doubt, it should ordinarily refer. As was indicated by BINGHAM J in the *Samex*[19] case, decisions of English courts on European law should be "communautaire", a prospect that has been described as "intimidating to an English judge."[20]

c The discretion to refer

The discretion to refer is that of the national court or tribunal, and will not be reviewable by the Court of Justice, unless the reference is in effect is spurious or an abuse of process.[1] It will be for the national court to formulate the question to be answered, though the Court of Justice will refine the question if it is clear exactly what the question for interpretation actually is. The decision to make a reference cannot be removed from a

---

16 See p 95, *ante. Firma Foto-Frost v Hauptzollampt Lübeck-Ost* Case 314/85 [1987] ECR 4199.
17 [1987] 3 CMLR 951.
18 [1993] QB 534, [1993] 1 All ER 420.
19 *Customs and Excise Commissioners v ApS Samex* [1983] 1 All ER 1042.
20 *R v Secretary of State for Transport, ex parte Factortame (No 2)* [1990] 3 CMLR 1.
 1 *Foglia v Novello* Case 104/79, [1980] ECR 745; *Foglia v Novello (No 2)* Case 244/80; [1981] ECR 3045.

court or tribunal by domestic law, though the decision not to make a reference will be a matter subject to such appeal as exist in the particular case.[2]

Guidelines for the exercise of the discretion by English courts were set out by LORD DENNING in *Bulmer v Bollinger*.[3] They can, though, be no more than guidelines and have been stated not to be binding. They should be compared with the various statements on Article 177 by the Court of Justice. The following factors were considered by LORD DENNING to be relevant:

(i)   the time needed to obtain a ruling;
(ii) the importance of not overloading the European Court with references;
(iii) the difficulty and importance of the point;
(iv) the expense involved;
(v)   the wishes of the parties.

He also stated that the facts should be established first, an "injunction of obvious merit".[4] The importance of deciding the facts first is that they provide the legal context for the point at issue, and indeed may determine whether or not a reference is in fact "necessary". However, as the Court of Justice stated in *Irish Creamery Milk Suppliers Association v Ireland*,[5] it is the national court which has responsibility for giving judgment in the case and is therefore in the best position to judge at what stage in the proceedings a reference is required. There is nothing to prevent a reference being made at an interlocutory stage. In the *Factortame* litigation important issues were raised and resolved under references at interlocutory stages.[6] In *Löwenbräu Münchin v Günhalle Lager Internationale*[7] GRAHAM J identified the following points to be borne in mind: (i) interlocutory proceedings do not fully dispose of the points at issue; (ii) it is not always clear what the matter in issue will be; (iii) whether the facts have been ascertained; (iv) the requirement for speedy determination. This will undoubtedly be for the judgment of the court.

Likewise in criminal cases the appropriate response and time for a reference may vary. In *Henn and Darby v Director of Public Prosecutions*[8] LORD DIPLOCK indicated that a reference should be dealt with if necessary after the trial, at the appellate stage. By contrast in *R v Goldstein*[9] the court indicated that where it is apparent at the outset of the case that a point of European law may well be determinative, the appropriate course is to make application to quash the indictment. The right approach may be to determine whether the interests of justice provided compelling reason for going ahead with the trial pending determination of a reference.[10]

In deciding whether or not to make a reference, the loading upon the

---

2 *Rheinmuhlen* case, Case 146/73; [1974] ECR 139; [1974] 1 CMLR 523.
3 See n 11, *ante*.
4 Per BINGHAM J in *Customs and Excise Commissioners v Samex*, n 15, *ante*.
5 Case 36,71/80, [1981] ECR 735; [1981] 2 CMLR 455.
6 *R v Secretary of State for Transport, ex parte Factortame (No 2)* [1990] 3 CMLR 1.
7 [1974] 1 CMLR 1.
8 [1980] AC 850; [1980] 2 All ER 166.
9 [1983] 1 AU ER 434; [1983] 1 WLR 151.
10 For criminal proceedings generally, see p 433 *et seq*, *post*.

Court of Justice appears not to be a relevant factor despite the dicta of LORD DENNING: the problems of the Court of Justice should not be resolved through the mechanisms of restricting reference. If a reference is indeed necessary, then such an approach in fact runs counter to the philosophy of the court in requiring references to be made. By contrast, expense is an important factor to be considered, to be weighed against other costs that are incurred in continuing the domestic proceedings with a possible or likely requirement to refer a later stage of the case. In *R v Pharmaceutical Society of Great Britain, ex parte Association of Pharmaceutical Importers*[11] KERR LJ expected the case to reach the House of Lords, which would therefore lead to a mandatory reference under Article 177(3), and considered that an immediate reference would therefore save considerable time and costs. As HODGSON J stated in the *Factortame* case: if a reference is going to be made "the sooner it is done the better."

The wishes of the parties will be a relevant but not decisive factor. The concept of "reference by consent" should not creep into the practice of the English courts, for it is the judgment of the court as to the necessity for and desirability of a reference that is important. However, where only one party wishes a reference there is no inevitability: it will usually be the case that a reference will assist one party only. Reference may be appropriate even against the wishes of both parties. The court may also take into account the fact that the matter is one upon which the European Commission has strong views.[12]

---

11 See n 17, *ante*.
12 *Ibid.*

PART II

The Administration of Justice

SUMMARY

CHAPTER 6

The Royal Prerogative and Judicial Review

A THE ROYAL PREROGATIVE

Historically the sovereign is the fountain of justice in England. For this reason the administration of justice is, strictly speaking, a prerogative of the Crown. This prerogative has, however, been substantially whittled away. Thus it was decided by COKE CJ in the case of *Prohibitions del Roy*[1] that the King (James I) could not, in his own person, judge any case. It is customarily accepted that the Crown no longer has a general power to create new courts by prerogative although it can, apparently, create courts to administer only the common law.[2] Nevertheless this power is worthless since any court so created would be powerless to apply any rules of law other than common law rules and would, presumably, have difficulty in obtaining Parliamentary authority for the finance required to maintain such a court. With the drastic curtailment of the immunity of the Crown in respect of civil proceedings (other than in a personal capacity) the position of the Crown is effectively formal. The remaining powers and privileges, though nominally vested in the Crown, are in reality those of its Ministers.[3]

Dicey defined the prerogative as follows:

> "The prerogative is the name for the remaining portion of the Crown's original authority, and is therefore, as already pointed out, the name for the residue of discretionary power left at any moment in the hands of the Crown, whether such power be in fact exercised by the King himself or by his Ministers."[4]

Most of the remaining vestiges of prerogative control over the administration of justice are formal rather than of substance. The superior courts are termed the "Queen's Courts" and the judges of those courts styled "Her

---

1 (1607) 12 Co Rep 63.
2 *Re Lord Bishop of Natal* (1864) 3 Moo PCC NS 115. The creation of the Criminal Injuries Compensation Board, is, however, a modern example of a tribunal created by prerogative act; see p 178, *post*.
3 In accordance with constitutional principle, exercisable by and on the advice of Ministers.
4 *Introduction to the Study of the Law of the Constitution* (8th Edn, 1915), p 421, cited with approval in *A-G v De Keyser's Royal Hotel Ltd* [1920] AC 508. See also: *Council of Civil Service Unions v Minister for the Civil Service* (the *GCHQ* case) [1985] AC 374; [1984] 3 All ER 935.

Majesty's Judges". Criminal proceedings, on indictment, are pursued in the name of the Queen and all criminal proceedings are conducted on behalf of the Crown. These so-called prerogatives are, however, illusory. Judges are appointed "on the advice of" the Lord Chancellor or, in some cases, the Prime Minister. There is no power in the Crown to intervene in civil proceedings and criminal proceedings may usually be commenced by any private individual. The parts of the royal prerogative which have continuing influence on the administration of justice are few. Among them may be included the power of the Attorney-General to stop a prosecution on indictment by entering a *nolle prosequi*, the power to pardon a convicted person and the prerogative of mercy under which the Crown may, through the Home Secretary, suspend, commute or remit any sentence.[5] The process of judicial review, though, provides an important mechanism for judicial scrutiny and control over parts of the administration of justice.

B   JUDICIAL REVIEW

1   Historical origins of the powers of the High Court

Historically, the superior common law courts controlled the conduct of inferior courts of record, in the name of the King and under the royal prerogative.[6] The existence of the prerogative itself was a matter claimed to be within the province of the common law courts. In the *Case of Proclamations*[7] the court stated that "the King hath no prerogative, but which the law of the land allows him." The errors of these courts, whether errors as to jurisdiction or errors of law within jurisdiction, were again controlled through the use of the prerogative.[8] This supervisory function was achieved through use of the prerogative writs. These were as follows:

(1) *prohibition*: inferior courts or administrative bodies could be prohibited from acting in excess of jurisdiction or unlawfully;
(2) *mandamus*: an inferior court could be ordered to exercise jurisdiction where it was declining to do so or an official ordered to perform a function which the law required of him;
(3) *certiorari*: the record of an inferior court could be examined by the King's Bench and the proceedings quashed on the ground of error of law, excess of jurisdiction or abuse of process;
(4) *habeas corpus*: requiring a person holding another in custody to justify the confinement to the court;
(5) *quo warranto*: enabling a party to challenge the jurisdiction of a court or person in public office purporting to exercise jurisdiction over him by means of a writ ordering the sheriff to summon the claimant to show by what authority (*quo warranto*) he asserted jurisdiction.

---

5 See p 124, *post*.
6 See p 133, *post*.
7 See n 1, *supra*.
8 See p 133, *post*.

Of the above, *quo warranto* fell into disuse long before its abolition in 1938.[9] The various forms of the writ of *habeas corpus* still exist and the writ of *habeas corpus ad subjiciendum* is still frequently used, often as a means of testing the validity of detention effected for the purpose of extradition. The remaining three writs were abolished in 1938 but replaced by *orders* of *prohibition, mandamus* and *certiorari*. They constitute the supervisory jurisdiction of the High Court and the procedure whereby this jurisdiction is invoked and exercised is now termed "judicial review".[10] An application for any of the orders named above, or for an injunction or declaration,[11] must be made by way of application for judicial review.

2   The scope of judicial review

This has widened greatly in recent years. Despite occasional judicial confusions, it was always clear that judicial review lay against any inferior court or tribunal, and against any body exercising statutory functions affecting the rights of individuals. This later developed to allow challenge to the actions of such a body affecting the legitimate expectations of an individual.[12] Doubt, though, remained about the reviewability of actions taken by or on behalf of the Crown under the royal prerogative. The traditional position was that though the court was entitled to rule as to the existence or extent of prerogative power, it was not entitled to review the exercise of such power.[13] Thus an attempt in *Hanratty v Lord Butler*[14] to challenge the exercise the prerogative power of mercy inevitably failed.[15]

Some evidence existed that this position was not absolute. In *R v Criminal Injuries Compensation Board, ex parte Lain*[16] the divisional court decided that *certiorari* could issue against decisions of that Board, a body established under prerogative power to administer a scheme for the provision of compensation to victims of crimes of violence. This, though, was not the review of prerogative power, but rather the review of actions taken by a body established under the prerogative. The issue arose more directly in *Laker Airways Ltd v Department of Trade*[17] where LORD DENNING observed, *obiter*, that he saw no reason why the exercise of prerogative powers should not be reviewable. The matter was effectively put beyond doubt by the House of Lords in *Council of Civil Service Unions v Minister for the Civil Service*.[18] The litigation arose out of an instruction by the Minister to the effect that the conditions of employment of staff at Government Communications Headquarters (GCHQ) would be revised so

---

9 By Administration of Justice (Miscellaneous Provisions) Act 1938, s 9, which provided that the remedy would, in effect, be replaced by injunction; see now Supreme Court Act 1981, s 30.

10 Under the Supreme Court Act 1981, s 31, and RSC Ord 53.

11 Available on judicial review since 1977: see RSC Ord 53, r 1.

12 See LORD DIPLOCK in the *GCHQ* case, *supra* n 4. The legitimate expectation can be either as to the receipt of a benefit, or of being treated procedurally in a particular way.

13 *Case of Saltpetre* (1606) 12 Co Rep 12; *Blackburn v A-G* [1971] 2 All ER 1380; [1971] 1 WLR 1037.

14 (1971) 115 Sol Jo 386.

15 But now see p 124, *post*.

16 [1967] 2 QB 864; [1967] 2 All ER 770; see p 178, *post*.

17 [1977] QB 643; [1977] 2 All ER 182.

18 See, n 4, *ante*.

as to prohibit membership of any trade union (other than an approved departmental staff association). This instruction was issued pursuant to power conferred upon the Minister by an order in council made under the royal prerogative.[19] The appellants applied for judicial review of the Minister's instruction. It was contended (*inter alia*) on behalf of the Minister that the instruction was not open to review by the courts because it was an emanation of the prerogative. In the event adjudication on this contention became unnecessary because the House of Lords held that the evidence disclosed the Minister's instruction to have been justified on the ground of national security. This being so, any observations by their Lordships upon the contention raised were necessarily *obiter*. However, the majority proceeded on the basis that the key question was not the source of the power, but rather whether it was of a nature suitable for judicial adjudication (*ie* justiciable). LORD ROSKILL identified certain prerogative powers as of a type not suitable for judicial determination. These included the making of treaties, the defence of the realm, the prerogative of mercy, the grant of honours, the dissolution of Parliament and the appointment of Ministers. More recent case law has shown, however, that even this list is not absolute, with a successful challenge being made to the exercise of the prerogative of mercy.[20]

The trend set by the *GCHQ* case has continued. Recent case law shows that it is now the nature of the function that matters, and which determines whether judicial review is available. In *R v Panel on Take-overs and Mergers, ex parte Datafin*[1] the court ruled that the absence of a statutory or prerogative power was not decisive: judicial review would lie in respect of any body performing a public law function.[2] In this case, the Take-Over Panel was acting "governmentally" in engaging in regulatory functions in the area of take-overs which would otherwise be performed by a statutory body on behalf of the State.[3]

The availability of judicial review is dependent, therefore, upon the nature of the particular power sought to be challenged. Many of the prerogative powers involving the administration of justice may be beyond judicial review, because of their unsuitability for judicial determination. The exercise of the prerogative of mercy might, in the light of the comments of LORD ROSKILL in the *GCHQ* case, be one example. However, in *R v Secretary of State for Home Affairs, ex parte Bentley*[4] a divisional court held that the courts have jurisdiction to review the exercise of the royal prerogative of mercy by the Home Secretary. The Home Secretary,

---

19 This is primary legislation, to be distinguished from the use of Orders in Council as delegated legislation.
20 See *Ex parte Bentley*, *infra*.
1 [1987] QB 815; [1987] 1 All ER 564.
2 Which is not created simply by the body concerned being a public body: see *R v East Berkshire Area Health Authority, ex parte Walsh* [1985] QB 152; [1984] 3 All ER 425. For the relevant principles, see *McClaren v Home Office* [1990] ICR 824, and p 279, *post*.
3 The effect of the *Datafin* decision appears weakened by subsequent cases; See *R v Chief Rabbi of the United Hebrew Congregations of Great Britain, ex parte Wachmann* [1992] 1 WLR 1036. In *R v Insurance Ombudsman Bureau & the Insurance Ombudsman, ex parte Aegon Life Assurance Ltd* (1993), unreported the court held that if the exercise of the power was consensual or contractual then it was not a public law matter, despite being woven into a system of governmental control.
4 [1993] 4 All ER 442.

in considering whether or not to grant a posthumous free pardon to B, a person hanged in 1952 for murder, had failed to have regard to the fact that such a pardon might be used in a variety of circumstances and take different forms. It might constitute a full pardon, or, as might have been appropriate in this case, a conditional pardon substituting a lesser sentence for that in fact imposed. The Secretary of State thus had made an error of law by failing to have regard to all relevant considerations, and therefore his refusal was unlawful.

In so deciding the court was applying the reasoning of the House of Lords in the *GCHQ* case. Even the exercise of the prerogative of mercy could be judicially reviewed if the grounds of challenge do not involve the court in the decision of policy questions. Thus, whilst the policy to be adopted for the granting of pardons was not justiciable, the present decision was, because the Secretary of State had failed to recognise the extent of his powers.

Even if a statutory basis exists, judicial review may be limited. The courts have held that actions of the police may be reviewed, but the scope of that review is restricted. An example of this is judicial review of the prosecution process. In *R v Commissioner of Police for the Metropolis, ex parte Blackburn*[5] the applicant sought an order of *mandamus* to compel the Commissioner of Police to reverse a policy statement which appeared to limit the enforcement of the gaming laws. The Court of Appeal held that *mandamus* might issue in an appropriate case, if there was what amounted to a complete failure to perform a duty imposed by law, but declined to make an order in the particular case before the court because the Commissioner had in fact reversed that policy. In a subsequent case involving the obscene publications laws,[6] the court stressed that the discretion was that of the Commissioner, the court only intervening where there was what amounted to an abdication of function.

Likewise with the discretion to prosecute. In *R v Chief Constable of Kent, ex parte L*[7] the divisional court stated, *obiter*, that judicial review of a decision to commence criminal proceedings is unlikely to be available. A different position exists in respect of young persons, where a policy exists in respect of cautioning: the decision to commence or discontinue criminal proceedings was subject to judicial review, but only where it could be shown that the decision was made regardless of, or contrary to, that policy.[8]

Moving to judicial review of the actions of the courts themselves, it is an effective means for the control of the inferior courts, ensuring a means of challenge where failures to comply with jurisdictional requirements, or principles of fair procedure, have occurred. It also provides a remedy where no right of appeal against a decision exists.[9] Similarly with the actions of other forms of judicial adjudication, such as tribunals or public

---

5 [1968] 2 QB 118; [1968] 1 All ER 763.
6 *R v Commissioner of Police for the Metropolis, ex parte Blackburn (No 3)* [1973] QB 241; [1973] 1 All ER 324.
7 [1993] 1 All ER 756,
8 *R v Havering Justices, ex parte Gould* (1993), unreported.
9 Judicial review can only be prevented by the clearest of words: *Anisminic Ltd v Foreign Compensation Commission* [1969] 2 AC 147; [1969] 1 All ER 208. It may be restricted: *R v Cornwall County Council, ex parte Huntington* [1992] 3 All ER 566.

inquiries. However, judicial review does not lie against superior courts. The Crown Court is a superior court of record. Despite this, it is amenable to judicial review when dealing with an appeal from a magistrates' court, for then it is exercising the jurisdiction of that court, an inferior court.[10] Its actions are also subject to review in any other case, subject to the important limitation contained in section 29(3) of the Supreme Court Act 1981 in respect of judicial review "in matters relating to trial on indictment". The reason for this provision is historical: the Crown Court took over the appellate jurisdiction of the old courts of Quarter Sessions, which were inferior courts and thus subject to judicial review. However, the application of section 29(3) has proved less than easy. In *R v Crown Court at Sheffield, ex parte Brownlow*[11] LORD DENNING sought to interpret the subsection as preventing judicial review of matters arising "in the course of trial on indictment". This extremely narrow construction was not adopted by the majority of the court, which concluded that section 29(3) prevented judicial review where a decision arose out of, or incidentally to, the jurisdiction to try cases on indictment. On this view, a decision by the trial judge as to information concerning the jury panel was held to be caught by section 29(3) and thus not judicially reviewable.

The approach taken by the majority has not been followed in subsequent cases. In *Smalley v Crown Court at Warwick*[12] the House of Lords considered a decision to forfeit a recognisance entered into by a witness to be judicially reviewable. LORD BRIDGE stressed the need to proceed on a case-by-case basis. He set out a working test: the limitation in section 29(3) applied to "any decision affecting the conduct of a trial on indictment". However, it has since been stressed that this is a guideline, and was not an attempt to re-write the words of the subsection.[13] In addition, the real difficulty is in applying the guidance given by LORD BRIDGE. Decisions to allow counts of an indictment effectively to remain untried, and applications to quash an indictment, are instances which have been held to be subject to the restrictions upon judicial review.[14]

The problem has recently been extensively considered by the House of Lords in two cases. The first was *R v Manchester Crown Court, ex parte Director of Public Prosecutions*[15] where the court held that an order of the Crown Court made upon an application to stay the proceedings for abuse of process[16] was an order affecting the conduct of the trial, and therefore fell within section 29(2). The second was *Director of Public Prosecutions v Crown Court at Manchester and Huckfield*,[17] where a decision by a circuit judge to quash an indictment for lack of jurisdiction was held to be a matter "relating to trial on indictment" and thus not judicially reviewable. One test is whether the decision sought to be reviewed arises in the issue between the Crown and the defendant formulated by the indictment,

10 See p 141, *post.*

11 [1980] QB 530; [1980] 2 All ER 444.

12 [1985] AC 622; [1985] 1 All ER 769.

13 *Per* LORD BRIDGE in *Sampson v Crown Court at Croydon*, [1987] 1 All ER 609; [1987] 1 WLR 194.

14 See *R v Central Criminal Court, ex parte Raymond* [1986] 2 All ER 379; [1986] 1 WLR 710.

15 [1994] AC 9; sub nom *Director of Public Prosecutions v Crown Court at Manchester and Ashton* [1993] 2 All ER 663.

16 See p 494, *post.*

17 [1993] NLJR 1711 (3 December 1993).

including issues relating to costs. If it does, then judicial review might well lead to delay in the trial, and therefore is probably caught by the restrictions imposed by section 29(3).

The House of Lords stressed that this test might not always be appropriate. In particular, the question was left open as to whether judicial review was available in respect of the procedures to be followed in cases of serious fraud.[18] However, the test formulated by the court would have the effect of permitting judicial review where an order was made affecting a person other than the defendant,[19] or where the court was acting under a different jurisdiction.[20]

3 Procedure

An application for any one of the prerogative orders, or for a declaration that a public law matter is unlawful, must be made by way of application for judicial review. This is the normal, though not exclusive, means of challenge where questions of public law arise. Matters relating to the administration of justice are likely to be public law matters.

Where in reality an action raises issues of public law, the normal procedure for determination of those questions is by an application for judicial review under Order 53 of the Rules of the Supreme Court, and a failure to use the Order 53 procedure may result subsequently in an application by the defendant to have the action struck out as an abuse of process of the court.[1] Prior to 1983 a choice as to which procedure was followed was open to the plaintiff or applicant. The Order 53 procedure that existed prior to 1977 had defects that often meant that proceeding by way of writ in the Queen's Bench Division was more attractive. Certain procedures such as discovery[2] and cross-examination of those who swore affidavits were not available on judicial review; nor was it open to a court dealing with such an application to make an award of damages, or issue a declaration.[3] These, and other, defects were remedied in 1977 when a revised Order 53 came into effect. As a result in 1981 the House of Lords in *O'Reilly v Mackman*[4] indicated firmly that the Order 53 procedure was to be the usual method of challenging public law actions or decisions. LORD DIPLOCK stressed the advantages of the limited time for challenge under Order 53, and the safeguard that the filter of requiring leave to apply creates. To seek to avoid these safeguards by proceeding by writ would amount in most cases to an abuse of process.

This distinction between public and private law matters, and the

---

18 In *R v Central Criminal Court, ex parte Serious Fraud Office* [1993] 2 All ER 399; [1993] 1 WLR 949 such proceedings were held not to be caught by the restriction in s 29(3). See also: *R v Crown Court at Southwark* [1993] 1 WLR 764. For procedures relating to serious fraud cases see p 482, *post*.

19 See *Smalley v Crown Court at Warwick*, n 12 *supra* (forfeiture of recognisance of third party); *R v Crown Court at Maidstone, ex parte Gill* [1987] 1 All ER 129 (forfeiture of property of third party).

20 See, eg, *R v Crown Court at Inner London, ex parte Benjamin* (1986) 85 Cr App Rep 267 (binding over of acquitted person).

1 *O'Reilly v Mackman, infra*. See p 316, *post*.

2 See p 348, *post*.

3 See now RSC Ord 53, r 1.

4 [1983] 2 AC 237; [1982] 3 All ER 1124; see also *Cocks v Thanet District Council* [1983] 2 AC 286; [1982] 3 All ER 1135.

procedures to be followed, has caused the courts considerable difficulty. Indeed, in *Doyle v Northumbria Probation Committee*[5] HENRY J observed as follows:

> "Looking at [the] authorities . . . there have been eight reported cases on this topic cited to me. Five of the eight went to the House of Lords . . . The principles that LORD DIPLOCK expected to emerge have clearly not yet been fully worked out, and the reason for this seems to me to be clear, namely that the circumstances in which there may be such a mixture of private and public law claims are infinitely variable and can arise in very disparate situations. But the wealth of authority on this point and the potential for expensive appeals on it leads one to conclude that there is potentially a formidable extra hurdle for plaintiffs in litigation where public and private law mix. It seems to me that this is at present an area of law where the forms of action abolished by the Common Law Procedure Act 1854 in the nineteenth century appear to be in danger of returning to rule us from their graves."

The position was somewhat clarified, if not entirely so, by the House of Lords in *Roy v Kensington and Chelsea and Westminster Family Practitioners Committee*.[6] In that case the plaintiff, a doctor, commenced an action by writ, seeking to obtain payments that he alleged were due to him, and being withheld by the defendant committee. The doctor's terms and conditions of employment were governed by regulation made pursuant to statute, and the committee sought to have the plaintiff's action struck out, arguing that the action raised public law matters which should be decided on an application for judicial review under Order 53. This application initially succeeded, but was rejected both by the Court of Appeal and by the House of Lords. The plaintiff was seeking to recover money allegedly owed to him. This raised private law rights, which could be enforced by private law action, even if they involved challenge to a public law decision. In his speech, LORD LOWRY sought carefully to limit the application of the principle in *O'Reilly v Mackman*, and preferred an approach which restricted the use of private law procedures to those cases involving no private law rights. Such an approach is consistent with a series of cases where a claim for money from a party was held to be a private law matter, even if the defence involved an assertion that the claim was invalid because it was made pursuant to an *ultra vires* action.[7] Simply because one party to an action is a public body does not turn the matter to be decided into a public law matter.[8]

The procedure under Order 53 requires that an application be made promptly and in any event within three months from the date when the grounds of the application first arose, unless the court considers that there is good reason for extending this period. The application is by originating motion, to a divisional court of the Queen's Bench Division in criminal matters, or to a judge sitting in open court in other cases. The applicant requires leave to apply for judicial review to be granted, and this is sought by *ex parte* application to a judge. The application is in a prescribed form,

---

5 [1991] 4 All ER 294; [1991] 1 WLR 340.
6 [1992] 1 AC 624; [1992] 1 All ER 705.
7 See in particular: *Wandsworth London Borough Council v Winder* [1985] AC 461; [1984] 3 All ER 976; *Davy v Spelthorne Borough Council* [1984] AC 262; [1983] 3 All ER 278.
8 *R v East Berkshire Area Health Authority, ex parte Walsh* [1985] QB 152; [1984] 3 All ER 425.

and must contain the relief sought and the grounds relied upon, and must be accompanied by an affidavit verifying the facts relied on. The judge may determine the application without a hearing (unless a hearing is requested in the notice of application). If the application for leave is refused the applicant may renew it by applying, in criminal cases to the divisional court or, in any other case, to a single judge sitting in open court or, if the court so directs, to the divisional court.

Applications for interlocutory orders, such as discovery, interrogatories, cross-examination of witnesses, may be made to a judge or master. However, it should be borne in mind that:

". . . in the ordinary way judicial review is designed to deal with matters which can be resolved without resorting to these procedures."[9]

On the hearing of the application for judicial review the court will hear any party served with the motion or summons and any other person who appears to be a proper person to be heard. The court has power to make orders of *prohibition*, *mandamus* or *certiorari*, to grant an injunction or declaration and to award damages if the applicant could have recovered damages had he proceeded by action, rather than application for judicial review.

The court has power to grant interim relief,[10] such as an interlocutory injunction. Where the relief sought is a declaration, an injunction or damages the court may, in certain circumstances, order the proceedings to continue as if they had been commenced by writ. As already observed, the essential feature of judicial review is that it applies to public law rather than private law matters. Thus it is not appropriate where the applicant's complaint is of a purely private nature, for example that he has been wrongfully dismissed by his employer, even where that employer is a public authority.[11] Conversely, if the applicant wishes to challenge a public-law decision he must proceed by way of application for judicial review and he cannot avoid the procedural requirements of Order 53 (notably the need for leave to move and the prescribed time limit) by bringing an ordinary action seeking a declaration or an injunction.

4   Grounds for judicial review

Judicial review is not a form of appeal. The High Court will not substitute its own decision for that of the court, tribunal or body below on the ground that it appears to be wrong, and, generally, is at pains to avoid doing so. The circumstances in which the court will interfere are want or excess of jurisdiction or failure to comply with the rules of natural justice and procedural fairness. These standards of procedural fairness vary from case to case but generally include the right of each party to state his case, the prohibition on a person being judge in his own cause, the right to be informed of the reasons for a decision and, in some cases, the right to legal representation before a tribunal.[12] In respect of inferior courts or tribunals,

---

9 *R v Derbyshire County Council, ex parte Noble* [1990] IRLR 332, *per* WOOLF LJ.
10 RSC Ord 53, r 3.
11 See *Ex parte Walsh, supra* n 8.
12 See *R v Board of Visitors of HM Prison, The Maze, ex parte Hone* [1988] AC 379, sub nom *Hone v Maze Prison Board of Prison Visitors* [1988] 1 All ER 321; *R v Secretary of State for the Home Department, ex parte Cheblak* [1991] 2 All ER 319; [1991] 1 WLR 890.

the court can intervene by way of judicial review if there is an error of law on the face of the record,[13] although this principle is of little practical importance given the wide interpretation the courts have given to the concept of excess of power or jurisdiction.[14]

In addition, in the case of an administrative person or body, the court will intervene when a discretion has been misused, or been fettered improperly, or otherwise used contrary to the principles of the enabling power. These are often known as the "*Wednesbury* principles".[15] Finally, if the body reaches a decision that no sensible authority could reach then it may be held to be invalid on the grounds of "*Wednesbury* unreasonableness".[16]

These grounds of judicial review were described by LORD DIPLOCK in *Council of Civil Service Unions v Minister for the Civil Service*[17] as (1) "illegality"; (2) "irrationality" (*viz Wednesbury* unreasonableness); and (3) "procedural impropriety". Whilst these terms have become widely accepted and used, it is important to recognise that they amount to no more than convenient labels,[18] and do not amount to the creation of new grounds of challenge. One possible extension of the grounds of challenge was canvassed by LORD DIPLOCK in the *GCHQ* case as "proportionality". This doctrine is important in European Community law,[19] but in *R v Secretary of State for the Home Department ex parte Brind*[20] the House of Lords concluded that no such ground existed as a general ground of challenge by judicial review, but rather formed part of the process by which allegations of breach of the *Wednesbury* principles, or of *Wednesbury* unreasonableness, would be judged. In any event, such a ground is more likely to be relevant to the review of administrative actions or discretions than to the judicial actions of inferior courts.

---

13 *R v Northumberland Compensation Appeal tribunal, ex parte Shaw* [1952] 1 KB 338; [1952] 1 All ER 122. This used to be confined to the record itself and excluded jurisdiction to correct errors in the reasons leading to the record but it is now held to extend to errors in reasons given in support of the recorded decision: *R v Crown Court at Knightsbridge, ex parte International Sporting Club (London) Ltd* [1982] QB 304; [1981] 3 All ER 417.

14 See *Anisminic Ltd v Foreign Compensation Commission*, p 125, *ante*, and LORD BROWNE-WILKINSON in *R v Lord President of the Privy Council, ex parte Page* [1993] AC 682.

15 *Associated Provincial Picture Houses Ltd v Wednesbury Corporation* [1948] 1 KB 223; [1947] 2 All ER 680.

16 For discussion, see *R v Secretary of State for the Home Department, ex parte Brind* [1991] 1 AC 696; [1990] 1 All ER 469, CA; [1991] 1 AC 696; [1991] 1 All ER 720, HL.

17 See p 123, *ante*.

18 *Per* LORD DONALDSON in *ex parte Brind, supra*.

19 See p 99, *ante*.

20 See, n 16, *supra*.

CHAPTER 7

The Courts

A   HISTORICAL INTRODUCTION

Some background as to the historical development of the courts is necessary
for an understanding of what in fact now exists, and why modern jurisdiction
is distributed in the way it is. As already noted[1] the basis underpinning the
development of the courts was the power of the monarch. This can in fact be
traced back to exercise of regal power, in the King's Council, the *Curia Regis*.

1   The Curia Regis

In medieval times legislative, executive and some judicial functions were
exercised by the King in Council. The King's Council is thus the predecessor
not only of Parliament but of the courts.

The medieval pattern was for courts to separate from the Council and
eventually acquire a jurisdiction independent of it. However the King at all
times retained a residual power deriving from his prerogative powers. Thus
the three main common law courts, the Court of Exchequer, the Court of
Common Pleas and the Court of King's Bench, split off from the Council and
their judges exercised jurisdiction to decide civil disputes and major criminal
cases in London and on assize. The King's justices assumed jurisdiction over
criminal offences. Nevertheless the undefined residual jurisdiction of the
King led to other courts deriving their jurisdiction from the Curia Regis,
notably the Court of Chancery and the Star Chamber. Indeed it was not until
the seventeenth century that the Council itself discontinued its judicial function. The functions of these courts were to remedy the procedural defects
and restrictions of the common law courts and to dispense justice where the
common law courts were for some reason unable to do so. The obvious
results of this ad hoc method of creating courts were clashes between them
and the common law courts over the extent of their respective jurisdiction.

2   The Court of Exchequer

This was the first of the three central common law courts to split off from the
Curia Regis. In the reign of Henry I the Exchequer became a separate
department of the Council dealing with the collection and distribution of

---

1 See p 4, *ante*.

royal revenue. By the reign of Henry II it had become a court, the judges of which were Exchequer Barons presided over by the Chief Baron who was, after the fourteenth century, always a lawyer, frequently of great distinction.

Originally the jurisdiction of the court was confined to disputes between subjects and the Crown concerning revenue. Later the court acquired jurisdiction over disputes between subjects, such as writs of debt and covenant,[2] through the fiction of "*quominus*". This depended upon a fictitious allegation of a debt owed by the plaintiff to the Crown which the plaintiff was the less able (*quominus*) to pay because of the debt owing to him by the defendant. This fictitious allegation enabled the court to determine the substantive issue between the parties.[3]

In addition the court appears, at least in its early days, to have exercised an equity jurisdiction, though its procedure was that of the common law courts rather than of the Court of Chancery.

When the court was finally abolished in 1875 its jurisdiction was transferred to the newly-formed High Court, its common law jurisdiction being exercised by the Queen's Bench Division after 1880, and its revenue jurisdiction by the Chancery Division. Its equity jurisdiction had been transferred by statute to the Chancery in 1841.[4]

3   The Court of Common Pleas

While the King was determining civil disputes in Council suitors were obliged to follow the court wherever it travelled. Because of the inconvenience this caused it became the practice for judges to remain permanently in Westminster Hall to try Common Pleas[5] and the Magna Carta, c 17, provided that the common pleas should be held in a "certain place" which was fixed at Westminster.

The judges of the court were full-time lawyers appointed from the ranks of the serjeants-at-law, the senior advocates who had an exclusive right of audience in the court. The serjeants were the leaders of the legal profession and consequently the most highly paid. This fact, coupled with the excessive formality of pleading attendant upon the real actions[6] (over which the court had a monopoly), made proceedings in the Common Pleas dilatory and expensive.

The jurisdiction of the court existed over disputes between subjects where the King's interest was not involved. Hence it tried all the real actions and the personal actions of debt, covenant and detinue. It also tried actions of trespass where the title to land was involved. It must be remembered that only wealthy landowners could afford to litigate in the royal courts so that most civil actions in the early Middle Ages in fact

---

2 These were the earliest personal actions recognised by the common law. Debt was an action for a fixed sum of money in return for consideration already given. Covenant lay for breach of any obligation entered into under seal. For more detailed discussion, see the 6th edition of this work, pp 22–29.

3 See Baker, *Introduction to English Legal History* (Butterworths, 3rd Edn, 1990).

4 5 Vict, c 5.

5 As opposed to Pleas of the Crown, which were based upon breaches of the King's peace, and usually involved fine or forfeiture. In modern terms, these were essentially criminal in nature.

6 Actions relating to land.

involved disputes over title to land. Thus the Common Pleas in the early period of the development of the common law exercised a far wider jurisdiction than the Exchequer or the King's Bench.

The court was abolished in 1875 and its jurisdiction transferred to the High Court, being exercised by the Queen's Bench Division after 1880.

4 The Court of King's Bench

This was the last of the three central courts to break away from the Council. Consequently it had always remained closer to the King than the Exchequer and the Common Pleas. This is not to say that the King's Bench was not separate from the Curia Regis. Although they were closely associated there is ample evidence that the judges of the King's Bench acted independently of the King[7] by the reign of Edward I and attempts by James I to sit in the court were defeated by Coke. However, because of its association with the King, it acquired jurisdiction to issue the prerogative writs (now "orders")[8] of mandamus, prohibition and certiorari, restraining excesses and abuses of jurisdiction by inferior courts and public officials.[9] In addition the writ of habeas corpus, which it had power to issue, was later of great constitutional importance in curbing the personal exercise by the King of his prerogative powers. Its wide appellate jurisdiction may also be traced to the exercise of the royal duty to correct deficiencies in cases tried in other courts.

The judicial function was exercised by the judges of the court presided over by the Chief Justice of England, an office ranking above that of Chief Justice of the Common Pleas.[10] This function was both original and appellate and both civil and criminal.

The original jurisdiction of the King's Bench was exercised principally in civil matters, although the judges of the court exercised original criminal jurisdiction in courts of assize. The civil jurisdiction, which derived from the Pleas of the Crown and in particular from the writ of trespass, developed in about 1250.[11] This operated to confer upon the court jurisdiction over most actions in tort since nearly all torts are offshoots of trespass. It did not acquire jurisdiction over contract until some time later.[12] However it filched jurisdiction from the Common Pleas over writs of debt by various procedural means.[13] The King's Bench had jurisdiction over all cases[14] where the defendant was in the custody of the warden of the King's Bench prison. Consequently the Sheriff of Middlesex was directed by bill to arrest the defendant for a trespass *vi et armis* and take him into custody. Since the court had jurisdiction over trespass actions it

---

7 See Plucknett, *A Concise History of the Common Law* (5th Edn), p 151.
8 See p 122, *ante*.
9 This jurisdiction is now exercised by the divisional court of the Queen's Bench Division by way of "judicial review" proceedings; see p 127, *ante*.
10 Coke, for example, was promoted from the latter office to the former.
11 Trespass was the link from early forms of action and later writs which provided the historical basis for the modern law or contract and tort. For its origins, see Woodbine, 'Origins of the Action of Trespass' 33 Yale LJ 799.
12 Until the late sixteenth century, upon the evolution of the writ of assumpsit.
13 For discussion, see 6th edition of this work, pp 8–9.
14 Excluding the real actions which remained in the exclusive jurisdiction of the Court of Common Pleas.

was able to try the real cause of action ancillary to the fictitious trespass suit which was in fact dropped. Other fictional devices were adopted in order to secure and extend the jurisdiction of the court.[15] By the sixteenth century the issue of these fictions were dispensed with, but the result was that the very existence of the Court of Common Pleas was threatened. Further disagreements eventually resulted in that latter court amending its procedures and jursidiction so as to remove some of the difficulties that had prevented actions in debt being dealt with in the Court of Common Pleas.[16]

The appellate jurisdiction of the King's Bench existed in both civil and criminal cases. However the right of appeal was based on an error in procedure in the court below.[17]

5   The Courts of Exchequer Chamber

There were, at different periods of history, no less than four courts bearing the title "Exchequer Chamber". The jurisdiction of all of them was appellate.

(1) The oldest was established by statute in 1357 as a result of the refusal of the Exchequer to submit to the appellate jurisdiction of the King's Bench. The court was created to sit in "any council room nigh the exchequer" (hence the name "Exchequer Chamber") and to consist of the Chancellor and the Treasurer with assistance from judges of the common law courts as assessors. Its jurisdiction was solely as a court of error from the Exchequer. Hence the business of the court was limited as it was also by the difficulty of getting the Chancellor and the Treasurer together, particularly when the latter office was vacant.

(2) There existed, even before 1357, a practice of judges reserving difficult points of law for consideration by a bench of judges drawn from all three common law courts and, later, the Chancery. These meetings were no doubt informal at first and the authority of the opinions delivered purely persuasive. They remained informal in the sense that no litigant had a right to require a judge to refer any point of law for consideration. However, the judgments were by the fifteenth century regarded as binding[18] and the informal meetings, by now usually held in the Exchequer Chamber, constituted the sitting of a court. Hence such a court was also termed a Court of Exchequer Chamber. Many of the leading cases of the common law were decided in this court before twelve judges and the court sat until the seventeenth century to determine civil cases and until the nineteenth century in criminal cases.

(3) A third Court of Exchequer Chamber was set up during the existence of the two already described by statute in 1585.[19] It was set up as a court of error from the King's Bench in cases of debt, detinue, covenant, account,

---

15 Principally the Bill of Middlesex procedure, whereby the court claimed jurisdiction where a person was taken into the custody of the Sheriff of Middlesex.

16 For a fuller account of this struggle for jurisdiction between the King's Bench and the Common Pleas, see Baker, *op cit.*

17 31 Edw 3, St 1, c 12.

18 In 1483 the Chief Justice of the Common Pleas followed a decision of the Exchequer Chamber even though he thought it wrong (YB 1 Ric 3, Michs, no 2).

19 31 Eliz 1, c 1.

action upon the case, ejectment or trespass commenced[20] in the King's Bench. It consisted of any six judges drawn from the Exchequer Barons and the justices of the Common Pleas. Thus there were at this time three courts of error; *viz* the Court of Exchequer Chamber (1357) from the Court of Exchequer, the King's Bench from the Common Pleas and the Court of Exchequer Chamber (1585) from the King's Bench. In addition error still lay direct from the King's Bench to the House of Lords. This somewhat complex hierarchy prevailed until the creation of the last Court of Exchequer Chamber in 1830.

(4) The court created in 1830[1] was the court of error from all three common law courts and was composed of judges of the two courts other than the one in which the trial at first instance took place. Appeal lay from the court to the House of Lords. The court existed until 1875 when its jurisdiction was transferred to the Court of Appeal.

6 Assizes

It was, during the Middle Ages, and indeed always has been, impossible to administer the criminal law on the basis of all trials taking place in London. Consequently, Norman and Plantagenet monarchs adopted the system, which appears to have existed even before the Conquest, of sending out royal justices throughout the kingdom to hold "assizes" (or sittings) of the royal courts. The jurisdiction of these assize courts, at first purely criminal, was later extended to civil proceedings.

The assize judges were generally the judges of the common law courts, but could also be serjeants-at-law or even prominent laymen. Consequently they exercised no jurisdiction by virtue of their office but only by reason of commissions issued by the Sovereign. The commissions conferring criminal jurisdiction were the commission of *Oyer and Terminer* and the commission of *Gaol Delivery*. The first directed the persons named in the commission to hear and determine all offences in respect of which the accused had been "presented" by the grand jury of the county.[2] The second directed them to deliver from the gaols of the county, and to try, all persons there awaiting trial.[3]

So successful and popular was the assize system that Edward I organised the circuits on the modern basis with each circuit consisting of a group of counties visited regularly three or four times a year by royal judges. In addition the Statute of Nisi Prius 1285 extended the system to certain civil actions. The basic reason for this extension was the difficulty of transporting local juries to Westminster. Consequently in those personal actions, such as trespass, triable in the King's Bench and Common Pleas with a jury, the sheriff was directed to secure the attendance of a jury at Westminster "unless before" (*nisi prius*) that day the justices of assize should visit that county.

---

20 This had the effect of confining it to proceedings commenced by bill since actions by writ were "commenced" in the Chancery.

1 11 Geo 4 & 1 Will 4, c 70.

2 See p 196, *post*.

3 These commissions were created by the Assizes of Clarendon 1166, and Northampton 1176 and continued to issue until their effective abolition under the provisions of the Courts Act 1971.

The system was extended in the fourteenth and fifteenth centuries to all types of civil action. It would, however, be incorrect to suppose that a trial at *nisi prius* was at this time a trial of the whole action. In fact only the issues of fact were tried at *nisi prius*. The pleading took place *in banc* (in Westminster) and the jury verdict was added to the record of the case to be sent back to Westminster for judgment to be entered since the commissioner of assize had no power to enter judgment. Later, when the commissioners were always lawyers and advocates went on circuit, the whole trial took place at the assize so that the trial of actions might take place in London or at an assize.[4]

7 Justices of the peace

Originally the office of justice of the peace was an administrative rather than a judicial office but a judicial function was given to it in the fourteenth century as a direct result of the declining criminal jurisdiction of the local courts and the inability of the assizes to deal with the growing number of offenders.

The origin of the justices of the peace is to be found in a royal proclamation of 1195 creating the knights of the peace to assist the sheriff in enforcing the law. This function was of an administrative and police character rather than of a judicial character. With the decline of the office of sheriff in the fourteenth century the "keepers of the peace" (*custodes pacis*) as they were by now known,[5] were given a judicial function in addition to their administrative tasks. The former function has increased as the latter has diminished. In 1330 the holders of this new office had become so powerful locally that they were given statutory power to punish the sheriff, if he abused his powers of granting bail to prisoners.

As a result of the effects of the Black Death on the labour market, Statutes of Labourers were passed from 1351 in an attempt to regulate prices and wages and to reorganise labour generally. The enforcement of these statutes was placed in the hands of "justices of labourers" who were, in 1361, included in the same commissions as the keepers of the peace. It is from this date that the office of JP in its modern sense originates. The new justices of the peace were laymen and not usually legally qualified, a tradition which for the most part continues to exist.[6] Their criminal jurisdiction was at first exercised solely in the sessions which they were, by statute,[7] compelled to hold in each county four times a year. These were the "quarter sessions" and in 1590 the justices in quarter sessions were given jurisdiction over all criminal offences not excluding capital felonies. It was, indeed, not until the Quarter Sessions Act 1842 that the jurisdiction

---

4 The assize system survived until 1st January 1972 – the date on which the Courts Act 1971 came into operation; s 1(2) provides that "all courts of assize are hereby abolished, and Commissions, whether ordinary or special, to hold any court of assize shall not be issued."

5 The nomenclature "justice of the peace" appears to date from about 1327, and to be an official title after 1361; Plucknett, *A Concise History of the Common Law* (5th Edn), p 168.

6 See p 162, *post*.

7 36 Edw 3, st 1, c 12.

of quarter sessions was limited to exclude treason, murder and felonies punishable with life imprisonment.

Later, in Tudor times, a number of statutes conferred jurisdiction on justices to try offences out of sessions. From these statutes, the first of which was passed in 1496,[8] stems the summary jurisdiction of the justices of the peace in "petty sessions". This summary jurisdiction, which is entirely statutory, is exercised without a jury and justices exercising this jurisdiction are now termed a "magistrates' court".[9]

As indicated earlier, the administrative jurisdiction of justices of the peace declined through the years as the criminal jurisdiction grew. Most of the administrative jurisdiction formerly exercised by justices is now in the hands of local authorities. However certain important functions remain. The common law power to issue warrants of arrest and summonses still exists. The important task of conducting preliminary investigations into indictable offences was conferred on justices of the peace by statutes of 1554 and 1555.[10]

8 The Star Chamber

The historical role of the Star Chamber should be noted, even though, strictly speaking it was not a common law court. It derived its jurisdiction from the King in the same way as the common law courts but it did not administer the common law and, more particularly, adopted a criminal and civil procedure repugnant to that obtaining in the common law courts. In addition, whereas the common law courts quite early in their existence became independent of the Council, the Star Chamber appears always to have retained the closest link with the Council. Hence it administered the royal prerogative rather than the common law although, by doing so, it added considerably to the scope of the criminal law.

Opinions differ as to the origins of the court. It seems to have originated from sittings of the Council in a chamber in Westminster known as the Star Chamber, possibly on account simply of its interior decor.[11] It consisted of members of the Council, the Chancellor, Treasurer and Privy Seal and common law judges, and had a miscellaneous civil jurisdiction over matters outside the common law such as mercantile and ecclesiastical disputes. It also assumed jurisdiction over matters within the scope of the common law courts and for this reason it fell into disfavour with common law judges. The growth of the Court of Chancery during the same period[12] effectively restricted the civil jurisdiction of the Star Chamber. It is the criminal jurisdiction of the Star Chamber which is of far greater interest and importance since it recognised and tried many new offences. Many of these were offences of a public nature such as riot, unlawful assembly, conspiracy, criminal libel, perjury, forgery and criminal attempts. All these crimes were created to fill gaps in the existing criminal law as administered in the assizes and quarter sessions.

---

8 11 Hen 7, c 3.

9 See p 162, *post*.

10 1 & 2 P & M, c 13 and 2 & 3 P & M, c 10.

11 An alternative theory, that the court was created by a statute of 1487 (*pro camera stellata*), is now discounted.

12 see p 138, *post*.

Procedure in the Star Chamber differed radically from procedure in the common law courts. The civil procedure resembled more closely Chancery procedure than the dilatory formality of the common law. Criminal procedure was even more fundamentally different. Proceedings were commenced, not by presentment by the grand jury, but by information filed by the Attorney-General. An inquisitorial procedure followed whereby the defendant was examined on oath, sometimes under torture. Witnesses' evidence was frequently given by affidavit thus denying the accused any opportunity of cross-examination. Finally, there was no jury, guilt being determined by the members of the court. In a modern situation such a procedure would be unthinkable and condemned as a total denial of justice. Nevertheless, it was at that time justifiable in the light of the influence on juries which certain persons exercised, the bitterness of the state trials for treason (which took place before juries) and, following the Wars of the Roses, the anarchic situation throughout the realm which the existing criminal law and courts could not remedy. Even Coke, that most noted champion of the common law, described the court as "the most honourable Court (our Parliament excepted) that is in the Christian world".[13] Nevertheless, in spite of its popularity in Tudor times, the accession of the Stuarts and, in particular, the Civil War resulted in the court becoming a symbol of prerogative power in the eyes of the Puritans and Parliamentarians and one of the first legislative acts of the Long Parliament was the abolition of the Star Chamber in 1641.

9   Court of Chancery

The development of principles of equity to supplement the common law, and remedy its weaknesses, has already been noted.[14] The Court of Chancery was the principal court of equity, and its most important jurisdiction was the recognition and enforcement of those principles, although it is a matter of debate whether the court developed to apply the Chancellor's jurisdiction to do equity, or, conversely, equity developed out of the jurisdiction of the Chancellor. What is clear is that the office of Chancellor and the principles of equity are, historically, inexorably linked. The nature and effectiveness of the court depended upon the characteristics of the particular Chancellor. The personal shortcomings of a Chancellor became ingrained in procedure in the court. Thus the court was brought into disrepute in the seventeenth century by the sale of offices in the court. All offices, including that of Master of the Rolls, were sold by the Chancellor.[15] Indeed so great was corruption in the court during this period that on the bursting of the South Sea Bubble in 1725 a deficiency of some £100,000 in court funds was discovered as a result of which Lord Macclesfield was impeached and fined.

A further defect in the Court of Chancery was the organisation of the court. There was an excess of court officials who attempted to extend the ambit of their duties so as to increase their revenue. Apart from the abuse which the sale of these clerkships created the proliferation of Chancery

---

13 4 Inst, p 65.
14 See p 6, *ante*.
15 The office of Master of the Rolls was apparently worth £6,000 in the eighteenth century. See *Ex parte the Six Clerks* (1798) 3 Ves 589.

clerks naturally made litigation in the court extremely slow and expensive. The excess of court officers was equalled only by the paucity of judges. At first the Chancellor himself was the only judge. In practice he was unable to hear all cases himself and by the sixteenth century was accustomed to delegate his judicial function to the Masters in Chancery although judgment was delivered only by the Chancellor himself. However this did little to speed up the conduct of litigation since the parties had a right to apply to the Chancellor for a rehearing. Arrears of work were handed down through successive Chancellors. Matters reached a head in the nineteenth century with the elevation of Lord Eldon to the office of Chancellor. Lord Eldon (1801–27) was a distinguished lawyer but unfortunately suffered from an excess of caution. He would not deliver any judgment or make any order without considering every available authority. There are records of judgments being reserved for months and even years. While this stabilised the court it also brought it into discredit with suitors and the backlog of cases pending became enormous. In 1813 Lord Eldon approved the appointment of a Vice-Chancellor as an additional judge of the Court but this brought little improvement since an appeal lay from his decisions to the Chancellor. Apart from this measure Lord Eldon stood fast against any reform and used the power of his office to thwart any attempt at reform of the judicial system. This obdurate conservatism contributed greatly to the welter of reform which in fact began shortly after his resignation from office in 1827. The Court of Chancery was finally abolished by the Judicature Acts 1873–75 and its jurisdiction substantially transferred to the Chancery Division of the High Court.

In addition to its equitable jurisdiction the court, because of its close association with the Crown, acquired jurisdiction over other miscellaneous matters. For example the Crown, as *parens patriae*, had protective custody of all infants within the realm; this jurisdiction, which comprised such matters as the power to appoint guardians, was assigned to the Court of Chancery but is now exercised by the Family Division.[16] A similar concept existed in relation to persons of unsound mind; since they too were in need of protection the Sovereign assumed responsibility for the care of lunatics and their property. This responsibility was, as with infants, delegated to the Chancellor and is today exercised, for the most part, by the Court of Protection, the judges of which are judges of the Chancery Division.[17]

Finally, note should be taken of the Court of Appeal in Chancery. This was established in 1851 to hear appeals from the Court of Chancery, but was abolished, along with that court, by the reforms in 1873–75 made by the Judicature Acts.

B   THE MODERN SYSTEM OF COURTS

The impact made by the Judicature Acts 1873–75 has already been noted, sweeping away many of the courts described above. It is clear from this analysis, and the more general introduction in Chapter 1 that the jurisdiction of High Court judges stems originally from the royal prerogative.

16 See p 154, *post*.
17 See p 175, *post*.

However, whilst the superior courts in England and Wales derive their jurisdiction, directly or indirectly, from the Crown, heavy regulation by statute now exists. In addition, many courts and tribunals of modern importance owe their origins not to the Crown, or to the historical development outlined above, but to statutory creation and intervention.

Courts can be classified in various ways. The two fundamental divisions of English courts are: (1) courts of record and courts not of record; and (2) superior and inferior courts. Before explaining further the significance of this classification it may be noted that there are other classifications, though these are not of universal application. Thus it is possible to classify courts according to their functions. The obvious classification in this repect would be into courts of civil and courts of criminal jurisdiction. This classification is not, however, a valid one since, although certain courts do exercise a purely civil or criminal jurisdiction, most English courts hear both civil and criminal cases. Thus the House of Lords, Court of Appeal, High Court, Crown Court and magistrates' courts exercise jurisdiction in both civil and criminal matters. A second classification would be into courts of original and courts of appellate jurisdiction. Nor is this division of general application. Although certain courts, such as the Court of Appeal and the House of Lords, exercise a purely appellate jurisdiction, while other courts, such as magistrates' courts, have no appellate jurisdiction, many courts, notably the High Court and the Crown Court, exercise both original and appellate jurisdiction.

The Court of Justice of the European Communities (the European Court) is, of course, *sui generis* since, although not an English court, it exercises jurisdiction within the English legal system. Its position within the system has already been seen.[18]

It may sometimes be a matter of dispute whether a particular tribunal is properly described as a "court" or not. This is not central to the question of whether the supervisory jurisdiction of the High Court extends to the body in question, since that jurisdiction is not limited to courts properly so called.[19] It is, however, important in the context of contempt of court[20] since the offence of contempt of court is, by definition, capable of commission only in relation to a "court". In *A-G v British Broadcasting Corporation*[1] the House of Lords (reversing the decision of the Court of Appeal) held that a valuation court constituted under section 88 of the General Rate Act 1967 was not "an inferior court", for the purposes of RSC Ord 52, r 1(2) since, although it was termed a court, its functions were essentially administrative and it was not a court of law established to exercise the judicial power of the state. The House was, however, divided on the question of whether it was a court at all (*viz* for any purpose other than contempt proceedings). This is no doubt of academic interest but it appears to be of no other practical significance whether a tribunal is properly describable as a "court" or not.

---

18 See p 111, *ante*.
19 See p 125, *ante*.
20 See p 191, *post*.
　1 [1981] AC 303; [1980] 3 All ER 161.

1 Superior and inferior courts

A traditional classification of English courts is their division into superior and inferior courts. The nature of superior courts is that their jurisdiction is limited neither by the value of the subject matter of an action nor geographically. The jurisdiction of inferior courts is limited both geographically and according to the value of the subject matter of the dispute.[2] The superior courts are the House of Lords, Court of Appeal, High Court, Crown Court, Judicial Committee of the Privy Council, Restrictive Practices Court and the Employment Appeal Tribunal. One of the distinctive features of inferior courts is that they are amenable to the supervisory jurisdiction of the High Court exercised by prerogative order,[3] though this applies also to the Crown Court in the exercise of its appellate jurisdiction even though the Crown Court is, as stated above, a superior court.[4] The most important of the inferior courts are county courts and magistrates' courts although all courts not listed above as superior are inferior courts. The distinction is also of importance in relation to contempt of court, since the penalties which may be imposed by inferior courts are far less than superior courts have power to inflict.[5]

2 Courts of record

An ancient division of courts is into courts of record and courts which are not courts of record. The basic historical distinction depended upon whether or not the court in question maintained a record of its proceedings. The records of courts of record are preserved in the Public Record Office. Courts of record may be inferior or superior. The essential characteristic of a court of record is no longer that it maintains a record; it is that it has power to punish for contempt. Consequently any court which has jurisdiction to punish contempt is a court of record. The powers of superior and inferior courts of record, and of magistrates' courts, to commit for contempt are now set out in the Contempt of Court Act 1981.[6] In addition the High Court has a common law jurisdiction to punish contempts committed before courts which are not courts of record.[7]

3 The principle of open justice

Before considering individually the constitution and jurisdiction of English courts attention may be drawn to the general principle of "open justice". The first aspect of this is that courts should sit in public. Ever since the

---

2 Whether a court is an inferior or a superior court can usually be ascertained by reference to the historical origins of the court or, if it was created by statute, by the terms of the statute creating it. However where the statute is silent it is necessary to look at the nature and powers of the court so as to decide whether they are analogous to those of a superior or an inferior court; see *R v Cripps, ex parte Muldoon* [1984] QB 68; [1983] 3 All ER 72 in which the Queen's Bench divisional court held an election court (under the Representation of the People Act) to be an inferior court.

3 See p 122, *ante*.

4 See p 140, *ante*.

5 See p 191, *post*.

6 See p 194, *post*.

7 *R v Davies* [1906] 1 KB 32; see p 194, *post*.

abolition of the Court of Star Chamber in 1641 English judges have rebelled against the notion of private sittings of courts. In the famous words of LORD HEWART CJ in *R v Sussex Justices, ex parte McCarthy*:[8]

> "... a long line of cases shows that it is not merely of some importance but is of fundamental importance that justice should not only be done, but should manifestly and undoubtedly be seen to be done."

The principle, and the circumstances which would justify departure from it, were set out by the House of Lords in *Scott v Scott*,[9] and more recently cogently explained by LORD DIPLOCK in *A-G v Leveller Magazine Ltd*,[10] as follows:

> "As a general rule the English system of administering justice does require that it be done in public: *Scott v Scott*. If the way the courts behave cannot be hidden from the public ear and eye this provides a safeguard against judicial arbitrariness or idiosyncrasy and maintains the public confidence in the administration of justice."

There are two aspects to the principle. One is that proceedings should be held in open court wherever possible. The other is that reports of proceedings should be permissible, provided they are fair and accurate, again wherever possible. These two principles should only be departed from where it is necessary to do so to protect the administration of justice itself, or where Parliament has specifically created an exception.

Several specific examples exist where Parliament has granted a power to sit *in camera*. These include wardship proceedings, proceedings involving a secret process, cases involving evidence of sexual capacity in suits for annulment of marriage, certain proceedings for injunctions,[11] youth court proceedings[12] and proceedings under the Official Secrets Acts.[13] A court may also sit *in camera* where the presence of the public would render the administration of justice impracticable. In deciding this question the court must take into account the effect of publicity on the parties only in so far as that affects the administration of justice. In *R v Malvern Justices, ex parte Evans*,[14] magistrates sat *in camera* in order to hear a plea in mitigation in respect of a driving offence. The mental health of the defendant was such that, if the court had not sat *in camera*, the defendant would have been inhibited in making her plea in mitigation. Whilst an appeal against the

---

8 [1924] 1 KB 256, at 259; see also *R v Denbigh Justices, ex parte Williams* [1974] QB 759; [1974] 2 All ER 1052; Supreme Court Act 1981, s 67.

9 [1913] AC 417.

10 [1979] AC 440; [1979] 1 All ER 745.

11 See *Practice Direction (Matrimonial Causes; Injunction)* [1974] 2 All ER 1119; [1974] 1 WLR 936; see also p 287, *post* as to hearing applications for *Anton Piller* orders.

12 Though *bona fide* representatives of the press may not be excluded: Children and Young Persons Act 1933, s 37. Any court may also prohibit the publication of the name of any child involved in legal proceedings: s 39. For the relevant principles, see *R v Leicester Crown Court, ex parte S* [1992] 2 All ER 659; cf *R v Lee* [1993] 2 All ER 170. Clause 37 of the Criminal Justice and Public Order Bill proposes amendments to the Children and Young Persons Act 1933, which restricts reports of proceedings in which children or young persons are concerned.

13 Official Secrets Act 1920, s 8.

14 [1988] QB 540; [1988] 1 All ER 371. See also *R v Evesham Justices, ex parte McDonagh* [1988] QB 553; [1988] 1 All ER 371, where a magistrates' court was held not entitled to prohibit publication of the defendant's address to save him possible harrassment from his ex-wife.

making of that order to sit in camera was dismissed, the divisional court observed that the occasions when it would be appropriate to make such an order would be rare, and in fact doubted whether on the facts of this particular case the magistrates had been correct to make the order they did.

The second aspect of the principle of open justice is that all the evidence should be communicated publicly and the third is that nothing should be done to discourage or prevent publication of fair and accurate reports of judicial proceedings. However, just as there are limitations on the principle that proceedings should be conducted in public, so are there circumstances which may justify a court restricting publicity of evidence, either within or outside the courtroom. To quote a common example, victims of blackmail are usually permitted to communicate their names and addresses in court by writing them down and to be referred to throughout the proceedings as "Mr X" or some such title. There are provisions in the Sexual Offences (Amendment) Act 1976 for preserving the anonymity of complainants and defendants in rape and similar offences.[15]

This area of the law was considered by the House of Lords in *A-G v Leveller Magazine Ltd*.[16] The House accepted that, in exercising its control over the proceedings before it, a court was entitled to derogate from the principle of open justice by sitting in private or permitting a witness not to disclose his name when giving evidence if it was necessary to do so in the interests of the due administration of justice. On the particular facts, the absence of a clear order restricting publication, and the fact that the identity of the witness in question was readily ascertainable from other evidence which was freely reportable, led to convictions for contempt of court being quashed.

Any such order will now be made pursuant to section 11 of the Contempt of Court Act 1981. This empowers the court to give "such directions . . . as appear to the court to be necessary" for giving effect to any order which it makes. It should be noted, however, that this section does not create a power to order a name or other matter to be withheld; it simply regulates the exercise of such power as the court may inherently possess. An appeal against the making of such an order exists.[17]

A third element relates to the postponement of the reporting of proceedings. Section 4(2) of the 1981 Act departs from the normal rule that fair and accurate reporting of legal proceedings, published contemporaneously with the case, is permissible. By section 4(2) a court may order the postponement of reporting where that is necessary in the interests of justice. If, however, these can be met in less restrictive ways,

---

15 Sexual Offences (Amendment) Act 1976, ss 4–6, as amended by Criminal Justice Act 1988 and Sexual Offences (Amendment) Act 1992; after a person has been "accused" (as to which, see s 4(6)) of a rape offence it is an offence to publish in a written publication or broadcast any matter likely to lead members of the public to identify a woman as the complainant; in each case a judge of the Crown Court has power, on application, to remove these restrictions in certain circumstances.

16 See n 10, *ante*; *R v Socialist Worker Printer and Publishers Ltd, ex parte A-G* [1975] QB 637; [1975] 1 All ER 142.

17 Criminal Justice Act 1988, s 159; *Re Crook* [1992] 2 All ER 687. The principles governing the making of such orders were set out in *Practice Direction (Contempt: Reporting Restrictions)* [1982] 1 WLR 1475.

then they should be so met.[18] The court has to balance the risk of substantial prejudice to the proceedings, and whether reporting restrictions are necessary and proportionate.[19]

C THE EUROPEAN COURT OF JUSTICE

This court plays an important role in the English legal system. Its nature, functions and powers have already been discussed.[20]

D THE HOUSE OF LORDS

1 Constitution and procedure

Parliament is the oldest court of the common law although it is not usual nowadays to refer to it as a court. Nevertheless reference is still made to the High Court of Parliament as a judicial body. Leaving aside the jurisdiction of each House to regulate its own procedure, the judicial function of Parliament is now exercised by the House of Lords.

In theory, though not in fact, an appeal to the House of Lords is an appeal to the whole House, not merely to those members who are in fact sitting to hear the appeal. Until the nineteenth century this was literally true in that any member of the House could and did vote in judicial sessions. Not unnaturally decisions of the House of Lords at that time enjoyed no very great authority, particularly since those peers who were lawyers and took the most prominent part in the exercise of the House's jurisdiction were by no means the senior and most respected judges of their day, a remark which also applies to certain Lord Chancellors of the nineteenth century. As a matter of practice puisne judges were frequently invited to advise their Lordships on the law. Indeed this is still possible though it does not appear to have been done since 1898.[1] However it was not until the Appellate Jurisdiction Act 1876 provided for the creation of salaried life peers to hear appeals that the convention against lay peers participating in judicial sittings of the House was firmly established.[2]

This Act provided that at the hearing of an appeal there should be present at least three of the following – the Lord Chancellor, the Lords of Appeal in Ordinary ("law lords") and such peers who hold or have held "high judicial office" as defined in the Act. In practice most appeals are heard solely by the Lords of Appeal in Ordinary. These are the senior members of the judiciary. They have the same rights as other peers but in practice they sit on the cross benches and take no part in political sittings of the House unless the matter concerns the administration of justice. By custom, one or two of the law lords are Scots and the Scottish members

---

18 In *Re Central Independent Television* [1991] 1 All ER 347 an order prohibiting radio or television reporting whilst a jury was staying overnight at a hotel was held excessive.
19 *R v Beck, ex parte Daily Telegraph plc* [1993] 2 All ER 177; *Ex parte Telegraph plc* [1993] 2 All ER 971; [1993] 1 WLR 980.
20 See p 111, *ante*.
 1 *Allen v Flood*, [1898] AC 1.
 2 An earlier attempt to create life peers by prerogative had been rejected by the House – *Wensleydale Peerage* case (1856) 5 HL Cas 958.

generally sit when the House is hearing appeals from the Court of Session, which is the Scottish equivalent of the Court of Appeal. The number of law lords, originally fixed at two, is now not less than seven nor more than eleven.[3]

Argument in appeals no longer takes place, as it used to do, in the chamber of the House. The appeal is argued in one of the committee rooms, their lordships sitting unrobed. The opinions of their lordships are not usually read in the chamber[4] although they retire to the chamber to state whether they would allow or dismiss the appeal. These opinions are not strictly "judgments" but speeches in support of the members' votes on the motion made by the Lord Chancellor or senior lord. Where the House is equally divided the appeal is dismissed. Equal division does not in practice occur because an uneven number of members invariably sits. Nevertheless the situation has arisen on a few occasions and arose in the case of *Kennedy v Spratt*.[5] In that case the appeal would have been dismissed by a majority of three to two but for the fact that one of the majority, LORD UPJOHN, died between the hearing of the appeal and the delivery of judgment having, however, recorded his opinion before his death. In the result, the votes being equal, the appeal was dismissed in any event.[6] The House of Lords has no power to pass judgment. It may only remit the case to the Court of Appeal or the trial judge with its recommendations which must then be translated by that court into a judgment.

2 Jurisdiction

a Original jurisdiction

The House of Lords has very little original jurisdiction. The right of a peer to be "tried by his peers", which was thought to have been created by Magna Carta, was finally abolished by the Criminal Justice Act 1948 and now all persons, whether peer or commoner, are subject to the ordinary jurisdiction of the English criminal courts.

Impeachment is a procedure whereby persons may be prosecuted by the House of Commons before the House of Lords. It has always been confined to the prosecution of political offenders. Although impeachment has not been abolished it is in practice obsolete and the jurisdiction has not been exercised since the impeachments of Warren Hastings and Viscount Melville in 1795 and 1805 respectively.

The Committee of Privileges, which is by convention composed of lawyers in the House, makes recommendations to the whole House arising

---

3 Appellate Jurisdiction Act 1947; Administration of Justice Act 1968, s 1(1)(a); this number may be increased by Order in Council (*ibid*, s 1(2)).
4 See *Practice Direction* [1963] 1 WLR 1382.
5 [1972] AC 83; [1971] 1 All ER 805.
6 See *Kennedy v Spratt (Background Note)* [1972] AC 99. Had LORD UPJOHN's written opinion indicated that he was in favour of allowing the appeal an anomalous situation would have arisen whereby his death would, in effect, have deprived the appellant of success. In such an event the members of the House would surely have changed their votes so that the appeal would be allowed or, possibly, taken no vote and had the appeal reheard by a differently constituted committee.

out of the Committee trying, at the instance of the Sovereign, a disputed claim to a peerage.[7]

Finally both the House of Lords and the House of Commons have jurisdiction over breaches of privilege, which include contempt of the House in question and wrongs committed within the precincts of each House. Either House may imprison the offender, who has no right of appeal and may not move for habeas corpus.

b   Appellate jurisdiction

The jurisdiction of the House of Lords is almost entirely appellate. In civil cases it hears appeals from the Court of Appeal but only with leave of either the Court of Appeal or the Appeals Committee of the House itself.[8] The ground of appeal does not have to be a point of law as it does in criminal cases but most cases which reach the House of Lords do in fact involve a point of law of public importance, in nine out of ten cases being concerned with the correct construction of Acts of Parliament.[9] The Administration of Justice Act 1969 introduced a "leap-frog" procedure whereby there can be an appeal direct from the trial court to the House of Lords without the need for a prior appeal to the Court of Appeal. Such an appeal lies subject to two conditions; first the trial judge must grant a certificate,[10] which he may do only if all parties consent and the case involves a point of law of general public importance which either relates wholly or mainly to the construction of an enactment or is one in respect of which the judge was bound by a previous decision of the Court of Appeal or House of Lords; secondly the House of Lords must grant leave.[11]

The appeal to the House of Lords in criminal cases is of modern origin. Although a writ of error was available before this century, there was no general right of appeal until the Criminal Appeal Act 1907, which provided for an appeal from the Court of Criminal Appeal[12] established by the Act. The right of appeal from the divisional court of the Queen's Bench Division was created by the Administration of Justice Act 1960 and the conditions for appealing to the House of Lords in a criminal matter are now contained in that Act. These conditions are discussed fully later in this book.[13] Appeal lies, subject to similar conditions, from the High Court and Court of Appeal of Northern Ireland and from the Courts-Martial Appeal Court.

---

7 The Committee sat, in 1976, to hear the celebrated *Ampthill Peerage* case [1977] AC 547; [1976] 2 All ER 411, when it consisted of nine peers, four of whom were law lords and delivered speeches, and again in 1985; *Annandale and Hartfell Peerage Claim* [1986] AC 319; [1985] 3 All ER 577 when, again, only the law lords delivered speeches.

8 Administration of Justice (Appeals) Act 1934. The House also hears appeals from the equivalent civil courts of Scotland (Court of Session) and Northern Ireland (Court of Appeal).

9 See observations of LORD HAILSHAM to this effect in *Johnson v Moreton* [1980] AC 37, at 53; [1978] 3 All ER 37, at 44.

10 Act of 1969, s 12(1); there is no appeal against the grant or refusal of a certificate (s 12(5)).

11 *Ibid*, s 13. The grant of leave precludes appeal to the Court of Appeal.

12 The jurisdiction of this court was transferred to the criminal division of the Court of Appeal by the Criminal Appeal Act 1966.

13 See p 524, *post*.

E THE COURT OF APPEAL

The Supreme Court of Judicature was the product of the complete reorganisation of the English superior courts effected by the Supreme Court of Judicature Acts 1873–75. These Acts are now consolidated in the Supreme Court Act 1981. The Acts created the Supreme Court of Judicature to which was transferred the original and appellate jurisdiction of the then existing superior courts of first instance and appeal.[14] The Supreme Court now consists of the Court of Appeal, the High Court and the Crown Court. The appellate jurisdiction of the superior courts of law and equity was transferred to the Court of Appeal, while the original jurisdiction was, broadly speaking, transferred to the High Court, the Crown Court having been added by the Courts Act 1971.[15]

1 Constitution

The Court of Appeal is composed of the Lord Chancellor, the Lord Chief Justice, the Master of the Rolls, the President of the Family Division of the High Court, the Vice-Chancellor,[16] former Lord Chancellors, the Lords of Appeal in Ordinary[17] (all the above being *ex officio* judges) and the Lords Justices of Appeal. Ordinarily, of the *ex officio* judges only the Master of the Rolls (in civil cases) and the Lord Chief Justice (in criminal cases) sit in the court. They are, in fact, the presidents of the civil and criminal divisions respectively. The Master of the Rolls was a first instance judge in the Court of Chancery, and, indeed, in the Chancery Division of the High Court until 1881. In modern times some of the greatest lawyers of their day have held the office of Master of the Rolls.

In addition to the regular judges of the court the Lord Chancellor may require any High Court judge, and may request any former judge of the High Court or of the Court of Appeal, to sit in the civil division and the Lord Chief Justice may require (or request as the case may be) any such judge or former judge to sit in the criminal division;[18] indeed, the criminal division more often than not contains a Queen's Bench Division judge and, in practice, the first court of the criminal division usually consists of the Lord Chief Justice, a Lord Justice of Appeal and one puisne judge while a second court comprises one Lord Justice of Appeal and two puisnes.

By section 3(5) of the Supreme Court Act 1981 any number of courts of either division of the Court of Appeal may sit at the same time. In the civil division the court is duly constituted if it consists of either two or an uneven number of judges not less than three.[19] The criminal division is duly constituted with either two or an uneven number of justices not less than

---

14 See p 132, *ante*.
15 See p 155, *post*.
16 The Vice-Chancellor became a judge of the Court of Appeal upon the implementation of the Supreme Court Act 1981.
17 The court has sometimes been composed of three law lords; see, for examples, *Mallett v Restormel Borough Council* [1978] 2 All ER 1057; *Re Amirteymour* [1978] 3 All ER 637; [1979] 1 WLR 63. Furthermore, in November 1979, the criminal division of the court sat at the law courts in Cardiff, the first time the court had sat outside London.
18 Supreme Court Act 1981, s 9.
19 *Ibid*, s 54; Court of Appeal (Civil Division) Order 1982; see p 420, *post* for details of procedure on appeals.

three, save that only a court of three or more can (a) determine an appeal against conviction or a verdict of not guilty by reason of insanity or a finding of unfitness to plead, an application for leave to appeal to the House of Lords; or (b) refuse an application for leave to appeal against conviction (or any such verdict or finding referred to above) other than an application which has been refused by a single judge.[20] In addition a single judge of the criminal division (who may be, and usually is, a High Court judge) has certain jurisdiction under the Criminal Appeal Act 1968, s 31 (as amended), notably to hear applications for leave to appeal. Occasionally a "full court" of five or more members is convened to hear appeals involving novel or difficult points of law in both the civil and criminal divisions, although such a court has no wider powers than the normal court.

2   Jurisdiction

Since 1 October 1966, the date upon which the Criminal Appeal Act 1966 came into operation, the Court of Appeal has consisted of a civil and a criminal division.

a   Civil division

The civil division exercises (a) all jurisdiction conferred on it by the Supreme Court Act 1981 or any other Act; and (b) all jurisdiction exercisable by it prior to the commencement of the 1981 Act.[1] It is sufficient to note at this stage that the civil division has no criminal jurisdiction and hardly any original jurisdiction. Its jurisdiction is entirely civil and almost entirely appellate. It hears appeals from the High Court, county courts, the Restrictive Practices Court, the Employment Appeal Tribunal and various tribunals, notably the Lands Tribunal. Appeal is by way of rehearing, except in the case of certain appeals from tribunals where it is by case stated.[2]

b   Criminal division

The criminal division of the Court of Appeal is the successor of the Court of Criminal Appeal, the jurisdiction of the latter being transferred to the former by section 1(1) of the Criminal Appeal Act 1966.

The Court of Criminal Appeal emerged as a result of the deficient system of criminal appeals which existed prior to 1907. The court was created by the Criminal Appeal Act 1907 and superseded the Court for Crown Cases Reserved and the right of appeal by writ of error to the Queen's Bench Division.

The jurisdiction of the criminal division is set out fully later.[3] Briefly, it hears appeals by persons convicted and, in certain cases, considers points of law referred to the court by the Attorney-General following acquittal,[4] following trial in the Crown Court, as well as references made to it by the

---

20 Supreme Court Act 1981, s 55; for details of procedure on appeal to the criminal division, see p 522, *post.*

1 *Ibid*, s 15(2).

2 Rules of the Supreme Court (Revision) 1965, Ord 61.

3 See p 512, *post.*

4 See p 516, *post.*

Attorney-General where a sentence imposed is considered to be unduly lenient.[5] It also hears appeals against sentence from the Crown Court. In addition the Home Secretary may refer a case to the division, under section 17 of the Criminal Appeal Act 1968, for assistance on any point or for determination as an appeal. The criminal division of the Court of Appeal has no civil jurisdiction and no original jurisdiction, its jurisdiction being solely appellate.

F THE HIGH COURT OF JUSTICE

The High Court was established by the Judicature Acts and to it was transferred the jurisdiction of the three superior common law courts of first instance, the Court of Chancery, the Courts of Admiralty, Probate, Divorce and Matrimonial Causes and other superior courts of civil and criminal jurisdiction (except the Chancery Courts of the Counties Palatine of Lancaster and Durham[6]). Its constitution and jurisdiction are now contained in the Supreme Court Act 1981. Prior to 1971 the High Court sat in the Royal Courts of Justice in the Strand, London, though High Court judges constituted a court of the High Court for all purposes when they tried cases on assize. Nevertheless their jurisdiction on assize derived not from their office but from the Commissions under which they sat. The Courts Act 1971 abolished all courts of assize but section 71 of the Supreme Court Act now provides that sittings of the High Court may be conducted at any place in England or Wales;[7] the centres at which sittings of the High Court are, in fact, held are determined in accordance with directions of the Lord Chancellor. Although there are standing directions, it is always open to the Lord Chancellor to give an ad hoc direction to enable a particular sitting to take place at a particular place if there is sufficient reason for it. Thus in *St Edmundsbury and Ipswich Diocesan Board of Finance v Clark*,[8] a case concerning a claim to a right of way over a disputed strip of land at Iken, a small village in Suffolk, a direction was given on behalf of the Lord Chancellor, at the request of the trial judge, MEGARRY J, authorising the court to sit at Iken.

The jurisdiction of the High Court is both civil and criminal and both original and appellate. It has virtually unlimited jurisdiction in civil actions, though this is not generally an exclusive jurisdiction. Most actions are brought in the county courts.

The High Court, when created, consisted of five divisions, but these were reduced in 1880 to the three which now exist[9] (save that the Probate,

---

5 See p 513, *post*.

6 These courts, which were superior courts, continued to exercise a Chancery jurisdiction equivalent to that of the High Court in the County Palatine of Lancaster and the County Borough of Teesside until their abolition by the Courts Act 1971, s 41 which merged them with the High Court.

7 Although evidence, including a view by the judge, may be taken outside the jurisdiction; cf *Tito v Waddell* [1975] 3 All ER 997; [1975] 1 WLR 1303.

8 [1973] Ch 323; [1973] 2 All ER 1155.

9 Under s 7 of the Supreme Court Act, Her Majesty may by Order in Council, on a recommendation of the Lord Chancellor, the Lord Chief Justice, the Master of the Rolls, the President of the Family Division and the Vice-Chancellor, increase or reduce the number of divisions.

Divorce and Admiralty Division has been re-named the Family Division[10]). Although all three divisions have equal competence each division, in fact, exercises a separate jurisdiction. This is not dictated by convenience but by the Rules of the Supreme Court which govern procedure and practice throughout the Supreme Court (except in the Crown Court where there are separate rules, the Crown Court Rules).[11] These Rules specify the manner in which an action or matter may be commenced and prosecuted in the High Court. Consequently certain types of action are confined to a particular division. Thus matrimonial causes in the High Court may only be heard in the Family Division and not in either of the two other divisions. In certain cases the jurisdiction of the divisions overlaps and it is possible to start certain proceedings in one or other of them. For example, two modern cases concerning similar conditions in similar contracts were tried within a short space of time. The first[12] was tried in the Chancery Division, the second[13] in the Queen's Bench Division. It is important to bear in mind that the divisions of the High Court are not different courts, so that the jurisdiction of any one High Court judge is exercisable by any other High Court judge, irrespective of the division to which he is assigned.[14] Furthermore the Lord Chancellor, with the concurrence of the Lord Chief Justice and the President of the Family Division, has directed that:

> ". . . any Division of the High Court to which a cause or matter is assigned shall have jurisdiction to grant in that cause or matter any remedy or relief arising out of or related to or connected with any claim made in the cause or matter notwithstanding that proceedings for such remedy or relief are assigned by or under any Act to another Division of the court."[15]

Nevertheless, as a matter of practice, the effect of statutes and rules of procedure is usually to confer upon each division jurisdiction which is independent of that exercised by the other two divisions.[16]

The jurisdiction of the High Court is both original and supervisory. The historic role of courts in supervising the actions of inferior bodies and tribunals has already been noted.[17] This function is now mainly performed by a divisional court of the Queen's Bench Division, which also has certain

---

10 Administration of Justice Act 1970, s 1. The same section also effected redistribution of business between the divisions as a consequence of the main purpose of the change which was to create a division which deals solely with family and domestic matters. Thus the Admiralty jurisdiction of the High Court was assigned to the Queen's Bench Division to be exercised by the new "Admiralty Court" created by s 2 of the Act, while contentious probate business was assigned to the Chancery Division, thereby eradicating the unsatisfactory duality of jurisdiction which had hitherto existed, whereby disputes concerning the validity of wills were heard in the Probate, Divorce and Admiralty Division, while questions of the construction of wills were determined in the Chancery Division.

11 See p 284, *post*; though the inherent jurisdiction of the High Court is exercisable by a judge of any Division; see *Re L* [1968] P 119; [1968] 1 All ER 20.

12 *Petrofina (Great Britain) Ltd v Martin* [1965] Ch 1073; [1965] 2 All ER 176.

13 *Esso Petroleum Co Ltd v Harper's Garage (Stourport) Ltd* [1966] 2 QB 514; [1965] 2 All ER 933.

14 See *Re Hastings (No 3)* [1959] Ch 368; [1959] 1 All ER 698; *Re Kray* [1965] Ch 736; [1965] 1 All ER 710; *Re L* [1968] P 119; [1968] 1 All ER 20.

15 *Practice Direction (High Court; Divisions)* [1973] 2 All ER 233; [1973] 1 WLR 627.

16 For the distribution of business between the divisions, see Supreme Court Act 1981, s 61 and Sch 1.

17 See p 122, *ante*.

appellate functions. Likewise, divisional courts of the Family Division have appellate functions. These are dealt with specifically below.[18]

a Chancery Division

The Chancery Division consists of the Lord Chancellor, who, although nominal head of the division, never sits at first instance, a Vice-Chancellor and such of the puisne judges as the Lord Chancellor may nominate.[19] Before 1972, sittings of the Chancery Division were held only in the Royal Courts of Justice and Chancery judges did not go on assize (though a concurrent Chancery jurisdiction was exercised by the now defunct Chancery Courts of the Counties Palatine of Lancaster and Durham). Although the Supreme Court Act authorises sittings of the High Court to be held at any place in England and Wales, in practice most Chancery business continues to be taken in London, members of the Chancery bench and bar not being noticeably peripatetic.[20] However the Vice-Chancellor of the County Palatine of Lancaster (who is now a circuit judge[1]) sits as a judge of the High Court[2] at Liverpool, Manchester and Preston and, time permitting, at Leeds and Newcastle-upon-Tyne for the hearing of proceedings assigned to the Chancery Division.

Original jurisdiction — Section 34 of the Judicature Act 1873 assigned to the Chancery Division jurisdiction over matters which were heard in the Court of Chancery prior to the abolition of that court in 1875. The distribution of High Court business between the divisions is now governed by section 61 of and Schedule 1 to the Supreme Court Act. Under that Schedule are assigned to the Chancery Division all causes and matters relating to:

(a) the sale, exchange or partition of land, or the raising of charges on land;
(b) the redemption or foreclosure of mortgages;
(c) the execution of trusts;
(d) the administration of estates of deceased persons;
(e) bankruptcy;
(f) the dissolution of partnerships or the taking of partnership or other accounts;
(g) the rectification, setting aside or cancellation of deeds or other instruments in writing;
(h) probate business, other than non-contentious or common form business;
(i) patents, trade marks, registered designs or copyright;
(j) the appointment of a guardian of a minor's estate, and all causes

---

18 See p 155, *post.*
19 Supreme Court Act 1981, s 5.
20 Although MEGARRY J (as he then was) cast doubt upon this belief, not only by conducting a sitting of his court at a village in Suffolk (*St Edmundsbury and Ipswich Diocesan Board of Finance v Clark* (*supra*)) but by visiting two islands in the western Pacific for the purpose of conducting a view (*Tito v Waddell* (*supra*), p 149).
 1 By virtue of the Courts Act 1971, s 16, Sch 2.
 2 Pursuant to the request of the Lord Chancellor made under s 9 of the Supreme Court Act 1981 under which section circuit judges or recorders may sit as judges of the High Court.

and matters involving the exercise of the High Court's jurisdiction under the enactments relating to companies.

This jurisdiction is augmented by statutes and rules of procedure. Thus the Chancery Division, in addition to the matters set out above, exercises jurisdiction over revenue matters, town and country planning and landlord and tenant disputes. Judges of the division when sitting as the Court of Protection[3] hear applications under the Mental Health Act 1983 concerning the management of the property and affairs of mental patients.

Patents Court — There are three "specialist courts" within the High Court, *viz* the Patents Court, the Admiralty Court and the Commercial Court.[4] Of these the first is part of the Chancery Division (the other two being part of the Queen's Bench Division). It was established by the Patents Act 1977 and consists of nominated judges of the division. It hears patent actions at first instance and on appeal from the Comptroller-General of Patents, Designs and Trade Marks, procedure being governed by RSC Order 104.

Probate jurisdiction and procedure — Probate procedure differs according to whether the deceased died testate, ie leaving a valid will, or intestate, ie leaving no will or leaving a will which is invalid, generally through failure to comply with the due formalities which are principally contained in the Wills Act 1837.

If a person dies testate his will should appoint one or more executors. These executors must first apply to the Principal Registry of the Family Division or to a District Probate Registry for a grant of probate. This application must be accompanied by the will itself, the executors' affidavit of undertaking to administer the estate, a statement of all the deceased's property for tax purposes and various other documents. In the overwhelming majority of cases no-one will dispute the validity of the will and the grant of probate will be made as a formality. However any person who disputes the validity of a will in respect of which a grant is sought may enter a *caveat* at the Registry in question. In that event the proceedings become contentious and there will have to be a trial as to the validity of the will.[5] This trial may take place in the county court for the district where the testator resided before his death if the net value of the estate is less than £30,000.[6]

If a person dies intestate a person will have to apply to be appointed an administrator of the estate. There will then be a grant of letters of administration rather than a grant of probate. The effect is similar in that it vests the deceased's property in the administrators who must then distribute it in accordance with the intestacy provisions.

Appellate jurisdiction — Although the jurisdiction of the Chancery Division is predominately original, there is some appellate jurisdiction. A single judge of the division has jurisdiction by statute to hear certain appeals, for example income tax appeals from the Commissioners of

---

3 See p 175, *post*. The wardship jurisdiction of the Chancery Division was assigned to the Family Division by the Administration of Justice Act 1970, s 1, Sch 1.

4 Supreme Court Act 1981, s 6.

5 The procedure is governed by RSC Ord 76; a probate action must be commenced by writ (Ord 76, r 2).

6 County Courts Act 1984, s 32; the limit may be raised by Order in Council (*ibid*, s 145).

Inland Revenue under section 56 of the Taxes Management Act 1970. A divisional court of the Chancery Division, comprising at least two judges of the division, has a limited jurisdiction, consisting of the hearing of appeals from county courts in bankruptcy and land registration matters. The Patents Court, as stated above, hears appeals from certain decisions of the Comptroller-General of Patents, Designs and Trade Marks.

b Queen's Bench Division

The jurisdiction of the Queen's Bench Division is wider in scope than that of the other two divisions of the High Court. It is both civil and criminal and both original and appellate. In addition it exercises the supervisory jurisdiction formerly exercised by the Court of King's Bench. The jurisdiction of the division is equivalent to the jurisdiction exercised by the three superior common law courts of first instance prior to 1875, as altered by subsequent statutes and rules. Procedure in this division is dealt with at length in Part III of this book.

Original civil jurisdiction — By far the most important aspect of the business of the division is its first instance jurisdiction over civil matters, principally actions in contract and tort. Jurisdiction over commercial matters is exercised in the Commercial Court, which is one of the lists in the division, maintained in London, and several regional centres.[7] Admiralty jurisdiction, assigned to the division by section 20 of the Supreme Court Act, is exercised by the "Admiralty Court", the judges of which are those judges nominated to be Admiralty judges by the Lord Chancellor.[8] Admiralty business includes actions to enforce a claim for damage, loss of life or personal injury arising out of a collision between ships, claims to the possession or ownership of ships, claims for loss of or damage to goods carried in a ship, towage claims and other specified proceedings.[9] When trying admiralty actions the judge often sits with lay assessors.

Appellate civil jurisdiction — The appellate jurisdiction of the Queen's Bench Division in civil matters is fairly minor. Appeal lies from an interlocutory order of a Queen's Bench Division master to a judge in chambers[10] and a single judge also has jurisdiction to hear certain appeals from tribunals, for example from the Pensions Appeal Tribunal.[11] A judge of the Commercial Court hears appeals from arbitrations and determines questions of law arising in the course of arbitrations in accordance with the provisions of the Arbitration Act 1979.[12] A divisional court of the Queen's Bench Division consisting of two or more judges of the division has a limited civil jurisdiction in hearing appeals by way of case stated from magistrates' courts, other than matrimonial proceedings, and the Crown Court, from the Solicitors Disciplinary Tribunal and in certain other cases.

---

7 As well as the Commercial lists heard in London, Liverpool and Manchester, Mercantile lists, for cases of a commercial or business character, have been created in Birmingham (see *Practice Note* [1993] 4 All ER 381) and Bristol (see *Practice Note* [1993] 4 All ER 1023, sub nom Practice Direction [1993] 1 WLR 1522). See further p 364, *post.*
8 Supreme Court Act 1981, s 6. Procedure in the Admiralty Court is governed by RSC, Ord 75; see p 365, *post.*
9 The full jurisdiction is listed in s 20 of the Supreme Court Act.
10 See p 419, *post.*
11 Pensions Appeal Tribunals Act 1943; Tribunals and Inquiries Act 1992, s 13.
12 See p 281, *post.*

Criminal and supervisory jurisdiction — The criminal jurisdiction of the High Court is exercised exclusively by the Queen's Bench Division. This is entirely appellate[13] and exercised by the divisional court consisting of at least two but often three judges of the division. The Lord Chief Justice often sits and the hearing will then take place in his own court in the Royal Courts of Justice. The jurisdiction is exercised over appeals by way of "case stated"[14] from magistrates' courts and the Crown Court (in the exercise of that court's appellate jurisdiction).

The supervisory jurisdiction of the division is also exercised by the divisional court. This includes jurisdiction to issue the prerogative writ of habeas corpus and to make orders of mandamus, prohibition and certiorari by which inferior courts and tribunals are compelled to exercise their powers properly and restrained from exceeding their jurisdiction. This jurisdiction, as has been seen,[15] is invoked by application for "judicial review", the procedure being governed by RSC Order 53. Such cases are dealt with as part of the Crown Office list, and heard by a group of judges who have become increasingly specialised in administrative law matters. This, together with a large increase in the number of cases brought, has led in effect to the development of a system of administrative law.[16]

Judges of the division exercise other functions. Thus, as has been seen, they discharge the bulk of the business of the criminal division of the Court of Appeal. They also sit in the Courts-Martial Appeal Court. Disputed Parliamentary elections are determined by an election court which consists of two judges of the Queen's Bench Division.[17]

It should be noted finally that the "first-tier" jurisdiction of the Crown Court is exercised principally by the judges of the Queen's Bench Division.[18] Judges of the Queen's Bench Division on average spend approximately half their time in the Royal Courts of Justice and half "on circuit".

c   Family Division

This division (formerly named the Probate, Divorce and Admiralty Division[19]) consists of the President and such of the puisne judges as the Lord Chancellor may nominate.[20] The jurisdiction of the division is set out in the First Schedule to the Administration of Justice Act 1970 and is both original and appellate.

---

13 Prior to 1972 the division exercised a limited original criminal jurisdiction in the form of a trial "at bar", a procedure adopted in the notorious case of *R v Casement* [1917] 1 KB 98; the jurisdiction was, however, virtually obsolete and was abolished by the Courts Act 1971, s 6 (now s 46(1) of the Supreme Court Act, which provides that all proceedings on indictment must be brought before the Crown Court).

14 For details of the procedure, see p 542, *post*.

15 See p 127, *ante*.

16 See the *dicta* of LORD DIPLOCK in *O'Reilly v Mackman* [1983] 2 AC 237 at 279; [1982] 3 All ER 1124.

17 Representation of the People Act 1983, ss 120 *et seq*. However, this is not part of the Queen's Bench Division and, indeed, is an inferior court and therefore subject to judicial review; *R v Cripps, ex parte Muldoon* [1984] QB 68; [1984] 3 All ER 72.

18 See p 159, *post*.

19 The division was re-named by the Administration of Justice Act 1970, s 1. The late Sir Alan Herbert described the jurisdiction as "wills, wives and wrecks"; of these, "wills" have gone to the Chancery Division and "wrecks" (other than the wrecks of marriages) to the Queen's Bench Division (*supra*).

20 Supreme Court Act 1981, s 5; there are at present sixteen.

Schedule 1 to the Supreme Court Act assigns to the Family Division:

(a) all High Court matrimonial causes and matters (whether at first instance or on appeal);

(b) all causes and matters (whether at first instance or on appeal) relating to:

  (i) legitimacy;
  (ii) the exercise of the inherent jurisdiction of the High Court with respect to minors, the maintenence of minors and any proceedings under the Children Act 1989, except proceedings solely for the appointment of a guardian of a minor's estate;
  (iii) adoption;
  (iv) non-contentious or common form probate business;

(c) applications for consent to the marriage of a minor;

(d) proceedings on appeal under section 13 of the Administration of Justice Act 1960 from an order or decision made under section 63(3) of the Magistrates' Courts Act 1980 to enforce an order of a magistrates' court made in matrimonial proceedings or with respect to the guardianship of a minor;

(e) certain proceedings under the Family Law Act 1986;

(f) proceedings under the Children Act 1989;

(g) proceedings under various statutory provisions.[1]

The general effect of these provisions is that the division has exclusive High Court jurisdiction over matrimonial disputes and children, thus avoiding the conflicts which, prior to 1970, arose between the Family and Chancery Divisions.[2] However, it should be noted that, under the Children Act 1989[3] a unified system for dealing with proceedings under that Act exists. Magistrates' courts, county courts and the Family Division each have jurisdiction, and the distribution of work between the three courts is governed by an order made by the Lord Chancellor,[4] which also provides for transfer of cases between the three courts.

The appellate business of the division comprises principally appeals from magistrates' courts and county courts, in respect of proceedings concerning matrimonial causes and children in magistrates' courts.

G THE CROWN COURT

1 Creation of the Crown Court

The Crown Court was created by the Courts Act 1971. In order to appreciate the jurisdiction of this court and its place in the hierarchy, it is necessary to examine briefly the system of courts that the Crown Court replaced.

Prior to 1 January 1972, the date upon which the Courts Act came into

---

1 Domestic Violence and Matrimonial Proceedings Act 1976; Child Abduction and Custody Act 1985; Family Law Act 1986; Human Fertilisation and Embryology Act 1990, s 30.
2 See, *eg*, *Hall v Hall* [1963] P 378; [1963] 2 All ER 140.
3 Section 92 of the Children Act 1989.
4 Children (Allocation of Proceedings) Order 1991, SI 1991/1677.

operation, trials on indictment took place either at quarter sessions or at assizes.[5] The essential characteristics of both quarter sessions and assizes was that their jurisdiction was local. This meant not only that the courts (as a rule) tried only offences committed within the locality of their jurisdiction but also that the administration of the courts was organised on a local basis, so that the methods of administration and organisation varied from area to area.

The most serious offences were tried at assizes before a court presided over by a judge sitting, not by virtue of his normal judicial office, but under royal commissions of *oyer and terminer* and *gaol delivery*; the persons named in the commissions usually included at least two High Court judges, almost invariably judges of the Queen's Bench Division, who would sit at the assize town for the duration of the assize. The jurisdiction of assizes was equivalent to that of the High Court since a commissioner when engaged in the exercise of his jurisdiction constituted a court of the High Court of Justice.[6]

All save the most serious offences tried on indictment were tried at quarter sessions of which there were almost 150 separate courts. Quarter sessions were of two kinds – county quarter sessions and borough quarter sessions. These courts, which as their name would indicate were held at least four times a year, were composed, in the case of county quarter sessions, by the justices of the peace of the county, almost invariably presided over by a legally qualified chairman, and in the case of borough quarter sessions, by a Recorder who sat alone and was a practising barrister of at least five years' standing. The jurisdiction of quarter sessions was both civil and criminal and original and appellate. The criminal jurisdiction comprised the trial of all indictable offences, save those which had, by statute, to be tried at assizes, jurisdiction to sentence persons committed for sentence following summary conviction and the hearing of appeals from the decisions of magistrates' courts. The whole of this jurisdiction has been transferred to the Crown Court together with the civil jurisdiction of quarter sessions which comprised principally matters concerned with various forms of licensing.[7]

Before leaving the pre-1972 system, mention must also be made of the Central Criminal Court and of the Crown Courts of Liverpool and Manchester. The Central Criminal Court, established by the Central Criminal Court Act 1834 and popularly known as the "Old Bailey" after the name of the street in London in which the court is situated, was the assize court exercising criminal jurisdiction in the Greater London area. The court was a court of the High Court and its jurisdiction extended over indictable offences committed in Greater London or on the high seas; the judges of the court sat under the commissions of *oyer and terminer* and *gaol*

---

5 Although trial "at bar" in the High Court was still theoretically possible; see p 154, n 13, *ante*.

6 In addition to the High Court judges, county court judges and Queen's Counsel were often included in the commissions; furthermore the Master of the Rolls, Lords Justices of Appeal and former Lords Justices and High Court judges might be included in the commissions but in practice were not. The Commissioners of Assize also tried civil cases as a court of the High Court.

7 Although certain administrative functions were transferred to local authorities (Courts Act 1971, ss 53, 56, Sch 8).

delivery and consisted of the Lord Chancellor, the Lord Mayor of the City of London, the Lord Chief Justice and the judges of the Queen's Bench Division, the Aldermen of the City of London, the Recorder and the Common Serjeant and a number of additional judges who had to be judges of at least ten years' standing; of these only the Queen's Bench Division judges, the Recorder, the Common Serjeant and the additional judges sat in practice.

The Criminal Justice Administration Act 1956 established, as something of an experimental innovation, Crown Courts in Liverpool and Manchester presided over by the Recorders of Liverpool and Manchester who were the full-time judges of the courts. The jurisdiction of these courts was solely criminal but was both original and appellate since the courts exercised the criminal jurisdiction of both assizes and quarter sessions within the area of their respective jurisdictions. These courts, which were abolished by the Courts Act 1971, must not be confused with the present Crown Court. Apart from the difference in the judiciary of the courts, the jurisdiction of the Crown Courts of Liverpool and Manchester was, as in the case of all quarter sessions and assize, local.

Of the system of courts described above one commentator observed:[8]

". . . not only have the courts been tied to geographical areas but their judges have been tied to them. This is true both of courts of quarter sessions in boroughs and counties and also of courts of assize where the judges of the High Court have been obliged to follow rigid itineraries which, since the beginning of the last century, have borne little relation to the volume of business to be dealt with or the populations which the assize towns were intended to serve. When populations are small, business is light and travelling slow, such a system has its obvious advantages and represents perhaps no more than a marginal waste of resources which is more than adequately offset by the benefit of having justice readily available on a local basis. The urbanisation of England from the late eighteenth century, together with the vast increase in population and the introduction of a rapid and efficient system of transport, have rendered a rigid system of locally organised justice no longer adequate to absorb the consequent increases in the volume of work."

In the result a Royal Commission was established under the chairmanship of Lord Beeching and the report[9] that followed contained recommendations which formed the basis for the system introduced by the Courts Act 1971.

The Courts Act 1971 abolished all courts of assize and quarter sessions and established in their place a single court to be known as the Crown Court. The constitution and jurisdiction of the Crown Court is now contained in the Supreme Court Act 1981. It is part of the Supreme Court and a superior court of record.[10] The Courts Act further abolished the

---

8 MD Huebner, 'An Outline of the New System' 121 New Law Journal, p 1136.

9 *Report of the Royal Commission on Assizes and Quarter Sessions* Cmnd 4153 of 1969.

10 Supreme Court Act 1981, ss 1, 45(1). This, however, appears to be largely a matter of terminology since, in the exercise of its appellate jurisdiction, the Crown Court (as were Quarter Sessions) is amenable to the supervisory jurisdiction of the High Court as if it were an inferior court (*ibid*, s 29(3); see p 126, *ante*), although it is not amenable to this jurisdiction in matters relating to trial on indictment: see p 126, *ante*. In addition s 151 of the Act, the interpretation section, provides that except where the context otherwise requires a reference in the Act, or in any other Act, to a judge of the Supreme Court shall

Crown Courts of Liverpool and Manchester and the Central Criminal Court, though the latter has been retained in name since it is expressly provided that when the Crown Court sits in the City of London it shall be known as the Central Criminal Court.[11]

As already indicated the essential feature of the Crown Court is that its jurisdiction is in no sense local. Section 78 of the Supreme Court Act 1981 provides that:

> "(1) Any Crown Court business may be conducted at any place in England or Wales, and the sittings of the Crown Court at any place may be continuous or intermittent or occasional.
> (2) Judges of the Crown Court may sit simultaneously to take any number of different cases in the same or different places, and may adjourn cases from place to place at any time."

Thus it is important to remember that there are not various Crown Courts throughout the country, in the way that there were various quarter sessions; there is one Crown Court,[12] sittings of which may be held anywhere at any time as indicated above.

2   Constitution

The judges of the Crown Court are all the judges of the High Court, the circuit judges and recorders; judges of the court sit alone as a rule, though there is provision for justices of the peace to sit, but only with one of the judges of the court.[13] This is in contrast to the former county quarter sessions which were composed entirely of justices of the peace, albeit almost always sitting with a legally qualified chairman. In addition to the

---

not include a reference to a judge of the Crown Court; cf *Sirros v Moore* [1975] QB 118; [1974] 3 All ER 776; see p 184, *post*.

11 Supreme Court Act 1981, s 8(3); the Lord Mayor of the City and any Alderman of the City are entitled to sit as judges of the Central Criminal Court with any High Court judge, circuit judge or recorder. The reasons behind the preservation of this obsolete tradition are not clear. There used to be a rule to the effect that an Alderman of the City had to be present in the court; although this rule has disappeared, the central seat in the No 1 court at the Old Bailey is still traditionally left vacant for the Lord Mayor. As a further concession to the City of London the 1971 Act provides that the holders of the offices of Recorder of London and Common Serjeant, although circuit judges *ex officio*, continue to be appointed and remunerated in accordance with the provisions of the City of London (Courts) Act 1964 rather than in accordance with the provisions of the 1971 Act, which govern the appointment and remuneration of all other circuit judges (s 16, Sch 2); finally judges sitting in the Central Criminal Court continue to be addressed as "my Lord" as opposed to "your Honour", which is the appropriate form of address for circuit judges, deputy circuit judges, recorders and assistant recorders (see *Practice Direction (Judge; mode of address)* [1982] 1 All ER 320; [1982] 1 WLR 101).

12 For an example of the relevance of this fundamental principle, see *R v Slatter* [1975] 3 All ER 215; [1975] 1 WLR 1084.

13 Supreme Court Act 1981, s 8. A further unimportant exception to the rule that the judges of the court sit alone is the right of the Lord Mayor and Aldermen of the City of London to sit in the Central Criminal Court (*supra*). Where justices do sit they are themselves judges of the Crown Court and must play a full part in all decisions of the court, whether on interlocutory matters or on sentence, so that in the event of disagreement the decision of the majority of the court prevails, even if the judge alone is in the minority. The summing-up and direction to the jury must, however, be given by the judge and where there is any ruling of law to be given that ruling must be determined by the judge alone; these principles were stated by the Court of Appeal in *R v Orpin* [1975] QB 283; [1974] 2 All ER 1121.

regular judges of the court any judge of the Court of Appeal and any former Court of Appeal or puisne judge may, on the request of the Lord Chancellor, sit and act as a judge and when so sitting and acting is regarded as a judge of the High Court.[14] There is also provision for the temporary appointment of deputy High Court and circuit judges and assistant-recorders.[15]

There are thus basically three tiers of judiciary. At the highest level are the High Court judges who, in practice, are almost invariably judges of the Queen's Bench Division and try principally those cases formerly heard at assizes.[16] Below High Court judges are circuit judges and recorders.[17]

Finally there are the provisions for justices of the peace to sit in the court. Their attendance is mandatory on the hearing by the Crown Court of any appeal or of proceedings on committal to the court for sentence, on the hearing of which proceedings the judge of the court sits with not less than two nor more than four justices of the peace. In addition any jurisdiction or power of the court may be exercised by a regular judge of the court sitting with not more than four justices.[18] Where justices sit the decision of the court is by majority and if the members of the court are equally divided the regular judge has a second and casting vote.[19] As a final illustration of the departure from the principle of localised jurisdiction, section 8(2) of the 1981 Act provides that a justice of the peace shall not be disqualified from acting as a judge of the Crown Court for the reason that the proceedings are not at a place within the area for which he was appointed as a justice, or because the proceedings are not related to that area in any way.

It will be noted that the judges of the Crown Court are not, as it were, full time criminal judges (as were the recorders of the former Crown Courts of Liverpool and Manchester). The High Court judges sit, of course, in civil cases in the High Court; the circuit judges, as well as exercising the very limited civil jurisdiction which the Crown Court inherited from quarter sessions, discharge the functions of county court judges;[20] Recorders sit mainly to try criminal cases though, as well as having the civil jurisdiction of the Crown Court, there is provision for recorders to sit as county court judges.

3 Jurisdiction and procedure

The Crown Court has exclusive jurisdiction over all trials on indictment for offences wherever committed, including proceedings on indictment for offences within the jurisdiction of the Admiralty in England.[1] In addition all jurisdiction formerly exercised by any court of quarter sessions was vested in the Crown Court.[2] This, as indicated above, includes the hearing

---

14 Supreme Court Act 1981, s 9.
15 Courts Act 1971, s 24.
16 As to the distribution of business, see p 469, *post.*
17 See p 182, *post.*
18 Supreme Court Act 1981, ss 74(1), 8(1)(c).
19 *Ibid*, s 73(3).
20 Courts Act 1971, s 20; see p 182, *post.*
 1 Supreme Court Act 1981, s 46.
 2 Courts Act 1971, s 8, Sch 1; this was subject to the provisions of Sch 8, Part I which transferred certain administrative functions of quarter sessions to local authorities.

of appeals by persons convicted summarily in magistrates' courts,[3] the sentencing of persons committed for sentence following summary conviction[4] and a limited civil jurisdiction, principally concerned with licensing appeals. Procedure in the court is governed by Crown Court rules.[5]

The Lord Chief Justice has power under section 75 of the Supreme Court Act 1981, with the concurrence of the Lord Chancellor, to give directions relating to the distribution of Crown Court business. The current directions[6] classify offences, for the purposes of distribution, into four classes,[7] the first of which, being the most serious, are to be tried by a High Court judge. Class 2 offences are to be tried by a High Court judge unless a particular case is released by or on the authority of a presiding judge, that is to say, a High Court judge assigned to have special responsibility for a particular circuit. All offences triable on indictment, other than those in classes, 1, 2 and 4 form Class 3 and may be listed for trial by a High Court judge, circuit judge or recorder, while certain indictable offences and all offences triable either way constitute Class 4 and may be tried by a High Court judge, circuit judge or Recorder but will normally be listed for trial by a circuit judge or recorder.[8]

H EMPLOYMENT APPEAL TRIBUNAL

1 History

In 1971 an attempt was made to create a specialist court to deal with matters relating to industrial relations. Section 99 of the Industrial Relations Act 1971, established the National Industrial Relations Court. The Act, together with the court itself, was extremely controversial, as was its jurisdiction and exercise of power. After a stormy and short life it was abolished in 1974. However, in 1976 the Employment Appeal Tribunal was established with similar objectives, but with different powers. The jurisdiction and functions of this tribunal are now governed by the Employment Protection (Consolidation Act) 1978.

2 Constitution

The constitution of the court comprises such number of judges as may be nominated from time to time by the Lord Chancellor from the judges of the High Court and the Court of Appeal, one of whom is appointed President, at

---

3 See p 540, *post.*

4 See p 535, *post.*

5 Section 86 of the 1981 Act (as amended by the Courts and Legal Services Act 1990) confers power to make Crown Court rules upon a Crown Court rule committee consisting of the Lord Chancellor together with any four or more of the following persons, namely the Lord Chief Justice, two other judges of the Supreme Court, two circuit judges, the registrar of criminal appeals, a justice of the peace, two person who have a Supreme Court qualification (see p 181, post) and two persons who have the right to conduct litigation (p 209, *post.* The current rules are the Crown Court Rules 1982.

6 See *Practice Direction (Crown Court Business: Classification)* [1987] 1 WLR 1671. The directions permit presiding judges to issue directions reserving particular cases for trial by a High Court judge.

7 For further details of the classification of offences and the distribution of business, see p 470, *post.*

8 As to when Class 4 offences will be tried by a High Court judge, see p 470, *post.*

least one nominated judge of the Court of Session and such other members as may be appointed from time to time by Her Majesty.[9] The additional members are persons having special knowledge or experience of industrial relations, either as representatives of employers or as representatives of workers, so that, although the President is a lawyer, the Tribunal consists of laymen with specialised knowledge of industrial relations. The members of the Tribunal may resign by notice in writing and may be removed by the Lord Chancellor after consultation with the Secretary of State on specified grounds, notably incapacity or misbehaviour.[10] The Tribunal, which is a superior court of record, has a central office in London and may sit at any time and in any place in Great Britain in any number of divisions concurrently. It is duly constituted when sitting with a judge and either two or four other members (or a judge and one other member by consent of the parties).[11]

3 Jurisdiction

The jurisdiction of the Tribunal is limited to that which is conferred upon it by the 1978 Act. In sharp contrast to the National Industrial Relations Court, the Tribunal does not have the original jurisdiction which that court had to deal, for example, with unfair industrial practices. Its jurisdiction is limited to hearing appeals; these lie on questions of law from industrial tribunals under the Equal Pay Act 1970, the Sex Discrimination Act 1975, the Race Relations Act 1976 and the various employment protection statutes.[12] In addition the Tribunal hears appeals on questions of fact or law arising in any proceedings before, or arising from any decision of, the Certification Officer under section 8 of the Trade Union and Labour Relations Act 1974 or under section 8 of the 1975 Act (under which a trade union may be certified as independent).[13]

4 Procedure

The Lord Chancellor has power to make rules of procedure, subject to which the Tribunal has power to regulate its own procedure.[14] The rules of procedure[15] aim at informality. Nevertheless any person appearing before the Tribunal may be represented by counsel or by a solicitor or, indeed, may appear in person or be represented by a representative of a trade union or employers' association or by any other person whom he desires to represent him.[16]

Procedure at hearings of the Tribunal is designed to combine informality with order. No-one appears robed, there is no bench or witness box, parties and their advisers sit at tables and may address the court seated. A

---

9 Employment Protection (Consolidation) Act 1978, s 135(2); in addition the Lord Chancellor has power to appoint temporary judges or members (*ibid*, Sch 11, Part I, paras 4–10).
10 *Ibid*, Sch 11, Part I, paras 1–3.
11 *Ibid*, Sch 11, Part I, paras 12–16.
12 See, in particular, Employment Protection (Consolidation) Act 1978.
13 *Ibid*, s 136(3).
14 *Ibid*, Sch 11, Part I, para 17.
15 Employment Appeal Tribunal Rules 1980, SI 1980/2035.
16 Act of 1978, Sch 11, Part I, para 20.

further departure from normal court practice is that no party is to be ordered to pay costs unless, in the opinion of the Tribunal, the proceedings were unnecessary, improper or vexatious or there has been unreasonable delay or other unreasonable conduct in bringing or conducting the proceedings.[17]

The Tribunal has powers in relation to compelling the attendance and examination of witnesses, the production and inspection of documents, the enforcement of its orders and all other matters incidental to its jurisdiction under the Act, save that no person can be punished for contempt except by, or with the consent of, a judge who is a member of the court.[18]

5   Appeals

Any decision of the Employment Appeal Tribunal on a question of fact is final (except in the case of committal for contempt) but appeal on a point of law lies to the Court of Appeal. The court, being a superior court of record, is not subject to the supervisory jurisdiction of the High Court.[19]

I   MAGISTRATES' COURTS

1   Constitution

A magistrates' court is defined by section 148 of the Magistrates' Courts Act 1980, as any justice or justices of the peace acting under any enactment or by virtue of his or their commission or under common law. Consequently magistrates' courts are composed of justices of the peace.[20] A magistrates' court must be composed of at least two and not more than seven justices of the peace in order to try an information summarily, hear a complaint or conduct an examination into the means of a person whom it is proposed to commit to prison for non-payment of a fine. However an exception is provided by the presence of a stipendiary magistrate who has all the powers of two lay justices.[1] A single lay justice has a limited jurisdiction and cannot order a person to pay more than one pound or impose imprisonment for more than fourteen days. It should be noted that a single justice may discharge the function of determining the mode of trial of an offence triable summarily or on indictment and of conducting a preliminary investigation.[2]

The jurisdiction of magistrates' courts is local. Every county, the London commission areas and the City of London have a separate commission of the peace, and a county will be divided into petty sessional divisions, which may be amended from time to time. The jurisdiction of the justices is generally confined to matters arising in or near these commission areas.[3]

---

17 Employment Protection (Consolidation) Act 1978, Sch 11, Part I, para 19.
18 *Ibid*, Sch 11, Part I, paras 18, 21, 22.
19 See p 125, *ante.*
20 See p 183, *post.*
 1 Justices of the Peace Act 1979, s 16.
 2 See p 462, *post.*
 3 Administration of Justice Act 1973; the commission areas are stated in accordance with the provisions of the Justices of the Peace Act 1979, ss 1, 2.

A magistrates courts' committee will oversee the performance and functioning of each county or commission area, comprising magistrates together with any co-opted members. They will appoint a justices' clerk who must have a five-year magistrates' courts qualification,[4] and be within any precribed age limits.[5] The duty of the justice's clerk is well described by section 28(3) of the Justices of the Peace Act 1979:

> "It is hereby declared that the functions of a justices' clerk include the giving to the justices to whom he is clerk or any of them, at the request of the justices or justice, of advice about law, practice or procedure on questions arising in connection with the discharge of their or his functions, including questions arising when the clerk is not personally attending on the justices or justice, and that the clerk may, at any time when he thinks he should do so, bring to the attention of the justices or justice any point of law, practice or procedure that is or may be involved in any question so arising."

The task of the clerk is therefore that of a legal adviser, though care must be taken to ensure that an appearance of interference with the magisterial function is avoided.[6] The clerk is also the permanent official and administrator of the court, who is responsible for the organisation of the court, the collection of fines, for dealing with applications for legal aid in criminal cases and other administrative work. Recent proposals in respect of the streamlining of the administrative and management functions of magistrates' courts have led to fears that the independent advisory function set out by section 28 might be put in jeopardy.[7] These proposals include the amalgamation of magistrates' courts committee areas, a requirement for approval by the Lord Chancellor of the chairman of such committees, the creation of a Chief Justices' Clerk to oversee the magistrates' courts service, the introduction of fixed-term contracts for justices' clerks, and an increased role for the Lord Chancellor in the recruitment process for senior staff.

2 Jurisdiction

It is common to suppose that the jurisdiction of the magistrates' courts is entirely criminal. This is very far from being true since magistrates have a wide and varied civil jurisdiction. The feature of both the civil and the criminal matters within the jurisdiction of the magistrates' courts is that they are matters of relatively minor importance compared with the civil matters heard in the High Court and the county courts and the criminal cases tried at the Crown Court. The compensating advantage of summary procedure is its cheapness and speed. The balance between the advantages of summary trial and Crown Court trial has led to repeated discussions as to the distribution of business between the two courts. This is discussed further in due course.[8]

Before examining more closely the civil and criminal jurisdiction of

---

4 Within the meaning of the Courts and Legal Services Act 1990, s 71.
5 Justices of the Peace Act 1979, s 26. When the clerk is represented in court by an assistant (as is often the case), the assistant clerk must fulfil the qualification requirements of the Justices Clerks (Qualification of Assistants) Rules 1979 (SI 1979/570).
6 See *Practice Direction (Justices Clerks)*[1953] 2 All ER 1306n [1953] 1 WLR 1416.
7 For the proposals, see *A New Framwework for Local Justice* (1993, HMSO.)
8 See p 452, *post.*

justices it should be remembered that sitting as magistrates' courts is not the only function of justices of the peace. They also sit in the Crown Court.[9] Furthermore such important functions as the conduct of preliminary investigations, the issue of summonses and warrants and the grant of bail are exercised by justices though not sitting as magistrates' "courts". It has only in recent years been confirmed that licensing sessions are "courts".[10]

a   Criminal jurisdiction

The criminal jurisdiction of the magistrates' courts exists principally over summary offences.[11] Such offences are offences triable without a jury and are all statutory offences since all summary jurisdiction derives from statute. These offences are of a minor character since the maximum penalty which can be imposed in respect of a summary offence is six months' imprisonment[12] and a fine limited in amount.[13] Nevertheless, the consequence of any conviction can often be significant, in terms of the loss of reputation, or of the consequences upon employment. In practice most summary offenders are convicted of motoring offences under the Road Traffic Acts and regulations made under those Acts. Indeed so numerous are the convictions for minor offences such as speeding and unauthorised parking that a new procedure was introduced by the Magistrates' Courts Act 1957 enabling persons to plead guilty to minor summary offences by post.[14] There are more than 2 million persons a year found guilty of summary offences in England and Wales.

In addition to their jurisdiction over summary offences magistrates' courts also have jurisdiction to try "offences triable either way"[15] and may, on conviction, impose penalties similar to those which may be imposed following conviction of summary offences.

b   Youth courts

Until 1991, these were known as juvenile courts,[16] and are magistrates' courts which exercise jurisdiction over offences committed by, and other matters concerning, children and young persons.[17] The aim of the procedure in these courts is to disassociate the juvenile offenders from the criminal atmosphere and environment of the ordinary magistrates' courts, and to avoid undue publicity. Thus a youth court must not sit in a room in which sittings of another court are held if a sitting of that other court has been or will be held there within an hour.

Proceedings are not open to the public and the only persons admitted to

---

9 See p 159, *ante*.

10 *Jeffrey v Evans*, [1964] 1 All ER 536; [1964] 1 WLR 505.

11 The jurisdiction appears to be exclusive: *R v East Powder Magistrates' Court, ex parte Lampshire* [1979] QB 616; [1979] 2 All ER 329, *post*.

12 Magistrates' Courts Act 1980, s 31(1).

13 See p 534, *post*.

14 See p 532, *post*.

15 See Magistrates' Courts Act 1980, s 17, Sch 1; for details of the procedure for determining the mode of trial of such offences, see p 448, *post*.

16 Criminal Justice Act 1991, s 70.

17 For these purposes a "child" is a person under 14 years, a "young person" aged 14–17 inclusive: Children and Young Persons Act 1933, s 107.

the court are the court officers, the parties to the case and their representatives, witnesses, *bona fide* members of the press and other persons authorised by the court to be present. In addition, to protect the young person, the press must not publish or broadcast the identity of any person under eighteen concerned in the proceedings, unless the court so orders. This restriction includes not only the accused, but also any witness under eighteen years of age.

A youth court consists of justices drawn from a special panel, the chairman of which sits permanently though the other members change by rotation. There must be three lay justices to form a youth court of whom one at least must be a woman.[18]

c Civil jurisdiction

This aspect of the magistrates' courts' jurisdiction is very varied. It extends over the recovery of certain civil debts such as income tax, national insurance contributions, electricity, gas and water charges, council tax, the grant, revocation and renewal of licences and domestic proceedings. The latter category is probably the most important aspect of the magistrates' civil jurisdiction; it is exercised principally under the Domestic Proceedings and Magistrates' Courts Act 1978 and Children Act 1989, in "family courts".

d Family courts

These courts were constituted under section 80 of the 1978 Act, and were known as domestic courts. Following a radical re-shaping of the law relating to children by the Children Act 1989, they were renamed "family courts".[19] They consist of justices drawn from a specially appointed panel to deal with such proceedings.[20] No person may be present during the proceedings except officers of the court, the parties and their legal representatives, witnesses and other persons directly concerned in the case, newspaper representatives and any other person whom the court may permit to be present.[1] There is provision for rules of court to be made requiring the magistrates to give and record reasons for their decisions (which they do not have to, and usually do not, do in ordinary proceedings) and for making available a copy of the record to prospective appellants.[2]

Under section 1 of the 1978 Act either party to a marriage[3] may apply for an order on the ground that the other "(a) has failed to provide reasonable maintenance for the applicant; or (b) has failed to provide, or to make a proper contribution towards, reasonable maintenance for any child of the family; or (c) has behaved in such a way that the applicant cannot reasonably be expected to live with the respondent; or (d) has deserted the

---

18 Youth Court (Constitution) Rules 1954, r 12 (SI 1954/1711, as amended).
19 Children Act 1989, s 92.
20 The formation of these panels and the composition of domestic courts is dealt with by rules of court made under s 67 of the Magistrates Courts' Act 1980; a stipendiary magistrate who is a member of a family court panel may sit alone (s 67(7)).
 1 *Ibid*, s 69(2).
 2 *Ibid*, s 74(1).
 3 It is to be noted that the provisions do not apply to unmarried cohabitees as do, for example, the provisions of the Domestic Violence and Matrimonial Proceedings Act 1976.

applicant." If any such ground is made out the court may order financial provision to or for the benefit of the applicant or any child of the family;[4] in addition the court may make orders as to custody or contact with children, and various orders, for example excluding one spouse from the matrimonial home, for the protection of spouses and children,[5] and various orders under the Children Act 1989.[6] An order made pursuant to that Act[7] requires many forms of proceedings to be commenced in the magistrates' court, subject to various powers of transfer to the county court or High Court.

Appeals from these orders lie to the Family Division, where they are usually heard by a divisional court, although in some cases they may be heard by a single judge.[8] Further appeal lies to the Court of Appeal and then to the House of Lords, in each case with leave.

J   COUNTY COURTS

The county courts are courts of exclusively civil jurisdiction dealing, in the main, with minor civil claims such as small debts. They were established by the County Courts Act 1846 to meet the need for a system of courts to deal with small claims. There are two important limitations to the extent of the county courts' jurisdiction. First, the jurisdiction is entirely statutory so that if, in any matter, statute provides no jurisdiction then none exists. Nevertheless statutes which are likely to affect a large section of the community frequently confer jurisdiction on the county courts. Modern examples are to be found in the Hire-Purchase Act 1965 and the Rent Act 1977. The general common law and equity jurisdiction of the county courts is contained in the County Courts Act 1984 and is principally limited by the value of the plaintiff's claim.[9]

The second limitation on the jurisdiction of the courts is geographical. The jurisdiction of county courts is local in nature so that there must be some connecting factor between the action and the county court district in which it is tried. There are about four hundred county court districts in England and Wales grouped into circuits, each of which has at least one circuit judge assigned to it. The administrative business of the court is supervised by the district judge who is a solicitor of at least seven years' standing and frequently holds the post of district registrar of the High Court. The district judge has a limited jurisdiction to try cases in which cases appeal lies to the judge. Apart from this, county courts have no appellate jurisdiction. Appeal lies from a county court to the Court of Appeal, subject to certain conditions, except in bankruptcy matters where appeal lies to a divisional court of the Chancery Division.

---

4 Act of 1978, s 2.
5 *Ibid*, s 16.
6 Which also gives jurisdiction on such matters to the county court (see p 397, *post*), and Family Division of the High Court (see p 155, *ante*).
7 Children (Allocation of Proceedings) Order 1991 (SI 1991/ 1677).
8 RSC, Ord 90, r 16.
9 Up until 1991 this was usually the determining factor. The changes implemented in 1990 give value a less determining role.

Details of jurisdiction and procedure in the county courts are discussed in due course.[10]

K CORONERS' COURTS

1 The office of coroner

This ancient office dates from the twelfth century when it principally concerned the custody of the King's revenue, particularly that revenue accruing from fines and forfeiture. In addition the coroner from time to time exercised the jurisdiction of the sheriff and enquired into such matters as deodands, treasure trove and unexplained deaths. Some of these functions, together with the administrative functions once exercised by coroners, have been removed.

The modern coroner's appointment and jurisdiction are governed by statute.[11] He must be a barrister, solicitor or registered medical practitioner of not less then five years' standing. He is removable by the Lord Chancellor for misbehaviour.

2 Jurisdiction

Although the coroner has jurisdiction over such matters as treasure trove and, in London, enquiring into the outbreak of fires, his jurisdiction is principally concerned with inquests into the death of persons whose bodies are "lying within his district"[12] where there is reasonable cause for suspecting that the person has died a violent or unnatural death, or a sudden death the cause of which is unknown, or has died in prison or that the death occurred while the deceased was in police custody, or resulted from an injury caused by a police officer in the purported execution of his duty.[13] In *R v West Yorkshire Coroner, ex parte Smith*[14] the Court of Appeal held that the phrase "lying within his jurisdiction" (which was the form of words used prior to the passing of the Coroners Act 1988) applied to a body brought into the district from abroad. This would appear to remain the position.

If the case falls within the terms of section 3 of the 1988 Act the coroner's duty is mandatory; he must hold an inquest.

To hold an inquest the coroner may, and in some cases must, summon a jury of between seven and eleven members. Witnesses attend and give evidence and the coroner may compel the attendance of a witness and fine a witness for failing to attend in answer to a summons. The procedure is entirely inquisitorial in that, although interested persons may be represented and may ask questions of the witnesses, it is the coroner who conducts the proceedings and there are no speeches made to the jury. The jury return their verdict which need not be unanimous provided there are

---

10 See p 396, *post*.
11 Coroners Act 1988 (a consolidation Act).
12 This form of words was used by Coroners Act 1988, s 8, in substitution for the phrase "lying within his jurisdiction".
13 1988 Act, s 8(3).
14 [1983] QB 335; [1982] 3 All ER 1098.

not more than two dissentients. This verdict is recorded in a document termed an "inquisition".

Prior to the passing of the Criminal Law Act 1977 the jury might return a verdict of murder, manslaughter or infanticide by a named person whereupon the coroner had power, without more, to commit that person for trial. In such a case the inquest took the place of a preliminary investigation by magistrates and the inquisition performed the function of an indictment.[15] This procedure, although rarely adopted, was an anachronism and it was abolished by section 56 of the 1977 Act. A coroner's inquisition cannot now charge a person with any offence. Where criminal proceedings are in hand in respect of a death which is the subject of an inquest or for an offence alleged to have been committed in circumstances connected with the death, there are provisions in section 1 of the Coroners Act 1988 for the adjournment of the inquest pending the resolution of the criminal proceedings, the decision ultimately resting with the Director of Public Prosecutions. After the conclusion of the relevant criminal proceedings the coroner will be notified of the outcome by the court concerned whereupon he may resume the inquest if in his opinion there is sufficient cause to do so. If he does, then the finding of the inquest as to the cause of death must not be inconsistent with the outcome of the relevant criminal proceedings.[16]

There is no appeal from a coroner's inquisition although the proceedings are subject to judicial review by the High Court and may be quashed by order of certiorari where, for example, the verdict cannot be supported by the evidence.[17]

Proceedings before a coroner's court are absolutely privileged for the purposes of defamation.[18]

L   JUDICIAL COMMITTEE OF THE PRIVY COUNCIL

1   Constitution

Prior to the Judicial Committee Act 1833 the jurisdiction of the Privy Council was exercised principally by laymen. This Act, as amended by the Judicial Committee Act 1844, the Appellate Jurisdiction Acts 1876–1947 and other Acts, created the Judicial Committee composed of the Lord President of the Council, the Lord Chancellor, ex-Lord Presidents, the Lords of Appeal in Ordinary and those members of the Privy Council who hold or have held high judicial office within the meaning of the Appellate Jurisdiction Acts 1876 and 1887. Membership has also been extended from time to time by Order in Council to persons who have held high judicial office in Commonwealth countries. In practice the Lord Chancellor and the Lords of Appeal in Ordinary are the members of the Committee who usually sit, with the result that decisions of the Privy Council enjoy great authority although they are not strictly binding on English courts.[19]

---

15 See p 473, *post.*
16 Coroners Act 1988, s 16(7).
17 See, generally, p 122, *ante.*
18 See p 190, *post.*
19 See p 64, *ante.*

The hearing of appeals takes place at the bar of the Privy Council before not less than three and usually five members of the Committee, although a greater number has been known.[20] The members of the Committee sit unrobed and procedure is similar to procedure in the House of Lords.

2 Jurisdiction

Although all English courts derive their jurisdiction directly or indirectly from the Sovereign, the Judicial Committee of the Privy Council is slightly different in that its jurisdiction is that of the Sovereign in Council. Consequently the Privy Council does not pass judgment. It merely tenders advice to the Sovereign in person. This is by convention followed and implemented by an Order in Council. For this reason only one opinion is usually read and dissents were until recently not recorded.[1] However it is now provided by Order in Council that dissenting opinions may be delivered in open court.[2]

The main aspects of the jurisdiction of the Privy Council are as follows.

(a) Appeals from courts outside the United Kingdom. Since the Sovereign is the fountain of justice for all her Dominions the Privy Council has jurisdiction to hear appeals from the Isle of Man, the Channel Islands, British Colonies and Protectorates and from the highest courts of independent Commonwealth countries. However, since the Statute of Westminster 1931 Commonwealth legislatures have been competent to pass legislation excluding appeal to the Privy Council and several have done so.[3] Thus the Privy Council held in 1947 that Canada could validly enact that the decision of its own Supreme Court be final and exclusive in civil and criminal matters.[4]

Leave to appeal in criminal matters is only given in exceptional cases. Misdirection will not suffice. There must be some "clear departure from the requirements of justice" or "something which, in the particular case, deprives the accused of the substance of fair trial and the protection of the law."[5]

(b) Admiralty jurisdiction. Prior to 1875 appeal lay from the High Court of Admiralty to the Privy Council. When the Judicature Acts assigned jurisdiction to hear appeals from the Probate, Divorce and Admiralty Division of the High Court to the newly formed Court of Appeal the jurisdiction of the Privy Council was virtually limited to appeals from that division when sitting as a "prize court".[6] The jurisdiction of the High Court

---

20 See, *eg, Pratt v A-G for Jamaica* [1993] 4 All ER 769; [1993] 3 WLR 995, where a court of seven judges declared gross delays in the carrying out of sentences of death to amount to inhuman and degrading treatment within the meaning of the Jamaican constitution.

1 *Cf*, judgment in the criminal division of the Court of Appeal where only one judgment is delivered as a rule, but for different reasons.

2 Judicial Committee (Dissenting Opinions) Order in Council 1966; for a particularly vigorous dissent, see *Abbot v R* [1977] AC 755; [1976] 3 All ER 140.

3 Including Aden, Botswana, Burma, Canada, Cyprus, Ghana, Guyana, India, Lesotho, Pakistan, Sierra Leone, Sri Lanka, Tanzania and Uganda.

4 *A-G for Ontario v A-G for Canada* [1947] AC 127; [1947] 1 All ER 137.

5 *Ibrahim v R* [1914] AC 599, at 614–615, *per* LORD SUMNER; see also *Prasad v R* [1981] 1 All ER 319; [1981] 1 WLR 469.

6 Now contained in Supreme Court Act 1981, s 16(2), although jurisdiction also exists to hear appeals from the Colonial Courts of Admiralty and from the Court of Admiralty of the Cinque Ports.

to sit as a prize court is now exercised, as with other Admiralty jurisdiction, by the Admiralty Court of the Queen's Bench Division.[7] A prize court is a court convened to determine issues concerning the ownership of ships and cargo and the validity of their capture by enemy warships.

(c) Appeals from ecclesiastical courts. Since the jurisdiction of the ecclesiastical courts was drastically curtailed in 1857[8] their jurisdiction has been confined to matters affecting members of the clergy and church buildings. The highest ecclesiastical courts are the Canterbury Court of Arches and the Chancery Court of York. Appeal from these courts lies to the Privy Council.[9] Although archbishops and bishops are not members of the Privy Council, whenever the Council is hearing an ecclesiastical appeal summonses are sent to one archbishop or the Bishop of London and four other bishops to sit as assessors, ie in an advisory capacity.

(d) Appeals from medical tribunals. The Privy Council hears appeals by persons who have had their names erased from the medical register by the Professional Conduct Committee of the General Medical Council under the Medical Act 1983.[10]

(e) Special references. Apart from its appellate jurisdiction outlined above, the Privy Council is sometimes required to advise on matters of law at the instance of the Sovereign.[11] In the exercise of this jurisdiction the Judicial Committee has advised on such diverse matters as the powers of colonial judges,[12] legislation in Jersey[13] and the eligibility of a person to sit and vote in the House of Commons.[14] The Secretary of State may recommend Her Majesty to refer to the Judicial Committee any question of whether a provision of any Measure of the Northern Ireland Assembly or Act of Parliament of Northern Ireland is void to the extent that it discriminates against any person or class of persons on the ground of religious belief or political opinion.[15]

M   COURTS OF PARTICULAR JURISDICTION

Prior to 1977 there were many courts of local jurisdiction which constituted exceptions to the normal hierarchy of courts in that their constitution and jurisdiction were controlled locally. However the judicial functions of the vast majority of such courts which actively exercised jurisdiction were abolished by the combined effect of the Courts Act 1971, the Local Government Act 1972 and the Administration of Justice Act 1977.[16] Certain courts are outside the ordinary hierarchy because their jurisdiction is concerned with matters wholly outside the scope of the ordinary civil and

---

7 Supreme Court Act 1981, s 20; see p 153, *ante*.
8 Court of Probate Act 1857; Matrimonial Causes Act 1857.
9 Ecclesiastical Jurisdiction Measure 1963, s 8.
10 Similar powers exist under the Dentists Act 1984, the Opticians Act 1989 and the Veterinary Surgeons Act 1966.
11 Judicial Committee Act 1833, s 4.
12 *Re Wells* (1840) 3 Moo PCC 216.
13 *Re Jersey States* (1853) 9 Moo PCC 185.
14 *Re Macmanaway* [1951] AC 161.
15 Northern Ireland Constitution Act 1973, s 18.
16 See p 11, *ante*; the few that remain are listed in para 23 of the Law Commission report, *Jurisdiction of Certain Ancient Courts* (Law Com No 72).

criminal law. Some of these courts, such as courts-martial, derive their jurisdiction from statute while others, notably the ecclesiastical courts, are autonomous although, of course, they are recognised by the Crown. The jurisdiction of these specialist courts is usually applicable only to certain members of society who have impliedly agreed to submit to their jurisdiction, though in some instances it extends to all members of the community.

1 Courts-martial

Courts-martial exercise jurisdiction over members of the armed forces. Their constitution, jurisdiction and procedure are governed by various statutes, principally the Army and Air Force Acts 1955, the Naval Discipline Act 1957 and the Armed Forces Act 1981.

Air Force and military courts-martial are similar in constitution and procedure.[17] The accused may be arrested for any offence against military law by a superior officer. In many instances his offence will only be a "summary" offence against Queen's Regulations in which case he will be tried by superior officers. In other cases the accused has a choice as to whether to be tried summarily or at a court-martial. Serious offences are always tried at courts-martial, except that murder, manslaughter, treason and rape committed within the United Kingdom cannot be tried at courts-martial but must be tried in the ordinary criminal courts. In all other cases the jurisdiction of civilian and military courts is concurrent. However a person who has already been convicted or acquitted by a civilian court cannot be subsequently tried at a military or Air Force court-martial, and vice versa.[18]

The trial of an offence at a court-martial is in many ways similar to a trial in the ordinary criminal courts. It is preceded by an inquiry which is similar to a preliminary investigation. The accused is sent for trial on a charge sheet which may be compared with an indictment. The trial will be before at least three (or five in the case of a general court-martial) officers who are assisted by a judge advocate from the Judge Advocate General's department[19] who is a lawyer and advises on the law. Proceedings are in open court and both counsel and solicitors have a right of audience. The prosecution case is conducted by an Army or Air Force officer either personally or through a civilian counsel. The order of proceedings and rules of evidence applicable are similar to those applicable in other criminal proceedings. The accused may appear in person or be represented by counsel, solicitor or a defending officer. There is no jury and at the conclusion of the evidence the judge advocate sums up and advises on the law, leaving the members of the court to arrive at their decision which is by majority, except that the court must be unanimous where sentence of death is to be imposed.[20] An acquittal is final whereas a finding of guilt is subject to confirmation by a superior officer. Prior to confirming the

---

17 Naval courts-martial differ slightly in their composition, although their jurisdiction and procedure are similar.
18 Armed Forces Act 1966, s 25.
19 The corresponding department in naval courts-martial is the Judge Advocate of the Fleet's department. The Judge Advocate General and the Judge Advocate of the Fleet are appointed by the Queen on the advice of the Lord Chancellor.
20 Army Act 1955, s 96.

finding of guilt the confirming authority may remit the finding to the court for reconsideration and may refuse to confirm the decision if it could not be supported by the evidence, was wrong in law or there was a miscarriage of justice.

The necessity for confirmation of a finding of guilt affords a safeguard to the accused against injustice. A further safeguard is provided by the power of the High Court to prevent excesses or abuses of jurisdiction by means of the prerogative orders of prohibition and certiorari and by habeas corpus.[1]

Although courts-martial cannot generally exercise jurisdiction over civilians this can be done where Her Majesty's forces are in armed occupation of hostile territory. In these circumstances a state of martial law may be declared by Her Majesty's commanders. A state of martial law may also be declared in time of insurrection although it is doubtful whether such a declaration would be valid within the United Kingdom. Furthermore civilians who are employed in the service of the forces on active service outside the United Kingdom are liable to trial in "standing civilian courts" which may be established outside the United Kingdom under section 6 of the Armed Forces Act 1976.

Courts-Martial Appeal Court — Until 1951 there was no appeal from conviction by a court-martial, the only remedy being a petition to the reviewing authority or, where an excess of jurisdiction was alleged, an application for prohibition, certiorari or habeas corpus.

The Courts-Martial (Appeals) Act 1951[2] created the Courts-Martial Appeal Court which is now composed of the *ex officio* and ordinary members of the Court of Appeal, judges of the Queen's Bench Division nominated by the Lord Chief Justice, certain Scottish and Irish judges and other persons of legal experience appointed by the Lord Chancellor. In practice the composition of the court resembles closely that of the criminal division of the Court of Appeal.[3] As in the latter court, there must be at least three judges. Only one judgment is delivered and procedure is similar to that in the criminal division of the Court of Appeal. The grounds of appeal to the Courts-Martial Appeal Court and the powers of that court on determining appeals are substantially similar to those of the Court of Appeal except that there is no right of appeal against sentence.

Appeal lies from the Courts-Martial Appeal Court to the House of Lords at the instance of the prosecutor or the defence subject to the conditions under which an appeal lies from the criminal division of the Court of Appeal to the House of Lords.[4]

2   Ecclesiastical courts

These courts have a history which is as old as the common law itself. Although they have been subject to control by the Sovereign since the reign of Henry VIII and although their jurisdiction over laymen has by stages been abolished there remains a hierarchy of courts within the Church of England. In addition the General Synod of the Church of

---

1 *R v Governor of Wormwood Scrubs Prison, ex parte Boydell* [1948] 2 KB 193; [1948] 1 All ER 438.
2 Now the Courts-Martial (Appeals) Act 1968.
3 See p 510, *post.*
4 See p 524, *post*; Courts-Martial (Appeals) Act 1968, s 39.

England has statutory power[5] to pass Measures concerning any matter affecting the Church of England and even concerning Acts of Parliament. These measures have statutory force upon receiving the Royal Assent. One such measure has been the Ecclesiastical Jurisdiction Measure 1963 which altered the hierarchy of ecclesiastical courts and abolished a large number of obsolete courts and their jurisdiction.

The ecclesiastical judicial system may now be summarised as follows. In each diocese there is a consistory court the judge of which is a chancellor appointed by the bishop. He must be at least 30-years-old and either be a barrister of seven years' standing or have held high judicial office. The consistory courts' jurisdiction[6] is principally concerned with investigating allegations of conduct unbecoming a clerk in Holy Orders and persistent neglect of duty. Appeal lies from the consistory courts to the Arches Court of Canterbury, presided over by the Dean of the Arches, or the Chancery Court of York, presided over by the Auditor, both officers being barristers of ten years' standing or persons who have held high judicial office. Appeal from these two courts lies to the Privy Council.[7]

Jurisdiction equivalent to that of the consistory courts is exercised over bishops and archbishops by Commissions of Convocation. Jurisdiction over all members of the clergy in matters involving "doctrine, ritual or ceremonial" is exercised by the Court of Ecclesiastical Causes Reserved composed of five judges appointed by Her Majesty including two persons who have held high judicial office and three diocesan bishops. Finally petition lies from both the Commissions of Convocation and the Court of Ecclesiastical Causes Reserved to a Commission of Review composed of three Lords of Appeal in Ordinary and two Lords Spiritual.

The penalties which ecclesiastical courts may impose range from rebuke to deprivation of Orders and disqualification from subsequent preferment. In addition such deprivation and disqualification are automatic where a priest or deacon is sentenced to imprisonment, has a decree of divorce or judicial separation pronounced against him on certain specified grounds, is found to have committed adultery in matrimonial proceedings or has had a magistrates' court order made against him in similar circumstances.[8]

Excesses of jurisdiction by the ecclesiastical courts may be controlled by the High Court by means of the prerogative orders of mandamus and prohibition. Certiorari does not, however, lie since these courts exercise and administer a different system of law.

3   Restrictive practices court

This court of record was created by the Restrictive Trade Practices Act 1956, now repealed and replaced by the consolidating Restrictive Practices Court Act 1976 and Restrictive Trade Practices Act 1976. The function of

---

5 Under the Church of England Assembly (Powers) Act 1919 as amended by the Synodical Government Measure 1969, s 2.

6 For a reported instance of the jurisdiction of consistory courts, see *Re St George's Church, Oakdale* [1976] Fam 210; [1975] 2 All ER 870.

7 See p 168, *ante*.

8 Ecclesiastical Jurisdiction Measure 1963, s 55 (substituted by Ecclesiastical Jurisdiction (Amendment) Measure 1974).

the court is to consider "restrictive agreements" and "information agreements" relating to the supply of goods or services.[9] Cases are referred to the court by the Director General of Fair Trading or by parties to such an agreement who have been ordered to furnish particulars to the court. The scope of the court's business was temporarily increased by the Resale Prices Act 1964 which restricted minimum resale price maintenance. Any supplier or trade association was able to apply to the Restrictive Practices Court for exemption for a class of goods on the grounds that this would be in the public interest.[10] The jurisdiction of the court was extended by the Fair Trading Act 1973 in that the Director General of Fair Trading may bring proceedings in the court against any person who either does not give or does not observe a written assurance that he will refrain from a course of conduct in the course of his business which appears to the Director to be detrimental to the interests of consumers in the United Kingdom and, in accordance with statutory criteria, unfair to consumers.[11]

The court consists of three judges of the High Court appointed by the Lord Chancellor, a judge of the Court of Session of Scotland, a judge of the Supreme Court of Northern Ireland and not more than ten lay members appointed by the Queen on the recommendation of the Lord Chancellor. The court is duly constituted with a presiding judge and two lay members except that in the case of proceedings involving only issues of law the court may consist of a single judge.[12] Appeal lies from the court on a question of law, and in proceedings under Part III of the Fair Trading Act 1973 (consumer protection) on a question of fact or law, to the Court of Appeal, the Court of Session or the Court of Appeal of Northern Ireland, as the case may be.[13]

4   Naval courts

A naval court may be summoned by an officer in command of one of Her Majesty's ships on any foreign station on a complaint to him by any member of the crew which appears to require immediate investigation, or where any British ship is wrecked, abandoned or lost in the area, or where the interests of the owner of any British ship or its cargo so require.[14] Such a court, consisting of naval officers, must investigate the matter judicially and may impose imprisonment or fine or forfeiture of wages, suspend or cancel officers' certificates, send an offender home for trial and order a ship to undergo a survey for unseaworthiness. Appeal lies from its decision to the divisional court of the Queen's Bench Division and thence, with leave, to the Court of Appeal.

---

9 Restrictive Trade Practices Act 1976, s 1; the extension to agreements relating to services was made by the Fair Trading Act 1973; for the definitions of "restrictive agreements" and "information agreements", see ss 6, 7, 11 and 12 of the 1976 Act.
10 Resale Prices Act 1964, s 5. All applications have long since been determined.
11 Fair Trading Act 1973, ss 34–35.
12 Restrictive Practices Court Act 1976, s 7.
13 *Ibid*, s 10.
14 Merchant Shipping Act 1894, s 480.

5 Court of Chivalry

The jurisdiction of an English court can only be removed by statute. Nevertheless the jurisdiction of most local courts and feudal courts has fallen into obsolescence. However a modern sitting was held of the Court of Chivalry, an ancient feudal court, to decide the entitlement of a theatre to display the coat of arms of the City of Manchester.[15] Prior to this case the court had not been convened since 1737. The court determines disputes over the right to use armorial bearings and ensigns. It is presided over by the Earl Marshal, although he appointed the Lord Chief Justice to sit as his deputy in the modern case in question. The court appears to have no power to enforce its decisions.[16]

6 Court of Protection

At common law the Sovereign has always assumed care and custody of persons of unsound mind and their property. As keeper of the Queen's conscience the Lord Chancellor was detailed to exercise this authority. At the present day the Lord Chancellor and the judges of the Chancery Division administer the property of persons of unsound mind within the meaning of the Mental Health Act 1983. When exercising this function the Chancery judge sits as the Court of Protection, the constitution and jurisdiction of which is now governed by the 1983 Act.[17]

The jurisdiction of the Court of Protection should not be confused with the jurisdiction of courts under various statutes to make orders for admission of persons to approved hospitals.[18]

N TRIBUNALS AND INQUIRIES

1 Statutory tribunals[19]

A large number of statutory tribunals has been created during the twentieth century to provide informal, relatively cheap mechanisms for the resolution of disputes, usually between the citizen and the State. This system of administrative justice has in the past caused some concern. The constitutional writer, Dicey,[20] rejected notions of a separate system of justice (*droit administratif*) for resolving disputes between citizen and the State. Such a view, even if true or tenable at the time it was expressed, is not tenable today: over the last 100 years Parliament has seen a greater need to confer jurisdiction upon bodies outside the ordinary jurisdiction of

---

15 *Manchester Corporation v Manchester Palace of Varieties Ltd* [1955] P 133; [1955] 1 All ER 387.

16 *Ibid*. Notwithstanding, the Law Commission report of 1976 (see p 170, n 16, *ante*) did not recommend the abolition of the court and it was one of the few courts of local and ancient jurisdiction which did not have its jurisdiction removed by the Administration of Justice Act 1977.

17 Though the power is exercisable in the High Court if the sum involved is a small one: *Re K's Settlement Trusts* [1969] 2 Ch 1; [1969] 1 All ER 194.

18 Eg, Mental Health Act 1983, s 37.

19 See, generally: Wade: *Administrative Law* (OUP).

20 *Introduction to the Study of the Constitution* (10th Edn 1964, MacMillan, at p 318).

the courts, and particularly in the context of social or welfare legislation. The reasons for the growth of a system of tribunals in this way reflect both the perceived disadvantages of the courts, in terms of formality, lack of speed, lack of expertise in some specialist areas of law, and cost. They also reflect the perceived advantages of tribunals as bodies which follow informal procedures, can hear cases relatively quickly, are cheap, and which have expertise in the particular subject matter.

Membership of tribunals often includes lawyers. Indeed, many chairmen will be legally qualified. Equally frequently, the members of tribunals will be laypersons with specific knowledge of the sphere of activity in question, but with little or no knowledge of the law.

Given the multiplicity of tribunals that exist, not all these perceived advantages or disadvantages operate in any given instance. Tribunals vary widely in terms of their composition, procedure, efficiency and formality. Examples include the Lands Tribunal (of almost court-like formality), industrial tribunals, rent tribunals, General and Special Commissioners of Income Tax, and social security appeals tribunals.

The industrial tribunals are in many ways a typical example. First established in 1964 with a very limited jurisdiction,[1] the jurisdiction of the industrial tribunals has been greatly enlarged by various statutes. Many of these provisions, notably those relating to complaints of unfair dismissal (which now constitute about two-thirds of the business of the tribunals) and claims for redundancy payment, are now consolidated in the Employment Protection (Consolidation) Act 1978.[2] The establishment of industrial tribunals is now governed by section 128 of the 1978 Act and regulations made thereunder. They have become an extremely important organ of the administration of justice; thus, although there is no fixed number of tribunals, since each may be convened as required, on average 75 tribunals currently sit in Great Britain every working day. Tribunals ordinarily consist of three members, one of whom is a legally qualified chairman, the decision being by majority. Members of tribunals are appointed because of their special knowledge and experience and they are entitled to draw on this in support of their decisions, although if evidence is given which is contrary to their knowledge and experience, the Employment Appeal Tribunal has stated that, while the tribunals are entitled to reject such evidence and to act on their own knowledge, they should first make this known to the parties and give witnesses the opportunity of dealing with it.[3]

Proceedings are relatively informal. The strict rules of evidence do not apply. Any person may appear before a tribunal in person or be represented by counsel or solicitor, or by a representative of a trade union or any employers' association or, indeed, "by any other person whom he desires to represent him".[4] Awards of costs are not usually made, unless a party has acted frivolously or vexatiously.[5]

---

1 See Industrial Training Act 1964, s 12.
2 Under s 131 of the 1978 Act, the appropriate Minister has power to confer upon tribunals jurisdiction over claims for damages for breach of a contract of employment, and related claims, and to modify other enactments for this purpose.
3 *Dugdale v Kraft Foods Ltd* [1977] 1 All ER 454; [1976] 1 WLR 1288.
4 Employment Protection (Consolidation) Act 1978, s 128, Sch 9, para 6.
5 Industrial Tribunals (Rules of Procedure) Regulations 1985, r 11 (SI 1985/16).

The jurisdiction of industrial tribunals extends over a wide range of aspects of industrial law, in addition to unfair dismissal and redundancy. Thus, for example, an employee may present a complaint to an industrial tribunal on the ground of the employer's failure to pay a "guarantee payment"[6] or maternity pay,[7] or on the ground that his employer has taken action for the purpose of preventing or deterring him from joining an "independent trade union"[8] or has failed to permit him to take time off as permitted by the Act.[9]

Following the abolition of the National Industrial Relations Court, appeal from industrial tribunals lay in all cases to the Queen's Bench Division. However appeal now lies to the Employment Appeal Tribunal in most cases.[10]

2 Domestic tribunals

There are a number of private or professional associations which have set up their own tribunals for resolving disputes between their own members or exercising control or discipline over them. The jurisdiction of these tribunals is based primarily on contract in that, by becoming a member of the association or professional body, a person contracts to accept the jurisdiction of the governing tribunal. Nevertheless in many cases these tribunals exist on a statutory basis with a right of appeal to the courts. Examples of domestic tribunals constituted under statute are the Solicitors Disciplinary Tribunal, under the Solicitors Act 1974,[11] and the Professional Conduct Committee of the General Medical Council, under the Medical Act 1983. Where the tribunal is not constituted under a statute then there is no appeal to the ordinary courts. However, the High Court exercises a supervisory jurisdiction over tribunals, even where their jurisdiction is not based on statute and will intervene to prevent an abuse of natural justice.[12]

3 Tribunals of inquiry

When a matter of urgent public importance arises Parliament may resolve to set up a tribunal to inquire into it. The tribunal is then set up by Her Majesty or a Secretary of State and upon the tribunal may be conferred many of the procedural powers of the High Court, such as summoning witnesses, compelling the production of documents and taking evidence on oath. If a witness refuses to answer a question put to him he may be reported to the High Court and punished for contempt of court.[13] A tribunal of inquiry must generally sit in public unless the public interest

---

6 Employment Protection (Consolidation) Act 1978, s 22.
7 *Ibid*, s 36.
8 *Ibid*, s 24.
9 *Ibid*, ss 27–29.
10 For details of the cases in which appeal lies to the Tribunal, see p 161, *ante*.
11 See p 215, *post*.
12 See p 130, *ante*.
13 Tribunals of Inquiry (Evidence) Act 1921, s 1; Contempt of Court Act 1981, s 20; cf *A-G v Clough* [1963] 1 QB 773; [1963] 1 All ER 420; *A-G v Mulholland* [1963] 2 QB 477; [1963] 1 All ER 767.

requires otherwise. The tribunal has discretion whether or not to allow representation by counsel or solicitor before it.

These tribunals of inquiry should not be confused with the frequent examples of governments appointing judges to head enquiries into particular issues.[14]

4   Local statutory inquiries

There are a number of statutes which confer jurisdiction upon Ministers to hold local inquiries. In practice these inquiries are conducted by inspectors but ultimately it is the Minister who assumes responsibility in Parliament. Inquiries of this nature often arise when objections are lodged against orders submitted by a local or public authority to a Minister for confirmation, or, sometimes, submitted by the Minister himself but subject to confirmation. The usual circumstance is the making of an order for the compulsory acquisition of land, or in respect of the refusal of planning permission.

Procedure at these inquiries is governed by the statute under which they are held. The extent of rights of appeal, usually on points of law only, is governed, again, by the particular statutory scheme. Furthermore, if procedural fairness is not observed (by, for example, the proper statement of reasons) judicial review may be an alternative course of action open to the aggrieved party.[15]

5   Criminal Injuries Compensation Board

Tribunals are sometimes established for the purpose of determining individuals' rights to compensation from public funds. The right to compensation arises where a person has suffered loss or damage, often by reason of an act of the legislature or the executive; compulsory acquisition of land is an obvious example.

A most important addition to compensation tribunals was the Criminal Injuries Compensation Board. The scheme was established as an experimental measure in 1964 and provides *ex gratia* compensation to victims of crimes of violence (or if the victim dies, his dependants). Compensation is assessed on the same basis as common law damages (where the application is by a dependant the principles of the Fatal Accidents Act apply) and takes the form of a lump sum payment. Although there is no right to compensation claims are determined by the Board consisting of a chairman and a number of qualified members.

Applications are in the first instance dealt with by a single member, the applicant having the right, if dissatisfied with the single member's decision, to a hearing before three other members of the Board. At the hearing the applicant must prove his case on a balance of probabilities; he may (as may the Board) call, examine and cross-examine witnesses. The procedure is informal and hearings are in private. Compensation will not be awarded unless the Board is satisfied (a) that the injury is one for which compensation of not less than £1,000 would be awarded; and (b) that the circumstances

---

14 See p 190, *post.*
15 See p 130, *ante.*

of the injury have been the subject of criminal proceedings, or were reported to the police without delay; and (c) that the applicant has given the Board all reasonable assistance, particularly in relation to any medical reports that they may require. The Board may reduce the amount of compensation or reject the application altogether if, having regard to the conduct of the victim and to his character and way of life, it is inappropriate that he should be granted a full award or any award at all.

The scheme extends, subject to restrictions, to victims of violence within the family.

The Board may reopen cases to take account of a serious change in a victim's medical condition within three years of the date of a final award.

An interesting feature of the Board is the method of its creation. Whereas tribunals are usually established by statute, the Board was set up by prerogative act. The government set out in a White Paper[16] the draft scheme, it was debated in both Houses of Parliament and, in an amended form, was announced by both Houses on 24 June 1964.[17]

Following recommendations made by various committees[18] the Criminal Justice Act 1988 placed the scheme on a statutory footing. These provisions have not yet been brought into force, but define what is a "qualifying injury", regulate the granting, witholding and reduction of compensation, and provide for a right of appeal to the High Court. There is, at present, no right of appeal from the Board, although its decisions are subject to judicial review by the High Court[19] and will be quashed if the Board misconstrues its mandate or if it must, on *Wednesbury* principles,[20] be deemed to have done so.[1]

6 Control by the courts of administrative tribunals and inquiries

Administrative justice can create dangers unless subject to effective safeguards and control. The Donoughmore Committee,[2] in 1932 recommended: firstly, that the supervisory jurisdiction of the High Court over tribunals be maintained; secondly, tribunals be compelled by the High Court to observe natural justice; thirdly, reports of statutory inquiries be published; finally, that there should be an appeal on a question of law. In 1957, the Franks Committee identified key principles of openness, fairness and impartiality. This report led to the Tribunals and Inquiries Act 1958.

The 1958 Act[3] created a Council on Tribunals consisting of not more than fifteen nor less than ten members appointed by the Secretary of State and Lord Chancellor.[4] The members are disqualified from membership of the House of Commons. The Council keeps under review the workings of

16 Cmnd 2323 of 1964.
17 Further amendments to the scheme were announced by the Home Secretary in 1965, 1969 and 1979.
18 Criminal Justice Act 1988, Sch 6.
19 *R v Criminal Injuries Compensation Board, ex parte Lain* [1967] 2 QB 864; [1967] 2 All ER 770.
20 See p 130, *ante*.
 1 *R v Criminal Injuries Compensation Board, ex parte Thompstone* [1984] 3 All ER 572; [1984] 1 WLR 1234.
 2 Committee on Ministers Powers (1932, Cm 4060, HMSO).
 3 See now the Tribunals and Inquiries Act 1992.
 4 *Ibid*, s 1.

tribunals and reports on them from time to time. The tribunals subject to the scrutiny of the Council are listed in the First Schedule to the Act and include agricultural lands tribunals, the lands tribunal, mental health review tribunals, rent tribunals and the General and Special Commissioners of Income Tax. In this way the Lord Chancellor, and through him, Parliament, is able to exercise direct extra-judicial control and supervision over some of the more important tribunals.

a   Supervisory control

The supervisory jurisdiction of the High Court, exercised in practice by the Queen's Bench Division, is a common law jurisdiction and does not depend upon statute. Any provision in an Act passed before August 1958 which excludes any of the powers of the High Court does not have effect so as to prevent the High Court from making orders of mandamus or certiorari. There are two ways in which the High Court may purport to exercise its supervisory control over tribunals. The usual method is by the issue of prerogative orders in judicial review proceedings; however these orders lie only against tribunals which are statutory, or at least of a public character and do not extend to tribunals exercising a purely voluntary jurisdiction. A person aggrieved by the decision of a voluntary tribunal may, however, invoke the High Court's supervisory jurisdiction by bringing an action against the officers of the tribunal, claiming an injunction or a declaration as to his rights.[5]

In recent years the High Court has shown an increased willingness to intervene in the affairs of trade and professional bodies which have the power to deprive individuals of their livelihood.[6]

b   Appeals from tribunals

An application for judicial review is not an appeal. There is no common law right of appeal from a tribunal so that an appeal only lies where statute so provides. The Tribunals and Inquiries Act 1992, section 11, provides for any party to appeal or to require the tribunal to state a case on a point of law from certain administrative tribunals to the High Court. These appeals are heard by the divisional court of the Queen's Bench Division. Other statutes provide rights of appeal to various branches of the Supreme Court and, in the case of doctors, dentists and opticians, to the Judicial Committee of the Privy Council.[7]

---

5 Under RSC Ord 15, r 16; see p 338, *post.*
6 *Bonsor v Musicians' Union* [1956] AC 104; [1955] 3 All ER 518; *Byrne v Kinematograph Renters Society Ltd* [1958] 2 All ER 579; [1958] 1 WLR 762; *Nagle v Feilden* [1966] 2 QB 633; [1966] 1 All ER 689.
7 See p 168, *ante.*

CHAPTER 8

The Judiciary

A APPOINTMENT AND CONDITIONS OF TENURE OF OFFICE

1 Appointment

The Lord Chancellor, the Lord Chief Justice, the Master of the Rolls, the President of the Family Division of the High Court, the Vice-Chancellor, the Lords of Appeal in Ordinary and the Lords Justices of Appeal are appointed by the Queen on the advice of the Prime Minister. Of these only the Lord Chancellor's appointment is made on a political basis. The *puisne* judges of the High Court, circuit judges and recorders are appointed by the Queen on the advice of the Lord Chancellor. Justices of the peace are appointed by the Lord Chancellor directly.

The law has generally limited judicial appointment to barristers of specified lengths of standing; solicitors were not, until recently, eligible for most judicial appointments – appointments as Crown Court recorders and as district judges in the county court being exceptions. The composition of the judiciary has mirrored that of the Bar in terms of gender and of racial or ethnic origin.[1] The Courts and Legal Services Act 1990 has removed these barriers, by relating qualification for judicial appointment to the new provisions in respect of rights of audience contained in the Act.[2]

Lords of Appeal in Ordinary are the senior members of the judiciary, and are generally appointed from the ranks of the Court of Appeal, although exceptionally a first instance judge may be elevated directly to the House of Lords. They must either have held judicial office for two years, or have a Supreme Court qualification.[3] The number of law lords, originally fixed at two, is now not less than seven nor more than eleven.

Lords Justice of Appeal are appointed by Her Majesty by letters patent. They must have been judges of the High Court or have a 10-year High Court qualification.[4] There must not be more than 23 Lords Justice of

---

1 See Pannick, *Judges*, (1987).
2 See Courts and Legal Services Act 1990, ss 26–27.
3 Appellate Jurisdiction Act 1876, as amended by the Courts and Legal Services Act 1990. A Supreme Court qualification is defined by the 1990 Act, s 71(3) as meaning that the person has a right of audience for all proceedings in the Supreme Court. See further p 210, *post*. The requirement does not apply to the officers, except the Lord Chancellor who is a Minister of the Crown.
4 Within the meaning of the 1990 Act, s 71(3): the person has a right of audience for all proceedings in the High Court. See further p 209, *post*.

Appeal. High Court judges are likewise appointed by the Crown. Some-times styled "puisne judges", they must have a 10-year High Court qualification. It is now possible for a solicitor to be appointed directly to the High Court bench. In addition, a circuit judge may be appointed to the High Court bench. High Court judges are appointed to a particular division by the Lord Chancellor, depending usually on the practice which the appointee had prior to appointment.

The office of circuit judge was created by the Courts Act 1971. Circuit judges are appointed by Her Majesty on the recommendation of the Lord Chancellor, and must have a ten-year Crown Court or ten-year county court qualification.[5] Again this permits a solicitor to be appointed directly to the circuit bench. Whereas circuit judges are full-time appointments, recorders are part-time judges of the Crown Court, appointed on a temporary basis. The terms of appointment will specify the duration of the appointment, and the number of occasions upon which they will be available to undertake judicial duties. Failure to comply with these requirements is a ground for removal of office.[6]

2 Tenure

Until Stuart times judges held office only during the King's pleasure and could be, and were, removed at the will of the King. Their position was altered in consequence of the Revolution settlement by the Act of Settlement 1700 which provided that;

> "Judges' commissions be made *quamdiu se bene gesserint*, and their salaries ascertained and established, but upon the address of both Houses of Parlia-ment it may be lawful to remove them."[7]

Thus, as long as they conducted themselves properly (*quamdiu se bene gesserint*) judges of the superior courts[8] could be removed only on an address by both Houses of Parliament. Presumably a judge who was guilty of serious neglect or misconduct could be removed by the Crown without the need for an address by Parliament.[9] This prohibition still applies to judges of the Supreme Court of Judicature,[10] except, however, for circuit judges and Recorders who are removable by the Lord Chancellor on the ground of incapacity or misbehaviour or, in the case of a recorder, failing to comply with the conditions of his appointment.[11]

Judges of the Supreme Court (excluding circuit judges and recorders) and Lords of Appeal in Ordinary must, unless appointed before 1959, retire at the age of 70, subject to limited rights of extension of office until

---

5 Within the meaning of the 1990 Act, s 71(3): the person has rights of audience for all purposes in the county court.

6 Courts Act 1971, ss 17(4), 21(6); see p 159, *ante*.

7 This does not apply to the Lord Chancellor, because he is a Minister of the Crown, and holds office at the Queen's pleasure.

8 See p 141, *ante*.

9 See *Earl of Shrewsbury's Case* (1610) 9 Co Rep 42a, at 50. No English judge has been removed under the Act of Settlement procedure, though an Irish judge was so removed in 1830.

10 It is now contained in s 11(3) of the Supreme Court Act 1981.

11 Courts Act 1971, ss 17(4), 21(6); see p 159, *ante*.

the age of 75 years.[12] Their salaries are determined by the Lord Chancellor, with the consent of the Minister for the Civil Service, and charged on the Consolidated Fund.

Justices of the peace may be removed from the commission by the Lord Chancellor without showing cause. Several justices have been so removed, generally for refusing to administer a law with which they were not in sympathy. Although there is no retiring age for justices of the peace they are put on the supplemental list at the age of 70,[13] which is *de facto* retirement in that they cease to be entitled to exercise judicial functions. Justices may be put on the supplemental list before they have reached this age, either at their own request or on the ground of "age or infirmity or other like cause" or on the ground that the justice declines or neglects to take a proper part in the exercise of his judicial functions.[14]

B   CONSTITUTIONAL POSITION

Much has been written on the question of whether judges are "servants" of the Crown. The better view seems to be that they are servants for they are appointed and, in certain circumstances, removable by the Queen and are paid out of the Consolidated Fund, although they cannot be controlled in the exercise of their office by the Queen or her Ministers. Generally the question of whether judges are properly describable as servants is unimportant though the question did arise in an acute form in 1931 when the National Economy Act of that year conferred power upon the Commissioners of Inland Revenue to reduce the remuneration of "persons in His Majesty's Service". The Commissioners purported to reduce judicial salaries. The validity of this measure, though strenuously disputed, was not decided since the Inland Revenue soon abolished these reductions under pressure of public opinion.

Whether judges are or are not Crown servants there is no doubt that the judicial function is not under the control of the legislature or the executive. Judicial independence is a fundamental of English constitutional law. If the courts are to perform their important function of judicial scrutiny and review of executive action, it is essential that this independence is maintained. The duty of the court may, for example, extend to declaring that a government Minister has acted unlawfully, or in disobedience to a binding order of the court. Thus, in *M v Home Office*[15] the Home Secretary was held to be in contempt of court for disobedience to an order of the court.

An offshoot of this principle of judicial independence is the doctrine of judicial immunity. Historically the degree of immunity has varied with the status of the judge. The old cases distinguish between judges of superior courts, who were held immune from action even if acting maliciously, and judges of inferior courts who enjoyed immunity only while acting within their jurisdiction. These principles operated somewhat capriciously; thus a

---

12 Judicial Pensions and Retirement Act 1993, s 26.
13 Justices of the Peace Act 1979, s 8. Stipendiary magistrates retire at 70 but may be retained in office up to the age of 72 (*ibid*, s 14).
14 1979 Act, s 8.
15 [1993] 3 All ER 537; sub nom *Re M* [1993] 3 WLR 433.

Recorder of London who unlawfully imprisoned the jurors at the trial of Penn and Meade for ignoring his direction to convict was held immune from suit[16] while an unfortunate county court judge in Lancashire was held liable in damages for a mistake of law as to his jurisdiction, made quite innocently and in good faith.[17]

Such rationale as there may have been behind this dichotomy may be thought to have little relevance to modern conditions and the Court of Appeal in *Sirros v Moore*,[18] rejected the principle whereby the degree of immunity depends upon the status of the court. LORD DENNING MR stated the position in straightforward terms:[19]

> "Every judge of the courts of this land – from the highest to the lowest – should be protected to the same degree, and liable to the same degree. If the reason underlying this immunity is to ensure 'that they may be free in thought and independent in judgment', it applies to every judge, whatever his rank. Each should be protected from liability to damages when he is acting judicially. Each should be able to do his work in complete independence and free from fear. He should not have to turn the pages of his books with trembling fingers, asking himself; 'If I do this, shall I be liable in damages?' So long as he does his work in the honest belief that it is within his jurisdiction, then he is not liable to an action. He may be mistaken in fact. He may be ignorant in law. What he does may be outside his jurisdiction – in fact or in law – but so long as he honestly believes it to be within his jurisdiction, he should not be liable . . . Nothing will make him liable except it be shown that he was not acting judicially, knowing that he had no jurisdiction to do it."

The result in the instant case was to render immune from liability a circuit judge, exercising the appellate jurisdiction of the Crown Court, who, without authority (but in good faith), ordered the arrest and detention of the plaintiff as the latter was lawfully leaving the court.

LORD DENNING, immediately after the passage quoted above, added:

> "This principle should cover the justices of the peace also. They should no longer be subject to 'strokes of the rodde or spur'. Aided by their clerks, they do their work with the highest degree of responsibility and competence – to the satisfaction of the entire community. They should have the same protection as the other judges."

However this dictum was rejected by the House of Lords in *McC v Mullan*[20] in which it was held that justices could be sued if they acted without or in excess of jurisdiction. The latter phrase, however, requires some elaboration. If justices have jurisdiction to entertain the proceedings then the mere fact that they impose a sentence or take some other course

---

16 *Hamond v Howell* (1677) 2 Mod Rep 218.
17 *Houlden v Smith* (1850) 14 QB 841.
18 [1975] QB 118, at 136; [1974] 3 All ER 776, at 785. The position of justices of the peace and their clerks is now set out in Part V of the Justices of the Peace Act 1979 (as amended). They cannot be held liable in respect of acts done within their jurisdiction (s 44). There is no similar protection as regards acts done in excess of jurisdiction if, but only if, it is proved that the justice or clerk acted in bad faith (s 45) but the justice is entitled to indemnity out of local funds, in respect of both damages and costs, if he acted "reasonably and in good faith" (s 53).
19 [1975] QB, at 136; [1974] 3 All ER, at 785.
20 [1985] AC 528; [1984] 3 All ER 908.

which is subsequently held to be wrong does not mean that they acted in excess of jurisdiction. They will only act without their jurisdiction if they impose a sentence or take a course which they have no power to do. In such a case they may be held liable for whatever form of trespass to the person, land or goods follows.

The House of Lords also doubted the correctness of the statements in *Sirros v Moore*[1] (including that quoted above) to the effect that the distinction between superior and inferior courts, for this purpose, no longer exists although it regarded the decision itself as defensible on narrower grounds.

The immunity which attaches to judicial proceedings is not personal to the judge. Thus no civil action lies in respect of words spoken in the course of proceedings by parties,[2] witnesses,[3] advocates[4] or in respect of the verdict of a jury.[5] Fair and accurate contemporaneous newspaper and broadcast reports of judicial proceedings in the United Kingdom are also absolutely privileged in the law of defamation.[6]

C THE JUDICIAL FUNCTION

Most of the work of the judges is judicial in the sense that they have to adjudicate upon disputes. To do this they are required, dispassionately, to find the facts upon the evidence presented to the court, to apply the law to the facts as found and then to give the "right decision". Appellate courts have repeatedly pointed out that the judicial function in the conduct of litigation goes no further than that. Thus, in relation to finding the facts, the court must act on the evidence before it; it has no duty to seek out some "independent truth" as LORD WILBERFORCE called it in the following interesting passage from his speech in a case concerning discovery of documents:[7]

> "In a contest purely between one litigant and another, such as the present, the task of the court is to do, and be seen to be doing, justice between the parties, a duty reflected by the word 'fairly' in the rule. There is no higher or additional duty to ascertain some independent truth. It often happens, from the imperfection of evidence, or the withholding of it, sometimes by the party in whose favour it would tell if presented, that an adjudication has to be made which is not, and is known not to be, the whole truth of the matter; yet, if the decision has been in accordance with the available evidence and with the law, justice will have been fairly done."

To this principle there is at least one important exception, namely, cases where the issue is the welfare of a child. Such cases are to be decided not on an adversarial basis, but rather upon what the court considers to be in

---

1 See n 18, *supra*.
2 *Astley v Younge* (1759) 2 Burr 807.
3 *Hargreaves v Bretherton* [1959] 1 QB 45; [1958] 3 All ER 122.
4 *Munster v Lamb* (1883) 11 QBD 588.
5 *Bushell's Case* (1670) Vaugh 135.
6 Defamation Act 1952, s 8.
7 *Air Canada v Secretary of State for Trade (No 2)* [1983] 2 AC 394, at 438; [1983] 1 All ER 910, at 919; see p 615, *post*.

the best interests of the child.[8] However, even in these cases a court must base its judgments upon evidence, and not infrequently such proceedings can often be highly adversarial.

Having found the facts, judges must apply the existing rules of law to those facts. There are two aspects of this function – the interpretation of statutes and the application of the doctrine of precedent. It is the duty of judges to ascertain the intention of the legislature, if the rule of law in question is statutory, or to apply the existing law where the rule of law in question is a rule of common law or equity. Different approaches to the interpretation of statutes have already been identified.[9] The traditional view is that judges are not competent to interpret a statute other than in accordance with the literal meaning of the words used, or to alter any existing rule of common law or equity. LORD DIPLOCK explained the rationale of this view, in relation to the interpretation of statutes, in a case concerning a trade dispute in the steel industry, in the following words:[10]

> "My Lords, at a time when more and more cases involve the application of legislation which gives effect to policies that are the subject of bitter public and parliamentary controversy, it cannot be too strongly emphasised that the British Constitution, though largely unwritten, is firmly based on the separation of powers; Parliament makes the laws, the judiciary interpret them. When Parliament legislates to remedy what the majority of its members at the time perceive to be a defect or a lacuna in the existing law (whether it be the written law enacted by existing statutes or the unwritten common law as it has been expounded by the judges in decided cases), the role of the judiciary is confined to ascertaining from the words that Parliament has approved as expressing its intention what that intention was, and to giving effect to it. Where the meaning of the statutory words is plain and unambiguous it is not for the judges to invent fancied ambiguities as an excuse for failing to give effect to its plain meaning because they themselves consider that the consequences of doing so would be inexpedient, or even unjust or immoral. In controversial matters such as are involved in industrial relations there is room for differences of opinion as to what is expedient, what is just and what is morally justifiable. Under our Constitution it is Parliament's opinion on these matters that is paramount."

To similar effect, but in relation to construction of a contract, are the words of LORD BRIDGE in a shipping case:[11]

> "The ideal at which the courts should aim, in construing such clauses, is to produce a result such that in any given situation both parties seeking legal advice as to their rights and obligations can expect the same clear and confident answer from their advisers and neither will be tempted to embark on long and expensive litigation in the belief that victory depends on winning the sympathy of the court. This ideal may never be fully attainable, but we shall certainly never even approximate to it unless we strive to follow clear

---

8 *Re B (A Minor)* [1989] 1 FLR 268.
9 See p 40, *ante*.
10 *Duport Steels Ltd v Sirs* [1980] 1 All ER 529, at 541; [1980] 1 WLR 142, at 157.
11 *AS Awilco v Fulvia SpA di Navigazione, The Chikuma* [1981] 1 All ER 652, at 659; [1981] 1 WLR 314, at 322. This decision was an appeal to the House of Lords from the Court of Appeal presided over by LORD DENNING MR as were both cases cited in the preceding two footnotes.

and consistent principles and steadfastly refuse to be blown off course by the supposed merits of individual cases."

Nevertheless strict adherence to this rule is not always possible since there is often uncertainty or ambiguity in the area of law being considered.[12] Indeed the rule cannot be applied in interpreting an Act of Parliament which makes no provision for the case in question or in deciding a case of "first impression", ie, a case for which there is no precedent. In such a case the judge must create new law. In cases of judicial review[13] this problem is particularly acute. The constitutional role of the courts is to ensure that executive bodies keep within the bounds of the power granted by Parliament. Inevitably that requires the court to engage in an interpretative function. However, in cases involving the exercise of discretionary powers, the grounds of challenge may require the court to search for a sometimes elusive parliamentary intention.[14] In such cases the court must take case to keep within its proper functions, namely, to decide questions of law and not to impinge upon the right of the executive body to make and apply policy.[15]

In relation to the development of common law principles, traditional views are changing. In *Jones v Secretary of State for Social Services*[16] LORD SIMON stated:

> "In this country it was long considered that judges were not makers of law but merely its discoverers and expounders. The theory was that every case was governed by a relevant rule of law, existing somewhere and discoverable somehow, provided sufficient learning and intellectual rigour were brought to bear. But once such a rule had been discovered, frequently the pretence was tacitly dropped that the rule was pre-existing, for example, cases like *Shelley*'s case,[17] *Merryweather v Nixan*[18] or *Priestley v Fowler*[19] were (rightly) regarded as new departures in the law. Nevertheless the theory, however unreal, had its value – in limiting the sphere of law-making by the judiciary (inevitably at some disadvantage in assessing the potential repercussions of any decision, and increasingly so in a complex modern industrial society), and thus also in emphasising that central feature of our constitution, the sovereignty of Parliament. But the true, even if limited, nature of judicial law-making has been more widely acknowledged of recent years."

Judges do sometimes create new law. For example, DENNING J (as he then was) virtually did this in *Central London Property Trust Ltd v High Trees House Ltd*,[20] in a judgment which created the doctrine of equitable estoppel. The important civil remedies of *Anton Piller* orders and *Mareva* injunctions[1] are both judge-made.

---

12 For a detailed discussion of the judicial approach to statutory interpretation and to the doctrine of judicial precedent, see pp 40, 57 *et seq, ante.*
13 See p 122, *ante.*
14 The intention of Parliament may on occasion be ascertained from the debates of proceedings in Parliament: see *Pepper v Hart* [1993] AC 593; [1993] 1 All ER 42.
15 See *R v Secretary of State for the Home Department, ex parte Brind* [1991] 1 AC 696; [1990] 1 All ER 469.
16 [1972] AC 944, at 1026; [1972] 1 All ER 145, at 198; see p 70, *ante.*
17 (1581) Moore KB 136.
18 (1799) 8 Term Rep 186.
19 (1837) 3 M & W 1.
20 [1947] KB 130; [1956] 1 All ER 256n.
 1 See p 289, *post.*

The self-assumed power of the House of Lords to depart from its own previous decisions[2] has had the effect of bringing into sharp relief the scope of the judicial function, for the members of the House are now free, in effect, to create new law. It is fair to say that certain judges deem it to be within their function to create new principles of law while others believe that any far-reaching change should be left to Parliament, which has greater facilities for testing the possible repercussions of law reform. The latter approach is exemplified by the following passage from the vigorous dissenting speech of Lord Simon in the leading case of *Miliangos v George Frank (Textiles) Ltd*:[3]

> "I am sure that an expert committee, including or taking evidence from departmental officials, would apprehend a great number of not immediately apparent repercussions of the decision which my noble and learned friends propose to take. Such a committee might conclude that the repercussions make the decision unacceptable. Or they might suggest some means of mitigating any adverse effect. Or they might advise that the repercussions were on balance acceptable. But at least the crucial decision would be taken in the light of all the consequences involved.
>
> By contrast, the training and qualification of a judge is to elucidate the problem immediately before him, so that its features stand out in stereoscopic clarity. But the beam of light which so illuminates the immediate scene seems to throw surrounding areas into greater obscurity; the whole landscape is distorted to the view. A penumbra can be apprehended, but not much beyond; so that when the searchlight shifts a quite unexpected scene may be disclosed. The very qualifications for the judicial process thus impose limitations on its use. This is why judicial advance should be gradual. 'I am not trained to see the distant scene; one step enough for me' should be the motto on the wall opposite the judge's desk. It is, I concede, a less spectacular method of progression than somersaults and cartwheels; but it is the one best suited to the capacity and resources of a judge.
>
> We are likely to perform better the duties society imposes on us if we recognise our limitations. Within the proper limits there is more than enough to be done which is of value to society."

Lord Simon was a lone dissenting voice in the case cited above, and the House of Lords did effect a radical reform of English law in holding that English courts have power to give judgments expressed in foreign currency.

On occasion, judicial restraint may be because the nature of the issues involved is such that resolution of a problem is best left to Parliament. Thus in *Malone v Metropolitan Police Commissioner (No 2)*[4] Sir Robert Megarry considered that the practice of interception of telephone communications "cried out" for legislation, but declined to develop common law rules to fill the vacuum that existed.

An important example of judicial law-making by the House of Lords is afforded by the cases of *WT Ramsey Ltd v Inland Revenue Commissioners*[5] and *Furniss v Dawson*[6] in which the House formulated and developed the principle whereby a series of prearranged steps or transactions, some of

---

2 See p 70, *ante*.
3 [1976] AC 443, at 481–482; [1975] 3 All ER 801, at 824–825.
4 [1979] Ch 344; [1979] 2 All ER 620.
5 [1982] AC 300; [1981] 1 All ER 865.
6 [1984] AC 474; [1984] 1 All ER 530.

which have no commercial purpose other than the avoidance or deferment of tax, fall to be looked at together so that liability to tax is determined according to the substance of the scheme as a whole and its end result. These cases amounted to a bombshell to the tax-avoidance industry.

In the realm of criminal law judges have occasionally regarded it as within their function to enforce public morality by creating new criminal offences. The earliest criminal offences were, of course, judge-made and even until the eighteenth century the scope of the criminal law was being extended judicially.[7] However, by the middle of the nineteenth century "times had changed and the pretensions of the judges to extend the criminal law had changed with them".[8] Accordingly it is universally accepted that judges have no power to create new criminal offences.[9] This principle has not prevented the courts on occasion from declaring that the common law recognises certain conduct to be criminal. Thus in *R v Manley*[10] the defendant had alleged falsely that she had been attacked and robbed. The police were put to considerable trouble and expense in investigating her story and members of the public were put under suspicion. She was convicted of public mischief and her appeal against conviction, on the ground that no such offence was known to the law, was dismissed. Equally striking is the decision of the House of Lords in *Shaw v Director of Public Prosecutions*,[11] to the effect that an agreement to publish the "Ladies Directory", containing names, addresses and photographs of persons willing to engage in prostitution and perversion, constituted a "conspiracy to corrupt public morals" which was a criminal offence. The following observation from the speech of VISCOUNT SIMONDS in that case has been widely quoted:[12]

"In the sphere of criminal law I entertain no doubt that there remains in the courts of law a residual power to enforce the supreme and fundamental purpose of the law, to conserve not only the safety and order but also the moral welfare of the State . . . The law must be related to the changing standards of life, not yielding to every shifting impulse of the popular will but having regard to fundamental assessments of human values and the purpose of society."

In *Knuller (Publishing, Printing and Promotions) Ltd v Director of Public Prosecutions*[13] a publication of a somewhat similar kind (although this time aimed at a homosexual market) was held to give rise to the same offence. Not only was *Shaw*'s case followed but a majority of the House (*obiter*) expressed the view that there were known to the criminal law further offences of outraging public decency and conspiring so to do.

---

7 The historical alteration in the function of the judiciary in relation to the development of criminal law is illuminatingly described in the speech of LORD DIPLOCK in *Knuller (Publishing, Printing and Promotions) Ltd v Director of Public Prosecutions* [1973] AC 435; [1972] 2 All ER 898.

8 *Knuller (Publishing, Printing and Promotions) Ltd v Director of Public Prosecutions* [1973] AC 435, at 474; [1972] 2 All ER 898, at 918, *per* LORD DIPLOCK.

9 This was virtually the only point upon which all five members of the House of Lords were agreed in *Knuller (supra)*; see also *Abbott v R* [1977] AC 755; [1976] 3 All ER 140.

10 [1973] 1 KB 529; her conduct would now amount to a summary offence under the Criminal Law Act 1967, s 5(2).

11 [1962] AC 220; [1961] 2 All ER 446.

12 [1962] AC at 267–268; [1961] 2 All ER, at 452.

13 [1973] AC 435; [1972] 2 All ER 898.

In the light of these authorities such comfort as may be drawn from the principle that judges have no power to create new criminal offences would appear to be more illusory than real. However, in the later case of *Director of Public Prosecutions v Withers*[14] the House of Lords to some extent redressed the balance by holding that conspiracy to effect a public mischief, in the sense of an agreement to do an act which, although not unlawful in itself, is injurious to the public, is not as such an offence known to the law; *a fortiori* there is no offence of public mischief as such. Conduct which has already been held to be criminal, such as that of the defendant in *R v Manley (supra)*, remains criminal but not simply because it falls within the general rubric of "public mischief" but rather because it is a specific form of conduct which, on the authorities, constitutes an established criminal offence.

Other areas in which the judicial function goes beyond the resolution of the dispute which the judge in question is determining are "guideline" authorities in which appellate courts lay down guidelines for the guidance of judges in approaching the exercise of discretionary powers. Thus the rates of interest to be awarded on damages in personal injury actions,[15] the principles to be applied in determining applications for interlocutory injunctions[16] and the circumstances in which judges should grant leave to appeal from arbitration awards[17] are all the subject of guidelines laid down by the House of Lords. Similarly in criminal cases the modern practice of the criminal division of the Court of Appeal is, on the hearing of one or more appeals against sentence relating to a particular type of offence, to give sentencing guidelines for the assistance of Crown Court judges in dealing with offences of the type.[18]

In addition to their judicial functions, judges are often asked to perform extra-judicial functions. Governments often appoint judges to head committees of inquiry or similar bodies, to investigate and report upon matters of public interest or controversy. The Denning Report into the Profumo scandal in the 1960s, the Wilberforce Report into an industrial dispute in the coal-mining industry, the Popplewell Report into a fire at Bradford City Football Club, and the Scott Inquiry into sales of arms to Iraq are all examples.[19] Since 1989, judges may also engage in informal and public discussion of matters of public interest, which may include the writing of books or articles, or appearances upon television or radio.[20]

Finally, judges exercise certain administrative functions. This is particularly true of justices of the peace who exercise many functions which are not properly termed judicial, such as licensing and the issue of summonses and warrants. Judges of the Chancery Division sitting as a Court of

---

14 [1975] AC 842; [1974] 3 All ER 984.

15 See p 374, *post*.

16 See p 326, *post*.

17 See p 283, *post*.

18 This practice seems to have originated in *R v Turner* (1975) 61 Cr App Rep 67 in relation to sentences for robbery and has since been followed in relation to many other sentencing areas; see, for example, *R v Clarke (Linda)* [1982] 3 All ER 232; [1982] 1 WLR 1090 (partially suspended sentences); *R v Aramah* (1982) 76 Cr App Rep 190 (drugs offences); *R v Boswell* [1984] 3 All ER 353; [1984] 1 WLR 1047 (causing death by reckless driving).

19 See also p 177, *ante*.

20 The Kilmuir rules, which prevented judges from making public comment on judicial matters, were abolished in 1989.

Protection supervise the affairs and administer the property of persons of unsound mind. The Lord Chancellor and all High Court judges are "visitors" of the Inns of Court and, as such, hear appeals from orders of the Senate of the Inns of Court and the Bar.[1] In addition much litigation in the courts is non-contentious and concerns such matters as the administration of trusts, the winding-up of companies, adoption and legitimacy. Finally sections 85 and 86 of the Supreme Court Act 1981 empower, respectively, the Supreme Court Rule Committee and the Crown Court Rule Committee to make rules of court for the purpose of regulating and prescribing the practice and procedure to be followed in the Supreme Court while in county courts the rule committee derives jurisdiction from section 75 of the County Courts Act 1984. All of these committees include judges. In addition the judiciary controls practice and procedure in the courts by the issue of Practice Directions.

D CONTEMPT OF COURT

1 General nature of contempt

Her Majesty's judges control the due administration of justice and have an inherent jurisdiction to punish conduct which is calculated to prejudice or interfere with the process of the law. Such conduct is termed a contempt of court. Contempt may be either of a criminal nature or of a civil nature. Criminal contempt is a common law offence punishable by fine or imprisonment. It can amount to contempt in the face of the court, where judicial proceedings are actually disrupted.[2] More commonly, offences of contempt comprise conduct which interferes more generally with the administration of justice. Provided that the conduct in question was intentional, there does not need to be an intent to interfere with the administration of justice if the conduct in fact has this effect.[3] For example, it is a criminal contempt to refuse to give evidence,[4] to use a tape-recorder in court without the leave of the court,[5] to fail to comply with a requirement to attend court under a subpoena, witness order or witness summons,[6] or to interfere with a juror or witness.[7]

The workings of the jury system are strongly protected by the law of contempt. Not only is interference with a juror a contempt, as well as a substantive criminal offence, by section 8 of the Contempt of Court Act 1981[8] a contempt is committed if any person obtains, discloses or solicits any particulars of statements made, opinions expressed, arguments advanced or votes cast by a member of a jury in the course of their

---

1 For this general jurisdiction, see *R v Visitors to the Inns of Court, ex parte Calder and Persaud* [1994] QB 1; [1993] 2 All ER 876.
2 See, eg, *Morris v Crown Office* [1970] 2 QB 114.
3 *A-G v News Group Newspapers plc* [1989] QB 110; [1988] 2 All ER 906.
4 *R v Phillips* (1983), 78 Cr App Rep 88.
5 Contempt of Court Act 1981, s 9; as to considerations relevant to the grant of leave, see *Practice Direction* [1981] 3 All ER 848; [1981] 1 WLR 1526.
6 Criminal Procedure (Attendance of Witnesses) Act 1965; see p 577, *post.*
7 *Re A-G's Application* [1963] 1 QB 696, sub nom *A-G v Butterworth* [1962] 3 All ER 326.
8 Passed in response to the judgments of the Divisional Court in *A-G v New Statesman and Nation Publishing Co Ltd* [1981] QB 1; [1980] 1 All ER 644.

deliberations. In *A-G v Associated Newspapers Ltd*[9] a divisional court held that the publication of the statements, opinions and arguments of jurors concerning their verdict in a high-profile fraud trial amounted to contempt of court, even though these had been obtained indirectly from transcripts of interviews conducted by a researcher, not newspaper staff.

Other examples of criminal contempt include the publication of the name of a party or witness where such publication is prohibited by statute, or is contrary to an order of the court.[10] It will also be a contempt of court for a journalist to refuse to disclose the source of his information, or to refuse to produce documents, when required to do so by a court,[11] or to place a party to litigation under improper pressure. Press vilification of a litigant is not permitted, although the law of contempt will not protect a litigant against fair and temperate criticism.[12]

Civil contempt will occur where a party fails to comply with an order of a court. Examples include the following: failure of a solicitor to comply with an undertaking,[13] failure to swear an account, refusal to comply with an order for discovery of documents or to answer interrogatories[14] and failure to comply with an injunction. Similarly mere failure to pay a judgment debt is not contempt, although wilful refusal to do so is.[15] However, if there is a reasonable alternative method available of securing compliance with a court order, the Court of Appeal has stated that that method should be adopted rather than committing the contemnor to prison.[16] A striking, and constitutionally important, example of civil contempt is the decision of the House of Lords in *M v Home Office*.[17] At the conclusion of a hearing of an application for leave to apply for judicial review brought by an individual who was claiming he was being deported illegally, a judge accepted what was understood to be a binding undertaking on behalf of the Home Secretary, and later made an order to the same effect. Under this undertaking and order the Home Secretary was under an obligation to ensure that the applicant was not deported, or, alternatively, returned to the jurisdiction. The evidence showed that the Home Secretary had failed to comply with this duty, and was found, in his official capacity, to be in contempt of court.

2   Strict liability contempt

It is possible for contempt to be committed in certain circumstances even in the absence of an intent to interfere with the administration of justice. This arises in respect of publications which are seriously prejudicial to a fair trial.

---

9 [1993] 2 All ER 535; [1993] 3 WLR 74.

10 *R v Socialist Worker Printers and Publishers Ltd, ex parte A-G* [1975] QB 637; [1975] 1 All ER 142; but there must be a clear direction and not merely a request: *A-G v Leveller Magazine Ltd* [1979] AC 440; [1979] 1 All ER 745.

11 In *Director of Public Prosecutions v Channel 4 Television Co Ltd* [1993] 2 All ER 517 fines totalling £75,000 were imposed on a defendant company for failure to comply with an order to produce documents.

12 *A-G v Times Newspapers Ltd* [1974] AC 273; [1973] 3 All ER 54, one of a number of actions resulting from the thalidomide tragedy which left a large group of children badly disabled.

13 *Re Kerly* [1901] 1 Ch 467.

14 See p 354, *post*.

15 Debtors Act 1869, as amended by Administration of Justice Act 1970, s 11.

16 *Danchevsky v Danchevsky* [1975] Fam 17; [1974] 3 All ER 934.

17 [1993] 3 All ER 537; sub nom *Re M* [1993] 3 WLR 433.

Up until 1981 the doctrine was very vague and ill-defined as to what test was to be applied, and as to the period of time during which the potential for commission of a strict liability contempt existed. The law was often criticised for its breadth, as well as uncertainty, and in 1973 the House of Lords went as far as deciding that any prejudgment of issues that were to be decided in a pending case amounted to contempt of court.[18] Following criticism of this decision, and in the light of an adverse ruling from the European Court of Human Rights,[19] the operation of the rule was radically changed by the Contempt of Court Act 1981.

This Act amends the strict liability rule. In particular the rule is: (1) limited to "publications" (as opposed to conduct); (2) applicable only to publications which create "a substantial risk that the course of justice in the proceedings in question will be seriously impeded or prejudiced"; and (3) applicable only if the proceedings in question are "active" (as determined by reference to Schedule 1 to the Act).[20] In addition the Act creates three statutory defences to the strict liability rule, *viz* innocent publication or distribution,[1] fair and accurate reports of legal proceedings held in public, published contemporaneously and in good faith[2] and discussion of public affairs or other matters of general public interest if the risk of impediment or prejudice to particular legal proceedings is merely incidental to the discussion.[3]

An illustration of how the defence of incidental discussion might work is the case of *A-G v English*[4] where the House of Lords decided that an article discussing the merits of mercy killing did not amount to contempt, even though at the time of publication a doctor was on trial accused of the mercy killing of a disabled child. LORD DIPLOCK observed:

> "Such gagging of *bona fides* public discussion in the press of controversial matters of general public interest, merely because there are in existence contemporaneous legal proceedings in which some instance of those controversial matters may be in issue, is what s 5 of the Contempt of Court Act 1981 was designed to prevent."

The application of the defence in section 5 will depend upon the nature of the subject matter of the discussion, and its relationship to the particular

---

18 See n 12, *supra*.

19 *Sunday Times v United Kingdom* (1979) 2 EHRR 245.

20 In criminal cases this will usually be from the date of the making of an arrest, the issue of a warrant for arrest or the issue of a summons. In civil proceedings, the relevant date usually will be the date of setting down for trial, or when the date for trial is fixed.

1 Contempt of Court Act 1981, s 3(1).

2 *Ibid*, s 4; but under s 4(2) the court may order publication to be postponed for the purpose of avoiding a substantial risk of prejudice to the administration of justice in those proceedings or in other proceedings pending or imminent; see *Practice Direction* [1982] 1 WLR 1475; breach of such order could be a contempt of court: *R v Horsham Justices, ex parte Farquharson* [1982] QB 762; [1982] 2 All ER 269.

3 *Ibid*, s 5.

4 [1983] 1 AC 116; [1982] 2 All ER 903. For application of the principles, see *A-G v Times Newspapers Ltd* (1983) Times, 12 February.

proceedings.[5] It should be noted, however, that it does not create a simple public interest discussion defence.[6]

3   Jurisdiction to punish contempt

Civil contempt was formerly punishable by writ of attachment but the Rules of the Supreme Court (Revision) 1965 abolished attachment so that civil contempt is now punishable by committal in the same way as criminal contempt.

The jurisdiction to punish for contempt, whether committed in or out of court, is inherent in superior courts of record. Such courts may commit for contempt and also punish contempt committed in the face of the court by immediate fine and imprisonment. Imprisonment must be for a fixed term not exceeding two years.[7]

Inferior courts of record have more limited powers. They can imprison for up to one month and impose a fine.[8] Although a county court is for all other purposes an inferior court it is treated as a superior court for this purpose.[9]

The powers of magistrates' courts to commit are contained in section 12 of the 1981 Act. Any person who (a) wilfully insults a justice, any witness before or officer of the court or any solicitor or counsel having business in the court, during his or their sitting or attendance in court or in going to or returning from the court; or (b) wilfully interrupts the proceedings or otherwise misbehaves in court is liable to be detained until the rising of the court and then to be committed for up to one month, or fined. Appeal lies to the Crown Court.

The Queen's Bench Division, as the successor of the Court of King's Bench, protects inferior courts against contempt by punishing contempts committed in inferior courts.[10]

Until 1960 there was no appeal against punishment for criminal contempt. The law was altered by the Administration of Justice Act 1960, section 13, which provides that the defendant shall have a right of appeal from any order or decision of a court or tribunal in the exercise of jurisdiction to punish for contempt, including criminal contempt. Appeal

---

5 *A-G v TVS Television Ltd* (1989) Times, 7 July.

6 And thus would not have assisted the defendants' newspapers in *A-G v Times Newspapers Ltd* [1974] AC 273; [1973] 3 All ER 54, because the intent in that instance was in fact to influence the conduct of particular proceedings. Cf *Re F (a minor) (publication of information)* [1977] Fam 58; [1977] 1 All ER 114.

7 Contempt of Court Act 1981, s 14(1); previously committal could be for an indefinite term. Where the contemnor is under 21 (but not less than 17) the committal is to detention: Criminal Justice Act 1982, s 9.

8 Contempt of Court Act 1981, s 14(1), (2).

9 *Ibid*, s 14(4A) (added by County Courts (Penalties for Contempt) Act 1983).

10 *R v Davies* [1906] 1 KB 32; *R v Daily Herald, ex parte Bishop of Norwich* [1932] 2 KB 402. The High Court also has statutory power under the Parliamentary Commissioner Act 1967 to deal with a person whom the Commissioner certifies as having been guilty of conduct in the nature of contempt in relation to an investigation held by the Commissioner under the Act. But this jurisdiction only extends to "courts" properly so called, and not to tribunals which are not courts; it may therefore be important to ascertain whether a particular tribunal is or is not a "court": *A-G v British Broadcasting Corporation* [1981] AC 303; [1980] 3 All ER 161; see p 140, *ante*. Note, however, that s 20 of the 1981 Act extends the jurisdiction to tribunals to which the Tribunals of Inquiry (Evidence) Act 1921 applies.

lies to the Court of Appeal, divisional court or House of Lords as the case may be.

Contempt is punishable, and is often punished, summarily; that is to say by a procedure which is far removed from the ordinary processes of the law. No precise charges are put, often the accused is given no opportunity of consulting lawyers or of an adjournment to prepare his defence. There is no jury and the decision is made by a judge who may himself have been the person insulted. Therefore the Court of Appeal has indicated that the summary jurisdiction should not be used where a more orthodox procedure could be adopted. In the words of LAWTON LJ:[11]

> "In my judgment this summary and draconian jurisdiction should only be used for the purpose of ensuring that a trial in progress or about to start can be brought to a proper and dignified end without disturbance and with a fair chance of a just verdict or judgment. Contempts which are not likely to disturb the trial or affect the verdict or judgment can be dealt with by a motion to commit under RSC Ord 52, or even by indictment."

It should be noted, in conclusion, that punishment for contempt of court is by no means the only legal sanction for abuse of legal process. Many forms of conduct which appear to have the characteristics of criminal contempt are not punishable as contempts because they are separate criminal offences. Where they cause damage to another person they may also be torts, although contempt of court is not in itself tortious. Thus a person who intimidates a witness commits a contempt of court but may not be sued by that witness in tort.[12]

---

11 *Balogh v St Albans Crown Court* [1975] QB 73, at 92–93; [1974] 3 All ER 283, at 295.
12 *Chapman v Honig* [1963] 2 QB 502; [1963] 2 All ER 513.

CHAPTER 9

Juries

A HISTORICAL GROWTH OF THE JURY SYSTEM

There is ample evidence that some forms of jury trial existed in England prior to the Norman Conquest. However, although the jury system was not the creation of the common law, it was certainly one of the cornerstones of common law procedure both in civil and criminal trials.

In criminal cases there were, until 1948, two juries. The first of these was the grand jury. The grand jury was not principally a trial jury in the modern sense. It originated in the jury of presentment of the hundred and its function was to present persons for trial before the royal judges at assizes or the justices in quarter sessions.[1] This function was later assumed by justices of the peace in the form of the modern system of preliminary investigation. For this reason the grand jury (of up to 23 members) ceased to be functional and its duties had been reduced virtually to formality long before its abolition. It was virtually abolished by the Administration of Justice (Miscellaneous Provisions) Act 1933, save for a few purposes, and entirely abolished by the Criminal Justice Act 1948.

The second jury in criminal cases was the petty jury (of 12 members). This was the equivalent of the modern trial jury. The trial of criminals by jury evolved in the thirteenth century to replace trial by ordeal, which the Church condemned in 1215.[2] Originally the grand jury of presentment also exercised the function of the trial jury but by the middle of the fourteenth century the petty jury had become distinct from its predecessor. The petty jury was originally summoned for its local knowledge and the members were really witnesses rather than judges of fact. Their function changed gradually as the practice grew of examining independent witnesses and by the fifteenth century the trial jury had assumed its modern function as judges of fact. Nevertheless not until *Bushell's* case in 1670[3] was it established that jurors could not be punished for returning a verdict contrary to the evidence or the direction of the trial judge.

In civil cases there was only ever one type of jury – the trial jury of 12 members, which had its origins in the Assize of Clarendon 1166.[4] By 1304

---

1 See p 135, *ante*.
2 Lateran Council 1215.
3 (1670) Vaugh 135.
4 See p 135, *ante*.

it was the rule of the common law courts that all trespass actions had to be tried with a jury. The result was that, with the decline of the real actions and the personal actions of debt and detinue,[5] virtually all actions in the common law courts came to be tried with a jury and this was the position until 1854 when the steady decline of the jury in civil cases began. The function of civil juries was, originally, that of witnesses but, as with criminal juries, a similar transition from witnesses to judges of fact took place.

B JURY TRIAL AT THE PRESENT DAY

Before the present century the jury system was widely pronounced to be one of the chief safeguards of the individual against the abuse of prerogative and judicial power. The vast majority of cases, both civil and criminal, were tried by a jury and this right was thought to be essential and inviolable. Blackstone, writing of the jury in criminal cases, saw the jury as a barrier between the liberties of the people and the prerogative of the Crown.[6] LORD CAMDEN, reflecting the mood of the age, observed:

> "Trial by jury is indeed the foundation of our free constitution; take that away, and the whole fabric will soon moulder into dust."[7]

By the middle of the nineteenth century this concept of the sanctity of jury trial was disappearing. Consequently the jury began to decline as a factor in the administration of justice in both civil and criminal cases. The principal reasons for this decline were the eclipse of the royal prerogative in the administration of justice, the rapid growth in the volume of litigation in civil cases, the even more rapid growth of summary jurisdiction in criminal cases and a general appreciation that juries were both unpredictable and fallible.

1 Criminal cases

In criminal cases the loss of faith in the jury system has been far less marked than in civil cases. The situation is still that a person aged eighteen or over[8] who has a common law right to jury trial cannot, subject to minor exceptions[9] be deprived of that right without his consent. Since all common law offences were triable by jury an accused person still has a right to claim trial by jury for any common law offence, subject to

---

5 See p 132, *ante*.
6 3 Comm 379.
7 See Jackson, *The Machinery of Justice in England* (8th Edn), pp 391 *et seq*.
8 There are special provisions for children and young persons; see p 451, *post*.
9 The exceptions are incitement to commit a summary offence (Magistrates' Courts Act 1980, s 45(1)) and offences of criminal damage, and associated offences, where the value involved does not exceed £200 (*ibid*, s 22(2)). The James Committee, which was established in 1973 and reported in 1975 (*The Distribution of Criminal Business between the Crown Court and Magistrates' Courts*; Cmnd 6323) recommended (inter alia) that theft and other related offences where the value of the property concerned was less than £20 should become summary offences; in the face of considerable public opposition provisions to this effect in the original Bill were removed during the passage of the Bill through Parliament; see further p 447, *post*.

those exceptions. However many offences which were formerly indictable are now triable "either way"[10] and most trials of such offences are, in fact, summary trials. Indeed the number of trials on indictment is very small compared with the number of summary trials. Modern legislation, especially that concerned with road traffic, has created a vast number of summary offences.

2   Civil proceedings

It is in civil actions that the decline of the jury has been most marked. Until 1854 most civil actions in the common law courts had to be tried before a jury. The Common Law Procedure Act 1854 provided for trial by a judge alone but only with the consent of both parties. This trend was continued by the Judicature Acts and by 1933 only about one half of civil actions in the Queen's Bench Division were tried with a jury. The Administration of Justice (Miscellaneous Provisions) Act 1933 was a landmark in the decline of the civil jury. By section 6 of that Act the right to claim a jury in a civil action was limited to cases of libel, slander, malicious prosecution, false imprisonment, seduction or breach of promise of marriage on the application of either party or on the application of a party against whom fraud was alleged.[11] The right to claim jury trial in the Queen's Bench Division in these cases is now contained in section 69 of the Supreme Court Act 1981.[12] Even in these cases a jury may be refused if the court considers that the trial will involve a prolonged examination of documents or accounts or a scientific or local investigation. In all other cases the grant of a jury is at the discretion of the court. It was once the case that this discretion was absolute or "completely untrammelled".[13] However in the leading case of *Ward v James*[14] the full Court of Appeal established that this was not so and that the discretion had, in the same way as any other discretion, to be exercised judicially. Furthermore, the Court of Appeal stated that in actions for damages for personal injuries trial should be by a judge alone in the absence of special circumstances, such as a substantial dispute on the facts. The basic reason for this opposition to jury trial in personal injury cases is the unpredictability of jury awards of damages. Juries, no doubt swayed by the knowledge that the substantive defendant in a "running-down" case is almost always an insurance company[15] with apparently bottomless resources, have sometimes made disproportionate awards to successful plaintiffs in this type of action. It was following two awards of £50,000 to victims in personal injury actions in 1963[16] that the courts became acutely aware of the unsuitability of juries in this type of case. Since the majority of actions in the Queen's Bench Division are actions for

---

10 Criminal Law Act 1977, s 16; see p 447, *post*.
11 Of these, actions for seduction and breach of promise of marriage were by the Law Reform (Miscellaneous Provisions) Act 1970.
12 See p 363, *post*. The right is confined to cases in the Queen's Bench Division.
13 *Hope v Great Western Rly Co* [1937] 2 KB 130; [1937] 1 All ER 625, *per* LORD WRIGHT MR.
14 [1966] 1 QB 273; [1965] 1 All ER 563.
15 Although the court should not be informed that the defendant in a personal injuries action is insured.
16 *Warren v King* [1963] 3 All ER 521; [1964] 1 WLR 1; *Morey v Woodfield (No 2)* [1964] 1 QB 1; [1963] 3 All ER 584. The sums at the time were extremely large.

damages for personal injuries,[17] *Ward v James* is a further landmark in the decline of the civil jury. Immediately before this decision approximately 2 per cent of trials in the Queen's Bench Division took place before a jury. The figure is now minimal.

Consequently, in little more than a century, jury trial in civil cases has virtually been superseded by trial by a judge alone, one noteable exception being trials for defamation. The role of juries in these cases has itself proved controversial, with extremely large awards of damages made by juries attracting considerable criticism.[18] Outside the Queen's Bench Division of the High Court juries are hardly ever encountered in civil actions. The Chancery Amendment Act 1858 provided power to summon a jury in the Court of Chancery. This power was transferred to the Chancery Division by the Judicature Acts but has been totally ignored. There may be a jury in defended divorce petitions and contentious probate proceedings though there seldom is in either type of case. A jury of eight may be summoned in the county court in the same circumstances as in the Queen's Bench Division but this is extremely unusual mainly because of the disproportionately high costs which it would entail. Juries may also be summoned in some of the courts of local jurisdiction. Finally coroners may, in certain cases, and in few cases must,[19] summon a jury of between seven and eleven persons.

Majority verdicts were permitted in criminal cases by the Criminal Justice Act 1967.[20] In civil cases majority verdicts (save by consent of the parties) were not receivable until the Courts Act 1971[1] which in effect extended the Criminal Justice Act provisions to civil cases.

C COMPOSITION OF JURIES

One of the most frequent criticisms of juries has related to their composition. Prior to the Juries Act 1974, eligibility for jury service depended upon the existence of a property qualification, which led in 1956 to LORD DEVLIN describing the jury as "predominantly male, middle-aged, middle-minded and middle-class".[2] This criticism was, to some extent, met by the Criminal Justice Act 1972 which both abolished the property qualification and extended the age limits for jurors. The relevant provisions are now contained in the Juries Act 1974, a consolidating statute. Under section 1 of this Act the basic provision is that every person is qualified to serve as a juror and liable, when summoned, to attend for jury service, if:

(a) he is registered as a parliamentary or local government elector and is not less than eighteen nor more than sixty-five years of age; and
(b) he has been ordinarily resident in the United Kingdom, the

---

17 Judicial Statistics, 1992 (HMSO).
18 See the comments of LORD DONALDSON MR in *Sutcliffe v Pressdram Ltd* [1991] 1 QB 153; [1990] 1 All ER 269.
19 See Coroners Act 1988, s 8(2), and p 166, *ante*.
20 The operative provisions are now contained in the Juries Act 1974, s 17; see p 494, *post* as to the procedure.
1 Courts Act 1971, s 39.
2 Devlin, *Trial By Jury*, p 20.

Channel Islands or the Isle of Man for any period of at least five years since attaining the age of thirteen.

There are, however, provisions relating to ineligibility, disqualification and excusal.[3] Thus the judiciary, members of the legal profession, court officers, police officers, ministers of religion and the mentally ill are ineligible[4] while persons who have in the last ten years served any part of a sentence of imprisonment, youth custody or detention, being a sentence of three months or more or have received a suspended sentence or had imposed on them a community service order or who have at any time been sentenced to custody for life or to a term of imprisonment or youth custody for a term of five years or more are disqualified from jury service.[5]

In addition to those who are ineligible or disqualified certain persons, notably members of Parliament, serving members of the armed forces and medical practitioners, may be excused from jury service if they so wish.[6] So too may others where there are "circumstances of personal hardship or conscientious objections to jury service".[7]

Thus the compositions of juries has radically changed; there are, for example, far more women sitting on juries nowadays as a result of the removal of the property qualification. Indeed, criticism is sometimes levelled at the youth or seeming lack of experience of some persons called to sit in judgment upon others as jurors. The key feature of the jury is, however, the randomly selected lay element that it provides in serious criminal cases. To this extent it mirrors the office of justice of the peace, which provides a lay element in summary trials. Whilst the oft-quoted right to "trial by peers" contained in clause 39 of Magna Carta 1215 never really related to trial by jury in the modern sense, the existence of a lay element can be regarded as an important means of ensuring that the law operates, and is applied, fairly.[8]

Some right to regulate this randomly selected lay element has always existed. The prosecution has always had the right to request that a juror "stand by for the Crown". The effect of this is that the juror stands down, and is not called upon for the purposes of the instant case unless the jury panel, from which the jury is selected, is exhausted. In reality it provides a mechanism for challenge not open to the defence. For this reason, the right to require a juror to "stand by" is one to be used "sparingly, and in very exceptional circumstances".[9]

---

3 The verdict of a jury is not void only because a juror was disqualified from jury service and no verdict can be challenged on the ground that a juror was not included in the relevant list of jurors or was misnamed or misdescribed or (unless objection was taken at the time) that the provisions of the Act as to the impanelling or selection of jurors has not been complied with (Juries Act 1974, s 18).

4 The full list is contained in Sch 1, Part 1 to the 1974 Act.

5 Act of 1974, Sch 1, Part II (as amended). Note that youth custody and detention centre orders were replaced by detention in young offenders institutions, by the Criminal Justice Act 1988, Sch 8.

6 For full details of the excusal provisions see Act of 1974, ss 8–9 and Sch 1, Part III.

7 See LORD LANE in *Practice Note: (Jury Service: Excusal)* [1988] 3 All ER 177, sub nom *Practice Direction* [1988] 1 WLR 1162.

8 Exclusion on religious grounds will only be granted if the religious belief will stand in the way of proper performance of the jury function: *R v Crown Court at Guildford, ex parte Siderfin* [1990] 2 QB 683; [1989] 3 All ER 7.

9 *R v Thomas* (1989) 88 Cr App Rep 370.

The prosecution are entitled to conduct checks upon potential jurors only in limited circumstances, set out in 1988 in *Attorney-General's Guidelines on Jury Checks*.[10] The permitted checks allow, broadly speaking, checks in respect of disqualified persons, and, in limited circumstances, security checks and checks upon extreme political views which might render the fair trial of a security or terrorist case virtually impossible. Such checks have to be authorised by the Attorney-General, and should be kept to an absolute minimum. The issues of principle were well described by LORD DENNING MR . . . when he observed as follows:[11]

> "To my mind it is unconstitutional for the police authorities to engage in jury vetting. So long as a person is eligible for jury service, and is not disqualified, I cannot think it right that, behind his back, the police should go through his record so as to enable him to be asked to "stand by for the Crown" or to be challenged for the defence.[12] If this sort of thing is to be allowed, what comes of a man's right of privacy? he is bound to serve on a jury when summoned. Is he therefore liable to have his past record raked up against him, and presented on a plate to prosecuting and defending lawyers who may use it to keep him out of the jury and, who knows, it may become known to his neighbours and those about him."

Challenge to the jury by the defence has in recent years been restricted. The right of the defence to challenge without being required to show cause was first reduced and then, in 1988, abolished.[13] The defence can now challenge only if it can show cause: ie good reason why the juror should not serve. A judge has an inherent power to intervene and prevent a person serving, where it is proper to do so.[14] For example, a judge might require a person who is manifestly unsuited, because of illiteracy, to stand down.

Juries are not generally selected on the basis of gender, race or ethnic origin, for that would run counter to the principle of randomness. In *R v Ford*[15] a judge refused to ensure a multi-racial jury in a case where racial motives were to be imputed to a police officer. An appeal against conviction was dismissed. Nevertheless, a trial judge who does in fact seek to achieve a particular balance is entitled to do so.[16]

D   THE MERITS OF JURY TRIAL

Jury trial has been the subject of significant criticism in recent years, particularly in respect of what some have seen as an unacceptably high acquittal rate.[17] Various research studies[18] have shown, however, that acquittal rates may reflect as much upon decisions to offer no evidence, or upon decisions by trial judges to withdraw a case from a jury as upon the nature of the jury, or upon jury trial.

---

10 [1988] 3 All ER 1086.
11 *R v Sheffield Crown Court, ex parte Brownlow* [1980] QB 530; [1980] 2 All ER 444.
12 Now abolished.
13 Criminal Justice Act 1988, s 118.
14 *Mansell v R* (1857) 8 E & B 54.
15 [1989] QB 868; [1989] 3 All ER 445.
16 *R v Danvers* [1982] Crim LR 680; *cf R v Bansall* [1985] Crim LR 151.
17 See, eg, Sir Robert Mark in the Dimbleby Lecture, 1973.
18 Baldwin & McConville, *Jury Trials* (1979, Clarendon Press); Vennard, 'The Outcome of Contested Trials', in *Managing Criminal Justice* (ed Moxon, 1985, HMSO).

The reality is that insufficient is known about how juries in fact work. Section 8 of the Contempt of Court Act 1981 prohibits investigations as to how juries reach their verdicts, whether or not of a serious academic nature. Breach of this rule amounts to contempt of court.[19] Despite this gap in knowledge the process of jury trial has come under challenge. The trial of serious offences by judges alone is not unknown in the United Kingdom: in Northern Ireland, trial of "scheduled offences"[20] has, since 1973, been by judge alone in so-called "Diplock courts".[1] More recently, the Report of the Fraud Trials Committee in 1986[2] recommended the abolition of jury trial in serious fraud cases, and its replacement by a fraud trial tribunal comprising a judge sitting with two lay assessors. The committee concluded that long fraud cases were so complex that it was not reasonable to expect juries to be able to cope with multiple defendants and charges, and the arcane nature of the evidence. This recommendation, opposed by many in the legal profession, has not been implemented, but the Royal Commission on Criminal Justice[3] has returned to the issue, recommending a limitation on rights to elect jury trial. These issues are discussed further in due course.[4]

The merits of jury trial are sometimes stated in terms of the deficiencies of alternative modes of trial. Summary process in the magistrates' courts is relatively quick, cheap, but by no means beyond criticism. Rightly or wrongly, it is often thought that jury trial favours an accused. Other advocates of jury trial rely upon the constitutional importance of jury trial, and the safeguards it is said to provide for an accused.[5]

Nevertheless, despite these criticisms, the jury remains a fundamental of the English legal system. LORD DENNING MR in *Ward v James*[6] explained the place of the modern jury as follows:

> "Let it not be supposed that this court is in any way opposed to trial by jury. It has been the bulwark of our liberties too long for any of us to seek to alter it. Whenever a man is on trial for serious crime, or when in a civil case a man's honour or integrity is at stake, or when one or other party must be deliberately lying, then trial by jury has no equal."

It was put more graphically by LORD DEVLIN, who described jury trial as "the lamp that shows that freedom lives".[7] Arguably, it provides some mechanism to prevent the unjust or oppressive use of the criminal law. This justification has not been regarded as convincing by all commentators,[8] and some point equally to the potentially random factors that may affect a jury's deliberations. The primacy of jury trial has also been used as

---

19 *A-G v New Statesman and Nation Publishing Co Ltd* [1981] QB1; [1980] 1 All ER 644.
20 Defined by Northern Ireland (Emergency Provisions) Act 1978, s 30 and Sch 4 to include murder, most serious offences of violence and offences related to the causing of explosions.
1 Following the recommendations of the Committee chaired by LORD DIPLOCK (1972, Cmd 5185, HMSO).
2 See p 463, *post*.
3 See p 434, *post*.
4 See p 453, *post*.
5 On this argument, see, generally: Cornish, *The Jury* (1968, Allen Lane).
6 [1966] 1 QB 273; [1965] 1 All ER 563.
7 Devlin, *op cit*.
8 See Darbyshire, 'The Lamp that Shows that Freedom Lives – Is It Worth the Candle?' [1991] Crim LR 740.

a justification for judicial non-interference with verdicts in alleged miscarriage of justice cases.[9]

---

9 See p 511, *post*.

CHAPTER 10

The Legal Profession

A INTRODUCTION

A distinctive feature of the English legal system is the division of the legal profession into two separate branches – solicitors and barristers. This precise division is unknown outside Britain and the Commonwealth. Elsewhere all practitioners are described as "lawyers", a word which has no particular application in England. The division of the legal profession dates back to about 1340, the time at which professional advocacy evolved.[1] The advocates with audience in the common law courts were the serjeants[2] and barristers while the preparatory stages of an action were carried through by officers of the court in question known as attorneys. There thus developed two classes of legal practitioner: serjeants and barristers on the one hand and attorneys who were, as solicitors still are, officers of the court. Solicitors, as distinct from attorneys, first appeared in the fifteenth century and practised in the Court of Chancery. They were, at first, inferior to attorneys and could not bind their clients as attorneys could. By the eighteenth century the offices of attorney and solicitor were frequently held by the same person and the distinction between them was finally abolished by the Judicature Act 1873.

The separation of barristers and solicitors was preserved by the Inns of Court. Barristers had to be members of one of the Inns of Court and these Inns, after the sixteenth century, refused to admit attorneys or solicitors to membership. As a result the latter banded together and by 1739 had formed their own professional organisation in London. This was styled "the Society of Gentlemen Practisers in the Courts of Law and Equity" and was the forerunner of The Law Society.

Thus the separation of the legal profession has an historical foundation as has the nature of the respective functions which barristers and solicitors perform. These structures, functions and divisions are, however, increasingly undergoing both challenge and change. Barristers are still primarily advocates, although many barristers in fact spend most of their time engaged in "paper-work" such as the drafting of pleadings, divorce

---

1 For details of the history of the emergence of both branches of the profession, see Baker, *An Introduction to English Legal History* (2nd Edn), pp 133–143.
2 Serjeants (*servientes regis ad legem*) were the senior advocates and had exclusive audience in the Court of Common Pleas. The rank of serjeant was abolished by the Judicature Act 1873.

petitions, complex settlements and opinions on specialised matters such as taxation and company law. Solicitors deal with the preparatory stages of litigation such as the preparation of evidence, interviewing witnesses, issuing writs and, usually, conducting interlocutory proceedings. Solicitors have had a right of audience in most courts and tribunals; this has not in the past extended to the Court of Appeal or to most proceedings in open court (as opposed to chambers) in the High Court, and rights of audience in the Crown Court are limited to such proceedings as the Lord Chancellor may direct.[3] In addition solicitors deal with a large number of non-litigious matters such as the drafting of wills, the supervision of trusts and settlements, the administration of estates and conveyancing.

There are other distinctions between the two branches of the profession. Solicitors may enter into partnerships, barristers may not. Barristers appear in court (other than magistrates' courts) in wig and gown; solicitors appear in gown in certain courts, notably the county court, but are never bewigged. Solicitors are instructed by their clients directly; barristers are generally instructed by a solicitor and not by a lay client direct.[4]

B   ROYAL COMMISSION ON LEGAL SERVICES

In 1976 a Royal Commission was set up to inquire into the law and practice relating to the provision of legal services in England, Wales and Northern Ireland to consider whether, and if so what, changes were desirable in the public interest in the structure, organisation, training, regulation of and entry to the legal profession.

The Commission produced its final report in October 1979.[5] Its conclusions and recommendations were (surprisingly, to some) basically favourable to the status quo, although it found that the distribution of legal services was uneven and the quality not uniform. The Commission summarised its observations on the quality of service in the following words:[6]

> "The evidence before us shows that year by year most legal work is transacted well and efficiently. Most clients are satisfied with the service they receive. The judiciary is in general able to rely on the quality of work performed in the courts. City institutions, including The Stock Exchange, the British Bankers' Association and the Committee on Invisible Exports told us that the legal

---

3 Supreme Court Act 1981, s 83; see *Practice Direction (Crown Court; Right of Audience)* [1972] 1 All ER 608; [1972] 1 WLR 307; *Practice Direction (Solicitors: Audience in the Crown Court* [1988] 3 All ER 717; [1988] 1 WLR 1427. This includes the hearing of appeals, and proceedings for committal for sentence where the solicitor (or his firm) represented the defendant at the magistrates' court. Full details of the courts and tribunals in which solicitors have a right of audience may be found in 44 *Halsbury's Laws* (4th Edn), paras 68–70.
4 This is a custom rather than a rule of law, and of fairly recent origin for, until the eighteenth century, it was customary for counsel to be instructed directly by lay clients. There are exceptions to this general rule: see *Halsbury's Laws* (4th Edn 3(1)) para 465. The Bar Council may permit barristers to act upon the instructions of other professions duly approved: Resolution of the Bar Council, 12 November 1985. See *Code of Conduct* 1990, paras 102, 901.
5 *Report of the Royal Commission on Legal Services* (Cmnd 7648, HMSO).
6 Report, para 22.16.

services available in London are of a high standard; this attracts legal and other business from abroad which contributes to our invisible exports."

Having said that, the Commission went on to point to certain shortcomings in the service and to suggest some remedies.[7] In particular it pointed to unacceptable delays in contentious business and noted that in the Queen's Bench Division the average lapse of time between cause of action and trial was four years. It decried "repetitious cross-examination, labouring points good and bad and general prolixity" and suggested that the remedy lay in good education and training, self-discipline, adequate research and careful preparation. It recommended *inter alia* that both solicitor and barrister should advise specifically on whether a conference before the day of trial was necessary for the proper presentation of a case (it being an occasional complaint of litigants, especially defendants in criminal cases, that they do not meet their counsel until shortly before the hearing on the day of trial), that measures should be taken to prevent parties being taken by surprise by offers of settlement at the door of the court, that The Law Society should issue guidelines on methods of office administration, that practising solicitors should plan ahead to meet the increasing need for specialisation and that written professional standards should be issued by both branches of the profession, failure to observe which would involve disciplinary proceedings.

On the controversial issue of fusion of the two branches of the profession, the Commission recommended against it on the grounds that there would be an unacceptable reduction in the number and spread of smaller firms of solicitors and an increase in the proportion of large city firms, that while there might be some saving in small cases, in large ones the expense might be greater and, with regard to the administration of justice, that:

"A two-branch profession is more likely than a fused one to ensure the high quality of advocacy which is indispensable, so long as our system remains in its present form, to secure the proper quality of justice."[8]

As to solicitors' practising arrangements, the Commission recommended that partnership between solicitors and members of other professions should not be permitted, that incorporation of a solicitor's business with limited liability should not be permitted but that incorporation with unlimited liability should, subject to certain safeguards,[9] that legal executives should continue to perform their functions as the employees of solicitors, but not as independent practitioners,[10] that The Law Society should introduce duty solicitor schemes in all magistrates' courts,[11] that a system of citizens' law centres should be established to provide legal services, particularly in relation to social welfare law (but not to undertake community work and campaigns),[12] that the so-called "conveyancing

---

7 Report, paras 22.17–22.75.
8 *Ibid*, paras 17.45–17.46.
9 *Ibid*, paras 30.15–30.28.
10 *Ibid*, para 31.26.
11 *Ibid*, para 9.9. Such schemes now exist: see *Duty Solicitor Arrangements* 1992, and p 238, *post*.
12 *Ibid*, paras 8.15–8.38.

monopoly" should be retained but with a reversion to scale charges[13] and that there should be no general extension of solicitors' rights of audience.[14] Finally the Commission made detailed recommendations on the subject of disciplinary procedures,[15] in particular that The Law Society should take action when cases of bad professional work are brought to its notice, that The Law Society should ensure that independent legal advice is available for those who allege negligence against solicitors, that within The Law Society the processes of investigation and adjudication of complaints should be separated and that laymen should be involved in these processes; there are also recommendations on the subject of charges.[16]

Nor were the recommendations affecting barristers any more radical. Here again the Commission recommended that, in relation to disciplinary procedure, the processes of investigation and adjudication of complaints should be separated and that the Senate should have the responsibility of taking action when cases of bad professional work are brought to its notice.[17] It recommended that all barristers should be required to have professional indemnity insurance against negligence claims,[18] should not be compelled to have a clerk,[19] that the organisation and functions of the circuits should be reviewed[20] and that the existing restriction against partnership at the bar should be retained, as should the two-tier system of silks and juniors.[1]

C COURTS AND LEGAL SERVICES ACT 1990

1 Introduction

Although the Royal Commission on Legal Services did not generate immediate legislation, or impetus for change, the issues which it considered were the subject of considerable discussion and debate. The late 1980s saw a period of fundamental government reconsideration of the way legal services were being provided, and by whom, and of the rules and practices governing such provision. A series of White Papers on civil justice,[2] upon legal services,[3] upon the organisation of the legal profession,[4] upon contingency fees,[5] and upon conveyancing services[6] were published, and generated heated and full responses from professional

---

13 *Ibid*, paras 21.28–21.101.
14 *Ibid*, para 18.60. See now p 209, *post*.
15 *Ibid*, paras 25.8–25.45. See now p 215, *post*.
16 *Ibid*, paras 37.14–37.68.
17 *Ibid*, paras 26.13, 26.18.
18 *Ibid*, para 24.11. The Bar gave effect to this in 1983, since when failure to be properly insured has constituted professional misconduct.
19 *Ibid*, para 34.7.
20 *Ibid*, para 32.54.
 1 *Ibid*, paras 33.66, 33.84.
 2 *Report of the Review Body on Civil Justice* (Cm 394, 1988, HMSO).
 3 *Legal Services: A Framework for the Future* (Cm 740, 1989, HMSO).
 4 *The Workload and Organisation of the Legal Profession* (Cm 570, 1989, HMSO).
 5 *Contingency Fees* (Cm 571, 1989, HMSO).
 6 *Conveyancing By Authorised Practitioners* (Cm 572, 1989, HMSO).

bodies and other interested parties.[7] The result of the debate was legislation in the form of the Courts and Legal Services Act 1990, which adopted a much more radical approach than advocated by the Royal Commission, and which introduced fundamental change in major areas of the work of the profession.

The Act has a distinct philosophy. Section 17 sets out the objectives and principles upon which the Act is based, and which it seeks to achieve. The "statutory objective" is:

> "the development of legal services in England and Wales (and in particular the development of advocacy, litigation, conveyancing and probate services) by making provision for new or better ways of providing such services, and a wider choice of persons providing them, while maintaining the proper and efficient administration of justice."

The Act identifies "general principles". Rights of audience or rights to conduct litigation should be decided only on the basis of: (i) qualifications; (ii) membership of a professional body having effective and enforceable rules of conduct; (iii) whether rules satisfactorily provide requirements for ensuring that legal services are not withheld on the basis of the objectionable nature of the case, the views of the client or because of the source of finance; and (iv) generally, whether rules of conduct are appropriate in the interests of the administration of justice.

Whilst both the solicitor and barrister branches of the profession meet these criteria, and are recognised by the Act in various ways as doing so,[8] the intent of the Act is that others might in the future equally satisfy these criteria and thus be permitted to perform certain functions hitherto regarded as the exclusive preserve of the legal profession. For this reason, significant elements of the changes made by the Act were, and remain, controversial.[9]

The Act gives important powers in respect of these matters to the Lord Chancellor. In exercising powers, and performing functions under the Act, the Lord Chancellor is advised by the Advisory Committee on Legal Education and Training, created by section 19 of the 1990 Act. This committee comprises 2 members of the judiciary (in addition to being chaired by a judge of the Supreme Court or a Lord of Appeal in Ordinary), 2 practising barristers, 2 practising solicitors, 2 persons experienced in the teaching of law, and 9 other persons not falling within these categories. In the appointment of such persons, the Lord Chancellor is to have regard to experience or knowledge of the provision of legal services, civil or criminal proceedings or the working of the courts, of the maintenance of professional standards amongst the legal profession, of social conditions, consumer affairs or the maintenance of standards in other professional organisations.[10]

---

7 See, eg, Bar Council: *The Quality of Justice – The Bar's Response* (Butterworths, 1989); The Law Society: *Striking the Balance; The Green Papers – The Judges' Response* (1989).

8 Thus, ss 31–33 preserve the existing rights of audience of barristers and solicitors, and each is deemed to have in force the required qualification regulations and rules of conduct required by ss 27–28 (see p 210, *post*).

9 In particular the Bar and judiciary opposed rights of audience in higher courts for solicitors and others, as potentially weakening the quality of advocacy and expertise traditionally claimed by the Bar. Other areas of particular controversy included potential loss of independence of the judiciary and the potential for multi-disciplinary practices.

10 1990 Act, s 19(5).

The Act also created the office of Legal Services Ombudsman to supplement the arrangements for the handling of complaints against barristers and solicitors.[11] His functions relate to the investigation of allegations properly made to him about the way in which a complaint made to a professional body has been handled. In doing that, he may also investigate the original complaint, make a report and make recommendations.[12]

2 Rights to conduct litigation

The 1990 Act removed the virtual monopoly in the right to conduct litigation vested in solicitors.[13] This right is defined by section 119(1) as the right:

(a) to exercise all or any of the functions of issuing a writ or otherwise commencing proceedings before any court; and

(b) to perform any ancillary functions in relation to proceedings (such as entering appearances to actions).

The principle stated by section 28 is that any person should be entitled to conduct litigation where a right to do so has been conferred by an appropriate body. That body will be required to have appropriate rules regulations and qualification,[14] and these broadly must satisfy the general principles set out in section 17.[15] Other rights to conduct litigation may exist by virtue of specific statutory provision. Solicitors are deemed to have been granted such rights,[16] and other bodies may be granted the right to conduct litigation following the procedures set out in some detail in the Act. It should be noted that The Law Society has created specialist panels of solicitors considered to have expertise to conduct litigation in certain areas of law, such as cases involving children, and personal injury cases. This may have the effect of limiting the conduct of such cases to such practitioners.

3 Rights of audience

Closely connected with, but separate to, the right to conduct litigation is the question of rights of audience. It has already been noted that barristers have exclusive rights of audience in some courts, and significant discussion occurred as to the extent to which the preservation of such exclusive rights was necessary or desirable for the maintenance of a strong and effective Bar, and for the maintenance of high standards of advocacy.[17]

In any court a litigant may represent himself.[18] That litigant may also be assisted by a friend. In *R v Leicester City Justices, ex parte Barrow*[19] the

---

11 *Ibid*, ss 21–22.
12 *Ibid*, s 23.
13 *Ibid*, s 28. For the previous position, see Solicitors Act 1974, s 20.
14 *Ibid*, s 28(2).
15 See p 208, *ante*.
16 *Ibid*, s 33.
17 See the arguments marshalled by the Bar in its response, *op cit*, n 7 *ante*, particularly at pp 128–146.
18 And often will be given assistance by the court itself.
19 [1991] 2 QB 260; [1991] 3 All ER 935.

Court of Appeal stressed the duty of a court to permit a litigant in person to have all reasonable facilities for exercising his right to be heard in his own defence, including quiet and unobtrusive advice from another person.[20] The court could not require such a litigant to obtain the leave of the court, although it could restrain the use of such assistance if its use was not *bona fides*, was unreasonable, or amounted to a hindrance to the administration of justice.

Except in such situations, representation is by solicitor or counsel. Until recently solicitors have limited rights of audience in the Crown Court, and in certain High Court proceedings.[1] The advantages of such limitations upon rights of audience were identified by the Bar Council in 1989, as follows:

(1) the operation of the "cab-rank" principle at the Bar, whereby barristers are obliged to accept any brief in an area in which they practice provided they are available, and a proper fee is offered;

(2) the limited rights of audience enable the development and maintenance of specialist advocacy skills;

(3) the availability of skilled advocates working in competition with each other;

(4) the development of standards of practice and integrity through peer-group discipline. It is also argued sometimes that exclusive rights are important to ensure a viable and thriving Bar, which in turn produces a pool of potential judicial appointees.

Not all the above points were accepted by those who favour extension of rights of audience. They pointed to the undesirability of experienced solicitors having to hand over a case to possibly a less experienced advocate, that many solicitor advocates are highly skilled, that barristers often return briefs at the last minute, leading to cases being handled by persons unfamiliar with the case, and that principles such as the "cab-rank" principle often do not work effectively in practice given the demands upon the time of successful advocates.[2]

Original proposals in the White Paper would have given considerable power to the Lord Chancellor to determine rights of audience for individual courts.[3] By section 27 of the 1990 Act, existing rights of audience for solicitors and barristers are preserved, but a framework is created for the extension of those rights to those who are suitably qualified. This may occur after fulfilment of a complex procedure involving consultation with various persons and bodies, and requires the consent not only of the Lord Chancellor, but also of the "designated judges".[4] Section 71 identifies six classes of advocacy qualification: Supreme Court, High

---

20 Generally known as a "*McKenzie* friend" in the light of the decision in *McKenzie v McKenzie* [1971] P 33; [1970] 3 All ER 1034.

1 See *Practice Direction* [1986] 2 All ER 226; [1986] 1 WLR 545: a solicitor may represent his client in open court in an emergency, in formal or unopposed proceedings (ie where there is unlikely to be any argument and the court is not called upon to exercise any discretion), and when judgment is delivered in open court following a hearing in chambers at which the solicitor represented his client.

2 See The Law Society response, *op cit*.

3 Leading to arguments of potential interference in the judicial process.

4 The Lord Chief Justice, the Master of the Rolls, the President of the Family Division and the Vice-Chancellor: see 1990 Act, ss 29(1)(b), 119(1).

Court, general Crown Court, county court and magistrates' court. It is unclear how far rights of audience will be extended, but mooted changes permitting members of the Crown Prosecution Service[5] to conduct prosecutions in the Crown Court have generated fierce criticism from the Bar. The Lord Chancellor and the four senior designated judges have recently approved an application by The Law Society for rights of audience in the higher courts for solicitors in practice, but have deferred a decision on rights of audience for employed solicitors. Legal executives are also seeking increased rights of audience.[6]

4 Contingency and conditional fees

English law has always regarded "contingency fees" (that is to say, fees the amount or payment of which are contingent upon the result of litigation) as unlawful on the grounds of public policy.[7] Although the White Paper published by the government in 1989[8] did not consider the complete abolition of all restrictions on contingency fees to be in the public interest, some change was thought to be desirable, and possibly valuable in cases where difficulties in financing litigation currently exist.

Section 58 of the 1990 Act authorises the introduction of conditional fee agreements. Such an agreement is defined as follows:

"An agreement in writing between a person providing advocacy or litigation services and his client, which –

(a) does not relate [to certain proceedings relating to matrimonial or domestic violence questions, or involving children];
(b) provides for that person's fees and expenses, or any part of them, to be payable only in specified circumstances;
(c) complies with such requirements (if any) as may be prescribed by the Lord Chancellor;
(d) is not a contentious business agreement."[9]

The effect of the Act is that a fee may be increased by a specified percentage (in accordance with regulations to be made by the Lord Chancellor) provided that is specified in the agreement. The percentage increase cannot be recovered under an order of costs against an unsuccessful party.

The use of such agreements has yet to be determined, but is likely to involve some personal injury cases, and, possibly, actions in defamation for which legal aid is not available.[10] Such agreements are not available for use in criminal cases.

5 The conveyancing monopoly

The virtual monopoly of solicitors of the conduct for profit of conveyancing business has long been under challenge, but has continued subject only to the creation of licensed conveyancers by the Administration of Justice Act

---

5 See p 232, *post*.
6 See [1993] NLJR 1774.
7 See *Halsbury's Laws* (4th Edn).
8 See p 207, *ante*.
9 As defined by the Solicitors Act 1974, s 59.
10 See [1993] NLJR 1665.

1985, which allows members of the Council for Licensed Conveyancers, who have shown compliance with the educational requirements and practice rules of that Council to engage in conveyancing for profit, even though not qualified as solicitors.[11]

The 1990 Act[12] creates a new body, the Authorised Conveyancing Practitioners Board, comprising members to be appointed by the Lord Chancellor. It has a statutory duty:

(a) to seek to develop competition in the provision of legal services;
(b) to supervise the activities of authorised practitioners in connection with the provision of conveyancing services.

In the fulfilment of that duty the Board may authorise a person to be an authorised practitioner, but can refuse an application in some circumstances.[13] These will include the applicant not being a "fit and proper" person, the applicant not complying with requirements in respect of protection against risk, the treatment of complaints or the payment of compensation. An applicant must be a member of the Conveyancing Ombudsman scheme.[14] The Lord Chancellor may also make regulations in respect of the competence and conduct of authorised practitioners. There are also specific rules designed to prohibit "tying-in" arrangements, whereby a person's freedom to secure independent legal advice might be prejudiced by a property deal which contained inclusive legal services, or which required the use of certain legal services as a condition of a loan.[15] These are thought to be particular dangers if the right to offer conveyancing services is extended to include banks or building societies.

6   Probate services

These are likewise extended. Existing restrictions in section 23 of the Solicitors Act 1974, which prohibit the preparation for reward of papers for the grant of probate or letters of administration, other than by a solicitor, barrister or notary, are relaxed. Henceforth, the authorised persons will include the Public Trustee, Official Solicitor, authorised banks, building societies and insurance companies.

D   SOLICITORS

1   The Law Society

The controlling body in the case of solicitors is The Law Society, constituted under a Royal Charter of 1845 as amended by supplemental charters,[16] and being given the name "The Law Society" by the Supplemental Charter of 1903. Membership of the Society is voluntary although

---

11 Such Licensed Conveyancers are subject to detailed rules concerning professional indemnity, the keeping of accounts, and subject to a disciplinary process. The Council for Licensed Conveyancers has wide powers of intervention.
12 Section 34 (not yet in force).
13 *Ibid*, ss 37(1), 38(1).
14 *Ibid*, s 37(7)(e). For details of the scheme, see 1990 Act, Sch 7.
15 *Ibid*, ss 104–107.
16 In 1872, 1903, 1909 and 1954.

the vast majority of the solicitors currently in practice are, in fact, members of the Society. The Society is governed by the President, Vice-President and a Council of not more than 70 members, the latter being elected for a period of five years; at present there are 70 members, of whom 56 are elected to represent constituencies and 14 are elected by the Council itself as specialists.

The objects of the Society remain, as defined in the Charter of 1845, as "promoting professional improvement and facilitating the acquisition of legal knowledge". Notwithstanding its voluntary composition The Law Society has important regulatory powers in respect of all solicitors, deriving mainly from the Solicitors Act 1974, a consolidating statute.

By section 2 of the 1974 Act the Society may, with the concurrence of the Lord Chancellor, the Lord Chief Justice and the Master of the Rolls, make "training regulations" about education and training for persons seeking to be admitted or to practise as solicitors. Training regulations may relate to education and training, whether by service under articles or otherwise, to be undergone by persons seeking admission as solicitors or by persons who have already been admitted. A person wishing to enter into articles must satisfy the Society as to his character and suitability[17] and no person may be admitted as a solicitor until he has obtained a certificate that the Society is satisfied that he has complied with training regulations (which will involve satisfactory completion of articles, legal education and examinations) and is satisfied as to his character and his suitability to be a solicitor of the Supreme Court. The Society maintains the Roll of Solicitors and, in order to practise as a solicitor, a person must have his name on the Roll and hold a current practising certificate.

Section 32 of the Act requires the Council of The Law Society to make rules[18] governing the handling by solicitors of clients' and certain trust moneys and the right to interest thereon. Section 34 requires the Council to make rules governing the annual submission by solicitors of an accountant's report.[19] Section 31 empowers the Council to make rules regulating professional practice, conduct and discipline.[20]

As well as exercising these powers and duties The Law Society also looks after the welfare of solicitors generally and attempts to maintain good relations with other bodies and with the public. To this end the Council examines the activities of unqualified persons doing the work of solicitors and, in appropriate cases, institutes proceedings. It also performs educative and public relations activities.

In addition to its control over its own members and other solicitors the Society protects the interests of the public by the maintenance of a compensation fund[1] out of which it may make a hardship grant to any person who suffers hardship through the failure of a solicitor to account for money due in connection with his practice as a solicitor or with any trust of which he is a trustee. The result is that members of the public are

---

17 Qualifying Regulations 1979–86.
18 The present rules are the Solicitors' Accounts Rules 1991.
19 The present rules are the Accountant's Report Rules 1991.
20 See Solicitors Practice Rules 1990.
1 Solicitors Act 1974, s 36 and Sch 2. The fund is made up of special annual contributions payable by solicitors on application for practising certificates. The Royal Commission found the present compensation arrangements satisfactory (Report, para 23.15).

indemnified against loss which might be suffered as a result of any solicitor's default in the handling of their moneys. The Law Society then assumes, through the doctrine of subrogation, the rights and remedies of the person to whom the grant was made to the extent of the grant.

By way of further protection of the public, the Society has power to take over and reorganise the practice of any solicitor who cannot safely be relied upon to continue the handling of his clients' affairs,[2] while the Council may, with the concurrence of the Master of the Rolls, make "indemnity rules" providing for the indemnity of solicitors against professional liability by the establishment of a mutual fund, by commercial insurance effected by the Society, by requiring solicitors themselves to insure or by any combination of these methods.[3]

While the combined effect of the provisions outlined above is to provide a wide measure of protection against default or neglect, it is not intended to protect against all loss suffered by a client. The Law Society does not owe a duty of care to those who may suffer loss through its performance of regulatory functions: in *Wood v The Law Society*[4] it was held that no compensation could be recovered in respect of conduct by The Law Society found by the court to be inadequate. Negligent conduct by a solicitor is actionable in the normal way, by the aggrieved party against the solicitor. However, the relationship between the supervisory functions of The Law Society and its capacity to intervene in respect of inadequate work was brought closer in 1985 when The Law Society was given a power to reduce fees, to require rectification of an error or the taking of other action.[5] These powers were re-cast and extended by the Courts and Legal Services Act 1990. The Law Society may now, in addition to the steps described above, order the payment of compensation of up to £1,000.[6] In deciding whether to take action under these provisions, the Society must have regard to the existence of any civil remedy open to the client, and whether it is reasonable to expect the client to commence legal action against the solicitor.[7]

---

2 Solicitors Act 1974, s 35 and Sch 1; this important power was introduced by the Solicitors (Amendment) Act 1974. The circumstances in which the Society can intervene are detailed in Part I of Sch 1 (as amended by Courts and Legal Services Act 1990, s 91 and by Administration of Justice Act 1985, Sch 1) but can briefly be summarised as dishonesty, undue delay on the part of the personal representatives of a deceased solicitor, failure to comply with professional rules, bankruptcy, imprisonment, removal from or striking off the roll or suspension from practice, and incapacity or abandonment of practice by a sole practitioner.

3 *Ibid*, s 37; this was a further important innovation effected by the Solicitors (Amendment) Act 1974. The current rules are the Solicitors Indemnity Rules 1984 under which The Law Society maintains a "master policy" of indemnity insurance on behalf of all solicitors required to be insured, practising solicitors being required to make a fixed contribution annually by way of premium.

4 [1993] NLJR 1475.

5 Solicitors Act 1974, s 44A, introduced by Administration of Justice Act 1985, s 1.

6 By virtue of Solicitors Act 1974, s 37A (inserted in that Act by Courts and Legal Services Act 1990, s 93(2)) and a new Sch 1A (inserted by 1990 Act, Sch 15).

7 1974 Act, Sch 1A, para 1(3).

2 Liabilities of a solicitor

a Liability to disciplinary proceedings

Solicitors are, of course, subject to the general criminal law. However, conduct on the part of a solicitor which falls short of a criminal offence may still result in sanctions. These are usually enforced by the Solicitors Disciplinary Tribunal although, since solicitors are officers of the Supreme Court, the High Court and Court of Appeal have inherent jurisdiction to strike the name of a solicitor from the roll or suspend him for misconduct.[8] In addition to this inherent jurisdiction the High Court has a limited statutory jurisdiction in disciplinary matters. The High Court must strike off the Roll the name of a solicitor who wilfully and knowingly assists an unqualified person to practise or act as a solicitor;[9] it must strike off the Roll or suspend from practice a person who, without the written permission of The Law Society, knowingly employs a person who has been struck off the Roll involuntarily or suspended from practice.[10] However the Tribunal has, in all these cases, corresponding jurisdiction and, since it also has a wider jurisdiction than the High Court, proceedings are generally instituted before the Tribunal.

The Solicitors Disciplinary Tribunal is constituted by the Master of the Rolls from "solicitor members" who must be practising solicitors of not less than ten years' standing and "lay members" who must be neither solicitors nor barristers.[11] It is, nonetheless, independent of The Law Society. The Tribunal is a judicial tribunal and proceedings before it are absolutely privileged for the purposes of the law of defamation.[12] There is a quorum of three members of whom at least one must be a lay member, although the number of solicitor members present must exceed the number of lay members present; the Tribunal may receive evidence on oath and compel the attendance of witnesses by subpoena. It may also, with the concurrence of the Master of the Rolls, make rules regulating its own procedure.

Its jurisdiction is threefold. First, it hears applications to strike the name of a solicitor off the Roll, or to require him to answer allegations contained in an affidavit, or by a former solicitor whose name has been struck off the Roll or suspended to have his name restored to the Roll or suspension lifted.[13] Secondly, it hears complaints by another party against a solicitor based either upon common law disciplinary offences of professional misconduct or upon specific offences under the 1974 Act, such as failure to

---

8 This jurisdiction is preserved by the Solicitors Act 1974, s 50(2).
9 Solicitors Act 1974, s 39(2).
10 *Ibid*, s 41(4).
11 *Ibid*, s 46; the Tribunal is a successor of the Solicitors Disciplinary Committee which existed until 1974. The provision for "lay members" was to allay public criticism of the system whereby complaints against solicitors were investigated exclusively by solicitors; with the same object, s 45 of the Act permits the Lord Chancellor to appoint "lay observers" to examine written allegations made by members of the public concerning the Society's treatment of complaints made about solicitors or their employees.
12 *Addis v Crocker* [1961] 1 QB 11; [1960] 2 All ER 629.
13 Solicitors Act 1974, s 47(1), as substituted by Courts and Legal Services Act 1990, s 92.

comply with the Solicitors' Accounts Rules,[14] or making a false statement in a declaration for obtaining a practising certificate.[15]

Finally, the Tribunal hears applications by The Law Society under section 43 of the Act to restrain the employment by solicitors, without the written permission of The Law Society, of clerks who have been convicted of criminal offences of dishonesty rendering their employment in a solicitor's practice undesirable or have been parties to disciplinary offences by solicitors. The major part of the Tribunal's business is concerned with the second type of matter – complaints against solicitors in respect of professional misconduct or offences under the Solicitors Act 1974. In dealing with these applications the Tribunal may make such order as it thinks fit.[16] In particular it may strike the solicitor's name off the Roll, suspend him from practice either for a fixed period or indefinitely, order him to pay a penalty not exceeding £5,000, to be forfeit to Her Majesty, and order him to pay a reasonable contribution towards the costs of the proceedings.[17] It may also exclude the solicitor from legal aid work, where there is good reason to do so because of his conduct in connection with a legally assisted person or in relation to the giving of advice or assistance under the legal aid scheme.[18] The Tribunal also has jurisdiction to impose sanctions for inadequate professional services.[19]

Any party may appeal from the decision of the Solicitors Disciplinary Tribunal to a divisional court of the Queen's Bench Division[20] and thence, with leave of either that court or the Court of Appeal, to the Court of Appeal.[1] Where the application is to restrain the employment of a clerk under section 43, appeal lies only at the instance of the clerk and the decision of the High Court is final.

b   Liability as an officer of the court

As stated above, the Supreme Court has both an inherent and a limited statutory jurisdiction over solicitors since they are officers of the Supreme Court.[2] This jurisdiction is merged in the wider jurisdiction of the Disciplinary Tribunal. In addition to this jurisdiction, the sanction for which is striking off the Roll, the High Court has further powers to impose liability upon solicitors as court officers. Thus solicitors may be, and

---

14 Solicitors Act 1974, s 32(3).
15 *Ibid*, s 9(5).
16 *Ibid*, s 47(2).
17 *Ibid*, s 47(2). The Lord Chancellor may vary the sum of £5,000 by statutory instrument, having regard to any change in the value of money (*ibid*, s 47(4), (5), added by the Administration of Justice Act 1982, s 56).
18 *Ibid*, s 47(2A), as amended by the Courts and Legal Services Act 1990, s 92(2).
19 Solicitors Act 1974, s 47A, inserted by Administration of Justice Act 1985, s 3(2).
20 *Ibid*, s 49(1), save that appeal is to the Master of the Rolls against an order restoring or refusing to restore to the Roll the name of a solicitor who has been struck off or an order revoking or refusing to revoke an order made under s 43. The Law Society is entitled to appeal to the Master of the Rolls against a decision by the Tribunal to restore to the roll a person previously struck off: *R v Master of the Rolls, ex parte McKinnell* [1993] 1 All ER 193.
1 Supreme Court Act 1981, s 18(1)(e).
2 See *Holden v Crown Prosecution Service* [1990] 2 QB 261; [1990] 1 All ER 368 (inherent jurisdiction to order defence solicitor to pay prosecution costs where serious dereliction of duty); *Langley v North West Water Authority* [1991] 3 All ER 610 (solicitor personally liable for costs resulting from failure to comply with county court *Practice Direction*).

sometimes are, ordered to pay personally costs thrown away by their neglect or improperly incurred. These costs may be made payable either to the solicitor's own client or to a third party. The principles to be applied in such cases were fully discussed by the Court of Appeal in *Re A Barrister (Wasted Costs Order (No 1 of 1991))*.[3] A three-stage test is to be applied: (a) has the legal representative complained against acted improperly, unreasonably or negligently?; (b) if so, did such conduct cause the applicant to incur unnecessary costs?; (c) is it just for the legal representative to compensate the applicant? This provision is both punitive and compensatory so that a solicitor may be ordered to pay costs even where the defaulting party is his partner or a clerk.[4]

A solicitor may also be liable, as an officer of the court, for loss occasioned by his negligence or breach of duty.[5] This liability may be summarily enforced by any party who has suffered loss. This may be compared with the general civil liability of a solicitor to his client, discussed below, which is enforceable by civil proceedings.

A further way in which a solicitor may incur liability as an officer of the court is by giving an undertaking to the court or in his capacity as a solicitor. The court often makes an order, or refrains from making an order, on the faith of a personal undertaking by a solicitor appearing; for example, an undertaking to stamp a document or an unconditional undertaking not to issue execution if payment of a judgment debt is expedited. The court will enforce a solicitor's undertaking summarily, not as a contractual obligation but in order to secure the proper conduct of its officers. An undertaking to pay money is an obligation *sui generis* enforceable summarily by the court and is neither a contractual obligation nor a judgment debt.[6]

Finally a solicitor is liable to be committed for contempt of court. A solicitor's liability for contempt of court is basically no different from the liability of laymen. Nevertheless solicitors, because of their close association with the court, may be guilty of contempt in a wider variety of ways. Furthermore there are various statutes and rules which impose special liability to committal upon a solicitor, for example for neglecting to inform his client of a judgment against the latter or for defaulting on an order to pay costs personally for misconduct.[7] Failure to comply with an undertaking is a contempt of court, and professional misconduct, as well as rendering the solicitor liable to perform his undertaking.

---

3 [1993] QB 293; [1992] 3 All ER 429, dealing with the application of the Courts and Legal Services Act 1990, s 51(6). See further p 382, *post*. For further discussion of wasted costs orders see *Ridehalgh v Horsefield* (1994) Times, 28 January.

4 *Myers v Elman* [1940] AC 282; [1939] 4 All ER 484 where it was made clear that the jurisdiction ought only to be exercised in cases of "serious dereliction of duty" by a solicitor or his employee; cf *R and T Thew Ltd v Reeves (No 2)* [1982] QB 1283n; [1982] 3 All ER 1086.

5 *Marsh v Joseph* [1897] 1 Ch 213.

6 *Re Hudson* [1966] Ch 209; [1966] 1 All ER 110. However the obligation will only be enforced summarily in clear cases; in cases where there is a triable issue the plaintiff must bring an action in the normal way: *Silver and Drake v Baines* [1971] 1 QB 396; [1971] 1 All ER 473.

7 Debtors Act 1869, s 4(4).

c   Civil liability

The solicitor, by his position, may render himself liable to civil proceedings either at the suit of his client or of some third party, in a variety of ways. The duty which the solicitor owes to his own client is an incident of the solicitor-client relationship and is dealt with in the following section. There are, in addition, several ways in which a solicitor may incur civil liability to persons other than his own client. In contract the solicitor's liability to third parties is governed usually by the ordinary law of agency. Thus if the solicitor contracts on behalf of an undisclosed client, the other party may elect to sue either the solicitor or the client.[8] If the solicitor acts without authority on behalf of a client he may, in accordance with general principles, be sued for breach of warranty of authority.[9] An exception to the general law of agency is that the solicitor is personally responsible for certain items of expenditure even though incurred as agent for his client, such as experts' fees and the costs of a shorthand writer. A solicitor's liability in tort is governed by the general law of torts. Thus, for example, a solicitor who fraudulently induces a third party to buy an estate with a defective title commits the tort of deceit.

A solicitor may sometimes owe a duty not only to a client, or prospective client,[10] but also to a third party. An example was seen in *White v Jones*[11] where a solicitor was held liable for loss caused to a potential beneficiary under a will. Instructions for the drafting of a new will benefiting the plaintiff had been given, but not implemented, prior to the death of the testator.

3   Incidents of the solicitor-client relationship

a   Solicitor's duty of care to his client

A solicitor's authority derives from the retainer given to him by his client. The effect of this retainer is to create a contractual relationship between the solicitor and the client. In most respects this relationship is, therefore, subject to the ordinary law of contract and in particular to that part of contract law concerning agency since the relationship created is, for purposes within the scope of the retainer, a principal and agent relationship. Consequently the solicitor has a right to be indemnified by his client for acts done within the scope of his authority. The solicitor's duty subsists throughout the period of his retainer. The general rule is that when retained the solicitor undertakes to complete the transaction for which he is retained. For that reason the solicitor is not entitled to his remuneration

---

8 *Foster v Cranfield* (1911) 46 L Jo 314. A solicitor has ostensible authority to bind his client to compromise of an action (whether or not he has actual authority so to do). Consequently, if an action is compromised on terms the client is bound by those terms and the other party may enforce them; cf *Waugh v HB Clifford and Sons Ltd* [1982] Ch 374; [1982] 1 All ER 1095.

9 *Yonge v Toynbee* [1910] 1 KB 215.

10 *Ross v Caunters* [1980] Ch 297; cf *Robertson v Fleming* (1861) 4 Macq 167. The decision in *Ross v Caunters* survives the House of Lords decision in *Murphy v Brentwood District Council* [1991] 1 AC 398; [1990] 2 All ER 908, where it has held that, in general, no liability existed for pure economic loss: see *White v Jones* [1993] 3 All ER 481; [1993] 3 WLR 730.

11 [1993] 3 All ER 481.

until the transaction is completed (although he is entitled to be put in funds for disbursements) and if he wrongfully withdraws from the retainer he will not be entitled to a *quantum meruit* for the work he has done. However, it is now provided[12] that a solicitor engaged to conduct contentious business may require payment of a reasonable amount on account of costs and if the client refuses or fails to make that payment the solicitor may, upon giving reasonable notice to the client, withdraw from the retainer. The solicitor must then have his name withdrawn from the court record since until he does so he remains in the position of the party's solicitor so far as the court and the other parties to the action are concerned.

If the solicitor is negligent the client may have an action against him for damages. The action lies in contract and, almost certainly, in tort as well.[13] A solicitor owes a duty to instruct competent counsel, where instructed.[14] However, if the solicitor himself acts he is not liable in negligence for work which, if carried out by counsel, would not have attracted liability.[15]

b Fiduciary obligations

The solicitor-client relationship is regarded in equity as a fiduciary one. Several consequences flow from this. In general the solicitor must act in good faith in all dealings with his client. This involves making a full and honest disclosure of facts within the solicitor's knowledge in any financial transaction with his client. This principle derives from the equitable doctrine of fraud and has differing consequences which depend upon the nature of the transaction.

The principle is at its strongest in the case of gifts to the solicitor by his client. There is a presumption of undue influence in the case of such a gift, the effect of which is to make the gift voidable at the instance of the client. The solicitor can retain the gift only by showing that it was made after the fiduciary relationship had ceased, or that it was ratified by the client after the relationship had ceased or that the client had independent legal advice.[16]

This presumption of undue influence, which applies to gifts *inter vivos*, does not apply to gifts by will although any person may allege and prove actual undue influence by the solicitor. Nevertheless, where a solicitor prepares a will under which he receives a large benefit the court requires affirmative proof that the testator knew and fully approved of the contents of the will.[17] Where a client intends to give a large benefit to a solicitor in his will the latter should insist on the will being prepared by another solicitor.[18] A purchase by a solicitor from his client, or a sale to his client, is not necessarily bad but the solicitor must show that the bargain is as good as the client could have obtained with due diligence elsewhere in order to

---

12 By Solicitors Act 1974, s 65(2).
13 *Groom v Crocker* [1939] 1 KB 194; *Midland Bank Trust Co Ltd v Hett, Stubbs and Kemp* [1979] Ch 384; [1978] 3 All ER 571; *White v Jones, supra,* n 11.
14 *Re A (A Minor)* [1988] Fam Law 339.
15 See p 229, *post*.
16 *Gibson v Jeyes* (1801) 6 Ves 266; *Lancashire Loans Ltd v Black* [1934] 1 KB 380.
17 *Wintle v Nye* [1959] 1 All ER 552; [1959] 1 WLR 284.
18 Failure to comply with these fiduciary obligations will invariably be regarded as serious professional misconduct and the offending solicitor is liable to be struck off the Roll; see, for example, *Re A Solicitor* [1975] QB 475; [1974] 3 All ER 853.

rebut the presumption of undue influence. This means that the price must be fair and that the solicitor must make a full disclosure. In practice the solicitor should see that the client has independent advice. Similar conditions apply to loans between solicitor and client.[19]

c Obligations to preserve confidence

One particular aspect of the fiduciary relationship between solicitor and client is the confidential nature of communications between them. This gives rise to two types of privilege; privilege in the tort of defamation and privilege from disclosure in evidence. This latter privilege is discussed in due course.[20]

4 Remuneration

Solicitors are entitled to remuneration for their services. However the way in which this remuneration is assessed and recovered is not primarily governed by the ordinary law of contract even though the right to remuneration arises out of a contractual relationship. It is governed by various statutes and rules, passed generally for the benefit of clients, and is subject to the supervision of the courts. Even where solicitor and client make an agreement as to costs, the court may still examine its reasonableness. It should also be remembered that the parties may in the future have the right, in some circumstances, to enter into a conditional fee agreement.[1]

The way in which a solicitor's remuneration is assessed depends upon whether the business done on behalf of the client is contentious or non-contentious. "Contentious business" is defined by the Act[2] as:

> "Business done, whether as solicitor or advocate, in or for the purpose of proceedings begun before a court or before an arbitrator appointed under the Arbitration Act 1950, not being business which falls within the definition of non-contentious or common form probate business in the Supreme Court Act 1981, s 128."

The test is thus whether or not proceedings are begun. If they are, all business relating to these proceedings is contentious. If proceedings are not begun, as for example where a dispute is settled before a writ is issued, the proceedings are treated as non-contentious. Non-contentious business is any business which is not contentious within the above statutory definition and comprises a very wide range of matters including conveyancing, drafting wills and settlements, advice and many other matters. The basic difference between contentious and non-contentious business in relation to the assessment of remuneration is that in the former the amount is usually fixed by the court by taxation while in the latter it is not, being fixed in accordance with statutory orders.

---

19 See, generally, *Cordery on Solicitors* (7th Edn), pp 9–29; *cf Spector v Ageda* [1973] Ch 30; [1971] 3 All ER 417.
20 See p 596, *post.*
 1 See p 211, *ante.*
 2 Solicitors Act 1974, s 87(1) (as amended).

a   Assessment of remuneration in contentious business

The Solicitors Act 1974, section 59 expressly authorises a solicitor to enter into a written agreement with his client regulating remuneration in contentious business.[3] In the absence of such an agreement the solicitor may submit either a bill containing detailed items or one charging a gross sum.[4]

The client has a right to have this bill taxed, in which case the appropriate basis of taxation is (unless the bill is to be paid out of the Legal Aid Fund) the "indemnity" basis.[5] On this basis:

> "All costs shall be allowed except in so far as they are of an unreasonable amount or have been unreasonably incurred."[6]

All costs incurred with the express or implied approval of the client are conclusively presumed to have been reasonably incurred and, where the amount has been so approved, are presumed to have been reasonable in amount.[7] However the solicitor must expressly inform his client of any costs which are of an unusual nature and might not be allowed on a "party and party" taxation; otherwise such costs are deemed to be unreasonably incurred.[8] In certain cases costs are charged on a fixed scale[9] while in High Court cases, the actual amounts are within the discretion of the taxing officer.[10] These amounts are calculated in the light of various criteria, which are discussed later.[11]

An exception to the above basis of taxation applies where the client is legally aided. In such a case in the High Court the solicitor receives from the Legal Aid Fund only his disbursements and his costs taxed on a "standard" basis. On this basis, which is less liberal than the "indemnity" basis of taxation, there is allowed "a reasonable amount in respect of all costs reasonably incurred".[12]

b   Assessment of remuneration in non-contentious business

Whereas remuneration in contentious business is usually fixed by the court, remuneration in non-contentious business is controlled differently. Save in certain exceptional cases under specific enactments,[13] the mode and amount of remuneration are regulated by orders made under section 56 of the 1974 Act.[14]

---

3 See p 222, *post.*
4 Section 64.
5 See p 383, *post.*
6 RSC, Ord 62, r 12(2).
7 Ord 62, r 15(2).
8 *Ibid.*
9 Ord 62, Appendix 3.
10 Ord 62, Appendix 2.
11 See p 383.
12 Ord 62, r 12(1).
13 Preserved by s 75 of the 1974 Act.
14 These orders are made by a committee consisting of the Lord Chancellor, the Lord Chief Justice, the Master of the Rolls, the President of The Law Society, a nominated solicitor who is president of a local law society and (for the purpose only of business under the Land Registration Act 1925) the Chief Land Registrar (s 56(1)).

As to the mode of remuneration, orders made under section 56 may provide for remuneration: (a) according to a scale of rates of commission or a scale of percentages; or (b) by a gross sum; or (c) by a fixed sum for each document prepared or perused; or (d) in any other mode; or (e) partly in one mode and partly in another.

The amount of remuneration may be regulated by order with reference to the following, among other, considerations:

(a)   the position of the party for whom the solicitor is concerned, that is, whether he is vendor or purchaser, lessor or lessee, mortgagor or mortgagee or the like;

(b)   the place where, and the circumstances in which, the business was transacted;

(c)   the amount involved;

(d)   the skill, labour and responsibility involved on the part of the solicitor;

(e)   the number or importance of the documents prepared or perused.

The basis of remuneration under this order is a lump sum which is fair and reasonable having regard to all the circumstances of the case and in particular the complexity of the matter, the skill, specialised knowledge and responsibility involved, the number of documents, the time involved, the value of any property or amount of any sum involved, whether any land was registered, and the importance of the matter to the client.

The client has no right to have a lump sum bill itemised. He has, nevertheless, two safeguards against an excessive charge. First, he has a right to have the bill taxed and secondly, without prejudice to this right, he has a right to require the solicitor to obtain a certificate from The Law Society that the sum charged is fair and reasonable, or, if it is not, what is a fair and reasonable sum. It is for the solicitor to show that the charge is fair and reasonable. A solicitor can bring no proceedings on a lump sum bill until he has drawn his client's attention to the latter's rights which are set out above. The right to require the solicitor to obtain a certificate may be exercised within one month of his being informed by the solicitor of his rights as above, provided the bill has been neither taxed nor paid. If the taxing master allows less than one half the amount charged he must bring the facts of the case to the attention of The Law Society.[15]

c   Special agreements as to remuneration

Solicitor and client may, in both contentious and non-contentious business, agree the amount of the solicitor's remuneration. Such agreements are, however, not freely enforceable in the same way as commercial contracts since their enforceability is regulated by statute.

In contentious business solicitor and client may make an agreement in writing, providing for remuneration by a gross sum, or by a salary, or otherwise and whether at a higher or lower rate than that at which the solicitor would otherwise have been entitled to be remunerated.[16] There is no prescribed form for the agreement and it may, for example, be contained in letters passing between solicitor and client provided that the

---

15 Solicitors' Remuneration Order 1972, arts 3, 4.
16 Act of 1974, s 59(1).

terms of the agreement can be ascertained with certainty. However there are certain other restrictions attaching to such an agreement. Any provision exempting the solicitor from liability for negligence or any other responsibility is void. The agreement itself is void if it involves any purchase by a solicitor of any part of the interest of his client in the proceedings.[17] The agreement cannot prejudice the rights of third parties although it may indirectly benefit them since the client cannot recover more costs from a third party than he has agreed to pay his solicitor.[18]

A provision relating to remuneration in contentious business cannot be enforced by action,[19] even though the agreement as a whole can be so enforced. It may, however, be enforced summarily by the High Court or a county court on application.[20] The court may, if it considers the agreement unfair or unreasonable, declare it void and order the costs covered thereby to be taxed as if the agreement had never been made.[1]

An agreement for remuneration in non-contentious business must likewise be in writing.[2] It may specify either a gross sum or an hourly rate.[3] Such an agreement is subject to the ordinary law of contract and may be sued on in the ordinary way. Nevertheless the court has an inherent jurisdiction to order taxation in order to determine whether the gross sum agreed (but not an hourly rate) is fair and reasonable, and may cancel the agreement or reduce the amount payable if the taxing officer certifies that it is unfair or unreasonable.[4] An hourly rate is not reducible by the taxing master.

d Recovery of costs

By section 69 of the Solicitors Act 1974 no action shall be brought to recover any costs due to a solicitor until one month after delivery of a bill signed by the solicitor, or by a partner in the firm if the costs are due to a firm, or accompanied by a letter so signed and referring to the bill. However, the High Court may by order dispense with this requirement if there is probable cause for believing that the party chargeable is about to quit England and Wales, to become bankrupt or compound with his creditors or do any other act which would tend to prevent or delay the solicitor obtaining payment.

Within one month of the delivery of a bill the client has a right to have it taxed and no action may be commenced on the bill until the taxation is completed.[5] After one month has elapsed the court may, upon such terms as it thinks fit, order taxation on the application of solicitor or client and

---

17 Solicitors Act 1974, s 59(2). A solicitor is, however, justified in acting for an impoverished client on terms that he shall receive no costs or reduced costs unless the action succeeds.
18 *Ibid*, s 60(3).
19 *Ibid*, s 61(1).
20 The appropriate court is the one in which the business to which the agreement relates was done if this is the High Court or a county court, or, if not, the High Court in respect of agreements to pay more than £50 or the county court for sums of less than £50 (1974 Act, s 61(6)). Application to the High Court is usually by originating summons; application to a county court is by originating application.
1 Solicitors Act 1974, s 61(2), (4).
2 *Ibid*, s 57.
3 *Ibid*, s 57(5), as amended by the Courts and Legal Services Act 1990, s 98.
4 *Ibid*.
5 *Ibid*, s 70(1).

may stay proceedings on the bill, or order that no action shall be taken, until taxation is completed.[6] However, except in special circumstances, the client will not obtain an order for taxation more than twelve months after the delivery of the bill or after payment, and in no event will he obtain an order more than twelve months after payment. Unless the client does not appear on the solicitor's application to have the bill taxed or the order for taxation otherwise provides the costs of the taxation depend upon its outcome. If one-fifth of the amount of the bill is taxed off the solicitor pays the costs; otherwise the client pays the costs.[7]

Subject to the above restrictions the solicitor may proceed to recover his costs as a contractual debt. He may do so by action or by proving in the client's bankruptcy or in the liquidation of a client company. As an alternative to action the solicitor may exercise his common law lien.[8] He has a general lien over all of the client's personal property in the solicitor's possession except his will. This entitles the solicitor to retain the property until payment of the full amount due. The lien is often exercised in relation to case papers. However a solicitor's lien is subordinate to the public interest that justice be achieved in the suit. Consequently a lien over a client's papers is qualified in that the solicitor is bound to hand over the client's papers to his new solicitor on the latter's undertaking to preserve the lien.[9] In addition the solicitor has a particular lien over property, other than real property,[10] recovered or preserved or the proceeds of any judgment obtained in an action, for his costs in relation to that action.

It will be appreciated that in a long and expensive piece of litigation the solicitor may be in the position of having to wait a very long time in order to recover his remuneration. To remedy this section 65 of the Act enables the solicitor, in contentious business, to request payment of a reasonable sum of money on account of costs; if the client refuses or fails within a reasonable time to make that payment the solicitor may, upon giving reasonable notice, withdraw from the retainer. The solicitor will then have to apply to the court for removal of his name from the record.

E   BARRISTERS

1   General organisation of the Bar

a   The Inns of Court

Persons may only practise as counsel in England if they have been "called to the Bar" of one of the four Inns of Court: Lincoln's Inn, the Inner Temple, the Middle Temple and Gray's Inn. These Inns are as old as professional advocacy itself in England and appear to have originated as

---

6 *Ibid*, s 70(2).

7 *Ibid*, s 70.

8 See, generally, *Halvanon Insurance Co Ltd v Central Reinsurance Corporation* [1988] 3 All ER 857; [1988] 1 WLR 1122.

9 *Gamlen Chemical Co (UK) Ltd v Rochem Ltd* [1980] 1 All ER 1049; [1980] 1 WLR 614. *Cf A v B* [1984] 1 All ER 265.

10 But note s 73 of the 1974 Act which enables the court to make a charging order in favour of the solicitor over any property including real property.

living quarters for those legal practitioners who were not serjeants.[11] The Inns' jurisdiction is in no way statutory. It is derived from the judges (and thus indirectly from the Crown) and is subject to control by the judges.[12] One member of the Court of Appeal has explained the Inns' functions as follows:[13]

> "I would regard the Inns of Court in their disciplinary power in relation to the practising member of the Bar as equivalently established over the centuries by its practice and acceptance as if the power had been derived from statute and as unassailable. If the Inns of Court had not controlled the professional conduct of the Bar the judges themselves would have had to do so. The judges themselves, deriving their authority from the Crown, were minded in the distant past to delegate, and the undisputed view in Lord Mansfield's time was that the judges had delegated their disciplinary power over the Bar to the Inns of Court."

In the Inns of Court there are three classes of members: benchers, who are the governors of the Inn, barristers, who are called by the benchers, and students who are admitted to membership by the benchers. The benchers of an Inn, who are judges or senior members of the Bar, have absolute control over the admission of students and the call of barristers. There is an appeal from their decisions to the Lord Chancellor and the judges of the High Court sitting as "visitors", a domestic tribunal. They cannot, however, be sued in respect of any act done in their official capacity nor can they be compelled by mandamus to admit a person as a student or call a student to the Bar.[14] The principal conditions which a student must satisfy before applying for call to the Bar are payment of the requisite fees, passing the Bar Final Examination and keeping eight terms.[15] No person under the age of 21 can be called to the Bar. Before a barrister can practise he must serve a pupillage under a senior member of the Bar (not a Queen's Counsel) for not less than twelve months.[16]

b The Bar Council

In 1966 the Senate of the Inns of Court was established and, in its original or modified form,[17] existed until 1987 when the Bar Council was reconstituted. The Bar Council is the governing body of the Bar. It comprises certain *ex officio* members such as the Attorney-General, Solicitor-General, the Director of Public Prosecutions and various representative barristers, together with members nominated by the Benchers of the Inns of Court and by circuits. It also comprises elected members.

Its functions include the laying down and implementation of general

---

11 Serjeants had their own Inns ("Serjeants' Inns"). There were also several Chancery Inns (eg New Inn, Clifford's Inn). All these have ceased to exist.
12 *R v Gray's Inn* (1780) 1 Doug KB 353, *per* LORD MANSFIELD.
13 SELLERS LJ in *Lincoln v Daniels* [1962] 1 QB 237, at 250; [1961] 3 All ER 740, at 745; *cf Re S (a Barrister)* [1970] 1 QB 160; [1969] 1 All ER 949. See *R v Visitor of the Inns of Court, ex parte Calder* [1994] QB 1; [1993] 2 All ER 876.
14 *R v Lincoln's Inn Benchers* (1825) 4 B & C 855.
15 The latter obligation is not imposed upon solicitors wishing to become barristers. There are four dining terms a year in the Inns of Court; Michaelmas, Hilary, Easter and Trinity. A term is kept by dining in Hall on a number of occasions (usually three) during the term.
16 For the appointment of Queen's Counsel see p 226, *post.*
17 The original body constituted in 1966 was replaced in 1974 by the Senate of the Inns of Courts and the Bar.

policy affecting the Bar, the maintenance of standards, honour and independence of the Bar and the external relations of the Bar with other organisations.

c   The Council for Legal Education

The Council for Legal Education makes recommendations to the Bar Council on matters relating to legal education, pupillage and continuing legal education. It prescribes the content of the academic stage of legal education sufficient for entry to the Bar,[18] and provides a practical, skills-based vocational training course for Bar Finals, and which all those wishing to practise at the Bar must attend.

2   Practice at the Bar

Barristers in independent practice work in sets of chambers. These are associations of barristers, who share common facilities, and administrative support. The work of individual barristers is organised and arranged by the barrister's clerk, who will also play a key role in the re-allocation of work within chambers where the barrister briefed is unable to appear, because of other commitments. It is permissible for a barrister to be employed, but he cannot then, generally speaking, offer legal services to anyone other than that employer, and cannot appear in courts where barristers have had exclusive rights of audience.[19]

Barristers' chambers are not partnerships. No statutory provision exists prohibiting such partnerships: indeed, there are no statutory restrictions upon the establishment of multi-disciplinary and multi-national practices.[20] The Bar Council may, however, continue to restrict these.

Barristers are divided into junior counsel and Queen's Counsel, the latter called "silks" because they wear a silk gown as opposed to that of stuff worn by juniors. Queen's Counsel are appointed annually by the Crown on the advice of the Lord Chancellor, on the basis of ability, experience and seniority, although some disquiet has been expressed in recent years concerning the alleged secrecy of the appointments process.[1] The significance of appointment as a silk is two-fold. First, Queen's Counsel do not usually take on the pleading and drafting work in contentious proceedings. Secondly, they are often instructed in the most difficult, complex or important of cases, thus reflecting their expertise and standing within the profession.

Until 1977 Queen's Counsel were subject to particular rules whereby they were not permitted to appear without a junior (the "two counsel" rule), nor to do drafting work nor give written opinions on evidence. As a consequence of a recommendation of the Monopolies and Mergers Commission in 1976, the Bar Council abolished the two counsel rule, although Queen's Counsel should decline to appear without a junior if he would be

---

18 See Consolidated Regulations of the Four Inns of Court, reg 15–16.
19 See p 211, *ante*.
20 Courts and Legal Services Act 1990, s 65.
 1 See de Wilde in (1993) *Counsel*.

unable properly to conduct that case, or other cases, or to fulfil his professional commitments unless a junior were also instructed. In practice, it is still comparatively rare to find Queen's Counsel appearing without a junior. Furthermore, Queen's Counsel may now engage in non-contentious drafting work and may, if he has agreed to appear without a junior in a case, settle pleadings or draft other documents in that case.

The barrister's function is primarily advocacy although he deals also with such matters as drafting conveyances, pleadings and other legal documents and advising on the law. He has a right of audience in virtually all judicial proceedings and in the House of Lords, the Judicial Committee of the Privy Council, the Court of Appeal and the High Court of Justice this right is exclusive, except in interlocutory proceedings and bankruptcy proceedings where solicitors have a concurrent right. In criminal proceedings in the Crown Court, prosecutions must be conducted by barristers[2] and prosecutors cannot appear in person. All petitions of appeal to the House of Lords from the Court of Appeal must be signed by two counsel.

In addition to these rights and privileges barristers have various duties both to the court and to their clients. Their duties to the court are all based on professional etiquette. Barristers are not, in the way that solicitors are, officers of the court so that they are not strictly subject to control by the courts. It is doubtful whether the courts could exercise jurisdiction to suspend a barrister from practising, since this power is left by the judges to the Inns of Court. Nevertheless a barrister may clearly be fined or imprisoned for contempt of court to the same extent as a solicitor or, indeed, any other person. Counsel cannot, in general, be heard in court unless they are "robed", a term which includes the wearing of wig, gown and bands, a practice which continues despite some debate as to its utility.[3] A barrister may, however, appear unrobed in magistrates' courts and also when appearing as litigant in person.[4] Although counsel are not officers of the court they are officers of justice. This is particularly true in criminal proceedings so that prosecuting counsel's function is to assist the court, not to press for a conviction. Indeed, the duty of prosecuting counsel to ensure proper disclosure of unused material[5] shows that counsel owes a wider obligation to the proper administration of justice. Even in civil cases barristers are under a duty to draw to the attention of the court authorities which do not support their client's case. Furthermore, counsel must not mislead the court by actively concealing facts[6] from the court which are material to the case, nor must he set up any affirmative case or defence inconsistent with any admission or confession made to him by his client, nor should he take a point of law which he knows to be bad.

3   Relationship between counsel and client

Historically, a barrister could not enter into a contractual relationship for the provision of his services, except, of course, in respect of employed

---

2 Note the provisions of Supreme Court Act 1981, s 83, which permit the Lord Chancellor to confer unlimited rights of audience upon solicitors in proceedings in the Crown Court, and further p 210, *ante*.

3 In 1993, a decision was taken to retain the traditional court dress of wig and gown.

4 *Practice Note* [1961] 1 All ER 319.

5 See p 480, *post*.

6 *Meek v Fleming* [1961] 2 QB 366; [1961] 3 All ER 148.

barristers. This rule was abolished in 1990,[7] although the Bar Council can restrict or prohibit the entry into such contracts.

Members of the Bar may now enter into written agreements with solicitors as to the time barrister's fees will be paid. In the absence of such an agreement, fees should be paid by solicitors within three months of the delivery of a fee note. Continued failure by a solicitor to pay barrister's fees may entitle the Chairman of the Bar Council to issue a direction prohibiting the acceptance by barristers of instructions from the solicitor concerned, unless accompanied by an agreed brief fee. Clearly, if a contractual arrangement has been entered into, it can be enforced by normal legal action.

The corollary of the historic inability to sue for their fees is their immunity from being sued in contract for professional negligence. Barristers were historically immune from actions in negligence because such actions could only be based on contract and were thus not possible against a barrister, with whom the client could not enter into a contractual relationship.[8] In the leading case of *Rondel v Worsley*[9] the House of Lords, faced with the question whether a barrister might now be held liable in negligence, decided not and dismissed the plaintiff's appeal from an order that his statement of claim be struck out as disclosing no cause of action. Lord Denning MR, in the Court of Appeal, reviewed the authorities at length, and based counsel's immunity upon various grounds of public policy and upon long usage from which the public interest did not require a departure. The grounds of public policy to which Lord Denning adverted may be summarised as follows:[10]

(1) *Independence*—"that he may do his duty fearlessly and independently as he ought and to prevent him being harassed by vexatious actions . . . If a barrister is to be able to do his duty fearlessly and independently he must not be subject to the threat of an action for negligence."

(2) *Professional obligation to act*—"A barrister cannot pick or choose his clients. He is bound to accept a brief for any man who comes before the courts. No matter how great a rascal the man may be. No matter how given to complaining. No matter how undeserving or unpopular his cause. The barrister must defend him to the end."

(3) *Duty to the court*—"He has a duty to the court which is paramount. It is a mistake to suppose that he is the mouthpiece of his client to say what he wants; or his tool to do what he directs. He is none of these things. He owes allegiance to a higher cause. It is the cause of truth and justice . . .. He must disregard the most specific instructions of his client, if they conflict with his duty to the court."

(4) *Protraction of litigation*—"If a barrister could be sued for negligence, it would mean a retrial of the original case . . .. If this action were to be permitted, it would open the door to every disgruntled

---

7 Courts and Legal Services Act 1990. See also the statement of the General Council of the Bar, reported at LS Gazette, 28 September 1988, and summarised below.
8 See *supra*.
9 [1969] 1 AC 191; [1967] 3 All ER 993.
10 [1967] 1 QB at 501–504; [1966] 3 All ER, at 665–666.

client . . .. If this action is to go for trial, it will lead to dozens of like cases."

Although the appellant's claim was "clearly as devoid of merit as it was of any prospect of success"[11] the House of Lords gave leave to appeal in view of the importance of the question of law involved. In the event the House of Lords affirmed the decision of the Court of Appeal. While their lordships differed slightly as to the emphasis to be placed upon individual heads of public policy they concurred, in the result, in each of the above four heads adverted to by LORD DENNING in the Court of Appeal.

The House of Lords also considered, as the Court of Appeal had done, the question of whether barristers' immunity extended to work done in chambers in advising, settling documents and other matters which might never come before a court. Although the majority view of the Court of Appeal had been that the immunity did so extend the House of Lords, with the exception of LORD PEARCE who favoured the wider immunity, expressed the opinion that, while the immunity from action extended to pleadings and other work done while litigation was pending, it did not extend to advisory work or work done on documents outside the context of litigation. These opinions were, of course, no more than *obiter dicta* although of great weight. However, in *Saif Ali v Sydney Mitchell & Co*[12] the House of Lords were once again called upon to consider the scope of barristers' immunity, but this time in relation to work done in chambers in the course of litigation. The same procedure was adopted to bring the issue before the court as had been used in *Rondel v Worsley*, namely an application to strike out a pleading alleging negligence against a barrister on the ground that it disclosed no reasonable cause of action.The case went, again, to the House of Lords where the majority (LORD WILBER-FORCE, LORD DIPLOCK and LORD SALMON), in allowing the solicitors' appeal, limited the immunity to those matters of pre-trial work which were so intimately connected with the conduct of the cause in court that they could fairly be said to be preliminary decisions affecting the way that the cause was conducted when it came to a hearing. Since the barrister's advice and pleadings in the instant case had in fact prevented the plaintiff's cause from coming to court at all, it could not be said to be "intimately connected" with the conduct of the plaintiff's cause in court and was therefore not within the sphere of a barrister's immunity from actions for negligence.

The test approved was taken from a New Zealand Court of Appeal case[13] and is narrower than that which had been favoured *obiter* in *Rondel v Worsley*. The test may not, in practice, be easy to apply in subsequent cases. Thus if, for example, the negligent conduct was failure to plead a cause of action (rather than failure to join a party) the immunity would appear to apply, although it is difficult to see why the barrister should be liable in the one case and not in the other.

Other incidents of the barrister's relationship with his client which may be noted briefly are the former's obligation to preserve the latter's confidences and counsel's authority to conduct proceedings on behalf of

---

11 [1967] 1 QB at 516; [1966] 3 All ER, at 674, *per* SALMON LJ; [1969] 1 AC, at 226; [1967] 3 All ER, at 998, *per* LORD REID.
12 [1980] AC 198; [1978] 3 All ER 1033.   13 *Rees v Sinclair* [1974] 1 NZLR 180.

the client. The scope of this authority is determinable in accordance with ordinary principles of the law of agency and includes the authority to compromise proceedings on behalf of the client and the authority to make admissions on the latter's behalf in civil proceedings, though not to plead guilty in a criminal prosecution.

4   Professional conduct

The duties of solicitors towards their clients is governed both by statute and by their code of professional conduct. In the case of barristers the obligations are governed solely by self-imposed standards.[14] The rules of conduct may change from time to time and may be altered by the Bar Council.[15] In no case are the rules enforceable in any way other than by complaint to the Bar Council followed by disciplinary proceedings before a Disciplinary Tribunal which may result in the barrister being fined, disbarred or suspended from practising by his Inn of Court, appeal lying to the Visitors.

Certain important rules of conduct should be carefully noted. Perhaps the most important rule is that, subject to a few exceptional cases, counsel may accept instructions only from solicitors or other approved professional persons,[16] and not from a client direct.[17] Touting for business among solicitors is prohibited, but limited advertising must be permissible.[18] Counsel should not normally interview witnesses before or during a trial, nor should he consult with a client except in the presence of the solicitor. Note should also be taken of the "cab rank" principle, discussed earlier.[19]

F   LAW OFFICERS

The "law officers", legal advisers to the Crown, are the Attorney-General and the Solicitor-General. The Attorney-General is the head of the English Bar, though neither he nor the Solicitor-General may engage in private practice while they hold office. They are assisted by Junior Counsel to the Treasury who, holding no political office, are practising barristers.

---

14 See Code of Conduct of the Bar of England and Wales (1990).

15 See p 225, *ante.*

16 Barristers are required "to act only as consultants instructed by solicitors and other approved professional persons": 1990 Code, para 102(a)(ii). See also p 205, *ante.*

17 *Doe d Bennett v Hale* (1850) 15 QB 171. For an unsuccessful attempt to challenge this rule, see *Re T (a barrister)*, [1982] QB 430; [1981] 2 All ER 1105. In criminal cases the rule was, until 1980, subject to the exception of the "dock brief" whereby the defendant, on a trial on indictment, could instruct from the dock any barrister who was robed and sitting in court for the sum of £2.10. The dock brief became obsolete by reason of the extension of legal aid in criminal proceedings, but it may be noted that the litigation in *Rondel v Worsley (supra)* arose out of a dock brief, the plaintiff having been refused legal aid.

18 Principally limited to advertising areas of practice and expertise: see 1990 Code, para 307. A barrister must not comment to or in any news or current affairs media concerning the facts or issues arising in a particular case: para 604.

19 see p 210, *ante.*

Apart from his political duties, which include advising government departments and answering questions in the House of Commons, the Attorney-General represents the Crown in certain civil proceedings and, as a matter of practice, in trials for treason and other important offences with a political or constitutional element. In addition he exercises the prerogative power of staying prosecutions on indictment by the entry of a *nolle prosequi* and, by statute, leave of the Attorney-General is required for the commencement of certain criminal proceedings. Mention may also be made of "relator" proceedings in which the Attorney-General appears on behalf of a section of the public, for example to restrain a public nuisance.

Thus where there is a case of public nuisance, or some other interference with the public weal (not being a criminal offence) the rule is that an ordinary member of the public cannot sue; this rule is necessary in order to avoid multiplicity of actions. In such cases the Attorney-General has power to bring proceedings. His role has in one case been defined as follows:[20]

> "It is settled in our constitutional law that in matters which concern the public at large the Attorney-General is the guardian of the public interest. Although he is a member of the government of the day, it is his duty to represent the public interest with complete objectivity and detachment. He must act independently of any external pressure from whatever quarter it may come. As the guardian of the public interest, the Attorney-General has a special duty in regard to the enforcement of the law."

However, the Court of Appeal in that case suggested that there was an exception to the general rule so that, in the last resort, if the Attorney-General refused improperly or unreasonably to exercise his power to initiate proceedings, or if there was not sufficient time, a member of the public, aggrieved by non-observance of the law, could himself come to the courts and seek a declaration and, in a proper case, an injunction, joining the Attorney-General, if need be, as a defendant. This suggestion was, however, rejected firmly by the House of Lords in the important case of *Gouriet v Union of Post Office Workers*.[1] The defendant trade union had resolved to call on its members not to handle mail from this country to South Africa, in support of a political protest against apartheid policy. This action would have amounted to a criminal offence under section 58 of the Post Office Act 1953. The plaintiff applied to the Attorney-General for his consent to act as plaintiff in a relator action against the union for an injunction to restrain the union from acting as it threatened to do, and thereby breaking the law. The Attorney-General refused his consent. The plaintiff thereupon issued a writ in his own name claiming an injunction and the question at issue was whether he was entitled so to do. The Court of Appeal held that he was[2] but the House of Lords, after hearing ten days of argument, reversed the Court of Appeal's decision. The House held that it was a fundamental principle of English law that public rights could only be asserted in a civil action by the Attorney-General as an officer of the Crown representing the public and that, except where statute otherwise provided, a private person could only bring an action to restrain a

---

20 *Per* LORD DENNING MR in *A-G (ex rel McWhirter) v Independent Broadcasting Authority*, [1973] QB 629, at 646–647; [1973] 1 All ER 689, at 697; the case involved an unsuccessful attempt by the late Mr Ross McWhirter to prevent the showing of a television film about the American artist Andy Warhol.
1 [1978] AC 435; [1977] 3 All ER 70.   2 [1977] QB 729; [1977] 1 All ER 696.

threatened breach of the law if such breach would infringe his private rights or would inflict special damage on him. Moreover the refusal of the Attorney-General to give his consent to a relator action is not subject to review by the courts, any more than is the exercise by the Attorney-General of any other of the powers and duties vested in him.

Accordingly the plaintiff's action was struck out. It may be noted, however, that had the defendant union actually committed a criminal offence, the plaintiff (or any other private person) could have instituted and pursued a private prosecution – although the Attorney-General could have brought this to a halt by entering a *nolle prosequi*.

The Solicitor-General's position is basically that of the Attorney-General's deputy and he may exercise any power vested by statute in the Attorney-General (unless the statute in question otherwise provides) if the office of Attorney-General is vacant, the Attorney-General is unable to act through illness or the Attorney-General authorises the Solicitor-General to act.[3]

G   DIRECTOR OF PUBLIC PROSECUTIONS AND CROWN PROSECUTION SERVICE

The Director of Public Prosecutions is a barrister or solicitor of not less than ten years' standing appointed by the Attorney-General.[4] The Director is the head of the Crown Prosecution Service.

Up until 1985, no national system for the prosecution of offences existed, prosecutions often being handled by the police by prosecuting solicitors departments, or by solicitors acting for the police. The Director of Public Prosecutions had a supervisory and advisory role in respect of certain crimes.[5] The Royal Commission on Criminal Procedure[6] in 1980 concluded that a system of public prosecutions independent of the police was fundamental for the proper and effective functioning of the prosecution process.[7] The response of the government was the passage of the Prosecution of Offences Act 1985, which created a new Crown Prosecution Service.

Section 3 of the 1985 Act defines the duty of the Director of Public Prosecutions. It includes the following:

(a)   to take over the conduct of all criminal proceedings instituted on behalf of a police force (whether by a member of that force or some other person);

(b)   to institute and conduct criminal proceedings where the importance or difficulty of the case makes it appropriate that the Director should institute the proceedings;

(c)   to take over binding over proceedings brought by a police force;[8]

---

3 Law Officers Act 1944, s 1.
4 Prosecution of Offences Act 1979, s 1; there are also Assistant Directors, who must be barristers or solicitors of not less than seven years standing (s 1(2)).
5 For these, see Prosecution of Offences Regulations 1978, now no longer operative.
6 (1981) (Cm 8092, HMSO).
7 See ibid para 7.3.   8 See p 257, *post*.

(d) the giving of advice to police forces on all matters relating to criminal offences;

(e) to appear in certain appeals.

Thus, the Director, and the Crown Prosecution Service effectively control the prosecution process. They do not control the process of investigation. That is a matter for the police, although the Crown Prosecution Service may direct that certain enquiries be made.[9]

The Crown Prosecution Service is a national organisation, with offices in regional centres. Crown Prosecutors are legally qualified, aided by support staff, and have similar rights of audience as solicitors have. The Lord Chancellor has the power to extend these rights of audience,[10] a power viewed with some apprehension by the Bar. The powers of the Crown Prosecution Service in terms of the commencement, review and discontinuance of proceedings, and the criteria used, are each discussed in due course.[11]

Mention should also be made of the Serious Fraud Office. Created by the Criminal Justice Act 1987 to assist in the investigation and prosecution of cases of serious fraud,[12] it has wide powers that go beyond those normally available to the police and prosecuting authorities. These are discussed in due course. Its work has led to a series of high-profile prosecutions, many of which have proved unsuccessful, and raised many questions as to how the law should deal with cases of this type.

---

9 1985 Act, s 3(2)(c).
10 See p 211, *ante*.
11 See p 437, *post*.
12 Criminal Justice Act 1987, s 1.

CHAPTER 11

Legal Aid and Advice

A INTRODUCTION

Prior to 1949 there were various provisions to enable persons to sue or be sued *in forma pauperis* and to prosecute and defend both civil and criminal proceedings with the financial assistance of various societies and authorities. These provisions have now been almost totally replaced by statute. Schemes in respect of advice and assistance were introduced by the Legal Aid and Advice Act 1949, though never fully implemented,[1] and specific provision in respect of legal aid in criminal cases was made by the Criminal Justice Act 1967.[2] The aim of such schemes was to make the law accessible to all, despite lack of means. The nature of the means-tested schemes adopted, together with gaps in legal provision, inevitably meant that the impact of such schemes was partial, and was supplemented by a variety of mechanisms involving both the provision of legal advice by lawyers on a voluntary or nominal fee basis,[3] or the provision of advice and assistance by persons and organisations outside the legal profession.[4]

Responsibility for the statutory schemes of advice, and for representation in civil cases, was entrusted to The Law Society, which performed its statutory functions through area offices and committees, in consultation with the Bar and under the guidance of the Lord Chancellor. Administration of the scheme for legal assistance in criminal cases lay primarily with the magistrates' courts, and, in particular, with the justices' clerks.[5] The extent and quality of provision was considered by the Royal Commission on Legal Services,[6] which identified certain

---

1 The schemes established by the 1949 Act were based upon the reccommendations of the *Report of the Committee on Legal Aid & Advice* (The Rushcliffe Committee) (Cmd 6641, 1945, HMSO). In particular, the full scope of the scheme proposed was never implemented.

2 Implementing the recommendations of the Departmental Committee: *Legal Aid in Criminal Proceedings* (Cmnd 2934, 1966, HMSO).

3 The old "dock brief" scheme was abolished in 1980: see p 230, *ante*. For a modern example see the Free Representation Unit of the Bar.

4 Such as Trade Unions, Citizens Advice Bureaux, Welfare and Consumer Advice agencies, and Law and Legal Advice centres often funded, in whole or in part, by local authorities.

5 See p 163, *ante*.

6 (Cm 7648, 1979, HMSO). The Report of the Royal Commission on Legal Services, paras 8.15–8.38, recommended the establishment of a system of citizens' law centres, to provide

essential principles relating to the provision of legal services. These were:

(1) that there should be equal access to the courts;
(2) equal access demanded adequate legal services;
(3) financial assistance out of public funds should be available for every individual who, without it, would suffer an undue financial burden in properly pursuing or defending his rights;
(4) the standard of legal services should be the same irrespective of whether or not provided at the public expense;
(5) a free choice of available lawyer should be available to each individual.

Despite these principles, the proportions of persons eligible for state assistance for advice or representation diminished during the 1980s,[7] and the system itself was subjected to further review by the government in 1988, in a White Paper entitled *Legal Aid in England & Wales*.[8] These proposals formed the basis for the provisions of the Legal Aid Act 1988, although not without some changes.[9] The White Paper indicated that "the purpose of legal aid is to ensure that people of small or moderate means receive access to proper legal advice and justice." In an attempt to achieve that the Act establishes a Legal Aid Board, which has the "general function of securing that advice, assistance and representation are available . . ." and of administering the Act. The Board comprises no fewer than 11 and no more than 17 members, appointed in the light of their experience in, or knowledge of, the provision of legal services, the work of the court and social conditions, and of management.[10] The membership of the Board must contain at least two solicitors. Members hold office for a period not exceeding five years, and may be removed if they become unable or unfit to perform their functions, or fail to attend meetings for six consecutive months.[11]

The Board has sweeping powers. By section 4 of the 1988 Act it may do anything:

(a) which it considers necessary or desirable to provide or secure the provision of advice, assistance and representation under the Act, or
(b) which is calculated to facilitate, or is incidental or conducive to, the discharge of its functions.

Advice, assistance and representation are terms defined by the Act.[12] Each may be provided in different ways in different areas of the country, and in different ways in different fields of law.[13] Subject to the Lord Chancellor concurring, this can include the securing of advice or assistance by contracting with any body. Thus, agreements might be reached with Citizens Advice Bureaux or other information agencies, welfare rights

---

legal advice, assistance and representation to those in the locality; these recommendations have not been adopted.
7 Due to a failure to consistently upgrade the income and capital limits.
8 *Legal Aid in England and Wales – A New Framework* (Cmnd 118, HMSO, 1987).
9 Eg the functions and powers of the Legal Aid Board.
10 Legal Aid Act 1988, s 3(9).
11 *Ibid*, Sch 1.
12 *Ibid*, s 2(2)–(4).
13 *Ibid*, s 4(1).

organisations,[14] law centres, or, indeed, franchise arrangements reached with individual firms of solicitors.[14] It is also open to the board to secure legal representation in given circumstances by contract with individual firms of solicitors, a power that might be exercised in multi-party or class actions.[15]

In the exercise of its functions the Board must have regard to such matters as the Lord Chancellor may from time to time direct, and is under a duty to publish information and reports.

B   LEGAL ADVICE AND ASSISTANCE

1   Nature of advice and assistance (green form scheme)

The Legal Advice and Assistance Act 1972 introduced a completely new scheme for the giving of legal advice and assistance in relation to both civil and criminal matters. The aim of the scheme was to introduce a simple and effective method of providing legal advice and assistance so as to make these services more readily accessible to the public. The scheme, which is generally known as the "green form scheme", is now contained in the Legal Aid Act 1988. Under the scheme a solicitor, and so far as may be necessary counsel, may give oral or written advice on any question of English law and as to any steps which the applicant might appropriately take (whether by way of settling any claim, bringing or defending any proceedings, making an agreement, or other instrument or transaction, obtaining further legal or other advice or otherwise) having regard to the application of English law to his problem.[16] It may even be used to enable a solicitor to attend court to advise a litigant who is representing himself.[17] In addition, the 1979 Act added to the scheme "assistance by way of representation"[18] which means taking on a person's behalf any step in the institution or conduct of any proceedings, whether before a court or tribunal or in connection with a statutory enquiry, whether by representing him in those proceedings or otherwise. This provision is potentially of very far reaching effect because it extends the scope of legal aid to tribunals (which were, in general, outside the scope of the scheme prior to the 1979 Act). The scheme does not apply to advice or assistance given in connection with any proceedings in which there is already in existence a legal aid certificate or (in criminal proceedings) a legal aid order.[19] Regulations specify the proceedings to which the scheme applies. Under the regulations currently in operation[20] it extends to domestic proceedings in magistrates' courts, proceedings before a Mental Health Review

---

14 Section 2(6) permits advice to be given by persons other than solicitors or barristers. Section 4 authorised the contracting out of such advice services. The Legal Aid Board is currently putting into place franchise arrangements which will allow approved firms of solicitors to engage in work, and manage their work, on behalf of the Board.
15 Legal Aid Act 1988, s 4(5).
16 *Ibid*, s 2(2).
17 The solicitor is then, effectively, in a position of a "*McKenzie* friend": see p 210, *ante*.
18 Added to the scheme by Legal Aid Act 1979, s 1. See, now, Legal Aid Act 1988, s 2(3), 8(2).
19 1988 Act, s 8(5).
20 Legal Advice and Assistance (Scope) Regulations 1989 (SI 1989/550), reg 9.

Tribunal and to representation of a parent or guardian in certain child care proceedings. It has been extended to proceedings before boards of visitors of custodial institutions[1] in consequence of public disquiet as to the safeguards available to prisoners appearing before such bodies. It is also sometimes available in the county court.[2]

The normal services which are provided under the scheme comprise such matters as general advice, writing letters, negotiating settlements and the like. It does not, save in those cases to which "assistance by way of representation" applies, extend to taking any step in proceedings (other than negotiating settlement) since this is a matter for legal aid proper rather than for legal advice or assistance, nor does it cover advice from a person other than a "legal representative".[3] The 1988 Act permits[4] the scope of the scheme to be limited by regulations as to what may be undertaken, or who may undertake them. In particular conveyancing and wills are outside the scope of the scheme.[5] This is a power most likely in the future to be used to exclude types of work considered inappropriate for support under the scheme, or where advice has been provided in other ways.

2 Financial provisions

Legal advice and assistance under the scheme is available to applicants whose resources are within the limits specified in regulations made under the Act. If an applicant's disposable income and capital fall within the limits then advice, or assistance, can be given, subject where appropriate to the payment of a contribution. To calculate this, the applicant must complete a form (the "green form") which contains requirements as to details of his income and capital so that the solicitor can decide his eligibility for legal advice and assistance.[6] If he is within the financial limits the solicitor must assess the contribution (if any) to be paid by the applicant. No contribution is payable by an applicant who is in receipt of income support or family credit or has a low disposable income. Above this a contribution calculated by reference to income, but not capital, is payable. If the solicitor is properly entitled to any further charge or fee, he has a first charge upon money or property recovered (subject to exceptions) and, in relation to any further deficiency, he is entitled to be paid out of the legal aid fund, up to the cost of two hours' work,[7] in accordance with prescribed hourly rates, or in respect of assistance by way of representation, the sums agreed by the Legal Aid Board (whose approval is always sought in respect of assistance by way of representation).

The fact that the services of counsel or solicitor are given under the Act rather than under private instructions does not, of course, affect the

---

1 *Ibid*, reg 9(b).

2 Legal Advice and Assistance (Scope) Regulations 1989 (1989/340), r 8.

3 *R v Legal Aid Board, ex p Bruce* [1992] 1 All ER 133.

4 Legal Aid Act 1988, s 8(3).

5 *Ibid*, regs 3, 4.

6 Legal Advice and Assistance Regulations 1989, r 8(3). The 1989 regulations specify £61 per week as the disposable income limit, and £1,000 as that for disposable capital (or £3,000 for assistance by way of representation).

7 *Ibid*, r 4(c). The figure in divorce is three.

professional relationship and duties which spring from the relationship.[8] The solicitor must exercise the same degree of care and skill in giving advice as he would normally and he must preserve the applicant's confidence[9] (except that he must complete and forward to the legal aid office the appropriate forms and must give to the legal aid authority any additional information that it may require).

3   Criminal cases

Given the fact that in criminal cases a person's liberty is at stake, or has already been curtailed by police action, the importance of availability of advice and assistance in criminal cases is undoubted. Section 1 of the Legal Aid Act 1982 authorised the creation of a scheme for the provision of advice and representation by solicitors in attendance at magistrates' courts, and at police stations. The matter is now governed by the 1988 Act, and regulations made thereunder.

The relevant regulations[10] make provision for the giving of advice to suspects at police stations. Rotas are drawn up, and ensure that a solicitor will be available to attend a police station to advise a person in custody.[11] A solicitor is also available at a magistrates' court to offer assistance by way of representation for the purposes of a bail application, plea in mitigation (where the case is to be dealt with forthwith) or other immediate application to the court. The right does not extend to a person who has already received such assistance, or who has instructed a solicitor privately. Where such advice is given, the provision of advice, or assistance, is not subject to means or to the payment of a contribution.

C   LEGAL AID IN CIVIL PROCEEDINGS

1   Courts and proceedings in which legal aid is authorised by the Act

Legal aid is now available in connection with proceedings (unless specifically excepted) in the House of Lords, the Court of Appeal, the High Court, the Employment Appeal Tribunal, any county court, coroners' courts, proceedings in the Restrictive Practices Court under Part III of the Fair Trading Act 1973, and proceedings in the Lands Tribunal. It is also available in certain proceedings in magistrates' courts, notably proceedings under the Domestic Proceedings and Magistrates' Courts Act 1978, the Guardianship of Minors Acts 1971 and 1973 and in certain proceedings under the Children Act 1989.

There are, however, excepted proceedings in respect of which aid is not, at present, authorised under the Act. Of these the more important are proceedings wholly or partly in respect of defamation,[12] and undefended

---

8 See p 218, *ante*.

9 Legal Aid Act 1988, s 31(1). Note that legal representatives may disclose to the Legal Aid Board, or a person acting on the Board's authority, information relating to the case of clients or former clients who are, or were, legally aided: Legal Aid (Disclosure of Information) Regulations 1991 (SI 1991/1753).

10 Legal Advice and Assistance (Scope) Regulations 1989 (SI 1989/340), r 7. See Duty Solicitor Arrangements 1990.

11 See, further, p 269, *post*.

12 Legal Aid Act 1988, Sch 2, Part II, para 1.

matrimonial proceedings (that is to say proceedings for divorce or judicial separation).[13] Where a legal aid order is made for the purpose of proceedings, that order extends to the costs of a reference to the European Court of Justice[14] since the reference to that court is simply a step in the proceedings in which it is made.[15]

Legal aid is not available in proceedings before judicial and administrative tribunals, which most people[16] consider a notable omission in view of the increasing volume, and importance, of business dealt with therein, particularly in industrial tribunals. It is for this reason that the provisions described above for assistance by way of representation are potentially so important. Nor, of course, is legal aid available in arbitrations. This may seem to confer a considerable benefit upon defendants (especially where they have insurers behind them) who can invoke an arbitration clause thereby preventing an impecunious plaintiff from pursuing his rights with proper legal representation. The mere fact that the plaintiff is insolvent does not prevent the defendant from obtaining a stay,[17] although if it appears that his insolvency was caused by the defendant's breaches of contract a stay may be refused[18] (with the result that the action will proceed and the plaintiff may apply for legal aid).

2 Conditions under which aid may be granted

Any person, not being a body corporate or an unincorporated body,[19] may apply for legal aid irrespective of nationality or residence. He must, however, be within the prescribed financial limits, this being the first condition precedent to the grant of legal aid. His "disposable income" must not exceed the specified limit. Disposable income and disposable capital are assessed by the assessment officer of the Benefits Agency in the light of the Legal Aid (Assessment of Resources) Regulations 1989 as amended. These regulations are complex. It is important to note that disposable income[20] is far less than gross income. Deductions are prescribed in respect of the maintenance of dependents, income tax, interest on loans, rent and other matters. A spouse's resources are, as a rule, treated as the applicant's resources for these purposes, and regard may also be had to property of which the applicant has disposed.[1] A common criticism of the disposable capital limit is that it tends to penalise those who have been prudent enough to accumulate modest savings. The Royal Commission on Legal Services, among several recommendations concerning legal aid, advice and assistance, stated that the underlying principle should be that an assisted person "should not

---

13 See Civil Legal Aid (Matrimonial Proceedings) Regulations 1989 (SI 1989/549).
14 See p 111, *ante*.
15 *R v Marlborough Street Stipendiary Magistrate, ex parte Bouchereau* [1977] 3 All ER 365; [1977] 1 WLR 414.
16 For criticism of the current position, see Farmer, *Tribunals and Inquiries*.
17 *Smith v Pearl Assurance Co Ltd* [1939] 1 All ER 95.
18 *Fakes v Taylor Woodrow Construction Ltd* [1973] QB 436; [1973] 1 All ER 670.
19 Legal Aid Act 1988, s 2(10).
20 Receipts are "income" only if they have an element of recurrence so that ad hoc gifts are not income: *R v Supplementary Benefits Commission, ex parte Singer* [1973] 2 All ER 931; [1973] 1 WLR 713.
1 Civil Legal Aid (Assessment of Resources) Regulations 1989 (SI 1989/338), r 9.

suffer an undue financial burden in pursuing his legal rights",[2] that the eligibility limits be abolished, that the free limit of disposable income and capital should be increased, and that the contribution proportion above the free limits be reduced to one-fifth. This approach has not, generally, been adopted.

The second condition precedent to a grant of legal aid is that the applicant must show that he has reasonable grounds for taking, defending or being a party to the proceedings.[3] In particular a certificate will not be granted in respect of proceedings at first instance where it appears to the Board that the proceedings are too trivial or simple to warrant the assistance of a solicitor, that the applicant would gain only a trivial advantage from the proceedings, that the applicant could finance the proceedings from another source, or the applicant is a member of an organisation which might help him.[4]

If a certificate is granted it may be marked with a contribution payable by the assisted litigant. The maximum contribution in proceedings is all the assisted person's disposable capital above a prescribed figure and one-quarter of the amount by which his annual disposable income exceeds a prescribed figure.[5]

3 Application for a certificate

An application for a legal aid certificate must be made on one of the forms approved for the purpose. It may include an application for an "emergency certificate", which may be granted where delay would cause a risk of miscarriage of justice or an unreasonable degree of hardship or other problems in the handling of the case; emergency certificates will usually authorise only the taking of immediate steps in order to protect the interests of the applicant. Some time will usually elapse between the making of an application and its determination, this time being mainly attributable to the financial assessment, usually based on interview, which is undertaken by the legal aid assessment officers of the Department of Social Security. The area legal aid director office may grant a certificate, although only the area committee can refuse an application.[6]

Assuming that the applicant's means qualify him for legal aid, he must still satisfy other criteria before a certificate will be granted.[7] In particular he must be regarded as having a reasonable case on its merits (for which purpose the opinion of counsel is often required). The certificate may be, and often is, limited to the taking of certain steps in the action. Thus, in the first instance it is frequently limited to the taking of counsel's opinion, on the basis of which the Legal Aid Board will consider whether to amend the certificate so as to extend it to enable further steps to be taken in the action or, on the contrary, to discharge it. By these powers of amendment and

---

2 Report, para 12.28.
3 Civil Legal Aid (General) Regulations 1989 (SI 1989/339), reg 15(2),(3).
4 *Ibid*, rr 29, 30.
5 Legal Aid Act 1988, s 9(1). The figures are regularly varied by regulations under section 9, cf Civil Legal Aid (Assessment of Resources) Regulations 1989 (SI 1989/388).
6 Civil Legal Aid (General) Regulations, r 38(1)(a),(b).
7 See p 239, *ante*.

discharge it is possible for the Legal Aid Board to supervise the conduct of the litigation to some extent, or at least to see, as far as possible, that large amounts of costs are not expended in pursuing hopeless lost causes. There is, of course, a duty on both solicitors and counsel to advise against the pursuit of cases which do not justify the support of the legal aid fund.

4 The effects on the proceedings of a party being aided

a Relationship between the assisted litigant and his solicitor and counsel

The professional relationship of solicitor and client is not prejudiced by the fact of the client being in receipt of legal aid. The solicitor's general duties are still owed to the client and he has authority to act for the client, unless the act performed is not within the scope of the certificate. Thus it has been held[8] that a solicitor is under a duty not to instruct leading counsel, even though authorised by the legal aid authority so to do, without first obtaining the client's specific agreement and authority after informing him of the probable cost and the potential effect upon the client's assets having regard to the Board's charge on property recovered or preserved in the action (as to which see *infra*). The solicitor must preserve his client's confidences though he is in some cases obliged to furnish information to the legal aid committees which would normally be privileged.

The chief effect of legal aid on the solicitor-client relationship is upon costs. The solicitor has no right to any costs from the client and he must not charge or take any sum in respect of costs. It follows that any item of costs incurred by a solicitor which is not allowed under the legal aid order is irrecoverable so that a disbursement of this nature will have to be met by the solicitor personally. In most proceedings the court must order the assisted person's costs to be taxed, on a "standard" basis.[9]

After taxation the solicitor may recover from the fund the full amount allowed on taxation for disbursements and profit costs.[10] The relevant factors to be taken into account are discussed later.[11]. However taxation is not necessary where an assisted litigant is successful and the costs payable by the other party are agreed with the assisted party's solicitor and counsel (if any).[12]

b Assisted litigant's liability for costs

An assisted person has, as stated above, no liability for costs towards his own solicitor and counsel. His primary liability to the legal aid fund is limited to the amount of his contribution. However, if he loses his action he may be ordered to pay the costs of the other side. This does not mean that he must pay the full taxed costs of his opponent. His liabilities are limited to such amount (if any) which is a reasonable one for him to pay,

---

8 *Re Solicitors* [1982] 2 All ER 683; [1982] 1 WLR 745.
9 See Civil Legal Aid (General) Regulations 1989 (1989/339), reg 105, and p 383, *post.*
10 See, generally, *ibid*, regs 105, 107.
11 See p 383, *post.*
12 For remuneration agreements, see p 222, *ante.*

having regard to the means of all the parties and their conduct in connection with the dispute.[13] In determining this amount, the assisted person's dwelling house, household furniture and tools and implements of his trade are not to be taken into account.[14] In addition the order may direct payment by instalments or may suspend payment *sine die*. The order may, however, be varied within six years if circumstances change.

An assisted person cannot be required by the court to pay the costs of an unsuccessful interlocutory application forthwith.[15] Also, an assisted person is not usually ordered to give security for costs although such an order can be, and has been, made.[16]

If the assisted litigant is awarded costs, these are payable by his opponent in the ordinary way. These costs are paid directly into the legal aid fund maintained by the Board. If the sums paid out by the Board to the assisted person's solicitor and counsel exceed the amount paid in, comprising the assisted person's contribution and costs recovered from the other side, the Board has a first charge for the balance on any property recovered or preserved in the proceedings, with certain exemptions, notably maintenance in matrimonial proceedings.[17] Thus if an assisted person is successful the public will not (unless the other side is also legally aided) generally be the loser, which is the reason for the public cost of the legal aid scheme being relatively so low.

c   Unassisted person's rights to costs

It follows from the preceding paragraph that the unassisted litigant appearing against an assisted litigant is at a substantial disadvantage in the matter of costs. If he loses he pays full costs; if he wins he recovers only limited costs, or, as often as not, no costs at all. It was to remedy this serious abuse that the Legal Aid Act 1964 was passed. This Act (the relevant provisions of which are now contained in sections 13 and 18 of the 1988 Act) was at first interpreted and applied by the courts in a very restrictive manner,[18] so much so that over the period of three years after the passing of the Act, Parliament provided no less than £120,000 for the purposes of the Act, of which only £1,155 was used. However, in *Hanning v Maitland (No 2)*[19] the Court of Appeal laid down broader principles for the application of the Act, stating that if the legally aided party lost the action it was usually just and equitable that the unassisted party should recover his costs from public funds, unless, for example, he has done something to bring the action on himself or has been guilty of misconduct.

The 1988 Act now provides that an unassisted party appearing against an assisted party may be awarded the whole or any part of his costs out of the legal aid fund, provided that the proceedings are finally decided in favour of the unassisted party,[20] that those proceedings were instituted by the

---

13 Legal Aid Act 1988, ss 12, 17(1).

14 *Ibid*, s 17(3), and General Regulations (*supra*, n 9) reg 126a.

15 *Ibid*, reg 124.

16 *Wyld v Silver (No 2)* [1962] 2 All ER 809; [1962] 1 WLR 863.

17 1988 Act, s 16(6).

18 See *Nowotnik v Nowotnik* [1967] P 83; [1965] 3 All ER 167; *Re Spurling's Will Trusts* [1966] 1 All ER 745; [1966] 1 WLR 920; *Re SL (infants)* [1967] 3 All ER 538; [1967] 1 WLR 1379.

19 [1970] 1 QB 580; [1970] 1 All ER 812.   20 Legal Aid Act 1988, ss 13, 18.

assisted party in the court of first instance and provided "the court is satisfied that the unassisted party will suffer severe financial hardship unless the order is made".[1] "Severe financial hardship" is not, however, strictly interpreted so that in *Hanning v Maitland (No 2)*, LORD DENNING MR stated that the condition should not be construed so as to exclude people of modest income or modest capital who would find it hard to bear their own costs. A company may suffer "severe financial hardship".[2] Furthermore no order is to be made unless an order in favour of the unassisted party would be made apart from this Act; thus, in divorce suits a wife is not usually ordered to pay her husband's costs, unless she has sufficient separate estate. If an assisted wife would not be required to pay her unassisted husband's costs, the latter has no recourse to the fund.[3]

Apart from the above provisions, which affect costs, proceedings are not generally affected by one or more of the parties being legally aided. Indeed proceedings may be lengthened since litigants are naturally not anxious to compromise proceedings which they are fighting at the public expense. This is one of the principal criticisms of the scheme to which may be added the fact that legal aid is not available before most tribunals and the inequitable position of the unassisted litigant, particularly where he is a plaintiff (and therefore at any rate at first instance, outside the scope of the provisions for payment of his costs out of the fund). For this reason insurance companies in industrial injuries actions often make payments in settlement of unmeritorious claims by legally aided plaintiffs, simply because, in the long run, this will prove a less expensive expedient than contesting the case successfully. There is a further anomaly in that a successful assisted litigant appearing against another assisted litigant may well find himself in a worse position than if he were unassisted since an assisted party cannot obtain an order against the fund, whereas the property he recovers will be subject to the Legal Aid Board's statutory charge.

D   LEGAL AID IN CRIMINAL PROCEEDINGS

Legal aid in criminal cases is granted by the court. In contrast to civil proceedings, the order is made by the court. Either the court of trial or the magistrates' court committing a case for trial may grant legal aid, as may either the Court of Appeal (Criminal Division) or the Crown Court in dealing with an appeal.[4]

In most cases the grant of legal aid is discretionary.[5] The test to be

---

1 *Ibid.* The party will be entitled only to payment of that amount which would cause him hardship not to recover: see *Adams v Riley* [1988] QB 372; [1988] 1 All ER 89.

2 *R & T Thew Ltd v Reeves* [1982] QB 172; [1981] 2 All ER 964; in *Kelly v London Transport Executive (supra)* the Court of Appeal, with apparent reluctance, felt unable to accede to the defendants' bold contention that the loss of £8,000 in costs would amount to severe financial hardship. For the position of a local authority, see *R v Greenwich London Borough Council, ex parte Lovelace (No 2)* [1992] QB 155; [1992] 1 All ER 679 (no reason why local authority should not establish "severe hardship").

3 *Povey v Povey* [1972] Fam 40; [1970] 3 All ER 612.

4 Legal Aid Act 1988, ss 20(3), (6).

5 But a grant is compulsory if an application is made when a person has been committed for trial on a charge of murder, where the prosecution are appealing (or apply for leave to

applied is that is should appear to the court "to be desirable to do so in the interests of justice". In deciding that question, the court will have regard to certain factors:[6]

(1) whether, in the event of conviction, it is likely that the court would impose a sentence which would either deprive the accused of his liberty, or lead to loss of his livelihood, or seriously damage his reputation;

(2) whether the case may involve consideration of a substantial question of law;

(3) whether the accused may be unable to understand the proceedings or state his own case, either through lack of knowledge of English or through mental or physical disability;

(4) whether the nature of the defence is such as to involve the tracing and interviewing of potential defence witnesses or expert cross-examination of the prosecution witnesses; and

(5) whether it is in the interests of a person other than the accused that the accused should be represented.

Whilst any doubt should be resolved in favour of the accused,[7] it is clear that these criteria give considerable discretion to the deciding court.

Given the different time scale within which the criminal process works, any assessment of resources or contribution by the accused may take place after an order has been made. However a court, before it makes a legal aid order, must require the applicant to furnish a written statement of means and, if it appears from this statement that he will be required to make a contribution and has the means to make an immediate payment, may refuse an order unless the applicant first makes a payment on account.[8] In magistrates' courts the application is initially dealt with by the clerk to the justices. If he refuses legal aid, appeal may be to an area committee if the offence is triable on indictment or "either way"[9] or to the justices themselves in the case of summary offences. The legal aid order will be a "through" order which covers the Crown Court as well as the committal proceedings.[10] As well as hearing appeals from refusals of legal aid by a magistrates' court, criminal legal aid committees deal with two other matters; firstly, where there is an application to a magistrates' court for the assignment of counsel in proceedings in that court under a legal aid order the court, if it does not grant the application, must refer it to the committee; secondly, applications by solicitors for prior authority to incur expenditure on obtaining an expert's or other report, bespeaking transcripts of shorthand notes or tape recordings of any proceedings or "performing an act which is either unusual in its nature or involves unusually large expenditure" must be made direct to the committee.[11]

---

appeal) to the House of Lords, where a person is at risk of being remanded in custody for a second time and wishes representation, and where a person is kept in custody for the preparation of reports (1988 Act, s 21(3)).

6 Legal Aid Act 1988, s 22(2).

7 *Ibid*, s 21(7).   8 Ibid, s 24(1).

9 See p 447, *post.*

10 1988 Act, s 20(5).

11 Legal Aid in Criminal and Care Proceedings (General) Regulations 1989 (1989/344), reg 44(1).

As a rule legal aid consists of representation by a solicitor and counsel and includes advice on the preparation of the accused's case. However in magistrates' courts legal aid does not extend to representation by counsel except in the case of an unusually grave or difficult indictable offence, while in certain cases there is power to order legal aid to consist of representation by counsel only.[12]

An assisted person may be ordered by the court to pay such contribution as appears reasonable, having regard to his commitments and resources. A contribution may be ordered to be paid by instalments. If the assisted person fails to pay any contribution, or any instalment thereof, this may be recovered in a magistrates' court as a civil debt or enforced as a judgment debt in the High Court or a county court.[13]

---

12 *Ibid*, reg 44(1).
13 1988 Act, Sch 3, para 1.

CHAPTER 12

The Police and Law Enforcement[1]

A   THE LAW ENFORCEMENT FUNCTION

Law enforcement is primarily, but not exclusively, in the hands of the 43 police forces of England and Wales. Whilst individuals have both rights and duties in respect of law enforcement and keeping the peace, it would be idle to pretend that a police constable is simply "a citizen in uniform". Every police officer holds the office of constable,[2] and legal authority may stem from that fact, but the reality is that police officers form part of an organisation with its own command structure, and are governed by detailed regulations dealing with conditions of employment, personal conduct and discipline.[3]

Other organisations play a role in law enforcement. Besides the police forces that exist under the Police Act 1964, there are specialist police forces such as the Ministry of Defence Police, and British Transport Police. Officers of such forces likewise hold the office of constable.[4] Nor should the role of other investigatory agencies be overlooked. The Serious Fraud Office was created by the Criminal Justice Act 1987 to "investigate any suspected offence which appears . . . on reasonable grounds to involve serious or complex fraud." The Director of the Serious Fraud Office is given wide ranging legal powers to assist in the investigation and prosecution of such offences.[5] Likewise the Department of Trade and Industry has wide-ranging investigative powers under the Companies Acts. Other

---

1 The literature on the police is extensive. See, in particular, Royal Commission on Criminal Procedure, 1981, Cmnd 8092, and the various research studies undertaken (set out at Annex D to the Report). For the current law, see Bevan and Lidstone, *A Guide to Police Powers* (1991, Butterworths). For the police more generally see Lustgarten, *The Governance of Police* (1986, Sweet & Maxwell).

2 Police Act 1964, s 18.

3 Police Regulations 1987 (SI 1987/851); Police (Discipline) Regulations 1985 (SI 1985/1805).

4 See *Halsbury's Laws*, (4th edn), paras 211–219.

5 The extension of these powers has been controversial. See *Smith v Director of Serious Fraud Office* [1992] 3 All ER 456.

bodies such as the Inland Revenue, Customs & Excise,[6] Health and Safety Executive and local authorities have investigative powers of importance. Nevertheless it is the police who perform the bulk of investigatory and law enforcement work. On occasions that may be with the assistance of the armed forces. They are, however, acting in aid of the civil power, and have no special legal rights.[7]

1 The role of the individual

All individuals have a duty to preserve the peace, though this is a duty of "imperfect obligation"[8] in the sense that, generally, there is no sanction for breach of that duty. A citizen who without physical impossibility or lawful excuse fails to assist a constable to restore the peace when that constable has reasonable necessity for calling on that citizen for assistance is guilty of an offence at common law.[9] The duty, though, goes further. In *Albert v Lavin*[10] LORD DIPLOCK stated:

> ". . . every citizen in whose presence a breach of the peace is being, or reasonably appears to be about to be, committed has the right to take reasonable steps to make the person who is breaking or threatening to break the peace refrain from doing so; and those reasonable steps in appropriate cases will include detaining him against his will . . ."

An individual is not liable in law for failure to preserve the peace in this way. By contrast, a constable may be guilty of the offence of misconduct in a public office.[11] A citizen also has more limited powers of arrest than a constable in respect of arrestable offences which are in fact occurring, or where there are reasonable grounds to believe that they have occurred.[12] It is these powers that are used by so-called "store detectives", who are, in reality, no more than citizens relying on their individual rights under law.

Apart from the above, a citizen has, generally, no duty to assist the police. The law proceeds also on the basis of a "right to silence" of an individual. Generally, there is no obligation to answer police questions or to co-operate with the police, though there is certainly a duty not to mislead.[13] Occasionally, the exercise of the right to silence in an abusive way may come close to criminal conduct.[14]

---

6 For discussion of the powers of the Revenue Departments, see the Keith Report: *Enforcement Powers of the Revenue Departments* (1985, Cmnd 8822/9120/9440, HMSO).
7 *Charge to the Bristol Grand Jury* (1832) 172 ER 962; *A-G for Northern Ireland's Reference (No 1 of 1975)* [1977] AC 105; [1976] 2 All ER 937.
8 *Per* Lord Diplock in *Albert v Lavin*, n 10 below.
9 *R v Brown* (1841) Car & M 314; 174 ER 522.
10 [1982] AC 546; [1981] 3 All ER 878.
11 *R v Dytham* [1979] QB 722; [1979] 3 All ER 641.
12 See s 24 of the Police and Criminal Evidence Act 1984, and p 261, *post.*
13 *Rice v Connolly* [1966] 2 QB 414; [1966] 2 All ER 649.
14 *Ricketts v Cox* (1981) 74 Cr App Rep 298; *Green v Director of Public Prosecutions* (1991) 155 JP 816.

2   The organisation of the police

Police structures were radically changed by the Police Act 1964.[15] The Act reflects the historical basis of policing, which has essentially always been organised around local structures. Policing arrangements are, for the most part, on a local basis, with theoretical local autonomy, though this is sometimes challenged by calls for larger police organisations. Different policing arrangements exist for the Metropolis of London from the rest of England and Wales. In England and Wales, outside the Metropolis, a police authority has authority for the policing in its area. The police authority is generally a committee of the county council, but control is vested in a Chief Constable. By contrast in the Metropolis a Commissioner of Police acts in the role of Chief Constable, and the Home Secretary fulfils the function of police authority, answerable to Parliament.

The extent to which these formal arrangements are adequate has been keenly debated in recent years. Some argue that direct local accountability is desirable. The special arrangements for London have likewise been criticised. Historically they have been justified in the light of the function of London as the capital city with special responsibilities for royal, diplomatic and parliamentary protection as well as the ceremonial functions of state. The degree of local accountability in London is less than elsewhere.[16] Such attempts to "democratise" police structures have been rejected. Instead, section 106 of the Police and Criminal Evidence Act 1984 provides that:

> ". . . arrangements shall be made in each police area for obtaining the view of people in that area concerning the policing of that area and for obtaining their co-operation with the police in preventing crime in the area."[17]

The duty of the police authority is "to secure the maintenance of an adequate and efficient police force for its area . . .".[18] To achieve that the authority is required, subject to the approval of the Home Secretary, to appoint a Chief Constable and to determine the number of persons of each rank in that force.[19] It may, again with the consent of the Home Secretary, provide and maintain such buildings, structures and premises as may be required for such purposes. Vehicles, apparatus, clothing and other equipment may be provided and maintained for policing purposes.[20] This local autonomy vested in police authorities is not, however, quite what it seems.

---

15 Passed to implement the Report of the Royal Commission on the Police (1962, Cmnd 1728). For discussion of this, and of the historical development, see Lustgarten, *op cit*, pp 32–52.

16 For general comment, see Hewitt, *The Abuse of Power* (1982, Martin Robertson).

17 For alternative possibilities, see Police Act (Northern Ireland) 1970, commented upon by Dickson (1988, 39 NILQ) and Walker (1990, 41 NILQ 105).

18 Police Act 1964, s 4.

19 *Ibid*, s 4(2).

20 Section 41 of the Police Act 1964. For challenge to the power of the Home Secretary to supply such equipment at the request of a Chief Constable, but without the agreement of or request from the police authority, see *R v Secretary of State for Home Department, ex parte Northumbria Police Authority* [1989] QB 26; [1988] 1 All ER 556, Such action was held to be lawful under s 41 of the Police Act 1964, and by virtue of the royal prerogative.

a Police authorities and central government

The key role of the Home Secretary in approving the appointment of Chief Constables has already been seen. Approval is also required for the removal of a Chief Constable.[1] Nor are the rights of the authority in respect of information unfettered. A Chief Constable who is unwilling to disclose information in a report requested by the police authority may refer the request to the Secretary of State for decision.[2] In addition, the Home Secretary can, where it is expedient in the interests of justice, safety or public order that a police force be reinforced, direct that such re-inforcement or other assistance be given to enable that force to meet special demands on its resources.[3] That can be done on the application of the Chief Constable, and does not require the agreement of the police authority.

The Home Secretary has a wide range of powers under the Police Act 1964, which are to be exercised "in such manner and to such extent as appears to him to be best calculated to promote the efficiency of the police".[4] The compulsory retirement of a Chief Constable in the interests of efficiency can be required.[5] So too can reports on policing matters, as well as the Annual Report. An inquiry into any matter connected with the policing of any area can be called for.[6] It is to the Home Secretary that the Inspectorate of Constabulary report. Adverse comment and report may lead to the withholding of the whole or part of central government grant. That this is no trivial threat is demonstrated by the fact that some 50 per cent of all police expenditure is met by central government. The threat to withhold grant is a powerful one, and can be used as a lever to secure change in the way a force is run.[7]

In addition to this range of statutory powers, the existence of the royal prerogative should not be ignored. The prerogative allows all reasonably necessary steps to be taken to ensure the preservation of the Queen's peace. In *R v Secretary of State for the Home Department, ex parte Northumbria Police Authority*[8] the Court of Appeal ruled that section 41 of the Police Act 1964 (which authorises the Secretary of State to provide and maintain central services and other services deemed expedient for promoting the efficiency of the police) authorised the Home Secretary to supply riot control equipment from central stores without the approval of the police authority. Even if section 41 were not to be construed in this way, the action of the Home Secretary would be lawful under the prerogative. Effectively, therefore, the police authority was by-passed, its approval neither forthcoming nor necessary.

It would also be wrong to view police authorities as acting always in isolation. Chief constables can seek mutual aid from other forces. Regional

---

1 Police Act 1964, s 5(5).
2 *Ibid*, s 12(3).
3 *Ibid*, s 14(2).
4 *Ibid*, s 28.
5 *Ibid*, s 29(1).
6 *Ibid*, s 30(1).
7 Since in addition local authority expenditure will be supported by rate support grant, the actual percentage in reality will be higher. In 1992, adverse reports by the Inspectorate of Constabulary upon the Derbyshire Police led to significant changes in the running of that force.
8 [1989] QB 26; [1988] 1 All ER 556

organisations have from time to time been created, both formally (eg the anti-terrorism squad, regional crime squads) and informally. An instance of the latter was the existence of the National Reporting Centre during a controversial industrial dispute in the mid 1980s.[9] A national police force has, thus far, been rejected in England and Wales.[10] Critics point to the centralising nature of such arrangements, and to the danger of an element of political influence or control of the policing process. It is important that the policing function be seen to be independent of the political process, and it is in that context that the relationship between police authority and chief constable is fundamental.

b   Police authorities and Chief Constables

Chief Constables have a wide degree of autonomy. Despite the terms of section 106 of the 1984 Act[11] the degree of local influence on Chief Constables is limited. Police authorities have the right to require a report in writing on such matters as may be specified, being matters connected with the policing of their area.[12] That is, though, subject to the Chief Constable's right to refer the request to the Home Secretary if the Chief Constable considers that a report would contain information which ought not, in the public interest, to be disclosed. In addition, a wise Chief Constable will no doubt be at pains to create good working relations with the police authority. Nevertheless, its legal rights are limited. It sets the establishment, and the budget, but, as has been seen, it may be liable for expenditure over which it has no control.

It is sometimes said that Chief Constables cannot be challenged on operational matters. That is an over-simplification. The law recognises that it is the Chief Constable who determines strategy and decision-making. The courts have regarded the scope for judicial review of the actions of a Chief Constable to be extremely limited. The deployment of police resources, and individual policing decisions, are matters not for the courts. In *R v Commissioner of Police for the Metropolis, ex parte Blackburn*,[13] the Court of Appeal was considering an application for an order of mandamus to compel the Commissioner to reverse a policy statement which directed his officers not to enforce the Gaming Acts, except in certain circumstances. Lord Denning MR stated:

> "I hold it to be the duty of [the Commissioner] as it is of every Chief Constable, to enforce the law of the land. He must take steps so to post his men that crimes must be detected; and that honest citizens may go about their affairs in peace. He must decide whether or not suspected persons are to be prosecuted; and if need be bring the prosecution or see that it is brought. But in all these things he is not the servant of anyone, save of the law itself. No Minister of the Crown can tell him that he must, or must not, prosecute this man or that one. Nor can any police authority tell him to do so. The

---

9 The national strike in the coal industry in 1980. For comment on the legal issues, see Freeman 'Law and Order in 1984' [1984] CLP 175.

10 Calls for national provision are made from time to time. See the calls for national units to fight crime and terrorism: The Times, 22 July 1992.

11 Section 106 of the Police and Criminal Evidence Act 1984, which provides for the making of arrangements in each police area to obtain the views of the people of that area.

12 Police Act 1964, s 12(2).

13 [1968] 2 QB 118; [1968] 1 All ER 763.

responsibility for law enforcement lies on him. He is answerable to the law and to the law alone . . . [but] there are many fields in which they have a discretion with which the law will not interfere . . . it is [for him] to decide in any particular case whether inquiries should be pursued, or whether an arrest should be made . . . It must be for him to decide on the disposition of his force and the concentration of his resources on any particular crime or area. No court can or should give him direction on such a matter . . ."

The court went on to stress, however, that if what was in issue was, in effect, an abdication of duty then the court could intervene. The matter was not put to the test because the policy statement was withdrawn. Again, in *Holgate-Mohammed v Duke*[14] whilst the House of Lords accepted that police discretion could be the subject of judicial review, provided it was used for a legitimate purpose its use was for the individual officer, not the courts.

These cases, and others like them,[15] do not strictly speaking deal with the relationship between Chief Constable and police authority. Nor is the distinction between operational and non-operational matters set out in those terms. Yet both are implicit from the approach set out above. The courts will concern themselves with issues of legality. That includes not only the existence of the power itself, but also review of police discretion on normal judicial review grounds. Thus if a Chief Constable were to abdicate the exercise of a statutory function, close his mind to the genuine exercise of discretion, or use powers for irrelevant or improper purposes, or in bad faith, the courts could intervene. Within these parameters they will not, even at the instance of the police authority.

c Chief Constables and individual officers

Police power essentially derives from the office of constable. Section 19 of the Police Act 1964 provides that a member of a police force shall have all the powers and privileges of a constable throughout England and Wales. Constables are office holders under the Crown, though not Crown servants.[16] They are not employees of the local authority[17] nor of the Chief Constable. The consequence of all this is that the powers are those of the constable, although sometimes powers can only be exercised by a police officer holding a certain rank. Thus, an intimate search of a suspect requires authorisation by an officer at least the rank of superintendent.[18] Nor can the officer legally be directed to exercise power in a particular way. Whilst the reality is that a police force will have policing policies and instructions, to which the officer is entitled to have regard, the legal powers are those of the officer. In *Lindley v Rutter*[19] a police officer was held to be acting unlawfully by removing an item of underclothing from a drunken arrested woman. Though power existed at common law to justify such conduct, the officer had, wrongly, regarded a standing instruction as

14 [1984] AC 437; [1984] 1 All ER 1054.
15 See also *R v Commissioner of Police for the Metropolis, ex parte Blackburn (No 3)* [1973] QB 241; [1973] 1 All ER 324; *R v Chief Constable for Devon & Cornwall, ex parte Central Electricity Generating Board* [1982] QB 458; [1981] 3 All ER 826.
16 *A-G for New South Wales v Perpetual Trustee Co Ltd* [1955] AC 457; [1955] 1 All ER 846.
17 *Fisher v Oldham Corporation* [1930] 2 KB 364; [1930] All ER Rep 96.
18 Section 62 of the Police and Criminal Evidence Act 1984.
19 [1981] QB 128; [1980] 3 WLR 660.

depriving her of any discretion as to whether or not such garments were to be removed from a suspect. She did not therefore address her mind as to whether the legal conditions for the exercise of the power existed.

That is not to say that it is always improper to rely on a standing instruction.[20] The reality is different. Individual officers are members of a force hierarchical in nature, and subject to the rules, regulations and discipline of that force. The Chief Constable will set out standing orders and other force policy, compliance with which will be expected. Failure to comply with police discipline will be an offence.[1]

B   POLICE ACCOUNTABILITY

The extent to which Chief Constables are accountable to either police authorities or to the Home Secretary has already been discussed. In reality accountability of the police will be through a variety of other mechanisms.

1   Rules of evidence

English courts adhere to the principle that it is no part of the courts' task to exclude evidence in order to punish the police. In *R v Leatham* CROMPTON J observed that:

> "It matters not how you get it; if you steal it even, it would be admissible."[2]

However, in criminal cases there is a discretion under section 78 of the Police and Criminal Evidence Act 1984 to exclude evidence where to admit it would create unfairness to the proceedings.[3] The use of this discretion has meant that where police impropriety has led to potential unfairness in the proceedings then evidence may well be excluded. For this reason, failure to comply with the Codes of Practice which govern the exercise of police powers, or with the provisions of the law itself, have often led to the exclusion of evidence obtained by the police improperly.[4]

2   Criminal proceedings

Certain police misconduct may amount to a criminal offence. Thus, offences of perjury, or conspiracy to pervert the administration of justice are from time to time identified.[5] More commonly the legality of police conduct may be tested in a prosecution brought under section 51 of the Police Act 1964. This section makes it an offence to assault, or to resist or

---

20 Compare *Middleweek v Chief Constable of Merseyside* [1992] 1 AC 179n; [1990] 3 All ER 662.
 1 See Police (Discipline) Regulations 1985 (SI 1985/1805).
 2 (1861) 8 Cox CC498; 121 ER 589.
 3 Even in the use of discretion under s 78 of the Police and Criminal Evidence Act the courts have disclaimed any intention of using powers to discipline the police; see: *R v Parris* (1988) 89 Cr App Rep 68. This in reality may be the effect; see Birch at [1989] Crim LR 95.
 4 See p 556, *post*.
 5 The various cases involving miscarriages of justice have identified possible police misconduct. See *R v McIlkenny* [1992] 2 All ER 417; *R v Edwards* [1991] 2 All ER 266; [1991] 1 WLR 207.

wilfully obstruct, a constable acting in the execution of his duty. Whilst the duty of the police can be stated broadly,[6] the expression "execution of duty" within section 51 has a technical meaning: an officer who infringes the rights of an individual without being able to point to some legal authority justifying such infringement will have gone outside the execution of duty, and thus a prosecution under section 51 will fail. Thus a police officer who is a trespasser and against whom reasonable force is used to eject him will not succeed in a prosecution for a section 51 assault.[7] Similarly with an officer who is unlawfully restraining an individual: physical force to secure release from that detention would not amount to a section 51 assault.[8] The key to each of these situations is the concept of unlawful interference with individual rights. If there is no interference with individual rights, or if authority in fact exists, the constable remains within the execution of duty.

3 Civil actions[9]

A Chief Constable is liable for any torts committed by a police officer in the performance or purported performance of police functions.[10] The Chief Constable will be indemnified by the police authority. In addition, a police authority has a discretion to pay damages in respect of torts and other claims committed by a constable, even if committed otherwise than in the performance of public duties.[11]

What is within "the performance of police functions" was considered in *Makanjuola v Commissioner of Police for the Metropolis*,[12] where an off-duty officer used his warrant card to gain admission to the property, where he then committed a serious sexual assault on the plaintiff. The Chief Constable was held not liable in damages for the sexual assault, because it was not a fraudulent performance of what the constable had authority to do honestly. Exemplary damages were awarded against the constable. The fact remains, though, that the effectiveness of the civil law remedy may depend upon the liability of the Chief Constable, since an individual officer may be of modest means and not worth suing.

The action in tort might be for assault, trespass or false imprisonment. Alternatively, the writ of habeas corpus will be a means of testing the legality of police detention.

---

6 "It is part of the obligations and duties of a police constable to take all steps which appear to him to be necessary for keeping the peace, for preventing crime or for protecting property from criminal injury . . . [they] also further include the duty to detect crime and to bring an offender to justice." (*per* Parker LCJ in *Rice v Connolly* [1966] 2 QB 414; [1966] 2 All ER 649).

7 *Davis v Lisle* [1936] 2 KB 434; [1936] 2 All ER 213.

8 *Kenlin v Gardiner* [1967] 2 QB 510; [1966] 3 All ER 931; *Collins v Wilcock* [1984] 3 All ER 374; [1984] 1 WLR 1172.

9 For civil remedies, see Clayton and Tomlinson, *Civil Actions against the Police* (1992).

10 Police Act 1964, s 48(1).

11 *Ibid*, s 48(4).

12 [1992] 3 All ER 617.

4   Judicial review

It has already been seen[13] that police discretion is judicially reviewable. Given the restricted role of the court, however, this is not in practice a realistic way of testing the legality of police action. By contrast, the use of the writ of habeas corpus can be an effective means in some circumstances of testing legality.

5   Crown Prosecution Service

The Crown Prosecution Service has responsibility for the prosecution of offences.[14] If police misconduct affects admissibility of evidence this may affect the strength of the police case and lead to a prosecution not being brought.

6   Complaints against the police

The adequacy of mechanisms for dealing with complaints against the police has been a matter of considerable debate since the 1970s. The complaints system is the non-legal mechanism available to members of the public who are dissatisfied with the conduct of an individual officer. Section 49 of the Police Act 1964 introduced a scheme for the internal investigation of complaints, with the Deputy Chief Constable of a force investigating and reporting, where appropriate, to the Director of Public Prosecutions. Continued pressure for a more independent form of scrutiny led to the Police Act 1976 which established the Police Complaints Board. The creation of this body failed to satisfy critics, principally because complaints were essentially still investigated by the police. As LORD SCARMAN observed in his Report into the Disturbances at Brixton,[15]

> "The evidence . . . has convinced me that there is a widespread and dangerous lack of public confidence in the existing system for handling complaints against the police . . . unless there is a strengthening of the independent 'non-police' element, public confidence will continue to be lacking."

The Royal Commission on Criminal Procedure also supported proposals for change.[16]

The Police and Criminal Evidence Act 1984 established a new system, under the control of the Police Complaints Authority. Complaints are made initially by or on behalf of a complainant to "the appropriate authority".[17] In the Metropolis, this will always be the Commissioner. Outside the Metropolis, who fulfils this role depends upon the subject of the complaint. If it is against a senior officer, the complaint is made to the police authority. For other officers it is the Chief Officer.

(a)   Senior officers[18] — The police authority may deal with the complaint at its discretion, if it is satisfied that the conduct complained of, if

---

13 See p 250, *ante.*
14 See p 232, *ante.*
15 (1981, HMSO).
16 Cmnd 8092-I, 1981. Op cit, paras 4.118–4.119.
17 Police and Criminal Evidence Act 1984, s 84(4).
18 Defined by s 84(4) as holders of rank above that of Chief Superintendent.

proved, would not justify criminal or disciplinary charges. In other cases an officer, whether from the same or another force, will be appointed to investigate.

(b)   *Other officers* — The Chief Officer considers whether the complaint is suitable for informal resolution. This will be the case if the complainant consents, and the Chief Officer is satisfied that the conduct complained of would not justify criminal or disciplinary proceedings. In other situations an officer is appointed to investigate.

The authority[19] supervises the investigation of certain categories of complaint: (i) complaints alleging that the conduct complained of resulted in death or serious injury to some other person; (ii) other complaints specified in regulations; (iii) any complaint referred to it by the police; (iv) any complaint where the authority requires reference to itself. In addition, section 88 permits the police to refer any matter where it appears to the appropriate authority that an officer may have committed any act which amounts to a disciplinary offence. Such a reference does not have to be after the making of a complaint, but it must be considered by the appropriate authority that it ought to be referred because of the gravity of the matter or because of exceptional circumstances.

The appropriate authority receives the report of the investigation. If it discloses a criminal offence then, in the case of senior officers, a copy of the report must be referred to the Director of Public Prosecutions.[20] In relation to other officers the Assistant Chief Constable, if he considers that criminal proceedings ought to be brought, again must refer the matter to the DPP. The Police Complaints Authority has power to direct a Chief Constable to send a report to the DPP if it considers that an officer ought to be charged.[1] It can also direct that disciplinary proceedings be brought.

C   POLICE POWERS

Authority to act in a particular way is conferred on the police by a wide range of authority, both common law and statutory. The detail of such powers is beyond the scope of this book. Nevertheless, the key features of the general framework of power, particularly those in respect of the treatment of suspects, are important in assessing the effectiveness of the criminal process whilst maintaining safeguards for individuals. The need to secure this balance has been emphasised by several controversial cases involving wrongful conviction and improper police behaviour.[2]

Historically, police powers were piecemeal and ill-defined, creating problems for both the police, who were often forced to the borders of legality in order to take necessary action, and for suspects. Disquiet over certain miscarriages of justice which raised questions as to police conduct[3] led to the setting up in 1978 of the Royal Commission on Criminal

---

19 See n 17, *supra.*
20 See p 232, *ante.*
 1 1984 Act, s 84.
 2 See n 5, *ante.*
 3 See, in particular, *R v Lattimore* (the *Confait Case*), leading to the Fisher Report, HMSO, 1977).

Procedure. This reported in 1981,[4] having conducted a wide-ranging review into the investigative powers of the police, and the questioning and treatment of suspects. The Report's recommendations were not accepted in their entirety by government, but the Report provided a basis for other proposals, now contained in the Police and Criminal Evidence Act 1984. In addition the Report recommended a scheme dealing with the prosecution of offenders: this resulted in the Prosecution of Offences Act 1985.[5]

1   General considerations

Before consideration of the framework, certain key matters merit discussion: first, the common law powers in respect of breaches of the peace; secondly, the concepts of "reasonable suspicion" and "reasonable belief"; thirdly, the use of force in the exercise of police powers; finally, the role of the Codes of Practice.

a   Breaches of the peace

A police officer is entitled to take any action necessary to prevent the continuance of a breach of the peace that is in fact occurring, or which is about to occur.[6] Arguably the officer also has a power of arrest in respect of breaches which have in fact occurred if there is a likelihood of recurrence.[7]

Definitions of what constitutes a breach of the peace have varied. In *R v Chief Constable of Devon & Cornwall, ex parte Central Generating Electricity Board*,[8] LORD DENNING stated:

> "There is a breach of the peace whenever a person who is lawfully carrying out his work is unlawfully and physically prevented by another from doing it."

This definition was too wide, and was not approved by LAWTON and TEMPLEMAN LJJ. More accurately, in *R v Howell*[9] WATKINS LJ stated:

> "We cannot accept that there can be a breach of the peace unless there has been an act done or threatened to be done which either actually harms a person, or in his presence his property, or is likely to cause such harm, or which puts somebody in fear of such harm being done."

The likelihood of a breach of the peace gives rise to several consequences. It gives the officer authority to take necessary action to prevent that occurrence from happening or continuing. This may involve the restraint and temporary detention of an individual.[10] It may involve the removal of

---

4 Cmnd 8092. For a useful summary of the pre-1986 law, see Cmnd 8092-I: *The Investigation and Prosecution of Criminal Offences in England & Wales: Law and Procedure.*
5 See p 232, *ante.*
6 *Albert v Lavin* [1982] AC 546; [1981] 3 All ER 878. The power extends to acts occurring on private property: *McConnell v Chief Constable of the Greater Manchester Police* [1990] 1 All ER 423; [1990] 1 WLR 364.
7 *R v Howell* [1982] QB 416; [1981] 3 All ER 383.
8 [1982] QB 458; [1981] 3 All ER 826.
9 [1982] QB 416; [1981] 3 All ER 383. This definition was approved in *Parkin v Norman* [1983] QB 92; [1982] 2 All ER 583.
10 See *Albert v Lavin, supra.*

an article or item of apparel from that individual.[11] It may involve requiring an individual not to go to a certain place, to travel by a certain route,[12] to undertake proposed activity elsewhere or in a different way.[13] All of this can impinge upon conduct which in itself may be perfectly lawful, and provides a wide measure of discretionary power which supplements the statutory scheme described below. A threatened breach of the peace may also provide the basis for entry upon property.[14] Finally, it may provide the basis for the arrest of an individual with a view to taking an individual before a magistrates' court to be bound over to be of good behaviour and to keep the peace.[15]

b Reasonable suspicion and reasonable belief

Virtually all police powers depend for their rightful exercise upon the existence of a particular state of mind in the person exercising the power. Usually what will be required is "reasonable suspicion" of certain facts, but sometimes in relation to particularly serious powers it will be "reasonable cause to believe" that will be required. Belief essentially involves the acceptance of the suspicion in fact held.[16]

In *Shaaban Bin Hussein v Chong Fook Kam*,[17] LORD DEVLIN observed that "suspicion in its ordinary meaning is a state of conjecture or surmise where proof is lacking: 'I suspect but cannot prove'". More recently, in *Castorina v Chief Constable of Surrey*[18] the Court of Appeal stated that honest belief was not a necessary pre-condition. Whilst clearly a reasonable suspicion must in fact be held, whether or not reasonable suspicion exists is to be determined objectively by the court. The existence or non-existence of reasonable suspicion therefore is an important element of ex post facto scrutiny of police action.

Reasonable suspicion is a suspicion based upon evidence. However, that does not have to be evidence that will be acceptable in a court of law. A wide range of factors is therefore important. They must though be characteristics individual to the person whose conduct is being considered, and not amount to stereotyping.[19] Code of Practice A[20] states that whether reasonable suspicion exists will depend upon all the circumstances. There must be some objective basis for it, such as a description of an article being carried, or a person seen acting in a certain way, or carrying an article at an unusual time or in a place where there have been a number of burglaries.

---

11 *Humphries v Connor* (1864) 17 ICLR 1: removal of orange lily from the lapel of the plaintiff lawful, since the intent was to prevent breaches of the peace.

12 *Moss v McLachlan* (1984) 149 JP 167. There must be some proximity in terms of time and place to the apprehended breach of the peace. See also the powers of regulation in Public Order Act 1986.

13 *Duncan v Jones* [1936] 1 KB 218; [1935] All ER Rep 710. *Piddington v Bates* [1960] 3 All ER 660; [1961] 1 WLR 162.

14 *CEGB* case, n 8, *supra*.

15 For powers in relation to binding over, see Justice of the Peace Act 1361, discussed generally in *Hughes v Holley* (1986) 151 JP 233. For a review of the law, see Law Commission Working Paper 103.

16 *Baker v Oxford* [1980] RTR 315. See Bailey & Birch [1982] Crim LR 549.

17 [1970] AC 942; [1969] 3 All ER 1626.

18 [1988] NLJR 180.

19 *Shaaban Bin Hussein v Chong Fook Kam* [1970] AC 942; [1969] 3 All ER 1626.

20 Made pursuant to s 66 of the 1984 Act. See para 1.7.

Reasonable suspicion can never be supported on the basis of personal factors alone. For example a person's colour, age, hairstyle or manner of dress are matters which cannot be used alone, or in combination with each other, as the sole basis upon which to justify the exercise of the stop and search powers described below. In reality it was such stereotyping that brought stringent criticism of the exercise of stop and search powers, leading to their reform in the 1984 Act.

c Force

The law allows necessary and reasonable force to be used in the exercise of police powers. The use of force in the exercise of police powers generally is governed by section 3 of the Criminal Justice Act 1967. This states that a person may use such force as is reasonable in the circumstances in the prevention of crime, or in effecting or assisting in the lawful arrest of an offender or suspected offender or of persons unlawfully at large. In addition, section 117 of the Police and Criminal Evidence Act 1984 provides that any power under the Act may be exercised using no more force than is reasonably necessary.

The legal tests are the same no matter what type of force is used. Traditionally, force has been by police officers armed only with a truncheon. Increasingly, firearms, or access to them, are available. The use of such weapons will have to be justified by the user in the same way as any other force, judged by its necessity and its reasonableness in the circumstances identified by the court.[1]

d Codes of Practice

By section 66 of the Police and Criminal Evidence Act 1984 the Secretary of State is under a duty to issue various Codes of Practice. Under that power, Codes have been issued dealing with the exercise of stop and search powers, the detention, treatment, questioning and identification of suspects, and the search of premises and seizure of property.

These Codes of Practice have legal significance in two ways. First, breach of the Codes can form the basis for disciplinary action against the officer. Secondly, and in reality more importantly, breaches of the Codes of Practice are relevant in the decision of any matter in court. This is dealt with later,[2] but generally operates to ensure compliance with the Code.

2 Stop and search powers

Stop and search powers are amongst the most controversial of police powers. On the one hand they provide a mechanism for action claimed to be necessary to prevent crime and detect offenders. On the other, they provide the potential for misuse and harassment of minority groups, and the success rate is low.[3] The Royal Commission on Criminal Procedure

---

1 See *R v MacNaghton* [1975] NI 203; *A-G for Northern Ireland's Reference (No 1 of 1975)* [1977] AC 105 [1976] 2 All ER 937.
2 See p 630, *post.*
3 See Zander at (1989) 40 NILQ 319; for research into use of pre-PACE powers, see Willis 'The Use, Effectiveness and Impact of Police Stop & Search Powers' (Research Study 15, Home Office, 1983).

investigated a wide range of powers to stop and search individuals, exercisable on different criteria, in different circumstances and by different people. In addition local powers existed. Thus, section 66 of the Metropolitan Police Act 1839 provided a power to stop, search and detain "any vessel, boat, cart or carriage in or upon which there shall be reason to suspect that anything stolen or unlawfully obtained may be found and also any person who may be reasonably suspected of having or conveying in any manner anything stolen or unlawfully obtained."

These powers were vague, and not always focussed on true policing needs. More objectionably, they provided a basis for potential abuse by their use on a stereotypical basis, on the grounds of colour or race, age, hairstyle or other unconventional characteristics. The Royal Commission proposed rationalisation and repeal of many of these powers.[4]

Sections 1–4 of the Police and Criminal Evidence Act 1984 deal with these matters. Section 1 provides a power for a constable to detain persons or vehicles for the purpose of search. The constable must have reasonable suspicion that stolen or prohibited articles will be found. This means that the reasonable suspicion must exist prior to the detention, for that is a power to be exercised for the purposes of making the search the Act permits. Of course, there is nothing to prevent the initial contact and questioning to be by consent. The answers obtained may form part of the material upon which the reasonable suspicion can be based, but that suspicion must exist prior to the detention.

The articles that may be searched for are stolen and prohibited articles. The nature of the former is self-evident. Prohibited articles need further definition. They include offensive weapons, which are further defined as articles made or adapted for use for causing injury to any person, or any article intended by the person carrying it with him to cause injury. Also included are articles with a blade or point: these will often, but not always, be offensive weapons as well.[5] Prohibited articles also include articles made or adapted for use in the course of, or in connection with burglary, theft, taking a motor vehicle without authority and obtaining property by deception; or articles intended for use by the person carrying them for use in one of these ways. It will be appreciated that the range of articles potentially within these definitions is very large indeed.

The power to stop and search is exercisable in any place to which the public have access.[6] Any article found may be seized. This of course does not include items that go beyond those described above: it is not a power to seize any evidence of any crime. In reality, however, in these circumstances the officer will usually arrest, and then use the powers of search and seizure that flow from the fact of arrest.[7] Plainly, care has to be taken to ensure that such powers are not abused. The Act creates a wide range of safeguards. The constable must give certain information to the person prior to the search, certain records are to be kept, and there are limits as to what items of clothing may be required to be removed. In particular, there

---

4 Cmnd 8092, 1981, pp 10–11. See now: Criminal Justice and Public Order Bill 1994.
5 See ss 1(7), (8), as amended by Criminal Justice Act 1988, ss 139–140. The prohibition in respect of articles with a blade or point (subject to limited exceptions) obviates the necessity for the prosecution to prove the intent of the possessor of the article.
6 Section 1(1).
7 See ss 18, 32, and p 264, *post.*

is no power to require a person to remove in public any clothing other than an outer coat, jacket or gloves, and, to avoid conflict with those who wear headgear for religious or ethnic reasons, there is no power to require the removal of a hat. This of course could be achieved by consent. Note also that there is a requirement for the statement of reasons for the search. The wording of the section suggests this should be so in all cases, even if obvious.

The exercise of the power is governed by Code of Practice A. A strict approach to questions of "reasonable suspicion" is essential. The Code does not affect the capacity of an officer to speak to or question a person in the normal course of his duties (and in the absence of reasonable suspicion) without detaining him or exercising any element of compulsion. Frequently it will be such normal conduct and questioning that provide the reasonable suspicion needed to justify formal detention for the purposes of search. The converse is equally true. The Act allows reasonable suspicion to be eliminated by questioning, and in these circumstances there is no obligation to search. The power is not, though, a power to detain and question.[8]

The power includes a right to detain and search vehicles for such articles. Again, the reasonable suspicion must exist at the time of detention. The bringing of the vehicle to a rest will be achieved through the power existing under section 163 of the Road Traffic Act 1988: a constable in uniform may require a vehicle to halt. This does not provide a basis for detention. Whether the vehicle is obliged to remain at rest will depend upon the extent to which that power will be implied by the courts,[9] or the extent which it is authorised by section 1.[10]

3   Arrest

Arrest is a matter of fact, not a legal concept, though it has legal consequences. As VISCOUNT DILHORNE put it in *Spicer v Holt*[11] "'Arrest' is an ordinary English word . . . whether or not a person has been arrested depends not upon the legality of his arrest but on whether he has been deprived of his liberty to go where he pleases."

The essence of arrest is therefore the deprivation of liberty. Since it would be illogical to categorise any detention as an arrest, an arrest must therefore be the purported exercise of authority.[12] Whether or not the authority in fact exists is a different matter: it is not a contradiction in terms to speak of an "unlawful arrest".

---

8 For the general principles, see *Rice v Connolly* [1966] 2 QB 414; [1966] 2 All ER 649 (refusal to answer police questions not a wilful obstruction of a constable acting in the execution of duty, contrary to Police Act 1964, because an individual has lawful authority to do so).

9 See *Steel v Goacher* [1983] RTR 98; *Lodwick v Sanders* [1985] 1 All ER 577; *Sanders v Director of Public Prosecutions* [1988] Crim LR 605.

10 See s 1(2)(b), which confers a power to detain a person or vehicle for the purposes of the search.

11 [1977] AC 987; [1976] 3 All ER 71.

12 See the definition of an arrest by Blackstone (in Commentaries 1830, p 289) as "the apprehending or restraining of one's person in order to answer an allegation or suspected crime". Note however that arrest may be made for the purposes of questioning: see *infra*.

The nature of an arrest was explained by Lᴏʀᴅ Dɪᴘʟᴏᴄᴋ in *Holgate-Mohammed v Duke*:[13]

"First it shall be noted that arrest is a continuing act: it starts with the arrester taking a person into his custody (by action or words restraining him from moving elsewhere beyond the arrester's control) and it continues until the person so restrained is either released from custody, or, having been brought before a magistrate, is remanded in custody by the magistrate's judicial act."

In that case an officer exercised powers of arrest on reasonable suspicion of burglary in order that he could continue questioning the suspect in a police station. Given that the power to arrest existed, its use to facilitate questioning was a legitimate use of police discretion. Therefore, whilst detention for questioning is not lawful, arrest for questioning is.

For there to be a lawful use of arrest powers there must be: (a) the power to arrest, and (b) the use of that power in the procedurally correct way.

a Powers of arrest

An arrest may be either under warrant or without a warrant. In respect of the former the Magistrates' Courts Act 1980 confers a power to issue an arrest warrant. A constable is protected by law in relying on that warrant.[14] In relation to arrest without warrant, the Police and Criminal Evidence Act 1984 made radical changes. The Royal Commission on Criminal Procedure had identified a wide variety of such powers, in both general and local Acts.[15] Section 26 has the effect of repealing all statutory powers that authorise arrest without warrant by the constable, other than those preserved by Schedule 2. This identifies 21 statutory powers that are so preserved, covering a wide range of situations. The Act also leaves untouched powers of arrest without warrant that arise at common law.[16] This therefore means that the powers of the police in relation to breaches of the peace are preserved.

The Act then goes on to deal with powers of arrest for arrestable offences, and powers of arrest pursuant to the general arrest conditions. An arrestable offence is defined by section 24(1) as:

(a) offences for which the sentence is fixed by law. Murder, with its mandatory life sentence, is an example;

(b) offences for which a person aged 21 years or over can be sentenced to a term of imprisonment of five years or more. This relates to the maximum permitted sentence, not that likely to be imposed;

(c) certain other specified offences. These are set out in section 24(2), and comprise offences that, pre-Act, were arrestable but which do not fall within the definition of arrestable offence. This list will change from time to time, as amendments are made by subsequent legislation.[17]

The Act then defines powers of arrest in respect of arrestable offences. These can be summarised as follows:

---

13 [1984] AC 437; [1984] 1 All ER 1054.
14 Magistrates' Courts Act 1980.
15 Cmnd 8092, 1981, Appendix 9.
16 1984 Act, s 25(6).
17 See, as examples, Official Secrets Act 1989, Football (Offences) Act 1991.

(a) any person may arrest anyone in the act of committing an arrestable offence, or who is reasonably suspected to be committing such an offence (section 24(4));

(b) any person may arrest anyone who is reasonably suspected of having committed such an offence, or who in fact has done so (section 24(5)). The Act, however, preserves the pre-1984 Act ruling in *Walters v WH Smith & Son Ltd*[18] that an arrestable offence must in fact have been committed. In *R v Self*[19] the defendant was charged with assault to escape lawful arrest. The arrest had been made by a citizen assisting a store detective, but the defendant was able to show that he had not in fact stolen the goods in question. Since in these circumstances the arrest was not lawful, the defendant was not in law guilty of the offence charged. This restriction does not apply to the power under section 24(4), and is a trap for the unwary. It suggests that a prudent citizen may prefer to ask the police to make the arrest, for no such restriction exists for police officers exercising arrest power under section 24(6);

(c) a constable may arrest without warrant anyone who is about to commit an arrestable offence, or anyone who he has reasonable grounds for suspecting to be about to commit an arrestable offence (section 24(4));

(d) a constable may arrest without warrant where there are reasonable grounds to suspect a person of having committed an arrestable offence (section 24(6)).

Alternatively, a constable can rely on the general arrest conditions contained in section 25. These apply where a constable reasonably suspects the commission of a non-arrestable offence, or its attempt, or, alternatively, if it appears to him that the service of a summons is impracticable. The arrest conditions are:

(a) the name of the person is unknown to the constable and cannot readily be ascertained;[20]

(b) reasonable grounds for doubting whether a name furnished is the person's real name;

(c) the person has failed to furnish a satisfactory address for service of a summons, or the constable reasonably doubts whether an address furnished is a satisfactory address for service;

(d) the constable has reasonable grounds for believing that arrest is necessary to prevent the relevant person causing injury to himself or another; suffering physical injury; causing loss or damage to property; committing an offence against public decency; causing an unlawful obstruction of the highway;

(e) the constable has reasonable grounds for believing that an arrest is necessary to protect a child or other vulnerable person from the relevant person.

The powers at common law to arrest for a breach of the peace also should not be forgotten. A wide variety of powers thus is vested in the hands of the police.

---

18 [1914] 1 KB 595; [1911-13] All ER Rep 170.
19 [1992] 3 All ER 476; [1992] 1 WLR 657.
20 See *G v Director of Public Prosecutions* [1989] Crim LR 150.

It should be borne in mind that the existence of a power of arrest does not require its exercise. On many occasions involving minor breaches of the law a constable may choose simply to caution informally the suspect. Alternatively, details can be taken for report and possible summons. The vast majority of non-indictable offences, and a sizable proportion of indictable offences, are proceeded with by summons as opposed to arrest and charge.[1]

b   Mechanics of arrest

The existence of a power is not enough. It must in fact be used, and in the right way. An arrest is not lawful unless the person arrested is informed that he is under arrest as soon as practicable after his arrest.[2] The person must likewise be told of the grounds for the arrest at the time of, or as soon as practicable after, the arrest. These two rules apply even if the fact of, or ground for, the arrest is obvious.[3] Section 28 makes an exception for cases where it is not practicable because the arrested person escapes before the information can be given. A failure to state the reasons when it does become practicable will invalidate the arrest, but only from that time, for the failure does not invalidate the arrest retrospectively.[4] Conversely, when the reasons are in fact stated the arrest becomes lawful. In *Lewis v Chief Constable of the South Wales Constabulary*[5] the Court of Appeal identified arrest as a continuing act. For that reason the arrest becomes lawful as soon as the reasons for the arrest are in fact stated. Thus the claim for damages, based on the fact that the initial arrest was unlawful, failed. This does not, of course, validate the period between the fact of arrest and the proper statement of reasons.

The statement of reasons does not have to specify a particular crime, or give a technical definition of the offence charged. What is needed is sufficient information to enable the arrested person to know the substance of why his liberty is being interfered with. In a pre-1984 Act case, *Christie v Leachinsky*,[6] the statement of reasons was inadequate because the officer relied on a power that he knew did not apply because the relevant factual conditions were not satisfied. However, the limits of this ruling were shown in the more recent case of *Abbassy v Commissioner of Police*.[7] The plaintiff was told that he was being arrested for "unlawful possession" of a vehicle. He had been asked four times about ownership of the vehicle, but responded in a rude and abusive fashion. Police inquiries later showed that he was in fact authorised to drive the vehicle, and the plaintiff was later charged with an offence of wilful obstruction of a constable acting in the execution of his duty, contrary to section 51(3) of the Police Act 1964, a charge later dropped. In an action for damages for, *inter alia*, unlawful arrest and false imprisonment the court ruled that it had been made clear to the plaintiff that the basis of the arrest was unlawful possession of the vehicle. The fact that the officer did not specifically mention the vehicle in

---

1 See further p 443, *post*.
2 Section 28(2).
3 Section 28(3).
4 *Hawkins v Director of Public Prosecutions* [1988] 3 All ER 673; [1988] 1 WLR 1166.
5 [1991] 1 All ER 206.
6 [1947] AC 573; [1947] 1 All ER 567.
7 [1990] 1 All ER 193; [1990] 1 WLR 385.

the statement of reasons was irrelevant. The judge had therefore misdi-rected the jury on a mater of law, and a re-trial was ordered.

An arrest also has certain physical requirements. It comprises compul-sion and submission to that compulsion. There must either be a touching symbolic of seizure of the body, or alternatively, words of compulsion to which there is submission.[8]

c   The consequences of arrest

By section 30, an arrested person must be taken to a police station as soon as practicable after the arrest. However, nothing prevents a constable delaying taking that person to a police station if his presence elsewhere is necessary in order to carry out such investigations as it is reasonable to carry out immediately.[9] By section 32 an arrested person may be searched if the constable has reasonable grounds to believe that the arrested person may present a danger to himself or others, or if he has reasonable grounds to believe he may have concealed on him an article that may assist in escape from lawful custody, or which is evidence relating to an offence. That does not have to be the same offence for which the person has been arrested.[10] There are also powers of entry conferred by section 32(2)(b) in respect of the premises where the arrested person was immediately before he was arrested, and, under section 18, of certain other premises occupied or controlled by the arrested person.

4   Detention

The 1984 Act creates a complex structure of provisions dealing with the detention of the suspect after arrest. In this, and with the treatment and questioning of the suspect, the key role is that of the custody officer. A duty to appoint such officers for each designated police station is created by the Act,[11] and it is to such a designated police station that an arrested person would normally be taken. The functions of such officers are set out in section 39. It is the duty of the custody officer to ensure that the treatment of all detained persons is in accordance with the requirements of the Act and of the Codes of Practice, and that the record-keeping required by the Act in fact occurs. The Act imposes duties on the custody officer both before and after charge. If the requirements of the Act are not complied with the detention is likely to become unlawful.[12]

The position is therefore an important one. The Act envisages and requires a separation of function between the custody officer and those investigating the offence. Only through such division of function will the interests of the suspect be protected. Whether this concept is sustainable in reality is a moot point. Quite apart from the loyalties and pressures that

---

8 *Alderson v Booth* [1969] 2 QB 216; [1969] 2 All ER 271.

9 Section 30(10).

10 This should be contrasted with the power to search premises (described below), which is confined to a search for evidence in respect of the offence for which the arrest was made. Note also the power to search premises under s 18.

11 1984 Act, s 36. This does not require a chief constable to appoint more than one such officer for each designated police station: *Vince v Chief Constable of the Dorset Police* [1993] 2 All ER 321; [1993] 1 WLR 415.

12 For the evidential consequences, see p 628, *post*.

membership of the same force might create, the custody officer may find it difficult on occasion to curb a natural desire to assist the investigation by asking questions or using his own personal knowledge of the suspect.[13]

In determining the legality of detention, the process must be looked at at various stages:

(a) The arrested person will be taken to the police station, unless his presence elsewhere can be justified.[14] If a person attends the station voluntarily, then he should be told he is free to go. If he is not he should be arrested, and will thereafter be subject to the same regime of detention.[15]

(b) At arrival at the police station, various matters relating to the arrested person will occur. First amongst these will be the creation of a custody record, which will detail all actions taken in respect of the arrested person. In particular, it will constitute the record of the various times that will govern the length of permitted detention.

(c) It is the duty of the custody officer to decide whether sufficient evidence exists to charge the person with the offence for which the arrest was made. If there is the custody officer should do so.[16] During the period of detention various reviews of the detention will occur. These will occur as follows:[17]

1st review: Not later than 6 hours after detention.

2nd review: Not later than 9 hours after 1st review.

3rd and subsequent reviews: Not later than 9 hours after previous review. In other words, there will be at least three opportunities to consider release or charge within any 24-hour period.

In addition, when during questioning the investigating officer considers that there is sufficient evidence to charge, the arrested person must be taken before the custody officer.

(d) If there is sufficient evidence to charge, whether initially or at any of the stages outlined, the custody officer must do so. Whether the arrested person can then be detained further will depend upon whether bail is granted.

(e) If there is not sufficient evidence to charge an arrested person then the periods of detention cannot exceed those permitted by the Act. The basic rule is that detention shall not last longer than 24 hours from the time of arrest, or time of arrival at the police station, whichever is earlier. This 24-hour period may be extended by a further 12 hours (ie 36 in total) by a senior officer.[18] That officer must have reasonable grounds to believe that detention is necessary to secure or preserve evidence relating to the offence for which the arrest was made, or to obtain such evidence by questioning; and, that the offence is a serious arrestable offence; and, that the offence is being investigated diligently and expeditiously.

If the police wish to detain beyond that 36-hour period under

---

13 See eg, *R v Absolam* (1988) 88 Cr App Rep 332.
14 See 1984 Act, s 30(10).
15 *Ibid*, s 29, and Code C, para 3.15.
16 Code C, para 16.1.
17 1984 Act, ss 42–44.
18 Of the rank of superintendent or above: s 42(1).

section 43 a warrant of further detention must be obtained from the magistrates' court. That court may issue such a warrant on the same grounds as stated above for the extension of detention by a senior officer. The warrant is for such period as the court thinks fit, not exceeding 36 hours. The court may extend this still further by a period of not longer than 36 hours, ending no later than 96 hours after first detention or arrest. In short, 4 days is the maximum permitted period of detention without charge.[19]

(f)   After a person has been charged he will be released unless the grounds for detention under section 38 exist. These are: that his name or address cannot be ascertained, or is reasonably believed to be false; it is reasonably believed that detention is necessary for the protection of, or to prevent him from causing physical injury to, any other person, or damage to property; it is reasonably believed that the arrested person will fail to appear in court to answer bail, or detention is necessary to prevent him interfering with the administration of justice or with police investigations of that or other offences.

5   Treatment of suspects

The Police and Criminal Evidence Act 1984 contains provisions designed to give proper protection to a suspect in the police station. These are supplemented by Code C dealing with the detention, treatment and questioning of suspects. The objective is to ensure not only that suspects are treated in accordance with minimum standards, but also that admissions and other evidence are obtained in such a way that they can safely be relied upon in court. The courts also regard the right to silence as important, and the Code seeks to prevent improperly induced self-incrimination.[20] The provisions apply even if a person is at the police station voluntarily, since if it is decided that the suspect will not be allowed to leave then he must be informed at once that he is under arrest.

a   Search

When taken into custody, the custody officer may cause a search to be made of the person detained, although such a search is not obligatory. Much will depend upon how long a suspect is being detained, whether he is to be placed in the cells, and so forth. Section 54 imposes a duty to record everything a person has with him when he is brought to the police station. A search can occur, provided it is not an intimate search. A strip search (ie one involving the removal of more than outer garments) should not occur unless the custody officer considers it to be necessary to remove an article which the detained person would not be allowed to keep. A search may also be carried out at any time whilst the person is in custody to ascertain whether or not he has anything with him that could be used for the purposes set out in section 54(4).

Section 54(4) allows certain articles to be seized, if found on search. These are any articles that: (a) the custody officer believes the person may

---

19 Calculated in accordance with the criteria set out in s 41(2).
20 See p 271, *post*.

use (i) to cause physical injury to himself or to another person, (ii) to damage property, (iii) to interfere with evidence, (iv) to assist in escape, or (b) the custody officer has reasonable grounds to believe that they may be evidence in relation to an offence.[1]

Intimate searches are governed by different rules. Section 118 defines an intimate search as a search consisting "of the physical examination of a person's body orifices". Intimate searches can only be carried out under section 55. An officer of at least the rank of superintendent must have reasonable grounds to believe:

(a) that the arrested person may have concealed on him anything which he could use to cause physical injury to himself or others and might so use whilst in custody, or

(b) the arrested person may have Class A drugs concealed on him, with the requisite intent.[2]

In either case an intimate search is only permitted if it is believed that it cannot be found without such a search. The search must be conducted in accordance with Annex A of Code C.

b   Information about rights

The arrested person must be informed of the right to have someone informed of his arrest. Section 56 provides that a person held in custody may on request have one person known to him, or who is likely to take an interest in his welfare, notified at public expense of his whereabouts as soon as practicable. If that person is unobtainable, the arrested person may nominate two others, and the police may extend the right further if they wish. The right is an important one, to be denied only in limited circumstances where to grant it would interfere with the investigation. Even if the grounds for denying contact with an individual may exist, they are unlikely to apply to making contact with a solicitor.[3] The arrested person also has the right to consult the Codes of Practice.[4]

c   Fingerprinting

In the absence of consent, fingerprints can only be taken on the authorisation of a senior officer, on suspicion of involvement in a criminal offence, and where it is believed that fingerprints will tend to prove or disprove the suspect's involvement.[5] Alternatively, if the suspect has been charged with a recordable offence and has not had fingerprints taken in the course of the investigation, they may be taken.

d   Intimate samples

These are defined by section 65 as a sample of blood, semen or any other tissue fluid, urine, saliva or pubic hair, or a swab taken from a person's body orifices. These can, of course, be taken by consent, though it is

---

1 Compare with the pre-1984 Act position as stated in *Lindley v Rutter* [1981] QB 128; [1980] 3 WLR 660.
2 Eg with intent to supply: see s 55(17).
3 *R v Samuel* [1988] QB 615; [1988] 2 All ER 135.
4 Code C, para 4; *Director of Public Prosecutions v Skinner* [1990] RTR 254.
5 Section 61.

required to be in writing, and then only if section 63 applies. Again, it must be under the authorisation of a senior officer who reasonably suspects involvement in a serious arrestable offence. "Serious arrestable offences" are defined by the Act in a detailed way,[6] and are the more serious of arrestable offences, which justify the creation and use of intrusive and onerous police powers. The senior officer must believe that the sample will confirm or disprove involvement in the offence.

The Act makes it clear that no such sample shall be taken without consent. However, refusal to grant such consent can lead to adverse inferences being drawn.[7]

Non-intimate samples can be taken pursuant to section 63. These can be taken without consent on authorisation of a senior police officer, who reasonably suspects involvement of the suspect in a serious arrestable offence, and that the sample will tend to confirm or disprove involvement.

e   Conditions of detention

These are governed by Code C, and may in extreme cases in any event amount to breach of Article 10 of the Bill of Rights 1688 which prohibits "cruell and unusuall punishments".[8] Cells must be adequately heated, cleaned and ventilated. Clean bedding should be supplied. Access to toilet and washing facilities must be granted. Adequate replacement clothing for any item taken for investigation must be provided. Adequate meals must be provided. Brief outdoor exercise, if practicable, should be permitted. Suspects should be visited every hour, or every half-hour in the case of persons who are drunk. The custody officer is under a duty to call for medical treatment if a suspect appears to be ill or suffering from mental disorder, is injured, does not show signs of sensibility and awareness, fails to respond to questions or conversation, or otherwise appears to require medical attention.

f   Vulnerable suspects

Special rules apply to vulnerable persons. In respect of those who appear to be deaf, or where there is doubt about their hearing or speaking ability, or ability to understand English, and the custody officer cannot establish effective communications, the custody officer must as soon as possible call an interpreter. If the arrested person is a juvenile, the identity of the person responsible for his welfare must be ascertained and informed as soon as practicable. An "appropriate adult"[9] must be asked to come to the police station. Similar rules apply to those suffering from mental handicap or suffering mental disorder.

---

6 Section 116.
7 Section 62(10).
8 See *Middleweek v Chief Constable of Merseyside* [1992] 1 AC 179n; [1990] 3 All ER 662; *R v Deputy Governor of Parkhurst Prison, ex parte Hague* [1992] 1 AC 58; sub nom *Hague v Deputy Governor of Parkhurst Prison* [1991] 3 All ER 733.
9 See Code C, para 1.7.

6 Access to legal advice

The right to access to legal advice was, in *R v Samuel*,[10] described as "fundamental". Although the Judges Rules which, prior to the 1984 Act, governed such matters, recognised the importance of such access, they were frequently broken and poorly enforced by the courts.[11] The 1984 Act has greatly strengthened the right, and led to much more rigorous enforcement by the courts.

Section 58 provides that a "person who is in police detention shall be entitled, if he so requests, to consult a solicitor privately at any time". Delay in granting this right can only be authorised, in respect of a serious arrestable offence, by an officer of the rank of superintendent or above, on certain limited grounds. These are stated to be where the officer reasonably believes that the exercise of the right:

(a) will lead to interference with or harm to evidence connected with a serious arrestable offence or interference with or physical injury to other persons; or

(b) will lead to the alerting of other persons suspected of having committed such an offence but not yet arrested for it; or

(c) will hinder the recovery of any property obtained as a result of such an offence.

Certain other limited exceptions relating to drug trafficking and terrorist offences exist.

These powers of delay have been construed by the courts in a way that makes them extremely limited in scope. In *R v Samuel*,[12] the accused had been denied access to a solicitor on the grounds that the accused's companions were still at large and might be alerted by the solicitor, albeit unwittingly. The court stated that any decision to deny access had to be by reference to the individual features of each case. Here the police had failed to demonstrate a reasonable belief that the particular solicitor would engage in such conduct. Indeed, if a particular solicitor was shown to fall within these provisions, the appropriate response would be to request the nomination of another solicitor, or the calling of the duty solicitor. It is not a ground of delay under these provisions that the solicitor will advise silence, or make the investigation harder.[13]

The Code of Practice sets out the detailed provisions regarding these rights. A suspect under arrest at the police station must be informed clearly of his right to have someone informed, and of his right to consult privately with a solicitor free of charge. These are continuing rights which may be exercised at any time during the period in custody. The custody officer must give suspects a written notice of these rights, containing an explanation of the arrangements for obtaining legal advice. Posters advertising the right must be displayed prominently in the charging area of each police station, and at certain stages in the process the suspect must be reminded of the right to free legal advice.

---

10 [1988] QB 615; [1988] 2 All ER 135.
11 See the Fisher Report (1977, HC 90).
12 See n 10, *supra*.
13 *Ibid*. See also *R v Alladice* (1988) 87 Cr App Rep 380.

The right is one to receive legal advice if the suspect so requests. There is no obligation on the police to request a solicitor, though if the suspect's family does and the solicitor attends, the suspect has the right to see him. The police must not take action to discourage the exercise of the right, and must not misrepresent the position.[14] The Code does not specify how such advice is to be given. It may be given in person, or over the telephone. Once requested the police must generally wait until after such advice has been tendered before proceeding with an interview. If an interview is taking place, a solicitor may be asked to leave if his conduct is such that the investigating officer is unable properly to put questions to the suspect.

The right is the right to legal advice from a solicitor. In reality it may be a legal executive or clerk who attends at the police station. The Code permits refusal of access to such persons if an officer of the rank of inspector or above considers that such a visit would hinder the investigation of crime. In *R v Chief Constable of Avon and Somerset Constabulary, ex parte Robinson*[15] a circular setting out force policy in this respect was held lawful because it did not fetter the discretion of the individual decision-making officer. What is not permitted is for the police to make judgments based upon the quality of advice likely to be tendered, and the terms of the Code have been amended to specify clearly what is proper. What is important is that the clerk should be admitted unless identity or status have not been properly established, if the person is not of suitable character to give advice (eg because of a criminal record) and any other matters disclosed in the letter of authorisation. The quality of advice given will, however, be important: the very fact of presence of a legal representative may "cure" procedural irregularities committed by the police which were not objected to at the time.[16]

The effectiveness of the right under section 58 has been the subject of considerable research.[17] It depends in part upon adequate availability of suitably qualified legal advisers, compliance with the spirit of the rules by the police and adequate sanctions in the courts. In relation to the availability of advice, duty solicitor schemes exist, run under the auspices of the Legal Aid Board. Those who do not request a named solicitor, or whose named solicitor is unavailable, may seek free advice. This may often be initially by telephone. Whilst the duty solicitor, drawn from a rota amongst local practitioners, may choose to attend, the only obligation to do so is where the suspect is to be interviewed, an identification parade is being held, or where an allegation of serious police misconduct is being made. The effectiveness of the scheme also presupposes a sufficiently large group of solicitors undertaking criminal legal aid work.

The impact of the provisions has been mixed. Research shows that take-up rates have varied greatly between police stations.[18] Whilst direct denial of rights has been rare, it has been found that a variety of ploys, whether intentional or inadvertent, by the police can dissuade suspects

---

14 See *R v Beycan* [1990] Crim LR 185.
15 [1989] 2 All ER 15; [1989] 1 WLR 793.
16 See *R v Dunn* (1990) 91 Cr App Rep 237.
17 See, in particular, Sanders & Bridges, 'Access to Legal Advice and Police Malpractice' [1990] Crim LR 494.
18 *Ibid.*

from taking advantage of this legal right.[19] The revision of the Code of Practice in 1991 was designed to minimise this risk. It is also the case that the courts have taken a strong line in cases of breach of these legal advice provisions. Though not automatic breach is likely in most cases to lead to exclusion of a confession subsequently obtained.[20]

7 Interviews

One of the most serious problems identified in recent years is the possibility that confessions by suspects may not in fact be reliable. In addition allegations were frequently made against the police. The 1984 Act and Code of Practice created a detailed framework for the conduct and recording of interviews. These provisions are regarded by the courts as of the greatest importance, and breaches of them have led to confessions subsequently obtained being excluded. Their purpose was explained by LORD LANE CJ in *R v Canale*:[1]

"The object is two-fold: not merely to ensure . . . that the suspect's remarks are accurately recorded and that he has an opportunity when he goes through the contemporaneous record afterwards of checking each answer and initialling each answer, but likewise it is a protection for the police, to ensure, so far as possible, that it cannot be suggested that they induced the suspect to confess by improper approaches or improper promises. If the contemporaneous note is not made then each of those two laudable objects is apt to be stultified."

At the heart of these provisions is the definition of what amounts to an interview. The Act has resulted in widespread tape-recording of interviews conducted in police stations. A detailed Code of Practice[2] deals with those tape-recordings and how transcripts thereof may be used. In addition, rules governing the keeping and verification of notes of interviews exist. For that reason there was a danger on occasion that the police would seek to circumvent such provisions by conducting conversations and obtaining admissions outside the police station. Amendments to the Code have been made in an attempt to minimise this danger. The definition of interview is now stated to be: the questioning of a person regarding his involvement or suspected involvement in a criminal offence or offences.[3] Questioning a person only to obtain information or his explanation of the facts, or in the ordinary course of the officer's duties does not constitute an interview. Neither does questioning which is confined to the proper and effective conduct of a search. There are, however, difficulties in applying this in practice.[4]

---

19 The right is to be granted access on request.
20 See p 628, *post*.
 1 [1990] 2 All ER 187.
 2 Code C.
 3 For interpretation of this, see *R v Cox* (1992) 96 Cr App Rep 464.
 4 For the difficulties see *R v Absolam* (1988) 88 Cr App Rep 332; *R v Blackburn and Wade* (1992) Times, 1 December.

a   Cautions

A caution must be administered before questions about an offence are put to a person suspected of an offence for the purpose of obtaining evidence which may be given in court. A caution must likewise be administered on arrest. The caution states:

> "You do not have to say anything unless you wish to do so, but what you say may be given in evidence."

This will therefore be given at the commencement of each interview. If there is a break in an interview the arrested person must be reminded that he remains under caution.

b   Interviews

These must occur at a police station, unless delay would lead to interference with or harm to evidence connected with an offence or interference with or harm to other persons, would lead to the alerting of other persons suspected of committing an offence but not yet arrested for it, or hinder the recovery of property obtained in consequence of the commission of an offence. Prior to the holding of any interview the suspect should be reminded of his right to free legal advice.

c   Records of interviews

The Code requires accurate records of interviews to be kept. The record will state time and date, location, names of those present. Breaks in the interview must be recorded. In respect of tape-recorded records, special rules apply. In relation to other interviews, the suspect should be shown the notes of the interview, and given an opportunity to sign it as requested. If the suspect declines to do so this must itself be recorded. If the record is not kept contemporaneously, the reasons for that failure must be recorded, and the record completed as soon as practicable. The interview notes should then be shown to the suspect for verification. Any unsolicited comments by the suspect should likewise be recorded and verified.[5]

d   Conduct of interviews

The law will exclude as evidence any confession obtained by oppression or in circumstances likely to lead to unreliability.[6] The Code specifies detailed requirements about breaks from questioning, maximum periods of questioning, the giving of proper food and refreshment as appropriate.

e   Vulnerable suspects

The Codes recognise that certain groups need special protection. This is true in respect of those suffering mental disability,[7] and juveniles.[8] In respect of the former, those who suffer mental handicap or mental illness

---

5 See Code C, paras 11.5–11.13.
6 See p 625, *post.*
7 Code C, paras 3.9–3.10.
8 *Ibid*, paras 3.7–3.8.

should not be interviewed in the absence of an appropriate adult,[9] unless the rules in Annex C governing urgent interviews apply. These only permit an interview to be held where delay would involve an immediate risk of harm to persons or serious loss or serious damage to property. If such a person is interviewed in the absence of an appropriate adult, then not only may the confession resulting be excluded on the grounds of unreliability,[10] the provisions of section 77 of the 1984 Act, which will require any confession to be corroborated,[11] will apply. Whether a person falls within these provisions will be decided by the court.

Similar rules about the presence of an appropriate adult apply to juveniles.[12] In addition, those suffering temporary disability through drink, drugs or illness should not generally be interviewed until they are fit, though the courts seem willing to leave this judgment to the police themselves.[13]

8 Identification

The dangers of identification evidence are well known.[14] To minimise them the Codes of Practice set out specific rules as to how suspects are to be identified, since court identifications are not generally permissible.[15] Failure to comply with the Code is likely to lead to the exclusion of evidence of that identification.[16]

Where the identity of a suspect is not known, a witness may be taken to a particular locality to observe possible suspects, or may be shown photographs, provided certain safeguards are complied with. Once the identity of a suspect is known, however, then identification should proceed in accordance with set procedures. In such cases the preferred method of identification is through an identification parade. This will be held if the suspect consents, and either the investigating officer considers it would be useful, or the suspect requests a parade. Only if it is impracticable to secure sufficient similar looking participants can the parade be declined by the police. If a parade is held, it must be in accordance with the detailed procedures set out in the Code. Evidence of identification can be given not only by the witness, but also by officers who saw and heard the witness identify the suspect.[17]

Where no parade is held, because it is impracticable or because no consent is given, a group identification, video identification or a confrontation (in that preferred order) are the alternatives allowed by the Code.

---

9 Code C, para 1.7. A solicitor representing the suspect may not act as an appropriate adult.
10 See p 625, *post.*
11 See p 574, *post.*
12 *Supra*, n 8.
13 *R v Lamont* [1989] Crim LR 813; *R v Moss* (1990) 91 Cr App Rep 371.
14 See *R v Turnbull* [1977] QB 224; [1976] 3 All ER 549, and the Devlin Committee report (1976, HC 338).
15 *Ibid.*
16 See p 576, *post.*
17 *R v McCay* [1991] 1 All ER 232; [1990] 1 WLR 645.

PART III

Civil Procedure

SUMMARY

CHAPTER 13

Preliminary Considerations

A CHOICE OF COURT

It has already been noted that in some matters the jurisdiction of the High Court is exclusive.[1] However, in others the jurisdiction of the High Court and county court is concurrent, in the sense that an action may be commenced in either.

Historically, the jurisdiction of the county court in matters in respect of which the Queens Bench Division had jurisdiction was limited by the financial value of the claim. Prior to 1991, in contract or tort actions, the value of the claim had to be no greater than £5,000. In equity and property matters the figure was £30,000. If the amount of the claim exceeded the jurisdiction of the county court then the matter had to be dealt with by the High Court, subject to statutory powers of transfer between the two courts.[2] Proceedings in the county court were potentially cheaper, but the procedures followed in the county court were not always either speedy or effective. It was hardly surprising, therefore, that the Review Body on Civil Justice[3] found that much of the work tried at High Court level was not of sufficient importance, complexity and substance to justify the time and expense involved in High Court proceedings. It identified the types of cases that did in fact justify proceedings at High Court level. These included: (a) public law matters, to be dealt with by way of judicial review;[4] (b) those matters dealt with in specialist jurisdictions, especially the Commercial Court;[5] (c) ordinary cases, which were important, complex or which involved a substantial claim. The Review recommended changes to the jurisdiction of the county court, and improved mechanisms for transfer between the two jurisdictions.[6]

As a result of this Review, the Courts and Legal Services Act 1990 altered the whole basis of distribution of work between High Court and county court, although not adopting in their entirety the recommendations of the Review Body. Section 1 of the 1990 Act empowers the Lord Chancellor to make provision for the allocation of business between the

---

1 See p 149, *ante*.
2 See p 415, *post*.
3 *Report of the Review Body on Civil Justice* (Cm 394, 1988, HMSO).
4 See p 122, *ante*.
5 See p 153, *ante*.
6 Recommendation 1.

two courts, other than matters to be dealt with by judicial review. In 1991 the Lord Chancellor made the High Court and County Court Jurisdiction Order,[7] which adjusted fundamentally the distribution of work between the two courts. By virtue of this order, there is no longer any limit to the jurisdiction of the county court in contract or tort. The general principle is that a plaintiff is free to choose whichever court is preferred, although in deciding where in fact to commence an action a plaintiff will usually have regard to the court by which such an action will ultimately be tried.[8] The general principle of freedom of choice expressed above is subject to one important qualification: any action of a value less than £50,000[9] and which involves a claim for damages for personal injuries, must be commenced in the county court.[10]

Self-evidently, the ultimate choice of the appropriate court of trial is the key factor in deciding where an action should be commenced. Article 7 of the High Court and County Court Jurisdiction Order[11] creates a presumption that cases of a value less than £25,000 must be tried in the county court, and those of a value of £50,000 or more in the High Court. The position will be otherwise if application of certain criteria shows that a different court of trial is in fact appropriate. These criteria also apply in deciding in which court cases falling between these two financial figures should be tried.

The criteria mentioned above are set out in Article 7(5) of the order, which deals primarily with the transfer of cases between the two jurisdictions. However, they are equally relevant to the question of initial choice of jurisdiction. The factors identified are as follows:

(i)   the financial substance of the action, including that of any counter-claim;
(ii) whether the action is otherwise important, for example by raising issues of general public importance, or where the case will amount to a test case;
(iii) the complexity of the facts, legal issues, remedies or procedures involved. Complex cases are more suitable for High Court trial;
(iv) whether transfer of the case will lead to more speedy trial, although this alone should not be a determining factor.

In addition certain types of case may be particularly suitable for High Court trial.[12] These include claims of professional negligence, fatal accident claims, allegations of fraud or undue influence, defamation cases, claims based on allegations of malicious prosecution or false imprisonment, and claims against the police. In such cases it is likely that High Court trial will ultimately be ordered,[13] and that may be decisive in determining where such actions should be commenced.[14]

To facilitate the greater use of the county court jurisdiction, section 38 of

---

7 SI 1991/724.
8 See *infra*.
9 Actions above this figure must be commenced in the High Court.
10 1991 Order, art 5(1).
11 *Ibid*, art 7(2).
12 *Civil Justice Review*, n 3, *ante*.
13 In some of them jury trial is available: see p 363, *post*.
14 See *supra*.

the County Courts Act 1984[15] gives to the county court, generally speaking, the power to make any order which could be made by the High Court if the proceedings were in that court. That power is subject to any limitation imposed by regulations made by the Lord Chancellor,[16] and in fact regulations have been made specifically prohibiting a county court from making an *Anton Piller* order[17] or issuing a *Mareva* injunction.[18] In substantial cases where such orders may be crucial to the obtaining of information or prevention of dissipation of assets, these restrictions may conclusively influence the choice of High Court rather than county court jurisdiction.

Within this framework the solicitor will choose the appropriate jurisdiction. That choice may be influenced by tactical reasons. For example, High Court proceedings may create an impression of seriousness and importance and be regarded by some as more intimidating. The solicitor may prefer the procedures of the High Court to those of the county court, or, conversely, may prefer the geographical proximity of the county court. However, where a choice of High Court jurisdiction is wrongly made, the plaintiff may be penalised by suffering a reduction in the costs that may be awarded upon taxation.[19]

B PUBLIC OR PRIVATE LAW

A second preliminary factor of importance which must be considered is whether the proposed action involves questions of public law. Where in reality an action raises issues of public law, the normal procedure for determination of those questions is by an application for judicial review under Order 53 of the Rules of the Supreme Court, and a failure to use the Order 53 procedure may result subsequently in an application by the defendant to have the action struck out as an abuse of process of the court.[20]

Prior to 1983 a choice as to which procedure was followed was open to the plaintiff or applicant. The Order 53 procedure that existed prior to 1977 had defects that often meant that proceeding by way of writ in the Queens' Bench Division was more attractive. Certain procedures such as discovery and cross-examination of those who swore affadavits were not available on judicial review; nor was it open to a court dealing with such an application to make an award of damages, or issue a declaration.[21] These, and other, defects were remedied in 1977 when a revised Order 53 came into effect. As a result in 1981 the House of Lords in *O'Reilly v Mackman*[1] indicated firmly that the Order 53 procedure was to be the usual method of challenging public law actions of decisions. Lord Diplock stressed the

---

15 Inserted by the Courts and Legal Services Act 1990, s 3.
16 Supreme Court Act 1981, s 38(4).
17 County Court Remedies Regulations 1991, reg 3(3)(b).
18 *Ibid*.
19 See Supreme Court Act 1981, s 51(8), inserted by the Courts and Legal Services Act 1990, s 4. For wasted costs orders, see p 382, *post*.
20 See p 314. *post*.
21 For discussion of the defects of Ord 53, see the speech of Lord Diplock in *O'Reilly v Mackman, infra*.
  1 [1983] 2 AC 237.

advantages of the limited time for challenge under Order 53, and the safeguard that the filter of requiring leave to apply creates. To seek to avoid these safeguards by proceeding by writ would amount in most cases to an abuse of process.

This distinction between public and private law matters, and the procedures to be followed, has caused the courts considerable difficulty. The observations of HENRY J in *Doyle v Northumbria Probation Committee*[2] have already been noted.

In *O'Reilly v Mackman (infra)* LORD DIPLOCK had not ruled out totally private law process as a means of challenge of the actions of public bodies. The difficulty encountered was in identifying the cases that fell within the exception.

The position was somewhat clarified, if not entirely so, by the House of Lords in *Roy v Kensington and Chelsea and Westminster Family Practitioners Committee*.[3] In that case the plaintiff, a doctor, commenced an action by writ, seeking to obtain payments that he alleged were due to him, and being withheld by the defendant committee. The doctor's terms and conditions of employment were governed by regulation made pursuant to statute, and the committee sought to have the plaintiff's action struck out, arguing that the action raised public law matters which should be decided on an application for judicial review under Order 53. This application initially succeeded, but was rejected both by the Court of Appeal and by the House of Lords. The plaintiff was seeking to recover money allegedly owed to him. This raised private law rights, which could be enforced by private law action, even if they involved challenge to a public law decision. In his speech, LORD LOWRY sought to limit the application of the principle in *O'Reilly v Mackman*, and preferred an approach which restricted the use of private law procedures only in respect of those cases involving no private law rights. He quoted with approval the dictum of LORD WILBERFORCE in *Davy v Spelthorne Borough Council*:[4]

> "We have not yet reached the point at which mere characterisation of a claim as a claim in public law is sufficient to exclude it from consideration by the ordinary courts: to permit this would be to create a duel system of law with the rigidity and procedural hardship for plaintiffs which it was the purpose of the recent reforms to remove."

A court having jurisdiction ought to let a case be heard rather than entertain a debate concerning the form of the proceedings. Such an approach is consistent with a series of cases where a claim for money from a party was held to be a private law matter, even if the defence involved an assertion that the claim was invalid because it was made pursuant to an *ultra vires* action.[5] Simply because one party to an action is a public body does not turn the matter to be decided into a public law matter.[6]

---

2 [1991] 4 All ER 294; [1991] 1 WLR 340. See p 6, *ante*.
3 [1992] 1 AC 624; [1992] 1 All ER 705.
4 [1984] AC 262 at 276; [1983] 3 All ER 278 at 285.
5 See, eg, *Wandsworth London Borough Council v Winder* [1985] AC 461; [1984] 3 All ER 976.
6 *R v East Berkshire Area Health Authority, ex parte Walsh* [1985] QB 152; [1984] 3 All ER 425.

C ALTERNATIVE FORMS OF RESOLUTION

Increasingly those with disputes have sought alternative means of dispute resolution. Litigation, particularly in the High Court, is both time-consuming and expensive, and suffers the (to some) disadvantage of, generally, being conducted in public.[7] Arbitration has long been an accepted alternative to court procedures, particularly in the sphere of commerce and business, and involves a binding resolution of a dispute by an arbitrator. The principle of arbitration has now been adopted in respect of small claims in the county court,[8] although, of course, there is a key difference in that arbitration in the county court results in an enforceable court order.

In addition, there has begun a tendency to look for other, more informal forms of mechanism for the resolution of disputes, generally known as Alternative Dispute Resolution. Unlike arbitration, the characteristics of such mechanisms are those of conciliation and negotiation, and thus by their nature will not involve generally the imposition of the verdict or conclusion. Again, such means of avoiding full-scale litigation is particularly helpful to parties to disputes in the commercial or business sectors, but consideration is also being given to forms of such conciliation in divorce proceedings.[9]

1 References to arbitration

The jurisdiction of arbitrators usually arises out of contract, though there are numerous statutory provisions which provide for the reference of disputes to arbitration. An agreement to refer disputes to arbitration is a contract and, as such, is subject to the ordinary law of contract. Any provision purporting to oust the jurisdiction of the courts is void, as being contrary to public policy, though there is no objection to a clause which makes reference to arbitration a condition precedent to a right of action. The effect of such a clause, known as a *Scott v Avery*[10] clause, is that if a party does institute proceedings without referring the dispute to arbitration, the clause may be pleaded as a defence in those proceedings and the other party may, after acknowledging service of the writ but before taking any other step in the proceedings, apply to the court for an order staying the proceedings.[11] The order is discretionary but, in the absence of some good reason, the court will stay the proceedings.

Since legal aid is not available in arbitrations an impecunious plaintiff is at a severe disadvantage if proceedings (in which he would be eligible for legal aid) are stayed. The poverty or insolvency of a plaintiff is, as a rule, not a ground for refusing a stay; however, where there is a triable issue as

---

7 See p 141, *ante.*
8 See p 402, *post.*
9 Lord Chancellor's Consultation Paper, *Looking to the Future: Mediation and the Grounds for Divorce* (1993) – see 143 NLJ 1739.
10 (1856) 5 HL Cas 811.
11 Arbitration Act 1950, s 4(1). The Arbitration Act 1975, s 1(1) makes similar provision in relation to agreements which are not "domestic arbitration agreements" as defined by s 1(4). The Act provides for the enforcement of awards made in the territory of any state (other than the United Kingdom) which is a party to the New York Convention on the Recognition of Foreign Arbitral Awards.

to whether that poverty or insolvency has been brought about by the defendant's breach of contract, a stay may be refused so as to avoid a denial of justice by reason of the plaintiff being of insufficient means to pursue his cause of action effectively.[12]

2   Procedure

Procedure on arbitrations is governed (except, in relation to statutory references, where the statute in question otherwise provides) by the Arbitration Acts 1950 and 1979. The issues arising must (in the absence of contrary agreement) be decided according to the ordinary rules of English law and the normal judicial procedure will apply, including the rules of evidence (though these are often dispensed with by agreement). The arbitrator has implied power to examine witnesses, order the discovery and inspection of documents, pleadings, interrogatories and the like. Until 1990, an arbitrator had no power to dismiss an arbitration for want of prosecution.[13] However, by section 13A of the Arbitration Act 1950 (introduced in 1990),[14] an arbitrator can dismiss a claim where:

(a)   there has been inordinate and inexcusable delay on the part of the claimant in pursuing the claim; and

(b)   the delay (i) will give rise to a substantial risk that it is not possible to have a fair resolution of the issues in that claim; or (ii) has caused, or is likely to cause or have caused, serious prejudice to the respondent.[15]

3   Appointment and powers of arbitrators and umpires

In the absence of specific provision reference to arbitration connotes reference to a single arbitrator.[16] Where specific provision is made for the appointment of two arbitrators there is an implied term that, immediately after they are appointed, they shall appoint an umpire who, if the arbitrators cannot agree, may enter on the reference in their stead.[17] Under section 10 of the 1950 Act the High Court has various powers to appoint arbitrators and umpires in default of appointment by the parties.[18] The High Court also has power to revoke the authority of an arbitrator or umpire on the ground of delay, bias or improper conduct[19] and has inherent jurisdiction to stay arbitration proceedings by injunction.

There used to be provision whereby an arbitrator might, and, if directed by the court, had to state in the form of a "special case" for the opinion of the High Court, either his award or any question of law arising in the

---

12 *Fakes v Taylor Woodrow Construction Ltd* [1973] QB 436; [1973] 1 All ER 670.

13 *Bremer Vulkan Schiffbau und Maschinenfabrik v South India Shipping Corporation Ltd* [1981] AC 909; [1981] 1 All ER 289. The decision was much criticised but the House of Lords declined to depart from it in *Paal Wilson & Co A/S v Partenreederei Hannah Blumenthal* [1983] 1 AC 854; [1983] 1 All ER 34.

14 By the Courts and Legal Services Act 1990, s 102.

15 These conditions may be varied to keep them in line with the practice in respect of dismissal by the courts for want of prosecution: Arbitration Act 1950, s 13A(2).

16 Arbitration Act 1950, s 6.   17 *Ibid*, s 8.

18 As amended by the Courts and Legal Services Act 1990, s 101.

19 Arbitration Act 1950, s 23.

reference.[20] The power to apply for a special case was sometimes exercised by a party to delay unduly the resolution of the dispute and to add needlessly to costs. It was thus particularly unfortunate that the power could not be restricted by the terms of the agreement, ie the parties could not "contract out" of the special case procedure.[1] The 1979 Act altered this situation by providing[2] that the parties may enter into an "exclusion agreement", but only if they do so after the arbitration has commenced. There will then be no power in the High Court to consider a question of law arising in the course of the arbitration; nor will there be any right of appeal (*infra*). Therefore (subject to the limited power of the High Court to set aside or remit an award for misconduct (*infra*)) the arbitrator's decision will be final. Exclusion agreements entered into before the arbitration is commenced are effective only in a limited class of cases and, in particular, are invalid in the case of a "domestic arbitration agreement", that is, basically, an agreement which does not provide for arbitration outside the United Kingdom and is not one to which no United Kingdom national or resident is a party.[3]

The decision of the arbitrator is in the form of an "award", dealing with all the issues on which reference was made. The award may contain provision for the payment of money, costs or an order of specific performance (except of a contract relating to land).[4] As between the parties the award gives rise to an estoppel *in personam*[5] in relation to the issues decided, thus extinguishing any cause of action in relation thereto.

4   Intervention by the court

An arbitration award may, with leave of the High Court, be enforced in the same way as a judgment or order of that court and, where leave is granted, judgment may be entered in the terms of the award. In addition action may be brought on the award as a contractual debt.

The court's powers over arbitration proceedings were altered and extended by the 1979 Act. This created, for the first time, a right of appeal on any question of law arising out of an award made on an arbitration agreement[6] (unless excluded by a valid "exclusion agreement" (*supra*)) but only by consent of all parties or with leave of the court; the court may not grant leave unless it considers that the determination of the question of law could affect substantially the rights of the parties and it may attach conditions to the grant of leave (for example the provision of security for the amount claimed).

In addition to the right of appeal, there is jurisdiction in the High Court (save where there is a valid exclusion agreement) to determine any

---

20 *Ibid*, s 21.
 1 *Czarnikow v Roth, Schmidt & Co* [1922] 2 KB 478.
 2 Arbitration Act 1979, ss 3, 4.
 3 *Ibid*, s 3(6).
 4 Arbitration Act 1950, s 15.
 5 See p 564, *post*.
 6 Arbitration Act 1979, s 1(2); the appeal is by originating motion, must be brought within 21 days and is to a judge of the Commercial Court: Ord 73, rr 2(2), 5(2), 6.

question of law arising in the course of the reference,[7] but only with the consent of the arbitrator or of all the parties.

There is an appeal from the High Court to the Court of Appeal, from decisions under sections 1 and 2 of the 1979 Act, but only (a) with leave of the High Court; and (b) if the High Court certifies that the question of law is one of general public importance or one which for some other special reason should be considered by the Court of Appeal.[8]

Where an arbitrator has misconducted himself or the proceedings the court may remove him and may set aside the award, or may remit it for reconsideration.

The parties may nominate any person they wish to act as arbitrator. Members of the Bar are not infrequently appointed. In addition, by section 4 of the Administration of Justice Act 1970 a judge of the Commercial Court may, if in all the circumstances he thinks fit, accept appointment as sole arbitrator or as umpire where the dispute appears to him to be of a commercial character and provided the Lord Chief Justice has informed him that, having regard to the state of business in the High Court, he can be made available to do so. Similar powers now exist in respect of official referees.[9] Where a judge has acted as arbitrator or umpire under this section appeal lies by case stated to the Court of Appeal.[10]

D   RULES OF THE SUPREME COURT

Procedure in the Queen's Bench Division is governed by the Rules of the Supreme Court.[11] These Rules are delegated legislation, being made by a Rule Committee under powers conferred formerly by the Judicature Acts and currently contained in section 84 of the Supreme Court Act 1981.

The Rules themselves together with guides to their interpretation are to be found in the current edition of the *Supreme Court Practice* (the "White Book") which, formerly published annually, is now produced in a new edition every three years with periodical supplements. It must be stressed that the Rules are purely procedural and cannot affect substantive rules of law. In the words of a Master of the Rolls:

---

7 Arbitration Act 1979, s 2(1); the application must be made within 14 days and is to a judge of the Commercial Court: Ord 73, rr 5(3), 6.

8 *Ibid*, s 1(7); compare the conditions for leave to appeal to the House of Lords in criminal cases (p 512, *post*). For a summary of the principles which a judge ought to apply when considering whether to grant leave to appeal (1) to the High Court; and (2) to the Court of Appeal, see *Antaios Cia Naviera SA v Salen Rederierna AB* [1985] AC 191; [1984] 3 All ER 229. In practice appeals to the courts in arbitration cases are discouraged.

9 Arbitration Act 1950, s 11, substituted by the Courts and Legal Services Act 1990, s 99.

10 RSC, Ord 61, r 2(6).

11 The Rules of the Supreme Court have their source in the Common Law Procedure Acts 1852 and 1854 and the Court of Chancery Procedure Act 1852 (15 & 16 Vict, c 86). These were substantially reproduced in a Schedule to the Judicature Acts 1873–1875 and later embodied in the Rules of the Supreme Court 1883, a statutory instrument drawn up by the Rule Committee. The current Rules were made under s 99 of the Judicature Act 1925, the statutory predecessor of s 84 of the Supreme Court Act 1981.

". . . The relation of the rules of practice to the work of justice is intended to be that of handmaiden rather than mistress . . ."[12]

It should also be appreciated that the Rules are not an exhaustive code either of the jurisdiction of the Supreme Court or of the procedure to be followed. The Supreme Court has, as have all courts whose jurisdiction does not derive entirely from statute, inherent powers and jurisdiction which do not derive from statute and are not necessarily formulated in statutory enactments. Thus, by way of example, the Supreme Court has inherent power to prevent abuse of the process of the court by staying proceedings or striking out claims.[13] The power of a judge to refuse to hear persons who have no right of audience before the court, or counsel who are improperly dressed, or to sit *in camera*, or to abort a trial and start a new one where a procedural irregularity has occurred, or to adjourn the proceedings are all inherent powers. In recent years the important developments of *Mareva* injunctions[14] and *Anton Piller* orders[15] have derived from the inherent jurisdiction of the court and the judges have formulated their own procedural requirements ancillary to the exercise of their jurisdiction in these areas.

Likewise, the court has inherent power to regulate its own procedure. In *Langley v North West Water Authority*[16] the Court of Appeal held that a Liverpool solicitor was bound to comply with a Code of Practice issued by the Liverpool County Court. This amounted to a local Practice Direction which the court was entitled to issue under its inherent jurisdiction, except to the extent that it was concurrent with statute law or rules of court.

E PRE-COMMENCEMENT ORDERS AND PROCEDURES

Questions concerning discovery and inspection of documents and the inspection, preservation and the like of property are dealt with during the course of proceedings, usually after the close of pleadings, and these matters are dealt with below in that context.[17] However statutory provisions enable parties to obtain orders of this type prior to the commencement of proceedings. There are two distinct procedures of this type, set out below. There are also common law powers.

1 Discovery and inspection of documents

By section 33(2) of the Supreme Court Act 1981 a person who appears to the High Court to be likely to be a party to subsequent proceedings in respect of a claim of personal injuries or death may apply[18] for pre-trial discovery of

---

12 SIR RICHARD HENN-COLLINS MR in *Re Coles and Ravenshear* [1907] 1 KB 1, at 4.
13 See pp 314–318, *post*.   14 See pp 289–292, *post*.
15 See p 287, *post*.   16 [1991] 3 All ER 610; [1991] 1 WLR 697.
17 See pp 348–355, *post*.
18 The application is by originating summons supported by an affidavit which must (a) state the grounds upon which it is alleged that the applicant and the person against whom the order is sought are likely to be parties to subsequent proceedings of the type specified in section 33(2); and (b) specify or describe the documents concerned and show, if practicable by reference to a draft pleading, their relevance. The summons and copy affidavit are served on the other party and require him to make an affidavit stating whether any documents specified or described are or have been in his custody, possession or power and, if not then in his custody, possession or power what has become of them: Ord 24, r 7A (1), (3)–(5).

documents in the possession, custody or power of a person. That person must be a likely party to the proceedings; it is not enough that that person is a potential witness. That party may be ordered to disclose whether those documents are in his custody, possession and power and, if so, to produce them to the applicant, unless they are protected from disclosure by the doctrine of privilege.[19] It is immaterial that the likelihood of the claim being made is dependent upon the outcome of the discovery; the words "likely to be made" in the section are to be construed as meaning "may or may well be made" if, on discovery, the documents in question indicate that the applicant has a good cause of action.[20]

It will be noted that the above procedure is limited to personal injuries litigation. It may be utilised, for example, by a plaintiff to enable him to see his employer's accident reports or documents relating to the maintenance of a vehicle or machine which has proved defective.[1] The object of this provision is to enable personal injuries litigation to be conducted openly and with a view to early settlement if possible, the strength or otherwise of the potential claim being identified at the outset.

2 Inspection etc of property

Section 33(1) of the Supreme Court Act 1981[2] empowers the High Court, in some circumstances, to make an order providing for the inspection, photographing, preservation, custody or detention of property (including land or chattels) which appears to the court to be property which may become the subject matter of subsequent proceedings in the court, or as to which any question may arise in such proceedings, or for the taking of samples of any such property and the carrying out of any experiment on or with any such property. This is not limited to articles in the possession of a party, a position which may be contrasted with that that exists after

---

19 Ord 24, r 7A (6); see p 352, *post*.
20 *Dunning v United Liverpool Hospital's Board of Governors* [1973] 2 All ER 454; [1973] 1 WLR 586. This case concerned the disclosure of medical records. Applications under the rule are frequently made in this type of case, namely actions against doctors and hospitals for damages for professional negligence because, in the nature of things, a party (and his own expert witnesses) can hardly formulate his claim properly, nor can counsel advise upon merits, without knowing what took place while the plaintiff was being treated by the defendant, and this will almost always necessitate inspecting the medical records relating to the diagnosis and treatment of the plaintiff's medical condition. The standard form of order used to limit disclosure, in the first instance, to the applicant's medical adviser, but the rules do not provide for orders in this form and the House of Lords has held that they cannot properly be made; *McIvor v Southern Health and Social Services Board* [1978] 2 All ER 625; [1978] 1 WLR 757.
1 Cf *Shaw v Vauxhall Motors Ltd* [1974] 2 All ER 1185; [1974] 1 WLR 1035 in which an order was made for the discovery of documents relating to the inspection, maintenance and repair of a fork lift truck which was alleged to have caused an accident due to a braking defect (this being the applicant's only cause of complaint against his employers). The Court of Appeal, in the case, expressly took into account the fact that the proposed plaintiff was legally aided so that there was the public interest in saving costs to be considered.
2 Replacing Administration of Justice Act 1969, s 21.

commencement of proceedings.[3] The relationship between the power of inspection and that of discovery was examined in *Huddleston v Control Risks Information Services Ltd.*[4] The court drew a distinction between a party wishing to examine "the medium" (ie the document itself) as opposed to being concerned with "the message" (ie with the contents of the document). Section 33(1), inspection, applied to the former, section 33(2), discovery, to the latter. Since in this case the plaintiff's concern was for the contents, which were believed to be defamatory, what was being sought was discovery, for which the relevant conditions, described above, did not apply. The power of inspection could not be used to circumvent these criteria.

3   The Norwich Pharmacal principle

In addition to the statutory powers described above, a court may in some circumstances order discovery against a third party who has information. Whilst this will often be during litigation,[5] it may appropriate to obtain such discovery prior to action, in order to discover whether a basis of action exists, and against whom.

The principle, which was first stated by the court in *Norwich Pharmacal Co v Commissioners of Customs and Excise*,[6] does not permit discovery in all circumstances: it is only where the third party is in some way involved in the wrongdoing alleged that the court will order discovery against that third party.[7] However, the rule has been extended to cases where a third party has information necessary for locating and recovering missing funds.[8]

4   Anton Piller orders

The High Court has an inherent jurisdiction to order a defendant to permit a plaintiff to enter the defendant's premises in order to inspect, remove or make copies of documents belonging to the plaintiff or relating to the plaintiff's property. Such an order is known as an *Anton Piller* order, after the case in which the Court of Appeal first sanctioned this type of order.[9] An order may be obtained *ex parte* but will only be made where the plaintiff shows that there is a grave danger of property being smuggled away or vital evidence destroyed; it is usually applicable to infringement of copyright cases or cases of that sort.[10] An *Anton Piller* order may, at first

---

3 RSC Ord 29, r 2. *Douihech v Findlay* [1990] 3 All ER 118; [1990] 1 WLR 269.
4 [1987] 2 All ER 1035; [1987] 1 WLR 701.
5 See p 348, *post.*
6 [1974] AC 133; [1973] 2 All ER 943.
7 *Harrington v North London Polytechnic* [1984] 3 All ER 666; [1984] 1 WLR 1293. In *Ricci v Clow* [1987] 3 All ER 534; [1987] 1 WLR 1658, the Court of Appeal decided that discovery of the identity of the publisher and printer of an alleged defamatory article would not be ordered against the defendant, a person involved in no way in the publication, but who knew the publisher's name.
8 *Arab Monetary Fund v Hashim (No 5)* [1992] 2 All ER 911; *Bankers Trust Co v Shapiro* [1980] 3 All ER 353.
9 *Anton Piller KG v Manafacturing Processes Ltd* [1976] Ch 55; [1976] 1 All ER 779.
10 See, for example, *Ex parte Island Records Ltd* [1978] Ch 122; [1978] 3 All ER 824.

sight, appear to be in the nature of a search warrant issued to a private individual, but in fact it is not; it confers upon the plaintiff no right to enter the defendant's premises, but rather imposes a duty on a defendant to permit the plaintiff to enter his premises. Failure on the part of the defendant to comply will, however, be a contempt of court.

The *Anton Piller* application has become extremely popular with plaintiffs and their advisers. By its very nature it may enable a plaintiff to strike gold in relation to wrongful acts, such as misuse of confidential information or infringement of copyright, which but for the order the plaintiff might possibly never have been in a position to prove (defendants in these matters frequently being less than frank as to voluntary discovery); all that the plaintiff risks is having to pay his opponent's costs of the application and damages if any are caused.[11] In order to minimise speculative and oppressive applications the courts have formulated several procedural safeguards. Thus the plaintiff's solicitor should attend when the order is executed; if permission to enter premises is refused no force should be used; the defendant should have the opportunity to contact his solicitor and should be advised of his right to obtain legal advice.[12] The requirement to allow entry does not in fact operate immediately, despite the use of the word "forthwith" in an order, but operates only after there has been a reasonable period of time to obtain legal advice.[13] The applicant must make full disclosure to the court of all matters relevant to his application and if material facts are omitted the order will be discharged.[14]

The nature of the *Anton Piller* procedure is exceptional, and creates potential for abuse. In *Universal Thermosensors Ltd v Hibben*[15] SIR DONALD NICHOLLS VC identified certain key points:

(1) *Anton Piller* orders normally contain a term that, before compliance, the defendant may obtain legal advice, if this is done forthwith. If such a term is to be of use, generally such orders should be executed only on working days in office hours, when a solicitor can be expected to be available.

(2) If an *Anton Piller* order is to be executed on private premises and a woman may be at the house alone, the solicitor serving the order must be, or be accompanied by, a woman.

(3) The order should expressly provide that, unless seriously impracticable, a detailed list of the items being removed should be prepared at the time of removal, with the defendant being given the opportunity to check that list.

(4) Orders sometimes contain an injunction restraining those on whom they are served from informing others of the existence of the order for a limited period, subject to an exception in respect of communication with a lawyers to gain legal advice. The length of time governed by the injunction should not be an excessively long period. In the instant case, one week was too long.

---

11 The plaintiff applying for any form of interlocutory injunction has to give an undertaking as to damages and this undertaking is always written into the court order.
12 *International Electronics Ltd v Weigh Data Ltd* [1980] FSR 423.
13 *Bhimji v Chatwani* [1991] 1 All ER 705; [1991] 1 WLR 989.
14 *Thermax Ltd v Schott Industrial Glass Ltd* [1981] FSR 289.
15 [1992] 3 All ER 257; [1992] 1 WLR 840.

(5) An order should not be executed at business premises without a responsible officer or representative being present.

(6) Consideration should be given as to how a competitor of the business subject to the order can be prevented from having unlimited access to the documents of that business.

(7) An *Anton Piller* order should, where possible, be served by a solicitor other than a member of the firm of solicitors acting for the plaintiff. That solicitor should also have experience of the *Anton Piller* procedure.

The defendant against whom an *ex parte* order has been made may apply to have the order set aside (as can any litigant against whom an *ex parte* order is made);[16] he may even refuse compliance with the order and apply urgently to have it set aside but he does so at his peril since if his application fails he will be in contempt of court and liable to severe penalties if he has in the interim breached the order, for example by destroying records.[17]

It was held by the House of Lords in *Rank Film Distributors Ltd v Video Information Centre*[18] that defendants could resist the making of an order on the ground of privilege against self-incrimination.[19] This was a serious inroad into the scope of *Anton Piller* orders since, in the nature of things, persons against whom such orders are made are frequently engaged in fraudulent activity. To remedy this, section 72 of the Supreme Court Act 1981 withdrew the privilege in relation to High Court proceedings for infringement of rights pertaining to any intellectual property or for passing-off, including proceedings brought to prevent any apprehended such infringement or passing-off and proceedings brought to obtain disclosure of information relating thereto. Other exceptions to the privilege also exist.

The extent to which *Anton Piller*, and other, orders can be resisted on the grounds of the privilege against self-incrimination was considered by the House of Lords in *AT & T Istel Ltd v Tully*.[20] The House was of the opinion that the privilege, which itself in a civil case was an "archaic and unjustifiable survival from the past" only protected the defendant if compliance with the order would provide evidence against him in a criminal trial. If the defendant could be protected against being exposed to the reasonable risk of the information being disclosed being used in a criminal prosecution by other means, then the courts were entitled to rely on those other means. In that case the Crown Prosecution Service had agreed not to seek to use in criminal proceedings the documents disclosed.

5 Mareva injunctions

a Jurisdiction

It will be appreciated that the prospective plaintiff in an action for debt or damages faces two distinct obstacles. The first is to obtain a judgment (or settlement) in his favour; the second is to enforce that judgment. It is of little

---

16 Ord 8, r 2.
17 *WEA Records Ltd v Visions Channel 4 Ltd* [1983] 2 All ER 589; [1983] 1 WLR 721.
18 [1982] AC 380; [1981] 2 All ER 76.
19 See p 594, *post* for details of this privilege.
20 [1993] AC 45; [1992] 3 All ER 523. See p 594, *post*.

consolation to most litigants to succeed in the action and yet be unable to enforce the judgment. Regrettably, where a defendant is uninsured against his liability this is a situation which often arises. Where the defendant is simply insolvent this is a misfortune that the plaintiff must bear. However the courts can and will intervene to prevent a defendant from avoiding his liability to the plaintiff by disposing of his assets, and in particular removing them outside the jurisdiction of the English courts. An injunction to restrain a defendant from so doing is called a *Mareva* injunction, taking its name from the 1975 case in which the jurisdiction was first acknowledged by the Court of Appeal.[1] Since 1975 the development of this area of law and practice, particularly in the Commercial Court,[2] has been rapid. The injunction was originally confined to foreign defendants and to prohibiting removal of assets from the jurisdiction but was soon extended to United Kingdom residents and to the prohibition of dispositions of assets within the jurisdiction.

The jurisdiction to make such orders is now conferred by section 37(3) of the Supreme Court Act 1981 which provides:

> "The power of the High Court . . . to grant an interlocutory injunction restraining a party to any proceedings from removing from the jurisdiction of the High Court, or otherwise dealing with, assets located within that jurisdiction shall be exercisable in cases where that party is, as well as cases where he is not, domiciled, resident or present within that jurisdiction."

The words "dealing with" encompass disposing of, selling or charging assets.[3]

Until recently it had been thought that one important restriction on the court's power to grant a *Mareva* injunction lay in the fact that the injunction is *ancillary* to a cause of action; it is not a cause of action in itself. Thus, if a plaintiff's claim is not justiciable in the English courts he could not obtain an injunction. For example, if the defendant is domiciled in a country to which section 25 of the Civil Jurisdiction and Judgments Act 1982 does not apply, leave to serve a writ outside the jurisdiction will be required. If this was not granted, there would be no basis for a successful application for a *Mareva* injunction.[4] This view was supported by the Court of Appeal in *The Veracruz I*,[5] where it was stressed that the powers of the High Court to grant an injunction derived from section 37 of the Supreme Court Act 1981, and were to grant an injunction in all cases where it was just and convenient to do so. The right to obtain an interlocutory injunction was not a cause of action in itself. However, this conclusion is called into doubt by the decision of the House of Lords in *Channel Tunnel Group Ltd v Balfour Beatty Construction Ltd*.[6] In that case LORD MUSTILL indicated that the fact that proceedings in an English court could be the subject of a stay did not prevent the court from granting interlocutory relief. LORD

---

1 *Mareva Compania Naviera SA v International Bulkcarriers SA* [1980] 1 All ER 213n; [1975] 2 Lloyd's Rep 509.
2 As to which see p 364, *post*.
3 *CBS United Kingdom Ltd v Lambert* [1983] Ch 37; [1982] 3 All ER 237.
4 But see *infra*.
5 [1992] 1 Lloyd's Rep 353.
6 [1993] AC 334; [1993] 1 All ER 664; as to which see p 326, *post*.

BROWNE-WILKINSON doubted whether the authority on which this restriction was based[7] remained good law.[8]

b Procedure

An applicant for a *Mareva* injunction is well advised to act quickly. To this end the customary practice is to apply *ex parte* in the first instance, sometimes even before issuing a writ (in which case the plaintiff will be required to undertake to issue a writ within a specified period or "forthwith") whereupon an order will be made to take effect until the return date on the summons which the plaintiff will have issued or undertaken to issue. The plaintiff must swear an affidavit in support of his application. In *Third Chandris Shipping Corporation v Unimarine SA*[9] the Court of Appeal stated guidelines that judges should follow on such applications:

(i)   the plaintiff should make full and frank disclosure of all matters in his knowledge which are material for the judge to know;

(ii) the plaintiff should give particulars of his claim and the amount thereof and of the defendant's case against it;

(iii) the plaintiff should give some grounds for believing that the defendant has assets within the jurisdiction;

(iv) the plaintiff should give some grounds (not merely that the defendant is abroad) for believing that there is a risk of the assets of the defendant being removed before the judgment is satisfied;

(v)   the plaintiff should give an undertaking in damages, in a suitable case to be supported by a bond or security.

In the light of the fact that the injunction is no longer limited to restraining removal of assets from the jurisdiction,[10] (iv) above is clearly modified.

The court has power to order discovery of documents or to administer interrogatories as to the amount, whereabouts or other details of the defendant's assets, with a view to securing the efficacy of the injunction.[11]

Copies of the injunction will generally be served upon the defendant's bank or other body having custody of his assets, so as to fix such body with knowledge of the injunction (since such body would itself be guilty of contempt of court if it assisted the defendant to act in breach of the injunction, knowing that it is probable that the asset is being disposed of in breach of the injunction). The receipt by a bank of such notice overrides its customer's instructions, eg to honour cheques.

c Principles upon which the court acts

By section 37(1) of the Supreme Court Act 1981 the High Court may grant an injunction "in all cases in which it appears to the court to be just and convenient to do so". However, although not subject to statutory fetters,

---

7 *The Siskina* [1979] AC 210; [1977] 3 All ER 803. See also: *South Carolina Insurance Co v Assurantie Maatschap pij, de Zeven Provincien NV* [1987] AC 24; [1986] 3 All ER 487.
8 See n 5, *ante.*
9 [1979] QB 645; [1979] 2 All ER 972.
10 *A v C* [1981] QB 956n; [1980] 2 All ER 347.
11 *Bank Ellat v Kazmi* [1989] QB 541.

the courts have developed principles on the basis of which to grant or refuse injunctions.

The general principles affecting the discretion whether to grant or refuse an interlocutory injunction are those laid down by the House of Lords in *American Cyanamid Co v Ethicon Ltd*[12] and will be considered in due course.[13] However there are additional principles of particular application to *Mareva* applications. As a first step the plaintiff must satisfy the court (i) that he has at least a good arguable case; and (ii) that the refusal of an injunction would involve a real risk that a judgment or award in the plaintiff's favour would remain unsatisfied because of the defendant's removal of assets from the jurisdiction or dissipation of assets within the jurisdiction.[14] An injunction will not be granted merely for the purpose of providing a plaintiff with security for a claim, even where it appears likely to succeed and even where the granting of the injunction will not cause hardship to the defendant.[15]

An injunction will not be granted so as to give the plaintiff priority over other creditors, nor to prevent the defendant from paying his debts as they fall due or carrying on his legitimate business. It is also common for the injunction to be expressed so as to exclude periodical payments of reasonable amounts to provide for the living or other expenses of the defendant,[16] including amounts to be paid to his legal advisers to contest the litigation.

d   Position of third parties

It has been noted that service of a copy of the injunction upon a third party, such as a bank, operates in effect to freeze the account. This has led to problems and the courts are vigilant to ensure that banks and other third parties do not suffer in consequence of the grant of a *Mareva* injunction. Thus, a bank is entitled to a variation of the injunction to enable it to set off against any funds which it holds any right that it has in respect of facilities granted to the client, for example bank charges, interest or the balance on another account. Similarly an injunction will not be granted, or will be discharged, where the effect would be to interfere substantially with the business of a third party.[17] In *Polly Peck International plc v Nadir (No 2)*[18] the court indicated that a *Mareva* injunction ought not to be granted against a bank, except where that bank was likely to act so as to avoid judgment.

Where a bank or third party is compelled to enter the proceedings in order to obtain an order, or discharge of an order, the plaintiff will ordinarily be required to pay its cost on an indemnity basis.[19]

---

12 [1975] AC 396; [1975] 1 All ER 504.
13 See p 327, *post.*
14 *Ninemia Maritime Corporation v Trave Schiffahrtsgesellschaft mbH & Co KG* [1984] 1 All ER 398; [1983] 1 WLR 1412.
15 See *Polly Peck International plc v Nadir (No 2)* [1992] 4 All ER 769.
16 See, for examples, *PCW (Underwriting Agencies) Ltd v Dixon* [1983] 2 All ER 158.
17 *Galaxia Maritime SA v Mineralimportexport* [1982] 1 All ER 796; [1982] 1 WLR 539.
18 See n 15, *ante.*
19 *Z Ltd v A-Z* [1982] QB 558; [1982] 1 All ER 556.

F ALTERNATIVE METHODS OF COMMENCING A CIVIL ACTION

An action in the Queen's Bench Division[20] is in most cases commenced by writ of summons, generally referred to as a writ. However there are alternative methods of proceeding of which the most important is by originating summons.[1] The latter method is appropriate where the parties' dispute is such that it can be peremptorily determined. As the name indicates it is a summons which actually originates the action as opposed to the issue of an ordinary summons which is an interlocutory step in an action commenced by writ. The method which the plaintiff chooses is not in all cases optional. Thus the following proceedings in the Queen's Bench Division must be begun by writ:

(1) in which a claim is made by the plaintiff for any relief or remedy for any tort, other than trespass to land;

(2) in which a claim made by the plaintiff is based on an allegation of fraud;

(3) in which a claim is made by the plaintiff for damages for breach of duty where the damages claimed consist of or include damages in respect of the death of any person or in respect of personal injuries to any person or in respect of damage to any property;[2]

One type of action must be commenced by originating summons; where any Act requires an application to be made to the High Court other than an application in pending proceedings and no other method is prescribed.[3] A common example is an application, made before commencing an action, for discovery of documents under section 33(2) of the Supreme Court Act 1981.[4] All other actions may be commenced either by writ or by originating summons but the following proceedings are appropriate to be commenced by originating summons:

(1) in which the sole or principal question at issue is, or is likely to be, one of the construction of an Act, or of any instrument made under an Act, or of any deed, will, contract or other document, or some other question of law, or

(2) in which there is unlikely to be any substantial dispute of fact.[5]

Since these actions are not concerned with disputes as to fact it would be pedantic for the parties to have to exchange pleadings. The originating summons procedure is not, therefore, appropriate where there is a significant dispute upon the facts. Nor is it appropriate where the plaintiff intends to apply for summary judgment under Order 14, since this important order

---

20 By RSC, Ord 1, r 4A (a) "any reference to proceedings in the Queen's Bench Division shall be construed as including a reference to proceedings in the Commercial Court but not to proceedings in the Admiralty Court." The Admiralty Court is part of the Queen's Bench Division (Supreme Court Act 1981, s 62(2)) but procedure differs in many respects from procedure in the remainder of the Division and a code of procedure is prescribed by Order 75; see p 365, *post*.

1 The extension of originating summons procedure in the Queen's Bench Division was an important innovation of the 1962 Rules. Prior to 1964 originating summonses were far more common in the Chancery Division and, in the Queen's Bench Division, were confined mainly to applications under s 17 of the Married Women's Property Act 1882 (which are now assigned to the Family Division).

2 Ord 5, r 2.

3 Ord 5, r 3.

4 See p 285, *ante*.

5 Ord 5, r 4.

applies only to actions commenced by writ. The tort of trespass to land is excepted from those proceedings which must be begun by writ because this action frequently involves a dispute as to title which can be resolved by reference to a single deed or contract – the very type of case with which originating summons procedure is appropriate to deal.

The only other methods of commencing proceedings in the High Court are by originating motion or petition, but these methods are applicable if, and only if, expressly authorised by the rules or by any Act.[6] Proceedings by petition occur in both the Chancery Division (for example for the winding-up of companies) and the Family Division (for example judicial separation proceedings), but not in the Queen's Bench Division, with the exception of election petitions under the Representation of the People Act 1983.

Having considered which is the appropriate method of proceeding the plaintiff must, before issuing his writ, consider two further preliminary matters. First he must ensure that his cause of action has accrued since, in order to succeed in his action, the plaintiff must prove a cause of action which was complete at the date of the issue of the writ. So, for example, an action for the recovery of a debt would be bound to fail if the debt had not fallen due before the issue of the writ even though, when the action came to trial, the debt was clearly overdue. It is axiomatic that English courts will not adjudicate upon hypothetical, as opposed to actual, disputes.[7] The second matter which he must consider concerns the proper parties to the action.

G   PARTIES

1   Joinder of parties

The names of all intended parties must appear at the head of the writ. There may be any number of plaintiffs or defendants, or both, to the action. At common law the effect of misjoinder or non-joinder of proper parties was to defeat the plaintiff's claim but nowadays "no cause or matter shall be defeated by reason of the misjoinder or nonjoinder of any party".[8] However the plaintiff must still weigh carefully his choice of parties. On the one hand he may fail to join a party from whom he is entitled to relief in which case his whole action may fail. Alternatively he may add parties whose presence is unnecessary in which event he will usually have to pay the costs occasioned by his error.

---

6 Ord 5, r 5.
7 *Re Barnato* [1949] Ch 258; cf *Ealing London Borough Council v Race Relations Board* [1972] AC 342; [1972] 1 All ER 105 and authorities referred to therein. The power of the High Court to make a declaratory judgment or order (Ord 15, r 16; see p xxx, *post*) can be exercised in relation to future rights but is only so exercised in exceptional cases, for example where future rights affect the present situation. A declaration which relates to a purely hypothetical issue or which would serve no useful purpose will not be made; cf. *Mellstrom v Garner* [1970] 2 All ER 9; [1970] 1 WLR 603. If a writ is issued prematurely the defect is incurable by amendment since amendment dates back to the issue of the writ (*Eshelby v Federated European Bank* [1932] 1 KB 254); the plaintiff's only course is to apply to discontinue the action (see p 316, *post*).
8 Ord 15, r 6(1).

Subject to the court's power to order separate trials or add or strike out parties,[9] two or more persons may be joined as plaintiffs or defendants in the following circumstances:

(1) where:

    (a) if separate actions were brought by or against each of them, as the case may be, some common question of law or fact would arise in all the actions; and

    (b) all rights to relief claimed in the action (whether they are joint, several or alternative) are in respect or arise out of the same transaction or series of transactions; and

(2) in any other case with leave of the court.[10]

The plaintiff should join all potential defendants whether relief is alleged to exist against them jointly, severally or in the alternative, for even in the latter circumstance the plaintiff, although he obviously must fail against one or more defendant, may not suffer by it. The reason is that if the court is satisfied that it was a proper course for the plaintiff to join the defendants, it may order the costs of the successful defendant to be added to the costs payable by the unsuccessful defendant.[11] Thus if a plaintiff is injured in a "running down" case he should join the drivers of all the vehicles (unless the liability of one driver, to the exclusion of the others, is *prima facie* obvious, in which event a wise course is to sue only one driver and then to join, by amendment, such other persons as the defendant "blames" in his defence);[12] where he seeks an injunction to abate a nuisance he should join both the landlord and the tenant of the premises from which the alleged nuisance comes; where he is uncertain whether a woman has contracted with him as agent of her husband or as a principal he should join both the husband and wife.[13]

In addition, under Order 15, rule 6(2), at any stage of the proceedings the court may, of its own motion or on application (a) strike out any party who is not a necessary or proper party; or (b) add as a party any person whose presence is necessary to ensure that all matters in dispute may be effectively and completely determined or any person between whom and any party there may exist a question or issue connected with the action which in the opinion of the court it would be just and convenient to determine. Thus in *Gurtner v Circuit*[14] the Motor Insurers Bureau successfully applied to be added as a defendant to an action for damages by a pedestrian against a motor cyclist, on the basis that, since neither the original defendant nor his insurers could be traced, the Bureau might, by reason of its agreement with the Minister of Transport to satisfy all unpaid damages awarded against an uninsured motorist, have to pay any damages

---

9 Ord 15, rr 5(1), 6(2).

10 Ord 15, r 4.

11 See p 381, *post.*

12 Counsel who fails to bear these precepts in mind may be liable in negligence; *Saif Ali v Sydney Mitchell & Co* [1980] AC 198; [1978] 3 All ER 1033; see p 229, *ante.*

13 *Morel Brothers v Earl of Westmorland* [1904] AC 11; unless, of course, prior correspondence or negotiation has disclosed that there is no issue on the point.

14 [1968] 2 QB 587; [1968] 1 All ER 328; cf. *Sanders Lead Co Inc v Entores Metal Brokers Ltd* [1984] 1 All ER 857; [1984] 1 WLR 452.

awarded. This gave the Bureau a legal and pecuniary interest in the proceedings sufficient to justify its joinder, notwithstanding that the plaintiff had no cause of action against the Bureau.

As in all branches of the law there are special rules which apply only to certain classes of person, usually by reason of a status. The prospective plaintiff must in particular determine whether a prospective defendant is the subject of any of these special rules.

2   Special parties

a   The Crown[15]

Until 1948, as an offshoot of the principle of Crown immunity, the Crown could not be made a party to an action in the courts, the only redress being against Crown servants in their personal capacity. However, by the Crown Proceedings Act 1947 the Crown may now, subject to minor exceptions, be sued in contract or tort. The immunity now extends only to the reigning monarch, although there is still a rule of statutory interpretation that the Crown is not bound by a statute unless expressly named in it. An action is commenced by or against the Crown through its appropriate government department as named in a list issued by the Treasury and service is on the solicitor for that department. If there is no appropriate department proceedings are carried on in the name of the Attorney-General. Although the Crown now has few relics of substantive immunity it enjoys certain procedural advantages; for example that judgment in default cannot be entered against the Crown without leave, that judgment under Order 14 cannot be entered against the Crown and that the Crown is not liable to have any judgment enforced against it.

Action against the Crown pursuant to the provisions of the 1947 Act lies only in respect of liability arising in the United Kingdom.[16] In *Franklin v A-G*[17] Lawson J was faced with the difficult task of deciding what was the appropriate form of proceedings to enforce a right existing against the Bank of England in relation to the plaintiff's entitlement to interest on Southern Rhodesia stock. The method of enforcement prescribed by the Colonial Stock Act 1877, section 20 was petition of right, under the then Petitions of Right Act 1860. However, that 1860 Act had been repealed by the Crown Proceedings Act 1947 and, as noted above, no action lay under the 1947 Act since the liability of the Crown did not arise within the United Kingdom. It was held, by Lawson J, that the procedure was by petition of right but in the old form used prior to the Act of 1860. This would seem to be the only surviving instance of the ancient procedure of petition of right whereby the Sovereign is petitioned to "order that right be done in this matter".[18] The Sovereign then refers the petition to the Queen's Bench Division for consideration and the High Court then makes an order which

---

15 The special rules of procedure applicable in proceedings to which the Crown is a party are contained in Ord 77.
16 Crown Proceedings Act 1947, s 40(2).   17 [1974] QB 185; [1973] 1 All ER 879.
18 For the full form of the petition, see *Franklin v R* [1974] QB 202n; [1973] 3 All ER 861.

appears to have the effect of a judgment against the Crown.

b Foreign states

Foreign states, their sovereigns or other heads of state (in their public capacity), their governments and departments of government are immune from the jurisdiction of the courts of the United Kingdom, subject to the exceptions provided by the State Immunity Act 1978.[19] However, that does not mean that a foreign state cannot, or should not, be made a party to an action. It may submit to the jurisdiction by taking a step in the proceedings, for example acknowledging service, and a state is not immune if it intervenes or submits to the jurisdiction (unless it does so only for the purpose of claiming immunity or asserting an interest in property in circumstances in which it could have claimed immunity had it been sued, or it takes a step in ignorance of its entitlement to immunity, provided it claims immunity as soon as reasonably practicable).[20]

Moreover the immunity does not extend to proceedings in respect of commercial transactions,[1] contracts requiring performance in the United Kingdom, certain contracts of employment, death, personal injury or damage to property caused in the United Kingdom and certain other proceedings described in the Act.[2] The effect of the Act has therefore been to restrict considerably the immunity from suit which foreign states formerly enjoyed at common law. Quite apart from the Act, the House of Lords has held that the immunity does not extend to activities, trading, commercial or otherwise, of a private law character in which the state in question has chosen to engage, but is limited to sovereign or public acts.[3]

An international organisation created by treaty cannot sue or be sued, except in certain circumstances. In *Arab Monetary Fund v Hashim (No 3)*[4] the House of Lords held that, although such an organisation was not a corporate body, with capacity to sue or be sued in the English courts, the registration of the treaty in one of the sovereign states conferred legal personality on the organisation, which English courts should recognise, thus enabling it to maintain an action. This explained the earlier decision in *McClaine Watson v Department of Trade and Industry*,[5] with the effect that the member states who had established the Council could not be liable in law under the International Tin Agreement.

Writs and documents are served through the Foreign and Commonwealth Office to the Ministry of Foreign Affairs of the state. Foreign states enjoy certain procedural privileges under section 13 of the Act. Thus they are not liable to committal or fine for failure to disclose or produce documents and (subject to certain exceptions arising out of international conventions) the following remedies are not available against foreign states: injunctions, orders for specific performance, orders for the recovery of land or other property, all process against property of the state for the

---

19 Act of 1978, ss 1, 14.   20 *Ibid*, s 2.
1 *Ibid*, s 3(1)(a) affirming *Trendtex Trading Corporation Ltd v Central Bank of Nigeria* [1977] QB 529; [1977] 1 All ER 881; see p 59, *ante*.
2 *Ibid*, ss 2–11.
3 *I Congreso del Partido*; [1983] 1 AC 244; [1981] 2 All ER 1064.
4 [1991] 2 AC 114; [1991] 1 All ER 871.
5 [1990] 2 AC 418; [1989] 3 All ER 523.

enforcement of judgments,[6] orders for the arrest, detention and sale of the property of the state in actions *in rem*.

c   Incorporated associations

An association may be incorporated either by royal charter or under a statute, usually one of the Companies Acts. In either case the creation is a legal *persona* with an existence, for the purposes of the law, completely independent of its members.[7] It is this factor which distinguishes a corporation or company from an unincorporated association, which is merely a group of individuals referred to by a collective name. An incorporated association may enter into contracts and may commit torts and even crimes. As a legal personality it may sue and be sued in its corporate title or registered name. However, since it has no physical existence, it can only appear through a solicitor.[8] Service on a company is effected by delivering or posting the document to be served to the company's registered office.[9] In one respect a plaintiff company is at a disadvantage; if it has insufficient assets it may be required to give security for costs.[10]

d   Unincorporated associations

An association which is not incorporated, under royal charter or statute, has no legal existence independent of the members of the association. There are for procedural purposes three classes of unincorporated association: partnerships, registered associations and unregistered associations.

Partnerships — Partners may sue and be sued in the firm name.[11] However if suing in the firm name they must on request disclose the name and address of every member of the firm.[12] If they are sued in the firm name, the partners must acknowledge service in their own names individually although proceedings continue in the name of the firm. Any person who denies that he is or was a partner when the cause of action arose should so state in his acknowledgment of service.[13] A judgment against a partnership may be executed against partnership property or against any person who has acknowledged service of the writ as a partner or failed to acknowledge service having been served as a partner, has

---

6 See *Alcom Ltd v Republic of Colombia* [1984] AC 580; [1984] 2 All ER 6 although the House of Lords in that case stated that the property in question (the credit balance in a bank account) would not be immune if the plaintiff could prove that funds in the account were used solely to meet liabilities incurred in commercial transactions; since the ambassador's certificate to the contrary was conclusive by virtue of s 13(5) of the Act, the plaintiff was unable to surmount this obstacle.

7 *Salomon v A Salomon & Co Ltd* [1897] AC 22.

8 So that the litigant's right to appear in person (Ord 5, r 6) does not extend to corporations or companies. They may, however, acknowledge service (and give notice of intention to defend) by a duly authorised person instead of a solicitor (Ord 2, r 1(2)).

9 Companies Act 1985, s 725. Service on the company solicitor is also usual. Corporations are served by serving the appropriate officer, eg mayor, chief executive (Ord 65, r 3.)

10 Companies Act 1985, s 726.

11 Ord 81, r 1.

12 Ord 81, r 2.

13 Ord 81, r 4; he may then apply to the court to set aside service.

admitted in his pleading that he is a partner or has been adjudged to be a partner.[14]

Registered associations — Certain associations are by statute registrable. This does not affect the position of the members but it does enable the association to appear in its registered name. The most common examples of such associations are trade unions[15] and friendly societies.[16]

Other unincorporated associations — Where an association is unregistered and not a partnership it cannot appear in its group name, since that name is no more than a convenient label for the members collectively.[17] Frequently the proper parties to the action will be members of the association in their private capacity. Where, however, the right or liability is common to all the members it is inconvenient, although possible, to join them all as parties. The appropriate procedure is a "representative action". In a representative action, where numerous persons have the same interest in any proceedings, whether as plaintiffs or defendants, one or more persons may be authorised to appear on behalf of all persons so interested.[18] However a representative action is only appropriate where all the persons to be represented have a common grievance and will all benefit from the relief claimed if plaintiffs,[19] or are jointly liable if defendants.[20] Thus where the liability of defendants is several, for example in conspiracy[1] or defamation, they cannot be represented and must be sued in their own names. Nevertheless an action for negligence has been allowed to proceed against representatives of the members of a club on the ground that they were joint occupiers of the club premises.[2] A judgment against representative defendants is binding on them all. However it can be executed against the actual parties but not against the persons represented without leave. An order for costs cannot be made against a person represented. The writ must define clearly the parties and the names of persons represented. Thus an order to represent "all the persons who were members of the City Livery Club on June 29, 1949" was made in one case, being a sufficient identification of the persons represented as defendants.[3]

---

14 Ord 81, r 5; such a judgment may also be executed against the private property of any other partner, but only with leave.

15 Trade Union and Labour Relations Act 1974, s 2(1)(h) (replacing earlier legislation); an "employers' association" (as defined in s 28(2) of the Act of 1974) may likewise sue and be sued in its own name. In *Engineers' and Managers' Association v Advisory, Conciliation and Arbitration Service* [1979] 3 All ER 223; [1979] 1 WLR 1113 the Court of Appeal held that, in certain circumstances, a union might be permitted representation by one of its officers, so obviating the need for counsel to appear for it.

16 Friendly Societies Act 1974 (consolidating earlier legislation).

17 But see *London Association for Protection of Trade v Greenlands Ltd* [1916] 2 AC 15, where the rules of procedure appear to have been flouted.

18 Ord 15, r 12.

19 *Smith v Cardiff Corporation* [1954] 1 QB 210; [1953] 2 All ER 1373; distinguished in *John v Rees* [1970] Ch 345; [1969] 2 All ER 274.

20 *Mercantile Marine Service Association v Toms* [1916] 2 KB 243.

 1 *Hardie and Lane v Chiltern* [1928] 1 KB 663.

 2 *Campbell v Thompson* [1953] 1 QB 445; [1953] 1 All ER 831; see also *Wallersteiner v Moir (No 2)* [1975] QB 373; [1975] 1 All ER 849 where a minority shareholder's action was likened to a representative action on behalf of the company and it was stated by the Court of Appeal that the shareholder, after issuing proceedings, should in effect apply to the court for an order sanctioning the proceedings, the effect of which would be to give the shareholder a right to have the company pay his costs.

 3 See n 2, *supra*.

It is important to distinguish a representative action from a "test case". The latter is popular terminology for an action the function of which is to determine the legal position of numerous individuals who are not parties to the action; for example an action based on the interpretation of a Finance Act upon which depend the tax obligations of a large section of the populace. The expression "test case" has, however, no legal meaning and only the parties to a test case are bound by the judgment. However, rights are determined conclusively through the operation of the doctrine of precedent.

e   Persons under disability; infants and patients

A married woman has, since 1935, ceased to be a person under a disability[4] and that phrase now applies only to infants and patients. An infant is a person under the age of 18.[5] A patient is a person who, by reason of mental disorder within the meaning of the Mental Health Act 1983, is incapable of managing and administering his property and affairs.[6] Infants and patients cannot appear personally.

They sue by their "next friend".[7] In the case of an infant this is usually the father or person in *loco parentis*; in the case of a patient, his receiver. In any case where there is no person competent or willing to appear as next friend, the Official Solicitor will do so. The next friend is not a party to the action (though he may, of course, be a co-plaintiff in his own right). Nevertheless his name must appear on the writ, *viz* "AB an infant, by CD his (father and) next friend", and he is personally liable for costs with a right of indemnity from the infant or patient for costs properly incurred. Since he is not a party he cannot counterclaim in his personal capacity; nor can he be required to give security for costs.[8] The next friend cannot act in person and so must be represented by a solicitor[9] who must file two documents: (1) the next friend's written consent to act, and (2) a certificate that the next friend has no interest in the proceedings adverse to that of the infant or patient.[10]

They defend by a "guardian *ad litem*" who will be the same person as the next friend would have been, or the Official Solicitor. The solicitor must file the same two documents as above. However the guardian *ad litem* is not personally liable for costs except where he has been guilty of gross

---

4 Law Reform (Married Women and Tortfeasors) Act 1935, s 1; and see Law Reform (Husband and Wife) Act 1962.

5 Family Law Reform Act 1969, s 1(1); the terms "infant" and "minor" are synonymous (*ibid*, s 1(2)).

6 This definition of a "patient" in Ord 80, r 1 is narrower than the definition in s 145(1) of the Mental Health Act 1983, ie a person suffering or appearing to be suffering from mental disorder, but corresponds with the criteria under s 94 of that Act (which applies for the purpose of deciding whether a person is within the jurisdiction of the Court of Protection); where there are proceedings in the Court of Protection application for the appointment of a next friend should be made to that court: *Re S (F G) (Mental Health Patient)* [1973] 1 All ER 273; [1973] 1 WLR 178.

7 Ord 80, r 2(1).

8 Since he is not a "nominal plaintiff" within Ord 23, r 1(1)(b); *Fellows v Barrett* (1836) 1 Keen 119; see p 355, *post*. Nor can he give a receipt for money recovered in settlement of an action, *Leather v Kirby* [1965] 3 All ER 927n; [1965] 1 WLR 1489.

9 Ord 80, r 2(3).

10 Ord 80, r 3.

misconduct, and in this respect his position differs from that of the next friend.

The next friend or guardian *ad litem* must, of course, act in the best interests of the person he represents. If he does not the court has inherent power to remove him but this power will not be exercised simply because the course which a next friend is taking is opposed by a number of other litigants.[11]

(1) Judgment on failure to give notice of intention to defend cannot be entered against an infant or patient. The proper course is to apply to the court to appoint a guardian *ad litem*.[12]

(2) No settlement of an action on behalf of an infant or patient is valid unless approved by the court.[13]

(3) Any money recovered by or on behalf of an infant or patient must be dealt with in accordance with the court's direction.[14]

(4) Allegations in a statement of claim or counterclaim are not deemed to be admitted by an infant or patient by reason only of his failure to traverse them.[15]

f Estates of deceased persons

Prior to 1971, if at the commencement of proceedings a person named as a party was dead, the action by or against that person was a nullity and could not be cured by amendment to substitute executors as parties.[16] The action had to be brought by or against the executors or administrators. However section 87 of the Supreme Court Act 1981 (replacing the Proceedings Against Estates Act 1970) and Order 15, rule 6A enable an action to be brought against the estate of a deceased person[17] even though no grant of probate or administration has been made; the defendant should be named in the proceedings "the personal representative of AB deceased." The plaintiff must then, during the period of validity for service of the writ or originating summons, apply to the court for an order appointing a person to represent the deceased's estate or, if a grant of probate or administration has been made since the commencement of proceedings, an order that the personal representative be made a party.[18]

---

11 *Re Taylor's Application* [1972] 2 QB 369; [1972] 2 All ER 873 – one of the many actions arising out of the "thalidomide" tragedy.
12 Ord 80, r 6.
13 Ord 80, rr. 10, 11. If a settlement or compromise is reached before a writ is issued, the court's approval to it can be sought by originating summons in the expedited form (see p 375, *post*) (Ord 80, r 11). If a settlement is reached after proceedings have begun, the application for the approval of the court is by ordinary summons, or to the trial judge if the settlement is reached during the trial. It seems arguable that Ord 80, r 10 is *ultra vires* in that, insofar as it purports to declare certain contracts void, it is more than a rule of procedure, but such an argument was rejected by the House of Lords in *Dietz v Lennig Chemicals Ltd* [1969] 1 AC 170; [1967] 2 All ER 282.
14 Ord 80, r 12. In *Leather v Kirby* [1965] 3 All ER 927n; [1965] 1 WLR 1489, the House of Lords stated that the money should usually be paid into court or, in the case of a patient, to the Court of Protection.
15 Ord 80, r 8; see Ord 18, r 13(1); also p 339, *post*.
16 *Dawson (Bradford) Ltd v Dove* [1971] 1 QB 330; [1971] 1 All ER 554.
17 Proceedings commenced in the name of a deceased person as plaintiff are still a nullity.
18 Ord 15, r 6A(4). Where no grant of probate or administration has been made any judgment or order binds the estate as if a personal representative of the deceased had been a party to the proceedings (Ord 15, r 6A(7)).

Before making such order the court may require notice to be given to any insurer of the deceased who has an interest in the proceedings as well as to any other person having an interest in the estate. Judgment cannot be signed until personal representatives have been appointed and any judgment signed before that time will be a nullity.[19]

g   *Vexatious litigants*

By section 42(1) of the Supreme Court Act 1981 (as amended) the High Court may, on the application of the Attorney-General, make a "civil proceedings order" against any person who has habitually and persistently and without any reasonable ground instituted vexatious civil proceedings or made vexatious applications in any civil proceedings.

The effect of such an order is that the person against whom it has been made cannot institute or continue any civil proceedings without the leave of the High Court.[20]

---

19 *Re Amirteymour (decd)* [1978] 3 All ER 637; [1979] 1 WLR 63.
20 See, generally, *A-G v Jones* [1990] 2 All ER 636; [1990] 1 WLR 859.

CHAPTER 14

Commencing an Action by Writ

A   THE WRIT AND ITS CONTENTS

A writ of summons (1) notifies the defendant of the issue of the writ, (2) informs him that he must either satisfy the claim set out on the back of the writ or return to the Court Office the accompanying acknowledgment of service stating therein whether he intends to contest the proceedings, and (3) informs him that if he fails to satisfy the claim or return the acknowledgment within the time stated or without stating therein an intention to contest the proceedings, judgment may be entered against him.[1] The writ must state the names of all the intended parties to the action, whether plaintiffs or defendants, the persons on whose behalf they are appearing, if they are appearing in a representative capacity, and the division of the High Court in which the plaintiff is suing.[2] In addition the writ must bear certain indorsements. These are of two kinds: indorsements of the plaintiff's claims and formal indorsements.

1   Indorsements of claim

The writ must be indorsed either;

(1)   with a statement of claim.[3] In this event, the statement of claim on the writ will be the statement of claim in the action and the plaintiff may not serve another, except by way of amendment. The advantage is a saving of time for the plaintiff may proceed to apply for

---

1 RSC, App A, Form No 1 (substituted by the Rules of the Supreme Court (Writ and Appearance) 1979, with effect from 3 June 1980); the old form of writ was in the form of a royal command to the defendant to enter an appearance.

2 In commercial actions in the Commercial Court (London, Liverpool and Manchester) the writ may be marked in the top lefthand corner with the words "Commercial Court" whereupon the action will be automatically entered in the commercial list (Ord 72, r 4(1)); see p 364, *post*). Finally a writ or originating summons by which "official referees'" business is to be begun may be marked in the top lefthand corner with those words whereupon the cause will thereafter be treated as official referees' business (as to which, see p 365, *post*).

3 This is usually termed a "special indorsement", though this expression does not appear in the current Rules. The plaintiff may in one action claim relief against the same defendant in respect of more than one cause of action. However admiralty actions in rem and in personam cannot now be joined in one writ; *Practice Direction (Admiralty; Writs)* [1979] 2 All ER 155; [1979] 1 WLR 426.

summary judgment under Order 14 as soon as the defendant has given notice of intention to defend. Also where the plaintiff's claim is for an equitable remedy or a declaration, he cannot obtain judgment in default until he has served a statement of claim; or

(2) with a concise statement of the nature of the claim made or the relief or remedy required in the action.[4] In this case the plaintiff will have to serve his statement of claim, setting out his claim in detail, at the same time as service of the writ, or subsequently. However he must still indorse his writ with particulars which are sufficient to enable the defendant to identify the cause of action against him.[5] Thus "the plaintiff claims damages for breach of contract", or "the plaintiff claims damages for slander" are insufficient. The plaintiff must identify the contract which he alleges has been broken, or the publication which he alleges to defame him. In addition: in actions for libel the actual publication complained of must be identified;[6] in actions for wrongful interference with goods brought by a plaintiff who is one of two or more persons claiming any interest in the goods, unless he has the written authority of all of them to sue, the writ must be indorsed with (i) particulars of the plaintiff's title; and (ii) identification of every other person who, to his knowledge, has or claims any interest in the goods.[7] Where the claim is for possession of land the writ must be indorsed with a statement showing whether the claim relates to a dwelling house and, if it does, whether the rateable value of the premises on every day specified by section 4 of the Rent Act 1977 in relation to the premises exceeds the sum so specified.[8] Where the action is brought to enforce a right to recover possession of goods the writ must be indorsed with a statement showing the value of the goods.[9] Where the plaintiff seeks to obtain judgment in a foreign currency, he should state this in his writ and, unless the facts themselves clearly show this (*semble* the facts set out in the general indorsement) he should plead the facts relied on to support such a claim in his statement of claim.[10]

---

4 Usually described as a "general indorsement".
5 Although failure so to do does not render the writ a nullity. The defect may be cured by amendment, by service of a statement of claim, or even by the defendant's delay in applying to have the writ set aside: *Pontin v Wood* [1962] 1 QB 594; [1962] 1 All ER 294.
6 Ord 82, r 2.
7 Ord 15, r 10A.
8 Ord 6, r 2(1)(c). The application of the Act depends, in the case of teancies commencing after 1 April 1990, upon the amount of rent payable: Rating (Housing) Regulations 1990 (SI 1990/434). Where the tenant is within the protection of the Rent Act the landlord ought to issue his proceedings in a county court since, in the High Court, he can no longer sign judgment in default without leave and, furthermore, cannot recover any costs.
9 Ord 6, r 2(1)(d).
10 *Practice Direction (Judgment Foreign Currency) (No 2)* [1977] 1 All ER 544; [1977] 1 WLR 197.

2 Formal indorsements

a "Fourteen-day" costs

Where a plaintiff's claim is for a debt or liquidated demand[11] *only*, the writ must be indorsed with a claim for fixed costs,[12] the amount being determined by the amount of the claim, and a statement that further proceedings will be stayed if, within the time limit for acknowledging service, the defendant pays the amount claimed and costs. This indorsement is only made where the claim is for a debt or liquidated demand, ie a specific sum of money either ascertained or readily ascertainable by arithmetic. Thus such a claim cannot be made where the action is founded on tort since damages in tort are always unliquidated. Where the plaintiff claims interest, whether pursuant to contract or under section 35A of the Supreme Court Act 1981, he must include the amount of the claim for interest calculated to the date of issue of the writ and if the defendant pays this amount (together with the amount of the claim and fixed costs) within 14 days the action is stayed and no further interest is payable.[13]

b Solicitor and address

The writ must be indorsed with the plaintiff's address within the jurisdiction and his solicitor's name and address if the plaintiff has a solicitor.[14] The latter is essential if the plaintiff is a body corporate, an infant or patient or a person who has no address within the jurisdiction, since these plaintiffs, contrary to the general rule, cannot appear in person.

c District registry actions

Where the writ is issued out of a district registry and the cause of action arose wholly or in part in the district of that registry, the writ may be indorsed with a statement to that effect.[15] The effect is that the defendant cannot apply to have the action transferred to another registry or to the Royal Courts of Justice.[16]

d Capacity

Where the plaintiff sues in a representative capacity, or the defendant is sued in such a capacity, the writ must be indorsed with a statement of the capacity in which he sues or is sued.[17] Where a writ does not bear the

---

11 Where the claim is for a debt or liquidated demand in foreign currency, the sterling equivalent of the amount claimed (immediately preceding the issue of the writ) should be certified on the writ by the plaintiff or his solicitor; *Practice Direction (Judgment; Foreign Currency)* [1976] 1 All ER 669; [1976] 1 WLR 83; amended by [1977] 1 All ER 544; [1977] 1 WLR 197.

12 Ord 6, r 2(1)(b).

13 *Practice Direction* [1983] 1 All ER 934; sub nom *Practice Note* [1983] 1 WLR 377. Cf Supreme Court Act 1981, s 35A(3).

14 Ord 6, r 5.

15 Ord 6, r 4. There are in most large towns district registries which may be regarded as branch offices of the Central Office of the Supreme Court. The district judge exercises in his registry the same powers as the masters exercise in the Central Office (Ord 32, r 23).

16 As to which see p 310, *post*.

17 Ord 6, r 3(1).

proper formal indorsement it will not be issued until the defects have been corrected. Where, however, an indorsement of claim lacks particularity the writ will be issued and will be valid. The defect must then be cured by amendment unless the defendant acquiesces in the fault.

e Personal injuries

Where a personal injury action is commenced in the High Court, the writ must be endorsed with a statement that the case is not one that must be commenced in the county court.[18]

B   ISSUE AND SERVICE OF THE WRIT

1   Issue

The writ must be issued using the prescribed form, but that form is not a writ until it has been issued. To issue his writ the plaintiff takes or sends three copies of his form to the Central Office or a district registry where one copy (signed by the solicitor issuing it) is stamped with the court fee and filed, and the other two are sealed and returned to the plaintiff. The action has now been commenced for the purpose of any statute of limitation. Leave is not generally required to issue a writ but to this rule there are five exceptions of which the two more important are: (1) where the defendant is outside the jurisdiction;[19] and (2) where the plaintiff has been declared a vexatious litigant.[20]

2   Service

Once issued the writ is valid for four months beginning with the date of issue.[1] However it may on application be renewed for a further period not exceeding 12 months if the court is satisfied that it has not been possible to serve it during that period. Such an application is made ex parte (without giving notice to the other party) on affidavit. An extension will only be granted in exceptional circumstances,[2] generally where the defendant is untraceable; it is not an exceptional circumstance that the plaintiff failed to serve the writ through accident, mistake or a delay in obtaining a legal aid certificate[3] nor that settlement negotiations were in progress.[4] While in force the writ may be served at any time of the day or night although not on

---

18 Ord 6, r 2(1)(f); see *Practice Direction* (Personal Injuries Action: Indorsement on writ) [1991] 3 All ER 352; [1991] 1 WLR 642.

19 Ord 6, r 7(1); see p 308, *post.*

20 Supreme Court Act 1981, s 42. The other cases in which leave is required are under the Mental Health Act 1983, s 139(2), under the Leasehold Property (Repairs) Act 1938, s 1, under the Post Office Act 1969, s 30(3), and under Limitation Act 1980, s 32A.

1 Ord 6, r 8(1). The position differs in cases where leave to serve outside the jurisdiction has been granted, where the relevant period is 6 months.

2 For the relevant principles, see *Kleinwort Benson Ltd v Barbrak Ltd "The Myrto"*, [1987] AC 597; [1987] 2 All ER 289; *Waddon v Whitcroft-Scovill Ltd* [1988] 1 All ER 996; [1988] 1 WLR 309. A writ should be served promptly, but each case turns on its own circumstances.

3 *Baker v Bowkett's Cakes Ltd* [1966] 2 All ER 290; [1966] 1 WLR 861; *Stevens v Services Window and General Cleaning Co Ltd* [1967] 1 QB 359; [1967] 1 All ER 984.

4 *Easy v Universal Anchorage Co Ltd* [1974] 2 All ER 1105; [1974] 1 WLR 899.

Sunday expect, in case of urgency, with the leave of the court.[5] The following are permitted methods of service.

a   *Personal service or service by post*

Personal service involves the plaintiff or his agent tendering the defendant a sealed copy of the writ accompanied by the appropriate form of acknowledgment of service.[6] Personal service has not been obligatory since 1979. A writ for service within the jurisdiction may, instead of being served personally on him, be served:

(a) by sending a copy of the writ by ordinary first class post to the defendant at his usual or last known address; or
(b) if there is a letter box for that address, by inserting through the letter box a copy of the writ in a sealed envelope addressed to the defendant.[7]

In the case of a partnership, this service must be at the last known address of the parties, not the business address.[8]

Where the writ is served in accordance with the provisions set out above, it is deemed, unless the contrary is shown, to be served on the seventh day after the date on which the copy was sent to or inserted through the letter box for the address in question.[9]

b   *Service on the defendant's solicitor*

This is an alternative to personal service. The defendant's solicitor must indorse on the writ a statement that he accepts service on behalf of the defendant.[10] The fact that a person is represented by a solicitor is insufficient, unless that solicitor in facts accepts service.

c   *Acknowledgment of service*

Where the defendant acknowledges service of the writ, it is deemed, unless the contrary is shown, to have been duly served on him and to have been so served on the date on which he acknowledges service.[11]

d   *Substituted service*

Where the plaintiff is unable to effect service as above, he may apply *ex parte* on affidavit to a master for an order for substituted service.[12] The

---

5 Ord 65, r 10; formerly the Sunday Observance Act 1677 (repealed by the Statute Law (Repeals) Act 1969) contained an absolute prohibition against service of process on a Sunday.

6 Ord 65, r 2. If the person served will not accept the copy, it is sufficient to tell him of its content and leave it as nearly as possible in his possession.

7 Ord 10, r 1(2). The copy must be a sealed copy and must be accompanied by the appropriate form of acknowledgment of service (r 1(5)).

8 *Marsden v Kingswell Watts (a firm)* [1992] 2 All ER 239.

9 Ord 10, r 1(3).

10 Ord 10, r 1(4).

11 Ord 10, r 1(5); see *The Gniezno* [1968] P 418; [1967] 2 All ER 738.

12 Ord 65, r 4. An action in the Queen's Bench Division is assigned to one of the masters when the first summons in the action is issued. Masters have, with a few exceptions (set

master, if he makes such an order, will specify the form which substituted service must take, for example, service by registered or recorded delivery post to the defendant's last known address, service on the defendant's solicitor or agent or service by advertisement in the press.[13]

e   Service in pursuance of contract

The parties may by contract agree upon a method of service, in which case service in accordance with this method is sufficient.[14] However, a writ cannot be served by facscimile machine.[15]

f   Actions for the recovery of land

Where no person appears to be in possession of land, the plaintiff in an action for the recovery of that land may, with leave, serve the writ by affixing it to some conspicuous part of the land, such as the door. In summary proceedings for possession of land commenced by originating summons the summons may be served by leaving a copy at the premises and where the occupants are not identified, by affixing a copy of the summons to the main door or other conspicuous part of the premises.[16]

g   Service outside jurisdiction

No leave is required in respect of claims to which the Civil Jurisdiction and Judgments Act 1982 applies. This Act applies to proceedings against persons domiciled in a contracting state.[17] Such actions shall be commenced in the courts of that state. To that general rule there are exceptions,[18] of which the most important are proceedings in contract which can be brought within the jurisdiction appropriate for the performance of the contract, and in tort, where the wrong occurred. In other cases, leave is required. The jurisdiction of the English courts comprises England, Wales, Berwick-on-Tweed and such part of the sea as the Crown may from time to time claim as territorial waters.[19] Leave in any case is discretionary but can only be given in those cases specified in Order 11, rules 1 and 2. This important order lists some twenty cases in which leave may be granted, for example: where the subject matter of the action is land situate within the jurisdiction, where the defendant is domiciled or

---

out in Ord 32, r 11), all the powers of a judge in chambers in relation to interlocutory matters. In addition masters have jurisdiction to try cases, with the consent of the parties, to assess damages and to make final orders in interpleader and garnishee disputes.

13 *Porter v Freudenberg* [1915] 1 KB 857. Where the defendant is insured against his potential liability, service may be ordered on his insurers: *Gurtner v Circuit* [1968] 2 QB 587; [1968] 1 All ER 328.

14 Ord 10, r 3; see *British Controlled Oilfields Ltd v Stagg* (1921) 127 LT 209.

15 But other documents can: Ord 65, r 5. See *Hastie and Jenkerson v McMahon* [1991] 1 All ER 255; [1990] 1 WLR 1575.

16 Ord 113, r 4.

17 Under the Brussels Convention: Belgium, Denmark, France, Greece, Holland, Italy, Luxembourg, Republic of Ireland, Germany, United Kingdom.

18 Article 5.

19 *R v Kent Justices, ex parte Lye* [1967] 2 QB 153; [1967] 1 All ER 560.

ordinarily resident within the jurisdiction, where the action is founded on a tort committed within the jurisdiction or concerns a contract made or broken within the jurisdiction. Since the grant of leave is discretionary, leave may be refused if the court considers that another forum could more properly try the case.[20] This particularly applies where it is proposed to serve the writ in Scotland or Northern Ireland.[1]

If the defendant is in Scotland, Ireland, the Isle of Man, the Channel Islands or the Commonwealth the writ or notice of the writ may be served in accordance with the English methods of service. Elsewhere it must be served through the British consul, or the foreign government (where it is willing), or the foreign judicial authority in any country with which there is a Civil Procedure Convention, or the authority designated under the Hague Convention.[3]

Where leave to serve is required the relevant considerations as to whether it should be granted are those contained in the recent House of Lords decision in *Seaconsar Far East Ltd v Bank Markazi Jomhouri Islami Iran*.[4] These conditions were stated to be as follows:

(a) that there must be a serious issue to be tried on the merits of the plaintiff's claim;
(b) that there is a good arguable case that the claim falls within at least one of the grounds contained in Ord 11, r 1(1);[5] and
(c) that England must be the forum in which the case can be most suitably tried in the interests of all the parties and for the ends of justice (*forum conveniens*).

It may be noted that if a foreigner enters the jurisdiction he may be served, and the action proceed, irrespective of the fact that leave to serve him could not have been obtained had he remained outside the jurisdiction. Thus service of a writ upon an international art dealer at Ascot racecourse, was held in one case[6] to have been effective to confer jurisdiction upon the English courts. However a defendant may obtain a stay of proceedings if he can show that there is another forum in which justice could be done between the parties and that to refuse a stay would produce injustice.[7]

Where there are already proceedings pending between the parties in a foreign court which is a natural and appropriate forum for the resolution of the dispute between the parties, the court will stay a subsequent action

---

20 See *Spiliada Maritime Corporation v Cansulex Ltd, The Spiliada* [1986] AC 460; [1986] 3 All ER 843.
1 Leave cannot be granted under Ord 11, r 1(1)(n) (claims by Commissioners of Inland Revenue) if the defendant is domiciled in Scotland or Northern Ireland.
2 Ord 11, r 3.
3 Ord 11, rr 5, 6.
4 [1993] 4 All ER 456; [1993] 3 WLR 756.
5 The Order lists a wide range of circumstance in which leave might be appropriately granted.
6 *Maharanee Gaekwar of Baroda v Wildenstein* [1972] 2 QB 283; [1972] 2 All ER 689.
7 The principles applicable to "*forum non convenions*" applications were laid down by the House of Lords in *The Spiliada* (n 20, *supra*).

unless the plaintiff can establish objectively by cogent evidence that even-handed justice might not be accorded to him in the foreign jurisdiction or that there was some personal or juridical advantage only available to him in the English action and of such importance that it would be unjust to deprive him of that advantage.[8] Factors such as local knowledge, the availability of witnesses and other legal and practical issues are all relevant.

C   ACKNOWLEDGMENT OF SERVICE[9]

1   Mode of acknowledging service

The defendant must acknowledge service within 14 days of service (including the day of service) to avoid being in default.[10] This is done by delivering or posting[11] to the Central Office or district registry the prescribed form of acknowledgment, duly completed. This is not a defence but a formal document the function of which is to avoid the plaintiff obtaining judgment in default or, if liability is admitted, to obtain a stay of execution.

2   Contents of acknowledgment of service

The form which the defendant is required to complete (on the back of which are printed notes for guidance) contains four sections. In (1) he is required to state his name; in (2) he states (by ticking the appropriate box) whether he intends to contest the proceedings; in (3) he indicates (again by ticking a box) whether, if the claim is for a debt or liquidated demand and he does not intend to contest the proceedings, he intends to apply for a stay of execution; in (4) he states (by ticking boxes) whether, if the writ was issued out of a district registry, he applies for the transfer of the action to the Royal Courts of Justice or to some other district registry.[12] Finally he (or his solicitor) must sign the form.

---

8 *The Spiliada*, see n 20, *ante*; *The Abidin Daver* [1984] AC 398; [1984] 1 All ER 470.

9 Prior to 3 June 1980 the defendant was required, by the writ, to "enter an appearance" and, if he did not do so, the plaintiff could enter judgment in default of appearance. The Rules of the Supreme Court (Writ and Appearance) 1979 abolished this procedure and prescribed a procedure analogous to that previously applicable under the Matrimonial Causes Rules, namely that whereby the defendant is sent a form of acknowledgment of service on which he is invited to state whether he intends to contest the proceedings.

10 Where service is out of the jurisdiction extra time is allowed. In proceedings within the State Immunity Act 1978 the period is two months (*ibid*, s 12(2)).

11 The use of registered or recorded delivery post is not required. Ordinary pre-paid post is sufficient but it must be remembered that service is acknowledged when the document actually arrives at the court office, not when it is posted. In addition there are very detailed directions as to the precise procedure to be adopted for transacting this, and other classes, of business which may now be transacted by post; these are set out in *Practice Direction (Use of postal facilities; Queen's Bench Division)* [1976] 2 All ER 446; [1976] 1 WLR 516.

12 Such application can only be made where (a) the defendant does not reside or carry on business within the district of the registry out of which the writ was issued; and (b) there is no indorsement on the writ that the plaintiff's cause of action arose wholly or in part within that district (Ord 4, r 5(3)).

3 Dispute as to jurisdiction

Acknowledgment of service of a writ does not constitute waiver of any irregularity in the writ or notice or service thereof or in any order giving leave to serve the writ or notice out of the jurisdiction or extending the validity of the writ for the purpose of service.[13] A defendant who wishes to dispute the jurisdiction of the court on the ground of any such irregularity, or on any other ground, must give notice of intention to defend (in his acknowledgment of service) and must then within 14 days apply by summons to have the writ or an order for service set aside. The master may on this application try the issue of jurisdiction as a preliminary point. An acknowledgment of service may be withdrawn with leave of the court and may be amended, so as to change the defendant's statement that he does not intend to contest the proceedings, without leave before judgment is obtained.

4 Judgment on failure to give notice of intention to defend

If any defendant fails to give "notice of intention to defend" within the time limited the plaintiff is entitled to enter judgment in default. He must either file an affidavit of service proving due service of the writ on the defendant (which, if service was effected by post (*supra*) must contain a statement to the effect that in the deponent's opinion the copy of the writ will have come to the knowledge of the defendant within seven days thereafter and that the copy writ has not been returned through the post undelivered) or produce the writ indorsed with a statement by the defendant's solicitor that he accepts service on the defendant's behalf. In some cases leave must also be obtained; examples are cases where the defendant is the Crown[14] or has served notice to reopen a credit agreement under the Consumer Credit Act 1974,[15] or the action is a mortgage action[16] or an action in tort between spouses.[17] In addition judgment in default cannot be entered against an infant or patient.[18]

Where there are several defendants some of whom do not give notice, the plaintiff may enter judgment against those who do not appear without prejudice to his right to proceed against the others, if their liability is joint or several. However, where the liability of defendants is alternative, a judgment against one, albeit a default judgment, is a bar to a claim against any other.[19]

The type of default judgment which the plaintiff obtains depends upon the indorsements on the writ.

(1) Where the writ was indorsed with a claim for a debt or liquidated demand or for the recovery of land the plaintiff is entitled to *final*

---

13 Ord 12, rr 7, 8 (replacing the former procedure of entering "conditional appearance"); see, generally on this topic, *Carmel Exporters (Sales) Ltd v Sea-Land Services Inc* [1981] 1 All ER 984; [1981] 1 WLR 1068.
14 Ord 77, r 9.
15 Ord 83, r 3.
16 Ord 88, r 6.
17 Ord 89, r 2.
18 The plaintiff must first apply to have a guardian *ad litem* appointed; Ord 80, r 6.
19 *Morel Bros & Co Ltd v Earl of Westmorland*, [1903] 1 KB 64 (affirmed [1904] AC 11).

judgment in default for the amount claimed or the recovery of land and costs on a fixed scale.[20] Thus a final judgment is final both as to liability and as to *quantum*.

(2) Where the writ was indorsed with a claim for unliquidated damages, judgment in default can be entered only in respect of liability. The damages still need to be assessed by the court.[1]

(3) Where the writ was indorsed with any other claim, for example for an injunction, a declaration, a decree of specific performance, an account or the appointment of a receiver, the plaintiff cannot obtain judgment in default.[2] He must first serve a statement of claim, unless this was indorsed on the writ, and the action proceeds as if notice of intention to defend had been given. Then if the defendant does not serve a defence within the time limit, the plaintiff may apply for judgment in default of defence, for such relief as he appears entitled to on his statement of claim.[3]

5   Setting aside a default judgment[4]

If the default judgment was irregularly or fraudulently obtained or is for an amount larger than is due the defendant has a right to have it set aside. In any other case, he may apply to have it set aside but he will have to show why he has failed to give notice of intention to defend, and also that he has a triable defence, which he will normally have to disclose by affidavit. In addition a third party who is affected by the judgment may apply to have it set aside even though not a party to the action. Thus an insurance company may apply to have a judgment against the insured set aside,[5] so also may a person in possession of land which the plaintiff has recovered by default.

Where a judgment regularly obtained is set aside it will almost invariably be on condition that the defendant pay the extra costs incurred.

Where, after judgment has been entered against a defendant purporting to have been served by post, a copy of the writ is returned to the plaintiff through the post undelivered, the plaintiff, before taking any further step must either:

(a) request judgment to be set aside on the ground that the writ has not been duly served; or

(b) apply to the court for directions.[6]

---

20 Ord 13, rr 1, 4. Leave is required where the action is for possession of premises to which the Rent Act 1977 applies (Ord 13, r 4(2)) or a mortgage action (Ord 88, r 6).

1 Ord 13, rr 2, 3.

2 However the fact that there is a claim for a *Mareva* injunction in addition to a liquidated demand will not prevent the plaintiff from signing judgment in default for the sum claimed and then applying for his injunction; although this course is not envisaged by the Rules the court has inherent jurisdiction to control its own process and were it not to sanction this procedure a recalcitrant debtor could avoid a *Mareva* injunction against himself by simply failing to acknowledge service: *Stewart Chartering Ltd v C & O Managements SA* [1980] 1 All ER 718; [1980] 1 WLR 460.

3 Ord 19, r 7(1). The application may be by motion, but is usually by summons unless an injunction is sought (which is generally outside the master's jurisdiction; Ord 32, r 11).

4 Ord 13, r 9.

5 *Windsor v Chalcraft* [1939] 1 KB 279; [1938] 2 All ER 751.

6 Ord 13, r 7(3).

If he takes course (a) the court must set aside the judgment, whereas if he elects for course (b) the court may set the judgment aside or direct that the writ be treated as having been duly served or make such other order and give such other direction as the circumstances may require.[7] Accordingly, course (b) is preferable since, if there seems to be no reasonable prospect of ascertaining the defendant's whereabouts the court may order the judgment to stand or, perhaps, order some form of substituted service.

6 Application for stay of execution

It will be appreciated that, in order to avoid a default judgment, the defendant must return the form of acknowledgment of service containing a statement to the effect that he intends to contest the proceedings (by ticking the appropriate box). The acknowledgment of service then constitutes "notice of intention to defend".[8] If he does not intend to contest the proceedings, one might legitimately wonder why he should trouble to return the acknowledgment of service at all. The answer is that if the claim is for a debt or liquidated demand, he may state that he intends to apply for a stay of execution of the judgment and, if he does so state, execution is automatically stayed for 14 days from the acknowledgment of service and if within that time the defendant issues and serves a summons for such a stay, supported by an affidavit in accordance with Order 47, rule 1,[9] the stay continues until that summons is heard, unless the court otherwise directs.

Accordingly this procedure enables a debtor who has no defence to the claim to obtain a breathing space by means of stay of execution; his alternative (but more expensive) way of achieving delay is to give notice of intention to defend, thereby compelling the plaintiff to issue an Order 14 summons to obtain a judgment.[10]

---

7 Ord 13, r 7(4), (5).
8 Ord 1, r 4(1).
9 See p 385, n 20, *post.*
10 For details of Order 14 procedure, see p 319, *post.*

CHAPTER 15

Proceedings After
Acknowledgment of Service

After the defendant has acknowledged service (assuming he gives notice of intention to defend), the action will normally proceed to the stage where the parties disclose their respective cases by the exchange of pleadings; however there are several courses which the action may take before that stage is reached and the procedure applicable to each of these must be considered. The principal possibilities are as follows:

A   The proceedings may be stayed, discontinued or dismissed.
B   The proceedings may be settled.
C   There may be an application for summary judgment under Order 14.
D   There may be disposal of a case on a point of law.
E   There may be a summons for an account to be taken under Order 43, rule 1.
F   There may be an application for judgment on admissions of fact.
G   The defendant may make a payment into court.
H   There may be an application for a trial without pleadings under Order 18, rule 21.
I   There may be an application for interim relief.
J   The defendant may issue third party proceedings or may interplead.

Each of these courses merits individual consideration.

A   STAY, DISCONTINUANCE AND DISMISSAL

1   Stay

The power of the court to stay proceedings may exist: (a) by statute; (b) under the Rules of the Supreme Court; or (c) under the inherent jurisdiction of the High Court.

Certain Acts of Parliament contain specific provisions empowering or requiring the court to stay proceedings. Of these, the most commonly encountered, in practice, are the Arbitration Act 1950, section 4 (power to stay an action brought contrary to an arbitration agreement),[1] Insolvency

---

1 See p 282, *ante*.

Act 1986, section 285 (stay of proceedings against a debtor after presentation of a bankruptcy petition) and, sections 112, 126 (stay of proceedings against a company after the presentation of a winding-up petition or in a voluntary winding up).[2] The Rules contain some provisions empowering or requiring the court to stay proceedings, generally until a party complies with an order.[3]

The power to stay under the inherent jurisdiction is expressly acknowledged and preserved by section 49(3) of the Supreme Court Act 1981 and is exercisable in a wide range of circumstances. Thus the court may stay proceedings which are obviously frivolous, vexatious, groundless or an abuse of the process of the court. It is necessary for a stay for the applicant to show that the action could not possibly succeed. Commencing a second action while there is in being an action based on the same facts is *prima facie* an abuse of the process of the court.[4] Other circumstances in which the court may stay proceedings in the exercise of its inherent jurisdiction include the existence of concurrent proceedings in the courts of another country,[5] the fact that the case ought properly to be litigated in another country[6] (in particular where the dispute arises out of a contract containing a foreign jurisdiction clause[7]) or the fact that the subject matter of the action is *res judicata*.[8] In addition it appears that there is inherent jurisdiction to order a stay whenever it is just and reasonable to do so, even though no party has failed to comply with any specific obligation. This was done in *Edmeades v Thames Board Mills Ltd*.[9] The plaintiff, in an action for damages for personal injuries, refused to submit to a medical examination by the defendant's doctor for the purpose of enabling the defendant to check on the injuries which the plaintiff claimed to have sustained. The Court of Appeal ordered a stay of the action until the plaintiff submitted to such examination. The decision is a remarkable one, since there is no power in any court to order a person to submit to medical examination.[10] It is odd that a person should be denied the use of the legal process to enforce

---

2 See also the Law Reform (Husband and Wife) Act 1962, s 1(2) which enables actions in tort to be stayed if the court considers that no substantial benefit would accrue to either party if the continuation of the proceedings or that the dispute could more conveniently be disposed of under s 17 of the Married Women's Property Act 1882.

3 See, for example, Ord 18, r 19 (p 339, *post*); Ord 6, r 5; Ord 21, r 5; Ord 81, r 2. Note also Ord 114, r 4, whereby, on an order being made referring a question to the European Court for a preliminary ruling under Article 177 of the EC Treaty, proceedings are (unless the court otherwise orders) stayed until the European Court has given a preliminary ruling on the question before it; see p 374, *post*.

4 *Slough Estates Ltd v Slough Borough Council* [1968] Ch 299; [1967] 2 All ER 270.

5 *The Abidin Daver* [1984] A C 398; [1984] 1 All ER 470; see p 310, *ante*.

6 See p 309, *ante*. This ground is known as *forum non conveniens* and is expressly preserved by s 49 of the Civil Jurisdiction and Judgments Act 1982. The fact that some proceedings have already commenced is relevant: *Spiliada Maritime Corporation v Cansulex Ltd* [1987] AC 460; [1986] 3 All ER 843. The authorities are unclear as to how far the allocation of jurisdiction by the 1982 Act prevents the court issuing a stay on this basis: see *Re Harrods (Buenos Aires) Ltd* [1992] Ch 72; [1991] 4 All ER 334.

7 *The Eleftheria* [1970] P 94; [1969] 2 All ER 641.

8 See p 564, *post*.

9 [1969] 2 QB 67; [1969] 2 All ER 127.

10 Although the creation of such a power has been recommended: *Report of the Committee on Personal Injuries Litigation* (Cmnd 3691, 1968, HMSO), para 312.

his rights simply because he refuses to do that which he is in no way obliged to do.[11]

2   Discontinuance

The parties and their solicitors will, at every stage of the proceedings, be attempting to resolve their dispute without the expense of a trial. In fact very few actions come to trial. If the plaintiff is satisfied that his cause of action was misconceived or has ceased to exist he may at any time consent to judgment being entered against him with costs. The result will be to determine finally the issues he has raised on his writ and pleadings. However the plaintiff is better advised simply to discontinue his action since this course will not prevent him from suing again at a more convenient time. If he acts before a defence is served or within 14 days of service of a defence, the plaintiff may without leave serve a written notice on the defendant to the effect that he is discontinuing the whole or any part of his action.[12] He may serve a notice of discontinuance at a later stage of the action but only with leave (unless the defendant agrees in writing), and a condition of the grant of leave may be that the plaintiff shall take no further proceeding in the matter. Alternatively leave may be refused and judgment entered for the defendant.

If a defendant has served a defence, he may withdraw it in whole or in part by giving written notice to the plaintiff.[13] The plaintiff may then enter judgment in default of defence. If a subsequent action is brought in respect of a cause of action previously discontinued, the master may order the proceedings to be stayed until the costs of the discontinued action have been paid.[14]

3   Dismissal

In a case in which the court has inherent power to stay proceedings, it will sometimes make an order dismissing the action, and the courts do not usually in such cases simply stay the proceedings if, for example, they are an

---

11 This view was apparently shared by LAWSON J who, in holding in *Baugh v Delta Water Fittings Ltd* [1971] 3 All ER 258; [1971] 1 WLR 1295 that there was no power to require a widow to submit to medical examination by staying the action if she refused (at any rate in the absence of any reason for supposing that her medical condition was out of the ordinary), expressed the opinion that *Edmeades* was wrongly decided, an opinion which soon brought a sharp rebuke by the Court of Appeal in *Lane v Willis* [1972] 1 All ER 430; [1972] 1 WLR 326, in which case *Edmeades* was approved. Cf *Norman v Hardy* [1974] 1 All ER 1170; [1974] 1 WLR 1048 in which GOULDING J declined to stay a pending action, which was registered as such under the Land Charges Act 1972, on the ground that it was not right to stay an action in circumstances not covered by the Rules of the Supreme Court for the purpose of bringing about a vacation of the register which the judge had no power to effect by direct order.

12 Ord 21, r 2(1). However a party in whose favour an interim payment has been ordered (as to which see p 328, *post*) may not discontinue except with the leave of the court or the consent of all other parties (Ord 21, r 2(2A)). This Rule was introduced to remedy the omission which was disclosed in *Castanho v Brown & Root (UK) Ltd* [1981] AC 557; [1981] 1 All ER 143 in which case the plaintiff, having obtained interim payments totalling £27,250 in his personal injuries action, together with an admission of liability, then served notice of discontinuance with a view to commencing another action in the United States based on the same accident. This was held to be an abuse of the process of the court so that the court had jurisdiction to strike out the notice.

13 Ord 21, r 2(2)(a).

14 Ord 21, r 5.

abuse of the process of the court or are groundless. On the other hand if, of course, the ground upon which they are stayed is one that can be removed (for example by a party complying with a court order), then it will be appropriate for the court to stay the proceedings rather than to dismiss them.

Dismissal for want of prosecution — One particular occasion of the exercise of the court's power to dismiss actions under its inherent jurisdiction is encountered in cases where the plaintiff has been guilty of "want of prosecution". It is of great practical importance and covers two distinct circumstances: (a) cases where the plaintiff has failed to comply with a peremptory (or "unless") order of the court; in such cases the action is liable to be dismissed on account of the contumelious conduct of the party in failing to comply with the court's peremptory order; (b) cases in which the plaintiff has simply delayed getting on with the action; these are more common.

If the time-limits prescribed by the Rules were strictly observed most actions would be disposed of in a matter of months. In practice the time-limits are, for one reason or another, not observed and even the simplest actions often take an unconscionable time to come to trial. The blame for delay must, as a rule, rest with the plaintiff and the ultimate sanction is that the action may be dismissed for want of prosecution. A dismissal, not being an adjudication on the merits, does not estop the plaintiff from issuing a fresh writ founded on the same cause of action.[15] However in *Birkett v James*[16] the House of Lords held that in cases in which the limitation period had not expired (so that if the action were dismissed the plaintiff could simply issue a fresh writ), the court would not, save in rare and exceptional cases, dismiss an action for want of prosecution. The rare and exceptional cases contemplated are those in which the plaintiff's default has been contumelious or cases, such as *Spring Grove Services Ltd v Deane*[17] where some factors other than mere delay have prejudiced the defendant. In such cases, on the basis that the court would stay a second action as being an abuse of the process of the court, it may dismiss the first action notwithstanding the fact that the limitation period has not expired. As stated above, such cases are likely to be very rare.

There have in recent years been numerous reported cases on this topic, starting with *Allen v Sir Alfred McAlpine & Sons Ltd*[18] in which the Court of Appeal set out the principles on which the court would approach applications to dismiss. These are: (1) that the delay must be inordinate, (2) that it must be inexcusable, and (3) that the defendant must have been prejudiced by the delay. In considering whether delay has been inordinate, the whole history of the action is considered including delay prior to the issue of the writ and delay for which the defendant has been responsible. An inordinate delay will be inexcusable unless the plaintiff has some reason for it. Even if the delay is inordinate and inexcusable the action may not be struck out if the defendant has not been prejudiced, for example where liability is admitted.[19]

---

15 *Pople v Evans* [1969] 2 Ch 255; [1968] 2 All ER 743. However the court has power to strike out such an action as being an abuse of the process of the court. This has been done in a few reported cases, eg *Spring Grove Services Ltd v Deane* (1972) 116 Sol Jo 844, which case was exceptional in that the defence depended essentially on the evidence of two witnesses who were no longer available to the defendant when the second action was brought; cf *Department of Health and Social Security v Ereira* [1973] 3 All ER 421.

16 [1978] AC 297; [1977] 2 All ER 801.

17 See n 15, *ante*.

18 [1968] 2 QB 229; [1968] 1 All ER 543; approved in *Birkett v James* (*supra*).

19 *Marlton (an infant) v Lee-Leviten* [1968] 2 All ER 874; [1968] 1 WLR 1214.

Moreover, in *Birkett v James* the House of Lords held that prejudice occurring prior to the issue of the writ was not sufficient, since delay during this period is permitted by the Limitation Acts. Thus the plaintiff has to demonstrate new prejudice over and above that which has occurred due to permissible delay in instituting proceedings. It need not be great but it must be "more than minimal". Nevertheless actions may be, and have been, struck out even where liability has been admitted by the defendant (thus providing an unexpected windfall for the defendant or, more often, his insurers). Thus in *Paxton v Allsopp*[20] an action for damages for personal injuries arising out of a car accident was struck out even though liability had been admitted, and, indeed, an offer of £2,050 had been made by the defendant's solicitors and rejected some years earlier. The reason for striking out was that, not only was the delay inordinate and inexcusable, but the defendant was prejudiced in that oral examination of the medical witnesses would be impossible after such a length of time. The case was, it should be pointed out, an extreme one since the application to strike out was made more than 13 years after the accident.[1]

The prejudice to the defendant to be considered is not confined to prejudice affecting the actual trial. In *Department of Transport v Chris Smaller (Transport) Ltd*[2] the House of Lords observed, obiter, that prejudice to the defendant's business interests would suffice.[3] The court should, though, be cautious about going further. The mere fact of anxiety accompanying litigation would only be sufficient in an exceptional case.[4]

Without prejudice to the above, Order 3, rule 6 provides that where a year or more has elapsed since the last proceeding in an action, the party who desires to proceed must give to every other party not less than one month's notice of intention to proceed (whereupon the other party may, of course, apply to have the action dismissed for want of prosecution).

B SETTLEMENT

The parties (or their insurance companies) are likely to be in constant communication to effect a settlement of the action. This they may do with complete candour since letters which pass between them are privileged from production and any offer or admission of liability made therein is said to be made "without prejudice".[5] The nature of a settlement is that it is a contract whereby the parties abandon their previous rights and obligations in return for the creation of new rights and obligations. Since the new obligations are contractual, they must, in accordance with general principles, either be under seal or made for consideration. These

---

20 [1971] 3 All ER 370; [1971] 1 WLR 1310; see also *Gloria v Sokoloff* [1969] 1 All ER 204; *Sweeney v Sir Robert McAlpine & Sons Ltd* [1974] 1 All ER 474; [1974] 1 WLR 200; *Bremer Vulkan Schiffbau und Maschinenfabrik v South India Shipping Corporation Ltd* [1981] AC 909; [1981] 1 All ER 289.

1 See also *Biss v Lambeth, Southwark and Lewisham Area Health Authority* [1978] 2 All ER 125; [1978] 1 WLR 382.

2 [1989] AC 1197; [1989] 1 All ER 897.

3 For an example, see *Antcliffe v Gloucester Health Authority* [1992] 1 WLR 1044.

4 See *Biss v Lambeth, Southwark & Lewisham Area Health Authority*, *supra*, n 1.

5 For privilege generally, see p 596, *post*.

releases are termed, therefore, a "release under seal" and a "release by way of accord and satisfaction"; the latter is more common and has been defined as:[6]

> ". . . the purchase of a release from an obligation, whether arising under contract or tort, by means of any valuable consideration, not being the actual performance of the obligation itself. The accord is the agreement by which the obligation is discharged. The satisfaction is the consideration which makes the agreement operative."

The parties may effect a settlement without the consent of the court by giving notice of withdrawal before trial. Where an order of the court is required, which will usually be the case when the action is settled during the trial, the required terms will be drawn up and indorsed on counsels' briefs, or, more usually, the parties will submit to judgment on agreed terms. The settlement of any action on behalf of an infant or patient must be approved by the court.[7]

C   SUMMARY JUDGMENT UNDER ORDER 14

This procedure was introduced by the Judicature Acts 1873–75, and involves the only order which is universally recognised by number. It will be appreciated that the defendant's purpose in giving notice of intention to defend is frequently to gain time. Order 14 procedure enables the plaintiff to bring the matter to an early determination where the defendant has no triable defence to liability.[8]

The rule applies to every action in the Queen's Bench Division (or Chancery Division) begun by writ other than one which includes:

(a)   a claim by the plaintiff for libel, slander, malicious prosecution, false imprisonment; or,

(b)   an admiralty action *in rem*.[9]

Provided the defendant has given notice of intention to defend and the plaintiff has served a statement of claim, the plaintiff may issue the appropriate summons. To do so he or a person duly authorised by him must first swear an affidavit setting out his cause of action, the amount claimed, if liquidated, and his belief that there is no defence to his claim except as to the amount of damages. The plaintiff should not swear to this lightly, for if he issues an Order 14 summons where the case is not a proper one, or where he must have known that the defendant had a triable defence, the master may order him forthwith to pay the whole costs of the application.[10]

The plaintiff, having filed his affidavit, then takes out a summons which

6 *British Russian Gazette and Trade Outlook Ltd v Associated Newspapers Ltd* [1933] 2 KB 616, at 643–644.

7 Ord 80, rr 11, 12; see p 301, *ante*.

8 Ord 86 provides a procedure, similar to Ord 14, in actions commenced by writ in the Chancery Division for specific performance or rescission of agreements relating to land or for the forfeiture or return of any deposit made under such an agreement.

9 Ord 14, r 1(2).

10 Ord 14, r 7(1); except where the plaintiff is an assisted person. See the remarks of LORD GODDARD CJ in *M Pocock v ADAC Ltd* [1952] 1 TLR 29 (*infra*).

must be served on the defendant, together with a copy of his affidavit, not less than 10 clear days before the return day (ie the day appointed for the hearing of the summons).[11] The defendant, if he contests the summons, must attend on the return day and show that he has a triable defence. This is usually done by an affidavit, but it can be done "otherwise",[12] for example by oral testimony.

At the hearing of the summons the master[13] may make the following orders.

(1) He may give judgment for the plaintiff, final or interlocutory.[14] This must be done unless the defendant satisfies the court "that there is an issue or question in dispute which ought to be tried or that there ought for some other reason to be a trial."[15] If he has any defence on a question of law or fact then he must be given leave to defend the action, even if the master strongly doubts that the defence will succeed.

(2) He may give the defendant unconditional leave to defend the action. In this case the action will proceed to trial in the usual way.

(3) He may give the defendant conditional leave to defend. This may be done where the master is almost, but not quite, sure that there is no triable defence.[16] The effect is that the defendant may present his defence provided he makes a payment into court of the whole or part of the sum claimed. The court must not impose a condition with which it is impossible for the defendant to comply. If the defendant wishes to avoid or limit a financial condition on the ground of his own impecuniosity the onus is on him to make a full and frank disclosure of his means. Moreover he cannot complain because a financial condition is difficult for him to fulfil; he must prove that it will be impossible for him to fulfil.[17] The defendant may appeal to a judge in chambers against any condition imposed.

(4) He may give judgment for the plaintiff as to part and to the defendant leave to defend as to part of the claim.

---

11 Ord 14, r 2. As to the meaning of "clear days" in the Rules, see Ord 3, r 2(4).

12 Ord 14, r 4(1). The defendant must show that he has a triable defence, although he need not set out every element of that defence. A general denial of liability is not sufficient. There is no express requirement for the defendant to serve his affidavit on the plaintiff. However the summons contains a notice requiring the defendant to send a copy of his affidavit to the plaintiff to reach him not less than three days before the return day (so that the plaintiff may swear an affidavit in answer if he wishes). If the defendant sends his affidavit late or not at all, thereby necessitating an adjournment of the summons, he will usually have to pay the costs thrown away in any event; see *Practice Direction (Order 14; Return Date)* [1970] 1 All ER 343; [1970] 1 WLR 258.

13 The summons is almost always returnable before a master. However if an injunction is sought (which a master has no power to grant) the summons should be made returnable before a judge; *Shell-Mex and BP Ltd v Manchester Garages Ltd* [1971] 1 All ER 841; [1971] 1 WLR 612.

14 If the judgment is a money judgment, he may also award interest: *Gardner Steel Ltd v Sheffield Bros (Profiles) Ltd* [1978] 3 All ER 399; [1978] 1 WLR 916.

15 Ord 14, r 3(1); the latter part of this sub-rule is wide enough to enable leave to defend to be given where, even though the defendant cannot point to a specific defence, it is just that the plaintiff be put to strict proof of his case: *Miles v Bull* [1969] 1 QB 258; [1968] 3 All ER 632.

16 *Fieldrank Ltd v E Stein* [1961] 3 All ER 681n; [1961] 1 WLR 1287.

17 *M V Yorke Motors (a firm) v Edwards* [1982] 1 All ER 1024; [1982] 1 WLR 444.

(5) He may give judgment for the plaintiff with a stay of execution pending the trial of a counterclaim.

(6) If the application was not made in good faith or the case was not within the order, a libel action for example, the master may order the plaintiff to pay the costs of the application forthwith.[18] This is an extreme sanction which will rarely be invoked.

(7) If the master gives leave to defend or orders a stay of execution pending the trial of a counterclaim, he must give all directions as to the further conduct of the action as if the summons were a summons for directions; in particular he may, with the consent of all parties, order the action to be tried by himself or another master[19] or may transfer the action to a county court where it is transferable under the County Courts Act 1984.[20]

A defendant may apply for summary judgment on a counterclaim, provided it is not a claim which is outside the scope of the Order.[1] In addition any judgment under Order 14 may be set aside by the court on such terms as it thinks just.[2] This rather likens a judgment under Order 14 to a judgment on failure to give notice of intention to defend.

Order 14 proceedings constitute an invaluable means of combating delaying tactics on the part of a defendant who owes money but simply wishes to postpone the evil day of payment. However, in order to obtain a judgment for part of the sum claimed, the plaintiff has to identify a part of the claim which is separately quantifiable (for example, individual invoices in a claim for the balance of an account). If the plaintiff cannot do this, then there is no power under Order 14 to give judgment for any sum at all, even though there may be no doubt whatsoever but that a substantial sum is due. Thus in a claim for the balance of an account[3] or for unliquidated damages,[4] the defendant can keep the plaintiff out of his money pending a trial (or arbitration) simply by denying that the account is accurate (if he can raise a triable issue as to its accuracy) or by putting the plaintiff to proof of his damages. However the plaintiff may in such cases obtain an interim payment[5] and it is common for the plaintiff to apply for an interim payment as an alternative to summary judgment.

D   DISPOSAL OF A CASE ON A POINT OF LAW

By Order 14A, a district judge may determine any question of law or construction of a document summarily. In order for this power to be used, certain conditions have to be satisfied:

(a) the defendant must have given notice of intention to defend;
(b) the question of law or construction of the document must be issuable for determination without a full trial;

---

18 Ord 14, r 7(1).   19 Ord 14, r 6.
20 See p 415, *post*.   1 Ord 14, r 5.
2 Ord 14, r 11.
3 *Contract Discount Corporation Ltd v Furlong* [1948] 1 All ER 274.
4 *The Fuohsan Maru* [1978] 2 All ER 254.   5 See p 328, *post*.

(c) it must appear that such determination will finally determine the entire cause or matter or any claim or issue therein;

(d) the parties must have had an opportunity of being heard, or have consented to an order or judgment on such determination.

Any determination made will be final, subject to the usual right of appeal.

E   ACCOUNT SUMMONS

The plaintiff may indorse his writ with a claim for an account to be taken. This procedure dates back to the early days of the common law where it was available to the feudal lord against his bailiff or steward. It was extended in equity to any principal and agent relationship, such as landlord and rent-collector.[6] It is appropriate where the defendant is an accounting party that is to say a person who has received money on the plaintiff's behalf. The plaintiff is not in possession of sufficient details to frame an action for a debt. His remedy is to ask the court to compel his agent to account for moneys received and to pay them to the plaintiff.

To do so he may, at any time after the time limited for acknowledging service of the writ, or after the defendant has acknowledged service, take out a summons. The application is usually supported by an affidavit setting out the grounds on which the plaintiff relies. Unless the defendant can show that there is some preliminary issue to be tried or that he has already accounted, the master will order an account to be taken and the amount found due to be paid to the plaintiff within a specified time. The plaintiff's rights thus become crystallised into a judgment debt in the normal way. Simple accounts may be taken by a master in the Queen's Bench Division, but the proceedings are usually transferred to the Chancery Division or to an official referee.[7]

F   JUDGMENT ON ADMISSIONS OF FACT

Where admissions of fact are made by a party "either by his pleadings or otherwise" any other party may apply to the court for such judgment or order as upon those admissions he may be entitled to, without waiting for the determination of any other question between the parties, and the court may on the hearing of the application give such judgment or make such order as it thinks just.[8]

The admissions may be made in the pleadings in which event, of course, the application will not be made at the early stages of the proceedings presently being considered. On the other hand, they may be made "otherwise", as the wording of the rule indicates; so admissions might be made in an affidavit sworn in opposition to Order 14 proceedings; or in the course of correspondence prior to the issue of proceedings, provided this

---

6 See *London, Chatham and Dover Rly Co v South Eastern Rly Co* [1892] 1 Ch 120.

7 See p 365, *post*.

8 Ord 27, r 3; the application may be made by summons or motion, but in the Queen's Bench Division is in practice made by summons.

was not "without prejudice".[9] However, the power to give judgment on admissions will only be exercised in the clearest cases. So, for example, the fact that a defendant has pleaded guilty to manslaughter does not enable the widow of the deceased to obtain judgment in a Fatal Accidents Act claim, because the defendant might wish to raise, for example, a plea of contributory negligence or *volenti non fit injuria*.[10] So also where, in a personal injuries action, the defendants' solicitors wrote to the plaintiff a letter saying that they were authorised to inform him that "the defendants now admit that the incident alleged in...the statement of claim resulted from negligence for which they were responsible" the Court of Appeal, perhaps surprisingly, refused the plaintiff judgment on this admission since, although it amounted to an admission of negligence, it did not admit damage, which is an essential element of the tort of negligence.[11]

G   PAYMENT INTO COURT

1   Method of payment

In any action for debt or damages the defendant may, at any time[12] pay money into court in satisfaction of any or all of the plaintiff's claims.[13] To do so he deposits his payment at the Bank of England, Law Courts Branch, and serves a written notice to this effect on the plaintiff and on every co-defendant.[14] Where the plaintiff has included in his writ two or more claims the defendant may either: (1) make a separate payment in respect of each, or (2) make one payment in respect of any or all of those claims.[15] The latter course is usually disadvantageous to the plaintiff, since he must either continue with all of his claims or accept the payment and abandon them all. Accordingly where the payment in of a lump sum in respect of several causes of action embarrasses the plaintiff, he may apply to the court by summons for an order that the defendant apportion his payment in respect of the several causes of action.[16] However, the defendant will not be required to sever his payment in unless the causes of action are substantially different, ie where a jury might be directed to make separate awards of damages. Where the causes of action are technically different but substantially the same, for example several meanings of the same words in a defamation action, the defendant, if he makes one payment in respect of them all, will not be required to sever it.[17]

Where the defendant has a counterclaim for damages he may expressly

---

9 See p 318, *ante*.
10 *Murphy v Culhane* [1977] QB 94; [1976] 3 All ER 533.
11 *Rankine v Garton Sons & Co Ltd* [1979] 2 All ER 1185. The decision seems highly technical since if the plaintiff had gone under Order 14 it is difficult to see on what basis judgment could have been withheld.
12 Even before service of the writ.
13 Ord 22, r 1(1). This may be done after the trial of an action has begun.
14 For interest and other rules governing deposits, see Supreme Court Funds Rules 1975.
15 Ord 22, r 1(4). Until 1965 this was not possible in defamation actions.
16 Ord 22, r 1(5). This order cannot be made in relation to money paid into court after the trial or hearing of the action has begun (Ord 22, r 3(3)).
17 *Pedley v Cambridge Newspapers Ltd* [1964] 2 All ER 794; [1964] 1 WLR 988; decided under Ord 82, r 4, before that rule was amended; see n 16, supra.

take this into account when paying money into court;[18] thus if he values the plaintiff's claim at £1,000 and his counterclaim at £200, he will pay into court £800. It will be appreciated that where he values his counterclaim in excess of the plaintiff's claim, he should not take it into account when paying in since, as we shall see, the effect of the plaintiff accepting the payment will be that the defendant cannot proceed with his counterclaim.

If the claim is for a debt or liquidated demand in foreign currency the defendant may pay into court in that currency, whereupon the currency will be held in a special account.[19]

The plaintiff's cause of action is deemed to include such interest as might be awarded in the judgment.[20] Consequently it is incumbent upon the defendant to make a payment which takes account of the interest which will have notionally accrued on the debt or damages up to the date of payment in.

2   Effects of a payment into court

The plaintiff must, within three days of receiving the defendant's notice of payment in, acknowledge receipt. He may then within 21 days, or later with leave, take the money out of court in respect of any cause of action for which a payment in was made.[1] If the defendant made a general payment in the plaintiff must take "all or nothing". The effect is that all the causes of action in respect of which the plaintiff accepted a payment in are stayed, as is any counterclaim which the defendant took into account under Order 22, rule 2. The plaintiff may then;

> (1)   tax and sign judgment for his costs to the date of payment in (but only if his whole claim is satisfied);[2] and
>
> (2)   in actions for defamation, malicious presentation, or false imprisonment, apply to a judge in chambers by summons for leave to make in open court a statement in terms approved by the judge.[3] This is so that he may vindicate his reputation publicly.

Alternatively the plaintiff may leave the money in court and continue with his action. In this event the court must not be told of the existence of a

---

18   Ord 22, r 2.

19   *The Halcyon the Great* [1975] 1 All ER 882; [1975] 1 WLR 515; see *Practice Direction (Foreign Currency)* [1976] 1 All ER 669; [1976] 1 WLR 83.

20   Ord 22, r 1(8).

1   Ord 22, r 3. He requires, under Ord 22, r 4, an order of the court in some cases; viz (a) where the payment is made by some, but not all, defendants sued jointly or in the alternative by him, (b) where the payment in was made as part of a plea of tender before action, (c) in actions by an infant or patient (Ord 80, r 12), (d) in actions under the Fatal Accidents Act and the Law Reform (Miscellaneous Provisions) Act 1934, or under the Fatal Accidents Act alone where more than one person is entitled to the money. Where the payment in was made or increased after the trial has begun the plaintiff may accept the money within two days of receiving notice but before the judge begins to deliver judgment or sum up to the jury. Save by consent, an application for leave to take out of court a sum paid in after the time for acceptance has expired should not be made to the trial judge since this would necessitate disclosing to the judge the fact (and probably the amount) of a payment in, which is specifically prohibited by Ord 22, r 7 (*infra*); *Gaskins v British Aluminium Co Ltd* [1976] QB 524; [1976] 1 All ER 208.

2   Ord 62, r 5(4).

3   Ord 82, r 5(1). There are certain limited exceptions to this right: see *Honeyford v Commission for Racial Equality* (1991) Independent, 13 May.

payment into court until all questions of liability and damages have been determined.[4] This is especially so in jury actions, notably defamation, for if the jury knew of a substantial payment into court they would obviously be likely to look upon it as an admission of liability by the defendant, rather than a genuine attempt to effect a settlement. To this rule there are two exceptions – the defences of tender before action and apology under section 2 of the Libel Act 1843. In both these cases payment into court is an element in a defence and will therefore appear on the pleadings and be disclosed to the court.

As long as the plaintiff recovers more than the amount paid in the payment in will have been of no avail to the defendant. However, if he recovers less or no more than the amount paid in then, although costs are discretionary, the plaintiff will usually have to pay the whole costs of the action in respect of which payment was made, from the date of payment in.[5] The modern tendency of the courts is to look at the action as a whole and not as several causes of action tried together. Thus if the plaintiff does not recover in the aggregate more than the total payment in by the defendant he may have to pay the costs of the whole action from the date of payment in.[6] To put it simply, the plaintiff is gambling to "beat the payment in".[7]

Where the plaintiff beats the payment in only by reason of interest that has accrued since the date of payment in it is to be anticipated that he would not be regarded as having beaten the payment in at all and that the trial judge would therefore order him to pay the defendant's costs from the date of payment in. In such a case it will be necessary for the judge to make a calculation of what the interest would have been at the date of payment in.

Where a defendant claims an indemnity or contribution from a third party or tortfeasor liable in respect of the same damage, that third party or tortfeasor cannot make a payment into court. He can, however, obtain a similar advantage by making a written offer to the defendant to pay a specified contribution to any debt or damages recovered against the defendant. If the defendant refuses this offer it may be drawn to the attention of the trial judge, who may take it into account when making an order as to costs, as if the offer were a payment into court.[8]

Finally it should be noted that the plaintiff may make a payment into

---

4 Ord 22, r 7; *Monk v Redwing Aircraft Co* [1942] 1 KB 182; [1942] 1 All ER 133; *Millensted v Grosvenor House (Park Lane) Ltd* [1937] 1 KB 717; [1937] 1 All ER 736.

5 Ord 62, r 5. *Findlay v Railway Executive* [1950] 2 All ER 969.

6 *Hultquist v Universal Pattern and Precision Engineering Co Ltd* [1960] 2 QB 467; [1960] 2 All ER 266.

7 LORD DENNING MR in *Mason v Mason* [1965] 3 All ER 492n; [1966] 1 WLR 757 pointed out the desirability of a new rule which would have the effect of concealing the existence and amount of a payment in from the Court of Appeal so that the court would not be embarrassed by its knowledge of a payment in. With effect from 1 April 1976 such a rule was introduced (Ord 59, r 12A).

8 Ord 16, r 10; Ord 62, r 5; *Bragg v Crosville Motor Services Ltd* [1959] 1 All ER 613; [1959] 1 WLR 324. A similar course may be taken in proceedings such as matrimonial property disputes, where the Rules make no provision for payment into court; *Calderbank v Calderbank* [1976] Fam 93; [1975] 3 All ER 333 or in arbitrations where a "sealed offer" may be made.

court in respect of a counterclaim against him[9] and that a party may, with leave, withdraw a payment in.[10]

H   TRIAL WITHOUT PLEADINGS

This procedure enables either the plaintiff or the defendant to obtain a trial without pleadings or without further pleadings as the case may be. The application may be made in any action commenced by writ other than one which includes:

(a)   a claim by the plaintiff for libel, slander, malicious prosecution or false imprisonment; or

(b)   a claim by the plaintiff based on an allegation of fraud, provided that any defendant has given notice of intention to defend.[11]

The object of this procedure is to enable the parties to determine their dispute without the delay and expense of pleadings or other interlocutory applications. However it is only appropriate where there is no substantial dispute as to fact, as, for example, where the action turns on the construction of a document. In this respect, and also in the conduct of the proceedings, the procedure is very similar to originating summons procedure, except that it applies to a wider range of proceedings in the Queen's Bench Division, such as a negligence action where the sole issue is the assessment of damages.

Since there are no pleadings the parties must agree on a statement of the issues in dispute. This may be done by letter.[12] In a commercial case application for a trial without pleadings is frequently made in conjunction with an application for transfer to the Commercial Court.[13]

If the master makes an order for a trial without pleadings he must, and if he dismisses the application he may, give directions as to the further conduct of the action as if the summons were a summons for directions.

I   INTERIM RELIEF

1   Interlocutory injunction

The power of the High Court to grant injunctions is, of course, inherited from equity. In addition to the court's inherent power to grant an injunction by way of final remedy, section 37(1) of the Supreme Court Act 1981 empowers the court to grant an injunction by an interlocutory order "in all cases in which it appears to the court to be just or convenient so to do."[14] It may be noted that the injunction need not be directed at achieving the same relief as that which is sought by way of final relief in the

---

9 Ord 22, r 6.

10 Ord 22, r 1(3); cf *WA Sherratt Ltd v John Bley (Church Stretton) Ltd* [1985] QB 1038; [1985] 1 All ER 216.

11 Ord 18, r 21.

12 *Hill v Scott* [1895] 2 QB 371.

13 See p 364, *post*.

14 The position of the Crown was discussed in *Factortame v Secretary of State for Transport*, [1990] 2 AC 85; [1989] 2 All ER 692.

proceedings. The most obvious example of this is the *Mareva* injunction, which has already been considered in detail.[15]

It was formerly thought that, on an application for an interlocutory injunction, the most important consideration was the relative strength of the parties' cases so that, in order to obtain an interlocutory injunction, the plaintiff had first to establish that he had a strong *prima facie* case.[16] The disadvantage of this approach was that it necessitated a close examination of the merits as disclosed in the affidavits sworn on behalf of each side, sometimes amounting almost to a trial of the action.[17]

In the leading case of *American Cyanamid Co v Ethicon Ltd*[18] LORD DIPLOCK stated that the approach referred to above was incorrect and, in a speech with which the remainder of their Lordships agreed, laid down the following principles:[19]

(1) The plaintiff must first satisfy the court "that the claim is not frivolous or vexatious; in other words that there is a serious question to be tried".

(2) The court should then go on to consider the "balance of convenience".

(3) As to that, the court should first consider whether, if the plaintiff were to succeed at the trial in establishing his right to a permanent injunction, he would be adequately compensated by an award of damages for the loss he would have sustained by refusal of an interlocutory injunction.[20]

(4) If damages would not provide an adequate remedy (for example because the defendant may be impecunious) the court should consider whether the defendant would be adequately compensated by the plaintiff's undertaking as to damages (*infra*) in the event of an interlocutory injunction being granted but a permanent injunction being refused at the trial.

(5) Where other matters are equal, it is a "counsel of prudence to take such measures as are calculated to preserve the status quo".

(6) Finally, "if the extent of the uncompensatable disadvantage to each party would not differ widely, it may not be improper to take into account in tipping the balance the relative strength of each party's case as revealed by the affidavit evidence."

LORD DIPLOCK made it clear that there may be special factors which operate in "individual cases" in addition to the principles enumerated above. Nevertheless it is clear that the courts should not embark on anything resembling a trial of the action.

The Court of Appeal initially showed little enthusiasm for these new

---

15 See p 289, *ante*.

16 See *J T Stratford & Son Ltd v Lindley* [1965] AC 269; [1964] 3 All ER 102.

17 Although there was the correlative advantage that, very often, the parties would either agree to treat the hearing of the motion as the trial of the action or, in fact, compromise the action on the basis of the decision of the motion. Many "leading cases" were decided in this way; cf *Fellowes & Son v Fisher* [1976] QB 122, at p 133; [1975] 2 All ER 829, at 837.

18 [1975] AC 396; [1975] 1 All ER 504.

19 [1975] AC at 408–409; [1975] 1 All ER at 510–511.

20 *Donmar Productions Ltd v Bart* [1967] 2 All ER 338n; [1967] 1 WLR 740n; cf *Hampstead and Suburban Properties Ltd v Diomedous* [1969] 1 Ch 248; [1968] 3 All ER 545. In cases not involving monetary payment, for example, an application for an injunction to prevent publication of an article or broadcast of a programme, the court should assess the relative

principles and Lord Denning MR, in particular, was apt to treat cases before him as "individual cases" taking them outside the *American Cyanamid* case.[1] In *Cayne v Global Natural Resources plc*[2] the Court of Appeal pointed out that where the grant or refusal of an interlocutory injunction will have the practical effect of putting an end to the action the task of the court is to do its best to avoid injustice, and to balance the risk of doing an injustice to either party. In such cases the *American Cyanamid* guidelines cannot apply and unless the plaintiff can show an overwhelming case he will not be granted an injunction the effect of which would be tantamount to shutting the defendant out from contesting the action. May LJ justified this departure by observing:[3]

> "I think that one must be very careful to apply the relevant passages from Lord Diplock's familiar speech in the *Cyanamid* case not as rules but only as guidelines, which is what I am certain Lord Diplock intended them to be."

A master having no power to grant injunctions, application must be made to a judge. In cases of extreme urgency application can be made *ex parte* on affidavit, in which event an injunction will be granted for a very short period until an application by summons or motion can be brought before the court. Otherwise application is by summons to a judge in chambers in the Queen's Bench Division or by motion in open court in the Chancery Division.[4]

As an alternative to injunction the court will usually accept an undertaking from the defendant (which has precisely the same effect). In addition, as a condition of being granted an interlocutory injunction the plaintiff is customarily required to give his undertaking as to damages, that is an undertaking to indemnify the defendant in respect of any damages which the latter sustains by reason of the injunction in the event of the action failing.[5] For this reason it is generally improvident for a plaintiff to apply for an interlocutory injunction unless he has a strong case in circumstances in which the injunction will cause the defendant heavy expense, for example by delaying building works.

2   Interim payment of damages

One long-standing criticism of civil procedure in the English courts was that wholly innocent parties, such as injured passengers in road accidents, had to wait for long periods for their damages while disputes between other

---

merits of the case: *Cambridge Nutrition Ltd v British Broadcasting Corporation* [1990] 3 All ER 523; cf *A-G v Guardian Newspapers* [1987] 3 All ER 316; [1987] 1 WLR 1248, where the Court of Appeal appeared to adopt an "arguable case" approach.

1 *Fellowes & Son v Fisher (supra)*; *Hubbard v Pitt* [1976] QB 142; [1975] 3 All ER 1.

2 [1984] 1 All ER 225.

3 [1984] 1 All ER at 237. The *Cyanamid* principles do not apply to mandatory injunctions, which are only granted by way of interlocutory relief in exceptional cases: *Locabail International Finance Ltd v Agroexport* [1986] 1 All ER 901; [1986] 1 WLR 657.

4 Ord 29, r 1.

5 Where the Crown engages in litigation for the purpose of asserting a proprietary or contractual right, the ordinary rule applies; however where the Crown has commenced proceedings for an injunction for the purpose of enforcing the law in the manner prescribed by statute, no undertaking as to damages will be required; *Hoffman-La Roche & Co AG v Secretary of State for Trade and Industry* [1975] AC 295, at 329; [1974] 2 All ER 1128. This is a rule of discretion: see also *Kirklees Metropolitan Borough Council v*

parties, such as the car drivers (in fact, their insurers) were being resolved. *The Report of the Committee on Personal Injuries Litigation*[6] recommended that in such litigation, courts should have power to make interim payments and effect was given to this recommendation by the Administration of Justice Act 1969. This was replaced by section 32(1) of the Supreme Court Act 1981 which authorises rules of court enabling the High Court:

> "in such circumstances as may be prescribed to make an order requiring a party to the proceedings to make an interim payment of such amount as may be specified in the order, with provision for the payment to be made to such other party to the proceedings as may be so specified or, if the order so provides, by paying it into court."

The power was first exercised in personal injuries actions in 1970 and was extended in 1980 to all actions in which there is a money claim, whether by way of debt, damages, account, *quantum meruit* or whatever. The application for an interim payment may be made at any time after expiry of the time limited for acknowledgment of service and is by summons supported by an affidavit which must:

(a) verify the amount of the damages, debt or other sum to which the application relates and the grounds of the application;
(b) exhibit any documentary evidence relied on by the plaintiff in support of the application; and
(c) if the plaintiff's claim is made under the Fatal Accidents Act 1976, contain the particulars mentioned in section 2(4) of that Act.[7]

By Order 29, r 11 an interim payment in an action for damages may be ordered only in three circumstances:

(a) where the defendant has admitted liability;
(b) where the plaintiff has obtained judgment against the respondent to the application for damages to be assessed; or
(c) where if the action proceeded to trial the plaintiff would obtain judgment for substantial damages. Thus the power to order a payment on account of damages is limited to clear cases.[8]

The fact of the interim payment being made must not be pleaded nor disclosed to the court at the trial until all questions of liability and damages have been decided.[9] On giving final judgment the court may make an order so as to adjust the position between the parties in relation to sums already paid by way of interim payment; such an adjustment may involve repayment by the plaintiff or compensating payments between two or more defendants.[10] Where, after making an interim payment, a defendant pays

---

Wickes Building Supplies Ltd [1993] AC 227; [1992] 3 All ER 717, where no cross-undertaking in damages was required of a local authority seeking an interim injunction to prevent stores trading illegally on Sundays.
6 Cmnd 3691 of 1968 (the Pearson Committee).   7 Ord 29, r 10.
8 It is further limited in that, in personal injuries actions, no order can be made unless the defendant is insured against his liability, a public authority or a person whose means and resources are such as to enable him to make the interim payment; Ord 29, r 11(2).
9 Ord 29, r 15; cf the rules relating to payments into court, p 323, *ante.*
10 Ord 29, r 17.

money into court under Order 22, rule 1,[11] the notice of payment must state that the defendant has taken into account the interim payment.

Power to order interim payments extends to actions for possession of land; where it appears to the court that in the event of final judgment the defendant would be held liable to pay to the plaintiff a sum in respect of the defendant's use and occupation of the land during the pendency of the action, the court may order an interim payment on account of that sum.[12] The order may be for a lump sum or for periodical payments during the pendency of the action, or both.[13]

Those provisions enable, for example, a landlord to be awarded sums equivalent to rent against a tenant who is holding over at the end of his lease.

J THIRD PARTY AND INTERPLEADER PROCEEDINGS

1 Third party proceedings

Irrespective of his liability to the plaintiff, the defendant may have a right to relief from a third party which relates to the original subject matter of the action or which is substantially the same as the relief or remedy claimed by the plaintiff.[14] Thus if the plaintiff is a lessor and sues the defendant lessee for breach of covenant, the defendant may be able to claim relief from a sub-lessee.[15] Usually the right claimed by the defendant is to an indemnity or a contribution. A right to indemnity may exist by contract, by statute[16] or by a rule of common law or equity. A common example is the right of an agent to be indemnified by his principal in respect of acts performed within the scope of his authority.[17] A contribution is, in effect, a partial indemnity. It arises where a person is sued and there are other persons liable in respect of the same damage. The others, who may be joint trustees, joint debtors or joint tortfeasors, for example, have a duty to contribute.[18]

In any of the above cases the defendant may bring a separate action for the remedy sought against the third party. However he will save time and costs by issuing a third party notice. He may do this without leave before serving his defence and with leave thereafter.[19] The notice must contain particulars of the nature of the claim and the relief sought and must be served on the third party together with a copy of the statement of claim and all pleadings thus far served in the action.[20]

---

11 See p 323, *ante*.
12 Ord 29, r 12.
13 Ord 29, r 13.
14 Ord 16, r 1. Until Rules made in 1929, a third party notice could only be issued for a contribution or indemnity. It now applies to a much wider range of proceedings by virtue of the wide provisions of the present rule. Cf *Myers v N & J Sherick Ltd* [1974] 1 All ER 81; [1974] 1 WLR 31.
15 *Pontifex v Foord* (1884) 12 QBD 152.
16 Examples are; ss 76, 77 of and Sch 2 to the Law of Property Act 1925 (implied covenants); Civil Aviation Act 1982, s 76(3).
17 *Read v Anderson* (1882) 10 QBD 100; *Johnson v Kearley* [1908] 2 KB 514.
18 See Civil Liability (Contribution) Act 1978, s 1 (repealing and replacing Law Reform (Married Women and Tortfeasors) Act 1935, s 6).
19 Ord 16, rr 1, 2.
20 Ord 16, r 3. Note also Ord 15, r 10A(2) whereby a defendant to an action for wrongful interference with goods (under the Torts (Interference with Goods) Act 1977) who wishes

The effect of this procedure is to make the third party a defendant in relation to the original defendant. The action then proceeds between them as if the defendant had issued a writ against the third party in the ordinary way. Thus if the third party does not give notice of intention to defend, the defendant is entitled to sign judgment in default. If his claim was for an indemnity the extent of this judgment will be the amount that the plaintiff recovers from the defendant.[1]

The third party may counterclaim against the defendant, but not against the plaintiff.[2] He can, however, interrogate the plaintiff. Alternatively the third party may join a fourth party and so on.[3] Although the third party does not, strictly speaking, stand in any relationship to the plaintiff the court is enabled by Order 16, rules 8 and 9 to determine any issue arising between the third party and the plaintiff. Third party proceedings are independent of the main action to the extent that they may continue to trial even after the issue between the plaintiff and defendant has been disposed of by final order.[4]

2   Stakeholder's interpleader

This is a procedure which is appropriate where a person is under a liability in respect of a debt or in respect of any money, goods or chattels and he is, or expects to be, sued by two or more rival claimants.[5] For example, an estate agent who is holding a purchaser's deposit or a repairer in possession of goods may find that there is a claim by a third party other than the depositor, such as the vendor or a hire purchase finance company. If he delivers the money or goods to the claimant who turns out not to have been entitled, he is liable to the rightful owner in the tort of conversion. If he wrongly withholds possession he is liable for wrongful interference with goods. In this situation he should interplead.

To do this he takes out an ordinary summons, if an action is pending, or an originating summons, if not, which he serves on all the rival claimants calling upon them to appear before a master or district registrar and specify their claims. The stakeholder, when he takes out the summons, must swear an affidavit stating that he claims no interest in the subject matter in dispute other than for charges or costs, that he does not collude with any of the claimants and that he is willing to pay or transfer the subject matter

---

to set up the title of a third party against the plaintiff's claim (*jus tertii*) may, at any time after giving notice of intention to defend, apply for directions as to whether any such person should be joined in the action; the application is by summons which must be served on the third party in question and if the latter does not appear on the hearing of the summons the court may by order deprive him of any right of action he might otherwise have against the defendant; Ord 15, r 10A(4).

1 Ord 16, r 5. But it cannot, without leave, be enforced until the defendant has satisfied the judgment against himself; Ord 16, r 7(2).
2 *Barclays Bank Ltd v Tom* [1923] 1 KB 221.
3 Ord 16, r 9. The procedure between a third party and a fourth party is similar to the procedure between the defendant and the third party.
4 *Stott v West Yorkshire Road Car Co Ltd* [1971] 2 QB 651; [1971] 3 All ER 534.
5 Ord 17, r 1.

into court.[6] On the return day the court will, if the claimants appear, make an order in one of the following forms:[7]

(1) that any claimant be made a defendant in a pending action in addition to, or in substitution for, the stakeholder;

(2) that an issue between the claimants be stated and tried, directing which shall be plaintiff and which defendant;

(3) that the issue be determined by the master if both parties consent, or one requests, or the question is solely one of law;[8]

(4) that the proceedings be transferred to a county court if the subject matter or its value does not exceed the county court limit.[9]

In addition the master may order the money or goods in issue to be paid or deposited in court pending the determination of the issue.[10] If the subject matter is money the stakeholder may deduct his charges and his taxed costs. Otherwise these will be paid after the determination of the issue.

---

6 Ord 17, r 3.

7 Ord 17, r 5.

8 The Court of Appeal has stated that the issue should not, however, be determined summarily if there is a serious claim to chattels of considerable value or there is a prospect of difficult questions of law arising; in such a case a proper trial of the claim should be ordered: *Fredericks and Pelhams Timber Buildings v Wilkins Read, Claimant* [1971] 3 All ER 545; [1971] 1 WLR 1197.

9 County Courts Act 1984, s 44.

10 Under Ord 29, r 4 the court has power on the application of any party to order a sale of perishable property which is the subject matter of proceedings or as to which any question arises.

CHAPTER 16

Pleadings

A THE NATURE AND FUNCTION OF PLEADINGS

If the action has not been brought to an end in one of the ways referred to in the preceding chapter the parties must proceed to the exchange of pleadings. Before embarking upon consideration of this important topic it is important to bear in mind the distinction between modern pleadings and the pleadings which formed the basis of the writ system at common law. Pleadings at common law had to state a conclusion of law in one of the prescribed forms. Pleadings in Chancery went to the other extreme and simply set out en masse all the relevant facts leaving the judge to decide where equity lay. The modern system of pleading strikes a happy balance between the common law and Chancery systems. The modern system has its origins in the Common Law Procedure Acts 1852 and 1854 and the first set of Rules of the Supreme Court in 1875.[1]

Pleadings are written statements served by each party on his opponent, containing the allegations of fact on which the party pleadings relies. They serve various purposes. Principally they enable each party to determine exactly which facts are alleged against him. This may save a party from preparing evidence to meet allegations which are not being made against him. Also it enables parties to establish their "common ground", that is to say facts on which they are in agreement, thus saving the expense of proving these matters at the trial.

Secondly, the action is decided upon the pleadings. Thus the parties and their successors may, by reference to the pleadings, determine in the future exactly what the case decided, so that they may not have to, and indeed may not be allowed to, fight the same issues again. Similarly reference to the pleadings in an action may disclose the *ratio decidendi* of the case for the purpose of the doctrine of precedent, since any fact not pleaded will not usually be regarded as a fact upon which a judgment is based.

The classic definition of what pleadings must contain is now to be found in Order 18, rule 7(1):

> ". . . every pleading must contain, and contain only, a statement in a summary form of the material facts on which the party pleading relies for his claim or defence, as the case may be, but not the evidence by which those

---

1 Contained in the Schedule to the Judicature Act 1875.

facts are to be proved, and the statement must be as brief as the nature of the case admits . . ."

Thus pleadings must contain facts not law.[2] However, this only means that conclusions of law (such as the existence of a duty of care in negligence) need not be pleaded, not that a point of law cannot be raised on the pleadings.[3] Only material facts should be pleaded. Thus immaterial facts, such as character or motive, must not be pleaded since they form no part of a cause of action or defence.[4] Evidence should not be pleaded. However, the line between facts and evidence is by no means clearly defined. It is suggested that evidence be confined to its narrow meaning, *viz* the means of proof.[5] By way of exception to the rule that evidence need not be pleaded, Order 18, rule 7A provides that a party intending to adduce evidence of another party's conviction, pursuant to section 11 of the Civil Evidence Act 1968[6] must include in his pleading a statement of his intention with particulars of the conviction and the date thereof, the court which made the conviction and the issue in the proceedings to which the conviction is relevant. If the person convicted intends to deny the conviction, allege that it was erroneous or deny its relevance he must make the denial or allegation in his pleading.

Finally, pleadings must contain all the material facts. The reason is that at the trial a party will be confined to his pleadings and will not be allowed to raise any matter not pleaded since this would take his opponent by surprise, the very contingency which pleadings are designed to avoid.[7] Thus where, in an action based on negligence, the plaintiffs relied in their pleaded case upon vicarious liability, they were not allowed in the House of Lords to allege that the defendants were negligent personally, since this was an allegation which they had not pleaded.[8] On the other hand a variation from the pleaded case, as opposed to a complete departure, is permissible; thus where, in one case, the plaintiff in his statement of claim alleged that a large stone had struck him on the head, he was not prevented from showing at the trial that his injuries had in fact been caused by several stones.[9]

Without prejudice to the generality of the above principles the Rules prescribe certain criteria as to the contents of pleadings generally. The most important of these are as follows.

---

2 *North–Western Salt Co Ltd v Electrolytic Alkali Co Ltd* [1914] AC 461; *Gautret v Egerton* (1867) LR 2 CP 371.
3 Ord 18, r 11.
4 *Rassam v Budge* [1893] 1 QB 571; *Plato Films Ltd v Speidel* [1961] AC 1090; [1961] 1 All ER 876; but see *Goody v Odhams Press Ltd* [1967] 1 QB 333; [1966] 3 All ER 369.
5 *Davy v Garrett* (1878) 7 Ch D 473; *North–Western Salt Co Ltd v Electrolytic Alkali Co Ltd* [1914] AC 461; see p 549, *post.*
6 As to the admissibility and effect of such evidence, see p 608, *post.* The rule also applies to findings of adultery and paternity as evidence in civil proceedings under s 12 of the Civil Evidence Act 1968. This does not apply in respect of foreign jurisdictions: *Union Carbide Corporation v Naturin Ltd* [1987] FSR 538.
7 Although where a party has pleaded conclusions of law he is not precluded, at the trial, from seeking to draw different conclusions of law from the facts pleaded: *Re Vandervell's Trusts (No 2)* [1974] Ch 269; [1974] 3 All ER 205.
8 *Esso Petroleum Co Ltd v Southport Corporation* [1956] AC 218; [1955] 3 All ER 864.
9 *McCarron v Cementation Co Ltd* (1964) Times, 26 October; see also *Waghorn v George Wimpey & Co Ltd* [1970] 1 All ER 474; [1969] 1 WLR 1764; *Farrell v Secretary of State for Defence* [1980] 1 All ER 166; [1980] 1 WLR 172.

(1) Every pleading must contain the necessary particulars of any claim, defence or other matter pleaded, including particulars of any misrepresentation, fraud, breach of trust, wilful default or undue influence on which the party pleading relies.[10]

(2) A party must give particulars of any alleged condition of mind of any person other than knowledge (for example, fraudulent intention or malice).[11]

(3) A party must in any pleading *subsequent* to a statement of claim plead any matter, for example any relevant statute of limitation, fraud or other fact showing illegality which he alleges makes any claim or defence of the other party not maintainable or which if not specifically pleaded might take the other party by surprise or which raises issues of fact not arising out of the preceding pleading.[12]

Thus, for example, if in a "running down" action the defendant driver's case is that his vehicle had a latent mechanical defect which caused it to go out of control, he cannot simply deny negligence in his defence and then raise the specific suggestion of latent defect at the trial since this would take the other party by surprise. He must plead the defence of latent mechanical defect specifically so that the plaintiff can inspect the vehicle, or have it inspected by his own expert, and join the manufacturer or person who last repaired or serviced the vehicle as a second defendant.

It will be observed that the above rules are of two kinds: (3) relates to matters which must be pleaded, whereas (1) and (2) relate to particulars which must be given of matters which are pleaded. It should also be noted that special rules exist that require a plaintiff in personal injury cases to serve with his statement of claim a medical report and a statement of the special damages claimed.[13]

B   THE EXCHANGE OF PLEADINGS

1   Statement of claim[14]

The plaintiff may have indorsed his writ with a statement of claim. This is a pleading and the plaintiff may not serve another statement of claim except by way of amendment. If the writ was only generally indorsed the plaintiff may serve his statement of claim at any time before the defendant gives notice of

---

10 Ord 18, r 12(1)(a). If these matters are not pleaded, in view of their gravity, judges are very slow to allow a party to rely upon them, directly or indirectly; see, for example, *Belmont Finance Corporation Ltd v Williams Furniture Ltd* [1979] Ch 250; [1979] 1 All ER 118.

11 Ord 18, r 12(1)(b); *Fowler v Lanning* [1959] 1 QB 426; [1959] 1 All ER 290. "Condition of mind" includes the condition of mind of the party pleading, if he relies upon it; *Feeney v Rix* [1968] Ch 693; [1968] 3 All ER 22. Although the rule excludes "knowledge" it is necessary to give particulars of the facts alleged to give rise to knowledge; Ord 18, r 12(4); cf *Astrovlanis Compania Naviera SA v Linard* [1972] 2 QB 611; [1972] 2 All ER 647 in which the former practice of the Commercial Court not to order particulars of an allegation of "scuttling" (ie conniving at the loss of a vessel in order to make an insurance claim in respect thereof) was held to be wrong and inconsistent with Ord 18, r 12(1)(a).

12 Ord 18, r 8(1).

13 Ord 18, r 12(1A), (1B), (1C). For the relevant procedure where the medical condition changes, see *Owen v Grimsby & Cleethorpes Transport* (1991) Times, 14 February.

14 Before 1875 this was called a "declaration"; the modern defence was called a "plea" and the reply, a "replication".

intention to defend or within 14 days thereof. If he does not the defendant may (although he is not obliged so to do) apply to have the action dismissed for want of prosecution.

The statement of claim is a statement of all the facts which are alleged to constitute the plaintiff's cause of action, and a statement of the relief or remedy required. Thus if the action is for breach of contract, the statement of claim must set out the date, time and place at which the contract was made, the parties to the contract, the term alleged to have been broken and details of the breach. It is bad pleading to allege a breach of contract without alleging the existence of a contract, since that may be just what the defendant wishes to deny. Similarly in a tort action the plaintiff must allege all the elements of the tort in question, although he need not name the tort. Otherwise, his statement of claim discloses no cause of action. Thus a statement of claim that alleged, "laconically", that at a stated time and place "the defendant shot the plaintiff" was held to disclose no cause of action, since it did not allege a mental element which is an element in the tort of trespass to the person.[15] The one limitation on the contents of the statement of claim is that it must contain only allegations in respect of causes of action mentioned in the indorsement on the writ or arising from facts mentioned on the writ.[16]

In addition to the general criteria for the contents of pleadings, referred to above, there are certain other matters which the plaintiff must have in mind when preparing the statement of claim. The more important of these are as follows:

(1) In libel and slander the plaintiff must give particulars of facts to support any sense of the words other than their ordinary meaning (innuendo).[17]

(2) In actions under the Fatal Accidents Act 1976, the plaintiff must serve:

> "full particulars of the dependants for whom and on whose behalf such action shall be brought, and of the nature of the claim in respect of which damages are sought to be recovered".[18]

(3) The plaintiff should set out in his statement of claim all reliefs and remedies to which he claims to be entitled, though he need not specifically claim costs.[19] The reliefs and remedies which the plaintiff may claim merit some attention.

a Debt or damages

For procedural purposes there are only two kinds of damages – general and special.

General damages — These are such damages as the law will presume to

---

15 *Fowler v Lanning*, [1959] 1 QB 426; [1959] 1 All ER 290.

16 Ord 18, r 15(2). The rule is, however, of no great practical importance since the plaintiff can raise a new cause of action by amending the writ; see *Brickfield Properties Ltd v Newton* [1971] 3 All ER 328; [1971] 1 WLR 862.

17 Ord 82, r 3; *Grubb v Bristol United Press Ltd* [1963] 1 QB 309; [1962] 2 All ER 380; *Rubber Improvement Ltd v Daily Telegraph Ltd* [1964] AC 234, sub nom *Lewis v Daily Telegraph Ltd* [1963] 2 All ER 151. The precise words of the publications relied upon should be set out verbatim; *Collins v Jones* [1955] 1 QB 564; [1955] 2 All ER 145.

18 Fatal Accidents Act 1976, s 2(4).

19 Ord 18, r 15(1).

have resulted from the defendant's act. These damages (which include damages for pain, suffering, loss of amenities and inconvenience) need not be specifically pleaded and the plaintiff cannot as a rule be required to give particulars of them. However, where a plaintiff has suffered damage of an unusual character he must in his pleadings warn the defendant of the fact that damages will be claimed in respect of such damage, thus showing the defendant the case he has to meet and assisting him in computing a payment into court.[20] Once again the general rule is that the plaintiff must not take the defendant by surprise. So, for example, future loss of earnings in a personal injuries action are general damages; nevertheless a plaintiff who alleges a continuing or future loss of earnings must make this clear. A claim for exemplary damages must be specifically pleaded together with the facts on which the party pleading relies.[1] General damages are claimed generally by the words "and the plaintiff claims damages".

Special damages — These are such damages as the law will not presume in the plaintiff's favour, such as loss of earnings, loss of business profits, and medical expenses. These damages must be specifically pleaded and proved at the trial. Where special damage is an element in the plaintiff's cause of action, he must plead it or his statement of claim will disclose no cause of action. It is important to note that any special damage not pleaded cannot be recovered at the trial, unless leave to amend is given.

If the claim is for a debt or damages in a foreign currency the statement of claim should make this clear and should set out the facts relied upon to support such a claim.[2]

b   Interest

The High Court has power under section 35A of the Supreme Court Act 1981[3] to award simple interest on debts and damages. Apart from this provision the plaintiff may have a right to interest arising out of contract or under the Bills of Exchange Act 1882. In any of these cases the claim for interest must be specifically pleaded.[4] The statement of claim must plead (i) the cause of action, with particulars, the sum claimed and the date when payment was due; (ii) the rate of interest claimed and the amount claimed from the date when payment was due to the date of issue of the writ; (iii) a claim for further interest from the issue of the writ, showing the daily rate.[5]

c   Other relief

There are various other forms of relief available. Of these an order for the possession of land or delivery of a chattel, being common law remedies, are available as of right, whereas the equitable remedies of injunction,

---

20 *Perestrello e Companhia Limitada v United Paint Co Ltd* [1969] 3 All ER 479; [1969] 1 WLR 570. This requirement cuts across the traditional distinction between general and special damages.
1 Ord 18, r 8(3), negativing *Cassell & Co Ltd v Broome* [1972] AC 1027; [1972] 1 All ER 801.
2 *Practice Direction (Judgment; Foreign Currency)* [1977] 1 All ER 544; [1977] 1 WLR 197.
3 Added by Administration of Justice Act 1982, s 15(1), Sch 1.
4 Ord 18, r 8(4). But note *Edward Butler Vintners Ltd v Grange Seymour International Ltd* (1987) 131 Sol Jo 1188; *McDonald's Hamburgers Ltd v Burgerking (UK) Ltd* [1987] FSR 112.
5 *Practice Direction (Interest; Pleading)* [1983] 1 All ER 934; sub nom *Practice Note* [1983] 1 WLR 377.

specific performance, rectification, rescission, account and discovery are discretionary. Where an order, such as an injunction, is sought it is usual to plead the precise terms of the order sought.

d   Declaration

Where the plaintiff claims no relief, legal or equitable, but seeks an adjudication upon his rights he may simply claim a declaration. The power of the High Court to make declarations of right or title is an inherent one deriving from the practice of the Court of Chancery; it is now codified in Order 15, rule 16 and provides a useful means whereby a party may ascertain his legal position before embarking upon a course of action. However, it is axiomatic that the courts will not adjudicate upon hypothetical questions so that no declaration will be granted where the defendant has neither committed nor threatened any wrongful act.[6] The procedure of applying for a declaration is particularly appropriate where a party seeks the court's decision as to status; thus declarations are frequently sought and made on such issues as whether a person is legitimate or whether a foreign divorce decree has effectively dissolved an English marriage. However, if the proceedings are directed at challenging the decision of a public body the applicant must proceed for judicial review[7] and the courts will not allow him to proceed by way of action for a declaration, thereby avoiding the procedural restrictions of judicial review proceedings, in particular the three-month time-limit.[8]

2   Defence (and counterclaim)

The defendant must serve a defence on the plaintiff within 14 days of the expiration of the time limit for acknowledging service of the writ or of receiving the statement of claim, whichever is the later.[9] If he does not, the plaintiff may enter judgment, final or interlocutory, in default of defence.[10] The procedure is similar to judgment on failure to give notice of intention to defend and the same limitations apply. This time limit may, as may all time limits under the Rules, be extended by agreement or by order of the master. Before drafting his defence, there are preliminary matters which the defendant must consider. For example, the statement of claim served on him may disclose no cause of action, or may introduce a new cause of action not indorsed on the writ. In such a case the defendant may apply by summons to a master to strike out the statement

---

6 *Ealing London Borough v Race Relations Board* [1971] 1 QB 309; [1971] 1 All ER 424; *Mellstrom v Garner* [1970] 2 All ER 9; [1970] 1 WLR 603. *Naylor v Wrotham Park Settled Estates* (1987) Times, 6 March.

7 See p 122, *ante*.

8 *O'Reilly v Mackman*, [1983] 2 AC 237; [1983] 3 All ER 1124. But see further p 128, *ante*.

9 The effect of this is that where the statement of claim is indorsed on the writ, the defendant has 28 days in which to serve a defence. Unless the court otherwise directs, the time for serving pleadings does not run during the month of August (Ord 3, r 3). This Rule, introduced in 1982, effectively reduces the "long vacation" from two months to one and indeed there are now sittings of the High Court in London and elsewhere (albeit to a limited extent) in September.

10 The plaintiff or his solicitor must certify that the defendant is in default on the back of the court copy of the judgment which he tenders for entry; *Practice Direction (Judgment by Default)* [1979] 2 All ER 1062; [1979] 1 WLR 851.

of claim.[11] A less radical course is to apply for particulars.[12] There may be a third party from whom the defendant has a right to relief in respect of the subject matter of the action, the other driver in a running-down action for example. In this case the defendant should institute third party proceedings to join that party to the action.[13] Alternatively the defendant may have found himself in the midst of a dispute in which he has no interest; for example a garage owner may be in possession of a car which is claimed by a hire purchase finance company and by the hirer or an estate agent in possession of a deposit when a sale of property has fallen through. In such a case he should interplead.[14] However if the defendant wishes to serve a defence to the statement of claim, he may frame it in the following ways.

a Defence generally

The defendant must deal individually with each allegation in the statement of claim. A general denial of liability is insufficient and will result in the defendant having to give lengthy particulars, incurring extra costs. In particular it is expressly provided[15] that:

> "a party must in any pleading subsequent to a statement of claim plead specifically any matter, for example, performance, release, any relevant statute of limitation, fraud or any fact showing illegality:
>
> (a) which he alleges makes any claim or defence of the opposite party not maintainable; or
> (b) which, if not specifically pleaded, might take the opposite party by surprise; or
> (c) which raises issues of fact not arising out of the preceding pleadings."

In respect of each allegation in the statement of claim the defendant may:

(i)   admit; or,
(ii) traverse; and/or,
(iii) confess and avoid; and/or,
(iv) object in point of law.

Admissions — An admission on the pleadings may be express or implied. An admission is implied from a failure to traverse, since the Rules expressly provide that every allegation of fact in a statement of claim or counterclaim that is not traversed is deemed to be admitted, except against an infant or person under disability, and excepting also allegations as to

---

11 Ord 18, r 19. This is a most important rule. It enables the court to stay or dismiss an action, or strike out any pleading: "on the ground that (a) it discloses no reasonable cause of action or defence, as the case may be; or (b) it is scandalous, frivolous or vexatious; or (c) it may prejudice, embarrass or delay the fair trial of the action; or (d) it is otherwise an abuse of the process of the court". The jurisdiction is "sparingly exercised and only in very exceptional cases", *per* LORD HERSCHELL on *Lawrence v Lord Norreys* (1890) 15 App Cas 210 at 219; for a recent summary of the principles applicable, see the judgment of MILLETT J in *Lonrho plc v Fayed (No 2)* [1991] 4 All ER 961; [1992] 1 WLR 1. Apart from this rule the court has an inherent jurisdiction under which it can deal with any case within this rule.
12 See p 346, *post.*
13 See p 330, *ante.*
14 See p 331, *ante.*
15 Ord 18, r 8(1).

damages.[16] Admission should not be regarded as a sign of weakness on the part of the defendant. Indeed there is no point in denying facts which your opponent can easily prove against you, or which are purely formal. Thus, if the defendant's case is that his conduct does not amount to a breach of contract, there is no point in denying the existence of the contract. Similarly, in an action for malicious prosecution, where the dispute is invariably as to whether the defendant was malicious and whether he had a reasonable and probable cause for instigating a prosecution, it is pedantic to deny that there was a prosecution which terminated in favour of the plaintiff, since this can easily be proved. Indeed, a party who denies facts that he should properly admit may be penalised in the matter of costs.[17]

Traverses — A traverse is simply a denial. It is unnecessary to traverse allegations of law. On the other hand it is essential that the defendant traverse positively and unambiguously every allegation of fact in the statement of claim that he disputes.[18] A paragraph in the statement of claim may contain two allegations of fact; for example "the plaintiff paid the defendant £5,000." This incorporates two allegations; firstly, that the plaintiff paid the defendant a sum of money; secondly, that the sum was £5,000. Accordingly a traverse that "the plaintiff did not pay the defendant £5,000" is insufficient if the defendant contends that the plaintiff paid him nothing at all. A proper traverse would be: "the plaintiff did not pay the defendant £5,000 *or any other sum*".

Pleas in confession and avoidance — This form of defence involves admitting the literal truth of an allegation (confession), but at the same time setting up other facts which alter or nullify its effect (avoidance). Thus where the statement of claim alleges the existence of a contract, the defendant may wish to allege that that contract has been discharged or frustrated or that he has been released, or that the action is statute-barred. All these pleas are pleas in avoidance. Similarly, the defendant may be prepared to admit a battery on the plaintiff, but may allege that it was performed in self-defence or under a right conferred by law. It is perhaps unfortunate that the Rules allow a party to plead inconsistent defences. Thus the defendant may both traverse and confess and avoid the same facts. For example, he may deny that he struck the plaintiff at all and yet plead that he did so in self-defence.

Objections in point of law — As a rule no party is obliged to take a point of law in his pleadings. Thus even where the statement of claim contains an apparent defect in law or discloses no cause of action, the defendant may elect to remain silent until the trial.[19] Indeed there are occasions where it is politic to do so, since by that time it may be too late for the plaintiff to set his pleadings in order by amendment. However, where the point of law could effectively dispose of the whole question, the Rules provide the

---

16 Ord 18, r 13(1), (4); Ord 80, r 8.

17 Ord 62, r 6(7).

18 The defendant need not and should not traverse allegations which the plaintiff has not pleaded; although a general traverse is insufficient, it is common form for the defence to conclude with a general traverse in addition to the specific traverses, viz "save as hereinbefore specifically admitted, the defendant denies each and every allegation contained in the statement of claim as though the same were herein set out and traversed seriatim"; see *Warner v Sampson* [1959] 1 QB 297; [1959] 1 All ER 120.

19 *MacDougall v Knight* (1890) 25 QBD 1; *Independent Automatic Sales Ltd v Knowles and Foster* [1962] 3 All ER 27; [1962] 1 WLR 974.

means for the defendant to raise this point at an early stage in the proceedings, thus forestalling a trial. The defendant may apply by summons to have the point set down for trial as a preliminary point.[20] In an extreme case, as already noted, the defendant may apply to have the plaintiff's statement of claim struck out on the ground that it is frivolous, vexatious or discloses no cause of action or is otherwise an abuse of the process of the court.

b   Special defences; set-off and counterclaim

In addition to pleading to the statement of claim in any or all of the above ways, in certain cases the defendant may raise a defence which is peculiar to one type of action. Thus the defences of fair comment, justification and offer of amends are peculiar to actions for defamation. These defences must always be specifically pleaded. In particular, the defences of tender before action[1] and apology under the Libel Acts 1843–45[2] are interesting from a procedural standpoint in that both require payment into court as an element in the defence. The payment in differs from a payment under the Rules of the Supreme Court, Order 22 in that the latter can only affect costs[3] while the former is an element in a defence to liability.

At this stage it is appropriate to consider the defence of set-off and, more important still, counterclaim.

Set-off[4] — A defence may contain a set-off which may be pleaded to the whole or to any part of the plaintiff's claim. Thus it may be pleaded in conjunction with a plea of tender before action, whereby the defendant has tendered a sum less than the sum claimed by the plaintiff because he pleads a set-off in respect of the balance.

The common law courts prior to 1875 recognised the set-off although it was limited in its scope to cases where both the plaintiff's claim and the amount to be set off were liquidated. The defence was also recognised in equity, where its scope was, however, greater and extended to unliquidated claims. With the fusion of the administration of law and equity in 1875 the equitable set-off became available throughout the Supreme Court. This is still the case, as evidenced by the wide phrasing of the present Order 18, rule 17:

> ". . . where a claim by a defendant to a sum of money (whether of an ascertained amount or not) is relied on as a defence to the whole or part of a claim made by the plaintiff, it may be included in the defence and set off against the plaintiff's claim, whether or not it is also added as a counterclaim."

Thus, for example, in an action for the price of goods, it is well established that the defendant can plead by way of set-off a claim for damages in

---

20 Ord 33, rr 3, 4.
 1 Ord 18, r 16. This old common law defence can only be pleaded to an action for a debt or liquidated demand; it is that the defendant tendered the whole sum due before issue of the writ.
 2 This defence, which is obsolete, is available to a newspaper or other periodical which publishes a libel without actual malice or gross negligence. The defence is never used because it cannot be pleaded in conjunction with any other defence and, in any event, the defence of unintentional defamation under the Defamation Act 1952, s 4 is more favourable to the defendant.
 3 See p 323, *ante*.
 4 Ord 18, r 17.

respect of the defective state of the goods;[5] similarly in a landlord's action for rent the defendant tenant can raise a set-off in respect of defects in the premises which affect the tenant's enjoyment of them.[6] On the other hand the equitable set-off historically developed from the power of the Court of Chancery to restrain a litigant at common law from enforcing his rights in the common law courts (where, of course, the only set-off permitted was a legal set-off). Therefore it was not, and is not, available unless the defendant's claim by way of set-off is such that it would be inequitable for the plaintiff to obtain judgment without taking it into account. This will not be the case, in general, where the transactions giving rise to the plaintiff's claim and the defendant's purported set-off are wholly unconnected. Thus the House of Lords in two cases refused to permit a set-off for unliquidated damages against a claim on a bill of exchange[7] or for damages for short delivery of cargo against a claim for freight charges.[8]

In such cases the defendant's proper course is to counterclaim, and then to apply for a stay of execution[9] on the claim pending trial of the counterclaim.

It must also be noted that both the claim and the set-off must be monetary. Thus if the plaintiff seeks an injunction or a declaration of title, for example, there can be no set-off to these claims. There are other limitations to pleading a set-off, *viz*:

(1) Both claim and set-off must exist between the same parties in the same capacity. Thus, if the plaintiff sues as trustee or executor of an estate, the defendant cannot set off a debt owed to him by the plaintiff in the latter's personal capacity.[10]

(2) If the set-off overtops the plaintiff's claim the defendant cannot recover the excess except by way of counterclaim. Since a set-off is only a defence, it can only operate to extinguish or reduce *pro tanto* the plaintiff's claim.[11]

(3) If the original claim is settled or discontinued the set-off is *ipso facto* terminated, since it depends for its existence on the original claim.

(4) The amount to be set-off must have been due when the writ was issued.[12]

Counterclaim[13] — A counterclaim is not a defence but, since it is pleaded at this stage, it is conveniently considered here. A counterclaim is a cross-action and may best be regarded as the defendant's statement of claim. Thus the subject matter of a counterclaim can be anything which

---

5 In this particular instance the common law in fact permitted an "abatement of price" (*Mondel v Steel* (1841) 8 M & W 858) but now that there can be a set-off in any event the historical source of the defendant's remedy is unimportant.

6 *British Anzani (Felixstowe) Ltd v International Marine Management (UK) Ltd* [1980] QB 137; [1979] 2 All ER 1063.

7 *Nova (Jersey) Knit Ltd v Kammgarn Spinnerei GmbH* [1977] 2 All ER 463; [1977] 1 WLR 713.

8 *Aries Tanker Corporation v Total Transport Ltd* [1977] 1 All ER 398; [1977] 1 WLR 185. Claims which are both unliquidated and unconnected cannot be the subject of set-off; cf *Axel Johnson Petroleum AB v MG Mineral Group AG* [1992] 2 All ER 163; [1992] 1 WLR 270.

9 As to which, see p 385, *post*.

10 *Rees v Watts* (1855) 11 Exch 410; *Phillips v Howell* [1901] 2 Ch 773.

11 The balance should be claimed by counterclaim: *Stooke v Taylor* (1880) 5 QBD 569.

12 *Richards v James* (1848) 2 Exch 471.   13 Ord 18, r 18.

could be the subject matter of an action commenced by writ. It need not relate to the plaintiff's claim, nor indeed need it claim the same remedy as that sought by the plaintiff.[14] If the claim and counterclaim are of a totally different nature and cannot conveniently be tried together, the court may order the counterclaim to be tried separately, or even transferred to a county court. The counterclaim must exist against the plaintiff but not necessarily in the capacity in which he sues (provided that he is a party to the action and not, for example, an infant's next friend). Thus if the plaintiff sues as trustee or executor, the defendant may counterclaim either against the plaintiff personally or against the estate that the plaintiff is representing.[15] In addition the defendant by his counterclaim may join new parties to the action, who are in the position of defendants *quoad* the original defendant (though not *quoad* the plaintiff).[16]

If both claim and counterclaim succeed the court will usually make one order as to damages.[17] There is a discretion as to costs and the court may either make one order as to costs (in which case the counterclaim is in effect treated as if it were a set-off) or two orders as to costs. In the latter case the defendant would be entitled to the costs of his successful counterclaim but would be liable for the costs of the plaintiff's claim, since a counterclaim is not a defence. In practice, where the claim and counterclaim arise out of the same transaction or series of transactions, for example, trading debts between the parties, the court will make just one order as to costs – in favour of the party who recovers the balance between the claim and counterclaim.[18]

For almost all purposes the counterclaiming defendant is in the same position as a plaintiff. He may obtain judgment in default of defence to his counterclaim[19] (though not on failure to give notice of intention to defend except by third parties,[20] since acknowledgment by the plaintiff is not required); he may also obtain judgment under Order 14 on his counterclaim.[1] In certain situations the counterclaiming defendant is in a better position than he would be as plaintiff. Of these the most important, in practice, arises where the defendant's cause of action has become statute-barred. Provided the plaintiff has issued his writ within the limitation period the defendant may counterclaim notwithstanding that his cause of action would, if he were the plaintiff, be statute-barred.[2] The defendant cannot, however, counterclaim until he has been served with a statement of claim.[3]

---

14 Ord 15, r 2(1); *Beddall v Maitland* (1881) 17 Ch D 174.
15 *Re Richardson* [1933] WN 90; *Stumore v Campbell & Co* [1892] 1 QB 314.
16 Ord 15, r 3(1). There must, however, be a claim against the plaintiff as well; *Furness v Booth* (1877) 4 Ch D 586. It is permissible that the liability of the plaintiff and of the third party be alternative: *Smith v Buskell* [1919] 2 KB 362.
17 Ord 15, r 2(4).
18 *Provincial Bill Posting Co v Low Moor Iron Co* [1909] 2 KB 344; *Chell Engineering Ltd v Unit Tool and Engineering Co Ltd* [1950] 1 All ER 378; *Childs v Gibson* [1954] 2 All ER 243; [1954] 1 WLR 809.
19 Ord 19, r 8.
20 Ord 15, r 3(5), (5A).
 1 Ord 14, r 5.
 2 Limitation Act 1980, s 35; cf *Henriksens Rederi AS v Rolimpex* [1974] QB 233; [1973] 3 All ER 589 for an enlightening analysis of the nature of set-off and counterclaim, legal and equitable.
 3 See *The Gniezno* [1968] P 418; [1967] 2 All ER 738.

3 Defence to counterclaim and reply

If the defendant has raised a counterclaim, the plaintiff must serve a defence to it, or the defendant will be entitled to judgment in default on his counterclaim. This pleading must be drafted in the same way as a defence, although the plaintiff cannot himself counterclaim since he is confined to the causes of action raised in his statement of claim.

The plaintiff need not serve a reply to reaffirm the allegations in his statement of claim that the defendant has traversed. These are already in issue.[4] However he must serve a reply if he wishes to make admissions, rebut positive allegations in the defence or raise an objection in point of law in answer to a plea of confession and avoidance.

> ". . . the reply is the proper place for meeting the defence by confession and avoidance."[5]

Thus where the defendant has pleaded fair comment or qualified privilege in an action for defamation, the plaintiff may rebut the defence by proving malice. This will be alleged in his reply.[6] If the defence of a statute of limitation is raised, the plaintiff, in his reply, may plead fraud or a written acknowledgment, which prevent time from running. The plaintiff cannot, however, raise a new cause of action in his reply since this constitutes a "departure" which is expressly forbidden by Order 18, rule 10.

A reply or a defence to counterclaim must be served within 14 days. If both are pleaded they must be incorporated in the same document.[7]

4 Subsequent pleadings

No pleading subsequent to a reply or a defence to counterclaim shall be served except with the leave of the court.[8] A rejoinder (by the defendant) may be necessary to rebut affirmative allegations in a defence to counterclaim. Surrejoinder (by the plaintiff), rebutter (by the defendant) and surrebutter (by the plaintiff) are virtually obsolete because of the rule prohibiting departures in pleading.

C   AMENDMENT OF WRIT AND PLEADINGS

1 Writ

Where there is some defect in the writ or in any pleading it can almost always be cured by amendment. Nevertheless the party at fault should act quickly so as to avoid increasing the extra costs which he will have to pay. The plaintiff may amend the writ[9] *once* without leave before the close of pleadings. An amended writ must be served on the defendant. The writ does not include any statement of claim indorsed upon it, since this is a

---

4 Ord 18, r 14(1).
5 JAMES LJ in *Hall v Eve* (1876) 4 Ch D 341, at 345.
6 Ord 82, r 3(3).
7 Ord 18, r 3.
8 Ord 18, r 4.
9 Ord 20, r 1(1). See also: *Singh v Atombrook Ltd* [1989] 1 All ER 385; [1989] 1 WLR 810.

pleading and not part of the writ. Amendments to the writ can be of a technical nature, for example, correction of a misspelling or an incorrect date; moreover the writ can with leave be amended under Order 20 to correct the name of a party, even if this has the effect of substituting a new party, if the court is satisfied that the mistake was a genuine one and not misleading as to the true identity of the party intended;[10] similarly an amendment may be allowed which adds or substitutes a new cause of action provided it arises out of substantially the same facts as the original cause of action. Amendments to alter the parties to the action to add or substitute a new cause of action can be made without leave only before the writ has been served.[11] Leave may be granted to make these amendments even after the period of limitation current at the date of issue of the writ has expired, if the courts think it just. In this way a new statute-barred cause of action may be raised, or a party may be "brought in" by amendment at a time when he could no longer be sued in a fresh action.[12] Apart from the provisions of Order 20, new parties may be added by order of the court following an application by summons[13] but a new cause of action arising since the issue of the writ, against a defendant, can never be added. The proper procedure in this case is to issue a second writ and apply to have the actions consolidated. It will be appreciated, however, that in this case the Limitation Act comes into play since time will be deemed to have run up to the time of issue of the new writ.

2 Pleadings

Any party may amend his pleadings once without leave before the close of pleadings.[14] As long as the proposed amendment does not amount to pleading a completely new cause of action and causes no injustice to an opponent it is permissible. Thus a party will be allowed to withdraw an admission mistakenly made.[15] A plaintiff may be allowed to amend his statement of claim even where the original disclosed no cause of action. To adopt any other approach would be a regression to the formalism of pleading at common law. The court's attitude is well illustrated in the judgment of BOWEN LJ in *Cropper v Smith*:[16]

---

10 See *Evans Construction Co Ltd v Charrington & Co Ltd* [1983] QB 810; [1983] 1 All ER 310.
11 Ord 20, r 1(3).
12 See *Rodriguez v Parker* [1976] 1 QB 116; [1966] 2 All ER 349; *Mitchell v Harris Engineering Co Ltd* [1967] 2 QB 703; [1967] 2 All ER 682; *Chatsworth Investments Ltd v Cussins (Contractors) Ltd* [1969] 1 All ER 143; [1969] 1 WLR 1; *Sterman v EW and WJ Moore* [1970] 1 QB 596; [1970] 1 All ER 581; cf *Braniff v Holland and Hannen and Cubitts (Southern) Ltd* [1969] 3 All ER 959; [1969] 1 WLR 1533; *Brickfield Properties Ltd v Newton* [1971] 3 All ER 328; [1971] 1 WLR 862.
13 Under Ord 15, rr 6, 7. The court will not, however, grant an application so as to deprive the proposed defendant of a defence of limitation; therein lies the great advantage of adding a party under Ord 20 rather than under Ord 15 (where possible). By s 35 of the Limitation Act 1980 a new claim (including a new cause of action and a claim against an added or substituted party) is deemed to have been commenced on the same date as the original action.
14 Ord 20, r 1(1), subject to limits. The one amendment rule does not apply in the circumstances identified by Ord 20, r 1(3).
15 *Hollis v Burton* [1892] 3 Ch 226.
16 (1884) 26 Ch D 700, at 710–711.

"I know of no kind of error or mistake which, if not fraudulent or intended to overreach, the court ought not to correct, if it can be done without injustice to the other party. Courts do not exist for the sake of discipline, but for the sake of deciding matters in controversy, and I do not regard such amendment as a matter of favour or grace . . .. It seems to me that as soon as it appears that the way in which a party has framed his case will not lead to a decision of the real matter in controversy it is as much a matter of right on his part to have it corrected if it can be done without injustice, as anything else in the case is a matter of right."

The amended pleading must be served on the opponent who may himself serve an amended pleading to it within 14 days.[17] Alternatively he may allow his original pleading to stand, or he may apply to the master to disallow the amendment on the ground that it causes injustice.[18]

The writ and pleadings may be amended after the close of pleadings but only with leave.[19] The application is by summons, usually the summons for directions. Amendment may even be allowed at the trial if the judge is satisfied that no injustice is thereby caused.[20] If amendment is allowed it is almost always on terms that the party amending pays the costs thrown away in any event and if the amendment necessitates an adjournment of the trial he will usually be ordered to pay the costs thrown away by the adjournment.

D   PARTICULARS

If a pleading is vague or too general the party on whom it is served may apply for particulars. The application should first be by letter, and the court will not usually make an order until there has been an application to the other side by letter. If particulars are not forthcoming application may be made by summons for an order for further and better particulars.[1] The functions of particulars are broadly twofold. First they prevent the party giving them from framing his case too widely, since at the trial he will be confined to his particulars as if they had been incorporated in his pleading. Thus if he relies in his particulars on conduct which he alleges amounts to negligence, he cannot at the trial give evidence as to other conduct (unless he obtains leave to amend his particulars). Secondly the party who is served with particulars is thereby better acquainted with the case against him so that he will not be taken by surprise at the trial. Any particulars which ought to have been included in the pleadings may be ordered,[2] for example particulars of special damages. However particulars cannot be ordered of matters which have not been specifically pleaded, nor can particulars be required of a simple traverse.[3] Particulars are most often sought in respect of the statement of claim.

Particulars cannot be required of any matter not pleaded. In this respect

---

17 Ord 20, r 3.
18 Ord 20, r 4. The application is by summons and is usually made on the summons for directions.
19 Ord 20, r 5. The court may even amend a pleading on its own motion: see *Nottage v Jackson* (1883) 11 QBD 627.
20 *Ives v Brown* [1919] 2 Ch 314; but see *Esso Petroleum Co Ltd v Southport Corporation* [1956] AC 218; [1955] 3 All ER 864.
1 Ord 18, r 12(3), (6); *Milbank v Milbank* [1900] 1 Ch 376.
2 See p 334, *ante*.
3 *Weinberger v Inglis* [1918] 1 Ch 133; see also *Chapple v Electrical Trades Union* [1961] 3 All ER 612; [1961] 1 WLR 1290.

they differ from interrogatories which may, as we shall see, relate to any relevant matter whether pleaded or not.

E   THE CLOSE OF PLEADINGS

The pleadings are deemed to be closed:

(a) at the expiration of 14 days after service of the reply or defence to counterclaim, or

(b) if neither a reply nor a defence to counterclaim is served, at the expiration of 14 days after service of the defence.[4]

Where the time for serving any of these pleadings is extended with leave, the close of pleadings is postponed until the expiry of such further time. The close of pleadings is important for three purposes:

(1) subsequent amendment of the writ and pleadings may only be made with leave;

(2) there is an implied joinder of issue on the pleading last served (unless the last pleading was a counterclaim); and

(3) the time is fixed within which discovery of documents must be made and the summons for directions taken out. These are the next stages in the action.

---

4 Ord 18, r 20.

CHAPTER 17

Procedure from the Close of
Pleadings to the Trial

A DISCOVERY AND INSPECTION OF DOCUMENTS

Discovery of documents is the procedure whereby a party discloses, to the court or to any other party, the relevant documents in the action that he has, or has had, in his possession, custody or power.

Documentary evidence plays an important part in nearly all civil cases. In an action for breach of contract, for example, the transactions between the parties may be contained entirely in letters which have passed between them. One party's letters may not be intelligible unless read in conjunction with letters in the possession of the other party. Similarly, in an industrial injuries action, the employers are likely to have internal accident reports, machine maintenance records, records of complaints and the like which it is very much in the plaintiff's interests to see, while, on the other hand, the plaintiff may have documents relating to his medical condition, or to his earnings since the accident or state benefits which he has received, all of which may be highly relevant to the quantification of his claim by the defendants. Accordingly a party will want to have his opponent disclose which documents the latter has, or has had, in his possession (discovery), and, secondly, to inspect and take copies of those documents in his opponent's possession (inspection).[1] Sometimes a party may have documents which are relevant to the litigation, and therefore disclosable, but which he wishes to safeguard against circulation either to third parties, or occasionally to the plaintiff himself for extraneous reasons. As to this point, the position is that on discovery each party impliedly undertakes not to use the documents which are disclosed for any ulterior or improper purpose. The use of such documents in breach of that implied undertaking will amount to a contempt of court. Thus in *Home Office v Harman*[2] a solicitor who passed documents to a journalist to assist in the preparation

---

1 "Inspection" is not limited to ocular inspection but includes examination by any of the senses. Thus, a tape-recording is a document, inspection of which would be effected by playing the same upon a tape-recorder to the inspecting party: *Grant v Southwestern and County Properties Ltd* [1975] Ch 185; [1974] 2 All ER 465; similar considerations apply to untransmitted television film: *Senior v Holdsworth, ex parte Independent Television News Ltd* [1976] QB 23; [1975] 2 All ER 1009.
2 [1983] 1 AC 280; [1982] 1 All ER 532.

of an article was held to be in contempt, even though the documents had been read in open court. Nor can a party generally rely upon such documents in other proceedings. Thus where a plaintiff in proceedings against his employers obtained discovery of a memorandum about him which contained an alleged libel, the court held that he could not found a libel action on that publication since that would be an abuse of the process of the court.[3] In *Crest Homes plc v Marks*[4] the court indicated that it would release a party from that undertaking if the applicant could demonstrate "cogent and persuasive reasons" for such a release, and that the release did not cause injustice.

If there is a real risk of the plaintiff using documents for an improper collateral purpose, the court may restrict inspection, for example to a party's legal advisers.[5]

Discovery may take place in two ways, under the Rules.

1 Discovery without order

Until 1964 discovery of documents was dependent upon the order of a master, which was made in most cases on the summons for directions. While discovery by order still exists, one major alteration in procedure effected in 1962 was the introduction of "automatic" discovery. Parties must now in any action commenced by writ, with certain exceptions, make discovery by exchanging lists within 14 days of the close of pleadings.[6] The lists are in a prescribed form[7] and annexed are two schedules, as follows.

SCHEDULE 1

Part 1
Relevant documents, listed numerically, which the party has in his possession, custody or power[8] and which he does not object to produce.

Part 2
Relevant documents as above which he objects to produce.[9]

---

3 *Riddick v Thames Board Mills Ltd* [1977] QB 881; [1977] 3 All ER 677.
4 [1987] AC 829; [1987] 2 All ER 1074. Ord 24, r 4A now has the effect of removing the implied undertaking, once the document has been read or referred to in open court.
5 For a discussion of this power, and some illustrations of the difficulties involved in its exercise, see *Church of Scientology of California v Department of Health and Social Security* [1979] 3 All ER 97; [1979] 1 WLR 723.
6 Ord 24, r 2. If any party does not comply he may be ordered to do so and may also be ordered to file an affidavit verifying his list; Ord 24, r 3(2).
7 Ord 24, r 5(1).
8 This comprises documents of which a party has an enforceable right to obtain possession; for example a director of a company of which he is, in effect, the alter ego, would have the right to obtain possession of that company's documents (which he would, therefore, have to disclose) whereas a company director simpliciter, though he has a right to inspect the company's documents, has no right to possess them (so that he could not, in those circumstances, be required to disclose them); *B v B (Matrimonial Proceedings; Discovery)* [1978] Fam 181; [1979] 1 All ER 801.
9 The list must contain a sufficient statement of the grounds of the privilege claimed; Ord 24, r 5(2).

SCHEDULE 2

Relevant documents, listed as above, which have been, but at the date of service of the list are not, in the possession, custody or power of the party in question.[10]

Notice to inspect

A party serving a list of documents must also serve on his opponent a notice to inspect the documents in the list (other than those which he objects to produce) setting out a time within 7 days and place where the documents in Part 1 of the first schedule may be inspected.[11]

The right to inspect includes the right to take copies of the documents in question, although these will, as a matter of courtesy, be supplied on payment by the solicitors for the party in question.[12]

The foregoing provisions for automatic discovery do not apply to actions commenced by originating summons. There are certain other proceedings to which the procedure is not applicable; notably actions to which the Crown is a party, and actions arising out of an accident on land involving a vehicle, where the defendant must not make discovery unless ordered to do so.[13] In addition, the court may, on the application of any party, made by summons, waive discovery by all or any of the parties or restrict discovery to certain classes of documents for disposing fairly of the action or for saving costs.[14]

2   Discovery by order

There are two important circumstances in which an order for discovery will be required. The first is where the action is one of those to which the above rule relating to automatic discovery is not applicable or where any party has failed to comply with that rule. In such a case there must be an application for an order for discovery of all relevant documents, if discovery is required. The second case arises where a party is dissatisfied with his opponent's list. He may then apply for discovery of particular documents.

A party who is served with a list of documents may believe that relevant documents which the maker of the list has, or has had, in his possession, custody or power are not included in his list. This may be due to a *bona fide* belief on the maker's part that the document in question is not relevant to the action, or to an omission, accidental or deliberate. In either case application may be made by summons to the master for an order for discovery of the documents in question. This application must be accompanied by an affidavit setting out the grounds for the deponent's belief and identifying the documents of which discovery is required. If the other party admits the existence of the documents in question but denies their

---

10 He must state what has become of them and who is presently in possession of them.
11 Ord 24, r 9. As to the court's power to restrict inspection, see *Church of Scientology of California v Department of Health and Social Security* (p 349, n 5, *supra*); there is, however, no apparent power to withhold inspection entirely (*ibid*).
12 *Ormerod, Grierson & Co v St George's Ironworks Ltd* [1905] 1 Ch 505.
13 Ord 77, r 12(1); Ord 24, r 2(2).
14 Ord 24, r 2(5).

relevance, the master may inspect them in order to decide whether they are in fact relevant. In addition that party may be required to make an affidavit stating whether or not any particular document is, or has at any time been, in his possession, custody or power and, if it no longer is, what has become of it.[15]

Finally, independent of the above provisions, any party may at any time require inspection of any document referred to in any other party's pleadings or affidavits.[16]

If any party fails to comply with an order for discovery the master may order his statement of claim to be struck out, if he is a plaintiff, or his defence to be struck out and judgment entered against him, if a defendant. In a case of extreme and wilful disobedience the offender may be committed for contempt of court.[17]

There is another issue which may be raised in connection with discovery. This arises where a party refuses to produce a document in his possession, custody or power.

3   Documents privileged from production

The only circumstance in which a party may refuse to produce a document is where that document is one of a class which the law recognises as privileged. The privilege which attaches to documents must be carefully distinguished from privilege in the law of defamation. Thus a document which attracts qualified privilege for the purposes of defamation, the minutes of a company meeting for example, is not necessarily privileged from discovery. The former rule is a rule of law, the latter a rule of evidence or procedure, and discussed further in due course.[18]

A party who wishes to claim privilege for a document cannot merely omit to include it in his list. He must include it in the second part of the first schedule to his list, together with a statement in the body of the list of the ground upon which he claims privilege for it. The principal classes of documents which the law recognises as being privileged from production are: documents which relate solely to the deponent's own case, incriminating documents, documents attracting legal professional privilege and documents whose production would be injurious to the public interest.

4   Discovery and inspection against other persons

We have already examined the procedure introduced by the Administration of Justice Act 1970, whereby orders for discovery and inspection of documents against proposed parties may be made before the commencement of proceedings.[19]

---

15 Ord 14, r 7; *Astra-National Productions Ltd v Neo-Art Productions Ltd* [1928] WN 218.
16 Ord 24, r 10.
17 Ord 24, r 16. The object of this rule is to secure compliance with the rules and orders of the court, relating to discovery, and not to punish a party for non-compliance; thus where a summons is taken out for a punitive order under rule 16 and the defaulting party complies before the hearing of that summons, it is wrong to make an order requiring payment into court of the balance of the claim: *Husband's of Marchwood Ltd v Drummond Walker Developments Ltd* [1975] 2 All ER 30; [1975] 1 WLR 603.
18 See p 594, *post*.
19 See p 285, *ante*.

Under section 34 of the Supreme Court Act 1981 there is, in addition, power, in actions for damages for death or personal injuries, to order a person who is not a party to the proceedings and who appears to be likely to have or have had in his possession, custody or power any documents which are relevant to an issue arising out of the action to disclose whether these documents are in his possession, custody or power and to produce those which he has to the applicant.

This power is exercisable only after the commencement of proceedings, the application being by summons (which must be served on the person against whom the order is sought and on all parties to the action) supported by affidavit.[20] As stated above, the procedure is limited in its application to personal injuries litigation where it may be used, for example, by defendants to obtain a sight of the plaintiff's hospital notes or by plaintiffs to obtain copies of manufacturers' instructions for using and maintaining machines, reports by employers to the Health and Safety at Work Executive and documents of that type. It is not limited to parties to proceedings already commenced.

5   Action for discovery

Save for the limited exception, in personal injuries actions, discussed above there is, as a rule, no procedure for obtaining discovery against persons who are not parties to an action. They can, of course, be compelled to attend the trial and to produce, at that stage, documents in their possession (by means of *subpoena duces tecum*) but there is a rule, sometimes known as the "mere witness" rule, whereby discovery cannot be obtained against a person against whom no relief is sought but who might be a witness in an action. It follows that if a party wishes to inspect documents in the possession of a person against whom he has no cause of action, he cannot sue that person simply for the purpose of obtaining evidence, by way of discovery of documents, for use against the party against whom there is a cause of action. This rule appears to have little in the way of logic to commend it but it is, nevertheless, too firmly entrenched to be altered save by way of legislation.

However, it has already been seen that a limited exception to the rule was formulated by the House of Lords in the case of *Norwich Pharmacal Co v Customs and Excise Commissioners*.[1] The facts of the case were unusual. The appellants, who were the owners of a patent covering a chemical compound, learned from information published by the respondents that a number of consignments of the compound had been imported between 1960 and 1970, none of which had been licensed by the appellants. The appellants therefore knew that others were infringing their patent but did not know their identity. The respondents refused to disclose the identity of the importers whereupon the appellants brought an action against the respondents seeking an order for discovery of documents relating to the importations. The House of Lords granted such an order;

---

20 Ord 24, r 7A.
 1 [1974] AC 133; [1973] 2 All ER 943, applied in *Loose v Williamson* [1978] 3 All ER 89; [1978] 1 WLR 639.

the reasoning behind the decision was expressed by Lord Reid, as follows:[2]

> "... if through no fault of his own a person gets mixed up in the tortious acts of others so as to facilitate their wrong-doing he may incur no personal liability but he comes under a duty to assist the person who has been wronged by giving him full information and disclosing the identity of the wrongdoers."

B INSPECTION OF PROPERTY

1 Inspection of property inter partes

The court has power, on the application of any party, to make an order for the detention, custody or preservation of any property which is the subject-matter of the action or as to which any question may arise therein or for the inspection of any such property in the possession of a party to the action and, for the purpose of enabling such an order to be carried out, may authorise any person to enter a party's land or building.[3] The application is often made on the summons for directions but may, if need be, be made by summons at any stage of the proceedings. The procedure is widely used in personal injuries actions, usually to enable an expert engineer on behalf of the plaintiff to inspect the defendant's factory premises, but is not confined to such actions.

As has already been noted,[4] section 33(1) of the Supreme Court Act 1981 enables an order to be made before the commencement of proceedings.

2 Orders against third persons

Analogous to the power of the court to order discovery and inspection of documents against strangers to the proceedings is the power, now contained in section 34(3) of the Supreme Court Act 1981, to make orders for the inspection, photographing, preservation, custody or detention of property[5] which is not the property of, or in the possession of, any party to the proceedings but which is the subject matter of the proceedings or as to which any question arises in the proceedings; orders[6] may also be made for the taking of samples of any such property and the carrying out of any experiment in relation thereto.

Application for such an order is by summons supported by affidavit. No order will be made if it appears that compliance would result in the disclosure of information relating to a secret process, discovery or invention not in issue in the proceedings.[7] The courts will take particular care with applications to inspect computer databases, including ensuring

---

2 [1974] AC, at 175; [1973] 2 All ER, at 948; see also, on the *Norwich Pharmacal* principle, *Arab Monetary Fund v Hashim (No 5)* [1992] 2 All ER 911.
3 Ord 29, r 2. There is no express power to order photographing but this is obviously an oversight since inspection will often be worthless without a right to take photographs.
4 See p 286, *ante.*
5 "Property" includes any land, chattel or other corporeal property of any description: Supreme Court Act 1981, s 35(5).
6 See also p 287, *ante.*   7 Ord 29, r 7A(6).

that the information stored is not corrupted, and that the respondent's use of the database is not interfered with.[8]

C INTERROGATORIES

Interrogatories are questions answerable on oath which any party may administer to his opponent.[9] The purpose of interrogatories is twofold: first to obtain admissions, and secondly to limit the scope of one's opponent's case. It may thus seem that answers to interrogatories are similar to particulars. In fact, they differ in several important respects.

(1) The scope of particulars is limited to matters in question between the parties, and must be necessary either (a) for disposing fairly of the cause or matter, or (b) for securing costs. Thus particulars cannot be required of matters not pleaded. Interrogatories, on the other hand, may relate to any matter relevant to the action.[10] For example, in an action for defamation, a defendant cannot ask the plaintiff to give particulars of why the words complained of are untrue since it is no part of the plaintiff's case to allege or prove the falsity of the words in question. However, if the defendant pleads justification, he may administer interrogatories to the plaintiff the function of which is to elicit from the plaintiff how far the latter is prepared to admit that the words, or any part of them, are true.[11] Broadly speaking, any question which could be asked of a witness at the trial may be asked in the form of an interrogatory, with the notable exception of questions as to the witness's credit or credibility.[12]

(2) Particulars cannot relate to evidence. Interrogatories are usually aimed at evidential matters, although they cannot extend to asking a party to disclose his means of proof or to name his witnesses.[13]

(3) Particulars are not given on oath. Interrogatories must always be answered on affidavit (though parties often agree to accept answers by open letter, which answers can be put in at the trial in the same way as sworn answers).

(4) A party may apply for particulars by letter on his own initiative. Indeed he should do so. A party may also apply for leave to administer interrogatories[14] on any matter in question. This provision may be useful in cases where, prior to changes in the rules, leave has previously not been sought.

---

8 *Huddleston v Control Risks Information Services Ltd* [1987] 1 WLR 701.
9 Ord 26, r 1. Leave is not now required. A party has an automatic right, subject only to an order of the court disallowing the interrogatories. Rules introduced in 1990 provide for service of interrogatories without order, the party on whom they are served being obliged either to answer them or apply to the court for them to be varied or disallowed.
10 Ord 26, r 1(1) (a); *Nash v Leyton* [1911] 2 Ch 71.
11 *Marriott v Chamberlain* (1886) 17 QBD 154; *Peter Walker & Son Ltd v Hodgson* [1909] 1 KB 239.
12 *Kennedy v Dodson* [1895] 1 Ch 334.
13 *Marriott v Chamberlain* (*supra*); *Knapp v Harvey* [1911] 2 KB 725.
14 Ord 26, r 1(2).

The interrogatories must be answered on oath within the time prescribed, being not less than 28 days.[15] The only ground upon which a party may refuse to answer is that of privilege. The privilege must be claimed in the answer[16] and the grounds are the same as those for the privilege from production of documents. Other objections must be taken at the hearing of the summons at which the order for interrogatories is made, or the application to withdraw or vary them is made, or not at all. Answers to interrogatories are binding and the party administering them is in a position of advantage since he may put in evidence at the trial all *or any* of the answers. He cannot be compelled to put in any answer which does not favour his case.[17]

If a party's answers are evasive or ambiguous he may be ordered to make a further answer either on affidavit or by oral examination.[18] The final sanctions for failing to comply with an order for interrogatories are the same as for disobedience to any other interlocutory order. Thus the defaulter's statement of claim may be struck out if he is a plaintiff or his defence if a defendant. In an extreme case of wilful disobedience the offender may be committed for contempt of court.[19]

D   SECURITY FOR COSTS

As a rule no party can be required to deposit money or a bond as security for the costs of a pending action. This rule applies even if the party concerned is insolvent or even bankrupt.[20] However there are exceptions to this rule, as there are to most rules. In these exceptional cases the defendant may apply by summons, usually on the summons for directions, for an order that the plaintiff provide security for costs:

(a) where the plaintiff is ordinarily resident out of the jurisdiction.[1] However security will not be ordered on this ground if the plaintiff has substantial property within the jurisdiction out of which costs may be defrayed, since the basis of the exception is that the

---

15 See Ord 26, r 2.

16 Ord 26, r 5; *Dalgleish v Lowther* [1899] 2 QB 590.

17 Ord 26, r 7. The court may, however, order an answer to be put in where it is so closely connected with another answer which has been put in evidence that the court considers that one ought not to be used without the other.

18 Ord 26, r 5. The test is whether the answer is sufficient, not whether it is true; *Lyell v Kennedy (No 3)* (1884) 27 Ch D 1.

19 Ord 26. r 6.

20 *Cowell v Taylor* (1885) 31 Ch D 34; *Cook v Whellock* (1890) 24 QBD 658; *Rhodes v Dawson* (1886) 16 QBD 548.

1 Ord 23, r 1(1) (a). As to the meaning of the words "ordinarily resident", see *Levene v Inland Revenue Commissioners* [1928] AC 217 and *Inland Revenue Commissioners v Lysaght* [1928] AC 234. This rule does not conflict with the Treaty of Rome, but the court may take into account the fact that the plaintiff is an EC resident and refuse to order security: *Landi Den Hartog BV v Stopps* [1976] FSR 497. The High Court may by issue of the prerogative writ *ne exeat regno* restrain a defendant from leaving the jurisdiction, subject to the conditions contained in the Debtors Act 1869, s 6, of which the most important is that the defendant's absence will materially prejudice the plaintiff in prosecuting his action; see, generally, the judgment of MEGARRY J in *Felton v Callis* [1969] 1 QB 200; [1968] 3 All ER 673. Note also the power to grant Mareva injunctions (see p 289, *ante*).

defendant, if successful, would not be able to enforce an order for his costs;[2]

(b) where the plaintiff is a nominal plaintiff suing for the benefit of a third party and there is reason to believe that he would be unable to pay the defendant's costs if ordered to do so;[3] a person suing in a representative capacity is not a nominal plaintiff;

(c) where the plaintiff has deliberately misstated his address on the writ, or has changed his address since the issue of the writ in order to evade the consequences of litigation;[4]

(d) where a plaintiff company may not be able to pay costs awarded against it.[5]

In addition, orders for the disclosure of documents or the inspection of property before the commencement of proceedings, or for the disclosure of documents or the inspection of property in relation to persons who are not parties to the proceedings[6] may be made conditional upon the applicant's giving security for costs.[7] However, in these cases, unlike the above cases, no application for security is made.

These are the only cases in which security for costs, as such, may be ordered. However it is as well to bear in mind that under Order 14 a defendant may be ordered to pay a sum into court as a condition of being granted leave to defend the action[8] and that an applicant for a *Mareva* injunction may sometimes be required to support his cross-undertaking as to damages by a bond or security.[9]

A counterclaiming defendant may sometimes be ordered to give security for costs[10] but, otherwise, security cannot be ordered to be given by a defendant or someone compelled to litigate.

Application for security should first be made by letter and then, if this fails, by summons. In order to assist the court as to the appropriate amount of security, it is helpful for solicitors to prepare a skeleton bill of costs to date. The court will order such security as appears just in all the circumstances of the case. Normally a discount from the defendant's assessment will be made to take account of the court's expectation of any reduction by the taxing officer of the fees particularised, but there is not (as used to be thought) any justification for a "conventional approach" of fixing security at two-thirds of the estimated party and party costs.[11] A

---

2 See *Kevorkian v Burney (No 2)* [1937] 4 All ER 468.

3 Ord 23, r 1(1)(b). The next friend of a person under a disability is not a nominal plaintiff: *Fellows v Barrett* (1836) 1 Keen 119. An example of a nominal plaintiff is one who, before action, assigns to a third party any damages he may recover; see *Semler v Murphy* [1968] Ch 183; [1967] 2 All ER 185.

4 Ord 23, r 1(1)(c), (d); Ord 23, r 1(2); *Knight v Ponsonby* [1925] 1 KB 545.

5 Companies Act 1985, s 726(1).

6 Supreme Court Act 1981, ss 33–35; see pp 285, 286, *ante*.

7 Ord 24, r 7A(5); Ord 29, r 7A(6).

8 See p 320, *ante*.

9 *Third Chandris Shipping Corporation v Unimarine SA* [1979] QB 645; [1979] 2 All ER 972; see p xxx, *ante*.

10 When his counterclaim is in the nature of a cross-action rather than simply by way of a defence; cf *Visco v Minter* [1969] P 82; [1969] 2 All ER 714.

11 *Procon (GB) Ltd v Provincial Building Co Ltd* [1984] 2 All ER 368; [1984] 1 WLR 557, in which the principles are stated by the Court of Appeal.

party who has obtained security may apply for further security as the action proceeds and the costs increase.

E DIRECTIONS

1 Automatic directions

The majority of actions in the Queen's Bench Division are personal injury actions. Prior to 1980 a summons for directions had to be issued in all such actions even though the directions sought and obtained were in most cases standard. Following recommendations of the Cantley Working Party on Personal Injuries Litigation,[12] a system of automatic directions in personal injury actions was introduced as Order 25, rule 8. This rule applies to any action for personal injuries except (a) any Admiralty action; and (b) any action where the pleadings contain an allegation of negligent medical treatment. The effect of the rule is that when the pleadings are closed the following directions take effect automatically:

(a) save where liability is admitted or where the action arises out of a road accident (in which cases discovery is limited to disclosure by the plaintiff of documents relating to special damages) there must be discovery of documents within 14 days and inspection within seven days thereafter;

(b) where any party intends to rely on expert evidence he must within 10 weeks disclose the substance of that evidence to the other parties in the form of a written report, which shall be agreed if possible;[13]

(c) unless such reports are agreed, the parties shall be at liberty to call as expert witnesses those witnesses whose reports have been disclosed, limited to two medical experts and one expert of any other kind;

(d) photographs, a sketch plan and the contents of any police accident report book shall be receivable in evidence at the trial, and shall be agreed if possible;

(e) the action shall be tried at the trial centre of the place where the action is proceeding or at such other trial centre as the parties may in writing agree;[14]

(f) the action shall be tried by judge alone, as a case of substance or difficulty (Category B) and shall be set down within six months;

(g) the court shall be notified, on setting down, of the estimated length of the trial.

It should be noted that there is nothing to prevent any party from applying by summons for further or different directions or orders. In addition the court may elect to transfer the action to a county court.[15] In London every

---

12 Cmnd 1476 of 1979.
13 Where more than one party intends to rely on expert evidence, disclosure is by mutual exchange of reports (r 8(2)).
14 Except where the Crown is a party, since the Crown has a right to trial in London (Ord 77, r 13).
15 See p 415, *post*. Not that many such actions will in fact be commenced in the county court, by virtue of the High Court and County Courts Jurisdiction Order 1990.

action set down under automatic directions is forthwith examined by a master and if it appears to him that the question of transfer ought to be considered, the parties are directed to attend the master at a given date and time for this purpose.[16]

2   Summons for directions

In cases outside the automatic directions procedure, directions are given by the master or district judge on the hearing of a summons for directions.

The plaintiff must, within one month of the close of pleadings, take out a summons for directions returnable in not less than 14 days.[17] To do so he issues the summons, using the appropriate form, at the Central Office or a district registry, and serves it on all defendants to the action. If he does not do so the defendant has two courses open to him. He may apply to have the plaintiff's action dismissed for want of prosecution, or he may issue the summons himself and serve it on the plaintiff.[18] The plaintiff must issue a summons for directions in every action commenced by writ with a few exceptions, the chief of which are: automatic directions cases, cases where directions have already been given following an application for summary judgment under Order 14 or for a trial without pleadings under Order 18, rule 21, actions for an account and actions which have been referred to an official referee or transferred to the Commercial Court.[19]

The general functions of the summons for directions are summarised in Order 25, r 1(1), so that:

(a)   all matters which must or can be dealt with on interlocutory applications and have not already been dealt with may so far as possible be dealt with, and

(b)   such directions may be given as to the future course of the action as appear best adapted to secure the just, expeditious and economical disposal thereof.

The summons for directions has been described as a "stocktaking" of all the interlocutory matters in the action. It is possible for a party to issue a separate summons for each interlocutory application which he wishes to make, but to save time and expense it is generally prudent to await the summons for directions to apply for all the orders required.[20] The form on which the summons is issued sets out in outline matters on which directions may be given, leaving the parties to fill in their detailed requirements and

---

16 *Practice Direction* [1984] 2 All ER 672; [1984] 1 WLR 1023.

17 Ord 25, r 1(1). In Admiralty actions the period is seven weeks and the summons will be returnable before a judge of the Admiralty Court; Ord 75, r 25; see p 365, *post*. There is a lacuna in the Rules of the Supreme Court in that if no defence is served the close of pleadings never occurs and there is no provision for applying for directions; fortunately the High Court has an inherent power to give directions on application: *Austin v Wildig* [1969] 1 All ER 99n; [1969] 1 WLR 67.

18 Ord 25, r 1(4).

19 The full list of exceptions is embodied in Ord 25, r 1(2).

20 There is a general rule that particulars will not be ordered before the summons for directions; nevertheless in exceptional cases, for example cases where the pleading is so vague that the other party cannot properly ascertain the case against him, particulars may be ordered; *Cyril Leonard & Co v Simo Securities Trust Ltd* [1971] 3 All ER 1313; [1971] 1 WLR 80.

also to add any other application for which the form does not provide (such as an order for the admission of a certified copy of notes of evidence taken in other proceedings). The applicant must delete the number[1] of any paragraph on the form which contains a matter on which he does not require directions. On the return day, and on adjourned hearings, the master will give directions for which the parties have applied and will also give directions of his own motion on certain matters, such as the mode and place of trial, whether or not the parties have applied for them.[2]

3 Matters dealt with on the summons

The standard form lists some fourteen matters upon which the parties may apply for directions, and leaves space for any others not listed. Certain matters which are, in fact, dealt with on the summons for directions, such as particulars of pleading, amendment of writ and pleadings, discovery and inspection of documents, security for costs and interrogatories have already been encountered.[3] It remains to consider the other principal matters which may be dealt with at this important stage of the proceedings.

a Consolidation of actions[4]

This is a procedure which enables a party to have separate issues tried together, whether or not they could have been joined on one writ.[5] It arises, for example, in defamation actions where one plaintiff wishes to sue several defendants for separate publications of substantially the same defamatory matter.[6] The application to consolidate should be made as early as possible and will often be made before the summons for directions in which case a separate summons will be required. The plaintiffs in a consolidated action must generally be represented by one firm of solicitors, so that, where more than one firm has been instructed, consolidation will be impossible unless the plaintiffs agree to be represented by one of the firms alone.[7]

A simple alternative to consolidation is for the master to order separate actions to be set down for trial consecutively in the same list, so that they will come before the same judge on the same day. The effect is to avoid the duplication of such expenses as witness fees.

---

1 He must not, however, delete the text.
2 *Nagy v Co-operative Press Ltd* [1949] 2 KB 188; [1949] 1 All ER 1019. If the directions sought are uncontested or agreed (when it is still necessary to obtain directions as to the mode and place of trial, before the action can be set down for trial) the plaintiff can apply by post for the directions he requires and the order may be drawn in the High Court office, personal attendance being dispensed with: *Practice Direction (Use of Postal Facilities; Queen's Bench Division)* [1976] 2 All ER 312; [1976] 1 WLR 489.
3 See pp 348–357, *ante*.
4 Ord 4, r 9.
5 In fact cases are normally consolidated only where the parties could have been joined on one writ under Ord 15, r 4.
6 See Defamation Act 1952, s 13; *Stone v Press Association* [1897] 2 QB 159; *Daws v Daily Sketch and Sunday Graphic Ltd* [1960] 1 All ER 397; [1960] 1 WLR 126.
7 *Lewis v Daily Telegraph Ltd (No 2)* [1964] 2 QB 601; [1964] 1 All ER 705. This case indicates that there is a power to "deconsolidate" consolidated actions.

b   Evidence

Order 38, rule 1, provides that:

> ". . . subject to the provisions of these rules and of the Civil Evidence Act
> 1968 and the Civil Evidence Act 1972, and any other enactment relating to
> evidence, any fact required to be proved at the trial of any action begun by writ
> by the evidence of witnesses shall be proved by the examination of the
> witnesses orally and in open court."

Nevertheless the rules provide for enabling and even compelling parties to reduce costs, particularly witness fees, by adopting alternative methods of proof. The most common method of reducing costs is by the use of admissions. A party need produce no proof of any matter admitted in his favour. Admissions on the pleadings may be express or implied from a failure to traverse.[8] Admissions may also be made in answer to interrogatories. A useful means of compelling an opponent to admit a fact is to serve him with a "notice to admit facts", calling upon him to admit the facts listed in the notice.[9] If he will not admit these facts and they are proved at the trial, unless the court otherwise orders, he will bear the costs of proof.[10] This is, of course, a powerful weapon but it must not be abused. A party should not be asked to admit the facts in issue or any inference of fact, such as negligence. He should only, in practice, be asked to admit facts of a formal nature or facts which can easily be proved against him if he does not admit them. If admissions are made which clearly establish one party's liability the other party may, without waiting for a trial, apply for judgment based on those admissions.[11] Similar to such a notice is a "notice to admit documents", calling upon the party served to admit the authenticity of the documents listed, though not the truth of their contents. The effect of failure to admit is, again, that the party who was served with the notice has to pay the costs of proving the documents at the trial, unless the court otherwise orders, which may involve an extra witness, such as a handwriting expert.[12]

Wide powers are conferred on the master by Order 38 as to the means of proof. Thus he may order evidence to be given at the trial by affidavit or in any other specified manner.[13] For example, he may order the date on which an important event occurred to be proved by production of a newspaper containing a report of the event. In addition he may restrict the number of medical or other expert witnesses who may be called at the trial.[14]

c   Disclosure of experts' reports

Many actions involve the giving of expert evidence. Thus, for example, in actions for damages for personal injuries there is invariably medical evidence concerning the extent of the plaintiff's injuries. In practice the

---

8 Ord 18, r 13; see p 339, *ante.*
9 Ord 27, r 2.
10 Ord 62, r 6.
11 Ord 27, r 3; see p 322, *ante.*
12 Ord 27, r 5.
13 Ord 38, rr 1, 2.
14 Ord 38, r 4. Note the restrictions embodied in the automatic direction (c) (*supra*).

plaintiff's advisers will obtain a medical report (upon which the pleaded case will be based); thereafter the defendants will have the plaintiff medically examined and will in consequence obtain their own medical report. These reports, coming into existence as they do in contemplation of litigation, are privileged from disclosure[15] so that neither party can be directly compelled to disclose his expert evidence to the other side.[16] This was widely thought to be an unsatisfactory state of affairs, particularly in personal injuries actions where, not only might a party be taken by surprise at the trial, but also the ignorance of the strength or weakness of the other party's case may act as a factor inhibiting settlement of the claim or the making of a realistic payment into court. In the result, following recommendations made by various committees,[17] changes were introduced in 1972, designed to secure the disclosure of expert evidence.

The number of medical or other expert witnesses who may be called at a trial can be limited by order, usually made on the hearing of the summons for directions.[18] Although this does not give the power to the court to order exchange of reports, no party can adduce expert evidence except: (1) with leave of the court; or (2) where the parties agree; or (3) where evidence is given by affidavit; or (4) where an application has been made to the court to determine what disclosure should be made, and such directions have been complied with; or (5) the party has complied with automatic directions.

The court will direct disclosure of experts' reports unless special reasons not to exist. The court must have regard to all the circumstances but circumstances which may justify not ordering disclosure are that the evidence is or will be based upon a version of the facts which is in dispute between the parties, and where, for example, there are suspicions that disclosure will lead to dishonest claims being discovered.[19] The substance of the evidence has to be disclosed. This deals with the practice of part of the statement being edited, or evidence being in statements in two or more parts. In *Kenning v Eve Construction Ltd*[20] two unfavourable points were omitted by a consulting engineer from his report, but dealt with in an accompanying letter. The court held that both the report and letter should be disclosed. The court may also direct that "without prejudice" meetings of experts be held, for the purpose of identifying those parts of their evidence which were in issue.[21] Where such a meeting is held, they may prepare a joint statement indicating those parts of the evidence on which they are, and

---

15 See p 596, *post.*
16 *Causton v Mann Egerton (Johnsons) Ltd* [1974] 1 All ER 453; [1974] 1 WLR 162.
17 Report of Committee on Personal Injuries Litigation (Cmnd. 3691 of 1969); Seventeenth Report of the Law Reform Committee on Evidence of Opinion and Expert Evidence (Cmnd. 4489 of 1970).
18 Ord 38, r 4(1).
19 "Special reasons" are not defined. They may exist where there is evidence that surprise is necessary in the interests of justice. See *eg,* dicta in *Naylor v Preston Area Health Authority* [1987] 2 All ER 313.
20 [1989] 1 WLR 1189.
21 Ord 38, r 38.

are not, in agreement, thus facilitating the trial of the case with as limited a degree of expert disagreement as possible.

d   Disclosure of non-expert evidence

Order 38, rule 2A introduced a wide power in respect of the disclosure of all evidence. In its present form it requires the High Court to direct every party to serve on other parties copies of the written statements of the testimony of the witnesses upon whom they intend to rely at trial. This disclosure is intended to streamline the trial process by reducing "trial by ambush" and reducing the element of surprise. Disclosure is also intended to promote the potential for settlement of the case, or the making of admissions on points that hitherto might have been contested or in dispute right up to the trial itself. It is also intended to assist in defining the key issues for decision at trial.

The powers of the court are exercised for the purpose of disposing fairly and expeditiously of the action and saving costs.[1] Where the witness is not called at trial, the written statement may not be put in evidence by any other party. Where he is, then it may be ordered that the statement serve as the evidence-in-chief of the witness. The statements are required to be in a prescribed form.

e   Place of trial

The master sometimes exercises his power to transfer the action to another division of the High Court or to a county court.[2] In other cases he must direct where and in what manner the action is to be tried.[3] This must be the last matter upon which the master gives directions. The place of trial will be either London or a centre at which the Lord Chancellor has directed sittings of the High Court to be held, pursuant to section 71 of the Supreme Court Act 1981. No party, other than the Crown,[4] has a right to trial in London, and the place of trial will be fixed where it is most convenient for all parties having regard to such matters as the availability of witnesses. This will generally be London, if service was acknowledged in London, or the centre for the district in the registry of which service was acknowledged, though the place of acknowledgment of service is not conclusive since the jurisdiction of the High Court, unlike that of county courts, is in no way local.

f   Mode of trial

The master or district judge will determine the mode of trial. Order 33, rule 2 sets out the possible modes of trial, *viz* trial before:

  (a) a judge alone;
  (b) a judge with a jury;
  (c) a judge with the assistance of assessors;
  (d) an official referee with or without the assistance of assessors;

---

1 Ord 38, r 2A(1).
2 Ord 33, r 4.
3 Ord 77, r 13(1).
4 See *Practice Direction* [1981] 3 All ER 61; [1981] 1 WLR 1296. For directions outside London see *Practice Direction* [1972] 1 All ER 287; [1972] 1 WLR 5.

(e) a master;
(f) a special referee.

If the master orders trial in London, he must fix the list in which the case is to be set down for trial. There are six such lists in the Queen's Bench Division, *viz* Crown Office List, Jury List, Non-Jury List, Short Cause List, Commercial List, Arbitration Case List and Admiralty List.[5] Cases which are to be tried without a jury and which are not likely to last more than four hours are set down in the Short Cause List. Most actions are tried in the Non-Jury List by a judge sitting alone. Provisions relating to jury trial are now contained in section 69 of the Supreme Court Act 1981 which provides that the only cases in which either party has a right[6] to a jury are actions to be tried in the Queen's Bench Division where:

(a) a charge of fraud against the party; or
(b) a claim for libel, slander, malicious prosecution or false imprisonment is in issue

unless in either case the trial requires any prolonged examination of documents or accounts or any scientific or local investigation which cannot conveniently be made with a jury.[7] In any other case the master has a discretion whether or not to order a jury. In *Ward v James*,[8] the Court of Appeal formulated the principle that, in the absence of special circumstances, it is a wrong exercise of the master's discretion to order a jury in an action based on a claim for damages for personal injuries.

Thus the law is that the discretion as to the mode of trial is a judicial rather than an absolute one, and that, in the absence of special circumstances, it is a wrong exercise of that discretion to order a jury in a personal injuries action. In the result jury trial has virtually disappeared in personal injuries actions. However, in *H v Ministry of Defence*[9] the position was said to be different where a claim for exemplary damages was being made. Jury trial is extremely rare in any case other than those in which the right to jury trial has been preserved by statute. Thus in *Williams v Beesley*,[10] an action alleging professional

---

5 See p xxx, *post.*
6 The right must be claimed before the master first fixes the place and mode of trial (Ord 33, r 5). "Fraud", in this context, is limited to deceit: *Barclays Bank Ltd v Cole* [1967] 2 QB 738; [1966] 3 All ER 948.
7 Even though a case does, prima facie, fall within this exception, jury trial may be ordered where a party's honour or reputation is at stake: *Rothermere v Times Newspapers Ltd* [1973] 1 All ER 1013; [1973] 1 WLR 448. Note that the right to jury trial should not be extended by analogy: *Racz v Home Office* [1994] 1 All ER 97. Rules may provide for additional cases (Supreme Court Act 1981, s 69(1) (c)). It will be noted that the right to jury trial is limited to the Queen's Bench Division. If an action involving a charge of fraud is started in the Chancery Division, therefore, it will be tried by a judge alone; however an application could be made under Ord 4, r 3 to have the action transferred to the Queen's Bench Division and a transfer would be ordered if the Chancery master or judge considered the case suitable for jury trial; see *Stafford Winfield Cook & Partners Ltd v Winfield* [1980] 3 All ER 759; [1981] 1 WLR 458.
8 [1966] 1 QB 273; [1965] 1 All ER 563.
9 [1991] 2 QB 103; [1991] 2 All ER 834.
10 [1973] 3 All ER 144; [1973] 1 WLR 1295, an exceptional instance of leave being granted to appeal to the House of Lords on an interlocutory appeal.

negligence against a solicitor, the House of Lords refused to order trial by jury, Lord Diplock stating that:[11]

> ". . . the fact that a case involves issues of credibility is not a ground for departing from the usual rule that cases, other than those in which a prima facie right to trial by jury is conferred by statute, should be tried by judge alone."

The Commercial Court — A separate list is kept in London, Liverpool and Manchester to hear "commercial actions", which are defined by Order 72, rule 1(2) to include:

> "any cause arising out of the ordinary transactions of merchants and traders and, without prejudice to the generalty of the foregoing words, any cause relating to the construction of a mercantile document, the export or import of merchandise, affreightment, insurance, banking, mercantile agency and mercantile usage."

The judges of the Commercial Court are such of the *puisne* judges of the High Court as the Lord Chancellor may from time to time nominate[12] and are usually judges of the Queen's Bench Division with special experience in commercial matters. Except by consent their powers are no greater than those of any other judge. However, procedure in the court is more flexible than the normal procedure. Thus the pleadings must be in the form of points of claim, defence, counterclaim, defence to counterclaim or reply and must be as brief as possible. Applications for particulars are not allowed unless essential. By consent the strict rules of evidence are relaxed. Thus evidence is admitted which would generally be excluded, and witness fees may be saved by deciding the case on documentary evidence alone. Moreover the judges regard it as their duty to be available at short notice at any stage of the action on the initiative of either party, so that disputes being dealt with in the Commercial Court are dealt with as quickly as possible. However, such is the popularity of the Commercial Court that a date for a trial of any substance is currently liable to be fixed at between one and two years from the date of the application to fix. A summons for directions may be taken out before the pleadings are closed. Summonses are heard by the judges and in London the current practice is for all judges of the court to sit on Fridays for the sole purpose of dealing with summonses. In one case the Master of the Rolls, Sir John Donaldson (himself a sometime member of the court) paid it the following tribute:[13]

> ". . . it may be situated in London, but, unlike the courts of Kuwait, those of Scotland or other English courts (other perhaps than the Admiralty Court), it is far more than a national or domestic court; it is an international commercial court the overwhelming majority of whose judgments are concerned with the rights and obligations of foreign nationals. It is a court which has an unrivalled expertise in marine insurance where that insurance is governed by English law. This is the result of the sheer volume of work of this nature which comes to the

---

11 [1973] 3 All ER, at 146; [1973] 1 WLR, at 1298.
12 Supreme Court Act 1981, s 6. There are at present five at any one time.
13 *Amin Rasheed Shipping Corporation v Kuwait Insurance Co* [1983] 1 All ER 873, at 882; [1983] 1 WLR 228, at 240 (affirmed [1984] AC 50; [1983] 2 All ER 884).

court and to the practitioners from whom the judges of the court are appointed."

A writ or originating summons issued out of London, Liverpool or Manchester may be marked in the top left hand corner, with the words "Commercial Court" and on the issue of the writ or summons so marked, the action will be entered immediately in the commercial list.[14] Actions may be transferred to the Commercial Court apart from this rule and, indeed, actions commenced in the Commercial Court under the rule may be removed from the list. Any party who seeks the removal of an action from the Commercial Court, when it has been set down in that list, must apply within seven days of giving notice of intention to defend.[15]

Any party to an action in the Commercial Court may take out a summons for directions in the action before the close of pleadings, and should do so as early as possible in the action. This is principally because the directions required may, in fact, relate to the framing of the pleadings. The summons is heard by a commercial judge rather than a master.

Finally it should be noted that special Mercantile Courts have been created in both the Midlands and the South-West of England to deal with commercial cases. These amount to new Queen's Bench lists in the district registries concerned, and have the capacity to deal with a wide variety of commercial cases. Cases follow the rules of court relating to commercial practice.[16]

The Admiralty Court — The Admiralty jurisdiction of the High Court, assigned to the Queen's Bench Division by the Administration of Justice Act 1970, is administered by the Admiralty Court, created by that Act as part of the Queen's Bench Division and consisting of such of the *puisne* judges of the High Court as the Lord Chancellor may from time to time nominate to be Admiralty judges.[17] Procedure is governed by RSC Order 75. There are special forms of writ for the commencement of proceedings and special rules of procedure, depending upon the type of Admiralty proceeding. To take but one example, in actions to enforce a claim for damage, loss of life or personal injury arising out of a collision between ships, each party must lodge a document known as a "preliminary act" which contains a statement of the material facts relating to the collision including such matters as the state of the weather, the course steered and speed of the ships, the lights on the ships, alterations in course, the angle of the ships at the moment of contact and what sound signals were given and heard. The preliminary acts are sealed and are not opened before the close of pleadings.[18]

Official referees — The office and title of "official referee" was created by the Judicature Act 1873 and abolished by the Courts Act 1971. However the title survives and is used to describe those circuit judges who are nominated by the Lord Chancellor[19] to deal with "official

---

14 Ord 72, r 4.
15 Ord 72, r 6.
16 See [1993] 4 All ER 381, 1023.
17 Under s 68(1) of the Supreme Court Act 1981 (as amended); the Lord Chancellor may also nominate deputy circuit judges or recorders (ibid).
18 Ord 75, r 18.
19 Under s 68(1) of the Supreme Court Act 1981, as amended.

referees' business" which is defined by Order 36, rule 1(2) to include a cause or matter:

> "(a)   which involves a prolonged examination of documents or accounts, or a technical, scientific or local investigation such as could more conveniently be conducted by an official referee; or
>
> (b)   for which trial by an official referee is desirable in the interests of one or more of the parties on grounds of expedition, economy or convenience or otherwise."

In practice the bulk of the work of the official referees concerns building disputes, civil or mechanical engineering matters, actions against architects, engineers, surveyors and other professionals, for breach of duty, claims by and against local authorities relating to their statutory duties concerning building regulations and claims involving adjudication over lists of complaints or defects. In the latter type of case the pleadings often consist of or include a "Scott Schedule" (so named after a former official referee) which is a document containing a list of numbered items and divided across the page into a number of columns in which there are completed by the parties in turn, their respective contentions in respect of those items, the final column being left blank for the purpose of the judge completing his adjudication on that item.

As in the Commercial Court, actions may be allocated to an official referee at the time that the writ is issued (by marking it "official referees' business") or may subsequently be transferred to an official referee. Thereafter all summonses are heard by the official referee (rather than a master or district judge) to whom the case is allocated.

An application for directions (including an application to fix a date for trial) must be made by the plaintiff within 14 days of the giving of notice of intention to defend or the date of the order transferring the cause or matter, whichever is the later.[20] Unfortunately, as in the Commercial Court, the current state of the lists is such that the interval between the application and the fixed date is usually measured in years rather than months.

It should be noted that the court has power to order any issue to be tried before, at or after the trial of the action and may order different issues to be tried separately.[1] Thus the master can order the assessment of damages, for example, to be postponed until after the trial on the issues of liability.[2] Under these provisions a preliminary point of law is often tried before the facts where this may effectively dispose of the action.[3] However, in *Tilling v Whiteman*[4] the House of Lords stated that this course should only be

---

20 Ord 36, r 6.
 1 Ord 33, rr 3, 4(2).
 2 This power has been sparingly exercised; see observations of WINN LJ in *Stevens v William Nash Ltd* [1966] 3 All ER 156; [1966] 1 WLR 1550, and in *Hawkins v New Mendip Engineering Ltd* [1966] 3 All ER 228; [1966] 1 WLR 1341. Cf *Coenen v Payne* [1974] 2 All ER 1109; [1974] 1 WLR 984. One advantage of trying the issue of liability before damages is that a judgment on liability for damages to be assessed enables the plaintiff to apply for an interim payment; see p 328, *ante*.
 3 See, for example *Everett v Ribbands* [1952] 2 QB 198; [1952] 1 All ER 832; *Carl Zeiss Stiftung v Herbert Smith & Co* [1969] 1 Ch 93; [1968] 2 All ER 1002.
 4 [1980] AC 1; [1979] 1 All ER 737.

adopted where the facts are complicated and the legal issues short and easily decided, for otherwise (as happened in that case) very considerable costs may be incurred in litigating through the appellate courts a point of law based on hypothetical facts which might never have required determination if the facts of the case had first been found.

Having dealt with all the interlocutory matters raised on the summons for directions including, finally, the mode and place of trial, the master will give an estimate of the length of trial, together with a provisional assessment of the substance, difficulty or public importance of the case.[5] He will then fix a period within which the plaintiff must set the action down for trial. When the plaintiff has done so he must, within 24 hours, inform all the other parties.[6] The parties must then proceed to prepare their cases for trial.

F TRIAL

1 Preparation of evidence

At an early stage of the action the papers will usually have been sent to counsel. Counsel will normally settle the pleadings but, in any event, he will usually be instructed before the summons for directions so as to obtain his advice on interlocutory matters. Cases are won and lost in their preparation. Counsel will therefore wish to consider which applications should be made, whether the pleadings require amendment and similar matters.

The first consideration upon preparing an action for trial is on whom the burden of proof rests. The general rule is *quis affirmat debet probare*; thus where any allegation of fact is in issue the party who alleges that fact must prove it. The pleadings will disclose where the general burden lies. If an allegation in the statement of claim is admitted (expressly or impliedly) it need not be proved at all. If it is traversed then the burden rests on the plaintiff. If it is the subject of a plea in confession and avoidance, then the burden is on the defendant to prove the matters in avoidance. However, the burden may shift during the action by the effect of presumptions. If a presumption is raised in favour of a party, the effect is to shift the burden of disproving the matter presumed to his opponent.[7]

Having decided which matters he must prove, counsel will decide how

---

5 The assessment is as follows: "A"- cases of great substance or great difficulty or of public importance; "B"- cases of substance or difficulty; "C"- other cases; *Practice Direction (Summons for Directions)* [1972] 1 All ER 288; [1972] 1 WLR 3.

6 Ord 34, r 8. In addition, where the trial is set down for trial outside London, the plaintiff must, after giving to the defendant seven days' notice of his intention so to do, lodge with the district judge a certificate of readiness for trial containing certain particulars, notably whether the order made on the summons for directions has been complied with, and in particular whether medical or experts' reports have been submitted for agreement and, if so, whether they have been agreed (or if not how many medical or expert witnesses are to be called), whether plans and photographs have been agreed, an up-to-date estimate of the length of the trial and a statement that the plaintiff is ready and wishes the action to be brought on for trial: *Practice Direction (Trial out of London)* [1972] 1 All ER 287; [1972] 1 WLR 5.

7 See p 562, *post.*

he proposes to prove them. The two principal methods of proof are by witnesses and by documents.

a   Witnesses

Counsel will name the witnesses whom he requires. There is no property in a witness, so that there is no objection to interviewing or calling any witness even if he has been served with a subpoena by an opponent.[8] It is, of course, wrong to call a witness whose testimony is unlikely to support one's case, since a party cannot cross-examine a witness he has called, unless the court gives leave to treat the witness as hostile.[9] Also, to intimidate or otherwise tamper with a witness amounts to a contempt of court.[10]

Usually a witness will be prepared to attend voluntarily if he is tendered a reasonable fee. Where he will not, his attendance may be compelled by *subpoena ad testificandum*.[11] A witness who fails to comply may be committed for contempt of court. Where a witness will not, or may not, be able to attend the trial his testimony may, by order of the court, be taken before a special examiner.[12]

b   Documents

Documentary evidence, especially in contract cases, frequently forms the basis of a party's case. Where he is in possession of the documents himself, he is in no difficulty. However the documents which are needed by a party may be in the possession of an opponent or of a third party. If they are in the possession of a third party, the proper course is to serve him with a *subpoena duces tecum*, ie "attend and bring the document with you". If the documents are in the possession of an opponent he should be served with a "notice to produce" the documents required. This does not have the effect of a subpoena, but if he does not produce the document, he cannot use the document himself and the party who served the notice may give secondary evidence of its contents.[13] In addition, if he has served a list of documents under Order 24 he is deemed to have been served with a notice to produce all the documents in his list.[14]

Formal proof of a document may be dispensed with if one's opponent is prepared to admit the authenticity of the documents in question. Accordingly, he should be served with a "notice to admit" these documents.[15]

---

8 See observations of Lord Denning MR in *Fullam v Newcastle Chronicle and Journal Ltd* [1977] 3 All ER 32; [1977] 1 WLR 651; see also *Harmony Shipping Co SA v Davis* [1979] 3 All ER 177; [1979] 1 WLR 1380; see p 577, n 1, *post*.

9 See p 583, *post*.

10 *Chapman v Honig* [1963] 2 QB 502; [1963] 2 All ER 513.

11 Ord 38, r 14. Where the witness is a prisoner an order may be obtained for his attendance by an application ex parte to a judge in chambers under the Criminal Procedure Act 1853, s 9. Where he is in custody on civil process, his attendance is secured by writ of *habeas corpus ad testificandum* upon application ex parte on affidavit to a judge in chambers.

12 Ord 39. Where the witness is in another country a "letter of request" is issued to the judicial authorities of that country. A deposition taken under this Order may be put in evidence at the trial either by consent of the other side or on proof that the deponent is dead, outside the jurisdiction or unable from sickness or other infirmity to attend the trial (Ord 38, r 9).

13 Ord 27, r 5(4); *Sharpe v Lamb* (1840) 11 Ad & El 805.

14 Ord 27, r 4(3).   15 Ord 27, r 5(1).

However, a party who has been served with a list of documents is deemed to admit the authenticity of every document in his list[16] unless he serves express notice of non-admission within 21 days after inspection.

Since automatic discovery now takes place in nearly all actions commenced by writ, it follows that express notices to produce and notices to admit documents will rarely be necessary.

c   Special damage calculation

The obligation to plead special damages fully has already been noted.[17] However, by the time the action comes on for trial the special damage claim, particularly in personal injury actions, will usually be out of date in consequence of time off work since the statement of claim, increase in wage rates, further statutory benefits and so on. Much court time is taken up in investigating these matters and to avoid waste of time, it is now the practice[18] that in any personal injury action in which there is a claim for loss of earnings, loss of future earning capacity, medical or other expenses or loss of pension rights, particulars (where appropriate in the form of a schedule) must be served by the claimant on all other parties not later than seven days after the case appears in the Warned List in London. Within seven days thereafter every party served with particulars must indicate whether and to what extent each item claimed is agreed and, if not agreed, the reason why not and any counter-proposals. Where there is a fixed date for hearing, the plaintiff's particulars must be served not less than 28 days before that date and the answer not later than 14 days thereafter. In cases for hearing outside London the particulars must be served not later than the lodging of the certificate of readiness and the answer not later than 14 days thereafter.

Failure to comply with these directions may result in penalising the defaulting party in costs.

d   Notices under the Civil Evidence Act 1968

Where it is desired to put in evidence at the trial statements admissible under the provisions of the Civil Evidence Act 1968, the party desiring to do so must within 21 days after setting down serve on every other party a notice containing prescribed particulars of (if the statement is oral) the time, place and circumstances in which the statement was made, the persons by whom and to whom it was made and the substance of the statement or, if material, the words used.[19] In the case of written statements admissible by virtue of the Act, the notice must annex a copy of the

---

16 Ord 27, r 4(1).
17 See p 335, *ante.*
18 *Practice Direction* [1984] 3 All ER 165; [1984] 1 WLR 1127.
19 Ord 38, r 22(1).

document in question as well as containing certain prescribed particulars relating to the circumstances of its compilation.[1]

If the party giving the notice alleges that the maker cannot be called as a witness at the trial because he is dead, beyond the seas, unfit by reason of his bodily or mental condition to attend as a witness, cannot be found or cannot reasonably be expected to have any recollection of matters relevant to the accuracy of his statement, the notice must contain a statement to this effect;[2] otherwise a party served with a notice may within 21 days serve a counter-notice requiring the maker of any statement to be called as a witness by the party who served the original notice, in which event if that person is not called as a witness, his statement is not admissible under the 1968 Act.[3]

When the evidence for each side has been prepared the parties must await trial. Neither party need serve any notice of the date of trial on his opponent. Accordingly (unless the case has been given a fixed date) all parties must watch carefully the lists. The Week's List is published on Mondays and contains the cases expected to be tried in that week. Each day there is published a Daily Cause List containing the actions to be heard that day and a Warned List consisting of actions likely to be tried in the near future. Thus neither side has any excuse if his case is not ready when the action comes on for trial. If one party fails to appear the trial may proceed in his absence.[4] However, if application is made within seven days, a judgment obtained in the absence of a party may be set aside, generally on condition that he pay the costs thrown away.[5] Although adjournment is possible, last minute postponements are looked upon with disfavour by the judge in charge of the list and may result in the offending firm of solicitors being penalised personally with the extra costs incurred.[6]

2   Procedure at the trial

If the action is to be tried with a jury, a jury of 12 is sworn. The trial then begins.

a   Right to begin

If damages are unliquidated or the burden of proving any single issue on the pleadings rests on the plaintiff, then the plaintiff begins. Thus the only case where the defendant has the right to begin is a case in which the

---

1 Ord 38, rr 22(2), 23(1), 24.
2 Ord 38, rr 22(3), 23(2), 24(3), 25. Any issue as to whether these conditions are satisfied in relation to the maker of a statement may be determined conclusively before the trial on an application by summons (Ord 38, r 27). The conditions appear to be disjunctive so that if, for example, it is established that the witness is abroad, his statement is admissible and it is not necessary to prove, in addition, that he cannot be found; *Piermay Shipping Co SA v Chester* [1978] 1 All ER 1233; [1978] 1 WLR 411.
3 Ord 38, r 26. The court has, however, discretion to admit statements under the Civil Evidence Act 1968 in cases where the proper notice was not served but it will not exercise this discretion in favour of a party who, for example, has deliberately not served a notice in order to retain the possibility of surprising an opponent; cf *Ford v Lewis* [1971] 2 All ER 983; [1971] 1 WLR 623.
4 Ord 35, r 1.
5 Ord 35, r 2. There can be an appeal against such a judgment, though this is rarely appropriate: *Armour v Bate* [1891] 2 QB 233.
6 Ord 62, r 8.

plaintiff claims only liquidated damages and the defendant has not traversed any allegation in the statement of claim. The right to begin and the right to the last word are advantages which are probably exaggerated, especially in the absence of a jury.

b   Case for the plaintiff

Counsel for the plaintiff opens his case stating the facts on which the plaintiff relies in the order in which they appear on the pleadings, which should be chronological order. He should not rely upon any fact which he is not permitted to prove, which means, of course, that he cannot allege any fact not pleaded, although he may, even at this late stage, be allowed to amend the pleadings. Neither counsel must disclose the existence of any interim payment, nor of any payment into court, unless the defendant has raised one of the two defences in which the payment is an essential element.[7] The plaintiff's witnesses are then called and sworn. They are examined and may be cross-examined and re-examined.[8] In the course of cross-examining the plaintiff's witnesses, counsel for the defendant must "put his case" which includes making clear which part of the plaintiff's case is challenged and what positive allegations are being made in relation to the evidence of the plaintiff's witnesses, so that they may have the opportunity of dealing with those allegations. This is important to the efficient conduct of trials because if counsel for the plaintiff calls a witness whose evidence is not challenged on a particular point, then he is entitled to assume that the point is not in issue and he will not call any other witnesses to deal with it. If the defence lead evidence as to matters which should have been put but were not put to the plaintiff's witnesses, judicial rebuke is virtually inevitable and, unless counsel was responsible for the oversight (in which event he will, in the interests of his client, immediately accept responsibility for it), the judge is likely to infer, and find, that the evidence in question is a recent invention. His documents, including answers to interrogatories which he wishes to put in, are then put in evidence. Finally counsel argues the propositions of law upon which he relies, citing to the court all relevant authorities on the point whether they support his own case or that of his opponent. If they tend to support his opponent's case, he must attempt to distinguish them from the present case on their facts. He cannot, however, ignore them, since this would infringe his duty to the court.

c   Case for the defence

At the close of the plaintiff's case the defendant has the following courses open to him:

> (1)   he may submit "no case to answer". This is a submission that the plaintiff has failed to make out a *prima facie* case, or to establish the elements of a recognised cause of action. The submission is rare in a civil action since the objection will usually have been taken long

---

7 Ord 22, r 7; see p 323, *ante*.
8 See p 583, *post*. It is a matter for the judge's discretion as to whether he allows other witnesses to remain in court while evidence is being given; *Moore v Lambeth County Court Registrar* [1969] 1 All ER 782; [1969] 1 WLR 141.

before the trial. If it is made, the judge, before deciding, may require the defendant to "stand on his submission", which means that he can call no evidence if his submission fails, although this is not usual in jury actions.[9] Counsel for the plaintiff has a right to reply to the submission. If it succeeds, judgment is entered for the defendant. If it fails and the defendant has been put to his election, judgment is entered for the plaintiff.

(2) He may state that he intends to call no evidence, oral or documentary. Counsel for the plaintiff will then address the court followed by defence counsel who thus obtains the right to the last word.[10]

(3) In most cases the defence will be a mixture of law and fact and the defendant will want to put in some evidence. In this event defence counsel may make an opening speech outlining his defence. His witnesses give their evidence in the same way as those of the plaintiff followed by the defendant's documents and legal submissions. The plaintiff may be permitted to adduce evidence in rebuttal where the defence case has raised matters which could not reasonably have been foreseen. Defence counsel then makes a closing speech, following which counsel for the plaintiff has a right to make a closing speech in reply. Where a party in his closing speech raises any fresh point of law, the other party is entitled to reply but only in relation to that point.

d   Verdict and judgment

At the conclusion of all the evidence and the legal argument for both sides the judge sums up (if there is a jury) or either gives judgment or reserves his judgment if there is not. He must direct the jury (if there is one) as to the issues in the case, stating on whom the burden of proving the individual issues rests, and outlining the evidence in support of those issues. He must also direct upon the standard of proof required from the party on whom the burden rests. He will direct on the law applicable to the issues of fact, for example, whether the words are capable of bearing the defamatory meaning alleged or whether the defendant owes the plaintiff a duty of care in negligence. He must leave the actual issues of fact and the assessment of damages to the jury. While he can suggest a conclusion of fact to the jury, the judge should not tell the jury of the limits within which an award of damages should fall, since this would amount to an attempt by the judge to assess damages, although it is common in defamation cases to give oblique guidance as to the need to avoid disproportionate sums. A modern tendency is for the judge to pose a series of questions to the jury calling for their decision on the facts and, if they find for the plaintiff on any issue, the amount of damages.[11]

---

9 *Laurie v Raglan Building Co Ltd* [1942] 1 KB 152; [1941] 3 All ER 332; *Young v Rank* [1950] 2 KB 510; [1950] 2 All ER 166; *Storey v Storey* [1961] P 63; [1960] 3 All ER 279.

10 Ord 35, r 7. This rule applies expressly to jury actions, but, in the Queen's Bench Division, applies in practice to non-jury actions as well; see *Weller v O'Brien* [1962] 3 All ER 65; [1962] 1 WLR 885.

11 However where a jury delivers a general verdict, the judge is not then entitled to ask questions to ascertain the grounds for the verdict; *Arnold v Jeffreys* [1914] 1 KB 512; *Barnes v Hill* [1967] 1 QB 579; [1967] 1 All ER 347.

Where the plaintiff has sought an equitable remedy as an alternative or in addition to damages, the grant of this remedy is in the discretion of the judge.

It remains for judgment to be entered in accordance with the verdict. A judgment crystallises the rights of the parties in respect of the subject matter of the action. Thus they are estopped from litigating the same issues of fact again.[12] Even if fresh damage becomes apparent the plaintiff cannot sue because his right is extinguished.[13] Counsel for the unsuccessful party may apply for a stay of execution pending an appeal. This may be granted on terms. After judgment on the issues of liability and damages the judge may make orders as to interest and costs.

Damages — Historically damages have always been expressed in English currency. This has caused hardship in cases in which sterling has been devalued, so a party who bargained for payment in foreign currency has been awarded damages in sterling, the rate of exchange being calculated at the date upon which his entitlement to payment arose (the "breach-date" rule). Accordingly in 1975 the House of Lords changed this rule.[14] Since 1975 the English courts have shown an increasing willingness to give judgment in foreign currency. At first limited to contract actions where the sum was due under the contract in a foreign currency and the proper law of the contract was the law of that country in whose currency the obligation was expressed,[15] the power is now exercised in cases where the plaintiff's loss would be most truly expressed in a foreign currency, in which case judgment will be given in that currency,[16] and in tort actions, where damages may be awarded in a currency which the plaintiff has used to make good the loss which he has suffered.[17]

Nevertheless a judgment can only be enforced in terms of sterling. Accordingly if enforcement becomes necessary the judgment will be converted into its sterling equivalent at the date when leave is given to enforce the judgment.

Provisional damages — Finally, there is, save in personal injuries actions, no procedure for successive awards of damages in the same action. Damages have to be assessed once and for all at the trial. This may cause hardship to either side, since subsequent events may demonstrate the hypotheses upon which the award of damages were based to be false with the result that the damages were too high or too low. This is particularly so in personal injury actions where, for example, an award of damages for loss of future earning capacity must necessarily be highly speculative. To remedy this situation section 32A of the Supreme Court Act contains

---

12 Clerical mistakes in judgments or orders, or errors arising therein from any accidental slip or omission, may at any time be corrected by the court on motion or summons without an appeal (Ord 20, r 11 – the "slip rule").

13 There is an exception to this rule; if special damage is an element in a cause of action, fresh special damage arising out of the same cause of action may be the basis of a second action: *Darley Main Colliery Co v Mitchell* (1886) 11 App Cas 127; *West Leigh Colliery Co Ltd v Tunnicliffe and Hampson Ltd* [1908] AC 27.

14 *Miliangos v George Frank (Textiles) Ltd* [1976] AC 443; [1975] 3 All ER 80.

15 *Miliangos v George Frank (Textiles) Ltd* (*supra*), not following *Tomkinson v First Pensylvania Banking and Trust Co* [1961] AC 1007, sub nom *Re United Railways of Havana and Regla Warehouses Ltd* [1960] 2 All ER 332; for the significance of this decision in relation to the doctrine of judicial precedent, see p 65, *ante*.

16 *The Folias* [1979] AC 685; [1979] 1 All ER 421.

17 *The Despina R* [1979] AC 685; [1979] 1 All ER 421.

provision for "provisional damages" in personal injury actions. The procedure is governed by Ord 37, rr 7–10. In appropriate cases the court has power to make an "award of provisional damages", which is an assessment of the plaintiff's damages on the assumption that the plaintiff will not suffer a specified disease or deterioration. If the same subsequently occurs, within the period fixed by the court, the plaintiff may apply for a further award.

Interest — Section 35A of the Supreme Court Act 1981[18] empowers the court to award simple (but not compound) interest on debts or damages "at such rate as the court thinks fit or as rules of court may provide". In commercial cases the usual rate is 1 per cent above United Kingdom clearing banks' base rates over the relevant period.[19]

Different rules exist in respect of personal injury actions, where on most awards, the court must grant interest.[20]

(1) the plaintiff is awarded interest on general damages for pain, suffering and loss of amenities from the date of service of the writ to the date of trial at a conventional rate of 2 per cent per annum;

(2) the plaintiff is awarded interest on special damages from the date of the accident to the date of trial at half the rates which during that period were payable on money in court placed on special account;[1]

(3) no interest is awarded on future loss of earnings or other prospective financial losses.

e   References to the European Court of Justice

As has been noted[2] Article 177 of the EC Treaty (to which English courts are bound to give effect[3]) confers power, and sometimes imposes a duty, upon English judges to request the Court of Justice of the European Communities (the European Court) to give a preliminary ruling concerning: (a) the interpretation of the EC Treaty; (b) the validity and interpretation of acts of the institutions of the Community; (c) the interpretation of the statutes of bodies established by an act of the Council where those statutes so provide.[4]

The decision whether to refer a question for a preliminary ruling is within the discretion of the judge and the procedure on a reference is governed by Order 114. A master has no power to make such an order but a judge may do so either following application or of his own motion. If an order is made it should set out in a schedule the request for the preliminary ruling and the proceedings will, unless otherwise ordered, be stayed until the European Court has given its ruling.

---

18 Added by Administration of Justice Act 1982, s 15, Sch 1 and replacing s 3 of the Law Reform (Miscellaneous Provisions) Act 1934.

19 See *Polish Steam Ship Co v Atlantic Maritime Co* [1985] QB 41; [1984] 3 All ER 59.

20 The principles were laid down by the Court of Appeal in *Jefford v Gee* [1970] 2 QB 130; [1970] 1 All ER 1202 and restated with modification by the House of Lords in *Wright v British Railways Board* [1983] 2 AC 773; [1983] 2 All ER 698.

1 See *Dexter v Courtaulds Ltd* [1984] 1 All ER 70; [1984] 1 WLR 372.

2 See p 111, *ante*.

3 European Communities Act 1972, s 2(1).

4 Similar provisions are contained in Article 150 of the Euratom Treaty and in Article 41 of the ECSC Treaty.

CHAPTER 18

Originating Summonses, Motions and Petitions

A USES OF THE ORIGINATING SUMMONS

Although most actions in the Queen's Bench Division are commenced by writ, and many must be commenced in this way, the plaintiff may in some cases proceed by originating summons.[1] An originating summons is defined as "every summons other than a summons in a pending cause or matter".[2] The procedure is aptly named since it actually raises the point at issue in the first instance, thus dispensing with the need for pleadings. It is the proper method for making applications under certain statutes; for example, applications to approve the compromise of an action by an infant or patient, interpleader applications where an action is not pending and summary proceedings for possession of land occupied by trespassers.[3] In addition it is a streamlined method of obtaining the court's decision on a point of law or on the construction of a document or statute.

B ORIGINATING SUMMONS PROCEDURE

There are now three forms of originating summons:[4] (1) originating summons between parties, general form; (2) originating summons between parties, expedited form; (3) *ex parte* originating summons (this form is used mainly in the Chancery Division). The first form is the usual one in the Queen's Bench Division. The second form differs in that it makes provision for a date of hearing to be inserted (rather like an ordinary summons in a pending action) but it can only be used in a small number of

---

1 See p 293, *ante*.
2 Ord 1, r 4.
3 Ord 113. This Order was introduced to combat difficulties posed by "squatters" in cases in which it was not possible to identify by name the trespassers against whom an order was sought. The Order provides a swift and summary procedure whereby the plaintiff may proceed by originating summons, to which no acknowledgment of service is required, supported by affidavit; an order for possession may then be made by a judge without the necessity for a trial and a writ of possession issued without leave.
4 Ord 7, r 2 (as amended by Rules of the Supreme Court (Writ and Appearance) 1979).

cases, specified in the Rules. The summons is issued in the same way as a writ, out of the Central Office or a district registry. It remains in force and is renewable in the same way as a writ and must be served on the defendant as if it were a writ, leave being required to serve it outside the jurisdiction:

> ". . . every originating summons must include a statement of the questions on which the plaintiff seeks the determination or direction of the High Court or, as the case may be, a concise statement of the relief or remedy claimed in the proceedings begun by the originating summons with sufficient particulars to identify the cause or causes of action in respect of which the plaintiff claims that relief or remedy."[5]

Although an originating summons is not a pleading[6] it is in many ways similar to a statement of claim and it seems that the inherent jurisdiction of the court and under Order 18, rule 19 to strike out any pleading extends to an originating summons.[7]

The plaintiff must, within 14 days after any defendant has acknowledged service, file with the court the affidavit evidence on which he intends to rely (in the case of an *ex parte* summons he must file this not less than four clear days before the date fixed for the hearing) and must serve copies thereof on all defendants. A defendant who has acknowledged service must then within 28 days file and serve any affidavit evidence upon which he intends to rely and the plaintiff may within 14 days thereafter file and serve further affidavit evidence in reply.[8]

The plaintiff will then obtain an appointment for the attendance of the parties before the court for the hearing of the summons.[9] Any defendant who has acknowledged service may raise a counterclaim whether or not that counterclaim could have been commenced by originating summons had he been the plaintiff; if the court cannot conveniently hear the counterclaim with the originating summons, it may order that it be struck out or tried separately.[10]

C DIRECTIONS OF THE COURT

The first hearing of the summons will usually be before a master who may adopt the following courses:

(1) If the liability of the defendant in respect of the claim is established, the master may make such order against him as the case may require. The issues raised are thus determined. However, if such an order is made against a defendant who does not appear at the

---

5 Ord 7, r 3(1).
6 *Lewis v Packer* [1960] 1 All ER 720n; [1960] 1 WLR 452.
7 Ord 18, r 19(3); *Punton v Ministry of Pensions and National Insurance* [1963] 1 All ER 275; [1963] 1 WLR 186. Moreover, although Ord 18, r 19(2) provides that no evidence is admissible on an application to strike out a pleading as disclosing no reasonable cause of action, it appears that an affidavit sworn in support of an originating summons can be referred to on an application on this ground made in relation to an originating summons: *Re Caines* [1978] 2 All ER 1; [1978] 1 WLR 540.
8 Ord 28, r 1A. These time-limits are abridged where the summons is in the expedited form or is an *ex parte* originating summons (Ord 28, r 2(2)).
9 Ord 28, r 2.
10 Ord 28, r 7.

hearing, it may subsequently be varied or revoked by the court on such terms as the court thinks just.[11]

(2) The master may order the proceedings to continue as if the action had been begun by writ (whether or not it could have been begun by writ), and may order that any affidavit shall stand as a pleading. In this event the master will treat the summons as if it were a summons for directions and will, accordingly, give directions on such matters as discovery of documents and the mode and place of trial.[12]

(3) The master may order the action to be transferred to the appropriate county court.

(4) Unless one of the above orders is made, the court will "give such directions as to the further conduct of the proceedings as it thinks best adapted to secure the just, expeditious and economical disposal thereof".[13] This includes most directions which would be given on the hearing of the summons for directions in an action commenced by writ. In particular the court must determine the mode and place of trial. This will usually be before a judge in open court, the evidence being given in most cases by affidavit. In addition the court is bound to consider at as early a stage as practicable whether there is or may be a dispute as to fact and whether the summons should be heard on oral evidence. The court may, if it thinks fit, order that no further evidence shall be filed and that the summons shall be heard on oral evidence or partly on oral evidence and partly on affidavit evidence, with or without cross-examination of the deponents as it may direct.[14]

D ORIGINATING MOTIONS

After writs and originating summonses, the third possible method of commencing proceedings in the Queen's Bench Division (and, indeed, in the High Court generally) is by originating application. Relatively few classes of case are appropriately commenced in this way in the Queen's Bench Division. An application under any enactment for an order directing a Minister, tribunal or other person to state a case for determination by the High Court is by originating motion. So also is an appeal from an arbitration to a commercial judge under the Arbitration Act 1979[15] and an application for committal for contempt of court where there are no pending proceedings.[16] Perhaps the most important type of case dealt with under this procedure in this Division is an application for "judicial review".[17] The application for leave is made to a judge in chambers (in most cases) *ex parte* and, if leave is granted, the originating motion may be

---

11 Ord 28, r 4(1).

12 Ord 28, r 8. However an action based on an allegation of fraud (which must be commenced by writ; see p 293, *ante*) cannot be continued as if commenced by writ: *Re 462 Green Lane, Ilford, Gooding v Booland* [1971] 1 All ER 315; [1971] 1 WLR 138; cf *Re Deadman, Smith v Garland* [1971] 2 All ER 101; [1971] 1 WLR 426.

13 Ord 28, r 4(3).

14 Ord 28, r 4(4).

15 Ord 73, r 2(2); see p 281, *ante*.

16 Ord 52, r 3.

17 See p 279, *ante*. The procedure is governed by Ord 53.

issued. On the hearing the court (usually the divisional court) may make any one of the prerogative orders and may, in addition, award damages, or grant an injunction or a declaration (the applicant being permitted to join claims for such relief if they arise out of or are connected with the subject matter of his application[18]). Parties may make interlocutory applications, for example for discovery and interrogatories, in the course of proceedings for judicial review, and these may be made to a judge or master.[19]

In the case of originating motions, other than for judicial review, the motion must include a concise statement of the nature of the claim made or the relief or remedy required,[20] and must be issued out of the Central Office in proceedings in the Queen's Bench Division. It will be served on the respondents to the motion, who will attend before the court on the day fixed for the hearing of the motion, whereupon on that hearing, or future adjourned hearings of the motion, the issue in question will be tried, either on affidavit or on oral evidence as the parties may agree or the judge may direct.

E PETITIONS

The final method of commencing proceedings in the High Court is by petition. Many forms of proceedings in the other two Divisions are commenced in this way, and there are generally specific rules, for example in bankruptcy, winding-up of companies and matrimonial causes, relating to these proceedings.[1]

In the Queen's Bench Division the only proceedings commenced by petition appear to be election petitions under the Representation of the People Act 1983, concerning disputes arising out of the conduct of local government or Parliamentary elections. Such proceedings are, happily, rare.

---

18 Ord 53, r 2.
19 Ord 53, r 8.
20 Ord 8, r 3.
 1 Although, generally, see Ord 8, r 3.

CHAPTER 19

Costs and the Enforcement of Judgments

A COSTS

1 Who must pay costs?

There are two sets of costs. First there are the costs which each party will have to pay to his own solicitor. These must be paid irrespective of the outcome of the action and, subject to the Rules, depend upon the contract between solicitor and client. Secondly there are the costs which one side may be ordered to pay to his opponent. These must be assessed or "taxed" by the court and will very rarely cover the full amount that a party has to pay to his own solicitor. It follows that even a litigant who is completely successful will often have to pay some costs himself. These represent the difference between the amount he pays his solicitor and the amount he recovers from his opponent, and are sometimes described as "irrecoverable costs". If the judge makes no order as to costs each party pays his own costs. In most cases, however, the judge will order one side to pay all or a proportion of the costs of his opponent. At common law a successful litigant had a right to costs but this right has been virtually removed by legislation so that at the present day the award of costs is discretionary. It is not, of course, an absolute discretion and it is a wrong exercise of the discretion to deprive a party of his costs if he has been completely successful and guilty of no misconduct.[1] In addition there are statutory fetters on the exercise of this discretion, of which the following should be specially noted.[2]

a Costs should follow the event

Unless there are special factors present, a successful party may expect his costs from an unsuccessful opponent. Nevertheless there is clearly a power to deprive a successful party of his costs on the ground that he has conducted the litigation dishonestly or recovered only a small part of his

---

1 *Donald Campbell & Co Ltd v Pollak* [1927] AC 732. See remarks of Viscount Cave LC at 811–812.

2 Though mention may also be made of the Slander of Women Act 1891, s 1 and the Rent Act 1977, s 141(4).

claim.[3] In an an extreme case a successful plaintiff may have to pay the costs of the defendant.[4] There is jurisdiction to order a successful defendant to pay costs but this jurisdiction is only exercisable in the most exceptional circumstances.[5]

There has been a considerable volume of litigation as to what is "the event" in an action.[6] In a simple action involving one plaintiff, one defendant and a single issue, no difficulty arises; the event is judgment on that issue. However, where there are several parties or several issues the situation is more complex. It must be noted, however, that costs are completely within the discretion of the court. In *Aiden Shipping Co Ltd v Interbulk Ltd*[7] the House of Lords stressed that section 51 of the Supreme Court Act 1981 permitted the ordering of costs against non-parties, and that:

> "Courts of first instance are . . . well capable of exercising their discretion under the statute in accordance with reason and justice."[8]

It should, however, be noted that this was a case where a close relationship existed between the third party (who was in fact a party to a related action) and the parties to the cause in respect of which the costs were awarded.[9] Guidance as to how the power to award costs in such cases should be used was given by the Court of Appeal in *Symphony Group plc v Hodgson*:[10] it was exceptional for a non-party to be ordered to pay such costs, particularly if the party had a cause of action against the non-party. Fair procedures should be followed to ensure that the non-party had the opportunity to make representations, and to ensure that cross-examination of a non-party is not simply being directed to the issue as to whether the court should make a costs order against that non-party.

Several parties — Where a plaintiff properly joins several defendants and succeeds against some but fails against others, the court may, in its discretion, order the costs of a successful defendant to be paid directly or indirectly by an unsuccessful defendant.[11] Conversely, where one defendant is sued by several plaintiffs, some of whom succeed and some of whom fail, the defendant should make a special application for the extra costs he has incurred through the presence of an unsuccessful plaintiff.[12] It may also be that a "costs sharing order" is made pre-trial. This may require a plaintiff in a multi-party action to contribute to costs incurred either personally or through the legal aid fund whilst conducting lead actions.[13]

---

3 *Barnes v Maltby* (1889) 5 TLR 207; *O'Connor v Star Newspaper Co Ltd* (1893) 68 LT 146.
4 See *Alltrans Express Ltd v CVA Holdings Ltd* [1984] 1 All ER 685; [1984] 1 WLR 394.
5 *Knight v Clifton* [1971] Ch 700; [1971] 2 All ER 378. There was no such power prior to the Judicature Act 1890 (now Supreme Court Act 1981, s 51(1)). An order against a successful defendant was made in *Ottway v Jones* [1955] 2 All ER 585; [1955] 1 WLR 706.
6 See *Reid, Hewitt & Co v Joseph* [1918] AC 717.
7 [1986] AC 965; [1986] 2 All ER 409.
8 *Per* LORD GOFF [1986] AC at 981; [1986] 2 All ER at 416.
9 See [1986] 2 All ER at 416 *Steele Ford & Newton v Crown Prosecution Service* [1994] AC 22; [1993] 2 All ER 769; *Shah v Karanjia* [1993] 4 All ER 792.
10 [1994] QB 179; [1993] 4 All ER 143.
11 *Bullock v London General Omnibus Co* [1907] 1 KB 264; *Sanderson v Blyth Theatre Co* [1903] 2 KB 533.
12 *Keen v Towler* (1924) 41 TLR 86.
13 See *Davies v Eli Lilly & Co* [1987] 3 All ER 94; [1987] 1 WLR 1136. In that case the plaintiff was one of some 1,500 plaintiffs, of whom about 1,000 were legally aided,

Several causes of action — Where several causes of action are tried together the court will, if the issues are severable, order the costs of them to be taxed separately.[14] The effect is that the plaintiff will recover the costs of the causes of action upon which he succeeds, and the defendant will be awarded the costs of the others. However this method of taxation is not possible where the several causes of action arise out of the same transaction. In such cases the judge may order that the whole of the successful plaintiff's costs be taxed, but that he shall recover only a fixed proportion of the taxed costs from the defendant.[15]

Costs of interlocutory proceedings — There will be various interlocutory applications made by each party throughout the action. There are two forms of order with respect to the costs of these applications. The court may make a special order as to the costs of the individual application upon making or refusing an interlocutory order, that is to say that the costs be awarded to the plaintiff or defendant "in any event".[16] Alternatively the court may order that the costs of the application be "costs in the cause" which means that the party who is eventually successful will recover the costs of the application. A modification of the latter order is "plaintiff's costs in cause" or "defendant's costs in cause", the effect of which is that if the plaintiff, in the former case, or the defendant, in the latter, is eventually successful, he will be awarded his costs of the interlocutory application in question, whereas if he is ultimately unsuccessful, each party pays his own costs of the interlocutory application. A third possibility is "costs reserved", ie to be dealt with at some later stage, usually following the trial. On a summons for directions the normal order is "costs in cause", on the basis that there has to be a summons, irrespective of what orders are made on the summons.

b   Payment into court

It has been noted that a payment into court (unless it is an element in a substantive defence) can affect only costs and not liability or damages. The effect is that if the successful plaintiff recovers no more than the amount paid in, in respect of one or more causes of action, he will be ordered to pay the defendant's costs of those causes of action from the date of payment in. He will still be entitled to his costs to the date of payment in, though these are often small consolation by comparison.[17]

c   Supreme Court Act 1981, section 51

Where an action is commenced in the High Court which should, in the

---

bringing actions arising out of their treatment with the drug Opren. Certain "lead actions" were nominated to decide common issues. Such an order is probably not made under Ord 62 r 3(3).

14 As to what is an "issue", see *Howell v Dering* [1915] 1 KB 54, at 63; *Reid, Hewitt & Co v Joseph* [1918] AC 717. Any item of costs attributable to more than one issue will be divided between the issues.

15 *Cinema Press Ltd v Pictures and Pleasures Ltd* [1945] KB 356; [1945] 1 All ER 440; cf *Cassell & Co Ltd v Broome* [1972] AC 1027; [1972] 1 All ER 801.

16 Ord 62, r 3.

17 Ord 62, r 5; where a payment in is accepted, with other claims being abandoned, the plaintiff is entitled to his full costs: *Hudson v Elmbridge Borough Council* [1991] 4 All ER 55; [1991] 1 WLR 880.

opinion of the trial court, have been commenced in a county court, the costs awarded to the party may be reduced by up to 25 per cent.[18] This will chiefly be relevant to personal injuries claims,[19] which are required to be commenced in the county court unless the amount expected to be recovered is £50,000 or more.[20]

Section 51(6) of the 1981 Act (as substituted) also permits the court to make a "wasted costs" order against a legal or other representative.[1] It permits the court to disallow costs incurred, or to make an order requiring personal payment, as a result of improper, unreasonable or negligent acts or omissions by such representatives, or in respect of costs which, in the light of such an act or omission, it would be unreasonable to expect the party on whose behalf they were incurred to pay.

This provision has been the subject recently of judicial scrutiny and comment. In *Re a Barrister (Wasted Costs Order) (No 1 of 1991)*[2] the court identified a three-stage test:

(a) Had the legal representative of whom complaint was made acted improperly, unreasonably or negligently?
(b) If so, did such conduct cause the applicant to incur unnecessary costs?
(c) If so, was it in all the circumstances just to order the legal representative to compensate the applicant for the whole or part of the relevant costs?

However, in *Ridehalgh v Horsefield*[3] the court stressed that care should be taken not to create a new and costly form of satellite litigation. "Improper conduct" was conduct which would justify disciplinary action; "unreasonable", means not permitting of reasonable explanation; "negligent" bears the meaning of a failure to act with the competence to be reasonably expected of ordinary members of the profession. It is not improper to pursue a hopeless case, unless that amounts to an abuse of process. Nor is any distinction to be drawn between legally aided and self-financing litigants.[4] A wasted costs order may well be justified where an advocate's conduct of court proceedings is quite plainly unjustifiable. Above all, such applications should not be used as a means of intimidation, and should normally be dealt with at the conclusion of the trial.

Having considered the question of which side must pay costs, the judge must decide what is to be the basis of taxation, for this will determine how much of an opponent's costs the loser will have to pay.

---

18 Supreme Court Act 1981, s 51(8), (9), as substituted by the Courts and Legal Services Act 1990, s 4.
19 See p 278, *ante*.
20 See p 278, *ante*.
1 See p 217, *ante*.
2 [1993] QB 293; [1992] 3 All ER 429.
3 (1994) Times, 28 January.
4 See also *Symphony Group plc v Hodgson* (1994] QB 179; [1993] 4 All ER 143.

2 The taxation of costs

a Bases of taxation

It was stated at the beginning of this chapter that there are two sets of costs; costs as between a solicitor and his own client, and costs as between the parties. The bases upon which these bills are taxed differ.

Regarding costs between a solicitor and his own client, each party must pay his own solicitor's costs as a contractual debt.[5] Very often the client will simply pay the bill presented to him without knowing or wishing to know of his right to have it taxed.[6] He has, however, a right to have the bill taxed. In this case the bill will be taxed on the indemnity basis. This means that "all costs shall be allowed except in so far as they are unreasonable in amount or have been unreasonably incurred."[7] All costs incurred with the express or implied approval of the client are deemed to be reasonable.[8] The result is that the client must pay his solicitor all costs unless they are both unauthorised and certified by the taxing master to be unreasonable, in which case the solicitor will have to pay them personally.

There is one exception to this principle. Where a litigant is legally aided, his solicitor recovers from the fund his disbursements which may well be far less than the complete indemnity which a "solicitor and own client" taxation provides, which will be conducted on the standard basis (*infra*).[9] There is allowed, on this basis, a reasonable sum in respect of all costs reasonably incurred. Any doubts are resolved in favour of the Legal Aid Board. Reasonableness, both as to items and as to amount, depends upon all the circumstances of the case, such as its length, the sum involved and the complexity and novelty of the issues raised.

As to the costs between the parties, the court has jurisdiction to award a fixed sum by way of costs to be paid by a party to his opponent.[10] In any other case the costs must be taxed. There are now two possible bases of taxation which may be ordered:

(1) standard basis;
(2) indemnity basis.

---

5 A lay litigant appearing in person used not to be entitled to remuneration for the time and labour expended in preparation of his case, though a solicitor acting in person was so entitled: *Buckland v Watts* [1970] 1 QB 27; [1969] 2 All ER 985. This rule was, however, abrogated by the Litigants in Person (Costs and Expenses) Act 1975. A party employing a salaried solicitor is, generally, entitled to have his bill of costs taxed as though it were the bill of an independent solicitor: *Re Eastwood Lloyds Bank Ltd v Eastwood* [1975] Ch 112; [1974] 3 All ER 603.
6 Note also that there may be a contentious business agreement: Solicitors Act 1974, s 59, as amended by the Courts and Legal Services Act 1990, s 98. See further, p 223, *ante*.
7 Ord 62, r 12(2).
8 And be deemed to be reasonable in amount if that amount was agreed. Costs will be deemed to be unreasonably incurred if they are of an unusual nature, unless the client was informed that they might not be allowed on taxation.
9 In accordance with the Civil Legal Aid (General) Regulations 1989, r 107.
10 Ord 62, Appendix 3.

(1) "Standard basis" is the usual basis of taxation between the parties[11] and it is also the least generous to the party in whose favour the order is made. On this basis are allowed "all such costs as were reasonably incurred." Any doubts about whether costs were reasonably incurred are resolved in favour of the paying party.[12] The taxing master must decide not only which items are reasonable, but also what is a reasonable amount in respect of each item. As to items allowable the master will not allow costs which may be termed luxuries, or costs thrown away by neglect or excessive caution.[13] As to scale the taxing master will have regard to Order 62, Appendix 2, which lists factors to which the master must have regard. These include the complexity and novelty of the questions involved, the skill, specialised knowledge and responsibility required by the solicitor or counsel, the amount involved and similar considerations.

(2) Where a party has acted improperly or unreasonably, that party may have disallowed all or part of the costs that would otherwise have been awarded.[14]

(3) As regards costs between solicitor and client, the application of the indemnity basis has already been noted.[15]

The party in whose favour an order on the standard basis is made has to prove that the costs were reasonable in amount and reasonably incurred and the fact that they were incurred with his approval is not conclusive (as it is between a litigant and his own solicitor (*supra*)). Accordingly a party who is awarded costs on the standard basis must still pay the difference between indemnity costs, which is the basis of his personal liability, and standard basis taxation, which he receives from his opponent. The extent of this liability for extra costs will depend upon the degree of extravagance which he has authorised in the conduct of his case.

b   Review of taxation

Any party who is dissatisfied with a taxation of a bill of costs may apply in writing to the same taxing master for a review of his decision. The application must be made within 21 days and must set out the disputed items and a summary of the grounds of objection.[16] The taxing master will then review his taxation of those items and certify his grounds and reasons for allowing, disallowing or altering the amount of disputed items.[17] If still dissatisfied either party may apply within 14 days by summons to a judge in

---

11 *Billson v Residential Apartments Ltd* [1992] 1 AC 494; [1992] 1 All ER 141. Where the paying party's conduct has been without merit (*House of Spring Gardens Ltd v Waite* [1991] 1 QB 241; [1990] 2 All ER 990) or oppressive (*Singh v Observer Ltd* [1989] 3 All ER 777n.) the indemnity basis may be ordered.
12 Ord 62, r 12(1).
13 *Smith v Buller* (1875) LR 19 Eq 473, at 475.
14 Ord 62, r 28.
15 See p 221, *ante*.
16 Ord 62, r 33.
17 Ord 62, r 34; see *Re Fraser, Leach v Public Trustee* [1958] 1 All ER 26; [1958] 1 WLR 6.

chambers for an order for a further review. The judge may review the taxation himself or refer it to another taxing master.[18]

B ENFORCEMENT OF JUDGMENTS

1 Judgments for the payment of money

a Enforcement in the High Court

The judgment creditor's rights in respect of which he brought the action are extinguished by the judgment. In their place he has a judgment debt. He will wish to enforce this debt which may consist of an award of damages and taxed costs, in addition to which may be included interest at a statutory rate from the date of judgment.[19] The judgment creditor may proceed to enforce the judgment[20] by any of the following five methods prescribed by Order 45, rule 1:

   (i)   writ of *fieri facias*;
   (ii) garnishee proceedings;
   (iii) a charging order;
   (iv) the appointment of a receiver;
   (v) writ of sequestration.

Writ of fieri facias (fi-fa)[1] — This is directed to the sheriff of the county in which is situated the property which it is proposed to seize. Where the debtor has property in more than one county concurrent writs may be issued.[2] The writ commands the sheriff to cause to be made (*fieri facias*) in the name of Her Majesty out of the debtor's chattels a sum sufficient to satisfy the judgment debt and interest together with the costs of execution. The sheriff may enter the judgment debtor's land (although he may not effect a forcible entry)[3] or the land of a third party if the debtor's goods are to be found thereon. He may seize and sell chattels, choses in action such as banknotes or cheques, promissory notes and a lease belonging to the judgment debtor, which he may assign. He cannot, however, seize property which is exempt from execution. This comprises freehold

---

18 Ord 62, r 35.
19 Under the Judgments Act 1838, ss 17, 18 as amended by the Judgments Act 1838 (Judgments Debts (Rate of Interest)) Order 1985, made under the Administration of Justice Act 1970, s 44. This means the date upon which judgment is pronounced, not the date when it is perfected by entry in the appropriate record book: *Parsons v Mather and Platt Ltd* [1977] 2 All ER 715; [1977] 1 WLR 855.
20 A stay of execution, for example pending trial of a counterclaim or appeal, is often ordered by the court. However, although this operates to stay execution by fi-fa (*infra*) it does not prevent the judgment creditor proceeding by one or more of the other methods of enforcement since these do not constitute "execution"; they are alternatives to execution: *Berliner Industriebank Aktiengesellschaft v Jost* [1971] 2 QB 463; [1971] 2 All ER 1513. The Court of Appeal pointed out the need for some modification of the normal form of order.
1 High Court enforcement by this means, of judgments less than £2,000 in value, can only occur in respect of High Court judgments. The High Court may enforce by this means county court judgments between £2,000–£5,000, and all claims over that must be enforced in the High Court: High Court and County Courts Jurisdiction Order 1991, art 8.
2 Ord 47, r 2.
3 *Semayne's* case (1604) 5 Co Rep 91a.

interests in land, equitable interests in land or chattels, fixtures attached to land, wearing apparel, bedding and tools and implements of trade[4] and goods belonging to a third party. The latter provision operates to exempt property which is subject to a hire purchase agreement.

A writ of execution may be issued within the six years following the judgment or order, or later with leave.[5] It may be executed within 12 months of issue on any day not excepting Sunday.[6] There are several other cases in which leave is required, notably where the writ is to be executed against the property of a partner in a firm where the judgment is against the firm,[7] against any person not a party to the original proceedings such as an assignee and against persons represented in a representative action.[8]

It is not unusual for a sheriff to find that goods which he has seized or is about to seize in execution are claimed by a third party such as a hire purchase finance company. His proper course of action in such a situation is to interplead. To do this he issues an interpleader summons serving it on the execution creditor and the claimant.[9] All three parties attend before the master on the return day. The master may try the issue himself, direct an issue to be stated and tried or otherwise deal with the summons as he might deal with a stakeholder's interpleader summons.[10]

The sheriff must make arrangements for the sale of the property seized in execution. Such sale should normally be by public auction and should not take place on the judgment debtor's premises.[11] In practice the sheriff himself takes no part in enforcement and a local auctioneer, acting as a sheriff's officer, usually takes possession of the goods and arranges the auction, or they are left in the possession of the judgment debtor subject to periodic inspection by the sheriff's officers. This arrangement is termed "walking possession" of the goods. In practice the judgment debtor will invariably pay the debt if he can to avoid a sale of his property. Comparatively few sales take place because the court may stay execution on application if the applicant is unable from any cause to pay the money.[12]

Garnishee proceedings — The purpose of these proceedings is to enable the judgment creditor to have assigned to him the benefit of any debt owed

---

4 There is no longer a prescribed value above which such goods are unprotected.
5 Ord 46, r 2(1) (a).
6 The Sunday Observance Act 1677 having been repealed by the Statute Law (Repeals) Act 1969.
7 Ord 81, r 5(4).
8 Ord 15, r 12(3); p 299, *ante*.
9 Ord 17, r 1(1) (b).
10 See p 330, *ante*.
11 Ord 47, r 6; *Watson v Murray & Co* [1955] 2 QB 1; [1955] 1 All ER 350.
12 Ord 47, r 1(1)(b). It may also do so if there are special circumstances which render it inexpedient to enforce the judgment or order (Ord 47, r 1(a)); under this rule execution may be suspended where a debtor company has entered into an informal scheme of arrangement with the majority of its creditors and where not to stay execution would bring down the company and compel it into a winding up or, at least, a statutory scheme of arrangement: *Prestige Publications Ltd v Chelsea Football and Athletic Co Ltd* (1978) 122 Sol Jo 436. The case is a good illustration of the modern tendency of the courts not to permit one creditor to steal a march over other creditors of an insolvent debtor; see also *Rainbow v Moorgate Properties Ltd* [1975] 2 All ER 821; [1975] 1 WLR 788 (see p 389, *post*); *D Wilson (Birmingham) Ltd v Metropolitan Property Developments Ltd* [1975] 2 All ER 814; *Roberts Petroleum Ltd v Bernard Kenny Ltd* [1983] 2 AC 192; [1983] 1 All ER 564. In these cases similar principles were applied to prevent creditors obtaining and

by a third party (the garnishee) to the judgment debtor. A garnishee order will only issue in respect of a legal debt presently owing to the judgment debtor. A common object of garnishee proceedings is a credit balance at the judgment debtor's bank.[13] Earnings may be garnished but only where the right to them has accrued, so that future earnings cannot be garnished. There is, in fact, no way of seizing or intercepting the judgment debtor's future earnings in the Queen's Bench Division.[14]

The judgment debtor may be required to attend before a master to submit to an oral examination as to what debts are owing to him and as to what property or means, if any, he has of satisfying the judgment.[15] When these matters have been ascertained, by examination or otherwise, the judgment creditor may apply *ex parte* on affidavit for an order *nisi* which is served on the garnishee personally and, unless the court otherwise directs, on the judgment debtor.[16] This order calls upon the garnishee either to pay the debt, or so much of it as may be sufficient to satisfy the balance of the judgment debt, to the judgment creditor or show cause for not so doing. If the garnishee fails to comply or show cause the order is made absolute and execution may issue against the garnishee to the extent of his obligation, which is, in effect, assigned to the execution creditor.[17] If the garnishee disputes liability to pay the debt claimed to be due from him[18] the master may determine the question at issue summarily or determine the manner in which it shall be tried, no consent being required to trial before a master.[19]

Where money is standing to the credit of the judgment debtor in court, garnishee proceedings cannot be taken in respect of that money but the judgment creditor can apply by summons for an order for the payment out of all or any part of such money. This summons must be served on the judgment debtor at least seven days before the return day.[20]

Charging order — The judgment creditor may apply *ex parte* on affidavit for an order imposing a charge on property of the kind specified in section 2 of the Charging Orders Act 1979. This comprises any interest held by the debtor beneficially in: (1) land; (2) securities of various kinds; (3) funds in court; and (4) any interest under a trust. In addition where the debtor is a trustee of property his interest may be the subject of a charging order if the

---

enforcing garnishee orders and charging orders (as to which see *infra*) so as to obtain preference over other creditors.

13 *Rogers v Whitely* [1892] AC 118. The Supreme Court Act 1981, s 40 brought within the scope of garnishee orders "any deposit account with a bank or other deposit-taking institution"; this includes, for example, the National Savings Bank and the Post Office. A debt which is not assignable, such as state pension, maintenance or the pay of a member of the armed forces, cannot be attached.

14 *Mapelson v Sears* (1911) 105 LT 639. Future earnings may be attached in respect of a maintenance order under the Attachment of Earnings Act 1971, s 1. Attachment of earnings orders may be obtained in respect of judgment debts only by transferring the judgment to a county court; see p 409, *post*.

15 Ord 48, r 1.

16 Ord 49, r 3(1). The immediate effect of the order is to bind the debt specified in the order from the moment of service of the order.

17 Ord 49, r 4. The order absolute may be enforced in the same manner as any other order for the payment of money.

18 He may, for example, allege a counterclaim against the judgment debtor: *Hale v Victoria Plumbing Co Ltd and En-Tout-Cas Co Ltd* [1966] 2 QB 746; [1966] 2 All ER 672.

19 Ord 49, r 5.

20 Ord 49, r 9.

judgment or order was made against him in his capacity as trustee or the whole beneficial interest under the trust is his alone or shared with others who are all jointly liable to the creditor for the same debt. Thus, for example, if the property in question is a house in the joint names of husband and wife, the legal estate may be charged if both the husband and wife are liable to the judgment creditor, whereas if only one is liable, then all that can be charged is the beneficial interest of that one.

An order may also be made charging a partnership interest.

(1) If he discovers that the judgment debtor has land or an interest in land within the jurisdiction, the judgment creditor may apply for an order creating a charge over the land or over the interest in the land.[1] An order *nisi* is made in the first instance specifying the time and place for further consideration of the matter and imposing the charge until that time. Unless the judgment debtor pays the debt or shows cause at that time the order will be made absolute. The charge so created is a general equitable charge and the judgment creditor should register it in the Land Charges Registry under the provisions of the Land Charges Act 1925. There are two important advantages of registration: a purchaser takes the land subject to the charge (registration amounting to notice) and priority is obtained over subsequent chargees. A land charge may be enforced by an order for sale in the Chancery Division.[2]

(2) If the judgment debtor has government stock or stock or shares in any registered company these cannot be seized in execution of a writ of *fi-fa* because a share certificate is not a negotiable instrument. It is simply evidence of obligations owed by the company which has issued it to the person named in the certificate. The judgment creditor's proper course is to apply for an order *nisi* creating a charge over the shares.[3] The effect of such an order is that no subsequent disposition by the judgment debtor is valid as against the judgment creditor. Unless the judgment debtor shows cause the charging order is made absolute. There is no provision for registering a charge on securities corresponding to the registration of land charges. The judgment creditor, to prevent a disposition of the securities by the judgment debtor, must serve on the company in which the shares are held a "stop notice". The effect is that the company on whom the notice is served must not register a transfer of the shares without serving notice on the judgment creditor, who may apply to the Chancery Division for an order prohibiting the transfer.[4] After the expiration of six months from the charging order *nisi* the judgment creditor may proceed to realise his charge by an order for sale obtainable in the Chancery Division.

(3) The judgment debtor may have an interest in funds or securities in court. This might occur, for example, where the judgment debtor

---

1 Ord 50, r 1. This was introduced by the Administration of Justice Act 1956, s 35(1) to replace the old writ of elegit.

2 Ord 31, r 1. However, it seems that a charging order on an undivided share in land is not registrable; *Perry v Phoenix Assurance plc* [1988] 3 All ER 60; [1988] 1 WLR 940.

3 Charging Orders Act 1979, s 2(2)(b); the order may extend to any dividend or interest payable (*ibid*, s 2(3)).

4 Ord 50, r 15.

has made a payment into court as security for costs. The court may make a "stop order" prohibiting any dealing with the whole or any part of the funds in question. Application for such an order is by summons in the cause or matter relating to the funds in court or, if there is no such cause or matter, by originating summons.[5] The summons must be served on every person whose interest may be affected by the order and on the Accountant General. The judgment creditor may enforce his charge by applying by summons for an order for payment out of the money or so much of it as is sufficient to satisfy his charge.[6]

(4) In relation to partnership property the sheriff cannot levy execution upon property belonging to a partnership in which the debtor is a partner (unless the judgment is against the firm). Nonetheless the judgment creditor may apply by summons to the master for an order charging the partner's interest in the partnership property.[7] The jurisdiction to create such a charge derives from section 23 of the Partnership Act 1890. The creation of a charge on a partnership interest gives the other partners the option of purchasing the interest charged.[8] Failing this the judgment creditor may apply by summons for the appointment of a receiver who will receive on behalf of the judgment creditor money accruing from the debtor's interest in the partnership.[9]

The power of the court to make charging orders, and indeed garnishee orders, is a discretionary one. It will be appreciated that the effect of such orders is to give the plaintiff priority over unsecured creditors of the defendant. Accordingly such orders should not be made against an insolvent defendant so as to place the plaintiff at an advantage over other creditors if it would be inequitable so to do.[10]

Appointment of a receiver by way of equitable execution[11] — This is a method of enforcement directed at the interception of certain classes of income and profits before they reach the debtor so that he does not have the opportunity of disposing of them to the detriment of the judgment creditor. The judgment creditor may apply by summons or motion to the court to appoint some person as a receiver to receive income such as rents or profits in respect of any interest in land, legal or equitable, or of any interest in chattels which could not be reached by a writ of *fi-fa*.[12] It should be stressed, however, that a receiver cannot be appointed to receive the

---

5 Ord 50, r 10.
6 Ord 49, r 9. If the judgment debtor is insolvent the judgment creditor is in the position of a secured creditor to the extent of the sum in court; *WA Sherratt Ltd v John Bromley (Church Stretton) Ltd* [1985] QB 1038; [1985] 1 All ER 216.
7 Ord 81, r 10.
8 Partnership Act 1890, s 23(3).
9 Ord 51, r 3; Ord 30, *infra*.
10 *Rainbow v Moorgate Properties Ltd* [1975] 2 All ER 821; [1975] 1 WLR 788; *Roberts Petroleum Ltd v Bernard Kenny Ltd* [1983] 2 AC 192; [1983] 1 All ER 564 (p 386, n 12, *supra*); see also, to similar effect, Charging Orders Act 1979, s 1(5).
11 Ord 51, r 3. The expression "equitable execution" is explained by the fact that this method of enforcement originated in the Court of Chancery. It is, however, misleading since it is not confined to equitable interests, nor is it a method of execution. It is a method of enforcement alternative to execution; see *Re Shephard* (1889) 43 Ch D 131, at 137.
12 The power is now contained in Supreme Court Act 1981, s 37.

judgment debtor's future earnings of employment for, as stated earlier, there is no direct means of attaching earnings in the Queen's Bench Division.

Before appointing a receiver the court will consider whether the probable costs of the appointment are justified by the amount claimed and the amount likely to be recovered by the receiver, and may direct an enquiry on these matters before making an appointment.[13] The general powers and duties of receivers appointed by the court are contained in Order 30. The receiver is usually required to provide a guarantee as security for what he receives as receiver.[14] The receiver is allowed a proper remuneration which is fixed by court. His obligation is to submit accounts to the court for approval as and when ordered to do so and to pay into court the amounts shown by his accounts to be due.[15]

Prior to 1971, committal for contempt of court was an indirect means of enforcing a judgment debt. However section 11 of the Administration of Justice Act 1970 limited the jurisdiction of the High Court to commit to prison in respect of non-payment of a debt due under a judgment or order to cases of default in respect of maintenance orders. Since these orders are invariably made in the Family Division, committal in the Queen's Bench Division for non-payment of a debt is effectively abolished (though, as will be seen, it remains a sanction for failure to comply with orders other than orders for the payment of money).

There remains, however, one process of contempt in respect of failure to pay judgment debts – the procedure by writ of sequestration.

Writ of sequestration[16] — In cases of contempt of court a committal order is sometimes accompanied by a writ of sequestration. The two have much in common in that they are both indirect methods of enforcement being in the nature of punitive measures. As indicated above, although committal to prison in respect of a judgment debt (other than a maintenance order) has been abolished, a writ of sequestration may still issue in respect of continuous failure to comply with an order for the payment of money, although the procedure is very rarely used in such cases, save occasionally against corporate bodies. A writ of sequestration may issue in any case in which a person refuses or neglects to do an act within a specified time or disobeys an order requiring him to abstain from doing some act. The writ commissions not less than four persons[17] to enter upon and take possession of all the real and personal estate of the judgment debtor and to keep the same under sequestration until the debtor complies with the judgment. If a fine has been imposed for contempt of court and remains unpaid, a writ of sequestration may issue to enforce payment of the fine. The procedure on application is by notice of motion for leave to issue the writ stating the grounds of the application and accompanied by an affidavit in support.[18] The application must be heard in open court.[19]

---

13 Ord 51, r 1.
14 Ord 30, r 2.
15 Ord 30, rr 3–6.
16 Ord 45, r 5.
17 As to the position of sequestrators and their potential liability for negligence, see *Inland Revenue Commissioners v Hoogstraten* [1985] QB 1077; [1984] 3 All ER 25.
18 Ord 46, r 5.
19 Except in the special cases set out in Ord 52, r 6 where the application may be heard in private, notably where the case involves the wardship, adoption, guardianship, custody or maintenance of infants, proceedings relating to mental patients, cases where a secret

A writ of sequestration is a practical alternative to committal where the judgment debtor is a corporation and the writ may issue, with leave, against the property of any director or other officer of the body.

In relation to a writ of sequestration, the position of third parties is similar to that of third parties in relation to injunctions; although they are not directly bound by the order, they must not knowingly take any step which would obstruct enforcement of the order. Thus, for example, a bank is under a duty to disclose to sequestrators balances which are held to the credit of the contemner and to pay over such sums on demand (unless a third party, such as the bank itself, has a prior charge on the balance).[20]

b   Other methods of enforcing judgments for the payment of money

County court enforcement — A judgment of the High Court for the payment of money may be enforced in a county court as if it were a judgment of the county court only by transferring the action to a county court. However, even without such transfer, High Court judgments may be the subject of (1) judgment summons procedure; or (2) attachment of earnings in a county court.[1] The primary advantage of the judgment summons, as opposed to the power of the High Court to require a debtor to attend an examination as to his means under Order 48, rule 1, is that the county court has power to make an order for payment by instalments in the first instance. Secondly, an attachment of earnings order may now be obtained, under the provisions of the Attachment of Earnings Act 1971, in a county court in respect of a High Court judgment debt. Both of these methods of enforcement are extremely practical in relation to debtors who have insufficient assets to satisfy the judgment but who have earnings out of which the debt, or at least part of it, might be recoverable.[2]

Bankruptcy — Where the debtor's total debts exceed the "bankruptcy level" and he is unable to pay his debts, the judgment creditor may issue a bankruptcy petition.[3] Bankruptcy proceedings are, in general, an unsatisfactory method of enforcement though the mere threat of bankruptcy proceedings may be a sufficient sanction where the judgment debtor is a person, such as a solicitor, whose livelihood cannot survive bankruptcy.

---

process, discovery or invention is involved or where it appears to the court that in the interests of the administration of justice or for reasons of national security the application should be heard in private.

20 *Eckman v Midland Bank Ltd* [1973] QB 519; [1973] 1 All ER 609, a decision of the now defunct National Industrial Relations Court, arising out of the refusal of the Amalgamated Union of Engineering Workers to recognise or comply with orders of that court.

1 County Court Rules 1981, Ord 25, r 11, Ord 27, Ord 28, r 1.

2 For details of procedure see p 409, *post.*

3 Insolvency Act 1986, s 267.

2   Judgments and orders other than for the payment of money

a   *Judgments for possession of land*[4]

A judgment or order for the giving of possession of land may be enforced by any one or more of the following three methods:

(1) *writ of possession*. This is the direct method of enforcement. It directs the sheriff to enter the land and cause the plaintiff to have possession of it. The writ cannot be issued without leave,[5] application for which is *ex parte* on affidavit, and leave cannot be granted unless it is shown that every person in actual possession of the whole or any part of the land has received sufficient notice of the proceedings to enable him to apply to the court for any relief to which he may be entitled, such as relief against forfeiture.[6] In practice judgments or orders for the possession of land are always enforced in this way;

(2) *order of committal*; and

(3) *writ of sequestration*, in theory at least, is an indirect method of enforcement but is almost never employed in this context. The procedure on application for leave to issue a writ of sequestration has already been noted; committal procedure is considered below.

b   *Judgments for delivery of goods*[7]

The appropriate writ of execution for a judgment for the delivery of goods depends upon whether or not the judgment contains an alternative provision for payment of the assessed value of the goods.

Writ of specific delivery — This is the appropriate writ where the judgment orders the delivery of specific goods without an alternative provision for the payment of their assessed value. It directs the sheriff to seize the goods described in the writ and deliver them to the plaintiff.

Writ of delivery — This is appropriate where the judgment orders the delivery of goods with an alternative provision for payment of their assessed value. The writ directs the sheriff to seize the goods described and deliver them to the plaintiff and, if he cannot obtain the goods, to levy execution upon the goods and chattels of the defendant to an extent sufficient to realise the assessed value of the goods. If the alternative course is adopted the writ has the same effect as a writ of *fi-fa*.

Whether a writ of delivery or a writ of specific delivery is issued the sheriff is authorised to enforce by execution the payment of any money ordered to be paid by way of damages or costs by the judgment or order which is to be enforced by the writ together with the costs of execution and interest.

Orders of committal and *writs of sequestration* are theoretically available

---

4 Ord 45, r 3.

5 Except where the judgment or order was given or made in a mortgage action (Ord 45, r 3(2)) or where the order was made in summary proceedings for possession of land against trespassers following the issue of an originating summons under Order 113 (Ord 113, r 7); as to this procedure, see p 375, *ante*.

6 Ord 45, r 3(3).

7 Ord 45, r 4.

as indirect methods of enforcement but, as in the case of orders for the possession of land, their use is generally inappropriate in this context.

c Judgments to do or abstain from doing any act

Where the judgment or order requires the defendant to perform any act other than the payment of money or the delivery of goods or land or requires him to abstain from doing any act, it is enforceable only by: (1) *order of committal*; and (2) *writ of sequestration*.

The order to which these rules apply may have been, for example, an injunction[8] (mandatory or prohibitory), an order to deliver an account, an order to produce a document or an order to answer an interrogatory.

Procedure by writ of sequestration has already been noted. In cases of contempt a writ of sequestration is an appropriate method of enforcement against a corporate body and is often joined with a committal order in respect of the officers of the corporate body.[9]

Committal orders — A committal order is an order committing a person to prison for contempt of court. An order may be made where a person required by a judgment or order to do an act within a time specified in the judgment or order refuses or neglects to do it within that time,[10] or a person disobeys a judgment or order requiring him to abstain from doing an act. A master or registrar has no power to make a committal order. The order is made by a judge following a motion in open court.[11] Notice of motion must have been served on the person sought to be committed together with a copy of the affidavit which must support the application. Personal service is generally required.[12] Committal must be for a fixed period although earlier discharge may be ordered if the court deems that the contemner has "purged his contempt" and releases him, generally on his undertaking to perform (or abstain from repeating, as the case may be) the act in respect of which he was committed. As an alternative to imprisonment there is jurisdiction to impose a fine for contempt.

It was formerly held that a person might not be committed for a mere neglect as opposed to a "wilful and contumacious disobedience of a court order".[13] However in *Knight v Clifton*[14] the Court of Appeal rejected this principle and asserted that in proceedings for committal for breach of an order of the court there is no need to prove that the conduct in question was wilful or contumacious; when an injunction prohibits an act, the performance of that act is a contempt irrespective of questions of intention

---

8 An undertaking given to the court is equivalent to an injunction against the person giving the undertaking so that breach of the undertaking is contempt of court: cf *Biba Ltd v Stratford Investments Ltd* [1973] Ch 281; [1972] 3 All ER 1041.

9 See, for example, *Worthington v Ad–Lib Club Ltd* [1965] Ch 236; [1964] 3 All ER 674.

10 Save where the act is the payment of money, in which case (except in the case of maintenance orders) there is no power of committal (Administration of Justice Act 1970, s 11); see p 390, *ante*.

11 Except in the cases set out in Ord 52, r 6 in which the court may sit in private; see p 390, n 19, *ante*.

12 Ord 52, r 4.

13 See for example, *Worthington v Ad–Lib Club Ltd* [1965] Ch 236; [1964] 3 All ER 674.

14 [1971] Ch 700; [1971] 2 All ER 378, disapproving *Worthington v Ad–Lib Club Ltd* (*supra*); see also *Re Mileage Conference of the Tyre Manufacturers' Conference Ltd's Agreement* [1966] 2 All ER 849; [1966] 1 WLR 1137 in which breach of an undertaking was held to be contempt where the persons concerned had taken all reasonable care to avoid a breach.

unless otherwise stated on the face of the order. This authority was cited with apparent approval by the House of Lords in *Heaton's Transport (St Helens) Ltd v Transport and General Workers' Union*,[15] inasmuch as the House of Lords accepted that wilfulness was not an element in contempt of court; however it appeared also to accept that conduct which was "casual or accidental and unintentional" would not amount to contempt. To this extent the assertion in *Knight v Clifton* that questions of intention are irrelevant is probably too wide.

---

15 [1973] AC 15; [1972] 3 All ER 101.

CHAPTER 20

Procedure in County Courts

A CONSTITUTION AND JURISDICTION OF COUNTY COURTS

1 Origins and constitution

One of the principal deficiencies of the English legal system, until the reforms of the nineteenth century, was the lack of a system of courts to deal with civil actions involving only a small amount of money.[1] As a result, the modern county courts were established by the County Courts Act 1846. The upper limit of the new courts' jurisdiction was originally fixed at £20 but this figure has been progressively increased and presently stands at £50,000 in most cases. The jurisdiction of the county courts is now principally contained in the County Courts Act 1984 (as amended).

Procedure in the county courts is regulated by the County Court Rules made by a Rule Committee under powers conferred by the Act.[2] The rules presently in force are the County Court Rules 1981 (as amended). These and other rules relating to county court practice and procedure are to be found in the *County Court Practice* (the "Green Book") which, although not an official publication, is accepted as authoritative in the same way as the White Book is accepted in the Supreme Court.

England and Wales is divided into districts each having one or more county courts.[3] These courts are, for administrative convenience, grouped into circuits with one or more judges presiding over each circuit. Each court has a sitting at least once a month, and, of course, at busy centres often considerably more often.

a Judges of county courts

The office of county court judge, as such, was abolished by the Courts Act 1971 and on the date on which that Act came into operation, 1 January 1972, all existing county court judges automatically became

---

1 See p 131, *ante*.
2 Section 75. In any case not expressly provided for in the Act or Rules, the principles of High Court procedure apply (s 76); see *Williamson v Rider* [1963] 1 QB 89; [1962] 2 All ER 268. They also have inherent power to regulate their own procedure: see *Langley v North West Water Authority* [1991] 3 All ER 610; [1991] 1 WLR 697.
3 *Ibid*, ss 1, 2; the places at which county courts are to be held and the names of those courts are specified in the Civil Courts Order 1983; they are set out in the County Court Directory in the Appendix of the Green Book.

circuit judges.[4] Although every circuit judge is, by virtue of his office, enabled to sit in any county court the Lord Chancellor is bound to assign one or more circuit judges to each county court district.[5]

b District judges

These are appointed by the Lord Chancellor and must be appropriately qualified.[6] The district judge exercises both an administrative and a judicial function. In his administrative capacity he maintains the court records, arranges for the issue and service of summonses, accounts for money paid into court and exercises a large number of similar functions. In practice he delegates much of this work to subordinate court officers, notably the clerks and bailiffs. The scope of his judicial function is narrower than that of the judge. He has power to hear and determine (a) any action or matter in which the defendant fails to appear at the hearing or admits the claim; (b) any action or matter in which the sum claimed or the amount involved does not exceed £5,000; (c) actions in which mortgagees of land claim possession; and (d) by leave of the judge and with the consent of the parties, any other action or matter.[7] He also deals with interlocutory matters and the taxation of costs.

2 Jurisdiction

Because county courts are the creation of statute, their jurisdiction derives entirely from statute. The general jurisdiction of the county court is to be found in the County Courts Act 1984. Nevertheless extensive jurisdiction is conferred upon the county court by other statutes. This latter jurisdiction is usually concurrent with the High Court or magistrates' courts although in a few cases it is exclusive to the county court.[8]

a Jurisdiction under the County Courts Act 1984

The jurisdiction of the county court under the 1984 Act may be classified as follows:

(1) *Actions founded on contract or tort*. The fundamental changes to the distribution of cases between High Court and county court have already been noted.[9] In particular the presumption is that cases with a value of £50,000 or more will be tried in the High Court.

(2) *Actions for the recovery of land* or where the title to any hereditament or right over land is in question.

---

4 Courts Act 1971, s 16, Sch 2; as to the position of circuit judges, see p 182, *ante*.
5 County Courts Act 1984, s 5. In addition every judge of the Court of Appeal, every judge of the High Court and every Recorder is capable of sitting as a county court judge if he consents so to do and may be required, under s 5(3), so to act on such occasions as the Lord Chancellor considers desirable. It is difficult to envisage any judge of the Court of Appeal or High Court sitting as a county court judge.
6 *Ibid*, s 9; the Lord Chancellor may appoint assistant district judges (s 7) and deputy district judges (s 8), who must be similarly qualified.
7 CCR, Ord 21, r 5.
8 For example, under the Rent Act 1977, the Race Relations Act 1976 and the Domestic Violence and Matrimonial Proceedings Act 1976, s 1.
9 See p 277, *ante*.

(3) *Equity proceedings* where the sum involved does not exceed the county court limit (currently £30,000) or more by written memorandum signed by the parties or their solicitors, and then only where the proceedings fall within certain specified categories. These categories are set out in section 23 of the Act and include the administration of estates of deceased persons, the declaration and execution of trusts, the foreclosure and redemption of mortgages, the rectification or cancellation of deeds, the maintenance and advancement out of trust funds of infants and proceedings for relief against fraud or mistake.[10]

(4) *Admiralty proceedings*, but only in certain specified proceedings and only in county courts which have been appointed by the Lord Chancellor to exercise jurisdiction in admiralty matters.[11] All these courts, with the exception of the Mayor's and City of London Court, are on or near the coast. The admiralty proceedings in question are set out in section 27 of the Act. They include claims for damage to a ship or for damage to or loss of goods carried by sea, towage and pilotage disputes. The limit of jurisdiction is in each case £5,000 (or £15,000 in salvage claims), but this limit can be increased by memorandum of agreement, although the extent of the proceedings over which the county court has jurisdiction cannot be so increased.

(5) *Contentious probate proceedings* where there is an application for a grant or revocation of probate or letters of administration, where the net value of the estate at the time of death was less than the county court limit (currently £30,000). The applicant must swear an affidavit containing the value of the estate and also the place of abode of the deceased, since only the county court for that district has jurisdiction.[12]

b   Jurisdiction under other statutes

Apart from the County Courts Act 1984, there are more than 150 statutes which confer jurisdiction in certain matters either on the county courts generally, or upon particular county courts. Of these mention may be made of the Rent Act 1977 and the Consumer Credit Act 1974 both of which are fertile sources of county court litigation. Special attention should be drawn to the Matrimonial Causes Act 1967 which conferred jurisdiction upon those county courts nominated by the Lord Chancellor as "divorce county courts" to hear undefended matrimonial causes,[13] and to the Domestic Violence and Matrimonial Proceedings Act 1976 under which a county court judge may, by injunction, exercise powers which include restraining a party from molesting the other party or a child living with the

---

10 See also County Courts Act 1984, s 24 for other equity proceedings which may, by consent of the parties, be tried in a county court.
11 County Courts Act 1984, ss 26, 27.
12 *Ibid*, s 32.
13 See now: Matrimonial Causes Act 1973; Matrimonial and Family Proceedings Act 1984.

applicant, excluding one party from the "matrimonial home" or requiring him (or her) to permit the other to enter and remain in the home.[14]

B   PROCEDURE IN THE COUNTY COURT

1   Actions

a   *Choice of county court*

Unlike that of the High Court, the jurisdiction of county courts is local. This means that the plaintiff must usually commence proceedings;

(1) in the court for the district in which the defendant or one of the defendants resides or carries on business; or

(2) in the court for the district where the cause of action arose wholly or in part;

(3) in the case of a default action, in any county court.[15]

If the plaintiff commences proceedings in any other county court the judge of that court may transfer the proceedings to a court which does have jurisdiction, order them to be struck out, or allow them to continue in his court.[16]

b   *Parties*

The County Court Rules regulating the choice and joinder of parties are parallel to the provisions of the Rules of the Supreme Court. Thus two or more persons may be joined as plaintiffs or defendants if their rights or liabilities arise out of the same transaction or series of transactions and, if separate actions were brought, any common question of law or fact would arise.[17]

Parties to whom special rules of procedure apply in the High Court, such as partners, companies and persons under disability, are in a similar position in the county court. An infant must generally, as in the High Court, sue by his "next friend" who must file an undertaking to be responsible for costs.[18] However, an infant may sue in his own name for any sum not exceeding the county court limit which may be due to him for wages or piece work or for work as a servant.[19]

---

14 Act of 1976, s 1. The Act extends to men and women living together but not married to one another and "matrimonial home" is construed accordingly. Under s 2 the judge may attach to the injunction a "power of arrest" which gives to police officers a power to arrest without warrant persons whom they reasonably suspect of being in breach of such an injunction. Nor can the police grant bail in such a case, but the person arrested must be brought before a judge within 24 hours of his arrest.

15 Ord 4, r 2(1). Oddly enough the matrimonial jurisdiction of divorce county courts is not local; a petition may be filed in any divorce county court (Family Proceedings Rules 1991, SI 1991/1247, r 2.6).

16 Ord 16, r 2.

17 Ord 5, r 2.

18 Ord 10, r 2.

19 County Courts Act 1984, s 47.

c   Commencement of proceedings

All proceedings, the object of which is to obtain relief against any other person, must (subject to any express provision to the contrary) be brought by *action* and commenced by *plaint*.[20] An action in which a claim is made for any relief other than the payment of money is termed a "fixed date action"; every other action is a "default action".[1] The plaintiff or his solicitor commences a default or fixed date action by filing in the court office a request for the summons (formerly called a *praecipe*) setting out the names, addresses and descriptions of all parties and the nature and amount of the claim. He must also file particulars of claim and the sum claimed with a copy for each defendant. Upon filing these documents the registrar issues to the plaintiff a plaint note containing the title of the action, the reference number of the plaint and a date and time for the return day. He also prepares, from the plaintiff's request, and issues a summons to which are annexed the particulars of claim. The summons and particulars are then served on every defendant at least 21 clear days before the return day.[2] The defendant is also served with forms of admission, defence and counterclaim.

A county court summons may be served by the plaintiff or his agent, in which case he must file an affidavit of service,[3] but it is usually served by the county court bailiff. The summons may be served by an officer of the court sending it by first-class post to the defendant at the address stated in the request for the summons or, if the plaintiff so requests, by the plaintiff delivering the summons to the defendant personally.[4] The defendant's solicitor may accept service on the defendant's behalf, in which case he must indorse on the bailiff's copy summons a statement to this effect. Substituted service may be ordered by the district judge following application by the plaintiff on affidavit. A summons may not be served out of the jurisdiction without leave of the judge. The circumstances in which leave may be granted are similar (though not identical) to those contained in Order 11, rule 1 of the Rules of the Supreme Court.[5]

---

20 Ord 3, r 1.
 1 Ord 3, r 2.
 2 Ord 7, r 6.
 3 Ord 3, r 2.
 4 Ord 7, r 10. Service by post is deemed to be effected on the seventh day after the date on which the summons was sent (Ord 7, r 10). Consequently service may be deemed to be validly effected even though the defendant never actually receives the summons. The defendant's remedy is to apply to set aside judgment, though this is a matter of discretion rather than of right: see *Cooper v Scott-Farnell* [1969] 1 All ER 178; [1969] 1 WLR 120. However where a summons sent by post has been returned undelivered, notice of non-service is sent to the plaintiff who is informed that he may request bailiff service; if he so requests the court bailiff then effects service by (a) inserting the summons through the letterbox at the address stated in the request for the summons; or (b) delivering the summons to some person, apparently not less than 16 years' old, at that address; or (c) delivering the summons to the defendant personally (Ord 7, r 10).
 5 Ord 8, r 2; see p 306, *ante*. Service on a Sunday, Christmas Day or Good Friday is prohibited except, in case of urgency, with leave of the court; Ord 7, r 3.

d   Defence

A defendant who is served with a summons has open to him the following courses of action.[6]

(1) In any action for debt or damages he may within 14 days of service pay into court the whole amount of the claim; the action is then stayed and if the defendant also pays in the costs stated on the summons he will not be liable for any further costs unless the court otherwise orders.[7] Alternatively he may pay into court some lesser amount, either in satisfaction of the plaintiff's claims or on account of a sum admitted by him to be due to the plaintiff. In the former case the payment in operates in the same way as a payment into court in the High Court under RSC Order 22. Thus if the payment in is accepted, the proceedings are stayed in respect of the causes of action to which the payment in relates while if the plaintiff goes on but then, at the trial, fails to "beat the payment in" he will normally be held liable for all costs subsequent to the date of payment in.

(2) Where the defendant admits the whole or any part of the claim but desires time to pay he may, within 14 days, file the form of admission attached to the summons and state how he proposes to pay the admitted sum, for example by fixed instalments. The district judge sends notice of this admission to the plaintiff who must, within 14 days, inform the court office whether or not he accepts the offer. If he does accept, the district judge will enter judgment accordingly. If he does not accept, the district judge must inform the defendant whereupon the action proceeds.[8] If the defendant admits the whole or any part of the plaintiff's claim, the plaintiff may apply to the court for such judgment as he may be entitled to on the admission; an alternative course for the plaintiff is to apply for an interim payment.[9]

(3) If the defendant denies liability or wishes to plead a set-off or counterclaim he must, within 14 days, file the forms of defence and counterclaim if appropriate. The district judge will serve copies of these upon the plaintiff.

(4) In a default action[10] if the defendant takes none of the above courses, the plaintiff may obtain judgment for the amount of the claim (if the claim is liquidated[11]) or interlocutory judgment for damages to be assessed (if the claim is for unliquidated damages) together with costs. In a fixed date action (*viz* an action in which there is a claim for some relief other than the payment of money) the defendant may appear on the return day without having filed a defence and dispute the plaintiff's claim. However he will be

---

6 Ord 9.
7 Ord 11, rr 1, 2.
8 Ord 9, r 3.
9 Ord 13, r 12; this rule applies RSC, Ord 29 (subject to minor exceptions) to county court proceedings; for details of the High Court procedure, see p 328, *ante*.
10 See *ante* p 311.
11 In county courts a claim for the cost of repairs executed to a motor vehicle is treated as a liquidated claim unless the court otherwise orders (Ord 1, r 10).

ordered to pay any extra costs incurred by his failure to file a defence.

e   Pre-trial review and other interlocutory proceedings

In the case of a fixed date action (other than an action for recovery of land) the return day on the summons will be, unless the court otherwise directs, a day fixed for the preliminary consideration of the action by the district judge, known as a "pre-trial review". In the case of default action, where a defence or counterclaim is delivered the court will fix either a day for the hearing of the action or a day for a pre-trial review.[12] A pre-trial review may also be held where the district judge is of the opinion that the question of giving directions ought to be considered. The pre-trial review is analogous to the summons for directions in High Court actions[13] and the district judge is enjoined to "consider the course of the proceedings and give all such directions as appear to him necessary or desirable for securing the just, expeditious and economical disposal of the action".[14] In particular the district judge must endeavour to secure that the parties make all such admissions and agreements as ought reasonably to be made by them and may record in the order any admission or agreement so made or any refusal to make any admission or agreement. Evidence on the pre-trial review may be given by affidavit. If the defendant does not appear on the pre-trial review and has not delivered an admission or defence, the district judge may, if he thinks fit, enter judgment for the plaintiff; if the defendant does not appear on the pre-trial review and has delivered a defence, the plaintiff may proceed to prove his case (generally by affidavit) and may ask for judgment in the same way as if the defendant had not appeared at the trial.

Every party must apply on the pre-trial review for any interlocutory order which he seeks and if he does not and makes a subsequent interlocutory application, he will usually have to pay the extra costs incurred. Interlocutory orders are, in practice, required rather less frequently than in High Court actions.

The interlocutory orders which the county court has power to make are similar to the orders which may be made in the High Court, the following being frequently encountered – third party proceedings,[15] further and better particulars of claim,[16] discovery and inspection of documents,[17] interrogatories,[18] amendment of pleadings,[19] security for costs,[1] interim payments.[2] It may also include orders as to exchange of statements.[3] After giving all necessary directions the district judge must, if the action remains to be tried, fix a day for the trial and give notice thereof to every party.[4]

---

12 Ord 3, r 3 (fixed date); Ord 9, r 5 (default). See generally Ord 17, r 11 (automatic directions).
13 See p 358, *ante.*
14 Ord 17, r 1.
15 Ord 12.
16 Ord 6, r 7.
17 Ord 14, rr 1–10; the automatic discovery provisions in the High Court (p 357, *ante*) do not apply in county courts.
18 Ord 14, r 11.
19 Ord 15.
 1 Ord 13, r 8.
 2 Ord 13, r 12.
 3 Ord 20, r 12A.
 4 Ord 17, r 10.

The pre-trial review operates, therefore, both as a summons for directions in actions which are destined to proceed to trial and as a means of the plaintiff obtaining judgment (either by default or by proving his case, as above) in other cases, without the need of a proper trial in open court.

In other cases, a system of automatic directions operates.[5] This provides a timetable for service of lists of documents, inspection of documents, disclosure of expert reports, for the making of requests for a hearing, and for the preparation of documentation prior to trial.

f   Premature determination of proceedings

A high proportion of actions never come to trial, being prematurely determined by agreement, by the defendant admitting liability, by the plaintiff discontinuing his claim, or by a judgment or order given or made on a pre-trial review. In addition Order 9, rule 14 now, in effect, applies High Court Order 14 procedure to most actions.[6]

If the parties arrive at a settlement, the plaintiff must give notice of this to the district judge who notes it in the minute book. The action is thus determined. However the consent of the court is required to a settlement of an action by or on behalf of a person under disability.[7] Some actions are brought solely for obtaining the court's sanction for a settlement which has already been reached. The particulars of claim in such an action contain only an outline of the claim, the terms of the proposed settlement and a request for the court's approval, which will be given in chambers by the judge or district judge. The judge or district judge will direct how the money is to be dealt with; in the case of an infant the money is usually paid into court and invested or applied for his benefit until he attains his majority, when he can demand payment of the capital.

As has already been noted the defendant may pay money into court at any time before judgment. If the plaintiff takes the money out of court proceedings are stayed and the plaintiff may tax and sign judgment for his costs.

The plaintiff may, at any time before trial, discontinue his action by giving notice in the prescribed form to the district judge and to the defendant, who will be entitled to his costs incurred before receiving notice of discontinuance.[8]

g   References to arbitration or for inquiry and report or to the European Court

(1) *Arbitration*. Before 1973 the power of county courts to refer cases to arbitration was limited to those cases in which the parties consented. Accordingly it was exercised only rarely. However, the Administration of Justice Act 1973 created wide powers to refer proceedings to arbitration

---

5 Ord 17, r 11.
6 For details of Ord 14 procedure in the High Court, see p 319, *ante*; the rule does not apply to (a) actions which stand referred to arbitration, (b) actions for the possession of land, or involving title to land, or (c) claims for libel, slander, malicious prosecution or false imprisonment.
7 Ord 10, r 10.
8 Ord 18, rr 1, 2.

and the relevant provisions are now to be found in section 64 of the Act and Order 19 of the Rules. The position is that either party may apply by notice for the case to be referred to arbitration, which may be ordered to take place before the judge, district judge or an outside arbitrator. In addition any proceedings in which the sum claimed or the amount involved does not exceed £1,000 automatically stand referred for arbitration by the district judge[9] upon receipt by the court of a defence to the claim. However in such cases the district judge may on the application of any party rescind the reference if he is satisfied:

(a)   that a difficult question of law or a question of fact of exceptional complexity is involved; or

(b)   that a charge of fraud against a party is in issue; or

(c)   that the parties are agreed that the dispute should be tried in court; or

(d)   that it would be unreasonable for the claim to proceed to arbitration having regard to its subject matter, the circumstances of the parties or the interests of any other person likely to be affected by the award.[10]

The advantage of arbitration is that it provides a procedure for small claims which is not only expeditious but inexpensive and informal. Thus the hearing is informal and the strict rules of evidence do not apply, the arbitrator may adopt any procedure he wishes so as to afford each party a fair and equal opportunity to present his case and may, with the consent of the parties, consult any expert or call for an expert report on any matter in dispute or invite an expert to attend the hearing as assessor.[11] Furthermore since in cases automatically referred no solicitors' charges are usually allowed as between party and party, litigants in, for example, consumer disputes can freely take their case to the county court in the knowledge that they are not at risk for substantial costs. In these ways the county court is able to exercise its original function as a "small-claims" court, readily accessible to litigants in person. An individual may be represented by a person other than a lawyer, subject to certain controls left in the hands of the court to prevent demonstrably unsuitable persons from exercising that right.[12]

The order for reference will usually be made at the pre-trial review.

(2) *Inquiry and report.* Section 65 of the Act empowers the court to refer to the district judge or a referee for inquiry and report proceedings which require any prolonged examination of documents or any scientific or local investigation,[13] proceedings concerning matters of account, other proceedings with the consent of the parties and any question arising in any proceedings.

Such an order may be made either on application or by the court of its

---

9 But the district judge may, on the application of any party, refer the proceedings for arbitration by the judge or an outside arbitrator (Ord 19, r 2(3)).

10 Ord 19, r 2(4).

11 Ord 19, r 7.

12 Lay Representation (Rights of Audience) Order 1992, made under Courts and Legal Services Act 1990, s 11.

13 See p 353, *ante* for position in High Court.

own motion and, as will be apparent from the terms of the section, is usually appropriate in complex cases, such as building disputes, where there is a great deal of detailed or expert evidence to be heard; the reference may be to the district judge or to an independent referee who will conduct the inquiry and make a report to the court. The procedure differs from arbitration in that it does not, as arbitration does, involve the adjudication being made by the person to whom the reference is made – judgment will still be given by the judge (or district judge) trying the case.

(3) *Reference to European Court.* County courts, like the High Court and the Court of Appeal, have power to refer questions for a preliminary ruling under Article 177 of the Treaty of Rome. The circumstances in which such a reference may be made and the principles which govern the court's discretion whether or not to refer have been considered elsewhere in this work;[14] the rules applicable in county courts are substantially similar to those which apply in the High Court. In view of the costs involved there are few references to the European Court from county courts, although the terms of Article 177 have compelled the enactment of rules to deal with such a contingency.

h   Trial

Unless it is settled or discontinued or disposed of at the pre-trial review the action comes on for trial on the day fixed. If the plaintiff does not appear when the case is called his action will be struck out and he will have to apply to have it reinstated at another time. If the defendant does not appear the trial may proceed in his absence and judgment may be entered against him. The trial will be before the district judge, the judge or, very rarely, the judge and a jury. The county court jury is obsolescent. No party has a right to claim trial with a jury unless there is in issue a charge of fraud against him or claim in respect of libel, slander, malicious prosecution or false imprisonment unless the trial requires any prolonged examination of documents or accounts or any scientific or local investigation which cannot conveniently be made with a jury.[15]

In any other case he may be granted a jury, eight in number. In fact actions which would be heard by a jury are usually heard in the High Court.[16] The conduct of the trial is similar to that in the High Court. Solicitors, however, have a right of audience in the county court and frequently appear.[17] Also, if the action is not determined in one day, the district judge must fix another date to continue the hearing which will not necessarily be the next day.

If the defendant admits the plaintiff's claim or does not appear judgment will be entered for the plaintiff. Where this judgment is for the payment of money the court may order the sum to be paid forthwith or within a specified time, or may order payment by fixed instalments.[18]

If the plaintiff does not succeed in proving his case the court may either

---

14 See p 113, *ante*.
15 County Courts Act 1984, s 66. The application for an order for trial by jury must be made not less than 10 clear days before the return day; Ord 13, r 10.
16 See p 113, *ante*.
17 See also the Lay Representative (Rights of Audience) Order 1992, and generally as to the Lord Chancellor's powers, the Courts and Legal Services Act 1990, s 27, p 209, *ante*.
18 County Courts Act 1984, s 71.

give judgment for the defendant or non-suit the plaintiff. The non-suit has long been abolished in the High Court but still exists in the county court. It differs from a judgment for the defendant in that it does not decide the case affirmatively against the plaintiff, so that he is not estopped from bringing a subsequent action on the same facts. However a second action may be stayed until the plaintiff has complied with an order for costs made against him in the former action.[19]

2   Rent actions

Much of the time of the average county court is taken up by landlords' actions for the recovery of premises and arrears of rent from tenants. Indeed the jurisdiction of county courts in actions for the recovery of possession of dwellings which are within the rateable value limits of the Rent Act 1977 is virtually exclusive.

A new summary procedure for the recovery of arrears of rent from a tenant or former tenant who is still in occupation of the demised premises was introduced in 1972 and is now embodied in Order 24, rules 8–11. The action, known as a "rent action", is commenced by the filing of a special form of request for a summons in the court for the district in which the land is situated. The summons fixes a return day for the hearing, there being no pre-trial review, and must be served on the defendant not less than seven clear days before the return day. There is no provision for the defendant to serve a defence or counterclaim and the usual forms of admission, defence and counterclaim are not sent to the defendant; nor is there any provision for his making an admission and a written request for time to pay. The form of summons simply requires the defendant to pay into court the whole of the claim (or such part as he admits) or to attend court on the return day, failing which judgment may be given in his absence.

3   Proceedings other than actions

Where, subject to any Act or rule, the object of proceedings is to obtain relief against any person or to compel any person to do or abstain from doing any act, the proper method of proceeding is by action, the procedure for which has been described above. Proceedings in the county court which do not fall into this category are commenced by originating application unless any Act or rule requires that they be commenced otherwise.[20]

An originating application may be likened to an originating summons in the High Court. It is appropriate where the applicant seeks an order of the court which does not amount to a claim for relief from another person. Thus the person who seeks an adoption order, a declaration of legitimacy, or an order under the Landlord and Tenant Acts will commence proceedings by originating application. Notice of the application must be served on the proper respondent; for example, an application for a declaration of legitimacy must be served on the Attorney-General and all persons whose

---

19 Ord 21, r 2. For judicial discretion, see *Clack v Arthur's Engineering Ltd* [1959] 2 QB 211; [1959] 2 All ER 503.
20 Ord 3, r 4. Proceedings may also be by petition where any Act or rule so provides.

interests might be affected by the declaration. If the respondent wishes to resist the application he must file an answer, following which there will be a hearing before the judge or district judge. Since there is no plaint, but only an application, the parties are described not as "plaintiff" and "defendant" but as "applicant" and "respondent".

4   Costs in the county court

The position as to costs between a party and his own solicitor has already been considered in connection with High Court litigation. As between the parties, the court has a judicial discretion over costs,[1] but as a rule the successful party will recover his costs from his opponent, as in the High Court.

a   Scales of costs

The essential distinction between High Court and county court costs is that the latter are fixed in amount by reference to scales[2] according to the sum claimed or recovered in the action or, where the claim is not only a money claim, according to the discretion of the court.

For the regulation of solicitors' charges and disbursements, other than court fees, there are three scales of costs. If the plaintiff succeeds the scale is determined by the amount for which he recovers judgment. If the plaintiff fails the scale is determined by the amount of the plaintiff's claim. The court has a discretion to award costs on a higher or lower scale than the one applicable in certain cases, notably if the judge certifies that a difficult question of law or fact is involved.[3] Where the claim is less than £25 the court cannot allow any solicitors' charges unless the judge certifies that a "difficult question of law or a question of fact of exceptional complexity" is involved.[4] No fee for counsel can be awarded where the defendant, in an action for money alone, delivers no defence and does not appear at the hearing, unless the judge or district judge at the hearing otherwise orders.[5] The judge also has a power to award a fixed sum by way of costs.[6]

b   Assessment of costs

Certain items are fixed in amount. For example, when a summons is issued in an action where the only relief claimed is a sum of money liquidated or unliquidated, the court fee and the charges of the plaintiff's solicitor for the issue of the summons are fixed and are entered on the summons. Accordingly, if the defendant within 14 days of service pays the sum claimed and costs into court, or pays in a lesser sum with an admission of liability which the plaintiff accepts in satisfaction, the defendant is generally liable for no further costs beyond those stated on the summons. This

---

1 Ord 38, r 1.
2 These scales do not apply to bankruptcy, divorce or Companies Act proceedings (where special scales apply).
3 Ord 38, r 9.
4 Ord 38, r 4(6).
5 Ord 38, r 8(2).
6 Ord 38, r 3D.

may, of course, cause hardship to a plaintiff who has already incurred expense, for example by obtaining a medical report or by having particulars of claim settled by counsel. Where costs are on the lower scale they must be assessed as a lump sum.[7] In other cases the costs will be taxed according to the appropriate scale; the basis of taxation within the scale is similar to that applicable in the High Court so that taxation will almost always be on a "standard" basis.[8] The district judge may fix and allow costs without taxation if the successful party so requests. Otherwise they must be taxed unless the parties agree an amount of costs in lieu of taxation.[9]

c   Taxation of costs

The district judge is the taxing officer of the court. The successful party must, within three months of the order for costs, lodge a bill of costs with the registrar and obtain an appointment for taxation. He must serve a copy of this bill on his opponent and give him not less than 14 days' notice of the appointment.[10]

On taxation the district judge will allow, in accordance with the scale, a reasonable amount for each item incurred. The judge may, at the trial, expressly authorise the district judge to allow an amount in respect of certain items, such as counsel's fee, in excess of the scale maximum. In this event the district judge may allow such sum as he considers reasonable in respect of these items. Where an item is not provided for in the scales the district judge may or may not in his discretion make an allowance in respect of it. The district judge certifies the total amount due on taxation in his *allocatur* which is endorsed on the bill.

d   Review of taxation[11]

Any party not satisfied with a taxation may apply to the district judge to review his taxation; the application must set out the disputed items and the grounds of objection. The district judge will then certify in writing his reasons for allowing or disallowing the disputed items. If dissatisfied with this review, any party may apply to the judge for a review. The judge then has the equivalent powers of the district judge in his review. He cannot upset the discretion of the district judge unless the exercise of this discretion was based upon a wrong principle of law.[12] There is a further appeal to the Court of Appeal, with leave of the judge, if a question of legal principle is involved.[13]

5   Execution and enforcement of judgments

a   Judgments for the payment of money

Where the judgment or order directs the payment of money, the methods of enforcing the judgment are similar to those available in the High Court, ie execution against the debtor's personal property, garnishee proceedings,

---

7 Ord 38, r 19, App C. Because of the lower scale limit (£100), costs on this basis are rarely
   encountered.
8 See p 384, *ante*.   9 Ord 38, r 19.
10 Ord 38, r 20.   11 Ord 38, r 24.
12 *White v Altrincham Urban District Council* [1936] 2 KB 138; [1936] 1 All ER 923.
13 *Goodman v Blake* (1887) 19 QBD 77; Supreme Court Act 1981, s 18(1)(f).

appointment of a receiver, creation of a charge over the debtor's land, or partnership interest or other assets,[14] and bankruptcy proceedings. County court judgments used not to carry interest. This was an anomalous and unjust state of affairs since High Court judgments have carried interest since the Judgments Act 1838. It has now been remedied by order made under section 74 of the Act.[15] Furthermore the important jurisdiction to make attachment of earnings orders under the Attachment of Earnings Act 1971, which in the High Court is limited to the enforcement of maintenance orders, is, in county courts, exercisable in respect of maintenance orders, judgment debts of £15 or more and administration orders.[16]

Finally mention may be made of the judgment summons. This was, until relatively recently, a widely used procedure to enforce both county court and High Court judgments. However, as noted below, the drastic curtailment of the power to commit to prison for default in paying civil debts in favour of the power to make attachment of earnings orders has rendered judgment summonses inappropriate in all but a very few cases.

Execution — Execution is effected by warrant of execution issued to the county court bailiff which is in the nature of a writ of *fieri facias*.[17] The warrant directs the bailiff to execute upon the debtor's personal property for the judgment debt, costs and interest. The rules relating to property which is exempt from execution, method of execution and interpleader proceedings are similar to those in the High Court. A judgment creditor seeking the issue of a warrant of execution must file the appropriate request in the court office. A notice is usually sent to the defendant telling him that a warrant has been issued and that if he pays the debt there will be no need to execute the warrant. This often results in the warrant being paid out. As an alternative the plaintiff may agree to suspend the warrant on condition that the debt and costs are paid within a specified time or by instalments.[18] In fact most warrants are paid out or suspended in this way and only in a small proportion of cases does the warrant have to be executed. The warrant, once issued, remains in force for one year from the date of issue unless renewed. The bailiff seizes sufficient goods to satisfy the warrant and either deposits them in a proper place, such as a warehouse or auction room, or takes "walking possession" of them. There will then be a sale of such goods as are sufficient to satisfy the judgment debt including costs. In order that the bailiff does not sell too much, he will have the goods "appraised", usually by a local auctioneer who also deals with the storage and sale of the goods. The sale is usually by public auction

---

14 See p 387, *ante*.

15 Introduced by Supreme Court Act 1981; see County Courts (Interest on Judgment Debts) Order 1991 (SI 1991/1184).

16 Attachment of Earnings Act 1971, s 1(2); see p 409, *post*. Under the same section, magistrates' courts have power to make attachment of earnings orders in respect of maintenance orders, fines and analogous impositions and legal aid contributions; accordingly the use of attachment of earnings orders to enforce ordinary judgment debts is confined to county courts.

17 County Courts Act 1984, s 85.

18 If a suspended warrant has taken effect, there is no power to suspend it further: *Moore v Lambeth County Court Registrar* [1969] 1 All ER 782; [1969] 1 WLR 141; cf, however, *R v Bloomsbury and Marylebone County Court, ex parte Villerwest Ltd* [1976] 1 All ER 897; [1976] 1 WLR 362.

following advertisement and, where the execution is for a sum exceeding £20, must be by public auction unless the court directs otherwise.[19]

The jurisdiction of the county courts is local. This rule applies to the county courts' jurisdiction over the execution of warrants. Thus where the debtor has property outside the jurisdiction of the county court from which the warrant against him was issued (called the "home court"), the warrant must be sent to the district judge of the county court for that district for execution.[1]

Attachment of earnings — Prior to 1970, attachment of earnings orders could only be made in matrimonial causes under the provisions of the Maintenance Orders Act 1958. Following recommendations of the Payne Committee[2] the procedure was extended by the Administration of Justice Act 1970 to judgment debts generally in virtual substitution for the powers of committal to prison under the Debtors Act 1869, though, as noted below, the power of committal was retained in a few cases. The relevant provisions of the 1970 Act were repealed and consolidated by the Attachment of Earnings Act 1971.

An application for an attachment of earnings order may be made by the person entitled to the benefit of the judgment or order, where the relevant order is an administration order[3] by any of the creditors scheduled to the order or (where the application is for an order to secure maintenance payments) by the judgment debtor himself.[4] The application is generally to the court for the district in which the debtor resides and must be served, in the same manner as a fixed date summons, not less than 21 clear days before the return day. The debtor must then, within eight days of service, complete and return a form containing full details of his employment, pay and income, financial liabilities and proposals for payment of the debt,[5] which proposals are notified to the applicant. The district judge may by notice require any person appearing to have the debtor in his employment to supply particulars of the debtor's earnings.

The application is heard by the district judge who may hear it in chambers, evidence being given by affidavit. If the debtor does not attend, the district judge may adjourn the hearing and notify the debtor of the date of the adjourned hearing; if the debtor then fails to attend or attends but refuses to give evidence, he may be imprisoned by the judge for up to 14 days.

An attachment of earnings order may be made in respect of any sums

---

19 County Courts Act 1984, s 97.
 1 *Ibid*, s 103.
 2 Cmnd 3909 of 1969.
 3 *Infra*.
 4 Attachment of Earnings Act 1971, s 3(1).
 5 *Ibid*, s 14; Ord 25, r 81; Form N56. Failure to comply with this or other requirements under the Act is an offence punishable as a contempt of court with imprisonment for not more than 14 days (*ibid*, s 23).

payable by way of wages or salary or by way of pension.[6] The order requires the debtor's employer to make periodical deductions from the debtor's earnings and to pay them to the collecting officer of the court; the order specifies the "normal deduction rate" and the "protected earnings rate", the latter being the amount which the court decides the debtor must retain out of his earnings in any event.[7] It is the duty of both debtor and employer to notify the court of changes in the debtor's employment. As long as an attachment of earnings order is in force, no execution for the recovery of the judgment debt may issue without the leave of the court.[8]

Judgment summons — This is a method of enforcing a judgment for the payment of money in that it enables the court to ascertain the debtor's means, to order payment of the debt by instalments (where the debt is a High Court debt it is not likely that the debtor will have had an opportunity to pay by instalments) and, as a final sanction, to imprison the debtor.

Imprisonment for civil debt as such was abolished by the Debtors Act 1869, section 4. However there remained a few cases under that Act in which a defaulting judgment debtor might be committed to prison. These are contained in section 5 of the Act which empowers any court to commit to prison for a term not exceeding six weeks or until payment of the sum due any person who defaults in paying a debt, or instalment of a debt, due from him under any order of that or any other competent court. This power can only be exercised by a judge who must be satisfied that the defaulter has, or has had, since the date of the judgment against him, the means to pay. It does not, therefore, render a defaulter liable to imprisonment where he simply has not the means to pay. His conduct must be in the nature of a contempt.[9]

However the power to commit under section 5 of the Debtors Act was severely curtailed by the Administration of Justice Act 1970, and the power is now exercisable by county courts only in respect of High Court or county court maintenance orders and orders for the payment of certain debts of a public nature such as income tax and national insurance contributions.[10]

Imprisonment does not extinguish the debt, although the debtor cannot be committed twice in respect of the same debt (though he can be committed separately in respect of separate instalments of the same debt). Since the 1970 Act, imprisonment in respect of civil debt is extremely rare and the judgment summons is of far less practical importance than formerly. Furthermore on a judgment summons the court has power, instead of making a committal order, to make an attachment of earnings order.[11]

The plaintiff must file the appropriate request in the office of the county court for the district where the debtor resides or carries on business. Where the judgment in question is not a county court judgment he must also produce an office copy of the judgment or order, an affidavit verifying the

---

6 Attachment of Earnings Act 1971, s 24.
7 *Ibid*, s 6. There is provision for variation and discharge of orders in s 9–11 of the Act.
8 *Ibid*, s 8.
9 *Re Edgcome* [1902] 2 KB 403.
10 Administration of Justice Act 1970, s 11, Sch 4.
11 Attachment of Earnings Act 1971, s 3(4), (6).

amount due and a copy of the sheriff's return to any writ of execution issued in the High Court.[12] The county court will then issue a judgment summons which is served on the defendant not less than 14 days before the day fixed for the hearing.[13]

At the hearing there will be an enquiry into the debtor's means. The judgment creditor may give evidence, orally or by affidavit, as to the debtor's means and the debtor will also be required to undergo a sworn examination as to his means. If he does not appear at the hearing the judge may adjourn the hearing and order the defendant to attend the adjourned hearing. This order must be served personally on the defendant not less than five clear days before the date fixed for the adjourned hearing.[14] If he does not attend then the judge may commit him to prison for not more than 14 days.[15]

If the judge is satisfied that the debtor has had the means to pay the debt but has not done so he may commit the defendant to prison for a term not exceeding six weeks. In fact the judge usually makes an order for payment by instalments if this has not already been done. If the judgment summons was issued in respect of a default on an instalment the judge will more readily make a committal order but even then it will usually be suspended provided the debt is paid within a specified time.

Administration orders — The great advantage of attachment of earnings orders is that they provide a means of intercepting the earnings of judgment debtors and thereby ensuring, so far as possible, that the debtor with insufficient assets to justify execution process pays his debts, albeit slowly. By the nature of things it is often the case that a judgment debtor has outstanding against him not one but several judgment debts. In such a case there is provision in the Attachment of Earnings Act 1971[16] for the making of a "consolidated attachment order" which is an attachment of earnings order for the payment of two or more judgment debts.

An alternative procedure in the case of insolvent debtors lies in the power of county courts to make administration orders. An administration order is an order providing for the administration of the debtor's estate by the court. The court may make such an order, under section 112 of the County Courts Act 1984[17] on the application of a debtor, creditor who has obtained a judgment against the debtor or on the motion of the court itself. The court also has an independent power under section 4 of the Attachment of Earnings Act 1971 to make an administration order on an application for an attachment of earnings order to secure payment of a judgment debt if it is of the opinion that the case is one in which all the debtor's liabilities should be dealt with together; if of the opinion that it may be such a case the court may order the debtor to furnish to the court a list of all his creditors and the amounts which he owes to them and if it

---

12 Ord 25, r 11.

13 Ord 28, r 3.

14 Ord 27, r 8; Ord 28, r 4.

15 County Courts Act 1984, s 110.

16 Section 17. Application for a consolidated attachment order may be made by the debtor or by any person who has obtained or is entitled to apply for an attachment of earnings order or, in certain circumstances, the court may make such an order of its own motion. Payments made under the order are divided pro rata among the creditors (Ord 41, r 18).

17 As amended by Courts and Legal Services Act 1990, s 13(5). These amendments are not yet in force.

appears that his total indebtedness does not exceed the county court limit the court may make an administration order.

Where an administration order has been made, any creditor, on proof of his debt before the district judge, is entitled to be scheduled as a creditor of the debtor for the amount of his proof.[18] Where the debtor applies for an order, he must file a request, verified on oath.[19] Any person who becomes a creditor after the date of the order may be scheduled as a creditor but payment to him is deferred until those who were creditors before the making of the order have been paid.

The effect of an administration order is that no creditor has any remedy against the person or property of the debtor in respect of any debt which the debtor has notified to the court or which has been scheduled to the order except with leave of the court.[20] Furthermore no creditor whose name is included in the schedule may, without the leave of the county court, present or join in a bankruptcy petition unless his name was notified to the county court by the debtor, he is a creditor for a sum exceeding £400 and the petition is presented within 28 days of the creditor receiving notice that his name has been notified to the court.[1]

The court will, under the order, administer the debtor's estate and distribute his assets and instalments paid by him *pro rata* among his creditors. As has been noted, an administration order may itself be enforced by an attachment of earnings order. Further, if the debtor fails to make any payment which he is required to make by an administration order, the court may, if it thinks fit, revoke the administration order and make an order under section 429 of the Insolvency Act 1986.[2]

b   Other judgments

Warrants of delivery and possession — A judgment for the recovery of land or for the delivery of possession of land may be enforced by warrant of possession which corresponds to the writ of possession available in the High Court.[3]

Similarly, a judgment for the delivery of specific goods is enforced by warrant of delivery. There are different forms of warrant of delivery which enable the bailiff either to execute upon the defendant's goods to the value of the chattel, as if the warrant were a warrant of execution, or to seize the specific chattel which is the subject matter of the warrant.[4]

Committal — The power of county courts to commit a person for contempt of court may be compared with the power of committal in the High Court. Thus where a person has failed to comply with any order of the court, he may be committed. A copy of the order in question must be

---

18 County Courts Act 1984, s 113.
19 Ord 39, rr 1, 3.
20 County Courts Act 1984, s 114(1).
 1 *Ibid*, s 112(4).
 2 The effect of such an order is to restrict a person's entitlement to obtain credit or enter into business transactions (see s 429(3)).
 3 Ord 26, r 17. There is power to suspend warrants (and this is often exercised in landlord and tenant cases). If a suspended warrant has taken effect there is no power to suspend it further (*Moore v Lambeth County Court Registrar* [1969] 1 All ER 782; [1969] 1 WLR 141) except in Rent Act cases, where the power to suspend possession is indefinite (*Yates v Morris* [1951] 1 KB 77; [1950] 2 All ER 577).
 4 Ord 26, r 16.

served on the defendant personally, warning him of the consequences of his disobedience. If the defendant still fails to comply with the order he will be required to attend the court and show cause why he should not be committed to prison. If he does not show cause, the judge may order a warrant of committal to issue for his arrest and imprisonment.

There are various other penal sanctions available to the county court. Thus a person who assaults an officer of the court in the execution of his duty is liable to imprisonment for up to three months or to a fine not exceeding level 5 on the standard scale,[5] while a person who wilfully insults the judge, any juror or witness or any officer of the court or wilfully interrupts the proceedings or otherwise misbehaves in court may by order of the judge be taken into custody and detained until the rising of the court and thereafter is liable to be committed to prison for up to one month and to a fine not exceeding level 4 on the standard scale.[6] These provisions are additional to the general provisions of the Contempt of Court Act 1981.[7]

C   MATRIMONIAL CAUSES PROCEDURE

Both the county court and High Court have jurisdiction in matrimonial causes but generally divorce and other such proceedings should be commenced in one of the divorce county courts[8] unless by reason of their complexity, difficulty or gravity they ought to be commenced in the High Court.[9]

A matrimonial cause is commenced by filing a petition in any divorce county court.[10] The form of petition is prescribed by the Matrimonial Causes Rules 1977; in addition to various formal matters the petition must contain the names of the parties, details of the marriage, the names of all children of the family, particulars of previous proceedings between the parties and details of grounds upon which relief is sought. In a divorce suit the petition must state that "the said marriage has broken down irretrievably" and must then allege which of the five facts set out in section 1(2) of the Matrimonial Causes Act 1973 the petitioner relies upon as proof of breakdown. The petition concludes with a prayer for the relief sought, which, in the case of divorce, is "that the said marriage may be dissolved", including any claim for a financial provision, costs or custody of children of the family.

The petitioner must file copies of the petition for each person to be served and their names and addresses are annexed to the petition. With the petition the petitioner must file a written statement containing details of the present and proposed arrangements for the residence, education, financial provision and contact with all children of the family

---

5 County Courts Act 1984, s 14; as to the "standard scale" see p 384, *ante*.
6 *Ibid*, s 118.
7 See p 191, *ante*.
8 As nominated by Family Proceedings Rules 1991, r 2.2 (SI 1991/1247).
9 See *Practice Direction (Family Division: Distribution of Business)* [1992] 3 All ER 151; [1992] 1 WLR 586.
10 Family Proceedings Rules contain various provisions for transfer of matrimonial causes to the High Court. The Matrimonial and Family Proceedings Act 1984, s 39 confers an unrestricted power on county courts to transfer family proceedings to the High Court, either of the court's own motion or on the application of any part to the proceedings.

under 16.[11] In addition, where a solicitor is acting for a petitioner for divorce or judicial separation a certificate as to whether or not he has discussed with the petitioner the possibility of a reconciliation must be filed with the petition. Unless the petitioner otherwise requests the petition, together with forms of notice of proceedings and acknowledgment of service, is served by post through the court. There is no entry of appearance although a party may, within eight days of service, give "notice of intention to defend." Within 21 days of the time-limit for giving notice of intention to defend the respondent may file an answer. If an answer to the petition is filed the proceedings become defended.[12] The answer contains the respondent's defence to the allegations in the petition, together with any claim for relief which the respondent wishes to make. If an answer is filed the petitioner has 14 days in which to file a reply. The following interlocutory proceedings are similar to those in the Queen's Bench Division and may include such matters as particulars of pleading, discovery of documents and interrogatories. These are closed by the district judge giving "directions for trial"[13] whereupon the case is set down. The trial is similar to the trial of any other civil action and takes place before a judge who deals with the relief sought and ancillary matters such as custody and costs. Financial matters are usually dealt with by district judges, with a right of appeal to a judge, the appeal taking the form of a complete rehearing.[14]

Special procedure list

On 1 December 1973 a new procedure was introduced[15] for the granting of decrees nisi of divorce or decrees of judicial separation, virtually without a hearing. Originally limited to cases of two years' separation and consent, it now extends to undefended petitions for divorce or judicial separation on any ground.

In cases to which these rules apply there is a special form of application for directions for trial which must be lodged together with an affidavit of evidence by the petitioner (and by any corroborative witness) in the prescribed form. If the district judge is satisfied that the petitioner has sufficiently proved the contents of the petition and is entitled to a decree he files a certificate to this effect whereupon a day will be fixed for the pronouncement of a decree by a judge in open court, notification of the day and place fixed being given to the parties. Where there are children of the family to whom section 41 of the 1973 Act applies (in relation to whose welfare the court has certain duties of enquiry under that section) and the respondent has neither applied for custody of or access to the children, nor returned an acknowledgment of service stating that he objects to the

---

11 And those minor children over 16 who are receiving instruction at an educational establishment or undergoing training for a trade, profession or vocation: Family Proceedings Rules, r 8(2); Form 4.

12 Until the implementation of the Matrimonial and Family Proceedings Act 1984, this required the case to be transferred to the Family Division of the High Court. This is no longer the case.

13 FPR, r 33; cf the summons for directions in the Queen's Bench Division; see p 358, *ante*.

14 *G (formerly P) v P (ancillary relief; appeal)* [1978] 1 All ER 1099; [1978] 1 WLR 1376; cf appeals from masters (and district judges) to judges in the Queen's Bench Division (p 418, *post*).

15 Matrimonial Causes (Amendment No 2) Rules 1973.

petitioner's claim for custody or wishes to apply on his own account, nor filed a statement as to arrangements for children proposing arrangements which differ materially from the petitioner's proposals, the district judge will fix an appointment for a judge in chambers to consider the arrangements for the children and notify the parties of that appointment.

On the day fixed it is unnecessary for the petitioner to appear at court or be represented; the cases are called on in a group, and, if no cause is shown to the contrary, decrees are automatically pronounced.[16]

D TRANSFER OF PROCEEDINGS

1 From one county court to another

It must be remembered that the jurisdiction of the county courts is local, so that the plaintiff is restricted in his choice of venue. This must generally be in the court for the district in which the defendant or one of the defendants resides or carries on business, or where the cause of action wholly or in part arose. Where proceedings are commenced in the wrong county court, the judge of that court may transfer them to the court in which they ought to have been commenced.[17]

Where an action is commenced in the proper court it may still be transferred to another county court. The judge or district judge may transfer the proceedings to another court if he is satisfied that they can more conveniently or fairly be tried in that court. Secondly, where an action has been commenced in a county court against a defendant who does not reside or carry on business within the district of that court, the latter may after delivering a defence apply *ex parte* in writing for an order transferring the proceedings to the county court for the district in which he does reside or carry on business.[18]

Finally, a judgment summons can only be issued in the county court for the district in which the defendant resides or carries on business and certain other proceedings for enforcement are confined to the debtor's local court. Thus where the action in which the judgment was obtained took place in some other court, proceedings must be transferred to the court having jurisdiction over the enforcement proceedings. The action is then transferred for all purposes to the latter court, so that money paid by the defendant must be paid to the court to which the proceedings are transferred.[19]

2 Transfer between county court and the High Court

It was noted earlier[20] that the jurisdiction of county and High Court is now largely concurrent. The criteria determining the appropriate court of trial were noted, and these apply equally to issues of transfer as to the commencement of the action.[1]

---

16 See *Practice Direction (Matrimonial Causes; Special Procedure)* [1977] 1 All ER 845; [1977] 1 WLR 320.
17 See p 398, *ante*.
18 Ord 16, r 4(1). See p 399, *ante*.
19 Ord 25, r 2. The proceedings in question are judgment summonses, applications for charging orders under s 1 of the Charging Orders Act 1979, for attachment of earnings orders and for orders for the oral examination of a debtor under Ord 25, r 3.
20 See p 277, *ante*.
 1 See p 278, *ante*.

CHAPTER 21

Civil Appeals

A RIGHTS OF APPEAL

There is no common law right of appeal from a superior court. It was established in *Darlow v Shuttleworth*[1] that the common law jurisdiction of the Court of King's Bench to hear proceedings in error from the inferior courts of local jurisdiction was transferred by the Judicature Acts to the divisional court of the Queen's Bench Division. However since this right of appeal is confined to situations in which proceedings in error might have been brought at common law and since the local courts have ceased to function[2] common law rights of appeal are virtually obsolete. Apart from this all rights of appeal are statutory. The basic rights of appeal in the Supreme Court are now contained in the Supreme Court Act 1981 although numerous statutes create particular rights of appeal in special cases.

1 Appeal to the Court of Appeal; civil division

The fulcrum of the system of civil appeals is the civil division of the Court of Appeal. In a number of cases the Court of Appeal hears appeals directly from the decision of the court below. In other cases the appeal lies to the High Court in the first instance and then to the Court of Appeal.

Section 16(1) of the Supreme Court Act 1981 provides:

> "subject as otherwise provided by this or any other Act...the Court of Appeal shall have jurisdiction to hear and determine appeals from any judgment or order of the High Court."[3]

Appeals from county courts lie, subject to the conditions set out in section 77 of the County Courts Act 1984, to the Court of Appeal with the single exception of appeals from orders in bankruptcy matters which lie in the first instance to a divisional court of the Chancery Division and thence with special leave to the Court of Appeal.

The Court of Appeal also has jurisdiction to hear appeals from the

---

1 [1902] 1 KB 721.
2 See p 4, *ante*.
3 Where the House of Lords grants leave to appeal direct from the High Court to the House, appeal to the Court of Appeal is excluded (Administration of Justice Act 1969, s 13(2)).

Employment Appeal Tribunal,[4] the Restrictive Practices Court,[5] the Lands Tribunal[6] and certain other statutory tribunals[7] and from commercial judges sitting as arbitrators or umpires under section 4 of the Administration of Justice Act 1970.

a Leave to appeal

As a general rule appeal lies to the Court of Appeal as of right but in certain cases leave is required. The more important cases in which leave is required are:

(1) from the determination of an appeal by a divisional court of the High Court;[8] leave may be given either by the divisional court or by the Court of Appeal;

(2) from a consent order or an order which is solely an order as to costs which by law are left to the discretion of the court; leave can only be granted by the court below;[9]

(3) from an interlocutory order or judgment made or given by a judge (with certain exceptions, notably where the liberty of the subject or the custody of infants is involved or where an injunction or the appointment of a receiver has been granted or refused);[10]

(4) from the decision of a county court judge, where the value of the claim in contract, tort or certain other monetary claims does not exceed £5,000, or in other cases within the equity and probate

---

4 Employment Protection (Consolidation) Act 1978, s 136(4); appeal lies only on a point of law.

5 Restrictive Practices Court Act 1976, s 10.

6 Lands Tribunal Act 1949, s 3(4). Appeal from tribunals is by case stated on a point of law. The procedure is governed by Ord 61.

7 Transport Tribunal, Commons Commissioners, Foreign Compensation Commission.

8 Supreme Court Act 1981, s 18(1)(e). Leave may be granted by the House of Lords for an appeal direct to the House from the divisional court (Administration of Justice Act 1969, s 12(2)(c)). See also Tribunals and Inquiries Act 1992, s 13(4) as to appeals under that Act.

9 Supreme Court Act 1981, s 18(1)(f). Although the Court of Appeal will, despite this statutory restriction, entertain on appeal where it adjudges that the court below has in effect failed to exercise its discretion at all: see *Alltrans Express Ltd v CVA Holdings Ltd* [1984] 1 All ER 685; [1984] 1 WLR 394 and the cases cited therein. Where there are genuine grounds of appeal in addition to an appeal against an order as to costs the appeal is not as to costs only even if all the other grounds of appeal are unsuccessful: *Wheeler v Somerfield* [1966] 2 QB 94; [1966] 2 All ER 305.

10 Supreme Court Act 1981, s 18(1)(h). Whether an order is final or interlocutory depends on the nature of the application to the court rather than the nature of the order made. Thus, for example, the refusal of a county court judge to order a new trial is an interlocutory order as is an order dismissing an action for want of prosecution (see p 317, *ante*), even though the practical effect may be final in that the action is at an end; the test stated above was laid down by the Court of Appeal in *Salter Rex & Co v Ghosh* [1971] 2 QB 597; [1971] 2 All ER 865 and applied in *Moran v Lloyd's* [1983] QB 542; [1983] 2 All ER 200 and *White v Brunton* [1984] QB 570; [1984] 2 All ER 606. Order 59, r 1A (made under power conferred by s 60 of the Supreme Court Act 1981) lists orders which, for this purpose, are to be treated as final or interlocutory, as the case may be.

jurisdiction, does not exceed £15,000.[11] Leave is not required where the determination sought to be appealed from includes or preserves an injunction or relates to upbringing of a child;

(5) from the decision of a commercial judge on an arbitration appeal.[12]

b   Right of appeal excluded

Although section 16 of the Supreme Court Act 1981 confers a general right of appeal from the High Court to the Court of Appeal there are certain cases specified in the Act and in the Rules in which the right of appeal is excluded. Of these the most important are:

(1) from any judgment of the High Court in any criminal cause or matter.[13] In fact it is not true to say that these appeals do not lie to the Court of Appeal; they do not lie to the civil division of the Court of Appeal but they generally do lie to the criminal division with the notable exception of appeals from the divisional court of the Queen's Bench Division which lie, under the Administration of Justice Act 1960, direct to the House of Lords;[14]

(2) from a decision which is provided by any statute to be final;[15]

(3) from a decree absolute for dissolution or nullity of marriage provided that the party wishing to appeal had time and opportunity to appeal from the decree nisi;[16]

(4) from any judgment order or decision of a circuit judge in the course of official referees' business except as provided in Order 58, rule 4.[17]

c   Appeals from the registrar and the single judge

An application for leave to appeal to the Court of Appeal is determined by a single judge and there is no appeal from his decision.[18] Other applications are, according to their nature, heard either by the full court, or by a single judge or by the registrar of civil appeals. An appeal lies

---

11 For the complete list, see County Court Appeals Order 1981.

12 Arbitration Act 1979, s 1(7); in this case a second prerequisite is that the judge certify that the question of law to which his decision relates either is of general public importance or is one which for some other special reason should be considered by the Court of Appeal. Note also Ord 58, r 7 under which appeal of the summary determination by a judge of a stakeholder's interpleader lies only with leave.

13 Supreme Court Act 1981, s 18(1)(a). An appeal from, or application for leave for, an application for judicial review of a decision not to refer a conviction to the Court of Appeal (Criminal Division) under Criminal Appeal Act 1968, s 17 (see p 514, *post*) is a "criminal cause or matter": *R v Secretary of State for the Home Department, ex p Garner* ((1991) 3 Admin LR 33). The key issue is the nature of the matter being reviewed in the judicial review proceedings: *Carr v Atkinson* [1987] QB 963; [1987] 3 All ER 684.

14 See p 419, *post*.

15 Supreme Court Act 1981, s 18(1)(c); *Lane v Esdaile* [1891] AC 210. Statutes under which an appeal to the High Court is final are listed in Ord 94, r 6.

16 *Ibid*, s 18(1)(d).

17 Under Ord 58, r 4(1) an appeal lies from a decision of an official referee on a point of law or as to costs or, with the leave of the official referee or the Court of Appeal on any question of fact. There is, in addition, a right to appeal against a committal order made by an official referee under the Administration of Justice Act 1960, s 13.

18 Supreme Court Act 1981, s 54(6).

from the registrar to a single judge.[19] Appeal from decisions of a single judge (other than the determination of an application for leave to appeal) lies to the full court.[20]

2 Appeals from masters and district registrars

The general rule is that an appeal lies as of right from any order of a Queen's Bench Division master to a judge in chambers.[1] In certain exceptional cases, set out in Order 58, rule 2, appeal lies from a master direct to the Court of Appeal. These are appeals from any judgment, order or decision (other than an interlocutory judgment, order or decision) given or made:

   (a)   on the hearing or determination of any cause, matter, question or issue tried before or referred to him under Order 36, rule 11 (power to order trial by or reference of issues of fact to a master);
   (b)   on an assessment of damages or the value of goods .[2]

Appeals from masters and district registrars take the form of a complete rehearing; that is to say the issue which was argued below is argued out again *de novo* before the judge. Since it is a complete rehearing, the parties are not confined to the points which were taken before the master. Nor are they confined to the evidence which was before the master and it is quite common for further evidence, in the form of affidavits, to be put in before the judge.

3 Appeal to the House of Lords

In civil matters appeal lies from the civil division of the Court of Appeal to the House of Lords only with leave of the Court of Appeal or of the House of Lords.[3] There is no requirement that the appeal be based on a point of law, though almost always appeal to the House of Lords is based upon a point of law rather than on an issue of fact or an award of damages. Although leave is the only prerequisite for appealing, no appeal lies from the decision of the Court of Appeal where any statute expresses the decision of the Court of Appeal to be final. Thus, for example, the decision of the court is final on any appeal from a county court in probate proceedings[4] and from the determination by a divisional court of the Chancery Division of a bankruptcy appeal from a county court.[5]

The Administration of Justice Act 1969, Part II provides for a "leapfrog" appeal direct from the High Court to the House of Lords subject to the

---

19 Ord 59, r 14(11); the appeal is by way of fresh application made within 10 days of the district judge's determination (*ibid*) and the single judge approaches the matter de novo unfettered by the registrar's decision: *Van Stillevoldt (CM) BV v El Carriers Inc* [1983] 1 All ER 699; [1983] 1 WLR 207.
20 Ord 59, r 14(12); the appeal is by way of fresh application made within 10 days of the single judge's determination.
 1 Ord 58, r 1. Likewise, appeal from any order of a district judge (Ord 58, r 3).
 2 An appeal lies in respect of any other matter that requires determination in order to assess the damages or value: RSC (Amendment) 1992/638.
 3 Administration of Justice (Appeals) Act 1934, s 1.
 4 County Courts Act 1984, s 82.
 5 Insolvency Act 1986, s 375.

grant of a certificate by the trial judge and of leave by the House of Lords in any case in which appeal lies to the Court of Appeal (with or without leave).[6]

For the purpose of European Community law the House of Lords is clearly "a court or tribunal of a Member State, against whose decisions there is no judicial remedy under national law" within the meaning of Article 177(3) of the EC Treaty, so that where a question arises concerning (a) the interpretation of the Treaty; (b) the validity and interpretation of acts of the institutions of the Community; or (c) the interpretation of the statutes of bodies established by an Act of the Council, where those statutes so provide, the House of Lords is bound to refer that question to the European Court for a preliminary ruling (unless, of course, the High Court or Court of Appeal has already referred the question in the same case) and, having obtained the ruling, is bound to follow it.[7]

B   PROCEDURE IN THE COURT OF APPEAL

Substantial amendments to procedure in the Court of Appeal were made by the Supreme Court Act 1981 and, more particularly, by a revision of Order 59 in 1982. These changes, and the reasons for them, were fully explained at the time by the Master of the Rolls, SIR JOHN DONALDSON.[8] The most important changes were; the creation of a new office of registrar of civil appeals,[9] much wider use of two-judge courts, allocation of interlocutory applications to the registrar or to a single judge, standardisation of the time for appealing, alteration of the listing arrangements and the introduction of a practice of handing down written judgments.

An appeal is initiated by serving notice of motion in respect of the whole or any part of the judgment or order in respect of which the appeal is brought. This notice must set out the grounds of appeal shortly but with sufficient particularity to enable the respondent to ascertain exactly what issues are being raised against him. Thus, merely to complain that the trial judge misdirected the jury would be inadequate; the particular nature of the misdirection must be specified. The notice must also contain a statement of the order for which the appellant is applying to the court, and the list in which he proposes to set down the appeal. The notice must be served on all parties interested in the appeal.[10] Notice of appeal must be served within

---

6 See p 416, *ante*; the principal conditions precedent to the grant of a certificate are (1) the consent of all parties, and (2) that the case involves a point of law of general public importance either relating to the construction of an enactment or being a point on which the judge was bound by precedent: *American Cyanamid Co v Upjohn Co* [1970] 3 All ER 785; [1970] 1 WLR 1507, a case concerning a petition for revocation of a patent, was the first "leap-frog" appeal heard by the House of Lords.

7 See, generally, *HP Bulmer Ltd v J Bollinger, SA* [1974] Ch 401; [1974] 2 All ER 1226, and p 114, *ante*.

8 The statement is reported as *Practice Note* [1982] 3 All ER 376; [1982] 1 WLR 1312 and repays study.

9 Supreme Court Act 1981, s 89(1), Sch 2. His functions include supervising the listing of appeals, giving directions as to the conduct of pending appeals (under Ord 59, r 9(3), (4)) and hearing interlocutory applications such as applications for extension of time, leave to amend a notice of appeal, security for costs, leave to adduce further evidence, expedition and vacating a hearing date.

10 Ord 59, r 3. Appeals from tribunals to the Court of Appeal are by case stated, the procedure being governed by Ord 61.

four weeks[11] of the date upon which judgment in the court below was signed or entered, though this time may be extended either by the Court of Appeal or, if application is made before the time expires, by the court below. Having served the notice of appeal, the appellant must within seven days apply to set down the appeal. To do so he produces an office copy of the judgment or order appealed from, together with two copies of his notice of appeal, one of which must bear the appropriate judicature fee stamp and an office copy of any list of exhibits made at the hearing.[12] The appeal is then set down in the appropriate list to await hearing. The next stage in the procedure is that the appeal will appear in the List of Forthcoming Appeals. Then, within 14 days, the appellant must lodge with the registrar bundles of the copy documents which are going to be required for the use of the court on the hearing; these include the notice of appeal, any respondent's notice, the judgment or order of the court below, the pleadings, a transcript of the official shorthand note of the judge's reasons (or a note of them if there is no official shorthand note), such part of the transcript of the official shorthand note of the evidence (or the judge's note if there is no official shorthand note) as is relevant to the appeal and such affidavits and exhibits used below as are relevant to the appeal.[13]

After the documents have been lodged the registrar may give such directions "as appear best adapted to secure the just, expeditious and economical disposal of the appeal" and may summon the parties to appear before him for this purpose.[14]

Thereafter the appeal will appear in the list of forthcoming appeals and will be listed for hearing. In order to save the time of the court in recording counsel's arguments, and in order to enable the court to examine those arguments in advance of the hearing, counsel submit in advance of the hearing "skeleton arguments" containing a numbered list of the points which each counsel proposes to argue and the references to the material to which counsel will refer in support of these points.[15]

Appeals may be heard by two or three judges of the court.[16]

Except in the case of applications for a new trial or to set aside a verdict, appeal is "by way of rehearing". That is to say the court hears full legal argument from both sides and may substitute its own judgment for that of the court below. However it is not a complete rehearing, as it is before the judge in chambers or in the Crown Court in criminal cases,

---

11 Ord 59, r 4. The only exceptions to the standard four-week period are: (1) six weeks in the case of appeals under s 14 of the Social Security Act 1980 (Ord 59, r 21) (see now Social Security Administration Act 1992, s 24); and (2) 14 days in the case of appeal from an order referring a question to the European Court (Ord 114, r 6).

12 Ord 59, r 5.

13 Ord 59, r 9; see also *Practice Note* [1986] 3 All ER 416, sub nom *Practice Direction* [1986] 1 WLR 1318 for further directions as to the manner in which the bundles should be prepared, bound and paginated.

14 Ord 59, r 9(3), (4).

15 *Practice Note* (n 13, *supra*).

16 Supreme Court Act 1981, s 54; if they are equally divided the case must, on the application of any party, be re-argued before another court containing an uneven number of judges (*ibid*, s 54(5)). The Court of Appeal has indicated that in complex cases, where a difference of judicial opinion may be anticipated, counsel should apply for a hearing before an uneven number: *Wandsworth London Borough Council v Winder* [1985] AC 461; [1984] 3 All ER 83.

since the court does not, in practice, hear again the testimony of the trial witnesses, but merely sees transcripts of their evidence.[17]

In addition the appellant is normally confined to the points of law which he raised in the court below. He may in certain circumstances, discussed below, be allowed to take new points on appeal but he cannot, except with leave of the Court of Appeal, rely on any grounds of appeal or apply for any relief not specified in his notice of appeal.[18]

Cross-appeal

A respondent who, not having appealed from the decision of the court below, seeks to have the judgment or order of the court below either varied or affirmed on other grounds need not enter a separate notice of appeal. His proper course is to serve on the appellant, and on any other party directly affected, a "respondent's notice" specifying the grounds of his contention and any alteration in the judgment or order which he requests. Thus, for example, if the appellant is appealing against a finding as to his liability the respondent may, by his notice, appeal against his award of damages. A respondent's notice must be served within 21 days of service of the notice of appeal, and the respondent must, within two days after service of the notice, file two copies of the notice.[19]

C POWERS OF THE COURT OF APPEAL

The Court of Appeal has all the powers, authority and jurisdiction of the court or tribunal from which the appeal was brought in any matter before it.[20] The court has power to examine trial witnesses though it rarely does so, being content in most cases to rely upon the judge's note or a transcript of the official shorthand note. It has power to receive further evidence orally, by affidavit or by deposition taken before an examiner but, where there was a trial or hearing on the merits, the Court of Appeal will not admit further evidence (other than evidence as to matters which have occurred since the trial) except on special grounds.[1] In *Ladd v Marshall*[2] DENNING, LJ, prescribed the following three conditions for the reception of fresh evidence in the Court of Appeal:[3]

> "first, it must be shown that the evidence could not have been obtained with reasonable diligence for use at the trial; secondly, the evidence must be such that, if given, it would probably have an important influence on the result of

---

17 Ord 59, r 12.

18 Ord 59, r 3(3).

19 Ord 59, r 6.

20 Supreme Court Act 1981, s 15. These powers are both statutory and inherent. Thus the Court of Appeal may strike out a notice of appeal in the same way as the High Court may strike out a statement of claim either under Ord 18, r 19 or in exercise of its inherent power: *Aviagents Ltd v Balstravest Investments Ltd* [1966] 1 All ER 450; [1966] 1 WLR 150.

1 Ord 59, r 10(2). A hearing under Ord 14 (as to which see p 319, *ante*) is a "hearing on the merits" for this purpose; *Langdale v Danby* [1982] 3 All ER 129; [1982] 1 WLR 1123.

2 [1954] 3 All ER 745; [1954] 1 WLR 1489; applied in *Roe v Robert McGregor & Sons Ltd* [1968] 2 All ER 636; [1968] 1 WLR 925.

3 [1954] 3 All ER 745, at 748; [1954] 1 WLR 1489, at 1491.

the case, though it need not be decisive; thirdly, the evidence must be such as is presumably to be believed, or, in other words, it must be apparently credible though it need not be incontrovertible."[4]

This statement was approved by the House of Lords in *Skone v Skone*[5] where the evidence consisted of a bundle of love letters written by the co-respondent in a divorce suit to the wife which tended to prove adultery between them. The trial judge had dismissed the husband's petition and accepted the co-respondent's evidence to the effect that adultery had not taken place. It was argued that these letters (which were in the possession of the wife) could have been obtained by seeking discovery of documents from the wife. The House of Lords rejected this argument on the basis that the husband had no reason to suspect the existence of such letters, that the letters, if genuine, falsified the judge's finding to such an extent that it would be unjust to leave matters where they were and, furthermore, that there was a strong prima facie case of deception of the court.

It must be emphasised that these rigorous conditions need not be satisfied in respect of evidence of matters occurring after the trial. Evidence will be admitted of matters occurring after the trial where the basis on which the trial judge gave his decision has been clearly falsified by subsequent events.[6]

Since appeal to the Court of Appeal is "by way of rehearing" the Court of Appeal has full power to make any order which should have been made in the court below[7] and to substitute its own order as to liability, quantum or costs for that of the court below. In addition the Court of Appeal is not confined to the points raised in the notice of appeal or respondent's notice. It may, though it rarely does, take any point of law or fact so far as is necessary to ensure the determination on the merits of the real question in issue between the parties. Should the Court of Appeal wish to decide an issue of fact which has not been pleaded, an extremely infrequent contingency, it may allow the pleading to be amended.[8]

The court has power to order an appellant to give security for the costs of an appeal in any case in which he could be required to give security for costs under Order 23[9] and, in addition, in "special circumstances"[10] generally where the appellant would be unable to pay the costs of the appeal if unsuccessful. Although an appeal does not operate as a stay of execution the Court of Appeal has power to order a stay of execution though it will only do so if there is some good reason, since it inclines against depriving a person of the fruits of his litigation. If a stay of

---

4 Compare the somewhat wider provisions for the reception of fresh evidence in the criminal division of the Court of Appeal; see p 520, *post*.

5 [1971] 2 All ER 582; [1971] 1 WLR 812.

6 *Mulholland v Mitchell* [1971] AC 666; [1971] 1 All ER 307 (in which the plaintiff's condition had unexpectedly deteriorated between the trial and the hearing of the appeal) and *McCann v Sheppard* [1973] 2 All ER 881; [1973] 1 WLR 540 (in which the plaintiff had died while his appeal was pending). Where the fresh evidence becomes available to a party during the trial he must adduce it then and there, even though this may necessitate an adjournment. He must not disregard it and thereafter found an application for a new trial upon the fresh evidence: *Cowling v Matbro Ltd* [1969] 2 All ER 664; [1969] 1 WLR 598.

7 Ord 59, r 10(3).

8 See *Bell v Lever Brothers Ltd* [1932] AC 161, at 216.

9 See p 355, *ante*.

10 Ord 59, r 10(5).

execution is ordered on an appeal from the High Court, interest is allowed on the judgment debt unless there is an express order to the contrary.[11]

Special note should be taken of the power, which the High Court also possesses, to refer a question to the European Court for a preliminary ruling. The procedure is governed by Order 114 and the principles upon which the Court of Appeal act have already been examined.[12]

In addition to the powers of the Court of Appeal listed above there is an extremely important power which the High Court does not possess.[13] This is the power to order a new trial, the exercise of which is considered in detail below.

D   THE APPROACH OF THE COURT OF APPEAL TO THE DETERMINATION OF APPEALS

1   Appeal on a point of law

Most appeals to the Court of Appeal are based on a point of law. It has already been stated that, notwithstanding the general power of the Court of Appeal to take a point not raised therein, the court usually confines itself to the points raised in the notice of appeal or respondent's notice. Furthermore there is a general rule that a party cannot take on appeal a point which he did not take in the court below.[14] To this rule there are two important exceptions. The first occurs where the point of law was expressly reserved in the court below. This might occur where the court below was not free to consider the point because it was bound by precedent on that point, whereas the Court of Appeal might be free to reconsider the precedent in question. Secondly, the Court of Appeal will allow a point to be taken, and indeed will take the point itself, where not to do so would result in an abuse of the court's process. Thus the illegality of a contract may be raised on appeal even though the point was overlooked in the court below.[15]

2   Appeal against a finding of fact

Since the appeal is by way of rehearing the Court of Appeal has power to substitute its own finding of fact, direct or inferential, for that of the trial judge or jury. There are, however, three restrictions upon this general power to upset findings of fact made at the trial. First, the Court of Appeal in practice confines itself to issues of fact raised in the notice of appeal or

---

11 Ord 59, r 13.

12 See p 114, *ante*.

13 Although s 17(2) of the Supreme Court Act 1981 enables rules of court to provide for an application for a new trial to be determined by the High Court where the trial was by a judge alone and no error of the court at the trial is alleged.

14 The rule is not, however, invariable so that where all the findings of fact upon which the application of the point of law depends were made by the trial judge, the Court of Appeal may allow the point to be taken: *Donaghey v P O'Brien & Co* [1966] 2 All ER 822; [1966] 1 WLR 1170 (affirmed on this point, though reversed on another ground, sub nom *Donaghey v Boulton and Paul Ltd* [1968] AC 1; [1967] 2 All ER 1014); cf *Wilson v Liverpool City Council* [1971] 1 All ER 628; [1971] 1 WLR 302.

15 See *Snell v Unity Finance Ltd* [1964] 2 QB 203; [1963] 3 All ER 50; cf *Oscroft v Benabo* [1967] 2 All ER 548; [1967] 1 WLR 1087; *Brady v Brady* [1989] AC 755; [1988] 2 All ER 617.

respondent's notice. Secondly, the Court of Appeal cannot make a finding in relation to a fact not pleaded, although it can give leave to amend the pleadings.[16] Finally, the court does not as a rule upset direct findings of fact, whether they were made by a judge or by a jury. The reason for this is that, as stated earlier, the Court of Appeal does not have the advantage, which the judge and jury had, of seeing the trial witnesses and observing their demeanour.[17] Consequently the jurisdiction exercised by the Court of Appeal in relation to findings of fact is confined to inferential findings of fact. The court has power to substitute its own inference from the facts as found for that of the trial judge or jury and will not hesitate to do so. Thus, for example, in one case the Court of Appeal reduced a plaintiff's award of damages by half on the basis of his contributory negligence even though there had been no finding of contributory negligence at the trial.[18] Contributory negligence, like negligence, is an inference of fact to be drawn from the facts as found. In another medical negligence action, where the crucial issue of fact was whether a hospital registrar had pulled "too long and too hard" on the head of the infant plaintiff in the course of his birth, LORD BRIDGE explained his willingness to uphold an appeal from the trial judge's finding in the plaintiff's favour in the following words:[19]

> "My Lords, I recognise that this is a question of pure fact and that in the realm of fact, as the authorities repeatedly emphasise, the advantages which the judge derives from seeing and hearing the witnesses must always be respected by an appellate court. At the same time the importance of the part played by those advantages in assisting the judge to any particular conclusion of fact varies through a wide spectrum from, at one end, a straight conflict of primary fact between witnesses, where credibility is crucial and the appellate court can hardly ever interfere, to, at the other end, an inference from undisputed primary facts, where the appellate court is in just as good a position as the trial judge to make the decision."

Where a jury has returned a general verdict it is impossible to distinguish direct findings of fact from inferential findings and, indeed, the jury cannot be asked, after they have returned a general verdict, to state what their direct findings of fact were.[20] The Court of Appeal, therefore, can only upset the general verdict of a jury if it cannot be supported by the evidence or is a verdict which no reasonable men could have reached.[1]

3 Appeal against the exercise of a discretion

In many circumstances the judge has a discretion as to whether, and in what manner, to exercise his powers. Commonly encountered instances of judicial discretion are the discretion as to costs, the discretion whether to

---

16 See *Bell v Lever Brothers Ltd* [1932] AC 161.
17 The Court of Appeal feels no such inhibition when the evidence at the trial was given by written statement or deposition; see *Gallie v Lee* [1969] 1 All ER 1062, at 1079; [1969] 2 WLR 901, at 921 (affirmed sub nom *Saunders (Executrix of Will of Gallie) v Anglia Building Society* [1971] AC 1004; [1970] 3 All ER 961).
18 *Hicks v British Transport Commission* [1958] 2 All ER 39; [1958] 1 WLR 493; see also *Benmax v Austin Motor Co Ltd* [1955] AC 370; [1955] 1 All ER 326; *Qualcast (Wolverhampton) Ltd v Haynes* [1959] AC 743; [1959] 2 All ER 38.
19 *Whitehouse v Jordan* [1981] 1 All ER 267, at 286; [1981] 1 WLR 246, at 269.
20 *Barnes v Hill* [1967] 1 QB 579; [1967] 1 All ER 347.
1 *Mechanical and General Inventions Co Ltd v Austin* [1935] AC 347.

grant or refuse an injunction and the discretion as to the mode of trial, in particular in relation to the question of whether or not to order jury trial. However, no discretion is absolute[2] and there may be a successful appeal to the Court of Appeal in relation to the exercise of a judicial discretion if the appellant can show that the judge exercised his discretion under a mistake of law,[3] or under a misapprehension as to the facts, or that he took into account irrelevant matters or gave insufficient weight, or too much weight, to certain factors[4] or that he failed to exercise his discretion at all.[5] If the judge gives no reasons, or insufficient reasons for the exercise of his discretion, the court may infer that he has gone wrong in one respect or another.[6] The burden of proof is on the party who alleges that the discretion was wrongly exercised and, in any event, the Court of Appeal will only allow the appeal if satisfied that the judge's conclusion is one which involves injustice or was clearly wrong.[7] In *Hadmor Productions Ltd v Hamilton* LORD DIPLOCK explained the extent of the appellate court's powers as follows.[8]

> "Before adverting to the evidence that was before the judge and the additional evidence that was before the Court of Appeal, it is I think appropriate to remind your Lordships of the limited function of an appellate court in an appeal of this kind. An interlocutory injunction is a discretionary relief and the discretion whether or not to grant it is vested in the High Court judge by whom the application for it is heard. On an appeal from the judge's grant or refusal of an interlocutory injunction the function of an appellate court, whether it be the Court of Appeal or your Lordships' House, is not to exercise an independent discretion of its own. It must defer to the judge's exercise of his discretion and must not interfere with it merely on the ground that the members of the appellate court would have exercised the discretion differently. The function of the appellate court is initially one of review only. It may set aside the judge's exercise of his discretion on the ground that it was based on a misunderstanding of the law or of the evidence before him or on an inference that particular facts existed or did not exist, which, although it was one that might legitimately have been drawn on the evidence that was before the judge, can be demonstrated to be wrong by further evidence that has become available by the time of the appeal, or on the ground that there has been a change of circumstances after the judge made his order that would have justified his acceding to an application to vary it. Since reasons given by judges for granting or refusing interlocutory injunctions may sometimes be sketchy, there may

---

2 RSC (Revision) 1962, Ord 36, r 1 described the discretion as to the mode of trial as an "absolute one" but the Court of Appeal in *Ward v James* [1966] 1 QB 273, at 293; [1965] 1 All ER 563, at 568 stated that the word "absolute" either added nothing or, if it did, was ultra vires The current Ord 33 omits the reference to an "absolute" discretion.

3 *Evans v Bartlam* [1937] AC 473; [1937] 2 All ER 646.

4 *Re F (a minor) (wardship; appeal)* [1976] Fam 238; [1976] 1 All ER 417; *Birkett v James* [1978] AC 297; [1977] 2 All ER 801.

5 *Evans v Bartlam, supra.*

6 *Ward v James* [1966] 1 QB 273; [1965] 1 All ER 563; *Re a Debtor (No 12 of 1970)* [1971] 1 All ER 504; [1971] 1 WLR 261 (affirmed [1971] 2 All ER 1494; [1971] 1 WLR 1212).

7 *Beck v Value Capital Ltd (No 2)* [1976] 2 All ER 102; [1976] 1 WLR 572n.

8 [1983] 1 AC 191, at 220; [1982] 1 All ER 1042, at 1046. The appeal was from a decision of the Court of Appeal, presided over by the then Master of the Rolls, LORD DENNING, who was thought by some to be inclined to substitute his own discretion for that of the judge below rather more freely than precedent would allow. LORD DIPLOCK had occasion to repeat, almost verbatim, the passage quoted above, in *Garden Cottage Foods Ltd v Milk*

also be occasional cases where even though no erroneous assumption of law or fact can be identified the judge's decision to grant or refuse the injunction is so aberrant that it must be set aside on the ground that no reasonable judge regardful of his duty to act judicially could have reached it. It is only if and after the appellate court has reached the conclusion that the judge's exercise of his discretion must be set aside for one or other of these reasons that it becomes entitled to exercise an original discretion of its own."

4 Appeal against an award of damages

The approach adopted by the Court of Appeal when determining an appeal against an award of damages differs according to whether the award was made by a jury or by a judge sitting alone. Where unliquidated damages are claimed, historically the court has not interfered with the award of a jury unless the damages awarded were so large or, more rarely, so small that no jury could reasonably have given them.[9] The reason for this is that the assessment of damages is historically the province of the jury in any case. Thus juries know of no fixed scale of damages comparable to that applied by judges, and the law has not considered it desirable that they should be made aware of any such scale.[10] In the matter of damages: "the views of juries may form a valuable corrective to the views of judges".[11] However a new trial may be ordered if it appears to the court either that the jury took into account irrelevant factors or failed to consider matters which it ought to have considered and in consequence awarded damages which were excessive or inadequate. The case of *Lewis v Daily Telegraph Ltd*[12] provides a good example. In that case two national newspapers published on the same day paragraphs alleged to be defamatory of the plaintiffs. The jury in the first action awarded the plaintiffs a total of £100,000; in the second action two days later in which there were factors which a jury might be entitled to take into account as aggravating damages, a different jury awarded the plaintiffs a further £117,000. New trials of both actions were ordered on the ground (*inter alia*) that the damages in each case were excessive. The House of Lords, affirming the decision of the Court of Appeal, stated that in such a case, pursuant to section 12 of the Defamation Act 1952, each jury should be directed to consider how far the damage suffered can reasonably be attributed solely to the libel with which they are concerned, and how far it ought to be regarded as the joint result of the two libels, bearing in mind that the plaintiff ought not to be compensated twice for the same loss.

In *Rantzen v Mirror Group Newspapers (1986) Ltd*[13] the plaintiff, a well-known television presenter, had been awarded £250,000 damages for

---

Marketing Board [1984] AC 130; [1983] 2 All ER 770, once again in reversing the decision of the Court of Appeal presided over by LORD DENNING.

9 *Johnston v Great Western Rly Co* [1904] 2 KB 250. The award must be an "entirely erroneous" estimate; *Banbury v Bank of Montreal* [1918] AC 626, at 694. The principle was reaffirmed by the House of Lords in *Cassell & Co Ltd v Broome* [1972] AC 1027; [1972] 1 All ER 801 where the House, by a bare majority, upheld an award of £40,000 for libel although unanimous in regarding the sum as excessive.

10 The desirability of not informing juries of awards of damages in comparable cases was reiterated by LORD DENNING MR in *Ward v James (supra)*.

11 *Per* MORRIS LJ in *Scott v Musial* [1959] 2 QB 429; [1959] 3 All ER 193.

12 [1964] AC 234; [1963] 2 All ER 151.

13 [1993] 4 All ER 975; [1993] 3 WLR 953.

defamation. The defendant appealed, on the basis that the award was excessive, and sought an order under section 8 of the Courts and Legal Services Act 1990, which now provides that where the court has the power to order a new trial on the basis of excessive or inadequate damages, it may be given the power[14] to substitute the proper sum instead of ordering that new trial. The Court of Appeal concluded that this power had to be exercised in the context of Article 10 of the European Convention on Human Rights,[15] which permitted restrictions on freedom of expression only where they were necessary in a democratic society to meet a pressing social need. On this basis large awards of damages were to be subjected to very close scrutiny. The question now to be asked is whether a reasonable jury could have thought the award necessary to compensate the plaintiff. On the facts the award was excessive by any objective standard of reasonable compensation, and an award of £110,000 substituted for that of the jury.

Where the award of damages appealed against was made by a judge sitting alone the Court of Appeal will not hesitate to interfere with the assessment, not only on the ground that the judge applied a wrong principle of law in making the assessment, but also on the ground that the award is out of scale with awards in similar cases. There is, of course, no prescribed scale of damages in any type of action but, nevertheless, there is a certain degree of parity in awards in respect of similar types of damage particularly in actions for damages for personal injuries.[16] In such cases the Court of Appeal will not make small adjustments to the sum awarded though it will make a substantial adjustment if that is found necessary. In practice the court will rarely interfere unless an adjustment of at least 20 or 25 per cent is envisaged. It is this diversity of approach to awards of damages made by judges and juries respectively that has led to the virtual disappearance of jury trial in personal injuries actions.[17]

5   Exercise of the power to order a new trial

The Court of Appeal has power under section 17 of the Supreme Court Act 1981 and Order 59, rule 11 to order a new trial. It may exercise this power on an appeal from a judge and jury or from a judge alone just as it can on a motion for a new trial following a trial with a jury.[18] A new trial may be ordered on any one issue without disturbing the finding of the court below on any other issue. Thus the Court of Appeal may order a new trial on the issue of damages while affirming the decision on the question of liability. Indeed if the only ground of application is the amount of damages the court should limit the new trial to that issue and leave the findings as to liability undisturbed.[19] If there is a new trial that trial is completely independent of

---

14 Ord 59, r 11(4).
15 See p 13, *ante.*
16 See observations of LORD DENNING MR on scales of damages in personal injuries actions in *Ward v James* [1966] 1 QB 273, at 296 *et seq*; [1965] 1 All ER 563, at 572 *et seq*.
   For an illustration of the tendency to standardise damages see *Bastow v Bagley & Co Ltd* [1961] 3 All ER 1101; [1961] 1 WLR 1494. See also *Brown v Thompson* [1968] 2 All ER 708; [1968] 1 WLR 1003.
17 See p 363, *ante.*
18 Compare the very limited power of the Criminal Division of the Court of Appeal to order a new trial; see p 520, *post.*
19 *Tolley v JS Fry & Sons Ltd* [1931] AC 333, at 341.

the first trial. The mode of trial need not be the same, no estoppels arise as a result of the first trial and the parties may raise new points and may contest issues left uncontested at the first trial. The costs of the first trial are sometimes ordered to await the outcome of the new trial though, as a rule, the successful applicant ought to be allowed the costs of his application.[20]

There are several grounds upon which a new trial may be ordered of which the more important are set out below.

a Misdirection

The judge has a duty to provide the jury with an adequate direction as to what are the issues to be decided, what is the law applicable to those issues and what is the effect in law of the evidence received. If this is not done there is a misdirection. The expression "misdirection" includes a failure to direct at all.[1]

b Improper admission or rejection of evidence

c Wrongful withdrawal of a question from the jury

It is expressly provided by Order 59, rule 11(2) that the court is not bound to order a new trial on any of the above three grounds "unless in the opinion of the Court of Appeal some substantial wrong or miscarriage has been thereby occasioned".[2] There will not have been an operative miscarriage of justice unless the appellant has lost a chance of success which was fairly open to him. The burden is on the party supporting the verdict to show that, on the evidence, there has been no miscarriage of justice.

d Perverse jury verdict

The Court of Appeal is slow to order a new trial on this ground and there is a heavy burden on the applicant. He must show not merely that the verdict is one which reasonable men *ought* not to have reached but that it is one which no jury of reasonable men, properly directed, *could* have found upon the evidence. This may occur either because there was no evidence at all in support of a material fact or because such evidence as there was could not reasonably be believed.

e Jury verdict as to damages

The circumstances in which the Court of Appeal is prepared to upset a jury verdict as to damages have already been noted.[3] Where the Court of Appeal does decide that damages awarded by a jury are excessive or inadequate it now has the power to substitute its own award without the consent of all parties concerned, and may also increase or reduce an award in respect of any distinct head of damages erroneously included in

---

20 *Hamilton v Seal* [1904] 2 KB 262; cf *Bray v Ford* [1896] AC 44.
1 *Hobbs v CT Tinling & Co Ltd* [1929] 2 KB 1.
2 Compare the wording of the proviso to s 2(1) of the Criminal Appeal Act 1968; see p 518, *post*.
3 See p 427, *ante*.

or excluded from the sum awarded, with consent of the party who will be adversely affected by the increase or reduction.[4]

f Discovery of fresh evidence

The principles upon which the Court of Appeal acts when considering applications for a new trial on the ground of the discovery of fresh evidence are similar to those applicable where the court is asked to receive fresh evidence on the hearing of an appeal.[5]

A common example of fresh evidence which will justify a new trial is the discovery that one of the trial witnesses gave false evidence.[6]

g Misconduct or other irregularity at the trial

A new trial may be ordered on the ground of misconduct on the part of the judge, the jury, counsel, court officers or other persons, provided that the misconduct in question prevented either party from having a fair trial. It is not sufficient that either judge or jury expressed a strong opinion in favour of one party during the trial. However new trials have been ordered where the verdict of the jury was reached by drawing lots,[7] where the jury expressed a strong opinion in favour of the plaintiff before hearing the defendant's evidence,[8] where the court was misled by counsel[9] and where the judge's constant interruptions prevented one side from conducting an effective cross-examination.[10]

h Surprise

The applicant for a new trial on the ground of surprise must swear an affidavit setting out the facts on which he relies. He may allege, for example, that the action came on for trial unexpectedly when his witnesses were not available or that his opponent was allowed to present his case in a way for which the applicant was not prepared. Thus where, in a personal injuries action, the plaintiff at the end of the trial confronted the defendants with, and succeeded on, a case based on allegations which had not been pleaded and which the defendants had not come to the trial prepared to meet, a new trial was ordered.[11] The application will only succeed if the surprise has occasioned a substantial miscarriage of justice.

i Judgment obtained by fraud

There are alternative methods of challenging a judgment obtained by fraud. The first is by a motion for a new trial. Alternatively the party affected may bring an action to have the judgment set aside. In either case the party has the burden of particularising and proving the fraud alleged.[12]

---

4 Ord 59, r 11(4).
5 See p 520, *post*.
6 *Piotrowska v Piotrowski* [1958] 2 All ER 729n; [1958] 1 WLR 797. A new trial was ordered in *Skone v Skone* [1971] 2 All ER 582; [1971] 1 WLR 812; see p 423, *ante*.
7 *Harvey v Hewitt* (1840) 8 Dowl 598.
8 *Allum v Boultbee* (1854) 9 Exch 738.
9 *Meek v Fleming* [1961] 2 QB 366; [1961] 3 All ER 148.
10 *Jones v National Coal Board* [1957] 2 QB 55; [1957] 2 All ER 155.
11 *Lloyde v West Midlands Gas Board* [1971] 2 All ER 1240; [1971] 1 WLR 749.
12 *Hip Foong Hong v H Neotia & Co* [1918] AC 888.

PART IV

Criminal Proceedings

SUMMARY

CHAPTER 22

Criminal Proceedings

A INTRODUCTION

The English criminal process is, essentially, adversarial in nature.[1] The process of investigation and evidence-gathering is conducted by the police or other investigating body, with limited powers of supervision in the hands of the Crown Prosecution Service.[2] The courts play no significant part in the preparation of the case. The trial itself is not an investigation into events or allegations, but rather a hearing to decide, within a complex set of rules,[3] whether the defendant is proved to be guilty of the particular offences which the prosecution have charged him with.[4] By contrast, in many civil law jurisdictions the process is inquisitorial in nature. This term is used to describe systems where judges or magistrates supervise the pre-trial investigations and preparation of the case, to a greater or lesser extent, and play a significant part in the questioning of the witness at trial, and in the decisions as to what evidence should be considered by the court. Simply put, the trial is much more of an investigation than a contest.

This adversarial characteristic has often been viewed as a strength of the English system. These strengths were identified by the Court of Appeal in *R v McIlkenny*:[5]

> "Another feature of our law, which goes hand in hand with trial by jury, is the adversarial nature of criminal proceedings. Clearly a jury cannot embark on a judicial investigation. So the material must be placed before the jury. It is sometimes said that the adversarial system leaves too much power in the hands of the police. But that criticism has been met, at least in part, by the creation of the Crown Prosecution Service. The great advantage of the adversarial system is that it enables the defendant to test the prosecution case in open court. Once there is sufficient evidence to commit a defendant for trial, the prosecution has to prove the case against him by calling witnesses to give oral testimony in the presence of the jury. We doubt whether there is a

---

1 For assessment generally of the adversarial system, see the various submissions of evidence to the Royal Commission on Criminal Justice (1993, Cm 2263, HMSO).
2 See p 232, *ante*.
3 See p 549, *post*.
4 Whilst a judge has a discretion to call a witness not called by the prosecution or defence, this power should be sparingly used, and only where necessary in the interests of justice: *R v Roberts* (1984) 80 Cr App Rep 89.
5 [1992] 2 All ER 417 at 425–6.

better way of exposing the weaknesses in the prosecution case, whether the witness be a policeman, a scientist or a bystander, than by cross examination."

Yet, despite these perceived advantages, a series of *causes célèbres*[6] focussed attention on the very nature of the criminal process. The court in *R v McIlkenny* itself identified some of the weaknesses of the system, such as the imbalance in resources as between prosecution and defence, and the need for proper disclosure of prosecution evidence to the defence. Above all, the effectiveness of any system depends upon it not being abused by those who work within it.

Criticisms and concerns as to the way in which the adversarial system works go beyond the trial process itself, and include criticisms as to how criminal investigations are conducted and supervised. Many, though not all, of the difficulties encountered in a series of well-publicised miscarriages of justice stemmed not from the trial itself, but rather from the manner of investigation by the police, and from a failure to apply properly pre-trial procedures designed to ensure the fairness of the trial itself.[7] The situation was of such public concern that in 1991 the Home Secretary established a Royal Commission on Criminal Justice. Its terms of reference required it:

> "to examine the criminal justice system from the stage at which the police are investigating an alleged or reported criminal offence right through to the stage at which a defendant who has been found guilty of an offence has exhausted his or her rights of appeal."

Police powers were not within its terms of reference,[8] nor were rules relating to bail or sentencing. The Commission reported in June 1993,[9] making some 352 separate recommendations. It did not recommend a fundamental change of approach, doubting whether a general move away from an adversarial approach would be desirable. It believed that a system which kept separate the roles of police, prosecutor and judge "offers a better protection for the innocent defendant, including protection against the risk of unnecessarily prolonged detention prior to trial".[10] Instead, its recommendations are intended to make the existing system "more capable of serving the interests of justice and efficiency", and to deal with matters that seemed to the Commission at present to turn what ought to be a search for the truth into "a contest played between opposing lawyers according to a set of rules which the jury does not necessarily accept or even understand".[11]

---

6 *R v McIlkenny, supra*; *R v Maguire* [1992] QB 936; [1992] 2 All ER 433; *R v Silcott, Braithwaite and Raghip* (1991) Times, 9 December; *R v Kisco* (1992) unreported.

7 Many of the cases in question involved alleged police malpractice. See, eg, *R v Maguire, supra*.

8 They had been the subject of consideration by the Royal Commission on Criminal Procedure, 1981, Cmn 8292, and subsequent legislation in Police and Criminal Evidence Act 1984.

9 1993, Cmn 2263. The various Research Studies published by the Royal Commission are a valuable source of data and analysis of the trial system and the operation of the criminal justice system.

10 Ch 1, para 14.

11 Ch 1, para 11.

B THE DECISION TO COMMENCE PROCEEDINGS

1 The discretion to prosecute

The fact that an offence is believed to have been committed does not mean that the commencement of a prosecution is inevitable. Discretion exists at various stages in the criminal process as to whether a prosecution should be commenced, or the suspect cautioned formally or informally. The police and the Crown Prosecution Service or other prosecuting authority each have discretion at appropriate times.[12]

At the policing level, an individual officer has a discretion as to what action should be taken. An officer may informally caution, make an arrest[13] or formally report a suspect for prosecution. These judgments will often be reached in the light of the overall policies adopted by the police force of which the officer is a member. At a later stage, the police may have to decide whether an offender should be charged, and if so with what offence, or, alternatively, whether a formal caution should be administered.

The practice of formally cautioning, rather than prosecuting, offenders can be traced back to 1929, but has never had a statutory basis, and was first regularised by a Home Office Circular of 1978.[14] Studies showed that cautioning practices varied widely between individual police forces, despite attempts by the Home Office to achieve greater consistency.[15] The position regarding formal cautioning policies is now governed by Home Office Circular 59/1990, which encourages the police to caution formally rather than prosecute in some circumstances. In respect of juveniles and young adults, this can be seen as an attempt to keep them out of the criminal justice system for as long as possible, although on occasion the operation of this policy causes disquiet.

For a person to be cautioned, there must be evidence of the suspect's guilt sufficient to give a reasonable prospect of a conviction, the suspect must admit guilt, and be willing to be cautioned. The circular deals with how the cautioning power should be used. It states as follows:

(a) in deciding whether to charge or summons an offender, no account will be taken of any previous convictions, or of any earlier caution;

(b) the seriousness of the accused's action will determine whether a prosecution should take place. The police will take into account aggravating features, such as the age of the victim, and whether violence was used;

(c) the views of the victim may be important;

(d) there is a presumption in favour of a caution for juveniles, and a high probability of a caution for young adults, aged between 17 and 20 years;

---

12 The discretion may be reviewable in limited circumstances on normal judicial review principles: see pp 123.

13 Arrest for the purpose of cautioning will only be lawful if the grounds for arrest in fact exists. There is no power to arrest for cautioning: see *Collins v Wilcock* [1984] 1 WLR 1172.

14 Home Office Circular 70/1978, replaced by Circular 14/1985.

15 See: Wilkinson & Evans, 'Police Cautioning of Juveniles – The Impact of Home Office Circular 14/1985' [1990] Crim LR 165; Westwood, 'The Effects of Home Office Guidelines

(e) if a caution is appropriate, regard will then be had to the previous cautions or pending prosecutions of the offender.

There will also need to be taken into account criteria relating to the public interest. These will include the nature of the offence, the likely penalty, the offender's age and state of health, previous criminal history, and the offender's attitude towards the offence.

The total effect of these provisions is that the prosecution of a juvenile is a course of action of last resort, and that the cautioning of adults is often confined to elderly offenders, those suffering mental stress and young first offenders who have committed minor offences. In 1991, some 279,000 offenders were dealt with by way of caution. Of these, 179,000 related to indictable or either way offences.[16] The Royal Commission recommended an extension of the practice to more petty offenders. However, it also identified the need for a consistent approach nationwide, cautioning to operate within national guidelines and with information being available as to cautioning practices nationwide.[17] It recommended that consideration be given to combining cautions with other support, through social services or the probation service, but recognised that a failure to prosecute an individual itself can damage confidence in the criminal justice system.

Irrespective of whether the practice of cautioning is based on formal or informal criteria, the conduct of the police must not amount to an abdication of the duty of law enforcement. Such conduct would be outside the legitimate exercise of discretion, and be susceptible to judicial review.[18] There may also be situations in which the decision whether to caution may be questioned. In *R v Chief Constable of Kent County Constabulary, ex parte L*[19] the Divisional Court considered that a decision to prosecute a 12-year-old girl, which was claimed to be in breach of the policy for cautioning of juveniles, was susceptible to judicial review, although on the facts found to be a proper exercise of discretion. WATKINS LJ considered that the policy of cautioning, instead of prosecuting, was well-settled and played a prominent part in the process of decision-making in an individual case. Care should be taken, however, to avoid "the danger of opening too wide the door of review of the discretion to continue a prosecution", and the court considered that different considerations in respect of judicial review of these decisions to caution might apply to the exercise of the discretion in respect of adults.[20] More recently, another Divisional Court in *R v Inland Revenue Commissioners, ex parte Mead*[1] has stressed that decisions relating to adults are not beyond judicial review,

---

on the Cautioning of Offenders' [1991] Crim LR 591; Evans, 'Police Cautioning and the Young Adult Offender' [1991] Crim LR 598.

16 RCCJ: Ch 5, para 57.

17 *Ibid.*

18 *R v Commissioner of Police for the Metropolis, ex parte Blackburn* [1968] 2 QB 118; *R v Commissioner of Police for the Metropolis, ex parte Blackburn (No 3)* [1973] QB 241. In *Buckoke v Greater London Council* [1971] 1 Ch 655 a policy decision not to prosecute fire service drivers for crossing red traffic lights was held to be lawful. See, generally, Leigh, *Police Powers in England & Wales* (2nd Edn, 1985).

19 [1993] 1 All ER 756.

20 There are no strictly defined limits to judicial review of the decisions of a prosecuting authority: see WATKINS LJ in *R v General Council of the Bar, ex parte Percival* [1991] 1 QB 212; [1990] 3 All ER 137.

1 [1993] 1 All ER 772.

although the situations in which the courts would in fact intervene will be rare.[2]

Unless the decision to caution is taken, or unless the offence is one to which a fixed penalty attaches,[3] the commencement of a prosecution is the only other alternative.

2 The decision to prosecute

a Who institutes?

The commencement of criminal proceedings is theoretically in the hands of the police, although many other organisations have law enforcement powers as well.[4] It is in most cases the police who will charge individuals, take them into custody, or provide the information sufficient for the issue of a summons or a warrant for arrest. However, it is the duty of the Director of Public Prosecutions to take over the conduct of all criminal proceedings instituted on behalf of a police force.[5] The reality is, therefore, that the DPP and Crown Prosecution Service play a central role. The Crown Prosecution Service, which is independent of the police, does not have responsibility for the police investigation, but may be consulted on occasion by the police at the investigation stage.[6] The decision when the prosecution should be continued, and on what basis, is that of the Crown Prosecution Service, not the police.

In respect of prosecutions by others, the Royal Commission on Criminal Procedure in 1981 concluded it would be both impracticable and undesirable to bring all prosecutions within the ambit of the Crown prosecutions arrangements.[7] Section 6 of the Prosecution of Offences Act 1985 therefore states that nothing in that Act shall preclude any person from instituting any criminal proceedings to which the Director's duty under the Act does not apply. Private prosecutions can be brought. However, some controls are needed. By section 42 of the Supreme Court Act 1981,[8] if on the application of the Attorney-General the High Court is satisfied that any person has habitually and persistently and without any reasonable ground instituted vexatious prosecution (whether against the same or different persons) the court may make a criminal proceedings order. This has the effect that no information shall be laid before a justice of the peace, and no application for leave to prefer a bill of indictment shall be made, by that person without the leave of the court. Leave is not to be granted unless

---

2 The fact that there are alternative remedies, for example to challenge for abuse of process, does not prevent the exercise of discretion itself from being challenged by way of judicial review.

3 The Royal Commission recommended the extension of the fixed penalty system: see ch 5, para 62, and *Keeping Offenders Out of Court: Further Alternatives to Prosecution* (HMSO, 1983, Cmnd 8958). Such a scheme successfully operates in Scotland.

4 In respect of private prosecutions, see Lidstone, Hogg & Sutcliffe *Prosecution by Private Individuals & Non Police Agencies* (Royal Commission on Criminal Procedure Research Study No 10, HMSO, 1980).

5 Prosecution of Offences Act 1985, s 3(2)(a). In important, difficult or otherwise appropriate cases the DPP may institute proceedings: s 3(2)(b). For discussion of the office of DPP, see p 232, *ante*.

6 The Royal Commission recommends greater use of this practice: see ch 5, para 17.

7 Royal Commission on Criminal Procedure, paras 7.40–7.52 (Cmnd 8092–I, 1981).

8 Inserted by Prosecution of Offences Act 1985, s 24.

the High Court is satisfied that the institution of proceedings does not amount to an abuse of process. In addition, in some cases the consent of the Attorney-General or DPP is needed.[9]

b   The criteria

By section 10 of the 1985 Act the Director of Public Prosecutions is under a duty to issue a Code for Crown Prosecutors, giving guidance on the general principles to be applied by them in determining, in any case, whether proceedings should be instituted, discontinued, or what charges should be made. This Code is to be found set out in the Annual Reports of the DPP.

The first question to be decided is whether there is sufficient evidence. There must be admissible, substantial and reliable evidence that a criminal offence has been committed by an identifiable individual. In deciding this, a *prima facie* case is not enough: the test is whether there is a realistic prospect of conviction.[10] In deciding that, a careful study will be undertaken of the available evidence. The possibility that evidence might be inadmissible either in law, or excluded because of failure to comply with relevant rules, the possibility that admissions might be unreliable, the possibility that a witness may be hostile or likely to be unreliable or not likely to tell the truth, the impression a witness will make in court, the availability of all necessary witnesses, and the competence of young children are all relevant questions. The prosecutor will look at the overall weight of the case, whether dangers of concoction of evidence exist, whether a case can be sustained against more than one accused (if there is more than one), and whether the public might consider a prosecution to be oppressive.

Having decided whether prosecution can be justified on the evidence, the prosecutor is then required to consider the wider public interest, although the interests of the victim should also be borne in mind. The graver the offence the less likelihood there will be that the public interest will permit the case to be dealt with by anything other than prosecution, although the Code does urge prosecutors to strive to ensure that the spirit of the cautioning guidelines is observed, where the seriousness of the offence allows. In particular the following factors may provide an indication that prosecution may not be required:

(a)   where a court is likely to impose a nominal penalty only;

(b)   where the offences are stale. Where offences were committed more than three years before the probable date of trial, there may be a reluctance to prosecute unless an immediate custodial sentence is in any event likely to be imposed upon conviction. However, the staleness may have been caused by the offender himself, or by the need for a long complex investigation;

(c)   youth;

(d)   old age or infirmity;

(e)   mental disorder at the time of commission of the offence. Where the

---

9   See, eg, offences of incitement to racial hatred (Public Order Act 1986, s 27); offences under the Prevention of Terrorism (Temporary Provisions) Act 1989; homosexual offences where either or both the parties are under 21 years of age (Sexual Offences Act 1967, s 8).

10   The so-called "51 per cent" rule.

effect of proceedings upon the health of the accused is not outweighed by wider public interest in favour of prosecution, proceedings may not be commenced, or may be discontinued. In this type of case, other relevant factors will be the nature of the mental condition, and the likelihood of further offending;

(f) in sexual cases the respective ages and roles of the participants will be relevant. Offences against young children, or involving a serious personal violation, will almost always result in prosecution;

(g) changes in attitude by the complainant.

c Discontinuance

Under section 23 of the Prosecution of Offences Act 1985 notice of discontinuance can be issued, provided this is done in summary cases before the beginning of the hearing of the evidence, or in cases to be tried on indictment, before committal for trial. This can be done by correspondence, and without the expense and inconvenience of a court hearing. It does not replace the power of a prosecutor to go before a court and offer no evidence or to withdraw a charge, both of which remain options.[11] Nor does it interfere with the power of the Attorney-General to prevent proceedings from continuing by the issue of a writ of *nolle prosequi*.[12]

In deciding the use of these various powers it is the duty of prosecutors to keep a case under review. In the case of juveniles it may become clear that caution is the more appropriate way of dealing with the matter. In respect of those suffering illness the effect on health may make it appropriate for the case to be withdrawn.[13] In any event, this power of review has been shown to be important. Since the creation of the Crown Prosecution Service in 1985, the proportion of prosecutions for indictable offences which has been discontinued or withdrawn has risen rapidly, from 7 per cent in 1985 to 22 per cent in 1991,[14] emphasising the role of the Crown Prosecution Service in deciding whether a case is sufficient, and whether it is in the public interest to proceed.

The Royal Commission on Criminal Justice considered the exercise of this duty in the light of the research it received concerning ordered or directed acquittals in the Crown Court.[15] It considered that weak cases should be identified at an early stage as possible, before the defendant, victim and other witnesses are put to the trouble and expense of a court appearance. To that end, it recommended that the Crown Prosecution Service should have power to discontinue a case without obtaining the consent of the court at any time prior to the hearing itself.[16]

---

11 *R v Director of Public Prosecutions, ex parte Cook* (1991) 95 Cr App Rep 233.
12 For the powers of the Attorney-General, see Edwards, *The Law Officers of the Crown.*
13 This power to discontinue remains throughout the trial itself. In *R v Seelig* (1993) the accused was discharged because medically unable to cope with the strains of a long trial in which he was defending himself: see The Times, 15 February.
14 Criminal Statistics in England & Wales, 1991, para 6(2).
15 See Block, Corbett & Peay, *Ordered & Directed Acquittals in the Crown Court* (Royal Commission Research Study No 15, 1993).
16 Ch 5, para 37.

d   Time-limits for prosecution and abuse of process.

In general there is no time-limit on the prosecution of an indictable offence, although, by contrast, summary proceedings must be brought within a specified period.[17] Even in some cases triable on indictment Parliament has for reasons of policy imposed a time-limit; thus a prosecution for unlawful sexual intercourse with a girl under sixteen may not be commenced more than twelve months after the commission of the offence.[18] However, even when no specific time-limit exists the court is not powerless, and can intervene to prevent abuse of process occasioned by delay. A court can, as part of its inherent power, order a stay to prevent abuse of process.[19] Thus if the prosecution has manipulated or misused the process of the court:

> ". . . so as to deprive the defendant of a protection provided by the law or if there has been such delay so that prejudice or unfairness to the defendant arises"[20]

then the court can order that the prosecution not proceed. This doctrine of abuse of process has even been extended to cases where, though the fairness of the trial is not in question, nevertheless it would be unfair to the accused to try the accused because of the abuse that has occurred. In *R v Croydon Justices, ex parte Dean*[1] this was applied and a conviction quashed, the accused having been assured that he would not be prosecuted.

Dealing with a case involving delay VISCOUNT DILHORNE in *Director of Public Prosecutions v Humphrys*[2] warned that use of this power should occur only "in the most exceptional circumstances". This was an approach echoed by LORD LANE CJ in *A–G's Reference (No 1 of 1990)*,[3] where he stated that even if delay was unjustifiable the imposition of a stay:

> "should be the exception rather than the rule. Still more rare should be cases where a stay can properly be imposed in the absence of any fault on the part of the complainant or prosecution . . . ."

The defendant must show on the balance of probabilities that, owing to the delay, he will suffer serious prejudice to the extent that no fair trial can be held. In deciding this, the ability of the court through the rules of evidence to regulate what is placed before it, and the ability of the judge to warn and to give appropriate directions to the jury, should both be borne in mind.

Statute has created a framework within which prosecutors must work. By section 2 of the Prosecution of Offences Act 1985, and the regulations that have been made under that Act,[4] there are time-limits regulating how long a defendant may be kept in custody pending the start of summary trial, between first appearance at court and committal for trial, and

---

17 Six months from the date of commission or when matter of complaint arose: Magistrates Courts Act 1980, s 127. See p 527, *post.*
18 Sexual Offences Act 1956, s 37 and Sch 2.
19 *Connolly v Director of Public Prosecutions* [1964] AC 1254; 48 Cr App Rep 183.
20 *R v Derby Magistrates' Court, ex parte Brooks* (1984) 80 Cr App Rep 164.
 1 [1993] QB 769; [1993] 3 All ER 129; see also *R v Bow Street Stipendiary Magistrate, ex parte Director of Public Prosecutions* (1989) 91 Cr App Rep 283; *R v Crown Court at Norwich, ex parte Belsham* [1992] 1 All ER 394; [1992] 1 WLR 54.
 2 [1977] AC 1; [1976] 2 All ER 497.
 3 [1992] QB 630; [1992] 3 All ER 169.
 4 Prosecution of Offences (Custody Time Limits) Regulations 1987–91.

between committal for trial and the start of the trial. Application can be made for extension of these limits, and a right of appeal exists in respect of a decision of magistrates' court to extend, or a refusal to extend, these time limits. By contrast, no power exists in respect of such an order made by the Crown Court, but since this is not a matter "relating to trial on indictment"[5] the power of judicial review arises.

C BRINGING THE OFFENDER BEFORE THE COURT

A person accused or suspected of having committed an offence may be brought before the court in one of three ways:

(i) by summons; this is a document, sent to or served on the defendant, ordering him to appear in court;

(ii) by warrant for his arrest; this is an order to the police, or in certain circumstances to private persons, to arrest the defendant and bring him before the court;
(a summons and a warrant are generally known as "process")

(iii) by arrest without warrant, where permitted by law.

Although these three methods exist, their use varies widely. Whilst summary offences will most often be prosecuted by summons, research studies show[6] that in respect of offences that can be tried on indictment there is a strong tendency for the police to rely on arrest rather than summons. In one such study,[7] 76 per cent of those proceeded against for indictable offences had been arrested and charged, and a majority of those brought to court by way of summons for such offences had also at some point been arrested. It should be remembered in this context that arrest for the purposes of questioning is perfectly proper if the grounds for arrest on the facts exist.[8]

1 Information

Both a summons and a warrant are obtained by the laying of information before a magistrate:

> "an information is nothing more than what the word imports, namely the statement by which the magistrate is informed of the offence for which the summons or warrant is required . . . ."[9]

An information may be laid either by the person requiring issue of process, or by somebody authorised by that person to do so, usually that person's solicitor or barrister. The application may be made either orally or in

---

5 See p 126, *ante*.

6 See McConville, *Corroboration & Confessions* (Royal Commission Research Study No 13, HMSO, 1992).

7 Gemmill & Morgan Giles, *Arrest, Charge & Summons* (Royal Commission on Criminal Procedure Research Study No 9, HMSO 1980).

8 *Holgate–Mohammed v Duke* [1984] AC 437; [1984] 1 All ER 1054.

9 HUDDLESTON B, in *R v Hughes* (1879) 4 QBD 614, at 633; cited with approval by the House of Lords in *R v Manchester Stipendiary Magistrate, ex parte Hill* [1983] 1 AC 328; sub nom *Hill v Anderton* [1982] 2 All ER 963, in which it was held that the information was "laid" when received at the office of the clerk to the justices for the relevant area, and that

writing: if, however, a warrant is sought the information must be in writing and substantiated on oath.[10] Where consent or authority is required for the issue of process, the magistrate before whom information is laid should see that the consent or authority is produced before issuing process. In addition, every court may decline to hear proceedings if they amount to an abuse of the process of the court.[11]

The information should describe in ordinary language the specific offence, avoiding technical terms as far as possible, and should not charge more than one offence.[12] If it does so, it must be amended before the commencement of trial.[13] It is not necessary to set out in the information all the elements of the offence, and in particular it is not necessary to "specify or negative" any exemption or general defence;[14] however the information should give such particulars as may be necessary for explaining the nature of the charge and where the offence charged is statutory there should be a reference to the relevant section of the Act.[15]

Failure to comply with these rules will not necessarily mean that the issue of process is invalid, with possible liability under the tort of false imprisonment, since section 123(1) of the Magistrates' Courts Act 1980 provides that:

> ". . . no objection shall be allowed to any information...or to any summons or warrant . . . for any defect in it in substance or in form, or for any variance between it and the evidence adduced on behalf of the prosecutor."

The section indicates that:

> "technical objections to informations are not to prevail, even though they touch the substance of the charge. There have been, however, many decisions under that section which show that the section does not operate to prevent an objection being effective where the error alleged is fundamental . . . ."[16]

It is a question of fact and degree in each case whether the error is indeed fundamental. If an information charges an offence under a statute which has been repealed,[17] if it does not charge an offence at all,[18] or if it is bad for duplicity[19] then there is a fundamental defect which cannot be cured by the section, but only by amendment or dismissal of the summons.

If and when the defendant is committed for trial he is entitled to see the information, if it is sworn; before committal, and seemingly in any case where the information is not sworn, the defendant's only right is to apply

---

it was not necessary for it to be personally received by the clerk or any justice; it was sufficient that it was received by a member of staff expressly or impliedly authorised to receive it for onward transmission to a justice or the justices' clerk.

10 Magistrates' Courts Act 1980, s 1(1), (3).

11 *Price v Humphries* [1958] 2 QB 353, at 357; [1958] 2 All ER 725, at 727.

12 See p 528, *post*.

13 See p 528, *post*.

14 Magistrates Courts Rules, r 4(3). See p 528, *post*.

15 *Ibid*, r 4(3).

16 HUMPHREYS J in *Atterton v Browne* [1945] KB 122, at 127, dealing with a section of the Summary Jurisdiction Act 1848 in similar terms to s 123(1); cf Magistrates' Courts Rules 1981, r 4(1).

17 *Meek v Powell* [1952] 1 KB 164; [1952] 1 All ER 347. *Hunter v Coombs* [1962] 1 All ER 904; [1962] 1 WLR 573. *Quaere* whether the defendant could waive the irregularity.

18 *Garman v Plaice* [1969] 1 All ER 62, at 64; [1969] 1 WLR 19, at 23.

19 For the meaning of this, see p 528 *post*.

for particulars of the charge to be given. This may be done at any time, application being in the first instance to the prosecutor, although application may be made to the magistrates' court for an order if particulars are refused or those given are thought to be insufficient.[20]

2 Conditions for issue of process

Before issuing process, a magistrate must be satisfied as to two matters:

(a) that jurisdiction to do so exists. It will do so if the person accused resides in that petty sessions area, or is believed to do so; if the alleged offence was committed in that area; or if it is necessary or expedient for a person to be tried in the same area as another person.[1] This may be because the offences should be tried together, perhaps because the offences are so closely connected that the same witnesses are involved.[2]

(b) the evidence is sufficient to do so. The issue of process is discretionary, subject to challenge in the normal way by means of judicial review.

If process is to be issued, the decision remains as to whether to issue a summons or a warrant, a decision which is a judicial one to be exercised personally by the magistrate. No defect in the summons or warrant issued will invalidate any trial that follows, provided it is based upon a valid information.[3]

3 Summons

> "A summons is a citation proceeding upon an information . . . laid before the magistrate who issues the summons, and conveying to the person cited the fact that the magistrate is satisfied that there is a prima facie case against him."[4]

A summons must state shortly the matter of the information and then set out the time and place at which the defendant is required by the summons to appear. A single summons may be issued in respect of several informations, but must state the matter of each information separately and has effect as several summonses, one for each information. In all cases the summons must either be signed by the magistrate issuing it or must state his name, with the signature of the clerk of the court to authenticate it in either event.[5]

The summons must then be served on the defendant; this may be effected by: (1) delivering it to him; (2) leaving it for him with some person

---

20 *R v Aylesbury Justices, ex parte Wisbey* [1965] 1 All ER 602; [1965] 1 WLR 339. It was held that the defendant was entitled to particulars of an information charging perjury on a particular day, since it did not state what piece of evidence was alleged to be false.
1 Magistrates' Courts Act 1980, s 1(2).
2 See eg *R v Blandford, R v Freestone* [1955] 1 All ER 681; [1955] 1 WLR 331.
3 *R v Manchester Stipendiary Magistrates, ex parte Hill* [1983] 1 AC 328; sub nom *Hill v Anderton* [1982] 2 All ER 963.
4 MATHEW J in *Dixon v Wells* (1890) 25 QBD 249, at 257.
5 In *R v Fairford Justices, ex parte Brewster* [1976] QB 600; [1975] 2 All ER 757 the court indicated that no challenge can be made to the hearing of a valid information, even if followed by an invalid summons.

at his last known or usual place of abode; or (3) sending it by post in a letter addressed to him at his last known or usual place of abode.[6] If a person summoned for an indictable offence fails to appear at the trial, service of the summons by methods (2) or (3) above must not be treated as proved unless it is first shown that the summons came to the defendant's knowledge; for this purpose, however, a letter or other communication purporting to be written by or on behalf of the defendant and giving rise to the reasonable inference that the summons came to his knowledge shall be admissible as evidence of that fact.[7]

This limitation does not apply to a summary offence, but where a summons has been issued under section 1 of the Act of 1980, and the court has begun to try the information to which the summons relates, the defendant may at any time during or after the hearing make a statutory declaration[8] that he did not know of the summons until a date specified by him. Thereafter the information remains valid (with the result that subsequent proceedings will not be barred by lapse of time),[9] but all subsequent proceedings are void. There may be a fresh trial but not before any of the same magistrates.[10] A summons remains in force even though the magistrate who issued it ceases for any reason to be a magistrate and with certain exceptions it may be served at any time after issue.

4 Warrant[11]

A warrant, unlike a summons, is an order for the arrest of the defendant. It contains a statement of the offence charged, is (like a summons) signed by the issuing magistrate or justices' clerk, but (unlike a summons) is an order for arrest. It is addressed to the officers of the police area in which the warrant is issued and such other persons as are named in the warrant, and directs them to arrest a particular person. That person must be mentioned by name or otherwise described; general warrants, ie warrants which do not name the person to be arrested, have been held to be illegal at common law ever since a series of famous cases[12] in the eighteenth century.

A warrant may be executed (ie the arrest effected) anywhere in the United Kingdom, at any time,[13] by any person to whom the warrant is directed or by any police officer acting within his police area;[14] an officer making the arrest need not have the warrant in his possession at the time but must show it to the defendant as soon as is practicable, if the defendant demands to see it.[15] This duty is equivalent to the duty imposed on a

---

6 Magistrates' Courts Rules 1981, r 99.
7 *Ibid*, r 99(2).
8 Under the Magistrates' Courts Act 1980, s 14.
9 *Ibid*, s 127.
10 *Ibid*, s 14(4).
11 Strictly called "a warrant of arrest" there being various other types of warrant, such as a search warrant.
12 Notably *Money v Leach* (1765) 3 Burr 1742; *Entick v Carrington* (1765) 19 State Tr 1029, 95 ER 807.
13 Until withdrawn; Magistrates' Courts Act 1980, s 125(1).
14 *Ibid*, s 125(2).
15 *Ibid*, s 125(3). This is reasonable from the point of view of the police (since there may be many police seeking to make the arrest, but only one warrant) and also for the purpose of protecting the liberty of the subject.

person making an arrest without warrant to inform the defendant of the reason for his arrest.

When a magistrate issues a warrant he may at the same time endorse it with a direction that the person named in the warrant shall, on arrest, be released on bail, on such terms as may be specified in the endorsement. The warrant is then said to be "backed for bail", and the officer in charge of the police station to which the defendant is taken after arrest must release him (subject to approving any surety tendered in compliance with the endorsement).[16]

A magistrate's discretion as to whether to issue a summons or a warrant is limited, by section 1(4) of the Magistrates' Courts Act 1980. No warrant may be issued against a person who is seventeen or over, unless the offence is indictable or punishable with imprisonment, or unless the defendant's address is not "sufficiently established" for a summons to be served on him.

5 Arrest without warrant

Finally, the defendant may be arrested without warrant, under the powers earlier discussed.[17] The purpose of an arrest in such circumstances is to commence the criminal process, but the motive may in fact be to secure the lawful detention of the arrested person, so that the questioning may occur in the police station[18] and the arrested person must be brought before a court within the relevant statutory period, or released on bail.

D CLASSIFICATION OF OFFENCES

Prior to the implementation of Part III of the Criminal Law Act 1977 the law relating to the classification of criminal offences and the determination of the appropriate mode of trial, summary or on indictment, was complex. Thus there were provisions for summary offences to be tried on indictment and for indictable offences to be tried summarily, while there was a third class of offences, colloquially (though not by statute) called "hybrid" offences which might take on the character of either summary offences or indictable offences according to the election of the parties. These classifications were reviewed by the James Committee in 1975,[19] which had as its twin aims a simplification of the procedure and possible reduction in the case loads of the Crown Court. Its recommendations were in part controversial, but the majority of them were adopted, and implemented by Part III of the Criminal Law Act 1977.

---

16 *Ibid*, s 117. Special provisions relate to the execution of warrants in Eire: see the Backing of Warrants (Republic of Ireland) Act 1965 which resolved the difficulties revealed by the decision of the House of Lords in *Metropolitan Police Commissioner v Hammond* [1965] AC 810; [1964] 2 All ER 722.
17 See p 261, *ante*.
18 *Holgate-Mohammed v Duke* [1984] AC 437; [1984] 1 All ER 1054.
19 *The Distribution of Criminal Business between the Crown Court and Magistrates' Courts*, Cmnd 6323, HMSO.

As regards mode of trial there are now three classes of offence,[20] namely:

(a) offences triable only on indictment;[1]
(b) offences triable only summarily;[2] and
(c) offences triable either way.[3]

1   Offences triable only on indictment

Since offences can only fall within one of the other two categories if statute so provides, it follows that where there is no express statutory provision an offence is triable only on indictment. This involves a trial by judge and jury in the Crown Court, usually preceded by a hearing in the magistrates' court; this is not a trial, but merely an enquiry, known as a "preliminary enquiry" or, more generally, "committal proceedings".[4]

In practice only the gravest indictable offences are triable only on indictment; these include any offences for which a person may be sentenced to death, murder, genocide, manslaughter, infanticide, child destruction, abortion, rape, sexual intercourse with a girl under thirteen, sedition, mutiny, piracy, offences under section 1 of the Official Secrets Act 1911, robbery, wounding or causing grievous bodily harm "with intent", blackmail, assault with intent to rob, aggravated burglary and burglary comprising the commission of, or an intention to commit, an offence triable only on indictment. It will, however, be recalled that these are triable only on indictment if committed by an adult; as we shall see, in the case of children and young persons, all indictable offences (other than homicide) may, and in most cases must, be tried summarily.

2   Offences triable only summarily

The expressions "summary offence" and "offence triable only summarily" may be taken as synonymous. A statute creating a summary offence will first define the offence and then state that it is punishable "on summary conviction" with a particular penalty, thereby indicating that the offence is a summary one. In addition a number of offences which, prior to the Criminal Law Act 1977, were not summary offences according to the statute creating them, became so.[5]

Special rules apply to some offences under the Criminal Damage Act 1971: offences under section 1 of this Act (excluding arson) are triable only summarily if the "value involved" does not exceed £2,000.[6] Section 22 of

---

20 Criminal Law Act 1977, s 14.

1 This should be distinguished from the phrase "indictable offences", which means offences which, if committed by an adult, are triable on indictment, either exclusively or because they are "either way" offences: Interpretation Act 1978, s 5, Sch 1.

2 A "summary offence" means an offence which, if committed by an adult, is triable only summarily.

3 An "offence triable either way" means an offence which, if committed by an adult, is triable either on indictment or summarily.

4 See p 262, *post.*

5 See Criminal Law Act 1977, s 15. These comprise offences mentioned in Sch 1 to that Act, and which were formerly hybrid offences.

6 "The relevant sum" was fixed at this amount by the 1980 Act.

the Magistrates' Courts Act 1980 prescribes a procedure for determining whether such offences are to be regarded as summary or as triable either way (if the value involved exceeds £2,000). The court begins by hearing any representations made by the prosecutor or the accused as to the value involved; if it appears to the court clear that the value involved does not exceed the prescribed sum, it will proceed to summary trial. If it is clear that it does exceed that sum, then it will treat the offence as triable either way (which, of course, it then is[7]). If it is not clear whether or not the value involved does exceed the prescribed sum, then the accused is given the choice and told that if he consents to summary trial, his liability to imprisonment or to a fine will be limited to the maximum that magistrates have power to impose; the nature of the offence will then be determined in accordance with the accused's decision. If a person is convicted, either by a magistrates' court or by the Crown Court, he cannot appeal on the ground that the magistrates were mistaken as to the value involved.[8]

3 Offences triable either way

The third class of offence is offences triable either way. Those made so triable under the 1977 Act are now listed in Schedule 1 to the Magistrates' Courts Act 1980, which consists of 35 paragraphs incorporating some 66 separate offences; these include unlawful wounding or inflicting grievous bodily harm, with or without a weapon, assault occasioning actual bodily harm, common assault, bigamy, certain forms of perjury and forgery, unlawful sexual intercourse with a girl under 16, all indictable offences under the Theft Act 1968 (except robbery, blackmail, assault with intent to rob and certain burglaries), arson, offences under section 1 of the Criminal Damage Act 1971 where the value exceeds £2,000 (*supra*) and indecent assault. In addition many other statutes expressly provide for an offence to be triable either summarily or on indictment (the former "hybrid" offences) and these are now triable either way.[9]

Possible reform

The classification of offences described above has proved controversial. The James Committee proposed to reclassify offences of low value theft as summary offences, thus restricting the right to jury trial.[10] This proposal met strong resistance, because of the impact any conviction for theft can have upon a person's reputation and career, and was not implemented. The reclassification of offences was considered further by the Royal Commission on Criminal Justice, which did not believe the current distribution of cases between magistrates' courts and Crown Court was

---

7 The court must hear "representations", meaning submissions, assertions of fact and sometimes production of documents; however the court is not bound to hear evidence of the value involved: *R v Canterbury and St Augustine Justices, ex parte Klisiak* [1982] QB 398; [1981] 2 All ER 129; moreover it is permissible in cases of doubt for the prosecution to limit the charge to certain items clearly below the prescribed value, even though in fact other damaged items would take the value above the prescribed value (so as to ensure summary trial) (*ibid*).
8 Criminal Law Act 1977, s 22(8).
9 *Ibid*, s 17(2).
10 Cmnd 6323.

either always rational, or amounted to an efficient use of resources.[11] It did not, however, seek to resolve this perceived problem by reclassifying the offences themselves, but instead considered how, and on what grounds, the decision as to mode of trial of either way offences was taken. This is discussed later.[12]

E   PROCEDURE FOR DETERMINING MODE OF TRIAL

The procedure for determining the mode of trial differs according to whether or not the accused is an adult. If he is, then, as has been noted, he will always be tried on indictment for an offence triable only on indictment and will always be tried summarily for a summary offence; only in the case of an "either way" offence are there alternative possibilities. In the case of children and young persons the position is quite different. Before considering these procedures it should be noted that if magistrates mistakenly adopt a procedure which is not permitted, for example by "trying" a case which is triable only on indictment or by committing for trial in the case of an offence triable only summarily, then their "trial" or "committal" will be a complete nullity. Even if the defendant has been "sentenced" he may later be committed for trial and properly tried, if the offence was triable only on indictment.[13]

The choice of charge is that of the prosecution. If the charge preferred is appropriate on the facts given their seriousness, then the defence cannot challenge that charge on the basis that the preferment of another, different charge would have permitted trial on indictment.[14] Problems may also arise where fresh charges are levelled by the prosecutor, which, in reality, amount to attempts to deprive the justices of jurisdiction to try the case themselves. In *R v Brooks (Christopher)*[15] the appellant appeared before magistrates on a charge under section 20 of the Offences against the Person Act 1861. The appellant was content to be tried summarily, and the justices so ordered. The chief prosecuting solicitor then advised the bringing of a new charge under section 18 of the 1861 Act. In quashing the conviction obtained on such a charge O'CONNOR LJ observed that the prosecutor was seeking "to act as an appellate tribunal from the justices. There is no other explanation for it, and he said as much . . .". However, in *R v Redbridge Justices, ex parte Whitehouse*[16] it was made clear that it was the abuse of power that lead to the irregularity in *Brooks*. If the facts are capable of supporting a fresh charge, the justices must decide whether it is both proper and appropriate. If they have already decided on summary trial, any further charge which would have the effect of making summary trial impossible should be scrutinised with care, but is not totally prohibited. The operation of this principle was seen in *R v Sheffield Justices, ex parte Director of Public Prosecutions*[17] where the defendant elected trial on a

---

11 Ch 6, para 13–19.
12 See p 453, *post*.
13 See eg *R v West* [1964] 1 QB 15; [1962] 2 All ER 624.
14 *R v Canterbury & St Augustine Justices, ex parte Klisiak*, n 7, *supra*.
15 [1985] Crim LR 385.
16 (1991) 94 Cr App Rep 332.
17 [1993] Crim LR 136.

charge of assault occasioning actual bodily harm. The Crown then substituted a charge of common assault. Upon the magistrates staying the proceedings, the prosecutor successfully applied for judicial review. The substitution was a proper one, despite the fact that it deprived the accused of his right to trial by jury. There was no evidence of manipulation, and the defence had been notified of the proposal at an earlier stage. It was an appropriate charge on the facts.

1 Adults charged with "either way" offences

Before any evidence is called, a magistrates' court before whom a person aged seventeen or over appears charged with an offence triable either way must adopt the following procedure:

(1) If the prosecution is being carried on by the Attorney-General, the Solicitor-General or the Director of Public Prosecutions and he applies for the offence to be tried on indictment, then it must be tried in that way and the court must proceed as examining justices.[18] In any other case the following steps apply.

(2) The court must first cause the charge to be written down, if this has not already been done, and read to the accused.

(3) First the prosecutor and then the accused are given an opportunity to make representations as to which mode of trial would be more suitable.

(4) The court then considers whether the offence appears more suitable for summary trial or for trial on indictment, having regard to the representations referred to in (3) above, to the nature of the case, whether the circumstances make the offence one of serious character, whether the punishment which a magistrates' court would have power to inflict for it would be adequate and

"any other circumstances which appear to the court to make it more suitable for the offence to be tried in one way rather than the other."[19]

Although the Act is silent on the point, it is clear on principle that the "circumstances" to be taken into account by the justices in reaching their decision cannot include the accused's past record, unless, presumably, the accused himself relies upon this. It would be invidious to permit the prosecution to make representations concerning the accused's past record because the justices would then (improperly) know of it when conducting the ensuing trial or committal proceedings as the case may be. This is recognised by the National Mode of Trial Guidelines.[20]

(5) If, following consideration as above, it appears to the court that the offence is more suitable for trial on indictment, then it must tell the accused that it has so decided and will then proceed as examining justices, the accused having no power to prevent this course even if neither he nor the prosecution has requested it.[1]

---

18 A single justice may discharge this function, but could not (unless a stipendiary) go on to conduct a summary trial; Magistrates' Courts Act 1980, s 18(5).
19 *Ibid*, s 19(4).
20 See *infra*.
1 Magistrates' Courts Act 1980, s 19(3).

(6) If, on the other hand, "it appears to the court that the offence is more suitable for summary trial", then the court must explain to the accused in ordinary language that he can either consent to summary trial or, if he wishes, be tried by a jury and that if he is tried summarily and convicted he may be committed for sentence to the Crown Court under section 38 of the Magistrates' Courts Act 1980.[2]

(7) After explaining to the accused, as provided under (6) above, his options, the court asks him whether he consents to be tried summarily or wishes to be tried by a jury. If he consents to summary trial, the magistrates proceed to try him; if he does not consent, they proceed as examining justices.[3]

(8) There are provisions in section 25 of the Act whereby the magistrates may change from summary trial to committal proceedings and *vice versa*. Where the court has begun to try an either way offence summarily it may, at any time before the conclusion of the evidence for the prosecution, discontinue the summary trial and proceed as examining justices.[4] This will necessitate starting all over again and the court may adjourn the hearing without remanding the accused.

Conversely, if the court has already begun proceedings as a preliminary enquiry it may at any time, if it appears to the court having regard to any representations made by prosecutor or accused with consent of the accused (and with the consent of the Attorney-General, the Solicitor-General or the Director of Public Prosecutions if any of them is the prosecutor) proceed to try the information summarily.[5] As indicated, this can only be done with the accused's consent and, before asking him whether he consents, the court must in ordinary language explain to him what is proposed, that it can only be done with his consent and (unless it has already done so) must explain the court's power to commit to the Crown Court for sentence.[6] If the magistrates do change from a preliminary enquiry to a summary trial evidence already given is deemed to have been given in and for the purposes of the summary trial.[7] Where, however, the defendant pleads not guilty the court must recall for cross-examination any witness who has already given evidence, unless not required by either side for that purpose.[8] The reason for this is that at a preliminary enquiry the defence will usually be reserved completely, or at any rate hardly pressed, and cross-examination of the same witness may vary very much according to whether proceedings are to be regarded as the preliminary enquiry or the trial proper.

---

2 As amended by Criminal Justice Act 1991, s 25. See further, p 535, *post*. A failure to warn an accused person of the liability to committal for sentence renders the conviction and committal bad, as from the moment of that failure. A fresh charge may still be brought: Magistrates' Courts Act 1980, s 20.
3 Magistrates' Courts Act 1980, s 20(3).
4 *Ibid*, s 25(2). This cannot be done following a plea of guilty: *Re Gillard* [1986] AC 442.
5 *Ibid*, s 25(3).
6 *Ibid*, s 25(4).
7 *Ibid*, s 28.
8 Magistrates' Courts Rules 1981, r 21.

The accused must usually be present in court in person during the proceedings at which the mode of trial is determined.[9] However, the court may proceed in the absence of the accused if they consider that by reason of his disorderly conduct before them it is not practicable for the proceedings to be conducted in his presence. In addition, where the accused is represented by counsel or a solicitor who in his absence signifies to the court the accused's consent to the proceedings for determining how he is to be tried for the offence being conducted in his absence, and the court is satisfied that there is good reason for proceeding in the absence of the accused, then the court may proceed in the accused's absence.[10] In either case the consents required either to summary trial under (6) above (in this case there is no need for the court to explain its power to commit for sentence) or to summary trial of an offence under section 1 of the Criminal Damage Act 1971 (where it is not clear whether the value involved exceeds the prescribed limit)[11] may be given by the accused's counsel or solicitor.[12]

2 Children and young persons

The law has given significant protection to children and young persons. An attempt was made by the Children and Young Persons Act 1969 to prohibit the prosecution of children[13] for all crimes except murder, and severely limit the prosecution of young persons. However, these provisions were never brought into force, and were repealed in 1991,[14] leaving children and young persons open to prosecution, but with restrictions as to how proceedings shall be heard.

Whenever a child or young person appears before a magistrates' court charged with any indictable offence except "homicide" he must, subject to certain exceptions, be tried summarily.[15] This rule does not apply to an offence of homicide. Nor does it apply:

(a) in the case of a young person charged with an offence for which the penalty is in the case of an adult fourteen years' imprisonment or more,[16] not being an offence for which the sentence is fixed by law, and the court considers that if he is found guilty it ought to be possible to sentence him to detention under section 53(2) of the Children and Young Persons Act 1933; or

(b) in the case of a child or young person charged jointly with an adult (eighteen or over) if the court considers it necessary in the interests of justice to commit them both for trial.[17] In this case the court may

---

9 Magistrates' Courts Act 1980, s 18(2).
10 *Ibid*, ss 18(3), 23(1).
11 See p 447, *ante*.
12 Magistrates' Courts Act 1980, ss 23(3), (4).
13 A "child" is a person aged 10–13 inclusive. A "young person" is a person aged 14–17.
14 Criminal Justice Act 1991, Sch 13.
15 Magistrates' Courts Act 1980, s 24(1); "appears" means appears or is brought before the court when the court makes its decision as to the mode of trial so that an accused who attains the age of eighteen before this occasion is treated as an adult notwithstanding that he was a young person when he appeared at an earlier remand hearing; *R v Islington North Juvenile Court, ex parte Daley* [1983] 1 AC 347; sub nom *Re Daley* [1982] 2 All ER 974.
16 See p 504, *post*.
17 Magistrates' Courts Act 1980, s 24.

also commit the child or young person for any other indictable offence with which he is charged at the same time (whether jointly with an adult or not) if that other offence arises out of circumstances which are the same as or connected with those giving rise to the first offence.[18]

A child or young person not accused jointly with an adult will be tried in a youth court.[19] However, if charged jointly with an adult he will be tried in an ordinary magistrates' court unless the adult pleads guilty or is not tried summarily (so that they are no longer jointly charged) in which event the court may before any evidence is called in the case of the child or young person remit him to a youth court for trial.[20]

3   Factors that influence mode of trial.

It has been noted that, in respect of "either way" offences, the mode of trial is determined both by the magistrates' court and by the accused. Magistrates are given specific guidance as to how these powers should be used by the 'National Mode of Trial Guidelines' set out in a *Practice Note*.[1] The Note, having identified the requirements of section 19 of the Magistrates Courts' Act 1980, states:

  (a) the court should never make a decision on the ground of convenience or expedition;
  (b) the court should assume that the prosecution version of the facts is correct;
  (c) the defendant's antecedents and personal mitigating circumstances are irrelevant;
  (d) the fact that the offences are specimen charges is relevant. By contrast, the fact that the defendant will be asking for other offences to be taken into consideration is not;
  (e) where complex questions of fact, or difficult points of law, arise, the court should consider committal for trial;
  (f) a juvenile should only be committed with a co-accused aged 18 or over if it is necessary in the interests of justice. In addition the guidelines suggested that where there is more than one defendant, and one elects trial on indictment the court should proceed to deal with all the defendants as examining magistrates. However, this can no longer be regarded as sound in the light of the decision of the House of Lords in *R v Brentwood Justices, ex parte Nicholls*.[2] The House there was of the opinion that where there is more than one defendant, each has the individual right to elect the mode of trial, irrespective of the election made by the co- defendants;
  (g) either way offences should be tried summarily unless the particular case has one of the specified features, and the court considers that its sentencing powers are insufficient.

---

18 *Ibid*, s 24(2).
19 See p 164, *ante*.
20 Magistrates' Courts Act 1980, s 29.
 1 [1990] 3 All ER 979; [1990] 1 WLR 1439.
 2 [1992] 1 AC 1; sub nom *Nicholls v Brentwood Justices* [1991] 3 All ER 516.

The Note then goes into considerable detail, and in respect of each offence identifies relevant factors that may indicate that it ought to be tried on indictment. Thus, for example, burglary is made more serious if it is at night, or if during a daytime burglary persons are present on the property, if soiling or vandalism occurs, if the burglary displays professional hall-marks or is one of a series of similar offences.

Statistics show that the proportion of cases involving persons aged 17 years or over being committed for trial in 1991 was 23 per cent.[3] Only about one in five of cases dealt with in the Crown Court are in fact triable only on indictment, the rest being triable either way, and some evidence exists to show that the key decisions are made by the magistrates rather than defendants. In one study[4] the research team found that about 64 per cent of cases at Crown Court had been sent there because magistrates had declined jurisdiction.[5] The research period in question was prior to the introduction of the 'National Mode of Trial Guidelines', and it is not clear what impact they have had on these decisions. In terms of those who elect trial, the same research study identified as important factors a belief in the better prospect of acquittal at Crown Court than on summary trial, and the possibility of receiving a lighter sentence especially in the light of the negotiations between prosecution and defence as to the charges proceeded with.[6] Yet some 70 per cent of defendants electing trial at the Crown Court end up pleading guilty.[7]

This was not regarded as a satisfactory state of affairs by the Royal Commission on Criminal Justice. It believed that there should be a more rational division of either way cases, to be achieved by modification of the procedures for determining mode of trial.[8] The decision should not be left to the defendant, but ultimately should be that of the court unless both prosecution and defence were able to reach agreement.[9] In cases where that was not possible the court itself should decide, bearing in mind the gravity of the offence, the past record of the defendant, the complexity of the case, and its likely effect on the defendant were he to be convicted.[10]

These proposals have proved controversial.[11] The Royal Commission believes that the fact that a defendant anticipates a fairer trial on indictment, or a better chance of acquittal, does not provide a rational

---

3 *Criminal Statistics for England & Wales*, 1991, para 6.4.

4 Hedderman and Moxon, *Magistrates Court or Crown Court – Mode of Trial Decisions and Sentencing* (Home Office Research Study No 125, 1992). The Royal Commission on Criminal Justice quotes figures of 52 per cent of cases being tried on indictment by magistrates' direction, with a further 30 per cent by way of election by the defendant: Ch 6, para 5.

5 The same study found that in 62 per cent of these cases, the sentence imposed was within the power of the magistrates' court to impose.

6 *Ibid*, Table 3.1. This perception is confirmed by Zander and Henderson, *The Crown Court Study* (Royal Commission Research Study No 19, HMSO, 1993). For other research, see Bottoms and McClean, *Defendants in the Criminal Process* (Routledge & Kegan, 1976); Vennard, 'The Outcome of Contested Trials' in *Managing Criminal Justice* (ed Moxon, HMSO, 1985). See also p 439, *ante*.

7 *Ibid*.

8 Ch 6, para 13.

9 *Ibid*.

10 *Ibid*, para 13.

11 See in particular, Ashworth, "Plea, Venue and Discontinuance" [1993] Crim LR 830, and the sources therein cited.

basis for determining the court of trial. By contrast, loss of reputation is regarded as an important, though not decisive, factor. The Commission also regarded the reductions of the work-load pressures on the Crown Court as a desirable objective.[12] By contrast, critics have attacked the principle of limiting jury trial further, and have pointed in particular to the unfair impact the Royal Commission's proposals will have upon those who have previous convictions, and, as a result, are more likely to be deprived of jury trial. It remains to be seen how far the Royal Commission's proposals in this respect are included in forthcoming legislation.

F BAIL

1 Nature of bail

A person is "granted bail" when he is released from the custody of the law subject to a duty to surrender to custody at some future time. The "custody" is the custody of a court unless bail was granted by a police officer, in which event it is the custody of the officer. Considerable changes in the law were effected by the Bail Act 1976, which gave effect to many, though not all, of the recommendations of a Home Office Working Party Report which identified the deficiencies of the old law.[13] Previously bail involved entering into a "recognisance" which is an acknowledgment of a debt to the Queen payable on default of compliance with the conditions of the recognisance. The 1976 Act abolished personal recognisances from the accused[14] but preserved them for sureties (where these are required). If granted bail the accused is under a duty to surrender to custody when required; if he fails without reasonable cause to do so he commits an offence under section 6(1) of the 1976 Act, punishable either on summary conviction or as a contempt of court.[15]

Bail may be granted either unconditionally or, in some circumstances, subject to conditions. Before any conditions can be imposed it must appear to the court that such conditions are necessary to prevent a failure to surrender to custody, to prevent the commission of an offence while on bail, to prevent interference with witnesses or an obstruction of the course of justice, or to allow inquiries or reports to be made to assist the court in respect of the defendant's physical or mental state.[16] These are, in fact, similar to the factors a court may rely upon in refusing bail where the court believes that "substantial grounds" to believe that any of them apply exist,[17] and in *R v Mansfield Justices, ex parte Sharkey*[18] it was argued that "substantial grounds" likewise had to exist before a court could impose conditions. This argument was rejected by the Court of Appeal. It was enough that a court considered that there was a real and not fanciful risk of

---

12 Royal Commission on Criminal Justice: Ch 6, para 15.
13 *Bail Procedures in Magistrates' Courts* (1974).
14 Bail Act 1976, s 3(2).
15 *Ibid*, s 3(4).
16 *Ibid*, s 3(6). The reports referred to will almost always be into his physical or mental state.
17 *Ibid*, Sch 1, para 1.
18 [1985] QB 613; [1985] 1 All ER 193.

an offence being committed whilst the accused was on bail. In this case, the justices were entitled to impose conditions preventing the defendants from picketing or demonstrating at places other than their own places of work, during a major industrial dispute in the coal industry and where the court knew that disturbances at coal pits had occurred.

Where conditions can be imposed, they may cover a wide variety of matters. They may comprise the provision of a surety or sureties to secure the person's surrender to custody; the provision of security (if it appears that he is unlikely to remain in Great Britain until the time appointed for him to surrender to custody); requirements to secure that he surrenders to custody, does not commit any offence while on bail, does not interfere with witnesses or otherwise obstruct the course of justice or makes himself available for the purpose of enabling inquiries or a report to be made to assist the court in dealing with him for the offence.[19] Conditions commonly imposed include conditions of residence, as to surrender of passport, reporting to a police station at prescribed times, not visiting specified premises and not approaching specified persons. Conditions imposed by a court may be varied by that court on the application of the person bailed, the prosecutor or a constable.[20]

2   Occasions for the grant of bail

The question of when bail may be granted to a person may arise at various stages of his case, from the moment that he is arrested to the final determination of any appeal arising out of his conviction. Bail in cases of treason can only be granted by order of a High Court judge or the Home Secretary.[1] In other cases, bail may be granted as follows.

a   By the police

We have seen that a warrant of arrest may be "backed for bail" in which event the officer in charge of the station to which the defendant is taken after his arrest must release him, subject to approving any surety tendered in compliance with the endorsement on the warrant.[2] Also, where the arrest is without a warrant the police have certain powers and duties under section 43 of the Magistrates' Courts Act 1980 in relation to the grant of bail.[3] The lack of a power to grant bail subject to conditions may lead to unnecessary court appearances.[4]

---

19 Bail Act 1976, s 3(6); these conditions may be imposed only by a court (not by a police officer). In murder cases, unless satisfactory reports on the accused's mental condition have already been obtained, the court must impose as conditions of bail (a) a requirement that the accused shall undergo examination by two medical practitioners for the purpose of enabling such reports to be prepared; and (b) a requirement that he shall for that purpose attend such an institution or place as the court directs (*ibid*, s 3(6A)).
20 *Ibid*, s 3(8).
 1 Magistrates' Courts Act 1980, s 41.
 2 *Ibid*, s 117; see p 445, *ante*.
 3 See p 445, *ante*.
 4 For such conditions, see n 19, *ante*.

b   By magistrates

Magistrates have power to grant bail at various stages of proceedings. When an accused person is first brought before a magistrates' court charged with an offence it quite often happens that the prosecution is not ready to proceed in which event the proceedings are adjourned and the accused is remanded, either in custody or on bail. This may arise in the course of summary proceedings or where the offence is triable only on indictment (in which event the magistrates will eventually conduct a preliminary enquiry) or where it is triable "either way".[5]

Secondly, if, after holding a preliminary enquiry, magistrates decide to commit the accused to the Crown Court for trial, that committal may be in custody or on bail.[6]

Thirdly, following summary conviction, the magistrates have power if they commit the defendant to the Crown Court for sentence (where this is open to them)[7] to commit in custody or on bail.[8]

Finally, following conviction, if the magistrates adjourn for the purpose of considering sentence they may remand the defendant on bail or in custody[9] and, having imposed a custodial sentence, they may, if a person has given notice of appeal or applied to the magistrates to state a case,[10] grant bail.[11]

If bail is refused on a remand, the maximum period of remand is eight clear days[12] unless he is already serving a custodial sentence, in which event it is 28 clear days.[13] There may, of course, be further remands thereafter.[14]

Where magistrates adjourn a summary trial, committal proceedings or the determination of the method of trial of an either way offence and remand the accused in custody, they may, if the accused is an adult, order that he be brought up for any subsequent remands before an alternative magistrates' court nearer to the prison where he is to be confined on remand.[15]

Although successive applications for bail may be made to a magistrates' court (or to any court having power to grant bail), the Bail Act 1976

---

5 Magistrates' Courts Act 1980, s 18(4); see p 447, *ante*.

6 *Ibid*, s 6(3).

7 See pp 535–540, *post* for the cases in which they may do this.

8 Magistrates' Courts Act 1980, s 38 and the other provisions permitting committal, except Mental Health Act 1983, s 43.

9 Magistrates' Courts Act 1980, s 128(1); if the remand is for medical examination and report, it must not be for more than three weeks, if in custody, or four weeks, if on bail and, if on bail, conditions as to undergoing medical examination must be imposed (*ibid*, s 30).

10 As to this procedure, see p 542, *post*.

11 Magistrates' Courts Act 1980, s 113.

12 *Ibid*, s 128(6); "clear days" means omitting the day of the remand and the day fixed for appearance. But in certain circumstances this may be exceeded: see Magistrates' Courts Act 1980, s 128A (inserted by Criminal Justice Act 1988, s 155). The key condition is that a previous remand must have been made.

13 *Ibid*, s 131(1).

14 *Ibid*, s 129(1).

15 *Ibid*, s 130; this is a security measure introduced by the Criminal Law Act 1977 to minimise the risks inherent in transporting dangerous prisoners over long distances. There are provisions for remands to be made in the absence of the accused (ss 128, 129).

restricts the scope for continued applications.[16] If bail has been refused a second application for bail can be supported with any argument that is desired, whether or not put before the court before. At any subsequent hearings the court need not hear arguments as to fact or law that it has heard previously.[17]

Concern has arisen about offences being committed whilst on bail. As a result, the Bail (Amendment) Act 1993[18] will give a limited right of appeal to the prosecution, in cases where the accused is charged with an offence with a maximum punishment of at least five years' imprisonment, with taking a conveyance without consent, or with aggravated vehicle-taking.[19]

c By the Crown Court

The Crown Court may grant bail to any person:[20]

(a) who has been committed in custody for appearance (trial or sentence) before the Crown Court; or

(b) who is in custody pursuant to a sentence imposed by a magistrates' court and has appealed against conviction or sentence; or

(c) who is in the custody of the Crown Court pending the disposal of his case by the Crown Court; or

(d) who, after the decision of the Crown Court in his case, has applied to the Crown Court to state a case for the High Court;[1] or

(e) who has applied to the High Court for an order of certiorari, or for leave to apply, in respect of proceedings in the Crown Court;[2] or

(f) to whom the Crown Court has granted a certificate under the Criminal Appeal Act 1968 (case fit for appeal); or

(g) who has been remanded in custody by a magistrates' court, where he has been refused bail by that court after hearing full argument.[3]

The prosecution also has a limited right of appeal against the grant of bail.[4] For this right to exist the prosecution must have objected to bail at the hearing before the magistrates' court. The prosecution have to

---

16 Sch 1, Part IIA to the Bail Act 1976, inserted by Criminal Justice Act 1988, s 154. These provisions are designed to implement in statutory form the decision of the court in *R v Nottingham Justices, ex parte Davies* [1981] QB 38; [1980] 2 All ER 775.

17 Even if refused bail on remand, an accused is entitled to have his right to bail fully reviewed at the stage of committal for trial: *R v Reading Crown Court, ex parte Malik* [1981] QB 451; [1981] 1 All ER 249.

18 Section 1(2). This provision is not yet in force.

19 Under the Theft Act 1968, s 12, as amended by Aggravated Vehicle-Taking Act 1992.

20 Supreme Court Act 1981, s 81 (as amended).

1 See p 542, *post.*

2 This only applies to appellate proceedings in the Crown Court, because while it is sitting as a court of trial it is not amenable to prerogative order; see p xxx, *ante.*

3 Cases (f) and (g) were added by the Criminal Justice Act 1982. Previously the Crown Court had no power to grant bail pending appeal to the Court of Appeal, nor prior to committal for trial (in the former case application had to be made to the Court of Appeal, in the latter to a High Court judge in chambers).

4 See *supra.*

show that there is a risk to the public of serious harm if the accused is bailed. The appeal is by way of rehearing.[5] The Crown Court may remand the defendant in custody or on bail subject to such conditions as it thinks fit.

d   By the High Court

Whenever a magistrates' court withholds bail in criminal proceedings or imposes conditions in granting bail, the High Court may grant bail or vary the conditions.[6] The High Court may also grant bail pending any application for certiorari or for the statement of a case by the Crown Court or a magistrates' court, or pending appeal from the Queen's Bench divisional court to the House of Lords.[7]

The application for bail in the High Court is by summons to the prosecutor before a judge in chambers in the Queen's Bench Division to show cause why bail should not be granted, or why the variation in conditions of bail proposed by the applicant should not be made. If an applicant for bail in the High Court is refused bail by a judge in chambers, he cannot make fresh applications to any other judge or to the divisional court[8] and there is no appeal against the judge's decision.

e   By the Court of Appeal

The Court of Appeal has power to grant bail pending appeal to that court or pending a retrial ordered by that court following such an appeal[9] or pending appeal from that court to the House of Lords.[10] It is rare for the Court of Appeal to grant bail, but it occasionally does so, for example where the sentence appealed against is a short one so that it might be served by the time the appeal comes on for hearing, or where there is a strong *prima facie* likelihood of success.[11]

3   The right to bail

The marginal note to section 4 of the Bail Act 1976 is "General right to bail of accused persons and others" (the "others" being persons who are brought up for breach of the requirements of probation, community service or combination orders,[12] or persons who have been remanded following conviction for reports). The section created a statutory presumption in favour of granting bail and provides that, except as provided in

---

5 For the relevant procedure, see s 81(2) of the Supreme Court Act 1981. Where notice of appeal is given orally, the magistrates must remand the defendant in custody pending hearing of the appeal.

6 Criminal Justice Act 1967, s 22 (as amended by Bail Act 1976, Sch 2).

7 Administration of Justice Act 1960, s 4.

8 RSC, Ord 79, r 9(11); cf *Re Kray* [1965] Ch 736; [1965] 1 All ER 710.

9 Criminal Appeal Act 1968, ss 8(2), 19; the power may be exercised by the single judge (*ibid*, ss 31, 45(2)).

10 *Ibid*, s 36. By s 37, if the prosecutor is appealing to the House of Lords and, but for the decision of the Court of Appeal, the appellant would be liable to be detained, the Court of Appeal may make an order providing for his detention or directing that he shall not be released except on bail; there is similar provision on prosecution appeals from the Queen's Bench divisional court (Administration of Justice Act 1960, s 5).

11 *R v Watton* (1978) 68 Cr App Rep 293.

12 Section 4(3), as amended by the Criminal Justice Act 1991. For these orders, see p 507, *post*.

Schedule 1 to the Act, bail shall be granted to a person who appears before a magistrates' court or the Crown Court in the course of or in connection with proceedings or applies for bail in connection with proceedings. It does not apply (save in the case of remand for reports) after conviction.

Schedule 1 contains detailed provisions relating to circumstances in which bail may justifiably be withheld. These vary according to whether the accused is charged with an "imprisonable offence" or a "non-imprisonable offence", that is to say whether or not the offence is punishable with imprisonment (even if the accused himself, for example by reason of his age, would not be liable to be imprisoned for it).

If the offence is non-imprisonable the only circumstances in which bail may be withheld are:

(1) if the defendant having previously been granted bail, has failed to comply with his obligation to surrender to custody and the court believes that he would so fail again;

(2) if the court is satisfied that the defendant should be kept in custody for his own protection or, if he is a child or young person, for his own welfare;

(3) if he is already in custody pursuant to a court sentence;[13]

(4) if, having been granted bail in the instant proceedings, he has been arrested for absconding or breaking the conditions of his bail.[14]

If the offence is imprisonable, there is a much wider range of circumstances in which bail may be justifiably withheld, in addition to those listed above. These are as follows:

(5) if the court is satisfied that there are substantial grounds for believing that the defendant, if released on bail (whether subject to conditions or not) would:

   (a) fail to surrender to custody; or
   (b) commit an offence while on bail; or
   (c) interfere with witnesses or otherwise obstruct the course of justice;

(6) where it has not been practicable for want of time to obtain sufficient information to enable the court to make its decision;

(7) where a case is adjourned for inquiries or report and it appears that it would be impracticable to complete the inquiries or make the report without keeping the defendant in custody.[15]

In considering the grounds referred to under (5) above the court must have regard to the nature and seriousness of the offence or default, the character, antecedents, associations and community ties of the defendant, the defendant's record in relation to fulfilling his obligations under previous grants of bail in criminal proceedings, the strength of the evidence against him and any other considerations which appear to be relevant.[16]

The Act[17] contains detailed provisions for recording the decisions of

---

13 Or a sentence of an authority acting under the Army, Air Force or Naval Discipline Acts.
14 Bail Act 1976, Sch 1, Part II.
15 *Ibid*, Sch 1, Part I.
16 *Ibid*, Sch 1, Part I, para 9.
17 Section 5.

both courts and police officers in relation to bail and entitling defendants to copies of records of such decisions. Where a court withholds bail or imposes or varies conditions of bail in the case of a person who has a "right to bail" in criminal proceedings, it must give reasons and these are recorded with the record of the decision.[18]

Where a magistrates' court withholds bail from a person who is not represented by counsel or solicitor, the court must inform him of his right to apply to the High Court (and, on committal for trial, to the Crown Court) for bail.[19]

4   Sureties

As already noted, the 1976 Act abolished personal recognisances from defendants (although persons unlikely to remain in Great Britain may be required to provide security). Recognisances still exist, however, in relation to sureties; these are persons who are sometimes colloquially said to "stand bail" for the accused. If a person is granted bail subject to the provision of sureties, the court must fix the amounts of the sureties and must also be satisfied that the proposed sureties are suitable having regard to their financial resources, character and any previous convictions and proximity (whether in point of kinship, place of residence or otherwise) to the defendant.[20] In practice courts are usually guided by the police in matters relating to the suitability of proposed sureties.

Before sureties are taken it is the practice to explain the nature of the obligations being undertaken so as to ensure that the proposed surety understands them and to warn of the consequences of the defendant failing to answer to his bail. These are, *prima facie*, forfeiture of the amount of the recognisance and possible imprisonment in default. The court has power to order the surety, in the event of default by the defendant, to forfeit the whole of the amount of the recognisance or part thereof.[1] Before exercising its discretion the court must give the surety the opportunity to be heard and must take into account circumstances relating either to means or to the surety's culpability for the non-appearance of the defendant which might make it fair and just for the surety not to be ordered to forfeit the whole amount of the recognisance. Although not decisive, the conduct of the surety will be an important factor in the decision of the court as to whether or not to order forfeiture, either in whole or in part. In *R v Southampton Justices, ex parte Green*[2] LORD DENNING MR stated that if the surety was guilty of no want of diligence and used every effort to secure the appearance of the accused it might be proper to remit the sum entirely. Imprisonment may be ordered in default of payment, of up to twelve months.

It is an offence, punishable on summary conviction or as a contempt of court, to agree to indemnify a surety in criminal proceedings (or, in the case of the surety himself, to be indemnified).[3]

---

18 Bail Act 1976, s 5(3), (4).
19 *Ibid*, s 5(6).
20 *Ibid*, s 8(2).
 1 Magistrates' Courts Act 1980, s 120(3); Powers of Criminal Courts Act 1973, s 31.
 2 [1976] QB 11; [1975] 2 All ER 1073.
 3 Bail Act 1976, s 9; for powers of committal to the Crown Court for sentence, see p 535, *post*.

An order of the Crown Court estreating the recognisance of a surety for a defendant who has failed to surrender to his bail to stand trial is not a "matter relating to trial on indictment" (within section 29(3) of the Supreme Court Act 1981) so that the order is subject to judicial review.[4]

---

4 *Re Smalley* [1985] AC 622; sub nom *Smalley v Crown Court at Warwick* [1985] 1 All ER 769.

CHAPTER 23

Trial of an Indictable Offence

Trial of an indictable offence involves trial by judge and jury in the Crown Court, with the significant expenditure of both time and money. The nature of the jury system,[1] and the reasons for election of trial on indictment of either way offences[2] have already been discussed. In this Chapter we examine the procedures themselves that are involved in trial on indictment. These were the subject of significant discussion by the Royal Commission on Criminal Justice which reported in 1993,[3] and which sought to strike a balance between changes necessary to ensure a fair trial, and those necessary to make the system of trial of indictable offences more efficient.

A   PRELIMINARY INQUIRY

1   Introduction

The first stage of the trial of an indictable offence will be the preliminary inquiry before justices,[4] although increasingly this is of a formal nature, and in some cases dispensed with totally. Its purpose is to provide initial judicial scrutiny of the prosecution case against the accused, and to ensure that sufficient evidence exists to justify requiring the accused to stand trial on indictment, with the expense and personal suffering that inevitably arises.

Great changes to the nature of committal proceedings were made by the Criminal Justice Act 1967. Up until 1967, the preliminary inquiry was oral in nature: prosecution witnesses had to give evidence orally, and the magistrates had to go through the motions of satisfying themselves that there was sufficient evidence to put the defendant on trial by jury. This was the case even where the sufficiency of the prosecution evidence was not being questioned, even by the defendant. Furthermore, since the magistrates often sat in open court, the resulting publicity in notorious cases sometimes gave rise to the creation of a real risk of prejudice to the trial itself. The 1967 Act therefore introduced new procedures, allowing

---

1 See p 201, *ante*.
2 See p 452, *ante*.
3 Cm 2263, HMSO, 1993.
4 Otherwise known as committal proceedings.

committal without consideration of the evidence, thus saving much time and expense. It also introduced changes limiting the publicity that can be given to evidence, or details of the offence.[5]

The majority of committals are now by this procedure. The Royal Commission received evidence that full committal proceedings, involving a hearing, occurred in only about 8 per cent of all cases that are tried on indictment.[6] The need for committal proceedings at all has been the subject of debate in recent years. As already noted, most committals are a formality. Further, research undertaken for the Royal Commission on Criminal Justice identified the significant number of acquittals that occur as a result of a direction by the judge to jury to acquit.[7] One conclusion that could be drawn from that is that committal proceedings do not provide an effective filter to prevent weak cases being committed for trial. This was in fact the view of the Royal Commission on Criminal Procedure in 1981.[8] It took the view that committal proceedings did not operate as an effective filter to prevent weak cases from reaching the Crown Court, and proposed the abolition of full committal proceedings. Indeed, they proposed a new procedure, to be known as "application for discharge" whereby the defence would be given the option of a hearing before magistrates at which to make a submission of no case to answer after the prosecution case had been disclosed in writing. It also proposed the abolition of the paper committals introduced in 1967.

The matter was considered further by the Fraud Trials Committee in 1986.[9] The committee identified the following objections to committal proceedings:

(i) the length of time taken by full committals, and the subsequent delays that arose;

(ii) the potential for abuse, where proceedings are undertaken in the hope of acquiring material to use as a defence, in the hope that advantage could be gained if witnesses die, go abroad or suffer from fading memories;

(iii) the difficulties magistrates have in dealing with serious fraud cases;

(iv) the cost;

(v) the small number of defendants discharged in fraud cases.

The committee recommended an interim procedural reform, until action might be taken by government on the Royal Commission recommendations in respect of serious fraud cases. The resulting changes were introduced in the Criminal Justice Act 1987.[10]

More recently, Parliament has limited committal proceedings in some cases involving children,[11] and in cases involving war crimes.[12] Where these provisions apply, a notice of transfer can be served which effectively deprives the magistrates of jurisdiction and leads to automatic transfer to the Crown Court. These cases are discussed later.

---

5 See p 468, *post.*

6 Report, Ch 6, para 23.

7 See p 452, *ante*

8 Cmnd 8092, HMSO, 1981.

9 See p 202, *ante.*

10 Criminal Justice Act 1987, s 4. See p 471, *post.*

11 Criminal Justice Act 1991, s 53.

12 War Crimes Act 1991, s 1.

This approach commended itself to the Royal Commission on Criminal Justice.[13] It recommended the abolition of the full committal procedure, but with the defence being able to make oral submissions of no case to answer, to be considered on the evidence in the case papers. In either way offences, submissions would be to a magistrates' court, and be dealt with by a stipendiary magistrate, but in respect of offences triable only on indictment such submissions would be to the Crown Court.[14] The principle of these recommendations, though not the detail, has been accepted, and it is proposed to abolish committal proceedings in the Criminal Justice and Public Order Bill currently before Parliament. If enacted, the prosecution will apply for transfer of any case triable on indictment alone, or of an either way offence to be tried on indictment. The defence will then have a right to apply to a magistrates' court for dismissal of that charge.

2 Procedure

a   Committal without consideration of the evidence

Under the 1967 Act, it is open to the court to commit for trial "without consideration of the evidence" if all the evidence before it consists of written statements in the form required by the Act. Provided that all conditions are satisfied, the statements are admissible in committal proceedings to the same extent that oral evidence to the same effect, by the makers of statements, would be. Such statements will normally be those of the prosecution witnesses, the defence not revealing its case at this early stage.[15]

The procedure can only be used if the defendant is legally represented, and agrees. The court also has the right to require any or all of the witnesses to attend and give oral evidence. The statements must be signed with a declaration that the statement is true to the best of the maker's knowledge or belief; before it is tendered to the court a copy must be given to all other parties (ie, normally by the prosecution to the defence), none of whom must object to the statement being tendered to the court.[16] Normally, the prosecution will have ascertained in advance that there will be no objection, and would not use the procedure otherwise. They will also inform the court that all their evidence is in the form of written statements, copies of which have been given to the defence.

Thus far, statements having been tendered to the defence without objection, the court must cause the charge to be written down and read to the defendant if not already done, and then may itself receive the statements and commit for trial, at once, on the statements, without any consideration of the strength of the prosecution evidence contained in them, or even reading them.[17] The court will however consider the statements and will

---

13 Report, Ch 6, paras 26–32. The Criminal Justice and Public Order Bill may implement these provisions: see The Times, 8 February 1994.

14 The Royal Commission makes consequential recommendations about the appropriate court for an application for bail, and in respect of the time limits for making such applications of no case to answer: paras 31 and 29.

15 For disclosure of evidence, see p 479, *post.*

16 Magistrates' Courts Act 1980, s 102(2). Service on the solicitor for the defendant suffices, but where there is more than one defendant, there must be one copy of the statements for each defendant: *R v Bott, R v Baker* [1968] 1 All ER 1119; [1968] 1 WLR 583.

17 Magistrates' Courts Rules 1981, r 6(1)–(3).

therefore depart from this procedure if counsel or a solicitor for the defendant or any of the defendants submits that they contain insufficient evidence to put his client on trial by jury,[18] and, not unnaturally, cannot commit under this procedure if the defendant wishes to give evidence himself or call witnesses. In any event, the statements must be authenticated by a signature from one of the magistrates, either individually or by one single certificate.

b   "Old-style" committal

If the parties do not agree to the use of the section 6(2) procedure, or if the other conditions for its use are not satisfied, the court can only proceed with what is now called an "old-style" committal. On appearing, the defendant is not of course asked to plead, since this is not the trial of the charge against him; indeed it may well not be until a later stage in the inquiry (as will be seen) that any specific charge is recorded in writing.

The prosecutor may make an opening speech, outlining for the benefit of the justices the facts against the accused; it is a matter for his discretion whether he does so. He will then call his evidence, which may consist of witnesses giving evidence orally or of written statements. If witnesses give evidence orally their evidence must be given on oath, subject to any enactment or rule of law permitting or authorising the reception of unsworn evidence.[19] They will first be examined in chief by the prosecution; they will then be subject to cross-examination on behalf of the defence and, if cross-examined, to re-examination on behalf of the prosecution. As each witness for the prosecution gives his or her evidence it will be recorded by the court clerk; then, as soon as possible after the examination of the witness is concluded, the whole record of that witness's evidence must be read over to him in the presence and hearing of the defendant. After making any corrections that are necessary the witness must sign the document.[20] The record of the witness's evidence is called a "deposition"; as will be seen, depositions are documents of considerable importance in the general process of the trial of an indictable offence. A deposition must be authenticated in the same way as a written statement, by signature of a magistrate.

In all of the above process it is theoretically open to the defence to object to the admissibility of evidence. The prosecution cannot rely on inadmissible evidence, but the decision of examining magistrates to receive inadmissible evidence generally will not be interfered with by way of judicial review, except where manifest injustice would otherwise arise.[1] Whilst examining magistrates have a discretion to exclude evidence, they should not generally use it, but rather leave such matters to the court of trial.[2] Nor should committal proceedings be adjourned for the purposes of judicial review of the processes the court has followed in hearing the evidence.[3]

It is also open to the prosecution to tender written statements, in exactly

---

18 Magistrates' Courts Act 1980, s 6(2)(b).
19 *Ibid*, s 98.
20 Magistrates' Courts Rules 1981, r 7(2).
 1 *Neill v North Antrim Magistrates' Court* [1992] 4 All ER 846; [1992] 1 WLR 1220.
 2 *R v Kings' Lynn Magistrates' Court, ex parte Holland* [1993] 2 All ER 377; [1993] 1 WLR 324.
 3 *R v Wells Street Stipendiary Magistrates, ex parte Seillon* [1978] 3 All ER 257; [1978] 1 WLR 1002.

the same form as those used under the section 6(2) procedure. Again, copies must be given to each of the defendants before they are tendered to the court and none of the defendants must object to their use.[4] The court or any party has power to require the attendance of the maker. This procedure is very useful in the case of a witness, such as the owner of the property in many cases of theft or handling, whose evidence is not disputed by anyone but is necessary for the prosecution to prove their case. The statement must be read aloud unless the court otherwise directs, and the court may direct that an "account" be given of any part not read aloud.

The function of committal proceedings is simply to ensure that no-one shall stand trial unless there is a *prima facie* case against him. Accordingly there is no greater obligation upon the prosecution than to adduce sufficient evidence to establish a *prima facie* case. The prosecution is not obliged to call all of the witnesses who will be called at the trial and cannot be compelled to call any particular witness even if that witness is the principal witness against the accused,[5] although the prosecution should call the evidence of a witness upon whose identification of the accused the case wholly or substantially rests.[6]

After the whole of the evidence of the prosecution has been given the defence may submit that there is no case to answer, either on the charge brought against the accused (assuming that a specific charge has been formulated at this stage), or generally. In other words it may be submitted either that the charge brought should be reduced to a lesser charge (murder to manslaughter for example) or that the accused should be discharged altogether as being completely innocent of any crime. Such a submission is only likely to succeed in the clearest of cases, since, it will be recalled, the magistrates are not concerned at this stage to assess the actual guilt or innocence of the defendant; their only duty is to decide whether there is sufficient evidence against the accused to put him on trial for any indictable offence. If no submission of "no case" is made, or if it is rejected, the magistrates must cause the charge to be written down, if this has not already been done, and then, if he is not represented by counsel or a solicitor, read out to the defendant and its nature explained to him in ordinary language.[7] Then, before the defendant is allowed to say anything in answer to the charge the court must administer to him the statutory caution,[8] which is as follows:

> "You will have an opportunity to give evidence on oath before us and to call witnesses. But first I am going to ask you whether you wish to say anything in answer to the charge. You need not say anything unless you wish to do so; and you have nothing to hope from any promise, and nothing to fear from any threat, that may have been held out to induce you to make any admission or

---

4 Magistrates' Courts Act 1980, s 102.

5 *R v Epping and Harlow Justices, ex parte Massaro* [1973] QB 433; [1973] 1 All ER 1011. The witness in this case was a little girl who was the victim of an alleged sexual assault by the accused. Although the defence were anxious to cross-examine her at the committal proceedings the prosecution decided not to call her and the accused was committed for trial on other evidence. The divisional court refused an application for an order of *certiorari* and upheld the validity of the committal. Such problems in cases of this type no longer arise: see p 470, *post*. See also Magistrates' Courts Act 1980, s 103.

6 For identification evidence, see p 575, *post*.

7 Magistrates' Courts Rules 1981, r 7(6).

8 *Ibid*, r 7(7).

confession of guilt. Anything you say will be taken down and may be given in evidence at your trial. Do you wish to say anything in answer to the charge?"

Whatever the defendant says in answer to the charge, once the statutory caution is complete, must be taken down in writing, read over to him and signed by one of the examining justices and also by the defendant if he so wishes.[9] This statement may then be given in evidence at the trial of the defendant (assuming that he is committed for trial) without the need for further proof.

Once the defendant has made such answer as he wishes, within the acceptable boundary, to make in response to the statutory caution, the court must further give him an opportunity to give evidence himself and to call witnesses.[10] If he wishes to take this course he must be permitted to do so, even if he has already made an unsuccessful submission of no case to answer.[11] He can, therefore, have "two bites at the cherry" since he may again try to persuade the magistrates, at the conclusion of all the evidence, that there is no *prima facie* case to justify committal.

However, in practice, if a submission of no case fails, it is overwhelmingly likely that the magistrates will ultimately commit and, therefore, it may do the defendant no good, and indeed positive harm, tactically, to give evidence and thereby reveal his case at this stage, especially if there is no question of being committed on a lesser charge. The defendant frequently "reserves his defence".[12] If defence evidence is called at this stage, the procedure is as follows. It is unusual for the defendant's solicitor or counsel to make an opening speech, but he may do so, in his discretion; except in one case,[13] he has only one chance to address the court and as a matter of tactics he will usually take it after his evidence and not before. Defence evidence will then be called. Any evidence, whether that of the defendant himself or any of his witnesses, will be reproduced in the form of depositions, or may be by written statement, in exactly the same way as the evidence of prosecution witnesses except in the unusual circumstance of a character witness being called.

c   Time-limits

It has already been seen that the Prosecution of Offences Act 1985 imposes time-limits upon the length of time an accused person may be held in custody.[14] The effect of these is that committal proceedings will need to be commenced within the prescribed limits. If, for whatever reason, delay occurs, the prosecution will have to obtain an extension of time from the court under section 22(3) of the 1985 Act. For that to be granted the court will have to be convinced by the prosecution that it acted with all due

---

9 Magistrates' Courts Rules 1981, r 7(8).

10 *Ibid*, r 7(10).

11 *R v Horseferry Road Stipendiary Magistrate, ex parte Adams* [1977] 1 All ER 373; [1978] 1 WLR 1197, where the divisional court issued an order of *certiorari* quashing committal proceedings in which the magistrate had refused to permit the accused, following an unsuccessful submission of no case, to give evidence on his own behalf.

12 It is commonly (but strictly inaccurately) also stated that he "pleads not guilty".

13 Where the defendant gives evidence and witnesses are called on his behalf, then, with leave of the court, counsel or solicitor may address the court twice: Magistrates' Courts Rules 1981, r 7(11).

14 See p 440, *ante*

expedition, and that a good and sufficient reason for extension exists. The meaning of this was explained by JOWITT J in *R v Crown Court at Norwich, ex parte Parker*:[15]

> "What is appropriate at the pre-committal stage is all the expedition needed to bring the case to a sufficient state of affairs so that the committal papers can be served on the defence so as to leave the defendant's advisors adequate time to consider them and to decide still within the custody time limit whether a committal under section 6(1) or (2) of the Magistrates' Courts Act is appropriate and to have the matter before the court so that what type of committal there is to be can be ventilated."

d   Reporting of committal proceedings

Following a well-publicised murder trial where pre-trial publicity created a severe risk of prejudice to the trial itself,[16] restrictions on the reporting of committal proceedings were introduced in 1967,[17] and are now contained in the Magistrates' Courts Act 1980. By section 8, it is generally unlawful to publish any report of committal proceedings, apart from various formal matters such as the court, the names of the justices, defendants and advocates, a summary of the charges and the decision as to whether or not to commit. The evidence, called by either side, may not be published until the end of the trial,[18] if the defendant is committed, or the end of committal proceedings, if he is not. It is open to the defendants or any one of them to apply, and the court must then order that the restriction is not to apply if all defendants so require; if one or more objects to such an order the court will make an order only if it is in the interests of justice to do so.[19] The restrictions on publicity apply equally to proceedings in the magistrates' court before the court proceeds to inquire into the information as examining justices. This will apply where there are mode of trial proceedings leading to committal proceedings.[20]

In addition to the general restrictions imposed by the Act, it is open to the court to use its powers to postpone or limit reporting which exist under the Contempt of Court Act 1981.[1] Further, there are specific restrictions in rape cases imposed by the Sexual Offences (Amendment) Act 1976. Under that Act it is an offence to publish matter likely to lead members of the public to identify a woman as the complainant or the defendant as the person accused.[2] In relation to committal proceedings the accused can

---

15 (1992) 156 JP 818.

16 The trial of Doctor John Bodkin Adams, in 1957. DEVLIN J stated that it would have been far better if the preliminary proceedings had been held in private.

17 Criminal Justice Act 1967, implementing the recommendations of the Tucker Report (Cmnd 479, HMSO, 1958).

18 By which time it will have been superseded by evidence given at the trial and will be of no general interest. See also the court's powers under s 4 of the Contempt of Court Act 1981, *post*, p 143.

19 Magistrates' Courts Act 1980, s 8(2A), inserted by Criminal Justice (Amendment) Act 1981. All co-accused must be given a fair opportunity to make such representations: see *R v Wirral District Magistrates' Court, ex parte Meickle* (1990) 154 JP 1035.

20 *Ibid*, s 25; see p 448, *ante*.

 1 Contempt of Court Act 1981, ss 4, 11.

 2 Sexual Offences (Amendment) Act 1976, s 4. The Act applies to "rape offences", and not to cases of indecent assault or other sexual offences. The restrictions on publicity apply equally to the trial and subsequent proceedings.

apply to the court to remove the restriction relating to publicising his identity (but not that of the complainant).[3]

All the above applies to publicity in the press, and on radio and television. As regards admission of the public to committal proceedings, the Act expressly states that examining justices must sit in public unless (a) statute directs to the contrary or (b) the magistrates consider that the ends of justice would not be served by them sitting in open court, as regards the whole or any part of the committal proceedings.[4] Thus publicity is encouraged as regards the attendance of members of the public in court, but not as regards reports to a wider public in the press and on television. Further, where the defendant is committed, or discharged after decision not to commit, there must be published on that day or the next, in a part of the magistrates' court to which the public have access, certain details such as the defendant's name and address, the charge or charges and (if there is a committal) the court of trial.[5]

3 Committal for trial

On committal for trial, several questions arise: (a) what should the charge be? (b) to which location of the Crown Court should the defendant be committed? (c) should the defendant be committed in custody or on bail?

a Charges

In an "old-style" committal it is for the justices to consider, on all the evidence, what charge is appropriate, the only limitation being that it must be properly founded on evidence appearing in the depositions. As seen, their power to dismiss the charge completely only arises at the end of the prosecution evidence.

There is no power to reduce the charge on a section 6(2) committal; therefore, if such a committal is to be used, the prosecution may be wise to bring charges in the alternative. As already seen, so long as the section 6(2) procedure is used, no question of dismissing the charge arises.

b Court of trial

The structure of the Crown Court has already been dealt with.[6] It is not a single court but sits in a number of different locations. These are described

---

3 In addition he can apply to the Crown Court for a direction removing the restriction in relation to his own or the complainant's identity, but such a direction may only be given if required for the purpose of inducing likely witnesses to come forward and if the conduct of the applicant's defence at the trial is likely to be substantially prejudiced if the direction is not given (*ibid*, ss 4(2), 6(2)).

4 Magistrates' Courts Act 1980, s 4(2).

5 *Ibid*, s 6(5). It is not stated how long the notice must be displayed. But this has effect subject to the restrictions imposed by the Sexual Offences (Amendment) Act 1976 (*supra*) so that the name of the defendant will not be included, nor will any matter likely to lead members of the public to identify him or the complainant.

6 See p 158,*ante*.

as first-tier, second-tier and third-tier centres. First-tier centres deal with both civil and criminal cases and are visited by High Court and circuit judges; second-tier centres deal with criminal cases only but are visited by both High Court and circuit judges, while third-tier centres deal with criminal cases only and are visited only by circuit judges. Each circuit contains a number of each type of centre. Offences in turn are divided into four classes,[7] each containing a number of offences. Offences in Class 1 must normally be tried by a High Court judge although cases of murder may be released by the presiding judge, for trial by a circuit judge approved for that purpose by the Lord Chief Justice; examples are murder and the rare offences for which a person may be sentenced to death. Offences in Class 2 must be tried by a High Court judge unless a presiding judge of the circuit releases any particular case for trial by a circuit judge or recorder; examples are manslaughter, abortion and rape. Offences in Class 3 may be tried by a High Court judge, or by a circuit judge or recorder; these are all offences triable only on indictment not falling within any other class.

Offences in Class 4 will normally be tried by a circuit judge or recorder, although they may also be tried by a High Court judge; examples are wounding or causing grievous bodily harm with intent, conspiracy and all offences triable either way.

Therefore, when a magistrates' court commits for trial a person charged with any offence within Classes 1–3,[8] it must specify, as the place of trial, the location of the Crown Court where a High Court judge regularly sits.[9] In the case of an offence in Class 4 the magistrates' court must simply specify the most convenient location of the Crown Court. In selecting the most convenient location, the justices must have regard to the location of the Crown Court designated by the presiding judge as the location to which cases should normally be committed from their petty sessions area.[10] The magistrates will also need to have regard to whether live TV link facilities exist, if one of the witnesses is a child who is permitted to give evidence through such a link.[11]

c   Bail

The magistrates must consider whether to release the defendant on bail, or to commit in custody. Factors which must be considered, including the imposition of conditions, have already been explained.[12]

---

7 By the directions set out in *Practice Note* [1987] 3 All ER 1064; sub nom *Practice Direction* [1987] 1 WLR 1671; see p 160, *ante*.
8 See n 9, *infra*.
9 *Practice Direction*, para 2.
10 *Ibid*, para 3, and Magistrates' Courts Act 1980, s 7.
11 In cases involving child witnesses, the court will wish to consider the availability of live TV link facilities. See *Practice Note* (1992) 95 Cr App Rep 354.
12 See *ante*, p 459.

4 Securing the attendance of witnesses

The relevant provisions are contained in the Criminal Procedure (Attendance of Witnesses) Act 1965; it applies to all witnesses giving evidence before the magistrates except the defendant and any witness of his merely as to character. As soon as possible after the witness has signed his deposition[13] he must be handed a document called a witness order, commanding him to appear at the court of trial. No sum of money is liable to be forfeited if the witness fails to appear, but disobedience to a witness order is contempt of the trial court and as such is punishable summarily by imprisonment for a period not exceeding three months or by other penalty imposed by the court of trial, unless the witness can satisfy the court that he had "just excuse" for failure to attend.[14]

If, however, the magistrates consider that the evidence of a particular witness at the trial is unlikely to be disputed or even required they may make in the case of that witness a conditional witness order, which requires him to attend at the court of trial only if notice is given to him to do so. On committing the defendant for trial the court must inform him of his right to require the attendance at the trial of a witness in respect of whom a conditional witness order has been made, and the necessary steps which he must take.[15]

The depositions and a number of other documents will be forwarded to the trial court by the clerk to the justices.[16] The defendant's right to see the information has already been noted. The general importance of the depositions is that, subject to a notice of additional evidence being served, what is in the depositions will be the evidence called against the defendant at the trial; the indictment can only be drawn from material appearing in the depositions; prosecuting counsel at the trial must confine himself in his opening speech to what appears in them and any departure from a deposition is regarded as an appropriate subject for cross-examination of a witness.

The names of the witnesses to be called by the prosecution are listed on the back of the indictment.[17] The defendant is entitled to assume that all of those witnesses will be present at court so that he need take no step to secure the attendance of any of them at his trial. However, although it is the obligation of the prosecution to have at court all witnesses whose names are on the back of the indictment, the prosecution may in certain circumstances refrain from calling such a witness.[18]

B NOTICES OF TRANSFER AND VOLUNTARY BILLS

The abolition of committal proceedings in serious fraud cases has already been noted.[19] Sections 4–6 of the Criminal Justice Act 1987 provide for cases to be automatically transferred to the Crown Court. Where a person has

---

13 A term which includes in this context statements tendered for the purpose of section 6(2) committal proceedings.
14 Act of 1965, s 3.   15 *Ibid*, s 1(3).
16 See generally, Magistrates' Courts Rules 1981, r 11.
17 In fact the practice varies from court to court and there is no statutory requirement to this effect; if their names are not so listed the defendant is entitled to assume that those witnesses who were tendered at the committal stage will be called.
18 See p 496, *post*.   19 See p 463, *ante*.

been charged with an indictable offence, and in the opinion of an appropriate officer[20] there is sufficient evidence for the accused to be committed for trial and the evidence reveals a case of fraud of such seriousness and complexity[1] that it is appropriate that the management of the case should without delay be taken over by the Crown Court, then a notice of transfer can be served. This must be done before the magistrates' court begins committal proceedings, and when served the magistrates' court loses all jurisdiction. The decision to serve the notice of transfer appears to be beyond judicial challenge;[2] however, the Act creates a procedure whereby a person may make an application for dismissal of the transferred charge.[3] This application is not, though, the same as committal proceedings. Oral evidence can be adduced only with leave of the judge, and there is no opportunity for a submission of no case to answer. The grounds of the application are that the evidence that has been disclosed would not be sufficient for a jury properly to convict him.

The Criminal Justice Act 1991[4] introduced similar provisions in cases where a child was the victim of, or witnessed, certain offences of violence or of a sexual nature, and where the case should be taken over and proceeded with by the Crown Court to avoid prejudice to the welfare of the child. In these circumstances, the Director of Public Prosecutions can serve a notice of transfer. The evidence must be sufficient for the person charged to be committed for trial. Similar safeguards to those earlier described in the context of serious fraud cases apply. Likewise, similar provisions exist in respect of war crimes, introduced by the War Crimes Act 1991.[5]

It is anticipated that, if the recommendations of the Royal Commission on Criminal Justice concerning committal proceedings generally are implemented, then the cases currently dealt with by notice of transfer procedure will follow the general pattern.[6]

By a procedure known as the voluntary bill procedure, the prosecution can apply to a High Court judge[7] for leave to prefer a bill of indictment against the accused. The judge in his discretion grants or refuses leave,[8] with the result that if leave is granted the bill is preferred forthwith and there is no need for any committal proceedings. At the same time the defendant loses the advantage of knowing in advance the substance of the case against him. The applicant himself cannot attend unless permitted by the judge to do so, whilst the defendant is not entitled to attend at all. Even

---

20 This is given a wide meaning by s 4(2) and includes the DPP, Director of the Serious Fraud Office, Commissioners of Inland Revenue, Commissioners of Customs & Excise, and the Secretary of State.

1 The Royal Commission on Criminal Justice recommends that this be reworded to read "seriousness *or* complexity", bringing within the transfer provisions cases that are suitable for such treatment but which currently go through the committal process: Ch 7, para 60.

2 See Criminal Justice Act 1987, s 4(3); Criminal Justice Act 1991, s 53(4).

3 See Criminal Justice Act 1987, s 6(2); Criminal Justice Act 1987 (Dismissal of Transferred Charges) Rules 1988 (SI 1988/1695).

4 Criminal Justice Act 1991, s 53.

5 War Crimes Act 1991, Sch 1, para 4.

6 But *cf Criminal Justice* and Public Order Bill 1994.

7 A circuit judge has no power to give leave to prefer a bill of indictment: *R v Thompson* [1975] 2 All ER 1028; [1975] 1 WLR 1425.

8 See, eg, *Re Roberts* [1967] 1 WLR 474. The issue of a voluntary bill is not susceptible to judicial review: *R v Manchester Crown Court, ex parte Williams* (1990) 154 JP 589.

where there is a hearing it is not in open court.[9] Regular use of the voluntary bill procedure could therefore lead to hardship.

For these reasons, the voluntary bill procedure is to be regarded as exceptional. In a *Practice Direction* in 1990[10] it was stated as follows:

> "The usual means of bringing a defendant to trial on indictment is by committal for trial in the magistrates' court. A voluntary bill should only be granted where good reason to depart from the normal procedure is clearly shown and only where the interests of justice, rather than considerations of administrative convenience, require it."

It is impossible to define precisely when the voluntary bill procedure should be used. Its use may be appropriate where committal proceedings have been disrupted[11] or have failed[12] where the public interest justifies prosecution. It is a much quicker procedure than proceedings by way of preliminary inquiry, and it might be thought desirable to use it if certain co-defendants had already been committed for trial and were awaiting trial. By the voluntary bill procedure, considerable delay and hardship to them might be avoided. Nevertheless the requirement that the bill must state specifically why the present procedure is being used instead of committal proceedings (if such is the case) shows that indiscriminate use of the procedure is to be avoided.

C THE INDICTMENT

1 Introduction

A bill of indictment is a written or printed accusation of crime made at the suit of the Crown against one or more persons. A bill of indictment may be preferred by any person[13] against any other person before the Crown Court, generally within 28 days of committal or notice of transfer; however, a bill of indictment is of no legal validity in itself. It only becomes a legal document when it is turned into an indictment proper by being signed by the appropriate officer of the court, who in turn can only sign the draft bill if he is satisfied that the accused is validly before the court.[14] The judge of the court may direct the appropriate officer to sign the bill, either on his own motion or on the application of the prosecution. After it has been signed, the proper officer must on request supply to the defendant a copy free of charge.[15]

Where the bill is preferred on the authority of a committal for trial it may charge any offence which appears on the depositions, or statements, in addition to or in place of the offence or offences for which he was

---

9 See, generally: *R v Raymond* [1981] QB 910; [1981] 2 All ER 246, where an attempt to challenge the validity of the voluntary bill procedure (on the grounds that it was inconsistent with the *audi alteram partem* principle) was rejected by the Court of Appeal.

10 [1991] 1 All ER 288; [1990] 1 WLR 1633.

11 *R v Raymond*, n 9.

12 *R v Horshamm Justices, ex parte Reeves* (1980) 75 Cr App Rep 236n.

13 Except in those cases where a private person has no right to institute proceedings: see p 437, *ante*.

14 Through committal proceedings, notice of transfer, voluntary bill, or by direction of the Court of Appeal. An alternative procedure under the Perjury Act 1911, s 9, existed until abolished by the Prosecution of Offences Act 1985, s 28.

15 Indictment Rules 1971, r 10(1).

committed, subject to the normal rules as to joinder of offences.[16] It is immaterial that the "added" offences involve a higher penalty than the original charge or charges. This rule does not in any way destroy what has already been described as one of the main purposes or advantages of the preliminary inquiry, namely to give the defendant fair notice of the case against him, since he will necessarily have knowledge of the facts alleged to constitute the offence, if not of the precise charge based on those facts. However, there are obvious possibilities of injustice, and the Court of Appeal has said[17] that whenever it is decided to bring such "fresh" charges, the police ought to see the defendant and warn him of the charges under caution, so that he may make a statement in answer if he wishes.

The whole of the indictment may consist of such "substitute" charge or charges. If the defendant considers that one or more of such charges does not fairly arise out of the facts in the depositions he may move to quash the indictment. It is then for the trial judge to rule on the sufficiency of the indictment. Where however the defendant was committed for trial in respect of two offences which had been repealed by statute, it was held that he was never lawfully committed at all, and it was immaterial that the third count of the indictment was in respect of an offence which both existed and was disclosed by the depositions.[18]

Clearly, there is a certain risk of hardship to the defendant in this procedure, since he may go to trouble and expense to defeat a particular charge at the stage of committal proceedings, only to find (on the assumption that he is committed for trial in respect of other matters) that the same charge appears in the indictment.

> ". . . We think it right to say that . . . it is an undesirable practice and can easily in some cases work hardship on defendants, and the right to prefer in the indictment charges which the magistrate has rejected is one which ought to be very carefully regarded."[19]

2   Form and contents

The rules as to the form of indictments are now contained in the Indictments Act 1915 and the Indictment Rules 1971. The drafting of the indictment is the responsibility of counsel for the prosecution,[20] whose duty it is to ensure that it is in proper form for the particular case. In most cases, other than those of complexity or difficulty, the actual drafting will be undertaken by the Crown Prosecution Service.

An indictment is in three parts; introductory matters, statement of offence and particulars of offence. The introductory matters are twofold, first the court of trial and secondly the name of the defendant, appearing in the form:

THE QUEEN v [Defendant] . . . charged as follows:

---

16 See p 476, *post.*
17 In *R v Dickson* [1969] 1 All ER 729; [1969] 1 WLR 405, where the defendant's solicitors had six days' notice of "fresh" charges.
18 *R v Lamb* [1969] 1 All ER 45; [1968] 1 WLR 1946.
19 *Per* FINNEMORE J in *R v Dawson; R v Wenlock* [1960] 1 All ER 558 at 562; [1960] 1 WLR 163 at 168.
20 *R v Newland* [1988] QB 402; [1988] 2 All ER 891.

As regards the statement of offence and particulars of offence, the rules provide[1] that every indictment must contain, and need not contain more than, a statement of the specific offence with which the defendant is charged, describing the offence shortly, together with such particulars as are necessary to give reasonable information as to the nature of the charge. Where, however, the offence is created by statute, there must be a reference to the statute and to the relevant section, and all the essential elements of the offence must be disclosed in the particulars, unless the defendant is not prejudiced or embarrassed by failure to describe any such element.[2] The fact that an indictment is defective does not render the trial a nullity. Whether a conviction obtained on an indictment that is deficient can stand will turn, ultimately, upon whether injustice or unfairness has been caused to the defendant.

Whether these provisions are effective is open to doubt. The Royal Commission on Criminal Justice observed[3] that indictments were largely formal in nature, giving little information. It found widespread evidence of a failure to comply with the duty to give reasonable information as to the nature of the charge, and agreed with the Law Commission when that body observed:

> "There are strong reasons of justice and efficiency why the particulars in each count in an indictment should contain sufficiently clear factual allegations to inform the jury of the issues it will have to decide, and more generally, to enable the indictment to operate as a practical agenda for the trial."[4]

3 Joinder; separate trials

Hitherto we have considered an indictment charging one offence only. However, within certain limits, a single indictment may charge more than one offence, or be drawn in respect of more than one defendant, or both. This is known as joinder.

a Joinder of offenders

The basic rule is that where two or more persons join in the commission of an offence, all or any number of them may be jointly indicted for that offence, or each may be indicted separately. If they are in fact indicted separately there would be no power in any court to order "consolidation" of the indictments, however desirable this might seem from the point of view of saving time and expense,[5] but, of course, the same result could be achieved through the use of the voluntary bill procedure[6] to supersede existing indictments. However, joinder is now very common. The matter is one of judicial discretion, and what is in the interests of justice. Where the individual offences of the different accused are related to each other by virtue of time or some other link, then it may well be appropriate for them

---

1 Indictment Rules 1971, r 5(1). Cf the rules for the content of an information: see p 528, *post*. There may also be approved forms of indictment for individual offences: *ibid*

2 *Ibid*, r 6. It is not necessary for the indictment to specify or negative any exception, exemption, excuse, proviso or qualification. There is, again, an analogy with the rules for the content of an information.

3 Ch 8, para 5. 4 *Counts in an Indictment* (Law Commission, 1992).

5 *Crane v Director of Public Prosecutions* [1921] 2 AC 299.

6 See p 472, *ante*.

to be tried together.[7] The fact that evidence against one accused is inadmissible against another will be a relevant factor, though not necessarily decisive. Another consideration will be the length of the trial that will ensue should they be tried together. This is returned to later.[8]

b Joinder of offences

The basic rule is to be found in rule 9 of the 1971 Rules:

> "Charges for any offences may be joined in the same indictment if those charges are founded on the same facts or form or are a part of a series of offences of the same or a similar character."

It should also be noted that in some limited circumstances summary offences may be tried with offences that are to be tried on indictment.[9]

It is a matter of fact and degree in each case as to whether this rule is satisfied, in accordance with principles set out in the cases. In *Ludlow v Metropolitan Police Commissioner*[10] the House of Lords indicated that in deciding whether offences were of a similar character regard should be had both to their legal and factual characteristics. To show a "series of offences" the prosecution must be able to show some nexus between them, a "feature of similarity which in all the circumstances of the case enables the offences to be tried together". It is not necessary that the evidence in respect of one charge should be admissible on another.

The application of the principle was seen in *R v Cannan*,[11] where the Court of Appeal held that a trial judge was entitled in his discretion to order the trial together of six offences involving three separate women. Three counts involved abduction, rape and buggery against one woman, another alleged attempted kidnapping against a second, and two more counts alleged abduction and murder of a third.

The position in sexual cases is particularly difficult because of the prejudice that may arise. In *Director of Public Prosecutions v Boardman*[12] Lord Cross seemed to equate the test for joinder of offences with their admissibility as evidence under the similar fact evidence rule.[13] He stated that if each count was inadmissible in respect of the other offences then they ought to be tried separately. It is, he said, asking too much of any jury to disregard the other charges when considering each individual charge. This approach has been criticised as being contrary to the wording of rule 9. More recently the question was again before the House of Lords. In *Director of Public Prosecutions v P*[14] the House was asked to consider whether charges must be tried separately in the absence of striking similarity, then believed to be the key test for admissibility of similar fact

---

7 *R v Assim* [1966] 2 QB 249; [1966] 2 All ER 881.

8 See *post*, p 477.

9 Criminal Justice Act 1988, s 40. The charge must be founded on the same facts or evidence, or be part of a series of offences.

10 [1971] AC 29; [1970] 1 All ER 567. The House was considering the appropriate provision of the 1915 Rules, which were materially the same as r 9. See also: *R v Kray* [1970] 1 QB 125; [1969] 3 All ER 941.

11 (1990) 92 Cr App Rep 16.

12 [1975] AC 421; sub nom *Boardman v Director of Public Prosecutions* [1974] 3 All ER 887.

13 See p 600, *post*.

14 [1991] 2 AC 447; sub nom *R v P* [1991] 3 All ER 337.

evidence. This question was answered "No" by LORD MACKAY, but since the court in any event rejected the "striking similarity" approach, it remains unclear as to whether the court was rejecting the striking similarity test, or intending to treat the tests for severance and admissibility as one and the same.[15]

4 Long trials: the number of counts and accused

It has already been seen that the joinder of offenders, and of charges, is permissible. The danger exists that an indictment may become so overloaded that, as a result, the trial becomes too complex in terms of the issues the jury has to comprehend and decide, or unmanageable in terms of time. On many occasions the courts have complained of indictments which are overloaded.

In *R v Novac*,[16] where a large number of counts of sexual offences were laid against four defendants, BRIDGE LJ observed:

> ". . . whatever advantages were expected to accrue from one long trial . . .
> they were heavily outweighed by the disadvantages. A trial of such dimen-
> sions puts an immense burden on both judge and jury. In the course of a four
> or five day summing up the most careful and conscientious judge may so
> easily overlook some essential matter. Even if the summing up is faultless, it
> is by no means cynical to doubt whether the average juror can be expected to
> take it all in and apply all the directions given. Some criminal prosecutions
> involve considerations of matters so plainly inextricable and indivisible that a
> long and complex trial is an ineluctable necessity. But we are convinced that
> nothing short of the criterion of absolute necessity can justify the imposition
> of the burden of a very long trial on the court."

The problem has arisen particularly in two different situations. The first concerns the use of conspiracy charges. There may be both evidential and tactical reasons why prosecutors may wish to lay a count of conspiracy in addition to counts alleging specific offences. This practice was disapproved in a *Practice Note* in 1977.[17] The onus is on the prosecution to justify a joinder of a conspiracy charge with other substantive offences. If it cannot, it must elect to proceed either upon the conspiracy charge or the substantive offences. Justification might exist where the substantive offences which the prosecution is in a position to prove do not adequately reflect the extent and persistence of the defendants' criminality. Thus, for example, there might be evidence to show that a person had been engaged for some time in the importation of drugs of various kinds, although the prosecution might only be able to prove one specific importation.

Secondly, a number of long complex fraud cases has placed great strain upon the jury trial system.[18] In *R v Cohen*[19] the trial was so long that the judge's summing-up (itself of considerable length) dealt only with one of

---

15 See *R v Tickner* [1992] Crim LR 444.
16 (1976) 65 Cr App Rep 107.
17 [1977] 2 All ER 540; sub nom *Practice Direction* [1977] 1 WLR 537.
18 See, generally, the Roskill Committee, *op cit*, and Royal Commission on Criminal Justice Report, Ch 7, paras 59–67.
19 [1992] NLJR 1267. The jury retired on the 184th day of the trial.

the issues before the court. In passing sentence following convictions, later quashed on appeal, McKINNON J observed:

> "All involved in this case have been called upon to achieve what no-one in our courts should be asked to achieve. That applies to the defendants, to the jury and to me."

The solution to the problem has not proved easy. The Roskill Report on Fraud Trials[20] advocated the abolition of jury trial in complex fraud cases, to be replaced by trial by judge and two specialist assessors. Such recommendations are a response to a recognition that such trials are inevitably long, causing unacceptable disruption to the lives of jurors, and unduly complex, the evidence often being beyond the comprehension of jurors. Such claims are, of course, difficult to gauge in the light of the prohibition on study of how in fact juries reach their verdicts, and upon what evidence.[1]

By contrast, others argue for the simplification of such cases. In its evidence to the Royal Commission, The Law Society[2] argued that such trials should be simplified by not including superfluous counts, and by keeping prosecution evidence within strict limits, principally by limiting the number of accused in the indictment. The Royal Commission itself considered the restriction of jury trial to be beyond its scope, but echoed the calls set out above for the number of counts or particulars on an indictment to be kept to a minimum.[3] In that regard, its recommendation for a review of the relationship between the criminal law and non-criminal action by financial regulators may be important in reducing the scope of criminal trials in such cases.[4]

5 Duplicity

Where two or more offences are joined in one indictment each one must be alleged in a separate count or paragraph of the indictment.[5] If an indictment in fact charges more than one offence in a single count then it is bad for duplicity. This must be distinguished from the analogous situation which, more accurately, may be described as uncertainty. This arises where a statutory provision contains one offence, which may be committed by a variety of means, or by virtue of different states of mind. Whether a count in an indictment may charge simply by reference to the statutory provision, or must allege the specific ingredients in each count, charging more than one count if necessary, is a question of construction of the relevant statute.[6]

In deciding into which category the statutory provision falls regard should be had to the question of whether different maximum punishments exist according to the presence or absence of specific factual ingredients.[7]

---

20 See *ante*, n 18.
 1 Contempt of Court Act 1981, s 8. For discussion of jury trial generally, see p 201, *ante*.
 2 Evidence of the Law Society to the Royal Commission on Criminal Justice (1992).
 3 Ch 8, para 79.
 4 Ch 7, para 64. For consideration of serious fraud cases generally, see p 487, *post*.
 5 Indictment Rules 1971, r 4(2). Each count is equivalent to a speparate indictment. Counts must be numbered consecutively: r 4(2).
 6 See p 528, *post*, for similar issues in respect of duplicity of charges of summary offences.
 7 *R v Courtie* [1984] AC 463; [1984] 1 All ER 740.

Where that is so, it is likely that a court will consider the statute to create separate offences, which should therefore be indicted separately.

6 Objecting to the indictment: amendment

If the defendant desires to object to the validity of the indictment he should do so before he is arraigned. The grounds of objection have already been explained,[8] though the power of the court to quash an indictment to prevent abuse of the process of the court should also be noted.

The Court of Appeal does not readily hear objections to the validity of an indictment where the objection was not taken at the trial, although failure to take it is not insuperable. When objection is taken the court may (unless it rules against the objection altogether) either quash the indictment or amend it. The Indictments Act 1915 permits a court to make such order of amendment as it thinks necessary to meet the circumstances of the case, unless amendment cannot be made without injustice.[9]

A new count may be added before the defendant is arraigned, and even after arraignment a count can be added charging a completely new offence;[10] the question is one of degree depending on the facts of the particular case.[11]

Application for amendment may be made by either side and at any time. Since counsel for the prosecution has general responsibility for the correctness of the indictment he should not open his case without being satisfied on the point and should make any necessary application for amendment before the defendant is arraigned, having inspected the indictment for the purpose. Defending counsel should also inspect, in his own client's interests.

Amendment may be made by the judge of his own motion, but before doing so he should give both sides the opportunity of commenting on the proposed amendment.[12]

D DISCLOSURE OF EVIDENCE

The fact that the effective working of the adversarial system depends, in part, upon proper disclosure was noted earlier.[13] Unlike in civil proceedings where discovery generally is available,[14] the duties of disclosure pre-trial in criminal cases have been limited. The prosecution has always been under a duty to disclose at committal the evidence upon which it proposes to rely, subject only to the right to call additional evidence in some circumstances and subject to certain conditions.[15] These rules remain, but in recent years concern has mounted at the extent to which the

---

8 See p 474, *ante.*
9 S 5(1).
10 *R v Radley* (1973) 58 Cr App Rep 394, where the amendment was made at the conclusion of the prosecution opening; cf *R v Tirado* (1974) 59 Cr App Rep 80.
11 It seems that an amendment on immaterial matter may be made at or after verdict: *R v Dossi* (1918) 87 LJKB 1024.
12 *R v West* [1948] 1 KB 709; [1948] 1 All ER 718.
13 See p 434, *ante.* Note in particular *R v McIlkenny* [1992] 2 All ER 417.
14 See p 349, *ante.*
15 Service of the witness statements must occur.

prosecution may have in its possession evidence upon which it does not intend to rely, but which might be relevant or helpful to the defence.[16]

By contrast the defence have never had a duty to disclose. The so-called "right of silence"[17] has permitted the defence at any stage to adduce evidence without notice, and without adverse inferences being drawn in law from that non-disclosure. That rule was modified in 1967 in respect of evidence of alibi,[18] and, more recently, in respect of the adducing of expert evidence.[19] The general right to silence remains, but has been the subject of fierce debate since the 11th Report of the Criminal Law Revision Committee in 1972,[20] a debate that is continuing in the light of the report of the Royal Commission on Criminal Justice.[1]

a   Disclosure of "unused material"

The earliest reported authority for a duty to disclose evidence was *R v Bryant and Dickson*,[2] though in that case the defence were aware of a witness who had not been called by the prosecution, and therefore had no ground for complaint. Uncertainty as to whether disclosure of witness statements was required arose, and was the subject of judicial disagreement.[3] The Royal Commission on Criminal Procedure found the practice of police forces to be inconsistent and variable.[4] To deal with this uncertainty in 1981 the Attorney-General issued guidelines dealing with non-disclosure.[5] Although not having the force of law in the strict sense, an accused person is entitled to approach his trial on the basis that the prosecution will have complied with the guidelines, and it has been held that a failure to comply amounts to a "material irregularity."[6]

The Guidelines provide as follows:

(1)   They define "unused material" as including all witness statements and documents not included in the committal papers served on the defence, together with the statements of those giving oral evidence at committal, and the unedited versions of all statements.[7]

(2)   All unused material in cases committed for trial should normally be made available to the defence if it has some bearing on the offences

---

16 See *infra.*

17 For the various meanings of this term, see Lord Mustill in *R v Director of Serious Fraud Office, ex parte Smith* [1993] AC 1, sub nom *Smith v Director of Serious Fraud Office* [1992] 3 All ER 456.

18 Criminal Justice Act 1967, s 12. See further, p 485, *post.*

19 Crown Court (Advance Disclosure of Expert Evidence) Rules 1987. See p 483, *post.*

20 1972, Cmnd 4991 (HMSO).

1 *Op cit.*

2 (1946) 31 Cr App Rep 146.

3 Cf Lord Denning MR in *Dallison v Caffrey* [1965] 1 QB 348; [1964] 2 All ER 610, approved in *R v Lawson* (1989) 90 Cr App Rep 107.

4 Cmnd 8092 (HMSO, 1981).

5 (1981) 74 Cr App Rep 302.

6 *R v Maguire* [1992] QB 936; [1992] 2 All ER 433. For the position in respect of summary trial, see *R v Bolton Justices, ex parte Scally* [1991] 1 QB 537; [1991] 2 All ER 619, and p 546, *post.*

7 In *R v Saunders* (1991) (unreported) the phrase "unused material" was interpreted broadly to include a mass of notes, tape-recordings and drafts of statements. See Royal Commission, *op cit*, Ch 6, paras 38–41. The Royal Commission was informed that the police were in some cases incapable of complying with the duty of disclosure, given the complexity of some cases.

charged and the surrounding circumstances of the case. This disclosure should be made as soon as practicable, if possible before committal proceedings, for the material disclosed may have relevance to the decisions as to how those proceedings are to be conducted, and what form they should take.

(3) There is discretion to refuse disclosure in certain circumstances:

    (i) where disclosure might lead to an attempt being made to persuade a witness to make a statement retracting an earlier one, to change his story, not to appear in court or otherwise to intimidate him;

    (ii) the statement (eg from a relative or close friend) is believed to be wholly or partially untrue and might be of use in cross-examination if the witness should be called by the defence;

    (iii) the statement is favourable to the defence and believed to be substantially true, but there are grounds for fearing that the witness (due to feelings of loyalty or fear) might give the defence solicitor a quite different story;

    (iv) the statement is quite neutral or negative, and there is no reason to doubt truthfulness, but where there are grounds to believe that the witness may change his story.

In these cases the defence should be given the witness's name and address.

    (v) The document is a sensitive statement, and it is not in the public interest to disclose it. For example, it may deal with matters relating to national security, or reveal the identity of a member of security services who as a result would be of no further use to them; it might disclose the identity of an informant who might be put in danger, or of a witness who may be in danger of assault or intimidation; it may reveal details which might facilitate commission of other offences or alert someone that they may be a suspect.

If doubt exists under these guidelines, the advice of counsel should be sought. The balance needs to be strict in respect of sensitivity of material and the extent to which the information might assist the defence. Doubt should be resolved in favour of the defence. Ultimately, however, the decision is that of the court, not of the prosecution. In *R v Ward*[8] the court stressed that the role of the court in such cases is to monitor the views of the prosecution as to what should, or should not, be disclosed under the guidelines. If the prosecution wished to withhold unused material, the court should decide on an application, notice of which should be given to the defence. However, the procedure was reconsidered in *R v Davis*.[9] In that case the Court of Appeal stated that the prosecution should notify the defence of any application it wishes to make to withhold unused material. If the nature of the material is such that even to reveal its nature, or that an application is being made, would not be in the public interest then the prosecution need not reveal it to the defence. It should be borne in mind,

8 [1993] 2 All ER 577; [1993] 1 WLR 619.
9 [1993] 2 All ER 643; [1993] 1 WLR 613.

however, that the fact that evidence is confidential will not necessarily prevent the court ordering its disclosure.[10]

The Royal Commission on Criminal Justice approved the approach taken by the Court of Appeal in *Davis*, as striking a fair balance between the public interest in protecting sensitive material and the needs of the defence.[11] The Commission was less happy about the general scope of the obligation to disclose which has "created burdens for the prosecution that go beyond what is reasonable".[12] It therefore proposed a two-stage process of disclosure.

(1) Stage 1: primary disclosure, which would be automatic, subject only to appropriate exceptions. This would include copies of all material relevant to the offence, the offender or to the surrounding circumstances of the case, irrespective of whether the prosecution intended to rely upon it. This would include, for example, material of importance to the defence because it raised questions concerning the defendant's mental state.[13] The prosecution would also supply a list of other material obtained during the course of its inquiry.
(2) Stage 2: secondary disclosure. The defence would have to establish the relevance of such wider material to the case. To avoid unnecessary and limitless disclosure, the Commission proposed that the defence should be under an obligation to disclose its own case.[14] This would enable the defence to relate its requests for further disclosure to the substance of its case.

The detail of such a scheme should, the Royal Commission recommended, be governed by subordinate legislation or code of practice within a legislative framework, which would also deal with exemptions and with the mechanisms to ensure compliance.[15]

The guidelines apply only to lawyers. In that regard the Court of Appeal in *R v Maguire*[16] decided that the duty of disclosure went so far as to encompass expert witnesses, in that case involving evidence of tests conducted by forensic scientists. A failure by a forensic scientist to disclose material which he might know had some bearing on the offence charged was a "material irregularity", a principle confirmed and applied in the later case of *R v Ward*.[17] In *Ward* the court stressed that there was a common-law obligation on the prosecution to make available to the defence any witness who they did not propose to call but who they knew could give material evidence which tended either to weaken the prosecution case or strengthen the defence case. Government forensic scientists were under a clear duty to act impartially, and, independently of the 1987

---

10 See *R v K* [1993] Crim LR 281.
11 Report, Ch 6, para 47. This procedure should apply to sensitive material which does not attract public interest immunity. Such issues should also be dealt with by High Court or designated circuit judges.
12 *Ibid*, para 49.
13 This is often important for the purposes of dealing with the admissibility of evidence of confessions. See *R v Ward* (*supra*) and, more generally, p 628, *post*.
14 See p 485, *post*.
15 It is proposed that those involved in the various stages of compliance should be required to sign a certificate signifying such compliance.
16 [1992] QB 936; [1992] 2 All ER 433.
17 Note 8, *supra*.

Rules, to disclose any scientific evidence that might arguably assist the defence. Not only that, the obligation also existed to disclose evidence of any tests or experiments which he had carried out, or had knowledge of, which tended to cast doubt on an opinion he was expressing, and to bring the record of such tests or experiments to the notice of the solicitors instructing him, so that they might be disclosed to the other party.

b   Expert evidence[18]

Section 81 of the Police and Criminal Evidence Act 1984 authorises the making of rules regarding the disclosure of expert evidence. The Crown Court (Advance Notice of Expert Evidence) Rules 1987 have been made under that power, and apply to trials on indictment. Following committal for trial the party who is seeking to rely on expert evidence, whether of fact or opinion, must furnish to the other party a statement in writing of any finding or opinion upon which he proposes to rely, and, on request in writing, provide a copy of (or access to, if that is more practicable) the records of any observation, test, calculation, or other procedure in respect of which the finding or opinion is based. A failure to disclose means that the evidence cannot be adduced without the leave of the court.

This obligation of disclosure under the 1987 rules is not the only obligation. In *R v Ward*[19] the Court of Appeal stressed that there is a common-law obligation upon a government forensic scientist to act impartially, and to disclose any scientific evidence that might arguably assist the defence. Failure to comply with this obligation was one of the principal reasons for quashing the convictions of the defendant in that case.

It was failure to disclose fully in this way that caused problems in *R v Ward* and other cases.[20] Such obligation to disclose does not, however, meet the criticism of those who argue that the trial process is unfairly tilted in favour of the prosecution because of its command of forensic science and other scientific facilities,[1] and generally the imbalance of resources. Some argue that the court itself should appoint its own expert witnesses, to report impartially to the court.[2] The whole question was examined extensively by the Royal Commission on Criminal Justice.[3]

The Commission considered, but rejected, a proposal to create an independent forensic science agency, as opposed to being part of a government department or police authority. Instead, it proposed[4] the establishment of a Forensic Science Advisory Council to report to the Home Secretary on the performance, achievements and efficiency of the forensic science laboratories, in both the private and public sectors. Subject to a rule that the same laboratory should not take on work for both prosecution and

---

18 For the admissiblity of expert evidence, see p 590, *post*.
19 [1993] 2 All ER 577; [1993] 1 WLR 619.
20 See eg *R v Maguire* [1992] QB 936; [1992] 2 All ER 433.
 1 For a description of the organisation of forensic science facilities, see the Royal Commission on Criminal Justice *op cit*, Ch 7, para 6–36.
 2 See Spencer [1992] Crim LR.
 3 Report, Ch 9.
 4 Ch 7, para 3.2.

defence in the same case, public sector laboratories should look on themselves as equally available to defence and prosecution. This is important in the light of research findings[5] that defence solicitors sometimes encounter difficulty in finding suitable independent experts to interpret prosecution findings.[6] In respect of the general duty of disclosure, the Royal Commission welcomed the approach taken in *R v Ward*.[7] It also recommended streamlining legal aid provision to assist in this respect.

Of significance is the approach taken by the majority of the Commission towards a more inquisitorial system in respect of forensic science evidence. The Royal Commission found[8] that a sizeable minority of contested Crown Court cases involve scientific evidence. In approximately 25 per cent of such cases there was a defence challenge to such evidence, and in some 800 cases a year not only was such a challenge made but also expert evidence was called on behalf of the defence. In these cases the duty of disclosure applies equally to the defence as well as the prosecution. The defence, however, is under no duty to disclose the evidence it has obtained from experts who it does not intend to call, perhaps because it is unfavourable. Nor is there a duty to disclose expert evidence acquired by the defence for the purposes of discrediting prosecution evidence through cross-examination. To overcome this adversarial approach the Commission recommended as follows:

(1) The defence should not be required to disclose evidence it does not intend to call, since it must be for the defendant to decide what evidence to give.[9]

(2) When the defence is calling expert evidence, the expert witnesses on both sides should be required to meet, to draw up a report for the court setting out scientific facts and their interpretation by both sides. In cases of substantial disagreement a preparatory hearing[10] should be held to decide how such disputes could be clarified, possibly by additional tests.[11]

(3) Where the defence do not dispute scientific evidence counsel should certify this.[12]

(4) Where the defence do intend to dispute scientific evidence but do not intend to call expert evidence themselves, they should, after disclosure, indicate which matters are and are not admitted. This will enable the prosecution to see which areas of expert evidence are in dispute, and the matters that need further clarification at a preparatory hearing.[13]

---

5 Roberts and Willmore, *The Role of Forensic Science Evidence in Criminal Proceedings* (Royal Commission on Criminal Justice Research Study No 11, HMSO, 1992); Steventon, *The Ability to Challenge DNA Evidence* (Royal Commission on Criminal Justice Research Study No 9, HMSO, 1992).

6 See RCCJ, Ch 9, paras 50–53.

7 *Ibid*, para 47.

8 Crown Court Survey: see RCCJ para 57. The estimates ranged from 30–40 per cent of cases, in quantity some 10,000 cases per year.

9 *Ibid*, para 62.

10 See p 487, *post*.

11 *Ibid*, para 63.

12 *Ibid*, para 64.

13 *Ibid*.

(5) A minority of the Commission also favoured requiring defence experts to participate in pre-trial discussions.[14]

The Commission also made recommendations as to the handling of expert evidence at the trial.[15] It emphatically rejected the appointment of a court expert, or an assessor, whose views would not be susceptible to examination or cross-examination.

c   Disclosure by defence

At his trial a defendant will not be allowed to adduce evidence in support of an alibi,[16] except with leave of the court, unless he has given to the prosecutor particulars of the alibi within seven days from the end of the committal proceedings.[17] The purpose of the rule is to enable checks to be made by the prosecution as to the truth or otherwise of the claims of the accused that he was elsewhere at the time of the commission of the offence. If notice is not given then the leave of the trial court is required before such evidence may be called.

In cases of serious fraud where a preparatory hearing is held,[18] by section 9 of the Criminal Justice Act 1987 the defence may be required to disclose the general nature of its defence (though not the names of the witnesses it proposes to call), and the principal areas of disagreement.

Apart from these cases, and the obligation to disclose expert evidence, discussed above, there is no duty upon the defence to disclose in advance the nature and content of the defence upon which it is proposed to rely. The so-called "right to silence" does not permit a court to invite a jury to draw adverse inferences from a failure to disclose pre-trial the facts relied upon by the defence.

Various calls for change have been made in recent years. In 1972, the 11th Report of the Criminal Law Revision Committee recommended that a court should be permitted to draw inferences from silence in court, or from a failure to disclose facts subsequently relied upon by the defence.[19] The report was highly controversial,[20] and not acted upon. More recently, the Court of Appeal in *R v Alladice*[1] considered that it was "high time" that some change in the law was made. This was indeed recommended in 1988 by the Working Group on the Right to Silence,[2] established by the Home Secretary. It made various recommendations:

(1) the proposals of the 11th Report be implemented, subject to modifications which place greater emphasis on the safeguards provided for the suspect;
(2) the prosecution and trial judge should have the right to comment

---

14 Royal Commission Report, Appendix.
15 *Ibid*, Ch 9, para 4.
16 An "alibi" is an assertion that the accused person was elsewhere at the time of the commission of the offence.
17 Criminal Justice Act 1967, s 11.
18 See p 487, *post*
19 Cmnd 4991, HMSO, 1972.
20 See eg MacKenna at [1972] Crim LR 605.
 1 (1988) 87 Cr App Rep 380.
 2 See Zuckerman, 'Trial By Unfair Means – The Report of the Working Group on the Right to Silence' [1989] Crim LR 855.

about a defendant's failure to mention to the police a fact later
relied upon by the defence;

(3) a new set of measures to compel greater pre-trial disclosure of both
prosecution and defence cases, with greater powers of comment for
both prosecution and judge;

(4) a revised caution.

The question of defence disclosure was one of the most controversial issues
considered by the Royal Commission. It took the view that no change
should be made in respect of the "right to silence", except in respect of
disclosure of the defence proposed to be ·relied upon. The majority[3]
believed that those who intend to contest the charges against them should
be obliged to disclose the substance of their defence in advance of trial, or
indicate that they will not be calling any evidence but simply argue that the
prosecution has failed to prove its case.[4] A failure to do so, or an
explanation at trial different from the one given in advance, or the advancing
of mutually exclusive alternative defences, should be a matter from which
the jury could draw adverse inferences, subject to the discretion of the
court to prevent this where good reasons exist.[5] A defendant who did not
disclose would not generally be entitled to further disclosure of material
from the prosecution.[6]

The rationale for such proposals is a desire to reduce "trial by ambush"
involving springing a defence upon the prosecution without warning. The
Royal Commission did not consider the proposals to infringe the right of
defendants not to incriminate themselves,[7] but accepted that a problem
existed only in a minority of cases.[8] By contrast, the dissenting opinion in
essence questioned whether the fundamental right of the defence not to
respond until trial, and to require the prosecution to prove its case, should
be changed where no real problem exists. It also pointed to the ineffec-
tiveness of the advance disclosure powers in serious fraud cases.[9] The
dissenting opinion has been favoured by government in the Criminal
Justice and Public Order Bill currently before Parliament.[10] This does not
alter the disclosure rules, but will permit such inferences as appear proper
to be drawn from a failure by the defendant to mention to the police any
fact later relied upon in his defence which he could reasonably be expected
to mention when questioned about the offence or from a failure to give
evidence in his own defence.[11] Inferences will also be permitted to be
drawn from a failure to account for objects or substances in his possession,
or for marks on such articles, and from a failure or refusal to account for
his presence at a particular place.[12]

---

3 With one dissentient: see RCCJ, pp 221–235.

4 *Ibid*, Ch 6, paras 56–73.

5 The Criminal Justice and Public Order Bill 1994 allows inferences to be drawn. See
infra.

6 See n 4, *supra*.

7 *Ibid*.

8 Ch 4, para 19, relying on data from the Crown Court survey.

9 P 222, para 8, relying on Levi, *The Investigation, Prosecution and Trial of Serious Fraud*
(Royal Commision on Criminal Justice Research Study No 14, HMSO, 1993).

10 11 January 1994, 235 HC Official Report, cols 20–122.

11 For the compellability of an accused person as a witness, see p 577, *post*. The position will
remain unchanged.

12 See further p 594, *post*.

This difference of opinion highlights questions as to the very nature of the criminal trial, and whether any departure from the strict adversarial approach will in fact serve any useful purpose.

E   PRE-TRIAL REVIEW

No formal system for pre-trial review by the court of trial exists, although informal arrangements operate. Pre-trial reviews in fact occur in Crown Courts across the country, providing a basis for voluntary discussion of matters affecting a forthcoming trial, such as the plea to be entered, length of trial, points of law or admissibility of evidence.[13] Such reviews appear to occur in approximately 25 per cent of cases.[14]

The one exception to this are cases involving serious fraud. Under the Criminal Justice Act 1987,[15] a trial judge may order a preparatory hearing if the case is of such seriousness and complexity that substantial benefits are likely to accrue from it. The purposes of the hearing are: (a) to identify material issues to be decided at the trial; (b) to consider how the juries' comprehension of the issues can be assisted; (c) to expedite such proceedings; (d) to assist the judge's management of such issues.

Unlike the informal preparatory hearings in ordinary cases, which can only deal with matters relating to the indictment, these hearings in serious fraud cases can deal with questions both of law and of admissibility of evidence. The judge may make orders concerning the form of presentation of the prosecution case, can require the defence to set out in writing, and in general terms, the nature of the defence relied upon, and deal with various matters relating to the agreement of documents. An appeal lies against such decisions.[16]

The Royal Commission considered one trial project that has involved all cases being listed for a "pleas and directions" hearing.[17] The majority of the Commission considered such a scheme to be both unnecessary and impracticable. Instead it proposed a scheme based on the automatic completion of forms with details of plea. The disclosure obligations recommended by the Commission[18] would then occur, and both prosecution and defence would then indicate whether a preparatory hearing was needed and for what purpose.[19] Such hearings would occur in a minority of cases, usually those anticipated to last at least five days, although it would be open to the parties to require a hearing in shorter cases.[20] Such hearings would deal with plea, matters of evidence (including issues of admissibility) and expert opinion, matters generally relating to the trial. Such decisions would be binding on the trial judge and counsel. For this reason the Royal Commission was concerned that the practice of returned briefs be minimised as much as possible.

---

13 The Royal Commission on Criminal Justice (at Ch 7, para 10) identified also a scheme based on the exchange of forms, recommended by a Working Party chaired by WATKINS LJ. The results obtained in a pilot scheme were disappointing.
14 *Ibid*, para 11, relying on the Crown Court Survey.
15 S 7(1).
16 *Ibid*, s 9(10).
17 Working Group on Pre-trial Issues – Recommendation 92 (cited by RCCJ, Ch 7, para 12).
18 See p 486, *ante*.
19 RCCJ, para 20.
20 *Ibid*, para 17.

Sanctions for non-compliance would be needed, including the potential for report to professional bodies, orders relating to the taxation of fees, and wasted costs orders.[1]

F   ARRAIGNMENT AND PLEAS

1   Attendance of the accused

On the day fixed for the trial to begin the defendant, if he has been detained in custody, will be brought from the prison or remand centre where he has been detained and lodged in the cells. If he has been on bail he must surrender to his bail and will then be placed in the cells to await his trial. It may be that the defendant has been on bail and does not appear, in which case the court of trial may issue a warrant, called a "bench warrant" for the arrest of the defendant; this is a summary procedure and will not normally be used unless the arrest of the defendant is a matter of urgency.

Still further powers are provided by section 7(3) of the Bail Act 1976 by which a constable may arrest without warrant any person who has been released on bail in criminal proceedings if, *inter alia*, he has reasonable grounds for believing that the person is unlikely to appear at the time and place required.

2   Arraignment

Assuming that the defendant has appeared at, or has been brought to, the court, the first formal step in his trial will be the arraignment, which is the process of calling an accused forward to answer an indictment. The defendant will be brought from the cells into the dock[2] and the proper officer will first ask him his name. Assuming that he is the person named in the indictment he will then be asked to plead. The indictment will be read to him (omitting only the introductory matters) and he will be asked to plead to it; further, where the indictment contains more than one count, each should be put to the defendant separately and he should be asked to plead separately, for each count is equivalent to a separate indictment.[3]

On arraignment the defendant may, of course, simply say nothing. If this occurs, the first question is whether the defendant is mute of malice, that is to say, able to speak but refusing to do so, or whether he is mute by visitation of God, that is to say, temporarily or permanently unable to speak. If there is any doubt a jury must be sworn to try the issue. Witnesses may be called on either side and counsel may address the jury; the judge will then sum up the case to the jury, who will retire if necessary and then give a verdict.[4] If the finding is that the defendant is mute of malice the court may then order the proper officer of the court to enter a plea of not guilty on behalf of the defendant (assuming that he still declines to speak);[5]

---

1 *Ibid*, para 36.

2 The Royal Commission did not recommend that docks be abolished. It considered that they should be situated as near as possible to the accused's legal representatives: Ch 8, para 109.

3 *R v Boyle* [1954] 2 QB 292; [1954] 2 All ER 721.

4 This may in some circumstances be by a majority: see p 500, *post*.

5 Criminal Law Act 1967, s 6(1)(c).

the trial will then proceed as if the defendant had himself pleaded not guilty. If, however, the finding is that the defendant is mute by visitation of God, the defendant may yet be perfectly well able to defend himself, and a plea of not guilty should be entered by the court and the trial should proceed in the ordinary way.

However there may well be some question of whether the defendant is fit to plead, the test for which is whether he is fit to challenge jurors, instruct counsel, understand the evidence and give evidence himself.[6] The procedure to be followed is contained in the Criminal Procedure (Insanity) Act 1964.[7] A jury must be sworn to try the issue. Again, evidence may be called by either side and speeches will be made; the judge will direct the jury, who will return a verdict. If the finding is that the defendant is unfit to plead the trial does not proceed, but the defendant is not free to go; he is liable to be detained in hospital or made subject to various orders.[8] The court has power, in the interests of the accused, to postpone trial of the issue of fitness to plead until any time up to the opening of the case for the defence. If, before such time, the defendant is acquitted (on a submission of no case to answer) his fitness or otherwise will not be determined.[9] This is to ensure that the case against the person being detained is in fact tested, and to ensure that an innocent person is not subject to detention. If the finding is one of fitness to plead, the defendant will then be called upon to plead to the indictment; if he still declines to answer, a plea of not guilty will be entered on his behalf.

3 Pleas

Assuming that all questions of fitness to plead have been disposed of adversely to the defendant, in the sense that the trial on the substantive issues must go on, various pleas are open to the defendant. In the vast majority of cases the alternatives are pleas of guilty or not guilty.

The decision to accept a plea to a lesser charge is that of the prosecutor, and does not require the consent of the court unless the decision arises after the prosecution has called its evidence and a case to answer has been found.[10] Such decisions may often assist in avoiding the time and expense of a trial, and is one explanation for the problem of "cracked trials". These are cases that are listed for trial but where on the day of trial the defendant pleads guilty.[11]

By contrast, the holding of discussions informally with the trial judge to ascertain attitudes to likely sentence is a practice that has been heavily criticised by the Court of Appeal.[12] Out-of-court discussions with the trial

---

6 *R v Berry* (1977) 66 Cr App Rep 156; not whether he is able to defend himself properly or well: *R v Robertson* [1968] 3 All ER 557; [1968] 1 WLR 1767.

7 As amended by the Criminal Procedure (Insanity and Unfitness to Plead) Act 1991. See ss 4, 4a and 5 of the 1964 Act.

8 *Ibid*, s 5.

9 *Ibid*, s 4; see, for such a case, *R v Burles* [1970] 2 QB 191; [1970] 1 All ER 642.

10 *R v Grafton* [1993] QB 101; [1992] 4 All ER 609. The position is different if counsel expressly asks for the approval of the judge: *R v Broad* (1978) 68 Cr App Rep 281. See, generally, *Farquharson Committee Report* (1986) LS Gaz 3599.

11 RCCJ, Ch 7, para 13. The Crown Court Study showed that "cracked" trials were 26 per cent of all cases, creating serious problems (para 45).

12 *R v Turner* [1970] 2 QB 321; [1970] 2 All ER 281; *R v Coward* (1979) 70 Cr App Rep 70.

judge should not occur unless absolutely essential, and then subject to various conditions. The Royal Commission proposed[13] a modification to this rule, so that judges may indicate the highest sentence that they would impose at that point on the basis of the facts put to them.[14] This might occur at pre-hearing, and encourage an accused to plead guilty. There is, of course, a danger that some defendants might plead guilty when they were, in fact, innocent.[15] The Crown Court Survey[16] found some evidence of this, but the significance of the data obtained is open to doubt.[17]

In fact the majority of accused persons at Crown Court plead guilty.[18] Therefore they obtain a "discount" on the otherwise justified sentence.[19] The Royal Commission proposed a formalised system, of graduated discounts, to encourage early pleas of guilty.[20] On the other hand, the research shows that approximately 50 per cent of those pleading not guilty are in fact acquitted,[1] with a significant number of "non-jury" acquittals. These non-jury acquittals merit further mention: the statistical evidence suggests that discharge, usually where the prosecution offers no evidence, is far more common than judges directing a jury to enter a 'not guilty' verdict because of the inadequacy of the evidence before the court.[2]

a   Plea of guilty

On the assumption that the plea covers the whole indictment, counsel briefed for the prosecution will give a brief outline of the facts and then call a police officer to give the antecedent history of the defendant, in the form of a sheet setting out the defendant's home and educational background, previous jobs, criminal record and anything else thought to be relevant. He may be cross-examined by defending counsel. The court will then usually consider a pre-sentence report,[3] presented usually on behalf of a probation officer. Such a report must generally be considered before a custodial sentence can be imposed.[4] There is then a plea in mitigation made by counsel for the defence, sometimes supported by witnesses (very rarely the defendant). The defendant will then usually be given the opportunity of saying something himself to the court, after which sentence will be passed. If there are two defendants, one of whom is pleading guilty and the other not guilty, the one pleading guilty will not normally be sentenced until the trial of the other defendant is concluded.[5]

---

13 *Op cit.*
14 Report, Ch 7, para 50.
15 It is for this reason that an accused must plead personally, not through counsel.
16 See generally Ashworth 'Plea, Venue and Discontinuance' [1993] Crim LR 830.
17 *Op cit*, para 45.
18 *Op cit*, Ch 6.
19 See, eg, *R v Hollington and Emmens* (1985) 82 Cr App Rep 281.
20 *Ibid*, para 47.
1 Vennard, "The Outcome of Contested Trials" in Moxon (ed) *Managing Criminal Justice*.
2 *Ordered and Directed Acquittals in the Crown Court*, RCCJ Research Study No 15, HMSO, 1993.
3 Criminal Justice Act 1991, s 3. These were formerly known as Social Inquiry Reports.
4 Criminal Justice Act 1991, s 4.
5 *R v Weekes* (1982) 74 Cr App Rep 161. The position may be different if the accused is going to give evidence for the prosecution against his co-accused.

It is customary for the normal rules of evidence to be relaxed at proceedings following a plea of guilty. The rules of evidence do not apply to "antecedent evidence", which is invariably given by a single police officer on the basis of files concerning the defendant which the officer has in court. Nevertheless the officer should not make allegations against the defendant which he has reason to think that the latter would deny and which he cannot properly prove.[6] Of course, if matters of importance are disputed, then the court may require them to be formally proved. In addition, where despite the plea of guilty there is a factual dispute which will affect the basis upon which the court will sentence the accused, the trial judge will hear evidence to determine that question, a so called "Newton" hearing.[7]

If the defendant pleads guilty to some, but not all, counts or pleads guilty to a lesser offence, the prosecution must decide whether to proceed on the remaining counts or "accept" the defendant's pleas, in which event the counts to which he has not pleaded guilty will be left "on the file". Although the defendant will never have been in peril of conviction on those counts, so that he could theoretically be tried on them, in practice this would not be permitted without leave of the court and, indeed, the counts on the file are sometimes ordered to be marked with words such as "not to be proceeded with without the leave of this court or of the Court of Appeal". However, even if the prosecution is content to adopt this course, the judge must, if asked, consent to it and, if he does not, he may order the trial to proceed.[8]

b   Plea of not guilty

It should be noted that this is not necessarily a positive assertion that the defendant is innocent but merely a request or a challenge to the prosecution to prove the case against him.

A defendant may plead guilty to one count in the indictment but not guilty to another, or even admit part of an offence contained in a single count but not the rest of the offence.[9] He may also plead not guilty to the offence charged but guilty to some other offence of which he may lawfully be convicted by way of alternative verdict; thus he may plead not guilty to murder but guilty to manslaughter. The whole question of alternative verdicts is now regulated by section 6(3) of the Criminal Law Act 1967. This enables the jury to acquit of the offence charged, but to convict of another offence which the court has jurisdiction to try and which is expressly or by implication alleged in the indictment.[10]

The point arises, often acutely, when the judge comes to sum up the case to the jury. Where nothing appears on the depositions which can be said to reduce the crime charged to the lesser offence of which the defendant

---

6 Cf *R v Robinson* (1969) 53 Cr App Rep 314, where the officer described the defendant as the principal drug "pusher" in the Midlands, "evidence" the reception of which the Court of Appeal described as "a clear and obvious injustice". See also *R v Wilkins* (1977) 66 Cr App Rep 49.

7 *R v Newton* (1982) 77 Cr App Rep 13.

8 *R v Broad* (1978) 68 Cr App Rep 281.

9 *Machent v Quinn* [1970] 2 All ER 255.

10 What is included "by implication" is often difficult to decide. The test is whether the allegations in the indictment are capable of including the elements of the alternative

wishes to plead guilty, it is the duty of counsel for the Crown to present the offence charged in the indictment, leaving it to the jury "in the exercise of their undoubted prerogative" to return a verdict of guilty of the lesser offence.[11] Even where there is material on the depositions capable of sustaining a lesser charge, the prosecution is entitled to formulate its charges as it thinks fit. However, it is for the discretion of the trial judge whether to direct the jury as to the potential for an alternative verdict.

Secondly, the defendant may change his plea once the trial has started but in this case the appropriate verdict must be returned by the jury which will have been sworn to try the case;[12] it may seem a formality that if the defendant changes his plea, for example, from 'not guilty' to 'guilty' the foreman of the jury should be required to stand up and say that the defendant is guilty but:

> ". . . once a prisoner is in charge of a jury he can only be either convicted or discharged by the verdict of the jury".[13]

c   Autrefois acquit and autrefois convict

These are by far the most important of a number of so-called "special pleas in bar" which can be raised by the defendant when the indictment is put to him.[14] The substance of the pleas in bar is that there is some reason why the court should not proceed to try the defendant, which should be made the subject of immediate inquiry, so that if the reason is found to be a valid one the defendant should be released and further proceedings stayed.[15] The general principle of the two pleas of *autrefois acquit* and *autrefois convict* is that the same person should not be put in jeopardy twice for the same offence founded on the same facts – not merely for the same facts. The two pleas were extensively considered by the House of Lords in *Connelly v Director of Public Prosecutions.*[16] The following principles emerge from that and subsequent cases.

    (i)   A man cannot be tried for a crime in respect of which he has previously been convicted or acquitted. The reason for this is that an accused should not be put in peril twice. It is for this reason that the doctrine does not apply where the accused was never in fact in jeopardy. In *R v Dabhade*[17] a charge was formally dismissed, because in law it was defective. The accused was committed for trial on a substituted charge of theft. In dismissing an appeal against conviction, based upon the principle of *autrefois acquit*, the Court of Appeal indicated that where a charge was dismissed because it was

---

offence: *Metropolitan Police Commissioner v Wilson* [1984] AC 242; sub nom *R v Wilson* [1983] 3 All ER 448.

11 *R v Soanes* [1948] 1 All ER 289.

12 *R v Heyes* [1951] 1 KB 29; [1950] 2 All ER 587.

13 *Ibid per* Lord Goddard CJ [1951] 1 KB at 30; [1950] 2 All ER at 588.

14 Others are demurrer (that the facts alleged do not constitute the offence charged); plea to the jurisdiction (that the court has no jurisdiction to try); pardon (that a pardon has been granted). These are extremely rare.

15 See the remarks of Lord Goddard CJ in *R v County of London Quarter Sessions, ex parte Downes* [1954] 1 QB 1 at 5–6; [1953] 2 All ER at 750.

16 [1964] AC 1254; [1964] 2 All ER 401.

17 [1993] QB 329; [1992] 4 All ER 796.

defective, or because the evidence was insufficient to sustain a conviction, or because of a rationalisation of the prosecution case, the appellant was never in fact in jeopardy.

(ii) The same rule applies where a person could have been convicted of the alleged offence on a previous indictment. In this context the rule as to alternative verdict offences is of importance. As has already been seen,[18] a defendant on being charged with certain crimes may plead, or be found, guilty of certain other crimes and not guilty of the offence charged, without the need for a fresh indictment. Thus on a charge of murder the accused may be convicted of manslaughter. The doctrines of *autrefois acquit* and *autrefois convict* apply to any offence which was an alternative verdict offence to the original offence, and of which the accused was acquitted or convicted. Thus if the defendant is acquitted of murder, the defence of *autrefois acquit* will be open to him if charged with manslaughter or attempted murder arising out of the death of the same person.

(iii) The rule applies if the crime in respect of which he is charged is in effect, or substantially the same as, the crime of which he was earlier acquitted or could have been (or was) convicted. This is in reality a matter for the common sense of the court.

(iv) One test of when the rule applies is to ask whether the evidence necessary to support the second indictment, or whether the facts which constitute the second offence, would have been sufficient to procure a legal conviction on the first indictment either as to the offence charged or of an offence of which the accused could have been found guilty.

(v) The matter is not decided simply by comparing indictments, but on the overall facts. The accused may adduce evidence as to the identity of the persons involved, and as to dates and other facts necessary to show that the doctrine applies.

(vi) It is not within the doctrine that the facts under examination, or the witnesses being called in the later proceedings, are the same as those in the earlier proceedings.

(vii) Irrespective of the above, a person may be able to show that a matter has in fact been decided already by a court competent to decide it, in the sense of a finding or plea of guilty and a sentence passed pursuant to that finding or plea. The matter must, though, in fact have been decided. In *Richards v R*,[19] the accused pleaded guilty to manslaughter, but had not been sentenced. At a resumed hearing the prosecution was halted, and the appellant subsequently tried and convicted and sentenced to death[20] for murder. In dismissing the appeal against conviction the Privy Council was of the view that the plea of *autrefois convict* did not assist the accused, because the adjudication was not in fact complete.

---

18 See p 491, *ante*.
19 [1993] AC 217; [1992] 4 All ER 807.
20 It was a Privy Council appeal from Jamaica, where the death penalty still exists.

4   Motion to quash the indictment

Instead of entering any plea, general or special, the defendant may move to quash the indictment. This may be done on several grounds. If any of the rules, already described,[1] as to the framing of the indictment have not been followed this may be made the ground for a motion to quash; however it has already been seen that the court possesses ample power to amend the indictment and it will only be rarely that a motion to quash on this ground will succeed. It could only do so on the ground of some grave defect of substance, such as the insufficiency of the particulars of offence, or duplicity. An indictment may also be quashed on the ground that the offence charged in it is not one known to the law. Yet another ground is that the appropriate officer did not have jurisdiction to sign it; as has already been seen he can sign it only if certain conditions are satisfied. An indictment can also be quashed if it amounts to an abuse of the process of the court.[2]

5   Preliminary points of law

It sometimes happens that there is a point of law involved in a case the decision of which may effectively dispose of the whole case. Thus, for example, the basic facts alleged by the prosecution may be admitted by the defence, the sole issue being whether those admitted facts amount to the offence charged. In cases of this sort it is obviously a sterile exercise to go through the motions of trial by jury when the outcome of the case will depend entirely upon the judge's decision as to the law. Accordingly there is an informal but well recognised procedure whereby, following a plea of not guilty, the judge hears argument upon the law (before empanelling a jury); if a ruling is given which, in the view of the accused and his advisers, is fatal to the defence, the accused can then change his plea.[3] However it is necessary for a plea of not guilty to be taken before the point of law is argued and the Court of Appeal has discouraged the practice of hearing argument on agreed facts before the accused has even pleaded.[4] It should be remembered though that matters of law may be decided at a preliminary hearing in cases of serious fraud,[5] a practice the Royal Commission proposed should be extended.[6]

6   Empanelling the jury: challenges

Assuming that there is a plea of not guilty to some part of the indictment the next stage of the trial will be the swearing of the jury. The Juries Act confers on the Lord Chancellor general responsibility for the summoning

---

1 See p 473, *ante.*
2 See p 479, *ante.*
3 See, eg, *Director of Public Prosecutions v Doot* [1973] AC 807; [1973] 1 All ER 940. An accused who has pleaded guilty in such circumstances can appeal against his conviction on the ground that the preliminary point of law was wrongly decided against him. See p 479, *ante.*
4 *R v Vickers* [1975] 2 All ER 945; [1975] 1 WLR 811.
5 See p 487, *ante.*
6 See p 487, *ante.*

of jurors,[7] a function in reality performed locally. From all the jurors summoned, twelve will be chosen by ballot; a jury should be randomly selected[8] and a court has no power to interfere with the selection of a jury except in the rarest of cases, and for cause, for example relating to the physical or mental fitness of the proposed juror.[9] The selected jurors will take their places in the jury box. Before the jury is sworn the defendant is given the opportunity to challenge members of the jury for cause, either to the whole panel summoned or to an individual juror. The burden is on the party making the challenge to show such a cause, the issue being tried by the trial judge. Prior to 1988 an accused had a right of peremptory challenge of up to three jurors, which meant that, unlike for cause, the defendant did not have to state any reason for challenge. This right was abolished by the Criminal Justice Act 1988. By contrast the right of the Crown to require jurors to "stand by" still exists.[10] By this procedure, the juror is asked to stand down, but consideration of the cause of challenge (since a challenge by the Crown must be for cause) is postponed. It will usually then happen that there are enough "spare" jurors for a whole jury to be assembled, however many more challenges are made, so that the trial can proceed and the cause of the Crown's challenge is never made the subject of enquiry. The Crown will usually act on the basis of knowledge of a potential juror's criminal record[11] or, in exceptional cases of other matters disclosed on an authorised check of police records.[12]

Each member of the jury having been sworn individually, the appropriate officer of the court then tells the jury of the terms of the offences to which the defendant has pleaded not guilty and informs them that it is their duty, having heard the evidence, to say whether he is guilty or not. The trial judge may also explain certain features about a criminal trial to the jury.[13]

G COURSE OF THE TRIAL

1 Publicity

English law regards "open justice" as a fundamental principle,[14] which therefore means that the trial, including the process of arraignment described above, should be open to the public, and may be reported. Despite this, the principle is not unlimited, and may be departed from where necessary where openness or publicity would harm the interests of justice.[15] Powers exist to postpone the reporting of all or part of a trial,[16] to

---

7 Juries Act 1974, s 2.
8 See RCCJ, Ch 8, paras 52–64, and p 199, *ante*.
9 See p 201, *ante*.
10 See *Attorney General's Guidelines* (1989).
11 These may disqualify a juror from service: see p 199, *ante*.
12 *Attorney General's Guidelines on Jury Checks* [1988] 3 All ER 1086, and p 201, *ante*.
13 Royal Commission on Criminal Procedure, Cmnd 8092, 1981, para 67.
14 *Scott v Scott* [1913] AC 417; [1911–13] All ER Rep 1.
15 See p 141, *ante*.
16 Contempt of Court Act 1981, s 4(2). A right of appeal against such an order exists: Criminal Justice Act 1988, s 159.

prevent reporting,[17] or in some situations to sit *in camera*. In addition, a variety of statutory powers exist that limit the principle.[18]

2 Hearing

Prosecuting counsel starts by making an opening speech. This will be an outline of the allegations against the defendant and of the evidence which it is proposed to call in support of the allegations. No reference should be made to any item of evidence if counsel has been informed that there is going to be an objection to the admissibility of that evidence. Such objection will be tried by the judge, in the absence of the jury, at the time in the trial when the evidence would otherwise have been called. The institution of the opening speech has been criticised on the ground that counsel may make allegations which are not borne out by the evidence of his witnesses (even before they are the subject of cross-examination) yet the jury may recollect only the statements of counsel, since they came first.[19] It is a strict rule that prosecuting counsel should limit his observations to what appears in the depositions, or witness statements. The only exception arises in the case of those witnesses in respect of whom a notice of additional evidence has been served. Even this practice is not strictly required by law, but the court has an inherent discretion to prevent oppressive conduct towards the defendant[20] and it is most unlikely that a judge would allow additional evidence to be called unless a notice of additional evidence, setting out a summary of that witness's evidence, had been served on the defendant.

Prosecution witnesses will then be called[1] and will be subject to examination-in-chief by prosecuting counsel, cross-examination by defending counsel and re-examination by prosecuting counsel. In certain circumstances, however, the witness may not appear in person, but there are a number of statutory powers which permit a witness's written statement to be given in evidence.[2] Witnesses (usually children) may sometimes be permitted to give evidence through a live TV link,[3] whilst,

---

17 Contempt of Court Act 1981, s 11.

18 *Scott v Scott* (n 14, *supra*).

19 The Royal Commission recommended that opening speeches should not contain such statements: whether matters are proved will be decided during the trial. The RCCJ suggested opening speeches should be restricted to explanation of the issues (Ch 8, para 9), and that such speeches should be limited in length to fifteen minutes.

20 See the remarks of LORD DEVLIN in *Connolly v Director of Public Prosecutions* [1964] AC 1254 at 1346 et seq; [1964] 2 All ER 401 at 438 et seq.

 1 It is the duty of the prosecution to take all reasonable steps to secure the attendance at the trial of all witnesses (other than those subject to a conditional witness order) named on the back of the indictment (*R v Cavanagh* [1974] 2 All ER 704; [1972] 1 WLR 676). However the prosecution has a discretion whether to call a particular witness and, having called him, whether to adduce his evidence-in-chief or merely to tender him for cross-examination. Where the witness's evidence is capable of belief the prosecution should call him even though his evidence is unfavourable to the prosecution case and if they do not do so, the judge may intervene and direct that he be called; on the other hand if the witness's evidence does not appear to be capable of belief the prosecution need not call him and it will then be for the defence to call him if they wish to do so; *R v Oliva* [1965] 3 All ER 116; [1965] 1 WLR 1028.

 2 See p 635, post.

 3 Criminal Justice Act 1988, s 32. In some circumstances a video recording of an interview may be seen: *ibid*, s 32A (inserted by Criminal Justice Act 1991 s 54).

if the administration of justice requires it, a witness may be permitted to give evidence from behind screens, so as to restrict the view of the public, or even the accused.[4]

When all the witnesses for the prosecution have been examined, prosecuting counsel will close his case by saying "that is the case for the prosecution" or words to that effect. There may then be a submission by defending counsel that there is no case to answer as regards the whole or some part of the indictment. This may be put in two ways; first that there is no evidence that the crime alleged against the accused was committed by him; secondly that the evidence, taken at its highest, is so tenuous that a jury could not properly convict on it.[5] This is a matter for the judge to determine and, although there is no set rule, it is usually regarded as desirable that the argument on the submission should take place in the absence of the jury. Prosecuting counsel has, of course, a right to reply to defending counsel's submission. If the submission is upheld the trial will end as regards that part of the indictment at least, although the jury should be instructed to return a formal verdict of not guilty; this is analogous to the case where the defendant changes his plea to guilty in the course of the trial.[6] Even if no formal verdict is taken, the case, once withdrawn from the jury, is completely "dead" and cannot be revived by the defendant's own evidence or evidence given by a prosecution witness who is allowed to be recalled.[7] Similarly where two men are jointly charged, and a successful submission is made on behalf of one of them, he is to be regarded as no longer charged during what remains of the trial.[8]

The role of the judge at this stage is crucial. If the prosecution evidence is such that no properly directed jury could convict upon it then it is the duty of the judge to stop the case.[9] This is particularly the case where the prosecution rely wholly on the confession of a person who suffers a significant degree of mental handicap, the confession itself being unconvincing. Such a case should be withdrawn from the jury.[10] By contrast, if the case is one where the strengths or weaknesses of the case depend upon the view to be taken as to the reliability of a witness or other matters properly within the remit of the jury, then the case should be left to the jury to decide.[11]

If the submission is simply rejected the trial will proceed. Even if no submission is made the judge may at any time after the close of the prosecution's case ask the jury whether they think that the prosecution case has been proved and invite them to return a verdict of not guilty if they think that it has not;[12] the more desirable practice is for the

---

4 *R v X, Y and Z* (1989) 91 Cr App Rep 36.
5 *R v Galbraith* [1981] 2 All ER 1060; [1981] 1 WLR 1039.
6 See p 492, *ante*.
7 *R v Plain* [1967] 1 All ER 614; [1967] 1 WLR 565. The corollary of this is that if the submission is wrongly rejected the accused is entitled to have his subsequent conviction quashed by the Court of Appeal, even though evidence subsequently given would support that conviction; *R v Cockley* [1984] Crim LR 429.
8 *R v Meek* (1966) 110 Sol Jo 867.
9 *R v Galbraith* [1981] 2 All ER 1060; [1981] 1 WLR 1039.
10 *R v McKenzie* [1993] 1 WLR 453.
11 *R v Galbraith*, n 5, *supra*.
12 *R v Young* [1964] 2 All ER 480; [1964] 1 WLR 717.

judge to take the initiative and direct the jury to return a verdict of not guilty.

The defence case will then open, assuming that the trial is proceeding as to part or all of the indictment. Defence counsel has no right to make an opening speech to the jury unless he is calling witnesses as to fact other than the defendant (whether or not he is also calling the defendant); even then the matter is in his discretion.[13] Witnesses for the defence are then called. If the defendant is giving evidence it is the general rule that he must give evidence before other witnesses; he must be in court, and if he heard the evidence of other witnesses before him, he might be tempted to "trim" his own evidence.[14] A witness about whose evidence there could be no controversy may of course be taken before the defendant. What evidence is called for the defence depends on the nature of the case, but it has already been seen[15] that "evidence in support of an alibi" cannot be called, without leave, unless prior notice has been given.

All defence witnesses are subject to examination-in-chief, cross-examination and re-examination in the normal way.[16] Where there is more than one defendant, cross-examination of prosecution witnesses and speeches will normally be taken in the order in which the defendants' names appear on the indictment, although there is no fixed rule on the matter. Once the case for the defence has been closed the prosecution may be allowed to call rebutting evidence, in the discretion of the judge. This is a necessary right, since apart from the "alibi defence", and expert evidence, there is no obligation on the defendant to reveal his case until the actual presentation of it in court. However, the general rule is that rebutting evidence should be allowed only where evidence has been called on behalf of the defendant which could not fairly have been foreseen by the prosecution.[17] Rebutting evidence may be called at any time up to the conclusion of the summing-up and retirement of the jury and defending counsel has a right to cross-examine the witnesses called in rebuttal. Further, if evidence is called after the conclusion of the speeches, counsel may deliver supplemental speeches dealing with the new evidence.

The judge has a right to recall witnesses himself or even call witnesses whom neither side has called; he may also question witnesses to clarify matters of doubt or to probe further into matters which he thinks have not been sufficiently investigated. However, a judge must be careful not to overstep the mark. In *R v Grafton*[18] prosecuting counsel decided during his case to offer no further evidence. The trial judge disagreed with that decision, and called the one remaining prosecution witness. In quashing the resulting conviction, the Court of Appeal stressed that the judge's power to call witnesses should be used sparingly, and only to advance the ends of fairness and justice. Until the case for the Crown is complete it is the Crown's decision as to whether or not the prosecution should proceed.

---

13 The Royal Commission recommended that the right of the defence to make a speech at the commencement of the case should be extended to all cases, in substitution for the right here described.

14 Police and Criminal Evidence Act 1984, s 79.

15 See p 485, *ante*.

16 For the limits to cross-examination, see p 585, *post*.

17 *R v Pilcher* (1974) 60 Cr App Rep 1.

18 [1993] QB 101; [1992] 4 All ER 609.

However, the Royal Commission recommended that trial judges be more questioning of counsel (in the absence of the jury) as to why witnesses who are believed to have evidence of relevance have not been called.[19]

Closing speeches then follow. Each side may address the jury, except that where a defendant is unrepresented and either gives no evidence at all or only gives evidence himself the prosecution have no right to sum up their case.[20] In all cases the rule is that prosecuting counsel speaks first and is then followed by counsel for the defendant.[1] The judge will then sum up.

The purpose of the summing-up is to instruct the jury as to the burden and standard of proof,[2] the role of judge and jury, and to give directions on points of law where it is necessary to do so. The Judicial Studies Board[3] has prepared model directions on common issues and points of law for the benefit of judges. The judge will also usually give a summary of the facts: indeed, in *R v Gregory*[4] the Court of Appeal suggested that there must be a reminder of the facts in all cases. However, in *R v Wilson*[5] the Court of Appeal upheld a conviction in a case where a judge considered the trial so short that a summary of the facts was unnecessary.

Criticism of this part of the judicial function has from time to time been made,[6] that summings-up can unwittingly, and occasionally deliberately, influence the juries' view of the facts. Some suggested to the Royal Commission that, as in the United States, no summing-up of the facts should be given. This was rejected, but the Commission did disagree with the approach taken in *R v Gregory*, and indicated that it is in each case a question of fairness and balance.[7]

3 Verdict

No pressure should be placed on a jury to reach a verdict.[8] The jury generally retire to the jury room to consider their verdict. They are put in charge of officers of the court called jury bailiffs who must take an oath not, without the leave of the court, to allow any person to speak to the jury or to speak to them themselves without such leave, except only to ask them if they are agreed upon their verdict. Once they have retired to consider their verdict, the jury can separate only with leave of the court,

---

19 Report, Ch 8, para 18.
20 *R v Harrison* (1923) 17 Cr App Rep 156. Where the defendant is represented but calls no evidence, counsel for the prosecution has a right to make a closing speech but the Court of Appeal has stated that it is a right which it should rarely be necessary to exercise save in long and complex cases: *R v Bryant* [1979] QB 108; [1978] 2 All ER 689, an instructive case on the history of the procedure relating to speeches in criminal trials.
1 Criminal Procedure (Right of Reply) Act 1964.
2 See p 559, *post*.
3 Responsible for the training of the judiciary. Such model directions must be adapted to the needs of the particular case.
4 [1993] Crim LR 623.
5 [1991] Crim LR 838.
6 See RCCJ, Ch 8, para 20.
7 *Ibid*, para 22.
8 *R v McKenna* [1960] 1 QB 411; [1960] 1 All ER 326: judge told jury that they would be kept overnight if they failed to agree a verdict within 10 minutes. A guilty verdict was returned after 6 minutes. The resulting conviction was quashed on appeal. See also: *Bushell's case* (1670) Vaugh 135, 124 ER 1006.

which in turn can be given only in cases of "evident necessity"[9] such as a juror being taken ill in the course of the jury's deliberations. They do not have to stay in the same jury room until they have reached a conclusion, but they must not separate, subject to the very limited exception noted above, and it is desirable if not essential for them always to be in the custody of one of the court bailiffs while, for example, staying at a hotel overnight.[10] The jury may, of course, ask for further guidance from the judge upon any point of law or evidence arising in the case, but both the request for information and the answer to it must be given in open court; if the jury have asked for guidance in the form of a note sent to the judge, this note should be read out *verbatim* and then the answer given.[11]

When the jury have concluded their deliberations they will return to court and one of their number, whom they have appointed foreman, will stand up and, subject to the possibility of a majority verdict, in answer to questions put by the appropriate officer of the court, deliver the verdict of the jury.[12] The Criminal Justice Act 1967[13] introduced into English law the majority verdict. A verdict need not be unanimous if when there are not less than eleven jurors, ten agree on the verdict, and when there are ten, if nine agree.[14] The law cannot accept any majority verdict unless the jury have had not less than two hours of deliberation, or such longer period as the court thinks reasonable having regard to the nature and complexity of the case,[15] nor can the court accept a majority verdict of guilty unless the foreman of the jury states in open court the number of jurors who agreed on, and dissented from, the verdict.[16] A *Practice Direction*[17] contains procedure whereby it is hoped to conceal the fact that an acquittal was by a majority. In *R v Pigg*[18] the House of Lords held that the words "ten agreed" (in answer to the question how many agreed and how many dissented) was sufficient compliance with the statute. If after such discussion as is practicable in the circumstances the jury still cannot reach the necessary measure of agreement the judge has no option but to discharge

---

9 *R v Neal* [1949] 2 KB 590; [1949] 2 All ER 438. Breach of this rule will almost invariably amount to a material irregularity resulting in a subsequent conviction being quashed; *R v Goodson* [1975] 1 All ER 760; [1975] 1 WLR 549 (where a juror, after retirement, was permitted by the jury bailiff to leave the jury room, following which he was seen making a telephone call); but compare *R v Alexander* [1974] 1 All ER 539; [1974] 1 WLR 422 in which the irregularity was a trifling one (juror returned to court simply to collect one or more of the exhibits and was observed throughout) and was held to be of insufficient gravity to justify quashing the conviction.

10 It may be necessary to restrict their reading or television viewing: see *Re Central Independent Television* [1991] 1 All ER 347; [1991] 1 WLR 4.

11 *R v Green* [1950] 1 All ER 38.

12 Once a verdict is given in the presence and hearing of all the jury, their assent to it is conclusively presumed: *R v Roads* [1967] 2 QB 108; [1967] 2 All ER 84.

13 Section 13 (now Juries Act 1974, s 17).

14 Majority verdicts are not considered desirable in re-trials; cf *R v Mansfield* [1978] 1 All ER 134; [1977] 1 WLR 1102.

15 Juries Act 1974, s 17(4).

16 *Ibid*, s 17(3). The requirement of this subsection is mandatory so that if, for whatever reason, the foreman does not so state the conviction will inevitably be quashed: *R v Barry* [1975] 2 All ER 760; [1975] 1 WLR 1190.

17 *Practice Direction* [1967] 3 All ER 137; [1967] 1 WLR 1198. Errors in the summing-up should be corrected by counsel before the jury retire: *R v Southgate* [1963] 2 All ER 833; [1963] 1 WLR 809n.

18 [1983] 1 All ER 56; [1983] 1 WLR 6.

them. The defendant will then be remanded in custody or on bail to be tried afresh. Theoretically this could happen several times, but if successive juries disagree the practice is for the prosecution to offer no evidence at a third trial. On a re-trial, the fact that there has been a previous trial is usually irrelevant and inadmissible, but it may become necessary to refer to it, for example for the purpose of proving that the defendant or a witness made some particular statement or admission. Thus in *R v McGregor*[19] the defendant was charged with receiving. At an earlier, abortive, trial he had admitted possession. A police officer was allowed to give evidence of this admission.

Other circumstances in which the jury may be discharged are:

(1)   illness. If during the course of a criminal trial a juror falls ill he may be discharged by the judge from further service, and depending on the facts, normally will be so discharged. The judge may then discharge the whole jury, but does not have to do so; neither is discharge of the single juror fatal to the continuance of the trial, since statute now provides[20] that when, in the course of a trial, any member of the jury dies or is discharged the trial may nevertheless continue provided that the number of jurors does not fall below nine. If, however, the charge is murder or any offence punishable by death the prosecution and every accused must consent in writing to the trial continuing, even if only one juror is discharged or dies;

(2)   misconduct of a juror, such as holding improper conversations with a member of the public about the case or absenting himself from his colleagues at the time when the jury were in the course of retiring to consider their verdict; and

(3)   improper revelation to the jury of the defendant's past criminal record. In such a case the jury is frequently discharged in the defendant's own interest, although every case depends on its own facts.

H   SENTENCING

A judge will sentence on the basis of the guilty plea or verdict of the jury. If there is a significant dispute about what factually occurred, then, following a plea of guilty, unless the prosecution accepts the defence version, a hearing is held to decide any dispute.[1] However, if there is a verdict (as opposed to a plea) of guilty, the judge sentences on the basis of the facts as they appear to him.

1   Passing sentence

If the defendant has been found guilty on any part of the indictment the

---

19 [1968] 1 QB 371; [1967] 2 All ER 267.
20 Juries Act 1974, s 16. The judge may discharge a juror "whether as being through illness incapable of continuing to act or for any other reason" (s 16(1)). This is a matter left to the discretion of the trial judge, although the Court of Appeal will interfere if injustice has resulted. In *R v Hambery* [1977] QB 924; [1977] 3 All ER 561 the trial judge discharged a lady juror in order to permit her to go away on holiday, a course which the Court of Appeal saw no reason to criticise.
1 Known as a *Newton* hearing: *R v Newton* (1982) 77 Cr App Rep 13.

court will then proceed to sentence, in a similar manner to that following a plea of guilty.[2] There is first an inquiry into the defendant's antecedents. A pre-sentence report is then considered. The defendant is then customarily given an opportunity of making such observations as he wishes, in addition to his counsel's speech in mitigation. It should always be made clear whether separate sentences are intended to be consecutive or concurrent.[3] In the course of this part of the trial it not infrequently happens that the defendant asks for other offences to be taken into consideration. This practice is based on convention and has no statutory foundation; yet at the same time it is extremely convenient both from the point of view of the police and of the defendant. If there are other offences which the defendant has committed but which are still untried (or unknown), then the defendant may admit them to the court of trial and ask the judge to take them into consideration when sentencing him for the offence of which he has just been convicted. In practice he will probably tell the police well before the hearing that he wishes certain offences to be taken into consideration or the police may suggest the matter to him and he will then be supplied with an appropriate form of admission; however there seems to be nothing to prevent a court taking an offence into consideration even if the defendant does not either admit it or ask for it to be taken into consideration until the actual trial. However:

> "If justice is to be done it is essential that the practice should not be followed except with the express and unequivocal assent of the offender himself. Accordingly, he should be informed explicitly of each offence which the judge proposes to take into consideration; and should explicitly admit that he committed them and should state his desire that they should be taken into consideration in determining the sentence to be passed on him."[4]

Once the defendant has served his sentence he will not, by long established custom, be prosecuted in respect of any of the offences which have been taken into consideration, although if he were prosecuted the defence of *autrefois convict* would not be open to him, there having been no trial, let alone conviction, in respect of those offences.[5] If, however, his conviction were quashed, a prosecution might be brought.

The mere fact that the defendant asks for the offence to be taken into consideration does not, of course, compel the court to do so. Certain limitations have been laid down in the cases. Broadly, the offence to be taken into consideration should be of the same character as the offence of which the defendant has been convicted; if the defendant has already been separately committed for trial in respect of the offence to be taken into consideration the judge should obtain the consent of the prosecution before doing so.[6] Even if the prosecution does consent the judge ought to consider whether the public interest requires a separate inquiry. Neither ought the court to take into consideration an offence carrying disqualifica-

---

2 See p 490, *ante*.

3 *Practice Direction* [1962] 1 All ER 417; [1962] 1 WLR 191.

4 *Anderson v Director of Public Prosecutions* [1978] AC 964, at 977; sub nom *Director of Public Prosecutions v Anderson* [1978] 2 All ER 512, at 515–516, per LORD DIPLOCK.

5 *R v Nicholson* [1947] 2 All ER 535.

6 *R v McLean* [1911] 1 KB 332.

tion from driving.[7] The reason is that in very many cases it will be desirable if not obligatory to disqualify the defendant, yet there can only be a disqualification on conviction, and taking other offences into consideration does not amount to a conviction in respect of them.

A sentence takes effect from the beginning of the day on which it is imposed, unless the court otherwise directs. Any sentence imposed, or other order made, by the Crown Court may, under s 47(2) of the Supreme Court Act 1981, be varied or rescinded by the Crown Court within the period of 28 days from the date of such sentence or order.

2 Deferment of sentence

As an alternative to passing sentence immediately upon an offender, the judge has power to defer sentence "for the purpose of enabling the court or any other court to which it falls to deal with him to have regard, in dealing with him to his conduct after conviction (including, where appropriate, the making by him of reparation for his offence) or to any change in his circumstances".[8] The deferment can only be made if the offender consents and the court is satisfied, having regard to the nature of the offence and the character and circumstances of the offender, that it would be in the interests of justice so to do.

The power to defer sentence is intended for cases such as those in which a persistent offender has at last shown an inclination to settle down and work or those in which persons have, under domestic or financial pressure, stolen from their employers sums which they say they propose to repay. Accordingly it will not be appropriate to defer sentence where the offence is so minor that it would not merit a sentence of imprisonment in any event. Nor is it appropriate to do so where the offence is so serious that it must inevitably result in a substantial custodial sentence. This is because it would not be appropriate to impose a custodial sentence if the information before the court about his conduct during the period of deferment is favourable to him.[9]

The period of deferment may be anything up to six months and there must not be a further deferment on the specified date.[10] Furthermore, where sentence is deferred, all aspects of the sentence should be deferred; the sentence must not be "split" by, for example, imposing an immediate disqualification from driving, but deferring the remainder of the sentence.[11]

---

7 *R v Williams* [1962] 3 All ER 639; [1962] 1 WLR 1268.
8 Powers of the Criminal Courts Act 1973, s 1. For the principles governing the exercise of such power, see *R v George* [1984] 3 All ER 13; [1984] 1 WLR 1082.
9 *R v Gilby* [1975] 2 All ER 743; [1975] 1 WLR 924.
10 Powers of Criminal Courts Act 1973, s 1(2).
11 *R v Fairhead* [1975] 2 All ER 737. However, a restitution order may be made under the Theft Act 1968, even if the passing of sentence is in other respects deferred: Theft Act 1968, s 28(1) (as amended by the Criminal Law Act 1977, Sch 12).

I   SENTENCES AND ORDERS

1   Death

The death penalty was abolished for murder in 1965.[12] Death continues to be the penalty for treason and piracy with violence.[13]

2   Imprisonment and other custodial sentences

In cases of murder, a sentence of life imprisonment is mandatory. The trial judge may in open court declare the period[14] which in his view should elapse before the release of the accused on licence.[15] The recommendation is not binding on the Home Secretary, who, in consultation with the trial judge and Lord Chief Justice, will set a "tariff".[16] This tariff determines when the defendant's continued imprisonment will be reviewed by the Parole Board.[17] The question of release on licence is for the Home Secretary, after a recommendation for release by the Parole Board.

Apart from these cases, sentences of imprisonment, which may for some offences include life imprisonment,[18] may only be imposed if the criteria prescribed by law are satisfied. The Criminal Justice Act 1991 recast the rules relating to the imposition of terms of imprisonment. By section 1(2) of the 1991 Act, a court can only impose a custodial sentence if (1) the offence[19] is so serious that only such a sentence can be justified, or (2) the offence is a violent or sexual offence,[20] and only such a sentence would be adequate to protect the public from serious harm from the offender. The intent is that imprisonment should not be used as a punishment unless the seriousness of the offence, or the risk to the public, warrants it. Nevertheless, difficulties quickly arose with the detailed rules governing offence seriousness, and had to be amended in key respects.

Offence seriousness is to be assessed in the light of the offence for which the sentence is being passed, together with any associated offences.[1] This is a change from the law as originally conceived, which restricted the court to considering only *one* associated offence. An associated offence is an offence for which the offender is being dealt with on the same sentencing occasion, or which the offender is asking to be taken into consideration on that occasion.[2]

---

12 Murder (Abolition of Death Penalty) Act 1965. The provisions of that Act were expressed to be temporary, but Parliament decided in 1969 that abolition was to be permanent.

13 The death penalty for arson of Her Majesty's ships and dockyards was abolished by s 11(2) of the Criminal Damage Act 1971.

14 This can include a recommendation that a defendant never be released: *R v Skingle and Sparrow* (1971) Times 16 October (reported, but not on that point, at [1973] 2 All ER 129; [1973] 1 WLR 488, sub nom *R v Sparrow*).

15 This power only applies in mandatory life sentence cases, but in any event in all life imprisonment cases judges give recommendations of the necessary period of detention to meet the requirements of retribution and deterrence. See p 505, *post.*

16 See *supra*, n 15.

17 Established under Criminal Justice Act 1967.

18 Known as discretionary life sentences.

19 And any associated offences.

20 These terms are defined by Criminal Justice Act 1991, s 31(2). See also *R v Robinson* [1993] 2 All ER 1; [1993] 1 WLR 168.

1 S 1(2), as amended by Criminal Justice Act 1993, s 66.

2 *Ibid*, s 31.

Particular problems also arose in respect of whether an offence is aggravated by the fact that the offender has previous convictions. As originally enacted, section 29 of the Criminal Justice Act 1991 required a court to disregard previous convictions unless they demonstrated aggravating features of the offence for which sentence was being passed.[3] This led to difficulties in both interpretation and application.[4] As a result, changes were made which allow a court to take into account previous convictions.[5] A court may also treat the commission of an offence whilst on bail as an aggravating factor.[6]

In deciding offence seriousness, the courts have adopted an approach based upon whether "right thinking members of the public, knowing all the facts, feel that justice had not been done by passing of a sentence other than a custodial one."[7] Offences can be regarded as serious enough to warrant custody in the light of a person's previous convictions,[8] or in the light of the fact that the offence was committed whilst the offender was on bail.[9]

The imposition of a term of imprisonment does not mean that the term specified is that which the offender actually serves. With regard to discretionary life prisoners, the 1991 Act created new procedures governing early release.[10] A court may indicate the period that must expire before the offender may have his case considered by the Parole Board. If the Parole Board recommends release, then the Home Secretary is duty bound to release him.

In other cases of imprisonment, the 1991 Act created a complicated system, the effect of which is that short-term prisoners[11] are released, either unconditionally (if the sentence is for less than 12 months) or on licence (if for 12 months or more), after half-sentence, whilst long-term prisoners[12] are eligible for release on licence after half-sentence and automatic release after the service of two-thirds of the sentence.[13]

A sentence of imprisonment may be imposed but suspended, ie ordered not to take effect immediately.[14] The sentence must not be for more than two years and the period of suspension must be between one and two years.[15] The effect of a suspended sentence is that so far as that sentence is

---

3 S 29(1).
4 For a summary of the problems, see *R v Bexley* [1993] 2 All ER 23; [1993] 1 WLR 192.
5 Criminal Justice Act 1993, s 66(6).
6 S 29(2) (as amended).
7 *R v Bradbourn* (1985) 7 Cr App R (S) 180, dealing with the wording of Criminal Justice Act 1982, s 1(4A)(c) relating to the imprisonment of persons under 21 years of age. see *R v Cox (David)* [1993] 2 All ER 19; [1993] 1 WLR 188; *R v Cunningham* [1993] 2 All ER 15; [1993] 1 WLR 183; *R v Lewis (John)* (1993) Times, 29 March.
8 See n 5, *ante*.
9 S 29(2).
10 Criminal Justice Act 1991, s 34. This change followed a finding by the European Court of Human Rights that the law did not comply with art 5(4) of the Convention. See p 15, *ante*.
11 Ss 33(5), 31(1).
12 Ss 33(5), 31(2).
13 Ss 33(3).17. Criminal Justice Act 1991, s 34.
14 Powers of Criminal Courts Act 1973, ss 22–25.
15 Where the court passes a suspended sentence for a term of more than six months, it has power under section 26 to make a "suspended sentence supervision order" which places the offender under the supervision of a probation officer during the period of the suspended sentence. There is no power to make such an order when only a part of the sentence is suspended under the Criminal Law Act 1977, s 47 (*infra*).

concerned, the defendant is not liable to be imprisoned unless (i) during the period of suspension he commits another offence punishable with imprisonment, and thereafter (ii) a court orders that the sentence shall take effect.[16]

When suspended sentences were first introduced there was a tendency for courts to impose a suspended sentence upon persons who, but for the existence of the power to impose suspended sentences, would not have received a sentence of imprisonment at all. However, suspended sentences are custodial sentences,[17] and therefore the criteria for the imposition of a custodial sentence (*supra*) must be satisfied before the decision whether it should be suspended is taken.[18] In addition the Criminal Justice Act 1991 has made it harder for a court to impose a suspended sentence. Under the revised terms of section 22 of the Powers of Criminal Courts Act 1973[19] the power to suspend a sentence of imprisonment should only be used where the exceptional circumstances of the case justify it. The Act provides no guidance at to what might amount to exceptional circumstances for this purpose.

It has been noted earlier that whether a custodial sentence can be imposed depends upon offence seriousness. So too with the imposition of community sentences.[20] In either instance, offence seriousness is to be assessed in the light of the offence for which the sentence is being passed, together with any associated offences.[1] This is a change from the law as originally conceived, which restricted the court to considering only *one* associated offence.[2]

The length of any custodial sentence imposed will be such as is commensurate with the offence, in the light of any associated offences.[3] Alternatively, if the basis of a custodial sentence for a violent or sexual offence is a necessity to protect the public, the length may be such as is necessary for that purpose.[4]

If the offender is under 21 years of age, the power to impose a custodial sentence is extremely limited. Where an offender is not less than 15 years of age, and a custodial sentence is justified, he may be sentenced to detention in a young offender institution.[5] Generally, such a detention cannot be ordered unless he has been legally represented at the time of sentencing.[6]

3   Community sentences

If an offence is serious enough to warrant the passing of a community sentence, but not so serious so as to require a custodial sentence, the court may make one or more community orders.[7] These are as follows:

(1) Probation: where the offender is placed under the supervision of a probation officer for a period not exceeding three years.

---

16 Powers of Criminal Courts Act 1973, s 22(1).
17 *Ibid*, s 23.
18 See s 1(2).
19 Criminal Justice Act 1991, s 22(2), inserted by the Criminal Justice Act 1991, s 5(1).
20 See *infra*.
 1 Criminal Justice Act 1991, s 1(2) as amended by the Criminal Justice Act 1993, s 66(1).
 2 See p 504, *ante*.
 3 Criminal Justice Act 1991, s 2(1)(a).
 4 *Ibid*, s 2(1)(b).
 5 Criminal Justice Act 1982, s 1A.
 6 *Ibid*, s 3.
 7 Criminal Justice Act 1991, s 6(4). That Act also identifies a further community order, curfew orders. The power to make curfew orders, conferred by s 6(4), has not been brought into effect: see Criminal Justice Act (Commencement No 3) Order 1992 (SI 1992/333).

(2) Community service orders: where the offender is required to perform work in the community for periods not exceeding 240 hours;

(3) Combination orders: these are a combination of probation and community service orders, within specified limits.

(4) Supervision orders: used for the supervision of offenders under 18 years of age.

(5) Attendance centre orders: where the offender under 21 years is required to attend an attendance centre for a specified number of hours.

The idea behind these orders is that offenders should be both punished and rehabilitated within the community. The particular order or orders forming part of the sentence must be commensurate with the seriousness of the offence and other offences associated with it, and be the most suitable for the offender.[8] Failure to comply with the requirements of such orders can result in the offender being punished, or being re-sentenced for the original offence.[9]

4   Fines

A Crown Court may impose a fine in lieu of, or in addition to, dealing with him in any other way. Unless a limit is fixed by the statute prescribing the offence, there is no limit to the amount of the fine. The court is obliged to fix a period of imprisonment or detention in default of payment.

5   Absolute and conditional discharges

Where a court thinks it inappropriate to pass any sentence, or make a probation order, it may discharge the offender either absolutely, without any condition, or subject to the condition that he does not commit any further offence for a period fixed by the court, not exceeding three years.[10] If he commits another offence in that period he is liable to be sentenced for his original offence.

6   Compensation and restitution

Compensation — A court by or before which a person is convicted of an offence may, instead of or in addition to dealing with him in any other way, make an order requiring him to pay compensation for any personal injury, loss or damage resulting from that offence (or any other offence which is taken into consideration). However, no compensation order may be made in favour of the dependants of a deceased person in consequence of his death, nor in respect of injury, loss or damage due to a road accident. In

---

8 Criminal Justice Act 1991, s 6(2).
9 See, generally, the Criminal Justice Act 1991, Sch 2.
10 Powers of Criminal Courts Act 1973, s 1A.

determining whether to make an order and the amount of such order the court must have regard to the offender's means. In practice the power to make compensation orders has been exercised somewhat sparingly. In particular, the Court of Appeal has repeatedly stated that no order should be made where it might result in the accused committing further offences in order to discharge his obligations; for this reason a substantial compensation order will not usually be appropriate where the offender is imprisoned since the need to discharge the order may hinder his rehabilitation on his release.[11]

If there are subsequent civil proceedings, the damages are assessed without reference to the order, but the order is taken into account when enforcing the judgment.[12] Compensation is of such amount as the court considers appropriate, having regard to any evidence and to any representations made by or on behalf of the accused or the prosecutor.[13]

Restitution — Where goods have been stolen and either a person is convicted of any offence with reference to the theft or such offence is taken into consideration on conviction of any other offence, the court may order anyone in possession of the goods to restore them to any person entitled to recover them from him, or may order the restoration of any goods directly or indirectly representing the stolen goods (eg the proceeds of sale), or may order a sum not exceeding the value of the goods to be paid out of any money of the person convicted which was taken out of his possession on his apprehension.[14] However, it should be borne in mind that this provision does not give the police power to seize money or other property when apprehending someone, in anticipation of a compensation or restitution order being made in due course. The police may, however, justifiably take possession of money or other property which they reasonably believe to be material evidence in relation to crime.[15]

A restitution order, under the above provisions, should only be made in clear and obvious cases. If there is any serious dispute concerning the ownership of the goods in question, this should be left to be determined by a civil court in the normal way and no order should be made.[16]

7   Miscellaneous orders

The principal sentences and orders the court has power to make have been considered above. There are, in addition, various other forms of order

---

11 See *R v Oddy* [1974] 2 All ER 666; [1974] 1 WLR 1212 and cases cited therein.
12 For the detail of this, see s 38 of the 1973 Act. Where the offender is a child or young person, the court should normally order payment by his parent or guardian (Children and Young Persons Act 1969, s 3(6)).
13 Act of 1973, s 35(1A) (added by the Criminal Justice Act 1982).
14 Theft Act 1968, s 28 (as amended by the Criminal Justice Act 1972).
15 Police and Criminal Evidence Act 1984, s 19. This power is subject to some limitations. See, s 19(2)–(6).
16 *R v Ferguson* [1970] 2 All ER 820; [1970] 1 WLR 1246.

which may be made, detailed consideration of which is beyond the scope of this work. However, it may be noted that the Crown Court has, in addition to the powers detailed above, power to make orders for costs either out of central funds or *inter partes*,[17] orders depriving offenders of property used, or intended for use, for the purposes of crime,[18] orders disqualifying an offender from holding or obtaining a licence to drive a motor vehicle,[19] orders authorising the admission to and detention in specified hospitals of offenders suffering from mental illness, psychopathic disorder, subnormality or severe subnormality[20] and recommendations for deportation.[1] Significant powers of confiscation and forfeiture also exist under the Drug Trafficking Offences Act 1986.

Where the Crown Court imposes a fine, forfeits a recognisance or makes an order for costs, it may order the person concerned to be searched and any money found on him to be applied towards payment of the fine or other sum.[2]

---

17 Costs in Criminal Cases Act 1973, ss 3, 4.
18 Powers of Criminal Courts Act 1973, s 43. The power is limited to personal property and so cannot extend to the defendant's house: *R v Khan* [1982] 3 All ER 969; [1982] 1 WLR 1405, one of several unsuccessful attempts by the courts to relieve drug dealers of their ill-gotten gains; see also *R v Cuthbertson* [1981] AC 470; [1980] 2 All ER 401.
19 Road Traffic Offenders Act 1988, s 34.
20 Mental Health Act 1983, s 37.
1 Immigration Act 1971, s 6.
2 Powers of Criminal Courts Act 1973, s 34A. This section was added by the Criminal Law Act 1977, s 49; curiously the Crown Court did not previously have this power, although magistrates' courts did.

CHAPTER 24

Appeal Following Trial on Indictment

A INTRODUCTION

If a defendant is convicted on indictment at the Crown Court his appeal lies, if at all, to the Court of Appeal (Criminal Division). Appeals from the decisions of the magistrates' court acting summarily, and from the Crown Court acting in its appellate capacity, lie to the Divisional Court of the Queen's Bench Division, and will be dealt with later.

The role and powers of the Court of Appeal (Criminal Division) have been the subject of a great deal of debate in recent years,[1] largely generated by a series of cases where convictions have had to be overturned, often some years after conviction and subsequent appeal.[2] In particular, the question of when the court should be able to overturn a conviction, how it should treat fresh evidence, and whether it should have greater powers to order re-trials, have each been raised, and the subject of consideration by the Royal Commission on Criminal Justice.[3] However, it is important to remember that controversy about the criminal appellate system is not new.

1 The development of the Court of Appeal (Criminal Division)

Until 1907 there was, in fact, no right of appeal at all. Where points of law arose on trial on indictment the trial judge could, but was not obliged to, refer such points for consideration by a court known as the Court for Crown Cases Reserved. Not until the passage of the Criminal Appeal Act 1907 was a formal appellate system introduced, and that Act was passed largely in response to a miscarriage of justice caused by the mistaken identification of an accused.[4] The 1907 Act created the Court of Criminal Appeal, which was given powers to allow appeals against conviction if that conviction was unreasonable or could not be supported having regard to

---

1 See O'Connor, 'The Court of Appeal: Re-Trials & Tribulations' [1990] Crim LR 615; JUSTICE Report on Miscarriages of Justice (1989).
2 See eg *R v Maguire* [1992] QB 936; [1992] 2 All ER 433; *R v McIlkenny* [1992] 2 All ER 417.
3 Cm 2263, 1993, HMSO.
4 The *Adolph Beck* case.

the evidence, or if there was a wrong decision on a question of law. No power to order a re-trial existed at that time. The Criminal Appeal Act 1964 created a power to order a new trial, although only on the ground of "fresh evidence",[5] a restriction that was not removed until the passing of the Criminal Justice Act 1988.[6] By the Criminal Appeal Act 1966, the jurisdiction of the Court of Criminal Appeal was transferred to the Court of Appeal (Criminal Division).[7]

The whole of the pre-existing legislation was consolidated in the Criminal Appeal Act 1968.

Thus a framework of powers for the court to review and reconsider convictions was created. The substance of these powers is discussed in this chapter. However, three general points need to be remembered:

(a) The right of appeal is that of the accused, except in cases referred to the court by the Home Secretary.[8] The prosecution has no right of appeal against acquittal. although there is a limited power for points of law, and lenient sentences. to be referred to the Court of Appeal by the Attorney-General.[9]

(b) The court's powers derive solely from statute. The court has no inherent or residual power which entitle it to fill gaps in the statutory provisions. Criticism can fairly be made of the statutory provisions, not only in the obvious cases where the court's role has been limited, but also in other areas where gaps in the appellate system exist.

(c) The recent controversies about the actions of the court must be viewed in the light of the overall function and role of the court. This is dealt with below.

2 The role of the Court of Appeal

The court has been at pains to stress the limits of its powers. In *R v McIlkenny*,[10] LLOYD, MUSTILL and FARQUHARSON LJJ in a joint judgment observed:

> "Under jury trial juries not only find the facts; they also apply the law. Since they are not experts in the law, they are directed as to the relevant law by the judge. But the task of applying the law to the facts, and so reaching a verdict, belongs to the jury and the jury alone. The primacy of the jury in the English criminal justice system explains why, historically, the Court of Appeal had so limited a function... Since justice is as much concerned with the conviction of the guilty as the acquittal of the innocent, and the task of convicting the guilty belongs constitutionally to the jury, not to us, the role [of the court] is necessarily limited. Hence it is true to say that whereas the Civil Division of

---

5 Section 1, re-enacted in Criminal Appeal Act 1986, s 7.
6 See p 521, *post.*
7 Being one of two divisions of the Court of Appeal: Supreme Court Act 1981, s 3(1). For the Civil Division, see p 148, *ante.*
8 See p 514, *post.*
9 See p 513, *post.*
10 [1992] 2 All ER 417.

the Court of Appeal has appellate jurisdiction in the full sense, the Criminal Division is perhaps more accurately described as a court of review."

The point has also cogently been made that not only is the court subordinate to the jury; also the juries' role is itself limited.[11] It is not the task of the jury within the adversarial system to pronounce innocence or guilt, but rather whether it has been proved, according to law, that the accused is guilty as charged. The Royal Commission on Criminal Justice concluded that such considerations as to the role of the jury have too heavily influenced the court, and that the Court of Appeal should be "readier to overturn jury verdicts than it has shown itself in the past."[12] In particular it should be more prepared to consider arguments that a jury has made a mistake, and to admit evidence that might favour a defendant even if it was, or could have been, available at the trial.

For these reasons the Court of Appeal has considered itself constrained in dealing with appeals, particularly those based upon new evidence. The extent to which these constraints are justifiable, or in the public interest, is a matter for debate.

B   THE GROUNDS OF APPEAL

1   Appeal against conviction

By section 1 of the Criminal Appeal Act 1968, a person convicted on indictment may appeal to the Court of Appeal:

(a)   against his conviction, on any ground which involves a question of law alone;

(b)   with the leave of the Court of Appeal, against his conviction on any ground which involves a question of fact alone, or a question of mixed law and fact, or any other ground which appears to the court to be a sufficient ground of appeal.

Where leave to appeal is required, it may be granted in the first instance by a single judge of the court; if he refuses, the applicant may have his case considered by the court itself.[13] This process excludes a large proportion of cases. In 1992, of 1,552 applicants for leave to appeal 33 per cent had leave granted, the percentage rising to 36 per cent on application to the full court. Of those granted leave to appeal, 45 per cent succeeded.[14] The Royal Commission found that the chances of success are distinctly higher where the defendant is represented. In this regard the Commission found uneven and unsatisfactory provision for the giving of legal advice on appeal, which is part of the professional duty of solicitor and counsel. Initial advice after the case on appeal is within the scope of criminal legal aid (99 per cent of cases within the Crown Court). The research also found misunderstandings about the powers of the court regarding length of sentence. The Commission concluded that interpreter facilities should be made available by the Prison Service to facilitate the giving of advice to

---

11 See p 201, *ante*.
12 Report, Ch 10.
13 Criminal Appeal Act 1968, s 31(3).
14 See Royal Commission on Criminal Justice, Report, Ch 10, paras 1–26.

those who do not understand English. The present requirement to obtain leave should be kept, and legal aid extended to cover advice as to whether an application should be renewed.

The trial judge may also grant a certificate that the case is fit for appeal, on a question of fact or mixed law and fact. This should only be done where the trial judge is satisfied that there is a substantial point, and one worthy of consideration by the Court of Appeal.[15]

Nothing in the Act prevents an appeal against conviction in a case where the accused in fact pleaded guilty at his trial. However, an appeal in such circumstances will only succeed if:(i) the defendant did not appreciate the nature of the charge; or (ii) he did not intend to admit that he was guilty of it; or (iii) on the admitted facts, he could not in law have been guilty of the offence to which he pleaded guilty. Such cases are rare, but not unknown.[16] In *R v Boal*[17] the court was prepared to entertain an appeal where the defendant had pleaded guilty as a result of advice based upon a misunderstanding of the law by his barrister.

2 Appeal against sentence

The defendant may appeal against the sentence passed on him after conviction unless the sentence is one fixed by law. Such an appeal requires the leave of a single judge, or, if refused, of the full court.[18] The appeal can be not only against the sentence, but also against any order that forms part of the sentence, such as a compensation order,[19] disqualification from driving, a binding over order[1] or recommendation for deportation.[2] There is no right of appeal against a recommendation that a defendant convicted of murder should serve a certain number of years, because this is not a recommendation binding on the Home Secretary.[3] By contrast, if a judge makes an order, in respect of a discretionary life sentence, specifying what part of the sentence must expire before the offender is able to have his case referred to the Parole Board, this has legal consequences and would appear to be a matter which can be subject to an appeal.[4]

The prosecution also has the right to have the sentence of a court reviewed. By section 36 of the Criminal Justice Act 1988, if it appears to the Attorney-General that the sentencing of a person in a proceeding in the Crown Court has been unduly lenient, in respect of an offence triable only on indictment (or such other offence as the Secretary of State may order) then, with leave of the Court of Appeal, the case may be referred to them

---

15 *R v Eyles* (1963) 47 Cr App Rep 260; cf *R v Smith* [1974] QB 354; [1974] 1 All ER 632.
16 *R v Forde* [1923] 2 KB 400, at 403; *R v Gould* [1968] 2 QB 65; [1968] 1 All ER 849; cf *R v Vickers* [1975] 2 All ER 945; [1975] 1 WLR 811.
17 [1992] QB 591; [1992] 3 All ER 177.
18 Criminal Appeal Act 1968, s 11.
19 Powers of Criminal Courts Act 1973, s 36(3) (b).
 1 *R v Williams* [1982] 3 All ER 1092; [1982] 1 WLR 1398.
 2 See the Criminal Appeal Act 1968, s 50(1), defining sentence to include "any order make by a court when dealing with an offender".
 3 *R v Aitken* [1966] 2 All ER 453n; [1966] 1 WLR 1076.
 4 See the terms of Criminal Justice Act 1991, s 34(2).

for the sentence to be reviewed. The application must be made within 28 days of the sentence being passed.[5]

Concern was expressed at the time this power was introduced that a defendant is in jeopardy twice.[6] The power to review granted by the Act is in respect of a sentence perceived to be unduly lenient, not simply in respect of a sentence with which the court disagrees. The power is used where the judge has erred as a matter of sentencing principle, and thus is a means of achieving consistent application of sentencing policy.[7]

3   Application to the Home Secretary

Once the avenues of appeal outlined above have been exhausted then, unless a final appeal to the House of Lords is permitted,[8] the one remaining formal option open to an accused is the making of an application to the Home Secretary for review of the case. The Home Office has general responsibility for considering claims that there has been a miscarriage of justice, or other defect in the legal process, though it has from time to time been criticised for the manner in which these powers are in fact exercised, especially the speed of reconsideration, and on the emphasis upon the need for fresh evidence as a justification for the exercise of formal powers.[9]

By section 17(1) of the 1968 Act, any person convicted on indictment may apply to the Home Secretary, and the Home Secretary may refer the case to the Court of Appeal. The Home Secretary may make a reference even where no application has been made by the defendant. The case is then for all purposes treated as an appeal by the person convicted.[10] Alternatively, the Home Secretary may refer any point arising in the case to the Court of Appeal for consideration and the opinion of the court on that point.[11] This is what occurred in *R v Berry (No 2)*[12] where a finding on a point of law by the Court of Appeal led to that court quashing a conviction, the court not determining another ground of appeal that was before the court. On appeal to the House of Lords by the prosecution, the decision of the Court of Appeal was reversed. The Court of Appeal now being without jurisdiction to deal with this further point, the only way in which it could now be dealt with by the court was for the Home Secretary to make a reference under section 17, which is in fact what occurred.

The exercise of the Home Secretary's discretion is a matter for political and public scrutiny, subject to the operation of judicial review where the discretion is used, or not used, in a way that is legally improper.[13] The number of cases requesting reconsideration is high, and the capacity to deal with them clearly limited. Some argue for the right of applicants to go directly to the Court of Appeal, not currently permitted. Others see a way forward as the taking the review of cases out of the hands of the Court of

---

5 Criminal Justice Act 1988, Sch 3.
6 See [1988] Crim LR at p 103.
7 Through guideline judgments.
8 See p 524, *post.*
9 Royal Commission on Criminal Justice, Ch 11, Report, paras 1–6.
10 *R v Chard* [1984] AC 279; [1983] 3 All ER 637.
11 S 17 (1)(a).
12 [1991] 2 All ER 789; [1991] 1 WLR 125; for the resulting decision, see *R v Berry* (3 April 1992, unreported).
13 See p 122, *ante.*

Appeal and Home Secretary, entrusting it instead to an independent review body, to whom the Home Secretary would refer cases. It should be remembered, however, that this would still require an investigative and sifting procedure within the Home Office itself, since no review body could expect to cope with the large number of cases potentially involved.

The operation of section 17, and, generally the role of the Home Office, was considered by the Royal Commission on Criminal Justice.[14] It noted that the Royal prerogative of mercy in respect of trials on indictment was "seldom exercised",[15] and it noted also that section 17 references are made in only a small proportion of the cases of those brought to the attention of the Home Office by the parties, or by campaigning groups such as JUSTICE.[16] The restrictive nature of the test[17] used by the Home Secretary to decide whether a reference should be made had been identified by the May Committee,[18] and its view that there was a need for change was supported by the Royal Commission. It recommended that the Home secretary's power to make references under section 17 should be abolished. Instead, the role now performed by the Home Office should be given to an independent body, a new Criminal Cases Review Authority.[19] This authority, to comprise both lawyers and lay persons, would oversee any further investigations needed into cases referred to it by complainants, although it would not appear to have powers to instigate investigations on its own motion. The government has accepted in principle this recommendation.[20]

Where this new Authority found that there were reasons for believing a miscarriage of justice had occurred it would refer the case to the Court of Appeal. The central question as to whether the powers of that court were adequate or used effectively would thus remain. In that respect the Royal Commission recommended changes to section 23 of the Criminal Appeal Act.[1] It recommended that the wording of that section be changed to permit the admission of fresh evidence where such evidence was "capable of belief", not simply "likely to be credible."[2] It also recommended that the grounds for quashing a conviction[3] should be replaced with a single ground, whether the conviction "is or may be unsafe".

4 Reference following acquittal

The prosecution does not have any right to appeal against acquittal, unlike the position in cases of summary trial. However, the Criminal Justice Act

---

14 *Op cit*, Ch 11.
15 *Ibid*, para 3.
16 A campaigning organisation with a primary aim of investigation of, and campaigning against, miscarriages of justice.
17 Royal Commission Report, Chapter 11.
18 Established to report on the miscarriage of justice in the Guildford pub bombing case.
19 Royal Commission Report, Chapter 11, para 1.
20 Announced on 11 January 1994; 235 Official Report (HC), cols 20–122.
 1 Report, para 7.
 2 See p 516, *post*.
 3 See n 5, *post*.

1972[4] gives to the prosecution a limited right to have points of law which arose during a trial resulting in an acquittal reconsidered by the Court of Appeal. The nature of the procedure is that of a reference of a point of law, rather than an appeal, for the outcome of the reference has no effect on the acquittal in the case.

The Act and the rules made thereunder go to great length to protect the acquitted person. Not only is his acquittal unaffected, he may appear to present argument in the Court of Appeal, is entitled to be represented by counsel and have his costs paid out of central funds. His identity must not be disclosed during the proceedings in the Court of Appeal except by his consent.

The purpose of the power is to enable clarification of points of law which are important, and before wrong interpretations of law become entrenched at trial court level. The court may, of its own motion or on application, refer the point to the House of Lords.

C   POWERS OF THE COURT

1   Power to quash a conviction

By section 17 of the 1968 Act the court may allow an appeal against conviction if one of three criteria is satisfied. These are set out below, but it should be borne in mind that these are not mutually exclusive. The Royal Commission found that in almost half the cases studied the court made no reference to which of the three grounds it was applying. They may, and often will, overlap.

a   Under all the circumstances of the case the conviction[5] is unsafe and unsatisfactory

This formulation was adopted in substitution for the formula contained in the 1907 Act, "the verdict is unreasonable or cannot be supported having regard to the evidence". The change was made, on the recommendations of the Donovan Committee,[6] to overcome restrictive interpretations by the court, which treated the two parts of the test as being synonymous, and the court often refused to interfere with a conviction except where there was no evidence upon which the conviction could be based. This judicial attitude was based upon the premise that it was wrong for an appellate court to usurp the functions of the jury, where evidence existed to justify the jury's conclusion.[7]

---

4 Section 36(1); this provision came into operation on 1 October 1973 and the first reference under it was *Re A-G's Reference (No 1 of 1974)* [1974] QB 744; [1974] 2 All ER 899.

5 "Conviction" was substituted for "verdict of the jury" by the Criminal Law Act 1977, s 44. The previous wording appeared to preclude an appeal if the accused pleaded guilty, unless the count to which the accused pleaded guilty disclosed no offence known to the law or (perhaps) on the admitted facts he could not in point of law have been guilty of the offence; this, presumably erroneous, drafting in the 1968 Act went judicially unnoticed until *Director of Public Prosecutions v Shannon* [1975] AC 717; sub nom *R v Shannon* [1974] 2 All ER 1009, in which case LORD SALMON drew attention to the need for some amendment to s 2(1) of the 1968 Act.

6 *Report of the Interdepartmental Committee on the Court of Criminal Appeal* (Donovan Report) (Cmnd 2755, HMSO), para 164.

7 See observations of LORD WIDGERY CJ, in *R v Anderson* [1972] 1 QB 304 at 309; [1971] 3 All ER 1152, at 1156.

Despite this change, first made by the Criminal Appeal Act 1966, the power has not proved easy to apply. The court is concerned solely with whether the verdict of the jury can stand, and in deciding that question there is no one particular approach that must be applied. In *Stafford v Director of Public Prosecutions*,[8] VISCOUNT DILHORNE cited with approval a passage from the judgment of the court in *R v Cooper*:[9]

> "The court must in the end ask itself a subjective question, whether we are content to let the matter stand as it is, or whether there is not some lurking doubt in our minds which makes us wonder whether an injustice has been done. This is a reaction which may not be based strictly on the evidence as such; it is a reaction that can be produced by the general feeling of the case as the court experiences it to be."

The Royal Commission received conflicting evidence about the application of this "lurking doubt" approach. Research indicated that between 1968–89 only six cases applied the test, and in 1989 one out of 114 appeals. Yet the more recent research for the years 1991–1992 showed a greater use of this power (14 out of 102).[10] Yet the language of lurking doubt may not always be used. For the court to conclude that a verdict was unsatisfactory because of an injustice in the case and in the verdict is no different from an application of the "lurking doubt" test. The Royal Commission recommends that the Court of Appeal should quash a conviction notwithstanding that the jury had all the relevant evidence and without any error of law, where it concludes that the verdict may be unsafe.[11]

Nevertheless, the court in *R v Maguire* stressed that it is the words of the Act that have to be applied, not some other reformulation of the question.

Despite the fact that the word "or" is used, the weight of authority suggests that "unsafe" and "unsatisfactory" in fact will be regarded as bearing the same meaning.[12] This was a view supported by the Royal Commission. It recommended the section be redrafted to state one single category "it is or may be unsafe". If it is unsafe, then the conviction should be quashed outright. If it *may* be unsafe, then it should be quashed and, generally, a re-trial ordered, unless impracticable or undesirable.[13] By contrast, a minority considered that it should be redrafted to take into account two distinct categories:

(1) those claiming that the verdict was arrived at through an erroneous view of the evidence by the jury;
(2) those alleging material irregularities or errors of law or procedure. The occurrence of errors at trial is the most common ground of appeal (in 1992 82 per cent of successful appeals). The court generally quashes the conviction. Errors in summing up, misdirection on matters of law, a failure in appropriate cases to withdraw the case from the jury are all instances where section 17(1)(a) may

---

8 [1974] AC 878; [1973] 3 All ER 762.
9 [1969] 1 QB 267, at 271; [1969] 1 All ER 32, at 34, *per* WIDGERY LJ (as he then was).
10 Report, Ch 10 para 43.
11 *Ibid*, para 46.
12 *R v Maguire* [1992] QB 936; [1992] 2 All ER 433.
13 See O'Connor, *op cit*, n 1, p 510 *ante*.

operate. The problem that arises where fresh evidence is tendered, and the effect that it has, is discussed below.

The unsafeness of the conviction may have arisen because of the way the case was conducted. In respect of appeals based upon error by lawyers, the test identified in *R v Ensor*[14] was whether injustice had been suffered as a result of flagrantly incompetent advocacy. This was, in the view of the Royal Commission,[15] too narrow.

> "It cannot possibly be right that there should be defendants serving prison sentences for no other reason than that their lawyers made a decision which later turns out to have been mistaken. What matters is not the degree to which the lawyers were at fault, but whether the particular decision, whether reasonable or unreasonable, caused a miscarriage of justice."

b   There was a wrong decision on a point of law

This formula was part of the 1907 Act, and remains unchanged. It includes rulings on matters of law, such as the admissibility of evidence, and could include errors of law in the summing-up, though strictly speaking these fit better within section 17(1)(a), because there is in such circumstances no actual decision.

c   There was a material irregularity in the course of the trial

This formula was introduced in 1966,[16] replacing the words in the 1907 Act, "on any ground there was a miscarriage of justice". The revised wording has been held to cover a wide variety of errors, usually procedural, occurring in the course of the trial, such as unfair conduct or undue interruption by the judge, improper disclosure to the jury of the defendant's character, tampering with a juror, misconduct on the part of a juror and failure to inform an undefended person of his right to call witnesses. In *R v Maguire*[17] it was held that a failure to comply with the requirements concerning disclosure of unused material amounted to a "material irregularity".

Applying the proviso

On an appeal against conviction the court may dismiss the appeal, even though of the opinion that the point raised might be decided in favour of the appellant, if it is considered that no miscarriage of justice has actually occurred. Where the court exercises this power, it is said to "apply the proviso".[18] The test is whether a reasonable jury, after a proper summing-up, could have failed to convict the appellant:[19] in other words, the court is

---

14 [1989] 2 All ER 586; [1989] 1 WLR 497.
15 Report, para 59.
16 Now Criminal Appeal Act 1968, s 2(1)(c).
17 [1992] QB 936; [1992] 2 All ER 433.
18 Because the paragraph in question of the 1968 Act (and of the 1907 Act) begins "provided that . . .".
19 *Stirland v Director of Public Prosecutions* [1944] AC 315; [1944] 2 All ER 13; see also (among many cases) *R v Haddy* [1944] KB 442; [1944] 1 All ER 319. For the proper attitude to application of the proviso in a murder case, see *Anderson v R* [1972] AC 100; [1971] 3 All ER 768.

putting itself in the place of the jury. It is often applied where there has been a misdirection on a matter of law. Where the proviso is applied, the appeal is dismissed, the court having no power in such cases to substitute an alternative verdict.

The relationship between the proviso and the powers contained in section 2(1) of the 1968 Act discussed above is complex. If the conviction is found to be unsafe or unsatisfactory under section 2(1)(c) there is no room for the exercise of the proviso. In relation to the other grounds, the Court of Appeal in *R v Maguire*[20] equated the "no miscarriage of justice" test in the proviso with whether the conviction could be regarded as safe or satisfactory.

> "If the court is unable to hold that 'no miscarriage of justice has actually occurred' in a case of irregularity then the conviction is not 'safe'. If it does so hold then the court is effectively saying that the conviction is safe and satisfactory."

For this reason it has been argued that there is really only one test that the court should apply in deciding the use of section 2(1): has there been a miscarriage of justice?[1]

The majority of the Royal Commission took the view:[2]

(1) if a conviction was safe despite an error, then the appeal should be dismissed;

(2) if an error was made that rendered the conviction unsafe, then the conviction should be quashed;

(3) if an error may render a conviction unsafe, then the conviction should be quashed and a re-trial ordered. This would render the proviso redundant.

The majority took the view that this should be the case even where appeals are based upon pre-trial malpractice or procedural irregularity. It is not the purpose of the appellate process to discipline the police or prosecution – the judge will have excluded tainted evidence anyway.

2   Power to substitute an alternative verdict

Where the defendant has been convicted of an offence and (1) the jury could on the same indictment have found him guilty of some other offence; and (2) it appears to the Court of Appeal that the jury must have been satisfied of the facts proving him guilty of that other offence, the court may, instead of allowing or dismissing the appeal against conviction, substitute a verdict of guilty of that other offence and pass sentence on the defendant for it.[3] The sentence must not be greater than that passed on the defendant at the trial, and must not, of course, exceed the maximum permitted by law for the substituted offence.[4] The court exercises this power with care, particularly in the light of (2) above, which involves some

---

20 [1992] QB 936; [1992] 2 All ER 433.
1 See O'Connor [1990] Crim LR 615.
2 Report, Ch 10, para 38.
3 Criminal Appeal Act 1968, s 3(1).
4 *Ibid*, s 3(2).

consideration of a verdict of a jury for which no reasons are given. Further, it is a material, though not decisive, point against exercising the power if the jury were not given any direction as to the alternative offence.[5] Where the indictment contains counts for two offences (such as theft and handling) which are in the circumstances alternative to each other, and the jury convict of one but acquit of the other, the court cannot substitute a verdict of guilty of the latter, even if that seems the correct verdict, since the jury expressly acquitted. The proper course, if there is a conviction on one is for the jury to be discharged from giving a verdict on the other whereupon the Court of Appeal may substitute a verdict of guilty.[6] This may also be important from the point of view of a re-trial.

3   Power to receive fresh evidence and to order a new trial

The power to receive fresh evidence was contained in the 1907 Act, and is now to be found in section 23 of the 1968 Act. This section contains both a duty and a discretion. Section 23(2) imposes a duty to receive fresh evidence if:

    (a) the evidence is likely to be credible, and would have been admissible at the trial; and

    (b) there is a reasonable explanation for the evidence not being adduced at trial.

The court may decline to receive such evidence if it is satisfied that the evidence, if received, would not afford any ground for allowing the appeal.[7] In addition, under section 23(1) the court has a discretion to admit the evidence of any witness or document if it thinks it necessary or expedient in the interests of justice to do so. In this situation the evidence does not have to satisfy the criteria in section 23(2) of not being tendered at the trial. Thus, in *R v Lattimore*[8] some of the evidence was in fact given at the trial, and all of it was in fact available. It was allowed to be heard because it cast doubt upon the confession evidence upon which the prosecution case largely depended. The court will only exceptionally, allow the discretion to be used as a means of different defences being put forward at the appellate stage. In *R v Ahluwalia*[9] the court, exceptionally, allowed fresh medical evidence to be adduced to support a defence of diminished responsibility to the charge of murder of her husband, a defence which had not been raised at trial.

    Appeals on the grounds of fresh evidence are rare. The Royal Commission considered the powers contained in section 23 to be adequate, although it considered the court should take a broad view as to whether evidence was available at the time of trial, and, if so, if there was a reasonable explanation for it not being adduced at that time. In respect of changes of evidence by a witness, if there is some reasonable explanation

---

5 See, generally, *R v Caslin* [1961] 1 All ER 246; [1961] 1 WLR 59. This case was decided under the corresponding provisions of the Criminal Appeal Act 1907, but appears still to be good law.

6 *R v Melvin and Eden* [1953] 1 QB 481; [1953] 1 All ER 294.

7 Criminal Appeal Act 1968, s 23(2).

8 (1975) 62 Cr App Rep 53.

9 [1992] 4 All ER 889.

why a witness wishes to depart from previous evidence,[10] the court should receive it, if capable of belief.

Complementary to the power to receive fresh evidence is the power to order a new trial, first introduced in 1964.[11] If the court is satisfied that the evidence would have created a reasonable doubt in the minds of the jury, it must allow the appeal and quash the conviction, but may order a new trial if it considers that the interests of justice so require.[12] This power to order re-trial is not now confined to fresh evidence cases.[13] The power to order re-trials is at the heart of the debate as to how cases where fresh evidence comes to light should be dealt with. It has been argued by LORD DEVLIN[14] that a conviction should always be quashed where fresh evidence has been received, since a conviction is bound to be unsafe or unsatisfactory if not based on all the evidence. That, though, is not the approach of the courts. In *Stafford v Director of Public Prosecutions*[15] the House of Lords considered that the verdict should be quashed if the court itself considers the verdict to be unsafe or unsatisfactory, thus requiring the court to take a view of the effect of the fresh evidence tendered. This approach has been criticised as restricting the use of the re-trial powers.[16] During the period 1966–68 re-trials were ordered in only 9 out of 45 fresh evidence cases. During 1981–86 only 14 retrials were ordered.

In *R v McIlkenny*[17] the Court of Appeal described its approach as follows:

> "Nor is there any difficulty in fresh evidence cases, where the fresh evidence is discovered soon after the trial. If the evidence is incredible, or inadmissible, or would not afford a ground for allowing the appeal, we decline to receive it. If the fresh evidence surmounts that preliminary hurdle, we first quash the conviction, if we think it unsafe or unsatisfactory, and then order a retrial . . . if the interests of justice so require. Where new evidence is conclusive, we quash the conviction without ordering a retrial . . . The difficulty becomes acute when there is no contest. For then we have to make up our own minds whether the convictions are unsafe or unsatisfactory without having the benefit of having the evidence tested by cross-examination. Where a retrial is still possible, the quashing of the conviction is . . . only the first half of a two stage process. Where a retrial is no longer possible, it is the end of the road."

The position is regarded by many as unsatisfactory, bearing in mind that any of these cases will involve complex and disputed questions of fact. The question remains as to whether these are matters best dealt with by the appellate courts or by some other means.

What should the court do? The criticism notably by LORD DEVLIN accepted by the Royal Commission, which concluded[18] that once the court has received evidence that is relevant and capable of belief it should quash the conviction and order a re-trial unless that is not practicable or desirable.

---

10 *Ibid.*
11 Criminal Appeal Act 1964, s 1.
12 Criminal Appeal Act 1968, ss 7 and 8.
13 See amendments to s 7 by Criminal Justice Act 1988.
14 Royal Commission on Criminal Justice, Report, Ch 10, para 62.
15 [1974] AC 878; [1973] 3 All ER 762.
16 Royal Commission, Report, para 66.
17 [1992] 2 All ER 417.
18 Report, para 63.

The Court of Appeal has not seen or heard the other witnesses, and is not the appropriate tribunal to assess the ultimate credibility and effect on a jury of the fresh evidence. It should not normally decide the question of weight unless it is satisfied that the fresh evidence causes the verdict to be unsafe.

4   Venire de novo

The appeal court has always had the power to order a *venire de novo* where proceedings in the court of trial were so defective as to amount to a nullity. To the defendant this no doubt seems very like ordering a new trial, but strictly the court is ordering not a new trial but a proper one. It has not, unfortunately, been established what degree of irregularity suffices to render proceedings a nullity; there are only particular examples in the cases of proceedings which have been held to be a nullity. This has been held to be so where the judge at the trial was not properly qualified,[19] where the defendant specifically asked for but was denied his right of peremptory challenges,[20] or where a plea of not guilty was misheard and dealt with as a plea of guilty.[1]

5   Hospital orders

The court has certain powers to consider whether a hospital order was rightly made, and in some circumstances can substitute a verdict of guilty for an offence which was charged at the trial, of which the defendant could have been convicted, for the special verdict of not guilty by reason of insanity or against a finding of unfitness to plead reached at the trial.[2]

D   APPEALS AGAINST SENTENCE

On an appeal against sentence the court may reduce the sentence, or may vary it, by substituting one form of detention for another. The court will interfere with a sentence where it is "wrong in principle", an approach that applies also to references made by the Attorney-General. Where the sentence is against conviction only there is no power to interfere with the sentence in any way. Nor, except on an Attorney-General's reference, has the court the power to increase sentence, a power that once existed but was rarely used.[3]

E   PROCEDURE

Under section 9(d) and (e) of the Criminal Appeal Act 1907 the court had the power to appoint a special commissioner to conduct an inquiry into documents and to appoint assessors where their special expert knowledge

---

19 *R v Cronin* [1940] 1 All ER 618.
20 *R v Williams* (1925) 19 Cr App Rep 67. Such right no longer exists; see p 495, *ante*.
 1 *R v Scothern* [1961] Crim LR 326.
 2 See p 489, *ante*.
 3 Abolished by Criminal Appeal Act 1966, s 4(2).

was likely to be required for the determination of a case. These powers were little, if ever used, and not re-enacted by the 1968 Act. The Royal Commission considered that the Court of Appeal is not well constituted to supervise or direct police or other investigations. Nor should the same body exercise judicial and investigatory functions.[4]

As noted above, some appeals to the court may be brought without leave, but in most cases there must be an application to the court itself for leave. The time limit for giving notice of appeal, or application for leave to appeal, is 28 days from the date of conviction or sentence. This time may be extended by the court. Such application is made in the first instance to a single judge of the court, who considers it in private. A single judge has most of the powers of a court of three judges (besides, of course, the power to grant leave); exceptionally he does not have any of the powers relating to fresh evidence. An application may of course be abandoned, and notice of abandonment cannot be withdrawn although it may be treated as a nullity if the abandonment was not the result of a deliberate and informed decision in the sense that "the mind of the appellant did not go with his act of abandonment."[5] For example, where an application for leave to appeal was granted but, because of a postal strike, was not communicated to the applicant before he gave notice of abandonment, he was permitted to withdraw his notice.[6] If the single judge refuses leave to appeal (or to exercise any other of his powers) the applicant may be considered by a court of two judges.[7] Both the single judge and the court may grant legal aid and bail. Bail, for obvious reasons, is very rarely granted;[8] indeed almost the only cases where it will be granted are where the defendant has obtained (or does not need) leave to appeal and has a very good chance of succeeding on appeal, or where the defendant has been given a comparatively short sentence after a long and complex trial.[9] In the latter case he might otherwise have served much of his sentence before the appeal was heard.

Time spent on bail does not, of course, count as part of the sentence.[10] Conversely, time spent in custody pending the determination of the appeal now counts as part of the defendant's sentence, subject to any direction to the contrary (for which reasons must be given). No such direction may be given where the defendant obtained leave to appeal, from the Court of Appeal or the trial court, or where the case has been referred to the court by the Home Secretary.[11]

---

4 Report, Ch 11, para 11.
5 *R v Medway* [1976] QB 779; [1976] 1 All ER 527.
6 *R v Noble* [1971] 3 All ER 361; [1971] 1 WLR 1772.
7 Criminal Appeal Act 1968, s 31(2); Supreme Court Act 1981, s 55(4). The application must normally be made to the court within 14 days of communication of the notice of refusal by the single judge, but the court has jurisdiction to extend the time even though the further application is not made until after the 14 days have expired: *R v Ward* [1971] 3 All ER 619; [1971] 1 WLR 1450; *R v Doherty* [1971] 3 All ER 622n; [1971] 1 WLR 1454n.
8 If the appeal is dismissed, it may embarrass the court to order the defendant's return to prison. "The court is always anxious in such a case, because although a man may have been on bail, he will have had the appeal hanging over him for all this time": LORD PARKER CJ in *R v Cavendish* [1961] 2 All ER 856, at 858; [1961] 1 WLR 1083, at 1085.
9 *R v Walton* (1978) 68 Cr App Rep 293.
10 Criminal Appeal Act 1968, s 29.
11 See p 514, *ante*.

Once an appeal has been heard and dismissed, or a notice of appeal abandoned, it cannot be re-opened and the applicant's only recourse is to petition the Home Secretary (who, as seen, may refer the case to the court).

F   APPEAL TO THE HOUSE OF LORDS

A further appeal lies by either prosecution or defence from the Court of Appeal (Criminal Division) to the House of Lords if (1) the Court of Appeal certifies that a point of law of general public importance is involved in the decision; and (2) either the Court of Appeal or the House of Lords gives leave to appeal on the ground that the point is one which ought to be considered by the House. The certificate was considered a necessary condition, to avoid the House of Lords being inundated with hopeless applications. This justification was not accepted by the Royal Commission, which recommended its abolition.[12] If the Court of Appeal is satisfied that there is a point of law of general public importance involved it will give the certificate, as it were, automatically. There will always, nevertheless, be an element of discretion as to whether an appeal is allowed to proceed, since even if the point were of general public importance it might still not be worthy of consideration by the House of Lords in the particular case; for example it might already be the subject of clear and satisfactory decisions of lower courts. This element of discretion is preserved by the requirement that there must be leave to appeal. It will be observed that only the Court of Appeal can give the certificate, and if that court refuses the certificate there can be no further proceedings. On the other hand, the Court of Appeal may give a certificate and yet refuse leave, in which case a petition may be made to the House of Lords for leave to appeal, the petition being heard by the Appeals Committee of the House.

It is proper and convenient that the certificate should state what the point of law of general public importance is;[13] however, it seems likely that other points may be raised by either side once the case is before the House of Lords on the point certified.[14] However, the grant of a certificate on some point affecting the validity of the conviction does not enable the appellant to argue that the sentence is invalid.[15] The House of Lords may exercise similar powers to those of the court below. As to applying the proviso,[16] however, VISCOUNT SIMONDS said in *Jones v Director of Public Prosecutions*[17] that the House of Lords:

> ". . . may feel some difficulty about exercising a jurisdiction which demands an examination not only of the particular question of law that is raised but of all the circumstances of the case."

The procedure described above does not apply following the hearing of an Attorney-General's reference after acquittal.[18] In these cases the Court of Appeal may of its own motion or in pursuance of an application refer the

---

12 Report, Ch 10, para 79.
13 *Jones v Director of Public Prosecutions* [1962] AC 635; [1962] 1 All ER 569.
14 *A-G for Northern Ireland v Gallagher* [1963] AC 349; [1961] 3 All ER 299.
15 See p 522, *ante*.
16 S 2(1) of the 1968 Act; see pp 518, 519, *ante*.
17 [1962] AC 635, at 660; [1962] 1 All ER 569, at 573.
18 Under the Criminal Justice Act 1972, s 36; see p 516, *ante*.

point of law in the case to the House of Lords "if it appears to the court that the point ought to be considered by that House"[19] and there is, accordingly, no need for a certificate that a point of law of general public importance is involved. Indeed the point of law need not be a point of general public importance, although no doubt the Court of Appeal would only refer such a point to the House, as a matter of practice.

---

19 Criminal Justice Act 1972, s 36(3).

CHAPTER 25

Summary Procedure and Appeals

It has already been noted[1] that offences can be classified into three types. In this Chapter the procedures to be followed in respect of summary offences are discussed. These procedures are, of course, equally applicable in respect of offences which are triable "either way".[2]

A PROCESS

The rules as to process are the same as in the case of an indictable offence, except that a summons cannot be issued merely on the ground that the defendant resides, or is believed to reside or be, in the area in question and a warrant cannot be issued in any case where a summons has already been issued. In any event, as has already been noted,[3] a warrant cannot be issued for the arrest of an adult in the case of a summary offence, unless the offence is punishable with imprisonment or the defendant's address is "not sufficiently established" for a summons to be served on him. Even where a warrant may lawfully be issued, it is rarely thought necessary in the case of any summary offence. The position therefore is that a summons or a warrant may be issued if:

(a) the summary offence was committed or is suspected to have been committed within the area; or

(b) it appears to the magistrate issuing process necessary or expedient, with a view to the better administration of justice, that the person charged should be tried jointly with or in the same place as some other person who is charged with an offence and who is in custody or is to be proceeded against within the area; or

(c) the person charged resides, or is believed to reside or be within the area; or

(d) under any enactment the magistrates' court has jurisdiction to try the offence. In this context, there should be noted section 2(6) of

---

1 See p 446, *ante*.
2 See p 447, *ante*.
3 See p 444, *ante*.

the Magistrates' Courts Act 1980, permitting a magistrates' court to try a number of offences provided that it has jurisdiction to try any one of them;[4] or

(e) the offence was committed outside England and Wales and, where it is an offence exclusively punishable on summary conviction, if a magistrates' court for the area would have jurisdiction to try the offence if the offender were before it.[5]

B JURISDICTION

A magistrates' court for an area[6] has jurisdiction to try summary offences committed within that area. It also has jurisdiction as a court of trial in the following circumstances: (1) where a person is brought before the court on a summons or warrant issued under section 1(2)(b) of the Act (to be tried jointly with another person over whom the court has jurisdiction);[7] (2) in relation to either way offences, in any case where it has jurisdiction as examining justices;[8] (3) in relation to the trial of juveniles for indictable offences, in any case where it has jurisdiction as examining justices; (4) where it has jurisdiction to try an offender for a summary offence, it can also try him for any other summary offence.

C THE COURSE OF THE TRIAL

1 Time-limit

Unless expressly provided to the contrary a magistrates' court cannot try an information charging a summary offence unless the information was laid within six months from the time when the offence was committed.[9] However, it may try summarily an either way offence outside the period, since this statutory time-limit is confined to summary offences.[10] Time runs from the time of commission of the offence, not from the time of its discovery; however, it is sufficient if the information is laid within the six months, even if the trial takes place outside that time. It is in each case a question of construction of the statute whether the offence in question is a continuing offence, that is, committed each day that the act or state of affairs in question continues, or whether it is a "once and for all" offence in that it is committed on one day and one day only. Thus in *R v Wimbledon Justices, ex parte Derwent*[11] a statute made it an offence to let or offer to let a house in excess of a certain rent. The divisional court held that a person

---

4 See p 443, *ante*.
5 Magistrates' Courts Act 1980, s 1(2); see the rules as to offences committed on boundaries etc which also apply here, p 443, *ante*.
6 *Viz* a county, a London commission area or the City of London (Magistrates' Courts Act 1980, s 2(1)). The provisions as to offences committed on boundaries, etc (p 443, *ante*) also apply here.
7 See p 443, *ante*.
8 See p 462, *ante*.
9 Magistrates' Courts Act 1980, s 127(1).
10 *Ibid*, s 127(2).
11 [1953] 1 QB 380; [1953] 1 All ER 390.

lets a house once and for all when he demises it by means of a lease and that an information laid six months after the date of the demise was out of time. Proceedings could therefore be restrained by prohibition since:

> ". . . If in a case brought before justices it can be seen on the face of the proceedings that the offence is alleged to have been committed more than six months before the information was laid, justices have no power to enter upon the case at all, because they have no jurisdiction to sit on a court of summary jurisdiction in the case of an offence alleged to have been committed more than six months before the proceedings were instituted."[12]

Even where the offence is continuing it seems that the time-limit runs from each day, so that the magistrates cannot hear any information that charges the offence as occurring more than six months before the date of the information;[13] in other words the matter is to be regarded as if the defendant committed the offence once every day. Where an information is laid in time it may be amended to charge a different offence, after the expiry of six months from the commission of that offence, provided that this does not cause injustice.[14]

2 Number of offences

A magistrates' court must not proceed to the trial of an information which charges more than one offence.[15] This is a natural rule, since the information fulfils the same function in summary trial as the indictment in the case of trial at the Crown Court; the same considerations of, *inter alia*, fairness to the defendant, which prohibit duplicity in an indictment, also prohibit an information charging more than one offence. Thus in *Ware v Fox*[16] an information charged the defendant with being concerned in the management of premises which were used for the purpose of smoking cannabis or cannabis resin or dealing in cannabis or cannabis resin. The Queen's Bench divisional court held that on the proper construction of the relevant statute[17] the information alleged two offences, namely managing premises used for smoking and managing premises used for dealing and was bad for duplicity. By contrast, section 5 of the Public Order Act 1936 created[18] the offence of using "threatening, abusive or insulting words or behaviour . . . with intent to provoke a breach of the peace or whereby a breach of the peace is likely to be occasioned". It was held in *Vernon v Paddon*[19] that the section created one offence, the essential feature of which is conduct intended to provoke a breach of the peace or whereby such a breach was likely to be occasioned.

The issue as to whether an information is bad for duplicity is not always

---

12 [1953] 1 QB 380, at 385; [1953] 1 All ER 390, at 391, *per* LORD GODDARD CJ.
13 *R v Chertsey Justices, ex parte Franks* [1961] 2 QB 152; [1961] 1 All ER 825.
14 *R v Newcastle-upon-Tyne Justices, ex parte John Bryce (Contractors) Ltd* [1976] 2 All ER 611; [1976] 1 WLR 517.
15 Magistrates' Courts Rules 1981, r 12(1). However, two or more informations may be set out in a single document (*ibid*, r 12(2)); see *Shah v Swallow* [1984] 2 All ER 528; sub nom *Director of Public Prosecutions v Shah* [1984] 1 WLR 886.
16 [1967] 1 All ER 100; [1967] 1 WLR 379.
17 Dangerous Drugs Act 1965, s 5.
18 Now repealed and replaced by Public Order Act 1986, s 5.
19 [1973] 3 All ER 302; [1973] 1 WLR 663.

easy to decide. In *R v Courtie*[20] LORD DIPLOCK suggested that where one provision involved the imposition of different penalties depending on whether the prosecution established particular factual ingredients then Parliament had created two separate offences, and these should be the subject of separate informations. Applying this principle a divisional court in *Director of Public Prosecutions v Corcoran*[1] held that an information charging an offence of failure, without reasonable excuse, to provide a specimen of breath, blood or urine, contrary to section 7(6) of the Road Traffic Act 1988 was bad for duplicity, because the maximum punishment for this offence depended on the purpose for which the specimen was being sought. However, a short time later a differently constituted divisional court, in dismissing appeals in several cases,[2] overruled the earlier ruling and distinguished *R v Courtie*. On a construction of the statutory provisions, this was one offence; the question of punishment was relevant to sentence only.

Where an information is found to charge more than one offence the prosecutor should be called on to elect before the trial begins on which offence to proceed; if he declines to make his election the information should be dismissed.[3] It is essential that the matter should be put right at the outset, since, as will be noted below, the magistrates must state the substance of the information to the defendant and ask him to plead to it; therefore the information must be in order for a proper plea to be received, and the defendant cannot be required to plead to an information that is bad for duplicity. It is very doubtful whether this irregularity is one which can be cured by the operation of section 123 of the Magistrates' Courts Act.[4] In any event if the information is not amended:

> ". . . if a conviction is to be drawn up, how is it to be done? the information has to be dealt with as a whole. . . . To split it into halves and say that one bit is proved and another bit is disproved involves, to my mind, an operation as impossible as a few years ago splitting the atom was thought to be."[5]

To avoid the difficulty the information itself should always be in court from the beginning of proceedings.[6] It is however quite permissible, and indeed common, for two informations against the same defendant, or (where the cases are related) against different defendants, to be tried together. It was formerly thought that this could only be done by consent but the House of Lords in *Chief Constable of Norfolk v Clayton*[7] held that, although magistrates should first seek consent to such a course, they could nevertheless in the exercise of their discretion order a joint trial even without the consent of the parties, although they should not do so where it would not be fair and just to a defendant.

---

20 [1984] AC 463; [1984] 1 All ER 740.
1 [1993] 1 All ER 912.
2 *Shaw v Director of Public Prosecutions* (and other cases) [1993] 1 All ER 918.
3 *Edwards v Jones* [1947] KB 659; [1947] 1 All ER 830.
4 See p 442, *ante*.
5 [1947] KB 659, at 667; [1947] 1 All ER 830, at 834, per OLIVER J.
6 *Per* LORD PARKER CJ and SALMON J (as he then was) in *Hargreaves v Alderson* [1964] 2 QB 159; [1962] 3 All ER 1019; see also *Garman v Plaice* [1969] 1 All ER 62; [1969] 1 WLR 19.
7 [1983] 2 AC 473; sub nom *Clayton v Chief Constable of Norfolk* [1983] 1 All ER 984. This does not, however, enable a summons and cross-summons to be tried together; this cannot

Where there are informations charging an offence and an attempt to commit that offence, these may be ordered to be tried together without the consent of the defendant[8] and this will usually be done.

3 Hearing

If the defendant appears at the hearing the court must state to him the substance of the information and ask him whether he pleads guilty or not guilty. In spite of these words, the same pleas as are open to a defendant charged with an indictable offence may be raised by a defendant charged with a summary offence. If the plea is one of not guilty the prosecutor may make an opening speech, and will then call his evidence. Where the prosecutor is unrepresented, it is open to the magistrates, in their discretion, to permit their clerk to examine prosecution witnesses.[9] Section 98 of the Magistrates' Courts Act, already cited,[10] will apply, and the witnesses will be subject to cross-examination and re-examination according to the circumstances of the case. At the conclusion of the evidence for the prosecution the defendant may address the court, whether or not he calls evidence; if he is calling evidence it will follow at once. The defendant may then address the court a second time but only if he himself has given evidence, another witness has been called on his behalf, and the court gives leave.[11] If the defendant addresses the court twice the prosecutor has a right to address the court a second time immediately before the defendant's second speech. The court will then retire if necessary and convict the defendant or dismiss the charge. If on the other hand the defendant pleads guilty the court may convict him without hearing evidence.[12] The wording of the subsection shows that it is often desirable to hear some evidence, particularly where it is part of the prosecution's case that the offence was committed in circumstances of aggravation, or perhaps if a committal for sentence to the Crown Court is contemplated or if the plea of guilty tendered may be "equivocal".[13] In any event the court retains full power over the case until sentence is passed and has discretion to allow a change of plea until that time if justice so requires.[14] Whether there is a plea of guilty or finding of guilt, there will normally be such an inquiry into the past record of the defendant as follows conviction of an indictable offence; the court may then adjourn, for not more than four weeks at a time, for inquiries to be made or for the purpose of determining the best way to deal with the case.[15] When the court resumes it need not be composed of the same magistrates; if, however, there are any newcomers the court which sentences or deals with the offender must make such inquiry into the facts and circumstances of the case as are necessary to acquaint the newcomers

---

be done *semble* even by consent: *R v Epsom Justices, ex parte Gibbons* [1984] QB 574; [1983] 3 All ER 523.

8 Criminal Attempts Act 1981, s 4(2).

9 *Simms v Moore* [1970] 2 QB 327; [1970] 3 All ER 1.

10 See p 464, *ante*.

11 Magistrates' Courts Rules 1981, r 14.

12 Magistrates' Courts Act 1980, s 9(3).

13 See p 490, *ante*.

14 *S (An Infant) v Manchester City Recorder* [1971] AC 481; [1969] 3 All ER 1230.

15 Magistrates' Courts Act 1980, s 10(3); the period is three weeks if the defendant is in custody.

fully with those facts and circumstances.[16] This must be done even though the court will *ex hypothesi* have held some such inquiry before; the use of the words "the court" seems to prohibit the newcomers being given information privately before the court sits.[17]

Finally, note should be taken of the power which magistrates have under the Justices of the Peace Act 1361 to bind over a defendant to keep the peace or be of good behaviour even where he is acquitted.[18]

D   ABSENCES

1   General effects of absence[19]

It sometimes happens that one or both of the parties fails to appear at the trial or adjourned trial of the information. If the defendant does not appear the court may hear the case in his absence provided that, where a summons was issued, either the court is satisfied that the summons was served on the defendant within what appears to be a reasonable time before the hearing, or the defendant appeared on a previous occasion to answer the information.[20] Alternatively the court may adjourn the hearing, with or without issuing a warrant for the arrest of the defendant; but a warrant can only be issued if the court is satisfied as to the matters stated above, and if the information is substantiated on oath. There is a further restriction on the issue of a warrant; if the court adjourns the trial after hearing evidence, or convicting the defendant without hearing evidence on a plea of guilty, the court must not issue a warrant unless it thinks it undesirable, by reason of the gravity of the offence, to continue the hearing in his absence. In any event, a warrant cannot be issued unless the offence is punishable by imprisonment or unless the court, having convicted the defendant, proposes to disqualify him.

If the prosecutor fails to appear the court may dismiss the information or, if evidence has been received on a previous occasion, continue the hearing.[1] This is one example of the importance of the stage of the trial at which the justices begin to hear evidence. Alternatively the court may adjourn the trial, or may in an appropriate case dismiss the information for want of prosecution under section 15(1) of the Magistrates' Courts Act

---

16 Magistrates' Courts Act 1980, s 98(7). This is perhaps the nearest that English law comes to allowing special "sentencing tribunals".

17 In the event of a question arising which might require reference to the European Court for a preliminary ruling (as to which, see p 113, *ante*) the justices may, on application or otherwise, order the question to be referred and the hearing will then be adjourned pending receipt of the European Court's ruling; for a case in which this was done, and observations as to the approach which magistrates should adopt to this problem, see *R v Plymouth Justices, ex parte Rogers* [1982] QB 863; [1982] 2 All ER 175.

18 See *Veater v G* [1981] 2 All ER 304; [1981] 1 WLR 567; *Hughes v Holley* (1986) 86 Cr App Rep 130.

19 Magistrates' Courts Act 1980, ss 11–16. As to absence during the initial procedure on information for an offence triable either way, see p 451, *ante*.

20 The mode of service is prescribed by the Magistrates' Courts Rules 1981, r 99. If the court proceeds in the absence of the defendant in a case where he has not been duly served in accordance with this rule, the "hearing" is a complete nullity: *R v Seisdon Justices, ex parte Dougan* [1983] 1 All ER 6; [1982] 1 WLR 1476.

1 Magistrates' Courts Act 1980, s 15.

1980. However, this power should not be used for this purpose save in exceptional cases. In *R v Hendon Justices, ex parte Director of Public Prosecutions*[2] a magistrates' court dismissed an information for want of prosecution when the defendants, their advocates and the prosecution witnesses were all at court, but the prosecuting solicitor was not. This absence occurred because of an error in court administration, and the court was aware that a solicitor was on his way to rectify the position. In quashing the order of the justices the divisional court stressed that the duty of the magistrates' court is to hear informations properly brought before it. The prosecution had a right to be heard; the proper course was to adjourn until the hearing could proceed.

If neither side appears, the court may again dismiss the information or, if evidence has been received on a previous occasion, continue the hearing;[3] alternatively the hearing may simply be adjourned.

2 Pleading guilty by post

The Magistrates' Courts Act 1957 provided a new and convenient procedure whereby the defendant can plead guilty in cases where his appearance at court would be no more than a formality, if not a serious waste of time and money. It is now governed by section 12 of the 1980 Act. The procedure laid down by the Act is generally acknowledged to have worked well and is extensively used, particularly in motoring cases; however, it has no application at all to (1) youth court proceedings in respect of persons under 16 years;[4] (2) offences triable either way; or (3) offences for which the accused is liable to be sentenced to imprisonment for a term exceeding three months. Where the Act does apply, the procedure is as follows. The prosecutor will serve with the summons a notice in prescribed terms as to the effect of section 12 of the Act and a concise statement of such facts as he will place before the court if the defendant does decide to plead guilty by post. Although the Act is silent on the point it seems that it is entirely within the discretion of the prosecutor as to whether he will make use of the Act and serve the above documents with the summons, even on the assumption that the Act applies to the offence charged. Where, however, the prosecutor does elect to use the procedure, he must serve the documents and then inform the clerk to the justices that he has done so. It is then for the defendant or his solicitor to inform the clerk that he desires to plead guilty without appearing, if that is so, by sending, appropriately completed, the part of the notice described above. He does not, of course, have to use the procedure, and even if he does at first give notification that he is not going to appear he may change his mind and appear.

If, however, he does not appear the court may proceed to hear the case in his absence (whether or not the prosecutor is also absent) provided that it is satisfied that the notice and statement of facts were served on the defendant with the summons. Before accepting the plea of guilty and convicting the defendant in his absence the court must cause to be read out aloud the defendant's notification that he is going to plead guilty, the

2 [1994] QB 167; [1993] 1 All ER 411.
3 Magistrates' Courts Act 1980, s 16.
4 S 12, as amended by the Criminal Justice Act 1991, s 69.

statement of facts served on the defendant and any statement by way of mitigation which the defendant himself may have submitted. The statement of facts read out must be precisely the same as that served upon the defendant. These rules must be meticulously observed, and breach of them may be a ground for quashing the conviction by means of *certiorari*:

> "we all know that these matters have to be dealt with expeditiously. . . . It seems to me, however, to be quite clear that, before the magistrates can exercise jurisdiction in a case of this sort, they must strictly observe the conditions of the statute. Mere knowledge of the contents of the accused's submission, the mere reading of it themselves, is not sufficient; the submission must be read in open court."[5]

The rule that the precise statement of facts must be read out is also important, because after hearing it the magistrates may decide that the case is too grave to be dealt with in the way contemplated by the parties and may adjourn the case for the defendant to be present.

Assuming that, after hearing the notification of intention to plead guilty, the statement of facts and the submissions in mitigation, the magistrates accept the plea, they will record a conviction and (in the majority of cases to which the Act applies) impose a fine. Where they think it desirable to imprison the defendant or to impose any disqualification on him they must adjourn the hearing[6] without imposing any penalty whatever. There must then be sent to the defendant a notice stating the time and place of the adjourned hearing and the reason for the present adjournment (that is that the court is considering imprisonment or disqualification). If he chooses not to appear after receiving notice of what the court has in mind the court can proceed to disqualify him in his absence;[7] they cannot however sentence him to imprisonment or detention in his absence.[8] In such a case the proper course is to issue a warrant for the defendant's arrest.[9] Thus a person can never be sentenced to imprisonment in his absence and can only be disqualified in his absence following an adjournment for the purpose of giving him an opportunity to appear. However, a person may be committed to prison, for default in payment of a fine, in his absence.[10]

E SENTENCE

The types of sentence imposable by magistrates are basically similar to those available to the Crown Court, although the extent of magistrates' powers in relation to severity of sentence is more limited. They can

---

5 *R v Oldham Justices, ex parte Morrissey* [1958] 3 All ER 559n, at 560; [1959] 1 WLR 58, at 59, per LORD PARKER CJ.
6 Under the Magistrates' Courts Act 1980, s 10(3): see p 531, *ante*. This applies even if disqualification is mandatory under the "totting-up" provisions; further there may even in this case be grounds for mitigating the normal consequences of conviction, which the defendant should have the chance to state: *R v Llandrindod Wells Justices, ex parte Gibson* [1968] 2 All ER 20 [1968] 1 WLR 598.
7 *Ibid*, s 11(4).
8 *Ibid*, s 11(3).
9 *Ibid*, s 13(3).
10 *Ibid*, s 82(5); *R v Dudley Magistrates' Court, ex parte Payne* [1979] 2 All ER 1089; [1979] 1 WLR 891.

normally only sentence to imprisonment for up to six months in respect of any one offence[11] (or 12 months in the case of consecutive sentences).[12]

Their powers relating to the imposition of fines and the making of compensation orders are restricted. Since all summary jurisdiction derives from statute the amount of the maximum fine for any offence is prescribed by statute. However where a statute provides for imprisonment or other detention but makes no express provision for a fine, there is a general power to fine instead of imposing a custodial sentence.[13]

As a result of inflation statutory fines may quickly become too low and, to combat this phenomenon, the Criminal Justice Act 1982, section 37 introduced "the standard scale" of fines for summary offences. This scale consists of 5 levels and the ensuing sections of the 1982 Act provided for the substitution of a level on the standard scale for the figures prescribed by existing statutory provisions. Thus, for example, a summary offence formerly punishable with a fine of £100 became punishable with a fine up to level 3. To keep pace with inflation these levels may be increased by order of the Secretary of State,[14] although it should be remembered that the fine that may be imposed in respect of an either way offence will be determined by the terms of the specific statutory provision. The maximum compensation that magistrates can order under a compensation order is similarly limited.[15]

The position regarding the appropriate level of fines for summary offences has proved somewhat controversial. In an attempt to create some equal impact of fines upon those of different incomes, the Criminal Justice Act 1991 introduced[16] a system of "unit fines", whereby the actual amount of a fine depended upon a complex formula that sought to multiply an amount related to the seriousness of the offence with a a multiple reflecting the level of disposable income of the defendant. After widespead public concern, the scheme was abandoned. The position is now governed by a revised section 18 of the Criminal Justice Act 1991,[17] which requires the sentencing court to take into account both the seriousness of the offence and the ability of the defendant to pay.[18]

Finally, reference should be made to the provisions, now contained in section 39 of the 1980 Act, whereby a person 17 or over who has been convicted before different magistrates' courts of two or more offences punishable with imprisonment or disqualification from driving, may be remitted to be dealt with by one of the courts concerned.

---

11 Magistrates' Courts Act 1980, s 31(1); they can, of course, commit to the Crown Court for sentence in the circumstances noted at pp 535–540, *post*.

12 *Ibid*, s 133.

13 Magistrates' Courts Act 1980, s 34(3).

14 Magistrates' Courts Act 1980, s 143 (as amended by the Criminal Justice Act 1982, s 48). They were increased by the Criminal Justice Act 1991, s 17, under which the maximum fine for a level 5 offence is £5,000.

15 *Ibid*, s 40(1); s 143 applies to s 40(1).

16 Criminal Justice Act 1991, ss 18–19.

17 As substituted by Criminal Justice Act 1993, s 65(1).

18 1991 Act, s 18(2). For discussion of offence seriousness under the 1991 Act, see p 504, *ante*.

F COMMITTALS FOR SENTENCE

In some instances a defendant who has been tried in the magistrates' court may be committed to the Crown Court to be sentenced or otherwise dealt with. The case then becomes:

> ". . . a sort of composite case in which power is given to one court to convict and to another to give judgment; and until the judgment is given the hearing of the case is not complete."[19]

Although these instances vary in detail, there are basically three objects of committal for sentence, namely to ensure that (a) a defendant receives greater punishment than a magistrates' court has power to inflict, if thought to deserve it, (b) the same court which made an order should deal with its breach, and (c) generally, that there should be uniformity in sentencing. It may be noted at this stage that where the magistrates exercise their power under section 1(1) of the Powers of Criminal Courts Act 1973[20] to defer sentence, it is usually wrong when the defendant comes before them again to be dealt with to commit him for sentence.[1] Furthermore, if the justices do decide to commit the defendant for sentence they must be scrupulously careful to leave all questions associated with sentence to the Crown Court. They cannot therefore impose any order such as a compensation order and all matters relating to sentence are out of the justices' hands.[2]

1 Summary trial of an adult for an either way offence

If a magistrates' court tries an adult for an either way offence and convicts him, but considers:

   (a) that the offence, or the combination of the offence and other offences associated with it,[3] is so serious that greater punishment should be inflicted than the magistrates' court has power to impose; or
   (b) in the case of a violent or sexual offence[4] committed by a person not less than 21 years of age, that a term of imprisonment longer than the magistrates' court has power to impose is necessary to protect the public from serious harm from him;

it may commit the defendant to the Crown Court for sentence.

This power is contained in section 38 of the Magistrates' Courts Act 1980.[5] Although the power to commit extends to all either way offences tried summarily, it does not apply to cases under the Criminal Damage Act

---

19 LORD GODDARD CJ in *R v Norfolk Justices, ex parte Director of Public Prosecutions* [1950] 2 KB 558, at 568; sub nom *R v Greenhoe Justices, ex parte Director of Public Prosecutions* [1950] 2 All ER 42, at 46.
20 See p 503, *ante*
 1 *R v Gilby* [1975] 2 All ER 743; [1975] 1 WLR 924; *cf R v Harling* (1977) 65 Cr App Rep 320.
 2 *R v Brogan* [1975] 1 All ER 879; [1975] 1 WLR 393.
 3 See p 504, *ante*.
 4 Defined in the Criminal Justice Act 1991, s 31(1); see *R v Robinson* [1993] 2 All ER 1; [1993] 1 WLR 168.
 5 As substituted by Criminal Justice Act 1991, s 25.

1971 where the magistrates proceed to summary trial on the basis that the value involved does not exceed the relevant sum.[6]

Committal will normally be to the most convenient location of the Crown Court. In selecting this the justices must have regard to directions given by the presiding judge or judges of the circuit.[7] Committal may be in custody or on bail, but the Court of Appeal has indicated that:

> ". . . the cases must be rare when magistrates' courts can properly commit for [sentence] on bail because the whole purpose of the committal is to have the man sent to prison, and have him sent to prison for a longer period than the magistrates' court could impose."[8]

However, the defendant may give notice of appeal against conviction and may then, *qua* appellant, be released on bail, although, where a possibly severe sentence awaits him, bail will only be granted "with extreme care, and only in really exceptional cases".[9] There is no appeal against the order of committal as such;[10] if the defendant thinks that the committal was bad in law, for example because he was not warned that he might be committed, he should apply to a divisional court of the Queen's Bench Division for an order of *certiorari* or prohibition; the Crown Court will not, of course, sentence him until the result of his application is known, since the order of committal may be held to be a nullity. On such an application the divisional court can only hear argument as to the legality of the committal and cannot entertain any suggestion that the committal was too harsh a step to take having regard to the facts; this is an argument to be addressed (although not in so many words) to the Crown Court when the defendant appears there for sentence.

On such appearance, procedure is as if the defendant had been committed for trial to the Crown Court and had pleaded guilty to the charge. No actual plea will be taken, since that stage of the trial is concluded, but otherwise the position is as if the defendant had pleaded guilty at the Crown Court itself. Thus notices required to be served three days before the "trial" may be served three days before the hearing at the Crown Court,[11] and, if the defendant has been granted bail, but fails to surrender, the Crown Court may issue a bench warrant.[12] It might then be thought that the Crown Court could allow the defendant to withdraw his plea of guilty (if such was tendered) in the magistrates' court, before he was sentenced, and it is now clear from *R v Mutford and Lothingland Justices, ex parte Harber*,[13] following the decision of the House of Lords in *S (An Infant) v Manchester City Recorder*,[14] that this is permissible. The Crown Court certainly has such a power when trying a case on indictment.[15]

---

6 Magistrates' Courts Act 1980, s 33(1) (b); see p 446, *ante*.
7 See *Practice Direction (Crown Court Business: Classification)* [1987] 1 WLR 1671.
8 *R v Coe* [1969] 1 All ER 65, at 68; [1968] 1 WLR 1950, at 1954.
9 *Re Whitehouse* [1951] 1 KB 673, at 675; [1951] 1 All ER 353, at 354.
10 *R v London Sessions Appeal Committee, ex parte Rogers* [1951] 2 KB 74; [1951] 1 All ER 343.
11 *R v Grant* [1951] 1 KB 500; [1951] 1 All ER 28.
12 Bail Act 1976, s 7.
13 [1971] 2 QB 291; [1971] 1 All ER 81. The Crown Court can only take into consideration what took place in the magistrates' court: *R v Marylebone Justices, ex parte Westminster City Council* [1971] 1 All ER 1025; [1971] 1 WLR 567.
14 [1971] AC 481; [1969] 3 All ER 1230.
15 See p 491, *ante*.

At the hearing there should be formal identification by the police of the defendant as the person who appeared at the magistrates' court and was committed; if there is no police officer present who can give this information, the defendant may, it seems, be asked whether he was the person who appeared and was committed. The Crown Court will inquire into the circumstances of the case as it would following a plea of guilty before itself; prosecuting counsel will give the court an outline of the facts. It should be noted that if there is a dispute as to the facts of the offence upon which the defendant has been committed for sentence, the Crown Court can either resolve that matter itself, if necessary by hearing evidence, or can remit the case to the magistrates' court for such dispute to be resolved.[16] The court will then consider the defendant's antecedents, and usually a pre-sentence report;[17] defending counsel (or solicitor) will then address the court in mitigation. The Crown Court can then pass any sentence up to the maximum which the particular indictable offence carries and can deal with the defendant in any manner in which it could deal with him if he had just been convicted of the offence on indictment before the court.[18] The position as to appeal itself against this sentence has already been considered.[19]

If the defendant appeals against conviction, as well as being committed for sentence, the Crown Court will of course hear his appeal first, since, if this succeeds, there will be no cause to sentence him.

2   Young persons: Magistrates' Courts Act 1980, s 37[20]

The maximum period of detention in a young offender institution that a youth court has power to impose corresponds with its maximum power of imprisonment for an adult, *viz* 6 months or 12 months for consecutive sentences.[1] Section 37(1) of the 1980 Act provides:

> "where a person who is not less than 15 nor more than 17-years-old is convicted by a magistrates' court[2] of an offence punishable on conviction on indictment with a term of imprisonment exceeding six months, then, if the court is of opinion that he should be sentenced to a greater term of detention in a young offender institution than it has power to impose, the court may commit him in custody or on bail to the Crown Court for sentence."

Because an offender less than 18 cannot be sentenced to a term of detention exceeding 12 months in any event,[3] the power of committal under s 37 is of limited application.

---

16 *Munroe v Crown Prosecution Service* [1988] Crim LR 823.
17 See p 490, *ante*.
18 Powers of Criminal Courts Act 1973, s 42.
19 See p 522, *ante*.
20 In its original form this section (which was the successor to s 28 of the 1952 Act) provided for committal with a recommendation for Borstal training. Borstal training was abolished by s 1(3) of the Criminal Justice Act 1982 and the present s 37(1) was substituted by the 1982 Act (s 77, Sch 14).
 1 Magistrates' Courts Act 1980, s 133 (as amended).
 2 But an adult magistrates' court must remit the case to the youth court for sentence: Children and Young Persons Act 1969, s 7(8).
 3 Magistrates' Courts Act 1980, s 24(3).

3 Offences under the Bail Act 1976

The Bail Act 1976 created three new summary offences: the first two consist of failure of a person released on bail in criminal proceedings, without reasonable cause, to surrender to custody, or, having reasonable cause, to surrender at the appointed place as soon after the appointed time as reasonably practicable;[4] the third offence is that of agreeing to indemnify sureties in criminal proceedings.[5] Each of these offences is a summary offence (and therefore triable only summarily[6]); in each case the magistrates have power to impose imprisonment for up to three months or a fine of up to level 5 or both. However, exceptionally, the Act provides that in each case if the court thinks:

(a) that the circumstances of the offence are such that greater punishment should be inflicted for that offence than the court has power to inflict, or

(b) in a case where it commits that person for trial to the Crown Court for another offence, that it would be appropriate for him to be dealt with by that court for the bail offence,

it may commit him in custody or on bail to the Crown Court for sentence. In the Crown Court the convicted person is liable to imprisonment for up to 12 months or a fine or both.[7]

This form of statutory provision, namely one that provides for committal for sentence in the case of a purely summary offence, is wholly exceptional.

4 Committal under the Powers of Criminal Courts Act 1973[8]

Various powers exist to commit for sentence under the 1973 Act. An offender may be committed where his conviction puts him breach of a Crown Court community order,[9] Crown Court conditional discharge[10] or Crown Court suspended sentence.[11]

5 Committal under the Criminal Justice Act 1991;[12] prisoners on licence

Where a person released on licence is convicted by a magistrates' court of an offence punishable on indictment with imprisonment, the court may commit him for sentence to the Crown Court, in custody or on bail. That court may revoke the licence.[13]

---

4 Bail Act 1976, s 6(1); the marginal note refers to the offence as "absconding" although that word does not appear in the body of the section.

5 *Ibid*, s 9(1).

6 Although the offences under s 6 may alternatively be punished as contempts of court (s 6(5)).

7 Bail Act 1976, ss 6(7), 9(4).

8 As amended by the Criminal Justice Act 1991.

9 Criminal Justice Act 1991, Sch 2, para 7(2)(b).

10 Powers of Criminal Courts Act 1973, s 1B(5).

11 *Ibid*, s 24(2).

12 Section 40(3).

13 See further, Criminal Justice Act 1991, s 40.

6 Committal under the Mental Health Act 1983[14]

A magistrates' court may make an order under the Mental Health Act 1983 committing the defendant, if he is fourteen or over, to a hospital, but it cannot at the same time make an order restricting the defendant's discharge for a fixed number of years. If, therefore, the court considers that a hospital order is appropriate but that it must in the particular case be accompanied by restrictions on release, the magistrates' court may, instead of making a hospital or any other order, commit the defendant to the Crown Court to be dealt with. Committal must be in custody; if, however, the magistrates' court is satisfied that arrangements have been made by a hospital to receive the defendant in the event of the Crown Court making a hospital order, the court may itself direct the defendant to be admitted to that hospital and to be detained there, pending determination of the case by the Crown Court. The Crown Court may make a hospital order, with or without restrictions, or it may deal with the defendant in any way in which the magistrates' court could have done.

7 Incorrigible rogues

A person deemed to be an "incorrigible rogue", within the meaning of section 5 of the Vagrancy Act 1824, for one of the various causes there specified, may be committed to the "house of correction" – that is, in custody or on bail to the Crown Court for sentence. The Crown Court may impose up to a year's imprisonment. A person is deemed to be a rogue within section 5 if, inter alia, he breaks or escapes out of a place of legal confinement before the expiry of his sentence or if he is apprehended as a rogue and vagabond and violently resists the constable "or other peace officer" so arresting him.

It is not of course for every offence that the defendant can be committed for sentence. Thus the defendant may be convicted of two or more offences, and *prima facie* liable to be committed in respect of only one. Now, however, for the sake of uniformity, where a defendant is committed for sentence under any of the above cases, except section 43 of the Mental Health Act 1983, in respect of an offence, he may also be committed in respect of other offences.[15] If the offence in respect of which the committal is being made (the "relevant offence") is an offence triable either way, then the other offences may be any other offences whatsoever in respect of which the committing court has power to deal with him (being an offence of which he has been convicted by that or any other court[16]). If, on the other hand, the relevant offence is a summary offence, then the other offences are limited to offences of which the committing court has

---

14 Section 43.
15 Criminal Justice Act 1967, s 56(1) (as substituted by the Criminal Law Act 1977, s 46). This has, of course, no application to a committal of someone in respect of a community order since such a committal does not arise out of a subsequent conviction but simply out of failure to comply with the terms of the original order.
16 This could arise where the offender (if an adult) had been convicted of offences by other magistrates' courts and those courts had remitted him to the committing court to be dealt with for those offences under s 39 of the Magistrates' Courts Act.

convicted the defendant, being offences punishable with imprisonment or disqualification from driving, or in respect of which there is in existence a suspended sentence which the committing court has power to implement.[17] Where there is a committal in respect of the "second offence", the Crown Court can only deal with the defendant as the magistrates could have done; subject to this, they have all duties and powers of sentence transferred to them, except that the magistrates' court may impose an order of interim disqualification from driving, pending the defendant's appearance at the higher court.

G   APPEALS FOLLOWING SUMMARY TRIAL

A defendant convicted by a magistrates' court may appeal either (1) to the Crown Court, and thence by way of case stated to the Queen's Bench Division of the High Court; or (2) by case stated to the Queen's Bench Division of the High Court; (3) from the Queen's Bench Divisional Court to the House of Lords, in certain circumstances. In addition to those rights of appeal there is the possibility of applying for judicial review. Each of these will be considered in turn.

1   Appeal to the Crown Court

Where the defendant has been convicted in the magistrates' court of either a summary offence or an either way offence tried summarily he may appeal to the Crown Court, if he pleaded guilty against his sentence only, or if he pleaded not guilty against both conviction and sentence.[18] It will be seen that there is an express statutory prohibition against an appeal against conviction if the defendant pleaded guilty. This may be contrasted with the position following trial on indictment, where, as already noted,[19] there is nothing in the Criminal Appeal Act to prevent an appeal against conviction to the Court of Appeal even if the defendant pleaded guilty. It has been observed that the judges have laid down that appeals against conviction following a plea of guilty will only be entertained by the Court of Appeal in certain exceptional circumstances; so in the case of appeals to the Crown Court also, the judges have given a construction to the statute which evades the effect of the exact words used by Parliament, but on this occasion in favour of the defendant. It has been held that to make a plea of guilty binding and effective it must be unambiguous;[20] if therefore the defendant says the actual word "guilty" but adds to it a statement which, if true, amounts to a defence to the charge, or if from the circumstances it is clear that he is denying the charge but has pleaded guilty through ignorance of the law, a plea of guilty accepted in these circumstances is a nullity.[1] The Crown Court can, therefore, hear an appeal against the "conviction" which is equally a nullity, and under powers presently to be considered can remit the case to the magistrates with an expression of

---

17 Under s 24(1) of the Powers of Criminal Courts Act 1973.

18 Magistrates' Courts Act 1980, s 108(1).   19 See p 512, *ante.*

20 *R v Durham Quarter Sessions, ex parte Virgo* [1952] 2 QB 1; [1952] 1 All ER 466; *cf R v Ingleson*, cited at p 512, *ante.*

  1 *R v Blandford Justices, ex parte G* [1967] 1 QB 82; [1966] 1 All ER 1921.

opinion that a plea of not guilty ought to be entered. Where on the other hand there has been a deliberate and unequivocal plea of guilty no appeal against conviction can be entertained.[2]

The expression "sentence" includes any order made on conviction by a magistrates' court, with an exception in respect of an order for absolute or conditional discharge, although if on a later date sentence is passed in respect of the offence for which the order for conditional discharge was made, that is following "breach" of the order, there may be (1) an appeal against that later sentence; (2) an order for the payment of costs; (3) an order for the destruction of an animal, made under the Protection of Animals Act 1911; and (4) any order, if the court has no discretion as to the making of the order or its terms, for example if the court is bound to order endorsement of a driving licence.[3] It has already been noted[4] that there is no appeal against a committal for sentence, in the cases already discussed in which there may be such a committal, although there may be an appeal against the conviction on which the committal is based.

There is a right of appeal against an order to enter into recognisances to keep the peace or be of good behaviour,[5] and this right exists where such an order has been made following acquittal.[6]

With limited exceptions only the defendant may appeal. The procedure is that an appeal must be commenced by giving notice of appeal, to the clerk of the magistrates' court, and to the other party, within 21 days after the day on which the decision of the magistrates' court was given (meaning the day on which sentence is passed if there is an adjournment of the case after conviction). The Crown Court may extend the time, either in relation to a notice not yet given or to a notice already given but out of time.

Proceedings before the Crown Court on an appeal against conviction take the form of a complete rehearing of the case;[7] the prosecution must open the case and call its witnesses afresh and either side may introduce fresh evidence without any leave. This is of course in sharp contrast to proceedings in the Court of Appeal. The Crown Court may confirm, reverse or vary the decision of the magistrates' court,[8] or remit the case with an expression of their opinion;[9] as already seen this latter procedure will be appropriate where an "equivocal" plea of guilty has been entered, which in all the circumstances the Crown Court considers should have been treated as a plea of not guilty. As regards appeals against sentence, the Crown Court may impose any sentence which the magistrates' court could have passed, whether more or less severe than that which they actually passed. The court may also do this if the appeal is against conviction only.[10] Again, there is a sharp contrast between appeals to the Crown

2 *P Foster (Haulage) Ltd v Roberts* [1978] 2 All ER 751.
3 Magistrates' Courts Act 1980, s 108(3).
4 See p 536, *ante*.
5 Magistrates' Courts (Appeals from Binding Over Orders) Act 1956.
6 *Shaw v Hamilton* [1982] 2 All ER 718; [1982] 1 WLR 1308.
7 Supreme Court Act 1981, s 48. Although the prosecution cannot alter the case by amending the information (*Garfield v Maddocks* [1974] QB 7; [1973] 2 All ER 303).
8 Supreme Court Act 1981, s 48(2) (a).
9 *Ibid*, s 48(2) (b).
10 *Ibid*, s 9(4). However the Crown Court cannot impose a sentence which the magistrates could not have imposed. Thus an unrepresented defendant who has not previously been sentenced to imprisonment cannot (subject to minor exceptions) be sentenced to

Court and appeals to the Court of Appeal following trial on indictment, since the Court of Appeal never has had the power to interfere with the sentence in any way if the appeal is against conviction only and, in addition, cannot now increase sentence;[11] the Crown Court can do both. Finally, the Crown Court may:

> "make such other order in the matter as the court thinks just, and by such order exercise any power which the said authority might have exercised."[12]

The wording is liberal, but it was held[13] on an almost identical provision in the previous legislation, that quarter sessions had no power to vary the sentence by quashing the sentence passed at the magistrates' court and committing to itself for sentence. The reason lies in the point already noted[14] that committal for sentence is not itself a sentence; if therefore magistrates elect to sit as a sentencing court instead of as a committing court quarter sessions could not go behind that election. Their power was to interfere with a sentence, not a decision as to whether the defendant should be committed or sentenced. This is presumably still true for the Crown Court.

If the appeal is against sentence only it may proceed on the basis of the facts relevant to sentence produced before the magistrates, if counsel for the appellant agrees to that course; there will then be no need for any evidence whatever to be called before the Crown Court. The same strictness of proof is not demanded in matters relevant to sentence as in matters relevant to conviction. In fact proceedings on an appeal against sentence normally take the same course as if the defendant had just been convicted, or had pleaded guilty, before the court.[15]

From the Crown Court a further appeal lies by way of case stated to the Queen's Bench Division of the High Court; this will be considered below.

2   Appeal by case stated to the Queen's Bench Division from magistrates' courts and the Crown Court

a   Magistrates' courts

Any person who was a party to proceedings before a magistrates' court or (although not a party) is aggrieved by the conviction, order, determination or other proceeding may appeal against the proceeding on the ground that it is wrong in law or in excess of jurisdiction by applying to the magistrates' court to state a case for the opinion of a divisional court of the Queen's Bench Division of the High Court.[16] The power to appeal by way of case

---

imprisonment (Powers of Criminal Courts Act 1973, s 21(1)). Accordingly, on appeal in such a case, the Crown Court cannot impose a sentence of imprisonment even though the accused is legally represented on his appeal: *R v Birmingham Justices, ex parte Wyatt* [1975] 3 All ER 897; [1976] 1 WLR 260.

11 See p 522, *ante*.

12 Supreme Court Act 1981, s 48(2)(c). Note, in addition, the provisions as to ordering questions to be referred to the European Court for preliminary ruling (Crown Court (References to the European Court) Rules 1972); see p 113, *ante*.

13 In *R v Bullock* [1964] 1 QB 481; [1963] 3 All ER 506.

14 See p 535, *ante*.

15 See p 490, *ante*.

16 Magistrates' Courts Act 1980, s 111(1).

stated is not normally a proper way of challenging a sentence that has been imposed, the proper procedure for which is appeal to the Crown Court.[17] Only where the sentence is, by any acceptable standard, "astonishing" will proceedings by way of case stated be entertained.[18]

Thus, either the defendant or the prosecutor in a criminal case may make application for a case to be stated. Application may also be made by a person aggrieved, but:

> "the words 'person aggrieved' do not really mean a man who is disappointed of a benefit which he might have received if some other order had been made (still less does it mean someone having a merely sympathetic interest in the proceedings). A 'person aggrieved' must be a man who has suffered a legal grievance, a man against whom a decision has been pronounced which has wrongfully deprived him of something, or wrongfully refused him something, or wrongfully affected his title to something."[19]

A party to proceedings who has succeeded in part only may appeal against the incompleteness of his success. Executors of a person who has died since the hearing of the case in the magistrates' court are "interested", at any rate if a fine has been imposed, since the money to pay this would come out of the estate of the deceased; they may accordingly bring an appeal by way of case stated.[20] If the deceased had been sentenced to imprisonment the executors appear not to be "interested".[1]

Application must be made in writing, within 21 days after the day on which the decision of the magistrates' court was given;[2] again, if the magistrates adjourn after conviction, the day on which sentence is actually passed is the first day on which time begins to run.[3] The application should be delivered to the clerk of the magistrates' court whose decision is being questioned or sent to him by post; the names of the magistrates constituting the court do not have to be given and it is therefore immaterial that there is an error in their names.[4]

The application must identify the point of law on which the opinion of the High Court is sought.[5]

The magistrates may refuse to state a case only on the ground that the application is in their opinion frivolous, and may not refuse to state a case if the application is made by or under the direction of the Attorney-General, even in the unlikely event of such an application being considered frivolous.[6] On refusal the magistrates must give the applicant a certificate of refusal if he so requires; he may then apply to the High

---

17 *Tucker v Director of Public Prosecutions* [1992] 4 All ER 901.
18 *Ibid*, per PILL J.
19 *Ex parte Sidebotham* (1880) 14 Ch D 458, at 465, *per* JAMES LJ, described as "the best definition of the expression 'aggrieved'" in *R v London Sessions, ex parte Westminster Corporation* [1951] 2 KB 508, at 511; [1951] 1 All ER 1032, at 1033, *per* LORD GODDARD CJ.
20 *Hodgson v Lakeman* [1943] 1 KB 15. *Aliter* in an appeal following trial on indictment: *R v Jefferies* [1969] 1 QB 120; [1968] 3 All ER 238.
1 *R v Rowe* [1955] 1 QB 573; [1955] 2 All ER 234.
2 Magistrates' Courts Act 1980, s 111(2), (3).
3 *Ibid.*
4 *R v Oxford (Bullingdon) Justices, ex parte Bird* [1948] 1 KB 100.
5 Magistrates' Courts Rules 1981, r 76(1).
6 Magistrates' Courts Act 1980, s 111(5).

Court for an order of *mandamus* directing the justices to state a case.[7] On the making of the application, whether granted or refused, the applicant loses his right to appeal to the Crown Court.[8]

A "case" will normally contain a statement of the information as laid, the facts found, the contentions of the parties, the cases cited, the decision and the question or questions for the decision of the High Court. If one or other of the parties is contending that there was no evidence on which the magistrates could come to their decision, a statement of the evidence should be included. This form, originally settled by LORD GODDARD CJ, should always be used. The case may be stated by all the justices whose decision is questioned or by any two of them[9] and may be stated in relation to a number of different prosecutions, even against different defendants on different days, provided that they raise precisely the same point. Under no circumstances should the case state that the decision was that of a majority, if that was the position.[10] The case should in any event be submitted to both parties for their consideration and in the event of any difficulty it should be left to the parties themselves to produce a draft and submit it to the magistrates for their consideration.[11] If, in spite of this, a party to an appeal considers that the facts have been improperly stated in the case he may apply to the Queen's Bench Division for the case to be remitted to the justices for restatement of the facts, the application being accompanied by an affidavit setting out the facts which it is alleged should go in the case.[12] Periods of 21 days are allowed for delivering the draft case to the parties, for the parties to make representations and for the justices to prepare the final case.[13] These time-limits are not inflexible and may be extended, but in such event a written statement of the reasons for the delay must accompany the final case.[14]

On the hearing the court will hear and determine the questions of law arising, after argument by counsel for the parties. The court may allow argument on a point not raised in the court below or even take such a point itself,[15] provided that in each case the point is one of pure law, not requiring any evidence. The magistrates themselves may file an affidavit, setting out the grounds of the decision and any facts which they may consider to have a bearing on the issues;[16] in view of the existence of the case this procedure will rarely be appropriate. Unless misconduct is alleged there is no need for the justices to be represented by counsel. The court may reverse, affirm or amend the decision in respect of which the case has

---

7 Magistrates' Courts Act 1980, s 111(6).
8 *Ibid*, s 111(4).
9 Magistrates' Courts Rules 1981, r 78(2).
10 *More O'Ferrall Ltd v Harrow Urban District Council* [1947] KB 66, at 70; [1946] 2 All ER 489, at 491.
11 *Cowlishaw v Chalkley* [1955] 1 All ER 367n, [1955] 1 WLR 101.
12 *Spicer v Warbley* [1953] 1 All ER 284; [1953] 1 WLR 334.
13 Magistrates' Courts Rules 1981, rr 77, 78.
14 *Ibid*, r 79.
15 *Whitehead v Haines* [1965] 1 QB 200; [1964] 2 All ER 530.
16 Review of Justices Decisions Act 1872.

been stated, or may remit the matter to the magistrates with its opinion, or make such other order as it sees fit.[17]

2   The Crown Court

The Crown Court may also state a case for the opinion of the High Court. Either party to any order, judgment or other decision of the Crown Court, other than one relating solely to trial on indictment, may apply for a case to be stated on the ground that the decision is wrong in law or in excess of jurisdiction.[18] Thus, either party to an appeal from the magistrates' court, against conviction or sentence may apply, as (apparently) may a person sentenced at the Crown Court after committal for sentence from a magistrates' court. These provisions are in several respects an extension of the old law; however, a person aggrieved by the Crown Court's decision, but not a party, still has no right of appeal. Application should be made in writing to the appropriate officer of the Crown Court within 21 days after the decision; again, the Crown Court may only refuse to state a case if the application is considered frivolous.[19] The powers of the Queen's Bench Division appear to be the same as those exercisable on an appeal from the magistrates.[20]

3   Appeal to the House of Lords

Finally it should be noted that an appeal to the House of Lords may be made from the divisional court of the Queen's Bench Division, subject to the same conditions as those governing appeals from the Court of Appeal in the case of trial on indictment.[1] Thus there must be a certificate from the divisional court that a point of law of general public importance is involved in its decision and either the divisional court or the House of Lords must give leave to appeal on the ground that the point is one which ought to be considered by the House of Lords. In this way a summary offence may be

---

17 Summary Jurisdiction Act 1857, s 6. If a question arises which is appropriate to be referred to the European Court for a preliminary ruling (as to which, see p 113, *ante*) the court may, of its own motion or on application, make an order whereupon proceedings will be stayed pending receipt of the ruling, unless the divisional court otherwise orders: RSC, Ord 114. A rehearing is only appropriate where a fair trial is still possible; cf *Griffith v Jenkins* [1992] 2 AC 76; [1992] 1 All ER 76 in which case the House of Lords laid down guidelines as to the circumstances in which the power to order a rehearing should be exercised.
18 Supreme Court Act 1981, s 28. Certain decisions of the Crown Court are made final; see s 28(2)(b).
19 Crown Court Rules 1982, r 26.
20 The case of *Harris, Simon & Co Ltd v Manchester City Council* [1975] 1 All ER 412; [1975] 1 WLR 100 demonstrated a little known legal oddity whereby under the Manchester General Improvement Act 1851 an objection to the Manchester City Council's resolution to stop up two streets was made by way of appeal to the Crown Court (as successor to the jurisdiction of quarter sessions) where the objection is heard as an appeal by judge and jury. Since juries do not make detailed findings of fact, the divisional court on an appeal by way of case stated approached the case on the basis that the appeal could succeed only if the judge had misdirected the jury or if their conclusion was perverse, in the sense of being a conclusion which no reasonable jury could have reached. This instance of an appeal by way of case stated of the verdict of a jury appears to be unique.
1 Administration of Justice Act 1960, s 1.

considered by four courts; the magistrates' court, the Crown Court, the divisional court of the Queen's Bench Division and the House of Lords.[2]

H   JUDICIAL REVIEW

Magistrates' courts and the Crown Court, in the exercise of their jurisdiction over summary offences, are inferior courts and therefore their proceedings are amenable to judicial review by the High Court.[3] This procedure may be appropriate where there is no right of appeal. Thus, for example, it has been noted[4] that there is no right of appeal from an order for the payment of costs; nevertheless the High Court has on *Wednesbury* principles[5] been prepared to quash an order for costs which was so far outside the normal sum imposed as to involve an error of law.[6] Similarly, following an appeal against sentence from a magistrates' court to the Crown Court, there is no further appeal (except by way of case stated if a point of law is involved); nevertheless in *R v St Albans Crown Court, ex parte Cinnamond*[7] a disqualification of 18 months for careless driving, although within the jurisdiction of the court, was quashed as being so far outside the normal sentence imposed by courts for this offence as to enable the divisional court to hold that it must have involved an error of law.

---

2 *Spicer v Holt* [1977] AC 987; [1976] 3 All ER 71 is a case in which this happened. It might, in addition, be considered by the European Court, to the extent that a question arising in the proceedings was referred to that court for a preliminary ruling; see p 113, *ante*.
3 See p 122, *ante* for details of this jurisdiction and procedure.
4 See p 130, *ante*.
5 As to which see p 130, *ante*.
6 *R v Tottenham Justices, ex parte Joshi* [1982] 2 All ER 507; [1982] 1 WLR 631.
7 [1981] QB 480; [1981] 1 All ER 802.

PART V

Evidence

SUMMARY

CHAPTER 26

Nature of Judicial Evidence[1]

A   INTRODUCTION

It has already been noted that English trials are not inquisitorial investigations into an incident dispute or problem. Essentially they are adversarial in nature, with the court deciding the facts, and applying the law, relevant to the issues put before it. It is not the court that decides what those issues are. In a civil case it is the parties themselves, through the pleadings. In a criminal case the issues are decided by the nature of the charge. Thus, once a charge of murder has been brought the issues are clear: did the accused unlawfully kill the deceased, with the intent that the law requires. These are the "facts in issue". The role of the law of evidence is to determine what facts can be proved in respect of these issues, and how they may be proved.

It will be clear from this that the term "evidence" is capable of more than one meaning. In one sense it refers to *how* the facts in issue may be proved. It was in this sense that Blackstone defined evidence as:

> "that which demonstrates, makes clear, or ascertains the truth of the very fact or point in issue, either on the one side or on the other."[2]

There is, though, another, wider, meaning. It can be used to describe *what* facts may be proved. This will include matters not only that relate directly to the facts in issue, but also other facts from which the facts in issue may be inferred. This is "circumstantial evidence", and is discussed further below.

Whether evidence can be adduced in court will depend upon whether or not it is admissible. This is a question of law. Admissibility does not determine the weight such evidence should be given (ie its value). This is a question of fact. It quickly becomes clear, however, that the adversarial trial system plays an important part in determining the rules that govern admissibility: many of the technical rules of evidence that exist do so because it has been considered necessary to regulate the type of evidence that can properly be put before a jury, in order to ensure a fair trial. Yet the effect of this sometimes is to exclude evidence that many would consider important if a trial were an investigation in search of the truth.

---

1 See, generally, *Cross on Evidence* (7th Edn, 1991, Butterworths).
2 Comm 367.

Thus, in a trial for murder the fact that a third party confessed to the crime has been held to be inadmissible evidence.[3] Increasingly, the courts are uneasy with rules of evidence that prevent evidence which might be of value from being heard.

B CLASSIFICATIONS OF JUDICIAL EVIDENCE

Writers, and indeed judges, often classify evidence in various ways. These classifications are sometimes of no great practical significance, but awareness of the terminology is important. These classifications are not mutually exclusive: a piece of evidence may fall within more than one category. The following are the main classifications.

a *Direct and circumstantial evidence*

Direct evidence is evidence of the facts in issue themselves. It may, for example, consist of the perceptions of the witness, or consist of documentary or real evidence. It may be contrasted with circumstantial evidence, which, as explained above, is evidence from which another fact can be deduced. It should not automatically be assumed that direct evidence is necessarily of better quality than circumstantial evidence. For example, in a prosecution for murder the testimony of a witness who claims to have seen the killing is direct evidence since the killing of the deceased by the accused is a fact in issue. Yet the incident may have happened quickly, and in circumstances of poor visibility, thus making the identification poor.[4] In addition, in some cases the witness may have a motive to give false evidence. On the other hand, evidence that the accused purchased a gun, that his fingerprints were found on that gun, that the bullet which caused death was fired from the same gun and that the accused had previously threatened the deceased are all items of circumstantial evidence, the cogency of which may be overwhelming.

b *Original evidence and hearsay evidence*

Original evidence is to be distinguished from hearsay. Original evidence is sometimes, somewhat confusingly, called "direct evidence", but the former term avoids confusion. It describes evidence which deals with the direct perceptions and actions of the witness. The witness can describe what was seen, done, and, in some cases, said. Documents can be produced in court and are original evidence, though the use of the contents of those documents may be restricted by law. By contrast, hearsay evidence involves testimony as to statements that were made outside court. *Cross on Evidence* defines the hearsay rule as follows:

> "An assertion other than one made by a person while giving oral evidence in the proceedings is inadmissible as evidence of any fact asserted."[5]

The assertion may be oral. For that reason the rule often prevents a witness from giving evidence as to what was said by somebody else. Similarly with a document: it cannot be used as a means of proving the truth of the statements

---

3 *R v Turner* [1975] QB 834; [1975] 1 All ER 70.
4 See p 575, *post.*
5 *Op cit*, p 42. See p 617, *post.*

made in it, unless one of the exceptions to the hearsay rule applies. A common misconception, however, is that every out-of-court statement, whether oral or in a document, infringes the hearsay rule. Not so. It is only if the statement is being relied upon as proof of the truth of its contents that the hearsay rule is infringed. For example, if a letter is submitted to the court to prove not the truth of its contents, but merely the fact that it was written, it is original, not hearsay evidence. Likewise with oral testimony. The evidence of a witness that she heard X threaten Y may well be original, not hearsay evidence, because its purpose is to prove that a threat was made.

This classification is of great importance. Hearsay evidence is inadmissible unless one of the exceptions to the rule, either at common law or under statute, applies. Many other rules of evidence owe their justification to the existence of the hearsay rule.

c   Documentary evidence

Self-evidently, documentary evidence is the production of documents. This term is given a wide meaning, and includes almost all known forms of recording statements.[6] Whether a piece of evidence is documentary may determine whether one or more of the statutory exceptions to the hearsay rule applies.

d   Real evidence

Real evidence involves the production of physical objects for the inspection of the court, where these, in themselves, have evidential relevance. Evidence is regarded as real evidence where the fact sought to be proved is actually perceived by the court. A piece of evidence may be both real and documentary.

As an alternative to the production of an object in court, the judge and jury, or, on summary trial, magistrates, may leave the court to inspect an object or a site. Such an inspection is termed a "view" and may be classified as real evidence.[7] It is less easy to characterise the demeanour of witnesses. The court is undoubtedly entitled to have regard to the physical characteristics and demeanour of witnesses, particularly in assessing their cogency. It can be described as real evidence, but in reality is one attribute that allows assessment of the oral testimony given to occur. Where the physical characteristic of a witness is a fact in issue, such as facial disfigurement, it is undoubtedly a form of real evidence.[8]

e   Best evidence and secondary evidence

The "best evidence" rule is one of the oldest common law rules of evidence. It is self-explanatory; the best (or most direct) evidence of a fact must be adduced. Thus the best evidence of the contents or existence of a document is the production of the original; a copy is secondary evidence.

---

6 "Document" is widely defined by Civil Evidence Act 1968, s 10, and includes photographs, negatives, tapes, discs, and other devices capable of being reproduced therefrom.
7 *London General Omnibus Co Ltd v Lavell* [1901] 1 Ch 135; *Buckingham v Daily News Ltd* [1956] 2 QB 534; [1956] 2 All ER 904.
8 See *Cole v United Dairies (London) Ltd* [1941] 1 KB 100; [1940] 4 All ER 318.

The best evidence of the condition of a physical object is the production of that object to the court. The rule also used to operate (but no longer does) to exclude circumstantial evidence where direct evidence was available.[9] The best evidence rule is of declining importance, with a great variety of exceptions.

f   Fact and opinion

Generally, a witness may testify only as to acts which have been directly perceived. The witness may not state a belief in facts which is based on anything but direct perception. This is the rule excluding proof by opinion. The rationale of this rule of exclusion is that it is the function of the court, not of the witnesses, to draw conclusions from the facts proved.[10] The functions of witnesses, and indeed of any method of proof, is simply to place those facts before the court. The law, though, does draw a distinction between expert and non-expert opinion. Where the matter to be decided is within the special skill or knowledge of a person established as an expert, then in certain circumstances evidence of opinion based on that expertise may be given.[11]

Opinion as a means of proof must be distinguished from opinion as a fact in itself. Where a person's opinion is, in itself, a relevant fact, there is no rule excluding proof of that opinion. For example, in defamation actions where the defence of fair comment is raised the defendant's opinion is relevant. Similarly, in an action based on malicious prosecution the defendant's opinion as to whether there was a reasonable ground for the prosecution is a fact in issue. Again, on a prosecution for having unlawful sexual intercourse with a girl under the age of sixteen the accused's opinion that the girl was over sixteen is an element in a defence to that crime.[12]

C   THE DECISION-MAKING PROCESS

A distinction can be drawn between the "tribunal of law" and "tribunal of fact". Each has the decision-making power in respect of law and fact respectively. Whether evidence is admissible is a question of law; what weight it should be given is a question of fact. In reality these functions may be performed by the same people.

In criminal cases tried on indictment, and in the minority of civil cases tried with a jury,[13] it is the judge who is the "tribunal of law", and the jury which is the "tribunal of fact". In these cases the judge decides questions of law. Where there is a mixed point of law and fact the judge determines the point of law, leaving such factual matters as remain unresolved to the jury. Where a ruling on law conclusively determines the case, the matter must be withdrawn from the jury, though the formal verdict or finding will still be that of the jury. Thus in a civil action for defamation it will be for the

---

9 *Williams v East India Co* (1802) 3 East 192.
10 See *North Cheshire and Manchester Brewery Co v Manchester Brewery Co* [1899] AC 83.
11 The matter must be one accepted by the courts as appropriate to be the subject of expertise: see p 590, *post.*
12 Sexual Offences Act 1956, s 6(3).
13 See p 553, *post.*

judge to determine whether the words are capable of being defamatory, and the jury who decides whether, in fact, they are.[14] Plainly if the words are incapable in law of a defamatory meaning there remains no factual issue to be determined and it should be withdrawn from the jury.

The judge will have the duty of ruling whether in law there is sufficient evidence to support the case for the prosecution or plaintiff. If not, the case must be withdrawn from the jury, who will be directed to enter the appropriate verdict. The judge also rules on the admissibility of evidence, this being a matter of law. In performing this function it will be the task of the judge to decide matters of fact upon which the admissibility of evidence depends. Thus, it may be suggested that a confession in a criminal case is inadmissible because of police misconduct whilst that confession was being obtained. Whether or not this misconduct occurred will have to be determined by the judge in order to resolve the question of admissibility. In criminal cases this is usually, though not always done in the absence of the jury, for otherwise it might learn of highly prejudicial but ultimately inadmissible evidence. This process is known as a *voir dire*,[15] or, more colloquially, a "trial within a trial".

In civil cases tried without a jury the judge discharges the functions of both judge and jury, but the functions themselves remain distinct, and different considerations must be observed depending upon whether matters of fact or law are being determined. Likewise with summary trial in magistrates' courts. The magistrates decide both questions of fact and law, though in relation to matters of law, lay justices are dependent upon the advice of the legally trained clerk.[16]

D　RELEVANCE AND ADMISSIBILITY

The term "admissibility" is used in the law of evidence to describe what evidence is permitted to be given. "Evidence" in this context bears its wider meaning, so admissibility refers not only to what may be proved but also what evidence will be acceptable to the court in proving it.

In order for evidence to be admissible, it must be relevant. Evidence that is not relevant serves no purpose in the proceedings, and will not be admissible. *Stephen* defined the word "relevant" as meaning that:

> ". . . any two facts to which it is applied are so related to each other that according to the common course of events one either taken by itself or in connection with other facts proves or renders probable the past, present or future existence or non-existence of the other."[17]

Whether evidence has relevance cannot be decided in the abstract, but rather by reference to the issues to be decided. Evidence that relates directly to the facts in issue will clearly be relevant, as will evidence from which circumstantial

---

14 This practice constitutes an exception to the general rule that the construction of documents and the determination of the ordinary meaning of words are matters of law for the judge; the exception does not appear to be confined to defamation cases (*R v Sunair Holidays Ltd* [1973] 2 All ER 1233; [1973] 1 WLR 1105).

15 From the name given to the form of oath used in these circumstances.

16 Despite its artificial nature, a magistrates' court may be required to hold a "trial within a trial" to determine admissibility: see *R v Liverpool Juvenile Court, ex parte R* [1988] QB 1; [1987] 2 All ER 668.

17 *Digest of the Law of Evidence* (12th edn), art 1.

inferences can be drawn. As with all questions of admissibility, it is for the trial judge to decide whether or not one fact is capable of being logically probative of a fact in issue and therefore relevant as circumstantial evidence. Whether such inferences are to be drawn from such evidence is, of course, for the tribunal of fact.

Such inferences may arise from events prior to a fact in issue, contemporaneously with it or subsequent to it. Thus, if the speed of a vehicle at a given moment is a fact in issue, evidence may be received of the speed of the vehicle a few moments earlier.[18] Evidence is also admissible of facts which supply a motive for conduct, the existence of which is in issue. Thus familiarity between man and woman may be evidence in support of alleged subsequent adultery; the purchase of poison by a person accused of murder, or the financial standing of a person accused of arson may each be relevant in this way. These are each examples of circumstantial evidence existing prior to the facts in issue.

Circumstantial evidence may exist subsequent to the facts in issue. Thus a promise to marry the mother of an illegitimate child was admitted in *Lloyd v Powell Duffryn Steam Coal Co Ltd*[19] as evidence of the paternity of the child. Similarly an illegitimate child's physical appearance or bloodgroup would be evidence of paternity. Attempts by parties to suborn witnesses to commit perjury,[20] to tamper with evidence[1] or to give a false alibi to the police have all been held to be relevant to issues of guilt or liability.[2] The third class of circumstantial evidence consists of facts contemporaneous with the facts in issue. It is on this basis that the whereabouts of an accused person at the time of the alleged offence is relevant.

Whether such circumstantial inferences can legitimately be drawn from the fact of the use of words is often a difficult question. We have already seen that the hearsay rule often prevents out-of-court statements from being used in evidence. If the fact that a statement is made of itself has probative value, then there is no evidential problem: the statement is relevant and thus admissible. In *Lloyd v Powell Duffryn Steam Coal Co*, LORD ATKINSON stated that it was improbable:

> "that any man would make these statements, true or false, unless he believed himself to be the father of the child."[3]

However, the courts are often reluctant to accept that simply the fact that the words were used has probative value. In *R v Blastland*,[4] the defence in a murder trial sought to call evidence that a third party, M, made statements that indicated knowledge of the murder at a time when such knowledge was not generally available. The fact of such knowledge was not relevant: it could have been acquired in a wide variety of ways, and this was not a case where M's state of mind was in issue. Again, in *R v*

---

18 *Beresford v St Albans Justices* (1905) 22 TLR 1.
19 [1914] AC 733.
20 *Moriarty v London, Chatham and Dover Rail Co* (1870) LR 5 QB 314.
 1 *R v Palmer* (1856) unreported. See Stephen, *History of the Criminal Law*, III, p 389.
 2 *R v Knight* [1966] 1 All ER 647; [1966] 1 WLR 230. It must be shown that the lie told fulfills certain criteria, for a person may have reasons other than guilt to lie.
 3 [1914] AC at 741.
 4 [1986] AC 41; [1985] 2 All ER 1095.

Kearley,[5] the defendant was charged with the supplying of controlled drugs. The fact of telephone calls and visits by persons asking for drugs was not relevant: relevance would only exist if there was reliance upon the truth of the assertion which was implicit in the statement, namely, that the defendant was a dealer in drugs. To rely on the truth of a statement in that way infringes the hearsay rule, and such statements were thus inadmissible.[6]

Evidence that relates to the facts in issue plainly will be relevant. This will include things said or done as part of the events in issue, and are said to form part of the *res gestae*.[7] Usually the matter reaches the court in terms of the admissibility of words accompanying the events in issue. Thus in *Ratten v R*,[8] on a charge of murder by shooting the defence was one of accident. It was held to be relevant evidence to adduce testimony of a telephone operator that he received a telephone call from a woman in an agitated state asking for the police, very shortly before the incident occurred. The very fact that the call was made was relevant, showing a state of mind of fear and agitation, and allowing a circumstantial inference to rebut the defence of accidental shooting. However, the trial has to be kept within bounds. Evidence that is insufficiently relevant will not be admissible, for it takes the court into a multiplicity of issues. Thus in *Agassiz v London Tramway Co*,[9] a statement made shortly after an accident by the conductor to the effect that the driver had already been reported to his employer, had been off the tram line five or six times that day, and was new to the job, was held inadmissible. It was not relevant to the question in issue in the proceedings.

Lawyers tend to refer to relevant evidence as having "probative force". Evidence may have no probative force at all to the facts in issue. By contrast it may have some probative force, but insufficient to outweigh the prejudice it causes to a fair trial. In these circumstances the admissibility of evidence is often regulated by way of judicial discretion. Again, evidence may be relevant, not directly to the facts in issue, but rather to the credit of a witness giving evidence which affects the standing of that witness in the eyes of the court, and thus assists the court in determining the facts in issue themselves. Such matters are said to be relevant to credit, and are caught by a rule of evidence known as the collateral evidence rule,[10] which limits the scope of judicial inquiry into such matters. In other situations, the probative force of evidence may be outweighed by its prejudicial effects.[11]

---

5 [1992] 2 AC 228; [1992] 2 All ER 345
6 See, further, p 619, *post*. Whether or not relevance exists is not always easy to decide. In *Kearley*, of the judges who considered the question, three (the majority in the House of Lords) considered the evidence inadmissible, six (the minority plus the Court of Appeal and trial judge) considered it admissible.
7 This term has various meanings: see Lord Wilberforce in *Ratten v R*, n 8 *infra*, and also p 622, *post*.
8 [1972] AC 378; [1971] 3 All ER 801.
9 (1873) 21 WR 199.
10 See p 586, *post*.
11 This is illustrated by the discretion which exists to regulate the admission of evidence of bad character: see, p 612, *post*.

E ADMISSIBILITY AND DISCRETION

Even in cases where evidence is legally admissible, the law sometimes confers a discretion as to whether, nevertheless, it should be excluded. By discretion, we mean that the court has a choice which is its alone, not to be interfered with on appeal unless the court has exercised its discretion in a manner which is wrong in principle. Discretion must be carefully distinguished from judgment: there are many instances where the admissibility of evidence may depend upon the view the court takes of a certain matter: an example is section 2 of the Sexual Offences (Amendment) Act 1976 which prohibits the asking of questions of the alleged victim of a rape offence about her sexual experience with persons other than the accused. Section 2(2) states that such leave shall not be granted unless the court considers that to refuse to do so would be unfair to the accused. This is a judgment, not a discretion.[12] The court has to form a view as to unfairness, but, if it so concludes, then it has no choice in the matter: it must allow the questions to be put. The significance is that the appeal courts will be more willing to interfere with the exercise of judgment than with that of discretion.

The role of discretion differs widely according to whether the proceedings are civil or criminal. In civil cases the role of discretion is extremely limited, and there has been considerable judicial disagreement as to whether any discretion to exclude exists.[13] The basic rule is that if the evidence is relevant and admissible, it is not for the court to refuse to permit such evidence to be adduced, although it should also be borne in mind that discretion exists as to the extent of discovery of documents ordered, and on what terms.[14]

In criminal cases the role of discretion is far more significant. The existence of a discretion to exclude otherwise admissible evidence in criminal cases has long been accepted, in part to ensure the fairness of the trial, and also to protect the wider rights of an accused. The scope of the discretion extended not only to confessions and other evidence obtained from the accused, but also in relation to evidence which, though admissible, would have prejudicial effect out of proportion to its probative value. For example, in some circumstances evidence of the bad character of an accused is admissible. Nevertheless in many cases there is a danger that the prejudice created is far greater than any probative value it has in the trial. The trial judge therefore has a discretion as to whether, and to what extent, evidence of bad character should be allowed.[15]

The scope of the discretion to exclude was considered by the House of Lords in *R v Sang*.[16] It was held that the fact that the evidence may have been obtained through the use of an *agent provocateur*, or by the incitement of a police officer or informer to commit the crime, did not provide a ground for exclusion. Entrapment was not a defence to a criminal charge. That finding was sufficient in itself to decide the appeal,

---

12 *R v Viola* [1982] 3 All ER 73; [1982] 1 WLR 1138.
13 See *D v National Society for the Prevention of Cruelty to Children* [1978] AC 171; [1977] 1 All ER 589.
14 See p 614, *post*.
15 See p 612, *post*.
16 [1980] AC 402; [1979] 2 All ER 1222.

but the House of Lords went on to consider generally the scope of the discretion in a criminal case. Prior to this case it had always been believed that the court had a general discretion to exclude evidence in a criminal case. The House of Lords now stated that except (i) in cases where the prejudicial effect of evidence outweighed its probative value, and (ii) in respect of admissions, confessions and other evidence obtained from the accused after the commission of the offence, no discretion to exclude evidence existed. Rules of evidence were there to ensure a fair trial, not as a means of disciplining the police. Courts should be concerned generally with how evidence is used, not how it was obtained. The exceptions recognised by *R v Sang* merely preserved the wider principles of protection of the fairness of the trial, and in particular protection of the privilege against self-incrimination and the right to silence.[17]

The discretion to exclude otherwise admissible evidence in criminal cases was re-cast by the Police and Criminal Evidence Act 1984. Section 82(3) preserves the common law rule: any discretion existing by virtue of the decision in *R v Sang* thus remains. However, at a late stage during the passage of the Act, section 78 was introduced. This states:

> "(1) In any proceedings the court may refuse to allow evidence upon which the prosecution proposes to rely to be given if it appears to the court that, having regard to all the circumstances, including the circumstances in which the evidence was obtained, the admission of the evidence would have such an adverse effect on the fairness of the proceedings that the court ought not to admit it.
>
> (2) Nothing in this section shall prejudice any rule of law requiring a court to exclude evidence."

This being a codifying provision, its words are to be given their ordinary and natural meaning.[18] However, the wording of section 78 does not make clear the intended scope of the discretion conferred. Given the terms of section 82(3) it was plainly intended to alter, at least in part, the restrictive decision in *R v Sang*, for otherwise it would have served no useful purpose. In the event, the courts have chosen to use the discretion conferred by section 78 broadly. It applies both to confession and non-confession evidence,[19] and much of the case law has turned upon the use of the discretion to exclude confessions, and the relationship of section 78 to section 76(2), the section that deals with the legal admissibility of confessions. Its use, though, has not been confined to confessions. In *R v Quinn*,[20] LORD LANE CJ stated:

> "The function of the judge is therefore to protect the fairness of the proceedings, and normally proceedings are fair if a jury hears all relevant evidence which either side wishes to place before it, but proceedings may become unfair if, for example, one side is allowed to adduce evidence which, for one reason or another, the other side cannot properly challenge or meet, or where there has been an abuse of process, eg because evidence has been

---

17 See p 595, *post*. the House of Lords rejected any more general discretion to exclude improperly obtained evidence. For the earlier authorities, see Heydon 'Illegally Obtained Evidence' [1973] Crim LR 603, 690.

18 *R v Fulling* [1987] QB 426; [1987] 2 All ER 65. See, further, p 629, *post*.

19 *R v Mason* [1987] 3 All ER 481; [1988] 1 WLR 139.

20 [1990] Crim LR 581.

obtained in deliberate breach of procedures laid down in an official code of practice."

This approach should not be regarded as definitive, but reflects the principle that wrongdoing in the acquisition of evidence may itself create unfairness. To this extent, therefore the traditional focus of the courts upon relevance, and the fairness of the trial, rather than the method of acquisition, may have been modified. Amongst the areas in which it has been used are the exclusion of identification evidence obtained in breach of the Code of Practice,[1] the exclusion of evidence admissible by virtue of section 74,[2] the exclusion of evidence obtained by entrapment,[3] and in certain circumstances the exclusion of real evidence.[4]

---

1 See p 576, *post*.
2 See p 607, *post*.
3 *R v Smurthwaite and Gill* [1994] 1 All ER 898.
4 Where it had been obtained from the accused by unfair means.

CHAPTER 27

The Burden and Standard of Proof

A   INTRODUCTION

The term "burden of proof" describes the obligation of proving a fact or facts. Much consideration has been given to the various senses in which this term can and should be used. In essence the key distinction is between the legal burden of proof and the evidential burden of proof. The legal burden (sometimes called "the persuasive burden") describes upon whom is the duty to satisfy the court on that issue, to the standard of proof the law requires. In any case the allocation of the legal burden depends upon the substantive law: the party upon whom the burden is placed by the substantive law will succeed if that burden is discharged. However, the burden of proof may be allocated between the parties on different issues. The party upon whom it is placed must therefore satisfy the court on that issue to the requisite standard. Thus in a criminal trial for murder the legal burden is upon the prosecution. By contrast the legal burden of proving the defence of insanity is upon the defence. If that burden is discharged the defence succeeds, and the substantive law regards that as a complete answer to a charge of murder. But, even if it fails, conviction can only occur if the prosecution has discharged its burden. To speak of "shifting" burdens of proof is misleading. The question simply is: upon whom is the burden placed on any given question?

In a civil case, similar problems exist. In a negligence case the legal burden is upon the plaintiff: it will be for the plaintiff to establish the constituent elements of the tort, to the requisite standard. If, however, the defendant pleads contributory negligence then the legal burden will, to that extent, be upon the defendant.

By contrast the "evidential burden" describes the duty to adduce some evidence on an issue. The concept has its chief importance in jury trial, for, if the evidential burden is not satisfied, then that issue will not be left to the jury to decide. Often the evidential burden will be on the same party upon whom rests the legal burden. This, though, is not always the case. In a criminal case the legal burden will usually be upon the prosecution. However, if a defendant wishes to raise certain defences, such as provocation, automatism or self-defence, then the evidential burden is upon the defendant. Unless some evidence is adduced then the question will not be left to the jury. This does not alter the fact that the legal burden throughout remains on the prosecution.

In this context the effect of presumptions must be borne in mind. They do not alter the burden of proof, but rather assist in its discharge. This is discussed in more detail later in this Chapter.[1]

B   FACTS WHICH DO NOT HAVE TO BE PROVED

Generally facts must be proved. By whom and to what standard will be returned to. However, there are certain matters which do not require proof in this sense at all. Thus facts which are admitted by a party in civil or criminal cases need not be proved. Similarly English courts take judicial notice of a number of matters with the result that neither party need adduce proof of these matters. Other facts may be presumed. A fact which is presumed in favour of a party need not be proved by that party, although the presumption may depend upon a prior fact being proved. Whether or not the other party may disprove the fact depends upon the classification of the presumption as rebuttable or irrebuttable. Finally, a party may be prevented by estoppel from denying or asserting a fact.

1   Formal admissions

Formal admissions must be distinguished from informal admissions and confessions. Informal admissions (in civil cases) and confessions (in criminal cases) are means of proving the facts admitted or confessed, and are admissible evidence against the maker of the admission or confession. Although they are out of court statements, they are permitted as an exception to the hearsay rule. Thus, if a car driver, following an accident, admits that he was driving on the wrong side of the road and that he failed to give a proper signal, this statement may be put in evidence at the trial as a means of proving the facts stated by the driver. The driver may, however, attempt to explain away his statement at the trial and may produce evidence to contradict its truth. If, on the other hand, the driver in a civil action to which he is a party formally admits he was driving on the wrong side of the road his opponent need not prove that fact at all; it is admitted in his favour. Thus an informal admission is a means of proving the fact admitted whereas a formal admission dispenses with the need for proving that fact.

In criminal cases a plea of guilty is a formal admission of guilt which dispenses with the need for a trial. Short of that, section 10 of the Criminal Justice Act 1967 provides for formal admissions by or on behalf of either prosecution or defence. Such an admission may be made either at or before the trial, but if made other than in court, must be in writing. The admission may be withdrawn at any time, with leave of the court. Once made, it remains an admission for the purpose of any subsequent criminal proceedings, unless, of course, it is withdrawn.

In civil cases rules of court provide for the means by which formal admissions may be made. In the High Court the Rules of the Supreme

---

1 See p 562, *post.*

Court provide for formal admissions at various stages of the proceedings. Thus admissions may be made on the pleadings. An admission on the pleadings may be express or implied, in some circumstances, by a failure to traverse (deny) an allegation. Alternatively an admission may be made in answer to interrogatories or to a notice to admit facts or documents or on the hearing of the summons for directions.[2] Finally admissions may be made during the course of the trial. Counsel or solicitors acting as advocates have a general authority to make admissions binding upon their clients.[3]

2 Judicial notice

There are certain facts of which the court recognises the existence, in civil and criminal cases alike, without the need for proof. Such facts are said to be judicially noticed. The rationale of the principle of judicial notice is that there are matters which are so notorious or well known that it would be pedantic to require proof of them. Certain matters must, by statute, be judicially noticed. These include the authenticity of signatures on certain public or official documents[4] and the contents of every Act of Parliament passed after 1850 unless the contrary is provided by the Act.[5] Apart from these statutory provisions it is impossible to classify satisfactorily the innumerable facts of which the courts take judicial notice. Examples include the fact that a fortnight is an impossibly short period of human gestation,[6] that the value of money has declined since 1189,[7] that the streets of London are full of traffic,[8] and that the reception of television is a common feature of domestic life.[9]

In many cases the court will take judicial notice of a fact without inquiry. Nevertheless in some cases the judge will consult sources to which it is proper to refer before deciding whether to take judicial notice of a particular fact. These sources are examined for reference, rather than as evidence, and it is for this reason that the fact ascertained is regarded as judicially noticed rather than proved. For example, the court takes judicial notice of the meaning of ordinary English words but the judge may still wish to refer to a dictionary.[10] Again, the status of a foreign government, or other facts of a political nature concerning relations with foreign states, will be matters of judicial notice decided

---

2 See pp 358, *ante.*

3 *Swinfen v Lord Chelmsford* (1860) 5 H & N 890.

4 Evidence Act 1845, s 2; Bankruptcy Act 1914, s 142.

5 Interpretation Act 1978, ss 3, 22(1) and Sch 12. By s 3(2) of the European Communities Act 1972: "Judicial notice shall be taken of the Treaties, of the Official Journal of the Communities and of any decision of, or expression of opinion by, the European Court on any such questions as aforesaid; and the Official Journal shall be admissible as evidence of any instrument or other act thereby communicated of any of the Communities or of any Community institution."

6 *R v Luffe* (1807) 8 East 193.

7 *Bryant v Foot* (1868) LR 3 QB 497.

8 *Dennis v AJ White & Co* [1916] 2 KB 1.

9 *Bridlington Relay Ltd v Yorkshire Electricity Board* [1965] Ch 436; [1965] 1 All ER 264.

10 For an example of use of reference works, see *McQuaker v Goddard* [1940] 1 KB 687; [1940] 1 All ER 471 where a judge consulted reference books before deciding that a camel was a domestic animal.

after evidence, often in the form of a certificate, from a Secretary of State.[11] In such cases the dividing line between judicial notice and proof is sometimes a very thin one.

It is sometimes said that the courts take judicial notice of the law of England. This is merely an alternative method of saying that law normally need not be proved. However this principle only extends to English law and, in the House of Lords, to the law of Scotland and Northern Ireland.[12] Foreign law is, paradoxically, a question of fact and must be proved as such although it is a question of fact to be decided by the judge not by the jury.[13]

Closely related to judicial notice are matters within the personal knowledge of the court or jury. A judge, or magistrate, may rely upon personal knowledge relevant to a fact in issue, provided it does not go beyond what is common or local knowledge.[14] It would not be proper to draw on specialised or specific knowledge not generally known. Nor should a jury supplement the evidence in a case with its own personal knowledge of the matters in issue.[15]

3   Presumptions

In certain circumstances the court presumes a fact in favour of a party who is thereby relieved of the burden of proving it. In a few of these instances the law provides that the party against whom the fact is presumed cannot deny its existence. The presumption is then said to be irrebuttable. However, in most cases the presumption is rebuttable. Consequently the effect of a presumption is to satisfy the evidential burden in respect of such matters.

Certain presumptions define where the burden of proof shall lie, either generally or on a specific issue: the presumption of innocence and the presumption of sanity are examples. Thus in a criminal case the legal burden of proving guilt is upon the prosecution but of insanity, upon the defence. So too with the presumption that a child is legitimate: it will be for the party seeking to establish illegitimacy to prove that.

In some circumstances the presumption is irrebuttable: in reality these are not really presumptions but are rather rules of substantive law couched in presumptive terms. For example section 50 of the Children and Young Persons Act 1933[16] provides that "it shall be conclusively presumed that no child under the age of ten years can be guilty of any offence". Since the presumption is irrebuttable it is really a rule of law to the effect that a child under the age of ten cannot commit a crime.

More usually, presumptions are rebuttable. A rebuttable presumption of law is a rule of law compelling the court to infer the existence of the fact presumed. The direct presumptions of innocence and sanity mentioned

---

11 *Duff Development Co Ltd v Government of Kelantan* [1924] AC 797.
12 *Rockware Glass Ltd v MacShannon* [1978] AC 795; sub nom *MacShannon v Rockware Glass Ltd* [1978] 1 All ER 625.
13 Administration of Justice Act 1920, s 15; Supreme Court Act 1981, s 69(5). European Community law cannot for this purpose be regarded as foreign law, and such questions are decided by either domestic courts or the Court of Justice: see p 113, *ante*.
14 *Reynolds v Llanelly Associated Tinplate Co* [1948] 1 All ER 140; *Keane v Mount Vernon Colliery Co Ltd* [1933] AC 309.
15 *R v Rosser* (1836) 7 C & P 648.
16 As amended by the Children and Young Persons Act 1963.

above are rebuttable presumptions of law. Most rebuttable presumptions of law, however, depend upon a basic fact being proved. Examples include the presumption of legitimacy, the presumption of death from seven years' absence unheard of,[17] the presumption that a document proved or purporting to be not less than 20-years old and produced from proper custody has been duly executed,[18] the presumption that alterations to a deed have been made before execution and that alterations to a will have been made after execution,[19] and the equitable presumption that property purchased by a parent in his child's name constitutes a gift rather than the creation of a trust.[20] The presumption that official acts have been duly performed[1] (*omnia praesumuntur rite esse acta*) is particularly important. It has even been used to support the legality of a police officer's action and thus justify upholding a conviction for an assault on a police officer acting within the execution of his duty.[2] In all of these cases the court is bound, on proof of the basic fact, to give effect to the presumption and infer the existence of the fact presumed. The effect of this is to cast the burden of disproving the existence of the fact presumed upon the party against whom the presumption is raised.

The last category of presumptions are those of fact. Presumptions of fact are merely specific and frequently recurring instances of the operation of circumstantial evidence. The nature of circumstantial evidence is that it consists of facts from which other facts may be presumed to exist. The basic difference between a presumption of fact and a presumption of law is that in the case of the former there is no rule of law which compels the court to apply the presumption whereas in the latter case the court not only may, but must, apply the presumption. The variety of presumptions of fact is infinite.[3]

4   Presumptions and the burden of proof

A difficult question is whether rebuttable presumptions affect only the onus of proof or whether they are of some evidential weight in themselves. It will be appreciated that a presumption which is of no weight in itself, but which merely determines the onus of proof, ceases to have any effect when evidence one way or the other has been adduced because the court will then decide upon the evidence (unless it finds the evidence so finely balanced that it is not satisfied either way, in which event the party on whom the burden of proof lies will fail). This

---

17 *Chard v Chard* [1956] P 259; [1955] 3 All ER 721.
18 Evidence Act 1938, s 4.
19 *Doe d Tatum v Catomore* (1851) 16 QB 745.
20 This is termed the "presumption of advancement": *Shephard v Cartwright* [1955] AC 431; [1954] 3 All ER 649. It applies also to purchases made by a husband in his wife's name though it is nowadays easily rebutted.
1 There are innumerable variations of this presumption; examples include: that a marriage has been duly celebrated; that a licence has been duly granted; that a public officer has been duly appointed; that a public seal is authentic.
2 *Cooper v Rowlands* [1971] RTR 291. For a recent example, see *Bugg v Director of Public Prosecutions* [1993] QB 473; [1993] 2 All ER 815 where a presumption of validity of a byelaw was made on a prosecution under that byelaw.
3 In effect, they are particular examples of circumstancial inferences being drawn.

point was clearly made by LORD REID[4] when explaining the effect of the presumption of legitimacy:

> ". . . the presumption of legitimacy now merely determines the onus of proof. Once evidence has been led it must be weighed without using the presumption as a make-weight in the scale for legitimacy. So even weak evidence against legitimacy must prevail if there is not other evidence to counterbalance it. The presumption will only come in at that stage in the very rare case of the evidence being so evenly balanced that the court is unable to reach a decision on it. I cannot recollect ever having seen or heard a case of any kind where the court could not reach a decision on the evidence before it."

Despite this, REES J in *T (H) v T (E)*,[5] while expressly applying LORD REID's dictum, founded his decision on the presumption, being unable to accept the evidence of either the husband or the wife as constituting proof even on a balance of probabilities; accordingly the presumption of legitimacy prevailed. In *Stupple v Royal Insurance Co Ltd*[6] the Court of Appeal was called upon to consider the effect in a civil case of a conviction admissible by virtue of section 11 of the Civil Evidence Act 1968.[7] This section creates a presumption that a person has in fact committed an offence of which that person has previously been convicted. The court failed to lay down any principle as to whether the conviction merely operated to shift the onus of proof on to the party denying the correctness of the conviction or whether the conviction was of weight in itself. LORD DENNING MR and BUCKLEY LJ disagreed as to whether the conviction carried weight. In *Hunter v Chief Constable of West Midlands Police*,[8] LORD DENNING went further and expressed the view that a party to civil proceedings could only rebut the presumption raised by the conviction by proving that the conviction was obtained by fraud or collusion or by obtaining fresh evidence. Although the House of Lords expressly disagreed with this statement,[9] LORD DIPLOCK (with whom all the other law lords agreed) evidently accepted that the conviction was in itself of evidential weight, since he explained:[10]

> "section 11 makes the conviction *prima facie* evidence that the person convicted did commit the offence of which he was found guilty, but does not make it conclusive evidence; the defendant is permitted by the Act to prove the contrary if he can . . . The burden of proof of 'the contrary' that lies on a defendant under s 11 is the ordinary burden in a civil action, ie proof on a balance of probabilities, although in the face of a conviction after a full hearing this is likely to be an uphill task."

5 Estoppel

Estoppel is a rule of evidence whereby a party to a civil case is prohibited from asserting or denying a fact. Estoppels may arise in three ways, by record, by deed or by conduct. Whenever it does arise it has the effect of

---

4 *S v S, W v Official Solicitor (or W)* [1972] AC 24 at 41, [1970] 3 All ER 107 at 109.
5 [1971] 1 All ER 590; [1971] 1 WLR 429.
6 [1971] 1 QB 50; [1970] 3 All ER 230.
7 See p 608, *post.*
8 [1980] QB 283; [1980] 2 All ER 227.
9 [1982] AC 529; [1981] 3 All ER 727.
10 [1982] AC, at 544; [1981] 3 All ER, at 735–736.

rendering relevant facts inadmissible. Estoppel has sometimes been described as a rule of substantive law rather than a rule of evidence.[11] Indeed, it may have the effect of a rule of substantive law where it prevents a party from asserting or denying a fact in issue since it operates in such a case to create a right against the party estopped, by preventing him from denying that right. Nevertheless estoppel is a rule of evidence rather than a rule of substantive law, even though it may affect substantive rights and so have the same effect as a rule of law. Thus a party may waive an estoppel in his favour and, in any event, estoppel cannot be used as a cause of action but only as a defence.[12] It is also occasionally stated that estoppel is a rule of procedure or pleading. The reason for this proposition is that an estoppel must be expressly pleaded.[13] This is an exception to the general rule that evidence need not be pleaded. Failure to plead an estoppel may operate as a waiver of the benefit of the estoppel. Nevertheless it does not follow that estoppel is a rule of pleading merely because it must be expressly pleaded. The Limitation Acts must be expressly pleaded but these cannot be said to be rules of pleading. It is best to classify estoppel as a rule of evidence to which special rules of procedure apply.

Estoppel in criminal cases is restricted to the pleas of *autrefois acquit* and *autrefois convict*, which have already been discussed.[14]

C THE BURDEN OF PROOF

1 Civil cases

In civil cases the burden of proof generally in the case is upon the plaintiff. It is the plaintiff who has the burden of proving every fact alleged, but in practice many of these facts will be admitted by the defendant in which case they need not be proved.

The burden of proof on specific issues in civil cases depends upon substantive law and, where they exist, upon the pleadings.Thus the plaintiff must prove every fact which is an essential element in the cause of action. In addition the plaintiff must prove any positive allegation to rebut a defence or to show an exception to the defence pleaded. In terms of the pleadings the plaintiff must prove every fact in his statement of claim (unless, of course, the fact in question is judicially noticed, admitted or presumed in the plaintiff's favour) and every positive allegation in the reply served. Thus in a libel action the plaintiff must prove publication and, if the defendant pleads qualified privilege, malice. Similarly in an action for breach of contract where the defence of frustration is pleaded the plaintiff must prove a breach of contract and also negligence if that is alleged to negative the defence of frustration.[15] The defendant has the burden of proving any particular defence which he raises. If his defence to an

---

11 See, eg, the observations of LORD WRIGHT in *Canada and Dominion Sugar Co Ltd v Canadian National (West Indies) Steamships Ltd* [1947] AC 46 at 56.

12 *Coombe v Coombe* [1951] 2 KB 215; [1951] 1 All ER 767.

13 RSC, Ord 18, r 7(1).

14 See p 492, *ante*. For the the fact that issue estoppel has no place in criminal proceedings, see *Director of Public Prosecutions v Humphrys* [1977] AC 1; [1976] 2 All ER 497.

15 *Joseph Constantine Steamship Line Ltd v Imperial Smelting Corporation Ltd* [1942] AC 154; [1941] 2 All ER 165.

allegation made by the plaintiff is a mere traverse (denial) the effect is simply to put that fact in issue leaving the burden of proving that fact upon the plaintiff. If, however, the defendant raises positive allegations by way of defence, or confesses and avoids one of the plaintiff's allegations, then the burden is upon the defendant to prove the fact alleged or matter in avoidance. Thus if the defendant in a libel action merely denies publication no particular burden of proof is assumed by the defendant. However, if qualified privilege, justification, fair comment or unintentional defamation are pleaded, the burden of proving these positive allegations is upon the defendant. It follows that in civil cases the particular burdens on particular issues may be distributed between the parties. The burden of proof in the case as a whole remains on the plaintiff.

The burden of proof on a particular matter cannot be avoided by stating an allegation in negative rather than positive form. Thus in an action for malicious prosecution it is for the plaintiff to allege and prove that the defendant had no reasonable and probable cause for the prosecution.[16] Similarly, where the statutory defence of unintentional defamation is raised it is for the defendant to show absence of malice.[17] It follows that a party gains no advantage by couching a positive allegation in negative terms. Thus whether a landlord alleges that the tenant "did not repair" the premises in question or whether he alleges that the tenant "let the house become dilapidated" the burden of proving this fact is upon the landlord.[18]

Finally, where the admissibility of evidence is in issue the party who alleges that an item of evidence is admissible bears the burden of proving this fact. For example, a party who wishes to put in secondary evidence of a private document must account for the absence of the original; a party seeking to prove a dying declaration must prove that the declarant is dead, together with the other conditions of admissibility of such declarations.[19]

2   Criminal cases

In criminal proceedings the effect of the presumption of innocence is that the burden of proving guilt is upon the prosecution. In furtherance of this the prosecution must prove every element of the crime charged. This includes (subject to the exceptions noted below) the burden of disproving all defences of which there is some evidence. In *Woolmington v Director of Public Prosecutions*[20] the accused, charged with murdering his wife, claimed that the killing was an accident. The trial judge in his summing-up directed the jury that if the Crown proved that the accused killed the deceased the burden rested on the accused to prove provocation or accident. The conviction was quashed in the House of

---

16 *Abrath v North Eastern Rail Co* (1883) 11 QBD 440.
17 Defamation Act 1952, s 4.
18 *Soward v Leggatt* (1836) 7 C & P 613.
19 See p 631, *post*.
20 [1935] AC 462; *cf R v Bone* [1968] 2 All ER 644; [1968] 1 WLR 983 in which the defendant's conviction was quashed because of the trial judge's failure to direct that, in

Lords because of this misdirection. In the hallowed words of LORD
SANKEY LC:

> ". . . throughout the web of the English criminal law one golden thread is
> always to be seen, that it is the duty of the prosecution to prove the
> prisoner's guilt, subject to . . . the defence of insanity and subject also to any
> statutory exception."[1]

Nevertheless a legal burden is sometimes cast on the defence in criminal
cases. Basically there are few situations in which a legal (as opposed to an
evidential) burden of proof is on the defence:

(1) The burden of proving a special plea in bar is upon the accused.
Thus, if it is claimed that the accused has been previously
acquitted on the same charge, then the doctrine of *autrefois acquit*
will apply. The burden of proof on this point will be on the
accused.

(2) The burden of proving insanity is on the defence where this issue is
raised at the instance of the defence. This may be seen as the
effect of the presumption of sanity.[2] Similarly the burden of
proving diminished responsibility[3] or unfitness to plead[4] is upon
the accused where either of these issues is raised at the instance of
the defence.[5]

(3) Several statutory provisions impose a specific burden upon the
defence. The statutory defence of diminished responsibility has
already been mentioned. To this may be added certain statutes
which impose a burden on the accused only after the prosecution
has proved particular facts. For example, section 5(2) of the Road
Traffic Act 1988 provides that, on a prosecution for being in
charge of a motor vehicle on a road or other public place having
consumed alcohol in such a quantity that the proportion thereof in
his breath, blood or urine exceeds the prescribed limit, a person
shall not be convicted if he proves that there was no likelihood of
his driving it whilst the proportion of alcohol in his breath, blood
or urine remained likely to exceed the prescribed limit. Another
example is section 1 of the Prevention of Crime Act 1953, which
imposes the burden of proving lawful authority or reasonable
excuse for the possession of an offensive weapon upon the
accused.

(4) Section 102 of the Magistrates' Courts Act 1980 provides that, on
summary trial, where an enactment makes the commission of a
particular act an offence subject to a proviso, exception, excuse or
qualification, the burden of proving that the case falls within such

---

relation to the defence of duress, it was for the prosecution to disprove that defence rather
than for the defendant to prove it.

1 [1935] AC at 481.
2 *M'Naughton's* case (1843) 10 Cl & Fin 200.
3 Homicide Act 1957, s 2(2); *R v Dunbar* [1958] 1 QB 1; [1957] 2 All ER 737.
4 *R v Podola* [1960] 1 QB 325; [1959] 3 All ER 418.
5 Where insanity, diminished responsibility or unfitness to plead is raised at the instance of
the prosecution the burden of proof is presumably on the prosecution. Section 6 of the
Criminal Procedure (Insanity) Act 1964 permits the prosecution to allege insanity where
the accused raises the issue of diminished responsibility and *vice versa*.

proviso, exception, excuse or limitation is upon the defendant. In relation to proceedings on indictment, it was for some time thought that the rule was different.[6] However, in *R v Edwards*[7] the Court of Appeal dispelled any such notion by holding that section 102 did no more than set out the common law rule in statutory form. The approach of the Court of Appeal was confirmed as correct by the House of Lords in *R v Hunt*.[8] It was in each case a question of the construction of the relevant statutory provision, and in that process the court was entitled to have regard to the question as to which party would find it easier or more difficult to discharge the burden of proof. Thus on the facts, it was the prosecution who should have the burden of proof of the composition of substances seized as prohibited drugs, since only it was in a position to discharge that burden by analysis of the substances.

In addition to the exceptional circumstances listed above in which a legal burden is imposed upon the defence, there are many cases, not capable of classification, in which an evidential burden is cast upon the defence. These arise principally where the burden is upon the prosecution of disproving a possible defence. Thus in a case such as *Woolmington v Director of Public Prosecutions*, although the legal burden of disproving provocation or accident is upon the prosecution, there is a burden upon the defence to adduce some evidence in support of these defences if such evidence has not been given during the course of the prosecution case. This is a common-sense rule, for otherwise the prosecution would be faced with the intolerable task of disproving every conceivable defence, no matter how fanciful.

D   THE STANDARD OF PROOF

1   The two standards of proof

Once it is determined upon whom the burden of proof rests the question arises as to what standard of proof that party must satisfy in order to discharge that burden. If that burden is merely an evidential burden the question of standard of proof does not really arise since the burden is discharged merely by adducing credible evidence. Where the burden is a legal burden, the traditional view is that there are two alternative standards of proof: proof beyond reasonable doubt, which is the appropriate standard in criminal cases, and proof on a balance of probabilities, which is the standard in civil cases. This, though, is an oversimplification, overlooking the fact that even in civil cases the standard of proof may vary according to the nature of the matter to be proved: where an allegation is of a grave or serious nature, then the courts will require a higher standard of proof. Indeed, the standard of proof may vary even within the same

---

6 *R v Turner* (1816) 5 M & S 206; *cf John v Humphreys* [1955] 1 All ER 793; [1955] 1 WLR 325.

7 [1975] QB 27; [1974] 2 All ER 1085.

8 [1987] AC 352; [1987] 1 All ER 1. For discussion of the problems raised by this case, see Birch 'Hunting the Snark – The Elusive Statutory Exception' [1988] Crim LR 221; *cf* Mirfield 'An Ungrateful Reply' [1988] Crim LR 233.

case. In *R v Wolverhampton Coroner, ex parte McCurbin*,[9] an inquest had to decide whether the death of an individual whilst being arrested by the police amounted to unlawful killing by the police, or death by misadventure. In upholding the direction to the jury given by the coroner, the Divisional Court concluded that the standard of proof necessary to establish unlawful killing was the criminal standard of beyond reasonable doubt, whilst that for establishing death by misadventure was the civil standard of the balance of probabilities. Whether there are in fact two standards at all, or rather different levels of proof which vary according to what has to be proved is a moot point, but the Divisional Court was at pains to stress that such matters should not be approached in an artificial manner.

2   The standard of proof in civil cases

The standard of proof applicable in civil cases is proof on the balance of probabilities. However, as has been noted, the standard to be applied will vary according to the nature of what has to be proved. Authorities have shown that allegations of crime or other similar serious allegations have to be proved to the criminal standard of beyond reasonable doubt.[10] There are dicta to suggest this is not the right approach: in *Bater v Bater*,[11] DENNING J observed that a civil court:

> "does not adopt so high a degree as a criminal court, even when it is considering a charge of a criminal nature."

However, findings of suicide, and of unlawful killing in inquests have each been held to require proof beyond reasonable doubt.[12] In *Halford v Brooks*,[13] a civil case where the allegation against the defendant was, in effect, one of murder, ROUGIER J observed:

> "No-one, whether in a criminal or a civil court, should be declared guilty of murder, certainly not such a terrible crime as this, unless the tribunal was sure that the evidence does not admit of any other sensible conclusion . . ."

It should be noted that in the rare case where a judge is unable to say which version of events is to be preferred, then the claim will fail for the defendant will have failed to discharge the burden of proof.

---

9 [1990] 2 All ER 759; [1990] 1 WLR 719.

10 See *Hornal v Neuberger Products Ltd* [1957] 1 QB 247; [1956] 3 All ER 970. In *Khawaja v Secretary of State for the Home Department* [1984] AC 74; [1983] 1 All ER 765 LORD SCARMAN indicated that the criminal standard was appropriate to habeas corpus proceedings, where the liberty of the individual was at stake. The distinction was largely "a matter of words".

11 [1951] P 35, at 37; [1950] 2 All ER 458, at 459; approved in *Hornal v Neuberger Products, Ltd* [1957] 1 QB 247; [1956] 3 All ER 970, and in *Blyth v Blyth* [1966] AC 643; [1966] 1 All ER 524.

12 *R v West London Coroner, ex parte Gray* [1988] QB 467; [1987] 2 All ER 129.

13 (1991) Times, 3 October. The approach taken in *Bater v Bater* (n 11, *supra*) was said to be unhelpful.

3   The standard of proof in criminal cases

Proof beyond reasonable doubt is generally described as the criminal standard of proof. However, it is the standard of proof only where the burden of proof is upon the prosecution.[14] In the few cases in which the burden of proving a fact is upon the defence in a criminal case, the appropriate standard of proof is proof on a balance of probabilities – the civil standard.[15]

The words "beyond reasonable doubt" have been subjected to considerable judicial analysis. In *Miller v Minister of Pensions*,[16] DENNING J observed that:

> "proof beyond reasonable doubt does not mean proof beyond the shadow of a doubt . . . If the evidence is so strong against a man as to leave only a remote possibility in his favour, which can be dismissed with the sentence 'of course, it is possible but not in the least probable' the case is proved beyond reasonable doubt, but nothing short of that will suffice."

Several attempts have been made to change this hallowed formula "beyond reasonable doubt". LORD GODDARD CJ in *R v Summers*[17] deprecated those words and suggested that an appropriate direction to the jury might be that they should "feel sure" that the accused is guilty. In *R v Hepworth and Fearnley*[18] he reiterated this, suggesting, as a further alternative, "completely satisfied". Today, the most common direction to the jury is in the following (or very similar) terms: "Before you can convict the defendant you must be satisfied so that you are sure of his guilt." It is clear, though, that it is not the particular formula that matters, but the effect of the summing-up.

E   CORROBORATION

As a general rule, English law does not require evidence to be confirmed by other evidence. It is permissible for a court to rely on one piece of evidence alone, though often it would be extremely unwise to do so. The existence of several pieces of evidence supporting the same fact greatly increases the weight that can be attached to that piece of evidence, and allows it to be safely relied upon. Nevertheless, there are circumstances in which supporting evidence is required as a matter of law, or highly desirable as a matter of practice. That supporting evidence is known as corroboration.

In *Director of Public Prosecutions v Kilbourne*,[19] LORD REID stressed that the idea of corroboration was not a technical one. He said:

---

14 *R v Carr-Briant* [1943] KB 607; [1943] 2 All ER 156.
15 Once the issue placed on the defence is proved, the prosecution is required to prove its case to the full standard.
16 [1947] 2 All ER 372.
17 [1952] 1 All ER 1059.
18 [1955] 2 QB 600; [1955] 2 All ER 918. Whichever of these formulations is adopted, an appellate court will not interfere (*Walters v R* [1969] 2 AC 26) although expressions such as "reasonably sure" and "pretty sure" have been disapproved by the Court of Appeal; *cf R v Head and Warrener* (1961) 45 Cr App Rep 225.
19 [1973] AC 729; [1973] 1 All ER 440.

"When in the ordinary affairs of life one is doubtful whether or not to believe a particular statement one naturally looks to see whether it fits in with other statements or circumstances relating to the particular matter; the better it fits in the more inclined one is to believe it."

Whilst the idea of corroboration may be non-technical, the same cannot be said of the doctrine as developed by the courts. It has become highly technical and artificial, with strict rules as to when it is required, and what can amount to corroborative evidence. The current state of the law is regarded by many as unsatisfactory, with the Law Commission calling for the abolition of the doctrine in criminal cases.[20] This abolition is proposed by the Criminal Justice and Public Order Bill currently before Parliament.[1]

1   Corroboration as a matter of law

There are a few instances where the existence of corroboration is required as a matter of law. These include offences of speeding based on the opinion evidence of a witness as to the speed a vehicle was travelling;[2] offences of perjury,[3] where the evidence of one witness as to the falsity of a statement must be corroborated; and various offences of procuration of women under the Sexual Offences Act 1956, where a person is not to be convicted on the evidence of one witness only.[4]

2   Corroboration as a matter of practice

Far more important than the statutory rules set out above are the cases where corroboration is required as a matter of practice. This statement is misleading. What the law in fact requires is that the trial judge direct the jury that it is dangerous to convict the accused in the absence of corroboration. The reasons for this have to be explained, what can in law constitute corroboration must be defined, and the evidence that is capable of corroborating must be identified. Failure to direct a jury in this way will nearly always result in a conviction being quashed.[5] Provided the jury are properly directed in this way, however, it may decide that the evidence is such as to justify a conviction even in the absence of corroboration, although an appellate court might on occasion quash such a conviction as being unsafe or unsatisfactory.[6]

This corroboration requirement applies in two classes of case: the evidence of accomplices, and the evidence of complainants of sexual offences. The reasons for the requirement in those two classes of case were summarised by LORD ACKNER in *R v Spencer and Smails*:[7]

---

20 *Corroboration of Evidence in Criminal Trials* (Law Commission Report 202, HMSO 1991 Cm 1620). For comment on the Working Paper proposals, see Birch 'Corroboration in Criminal Trials' [1990] Crim LR 667.
1 *Cf* the recommendations of the Royal Commission on Criminal Justice, Cm 2263, HMSO, (1993) paras 65–76.
2 Road Traffic Regulation Act 1984, s 89.
3 Perjury Act 1911, s 13.
4 Sexual Offences Act 1956, ss 2, 3, 4, 22 and 23.
5 See generally Cross, *op cit*, at pp 255–257.
6 See *ante*, p 517.
7 [1987] AC 128; [1986] 2 All ER 928.

> ". . . in the . . . categories where the "full warning" is obligatory, the inherent unreliability of the witness would not be apparent to the jury . . . Complainants of sexual assaults do on occasion give false evidence for a variety of reasons, some of which may not have occurred to a jury. Accomplices may have hidden reasons for lying, and again this probability may not be apparent to the jury."

However, the fact is that while these dangers may exist in some cases, they do not inevitably exist in all, or even the majority. Conversely, there are many situations falling outside the two categories where equally there may be hidden dangers or motives for lying.[8] The law does not distinguish between cases within the categories where the dangers do exist, and those where they do not.

Accomplices were defined by LORD SIMONDS LC in *Davies v Director of Public Prosecutions*,[9] as follows:

(1) participants in the crime alleged, whatever the degree of participation;
(2) receivers of stolen goods in relation to those who are alleged to have stolen those goods;[10]
(3) parties to another crime alleged to have been committed by the accused and in respect of which "similar fact evidence" would be admissible.[11]

The facts of the *Davies* case were that the accused was charged with murder by stabbing the deceased, a member of a rival gang. The witness whose testimony was in question was a member of the same gang as the accused and had joined in an assault on the deceased. However, he had not been a party to the stabbing, and was not aware the accused had a knife. It was held that the witness was not an accomplice, so that the rule requiring the corroboration direction did not apply. LORD SIMONDS also indicated that it is only where an accomplice is giving evidence for the prosecution that the rule applies: a person indicted jointly with the accused and giving evidence against him is not to be regarded as an accomplice. Nevertheless, it has been held that the trial judge should, as a matter of discretion, consider giving the jury a similar warning in respect of the evidence of a co-accused.[12]

There has been a general trend against extending the formal requirement for a corroboration direction.[13] Firstly, the courts have declined to extend the doctrine beyond the established categories. Corroboration in the technical sense is not required in identification cases,[14] those involving dying declarations,[15] or the testimony of compulsory

---

8 See, p 575, *post.*
9 [1954] AC 378; [1954] 1 All ER 507.
10 Receiving stolen goods now has been replaced by the offence of handling stolen goods: Theft Act 1968, s 12. It is uncertain whether the converse applies: ie whether a thief of goods is an accomplice on the trial of the handler. See *R v Crane* (1912) 7 Cr App Rep 113; *R v Vernon* [1962] Crim LR 35.
11 See p 600, *post.*
12 There is no mandatory requirement; see *R v Cheema* [1994] 1 All ER 639.
13 For the reasons for this, see LORD ACKNER in *R v Spencer and Smails* (*infra,* n 16).
14 *R v Turnbull* [1977] QB 224; [1976] 3 All ER 549. See p 575, *post.*
15 *Nembhard v R* [1982] 1 All ER 183; [1981] 1 WLR 1515.

mental patients.[16] Despite concerns about the dangers of confession evidence, the courts have not sought to adopt a rule requiring the corroboration of confession evidence.[17] Indeed, such an extension of the doctrine was rejected by the Royal Commission on Criminal Justice in 1993.[18] However, the Royal Commission recommended that juries be warned of the need for great care in convicting on the basis of confession evidence alone, tailored to the circumstances of the individual case.[19] A jury might be directed to look for supporting evidence, as is currently the case in identification cases.[20]

Secondly, the courts have sought to confine the doctrine, even within the established categories. Thus, in *R v Chance*[1] the Court of Appeal ruled that no corroboration direction was required in a case of intruder rape where the only issue before the court was one of identification.

Finally, in accepting that there may be other groups of witnesses whose testimony is inherently suspect appellate courts have rejected the extension of the corroboration categories. Instead, they have left in the hands of the trial judge a discretion as to how to proceed with caution where a witness has a purpose of his own to serve.[2]

3 The definition of corroboration

For evidence to be used as corroboration, it must be admissible evidence that satisfies the test propounded by LORD ALVERSTONE in *R v Baskerville*:[3] it must be independent of the witness to be corroborated, it must implicate the accused, and do so in respect of the material particulars of the offence.

(a) The requirement of independence rules out as corroboration evidence from the witness to be corroborated. Thus in a sexual case, the recent complaint of the alleged victim will not be corroborative, no matter how cogent it might seem, because it is not independent of that witness.[4] Whether in such cases distress can corroborate will depend upon the circumstances. The courts will reject, as not independent, distress that is in reality part and parcel of the complaint.[5] If, however, it is deemed to be genuine, and in circumstances where the witness is unaware of being observed and thus unlikely to fabricate, then the courts have been prepared to treat that distress as independent.[6] In addition, the courts have taken the view that if the witness has knowledge not generally

---

16 *R v Spencer and Smails* [1987] AC 128; [1986] 2 All ER 928.
17 *Cf R v McKenzie* [1993] 1 WLR 453.
18 Report, paras 85–87.
19 para 87.
20 See p 575, *post*.
 1 [1988] QB 932; [1988] 3 All ER 225.
 2 *R v Prater* [1960] 2 QB 464; [1960] 1 All ER 298. This will include the evidence of a co-defendant who is not an accomplice: *R v Cheema* [1994] 1 All ER 639.
 3 [1916] 2 KB 658; [1916–17] All ER Rep 38.
 4 *R v Whitehead* [1929] 1 KB 99; [1928] All ER Rep 186. In that case, LORD HEWART CJ observed that if the position were otherwise "it is only necessary for her to repeat her story some twenty five times in order to get twenty five corroborations of it."
 5 *R v Redpath* (1962) 46 Cr App Rep 319; *R v Knight* [1966] 1 All ER 647; [1966] 1 WLR 230.
 6 See, eg *R v Chauhan* (1981) 73 Cr App Rep 232.

available, and which supports his testimony, then that "esoteric" knowledge ought to be able in law to amount to corroboration.[7]

(b) The evidence must implicate the accused. For example, on a charge of rape evidence may support the fact that sexual activity took place. That will not be enough: there will be a need to implicate the accused.[8] Frequently, whether it does so implicate will depend upon circumstantial inference from the corroborative testimony.

(c) The corroborative evidence must implicate the accused in the material particulars of the offence. Thus, again to use the offence of rape as an example, not only must the evidence confirm the fact of sexual relations, and that they were with the accused, but in addition it must confirm that such relations were without the consent of the woman.[9]

Corroborative evidence can come from a wide variety of sources, including the accused himself. An admission can corroborate whether in whole or in part. The fact that the accused gives a false alibi, runs away or lies (whether before or after the trial) can corroborate. In these circumstances, however, the lie must be demonstrated as such by a witness other than that to be corroborated, and the court must be satisfied that the reason for lying was out of a realisation of guilt and a desire to avoid conviction.[10] Silence can never corroborate, unless that silence amounts to an acceptance of an allegation put to him.[11] A refusal to give an intimate sample of blood, urine or other body fluid can corroborate.[12]

4   Cases where supporting evidence is required

It has already been seen that the courts have declined to extend the formal doctrine requiring a warning, and a search for *Baskerville* corroboration. Nevertheless there are several situations where the law expects there to be supporting evidence.

a   Section 77 of the Police and Criminal Evidence Act 1984

The need for mentally handicapped persons to be questioned in the presence of an independent adult has already been discussed. Where a confession was in fact obtained in the absence of such a person, then if the case against that person depends wholly or substantially upon that confession, the judge has to warn the jury of the special need for caution before convicting on the strength of that confession. Since a confession obtained in the absence of an appropriate adult is likely to be excluded under section 78 in any event,[13] the main effect of this requirement will be

---

7 *R v Nagy* [1990] Crim LR 187; *cf R v Willoughby* (1988) 88 Cr App Rep 91.

8 *James v R* (1970) 55 Cr App Rep 299.

9 *Cf R v Bailey* [1993] Crim LR 860, where a contrary view appears to have been taken, allowing evidence to corroborate which supported the credibility of the witness.

10 *R v Lucas* [1981] QB 720. These criteria apply whenever lies are used to support an inference of guilt: *R v Goodway* [1993] 4 All ER 894; *R v Richens* [1993] 4 All ER 877.

11 See *R v Chandler* [1976] 3 All ER 105; [1976] 1 WLR 585; *cf Hall v R* [1971] 1 All ER 322; [1971] 1 WLR 298.

12 Police and Criminal Evidence Act 1984, s 62(10).

13 See p 629, *post.*

in respect of confessions made during urgent interviews, which may be conducted in the absence of such an appropriate adult.[14]

Even if a confession made by a mental handicapped person is admitted, there may be, because of its contents, grounds to consider it suspect. In these circumstances if the case depends wholly upon that confession, which is not supported by other evidence, the trial judge should withdraw the case from the jury.[15]

b   Suspect witnesses

A body of authority has arisen in respect of suspect evidence falling outside the established categories of evidence requiring corroboration. In these cases the judge should warn the jury of the special need for caution in assessing the reliability of the testimony of such witnesses. In *R v Beck*[16] the witness, a director of a finance company, was not technically an accomplice but nevertheless had a purpose of his own to serve. The court held that the trial judge was right to give only a warning to proceed with great caution, not the full corroboration direction. Another example is *R v Lovell*,[17] where there were self-evident dangers in the testimony given by a witness against members of a family with whom there was a long standing feud.

The form of the warning in such a case is not always clear. In *R v Spencer and Smails*[18] the House of Lords stated that although it could often be convenient to use the words "danger" or "dangerous", the use of such words was not essential to an adequate warning, provided the jury were made fully aware of the dangers of convicting on such evidence.

c   Identification evidence

The dangers of reliance upon identification evidence are well known. A series of wrongful convictions led to the establishment of the Devlin Committee[19] to investigate how the law dealt with identification evidence. A specific corroboration requirement was rejected, but the Committee recommended that the trial judge should direct the jury not to convict on the testimony of an eye witness alone, unless the case was exceptional or the identification was supported by substantial other evidence. No legislation followed, but the Court of Appeal in *R v Turnbull*[20] laid down certain guidelines. The court rejected a rule prohibiting conviction on identification evidence alone, and focussed on the nature of the identification. Where the identification could be split into categories of good and poor quality identifications, the following guidelines were set:

(1)   In all cases where the case depends wholly or substantially upon the correctness of an identification the judge should direct the jury to proceed with special caution.

---

14 See *R v Moss* (1990) 91 Cr App Rep 371.
15 *R v McKenzie (Practice Note)* [1993] 1 WLR 453.
16 [1982] 1 All ER 807; [1982] 1 WLR 461.
17 [1990] Crim LR 111.
18 [1987] AC 128; [1986] 2 All ER 928.
19 *Report of the Departmental Committee on Evidence of Identification* (HMSO, Cmnd 338, 1976).
20 [1977] QB 224; [1976] 3 All ER 549

(2) The circumstances of the identification should be carefully considered. Where the quality of the identification is good, for example, made in good conditions of light, weather and with ample
opportunity to observe, then the case can safely be left to the jury
with the general warning. Where, however, the identification is of
poor quality (because for example of poor visibility or a fleeting
glance) then the case should be withdrawn from the jury unless
there is supporting evidence.

(3) The supporting evidence does not have to be corroboration in the
technical sense.

(4) The judge must identify for the jury the evidence capable of
supporting the identification. Whether or not it does so is of course
a matter for the jury.

Certain points should be noted. Recognition may be stronger than an
initial identification, but even recognition cases fall within the principles in
R v Turnbull, which was itself a recognition case.[1] Secondly, it only applies
to identification of humans. Identification of objects such as motor cars
appears not to be within the rule, though the possibilities of error remain
high.[2] Thirdly, note the procedures that have to be adopted in respect of
identification, under the Code of Practice.[3] Lastly, there is no difference in
principle between an identification resulting from a witness seeing a person
or incident, and a witness seeing the same person or thing on film or video
tape. In each case the witness is using his particular knowledge of a person
to identify him. In such cases the *Turnbull* guidelines apply.[4]

---

1 See also *R v Bowden* [1993] Crim LR 380; *cf R v Courtnell* [1990] Crim LR 115. The need
  for care was stressed in *R v Caldwell and Dixon* (1993) Times, 8 June.
2 *R v Browning* (1991) 94 Cr App Rep 109.
3 See p 273, *ante*.
4 *Taylor v Chief Constable of Cheshire* [1987] 1 All ER 225; [1986] 1 WLR 1479.

CHAPTER 28

The Means of Proof

Having decided what facts may be proved, upon whom the onus of proving those facts lies and the nature of this burden the question arises as to how these facts are to be proved. Assuming that the fact in question is not admitted, judicially noticed or presumed in favour of the party who would otherwise have to prove it there are three ways in which a fact may be proved: (1) by the testimony of witnesses; (2) by documentary evidence; (3) by "real" evidence. Each of these means of proof is considered below.

A WITNESSES

1 Competence and compellability

The general rule is that all persons are both competent and compellable as witnesses in judicial proceedings. This is so even if a statement or "proof of evidence" has been taken from that witness by an opposing party. Likewise, even if an expert has been retained by one party that does not prevent the expert being called by the other party. There is no property in a witness.[1]

The attendance of witnesses in magistrates' courts is compelled by summons or warrant.[2] Failure to comply with a summons entitles the court to issue an arrest warrant. A refusal without just excuse to give evidence is punishable by imprisonment or a fine. In criminal trials at the Crown Court attendance is compelled by witness order or witness summons – failure to comply with either of which is punishable as a contempt of the trial court, and a warrant of arrest may be issued.[3] Attendance in the High Court is compelled by subpoena; again, failure to comply is a contempt of court. In

---

1 *Harmony Shipping Co SA v Davis* [1979] 3 All ER 177; [1979] 1 WLR 1380: in that case a handwriting expert retained by the plaintiffs inadvertently gave advice to the defendants concerning the same documents. It was held that the defendants could compel him to give evidence. The principle applies equally in criminal cases. Thus in *R v King* [1983] 1 All ER 929; [1983] 1 WLR 411 the Crown subpoenaed a handwriting expert retained by the defence and obtained from him documents sent by the defendant which included a document which was highly prejudicial to the defence case. For the extent of protection of legal professional privilege, see p 596, *post*.
2 Magistrates' Courts Act 1980, s 97.
3 Criminal Procedure (Attendance of Witnesses) Act 1965, p 471, *ante*.

civil cases the court can neither compel a party to call any witness nor call a witness itself. In criminal proceedings and in proceedings for contempt of court,[4] however, the court may, of its own volition, call any witness without the consent of the parties.

As a general rule, if a witness cannot give coherent evidence then the witness may be discharged. In *R v Baines*[5] the judge exercised his discretion to adjourn proceedings over the weekend because the witness was too affected by drugs to comprehend the proceedings. If a witness who has been sworn appears to be of unsound mind or too incoherent or incapable of communication to make sense the judge may rule the witness incompetent.[6]

There are several exceptions to the general rule, stated above, that all persons are both competent and compellable as witnesses. The most important of these exceptions are set out below. It is important to note that compellability of a witness is a separate matter from any privilege which that witness may validly claim. Thus a witness does not cease to be compellable merely because he may claim privilege from answering any specific question or for the contents of a document.

a   Children

If a child is competent then that child is also compellable as a witness. Until recently, competence was determined by deciding whether the child had sufficient understanding to give sworn evidence. The test to be applied was stated as follows by BRIDGE LJ in *R v Hayes*:[7]

> ". . . [whether] the child has a sufficient appreciation of the solemnity of the occasion and the added responsibility to tell the truth, which is involved in taking an oath, over and above the duty to tell the truth which is an ordinary duty of normal social conduct."

If a child failed to satisfy this test in civil proceedings, then the child was not a competent witness. The impact of that is mitigated by more relaxed rules of hearsay permitting the child's out of court statement to be relied upon.[8] By contrast, the power existed in criminal proceedings to permit the unsworn testimony of a child to be heard.[9]

As a result of widespread concern about the way children's evidence was dealt with,[10] particularly where the child is the victim of abuse, changes were made to the rules governing the competence of children in criminal cases. Section 52 of the Criminal Justice Act 1991 states that the evidence of a child under fourteen years of age shall be given unsworn. A child is henceforth to be treated like any other witness: the court may in any given instance rule that the child is not competent. The criteria for this will be applicable to child and adult alike:[11] it must be clear to the court that some

---

4 *Yianni v Yianni* [1966] 1 All ER 231n; [1966] 1 WLR 120.
5 [1987] Crim LR 508.
6 *R v Whitehead* (1866) LR 1 CCR 33.
7 (1976) 64 Cr App Rep 82.
8 See the Children (Admissibility of Hearsay Evidence) Order 1991.
9 Children and Young Persons Act 1933, s 38. It was by no means clear in which respects this test differed from that for sworn testimony. It was in essence a question of degree.
10 See *Report of the Advisory Group on Video Evidence* (Home Office 1989) (the "Pigot Report").
11 Criminal Justice Act 1991, s 52.

coherent evidence can be given by the child.[12] The weight to be given to that evidence will depend upon the youth and maturity of the child.[13]

The law makes special provision for children who are competent to give evidence. Even if the child does give evidence, protection can be given by allowing the child to give evidence from behind screen, so as to avoid the scrutiny of the accused.[14] Alternatively, in cases involving offences of violence, or sexual offences, then a child may give evidence through a live television link.[15] The reason for the introduction of this power was the desire to minimise the effect the proceedings may have on the child witness in alleged child abuse cases. The power also applies to cases where an adult is outside the United Kingdom.[16] The use of such a link is subject to the leave of the court being granted. The 1991 Act also extends the range of circumstances in which the out-of-court statement of a child can be used.[17] In particular, it allows a video recording of an interview held with a child to be shown in evidence, with leave of the court. If such a video is shown, what the child says is evidence which can be used to prove the truth of the facts that the child speaks of, and thus this constitutes an exception to the hearsay rule. Leave will be granted unless (a) it appears to the court that the child witness will not be available for cross-examination, (b) rules of court requiring disclosure of the circumstances in which the recording was made have not been complied with to the satisfaction of the court, (c) the court is of the opinion that, in the interests of justice, the recording ought not to be admitted.[18]

In considering whether or not leave should be granted, the court must consider whether any prejudice to the accused which might result is outweighed by the desirability of showing the whole, or substantially the whole, of the video. This power applies to youth courts, or to Crown Courts, but not to proceedings in the magistrates' court.[19] The video will need to be considered in the light of the Memorandum of Good Practice adopted in relation to such matters by the Home Office.[20]

Section 103 of the Magistrates' Courts Act 1980 renders the statement of a child admissible in certain committal proceedings. This is subject to various exceptions, particularly where the defence objects, or where the prosecution requires attendance in order to establish identity. In addition, section 55 of the Criminal Justice Act 1991 allows in these cases the Director of Public Prosecutions to serve a notice of transfer, which results in the case going automatically to the Crown Court.[1]

---

12 See p 578, *ante*.
13 There is no minimum age below which a child cannot give evidence. The view expressed by LORD GODDARD CJ in *R v Wallwork* (1958) 42 Cr App Rep 153 that it was to be hoped that five-year-old children should not be called to give evidence was rejected by the Court of Appeal in *R v Z* [1990] 2 QB 355; [1990] 2 All ER 971. However, the younger the child the greater the need for caution.
14 *R v X, Y and Z* (1989) 91 Cr App Rep 36.
15 Criminal Justice Act 1988, s 32(1)(b).
16 *Ibid*.
17 Criminal Justice Act 1991, s 54, incoporating a new s 32A into the Criminal Justice Act 1988.
18 *Ibid*, s 32A(3).
19 *Ibid*, s 32A(1).
20 Home Office (HMSO, 1992).
 1 See p 471, *ante*.

b   Mentally handicapped persons

Persons of unsound mind who are not capable of understanding the oath and giving rational testimony are not competent witnesses. The test is whether the witness understands the nature of the oath.[2] In *R v Bellamy*,[3] the Court of Appeal held that the test to be applied was the same as that relating to children. An awareness of the divine sanction of the oath was unnecessary.[4] Medical evidence may be called to show that a witness suffers from some disease which affects the reliability of his evidence.[5]

c   Accused persons in criminal cases

An accused person is not a competent witness for the prosecution,[6] although the prosecution may rely on testimony given by the witness in his own defence. If the prosecution wishes to call to give evidence a person who is a participant in the offence, that person must not be an accused person in the same proceedings.[7] This can be achieved in various ways. The prosecution can simply elect not to charge a participant. Alternatively, even if that person has been jointly charged various mechanisms exist: the proceedings can be prevented from continuing by the Attorney-General entering a *nolle prosequi*,[8] by the person being formally acquitted (no evidence having been offered), by the severance of the indictment so that the person is separately tried,[9] or by that person pleading guilty.[10] Once that person ceases to be an accused, he is both competent and compellable. He remains, however, an accomplice, and the corroboration requirements still apply.[11]

Since 1898, an accused person has been a competent witness in his own defence, but the principle against self-incrimination means that he is not compellable.[12] Nor may the prosecution comment upon failure to give evidence,[13] though the judge may do so. The direction that is generally appropriate was set out by PARKER CJ in *R v Bathurst*:[14]

> "The accused is not bound to give evidence, that he can sit back and see if the prosecution have proved their case, and that, while the jury have been deprived of the opportunity of hearing his story tested in cross-examination, the one thing they must not do is to assume he is guilty because he has not gone into the witness box."

---

2 See p 578, *ante*.

3 (1985) 82 Cr App Rep 222.

4 See *R v Hayes* [1977] 2 All ER 288; [1977] 1 WLR 234.

2 *Toohey v Metropolitan Police Commissioner* [1965] AC 595; [1965] 1 All ER 506.

3 *R v Rhodes* [1899] 1 QB 77.

4 An accomplice who is to be tried separately should not generally be called as a prosecution witness unless the prosecution undertake to discontinue the proceedings against him: *R v Pipe* (1966) 51 Cr App Rep 17.

8 See p 439, *ante*.

9 See p 476, *ante*.

10 *R v Tomey* (1909) 2 Cr App Rep 329.

11 See p 570, *ante*.

12 Criminal Evidence Act 1898, s 1(a). This rule is preserved by the Criminal Justice and Public Order Bill.

13 *R v Rhodes* [1899] 1 QB 77.

14 [1968] 2 QB 99; [1968] 1 All ER 1175. See also: *R v Sparrow* [1973] 2 All ER 129; [1973] 1 WLR 488.

d Spouses

At common law spouses were incompetent to give evidence either for or against each other, in both civil and criminal cases. The position has been significantly amended by statute.

In civil cases the Evidence (Amendment) Act 1853 removed the common law restriction completely: spouses are both competent and compellable. By contrast in criminal cases special rules apply. These were significantly altered by section 80 of the Police and Criminal Evidence Act 1984, which sought to strike a balance between preserving the relationship of marriage on the one hand, and ensuring credible evidence is put before the court on the other. The rules can be stated as follows:

(a) Unless the spouse is jointly charged with the accused for the same offence,[15] that spouse is competent for the prosecution.
(b) The spouse is competent for the defence of the accused, or a co-accused, irrespective of whether the spouse is jointly charged.
(c) The spouse is compellable for the accused, unless jointly charged with the same offence.
(d) The spouse is compellable for the prosecution only in limited circumstances. These are:

   (i) where the offence charged involves an assault on, or injury or threat of injury to, the spouse or a person at the time of the offence under the age of 16 years;
   (ii) a sexual offence alleged to have been committed against a person under the age of 16 years;
   (iii) an offence of attempting, conspiring, aiding or abetting, counselling or inciting such an offence.

It should be noted that where the spouse is competent but not compellable the trial judge should inform the witness of the right not to give evidence, and that by taking the oath the witness is waiving the right not to give evidence.[16] Once sworn the witness may be treated as hostile, if the rules relating to hostility apply.

e Miscellaneous

The Sovereign is not a compellable witness; nor are foreign sovereigns, ambassadors, High Commissioners and various grades of diplomatic staff. In any legal proceedings to which a bank is not a party, a bank or bank officer cannot be compelled either to produce any bankers' book the contents of which can be proved by secondary evidence, or to prove any matter therein recorded.[17] In civil cases the court has a residual power to set aside a *subpoena* (which of course means that a witness is not compellable) if the court considers that it would be oppressive to compel a person to give evidence.[18]

---

15 The language of the section contemplates one charge. It does not make clear the approach to be adopted where the indictment comprises more than one charge, not all of which fall within the criteria set out in s 80.
16 *R v Pitt* [1983] QB 25; [1982] 3 All ER 63.
17 Bankers Books Evidence Act 1879, s 6.
18 *Morgan v Morgan* [1977] Fam 122; [1977] 2 All ER 515.

2 Oaths and affirmations

a Oaths

The general rule is that all witnesses must give evidence on oath. Any person having authority to hear evidence has power to administer an oath[19] but the oath is generally administered by the clerk of the court or other court official. The usual form of oath runs as follows:

> "I swear by Almighty God that the evidence which I shall give shall be the truth, the whole truth, and nothing but the truth."

The witness holds the New Testament, or in the case of Jews the Old Testament, in his uplifted hand.[20] This form of oath is appropriate only to members of the Christian and Jewish faiths. Any person who objects to taking the usual oath may take any other form of oath, according to his religious beliefs, which he declares to be binding on his conscience. The form of oath for use in youth courts and by children and young persons in other courts begins with the words "I promise before Almighty God" instead of "I swear by Almighty God that . . .".[1]

b Affirmations

As an alternative to an oath any person who objects to being sworn is permitted to "make his solemn affirmation" instead of taking an oath. This substitutes the words "I (name) do solemnly, sincerely and truly declare and affirm" for "I swear by Almighty God that . . .".[2] A witness is also permitted to affirm if it is not reasonably practicable without inconvenience or delay to administer the form of oath appropriate to the witness's religious beliefs (for example, because the book on which the witness wishes to swear is not available).[3] An affirmation is not unsworn testimony: it is equivalent to an oath and a false statement on affirmation amounts to perjury.[4]

3 The examination of witnesses

Two basic rules exist in relation to the giving of testimony by a witness. The first is that the testimony should be given orally. There are, however, numerous exceptions to this rule.[5] Oral testimony will generally be given in open court. The law, however, permits exceptions to this where it is essential for the administration of justice, or where statute specifically authorises.[6] In addition, it has already been seen that in some situations a child may give evidence from behind screens, or through a live television link.[7]

---

19 Evidence Act 1851, s 16.
20 Oaths Act 1978, s 1.
 1 Children and Young Persons Act 1963, s 28.
 2 Oaths Act 1978, s 6.
 3 *Ibid*, s 5(2).
 4 *Ibid*, s 5(4); Perjury Act 1911, s 15(2) (as amended).
 5 See pp 632, 635, *post*.
 6 See p 635, *post*.
 7 Criminal Justice Act 1988, s 32. See p 579, *ante*.

The second basic rule relating to the testimony of witnesses is that it must be confined to facts which the witness personally perceived. This rule operates to exclude opinions and hearsay as means of proof. The exceptions to this rule are discussed below.[8] Where a witness does give evidence at a trial, there are three stages to his examination: examination in chief, cross-examination, and re-examination. The two later stages need not always take place, and re-examination is, by definition, only possible where there has been cross-examination.

a Examination-in-chief

This is the first stage in the examination of a witness, and is carried out by the party calling the witness, generally through solicitor or counsel. There are a number of rules that must be observed. Leading questions must not be asked. A leading question is a question framed in such a way as to suggest the answer desired. "Did you then see the accused attack the deceased?" is an extreme example. It is sometimes said that any question that can be answered with a simple "Yes" or "No" is a leading question. This is often, though not invariably, true. Leading questions are often permitted on formal matters, such as name, address and occupation, and it is permissible for a party to lead a witness with the concurrence of the other parties and the court. It follows from the prohibition on leading questions that a party cannot cross-examine his own witness. No doubt counsel is frequently annoyed by the failure of a witness to give the answer desired, particularly if the witness has given the desired answer in a deposition or proof of evidence. Nevertheless the answers of a witness who does not "come up to proof" have to be accepted,[9] although there is nothing to prevent that party calling other witnesses, whose testimony may, of course, contradict that of the witness who has failed to "come up to proof".

A witness cannot be questioned by the party calling him upon a previous inconsistent statement. There is, however, one important exception to this rule; where the judge gives leave to treat a witness as "hostile" the party calling the witness may cross-examine him upon his previous inconsistent statement.[10] A witness is "hostile" if that witness is not desirous of telling the truth at the instance of the party calling him.[11] Some hostility or animosity is called for: it is not enough that the evidence is unfavourable to the party calling the witness. If a witness is hostile then, at common law, he may be asked leading questions by the party calling him and, under section 3 of the Criminal Procedure Act 1865, previous inconsistent statements may be put to him. In criminal cases this statement is not evidence of the truth of its contents, and serves only to weaken or destroy the credit of the witness.[12] However, in civil proceedings the statement, and any other statement adduced to rebut that statement, is admissible to the extent to which direct oral evidence by the maker would be admissible.[13] It should

---

8 See p 622, *post.*

9 *Ewer v Ambrose* (1825) 3 B & C 746.

10 This right stems from common law: *Clarke v Saffery* (1824) Ry & M 126. Most commonly now it arises pursuant to Criminal Procedure Act 1865, s 3, which applies in both criminal and civil proceedings.

11 *Ewer v Ambrose* (1825) 3 B & C 746.

12 *R v White* (1922) 17 Cr App Rep 60.

13 Civil Evidence Act 1968, s 2. See p 636, *post.*

be noted that the leave of the judge is required before a witness is treated as hostile. In practice it may well be the case that a witness is first given the opportunity to "refresh memory" from an earlier statement.[14] If a witness is hostile, then the weight to be given to the testimony of the witness is for the jury or magistrates: the reality is that in most cases the effect will be to destroy the credibility of the witness.[15]

In the light of these rules it might logically be supposed that in a criminal cases if a witness manifested his hostility by simply refusing to give any evidence at all, it would not be permissible to put his previous statement to him since, firstly, it cannot be evidence of the truth of its contents and, secondly, it cannot contradict evidence where none has been given. Section 3 of the Criminal Procedure Act 1865 would therefore not apply. Nonetheless, in *R v Thompson*[16] the Court of Appeal permitted this very course. The defendant was charged with incest with his daughter. She, when called by the prosecution, answered some preliminary questions but then indicated that she would not give evidence against her father. Thereupon prosecuting counsel successfully applied to put to her the statement that she had made previously to the police, the court relying on its common law power to declare a witness hostile and permit leading questions. It will be appreciated that if (as happened in *Thompson*) the witness admits authorship of the statement and confirms the truth of its contents, then the contents become part of the witness's evidence and the effect of the hostile witness's recalcitrance is nullified. If the witness had denied the statement it is doubtful if this could then have been put to her, since section 3 of the 1865 Act did not apply.

A witness may refresh memory from a statement before the witness gives evidence. Even during the giving of evidence the witness may be given an opportunity to refresh memory from such a statement made nearer the time of the events. In *R v Da Silva*[17] the court stated that the judge must be satisfied that the witness cannot otherwise recall the events, that the statement was made nearer the time of the events in question and represents the witness's recollection, that the witness has not read it before going into the witness box, and also wishes to consult the document. In these circumstances the judge might allow a witness to interrupt testimony for this purpose.

If, however, the witness wishes to refresh memory throughout his evidence, the document must be "contemporaneous". The cases have interpreted this phrase broadly: the document must have been brought into existence at a time when the events were still fresh in the mind of the witness,[18] although refreshing memory from a suitably authenticated copy of such a document will suffice.[19] This will often, say, allow police officers

---

14 See *infra*.

15 In *R v Pestano* [1981] Crim LR 397, the prosecution sought to rely on the truth of part of what a hostile witness said. The Court of Appeal ruled that whether weight was to be given to any part of the testimony was a matter for the jury, having been properly directed as to the dangers.

16 (1976) 64 Cr App Rep 96.

17 [1990] 1 All ER 29; [1990] 1 WLR 31.

18 *R v Richardson* [1971] 2 QB 484; [1971] 2 All ER 773.

19 *R v Cheng* (1976) 63 Cr App Rep 20. Athough it was held in *A-G's Reference (No 3 of 1979)* (1979) 69 Cr App Rep 411 that the copy had to be made at a time when the events recorded were still fresh in the mind, in *R v Chisnell* [1992] Crim LR 507 police officers

to refresh memories from their pocketbooks. If a document is used for memory-refreshing purposes, then in a criminal case it will not be evidence of the truth of its contents. This would infringe the hearsay rule. However, in civil proceedings any statement made in a document by a person who uses that document to refresh memory is admissible as evidence of any fact stated therein of which direct oral evidence would be admissible.[20]

Generally speaking, a previous consistent statement by a witness is not admissible. Such statements are self-serving, and in relation to their contents would infringe the hearsay rule. There are, however, exceptions. In criminal cases, evidence of the recent complaint of the victim of a sexual offence is admissible to show consistency and to negative consent.[1] In addition, in civil cases section 2 of the Civil Evidence Act 1968 allows a previous statement to be admissible as evidence of its truth. Generally, however, this can only be given in evidence after the witness has given evidence-in-chief:[2] thus the main use of such statement will be to bolster the evidence of a witness who has been cross-examined upon, for example, a previous inconsistent statement.

b Cross-examination

Following examination-in-chief the witness may be cross-examined by or on behalf of the opposing party or parties. Cross-examination may comprise a far wider range of questions than examination-in-chief. In addition, leading questions may be put to the witness. There are three possible lines of cross-examination. First, a witness may be cross-examined as to the facts in issue. The object of this line of questioning is to establish information concerning the facts in issue that is favourable to the cross-examining party. The object of the two remaining lines of questioning is to discredit the witness. This is achieved by cross-examination as to credit or credibility. It is also the duty of the advocate to "put" to the witness the facts or case which it is alleged differ from that being stated by the witness. This is so that the witness may have an opportunity to comment or respond to such differences or allegations.

A witness (other than an accused in a criminal case) may generally be asked any questions to show that the witness is a person who ought not to be believed. Questioning may extend to matters such as the witness's character, previous convictions, and general reputation. Likewise, questions that affect a witness's credibility are permissible, and will usually be directed at some physical or mental attribute. Thus questions to impeach credibility may relate to such matters as the witness's hearing, memory or eyesight.

Normally, any question relevant to issue will be allowed. Exceptions to this arise in the case of certain questions dealing with the interception of

---

were allowed to refresh their memory from notes transcribed many months earlier when the events were still fresh in the mind.

20 Civil Evidence Act 1968, s 3.

1 *R v Lillyman* [1896] 2 QB 167. If the witness does not give evidence, then there is, of course, no testimony to be consistent with and the out-of-court statement would not be admissible unless one of the exceptions to the hearsay rule applied: *R v Wright* (1987) 90 Cr App Rep 91.

2 See p 636, *post*.

telephone conversations,[3] and (to the extent to which information can be required to be disclosed) journalistic sources,[4] and matters affected by privilege or public interest immunity.[5] By contrast, the law imposes limits on questioning affecting credit or credibility. In *R v Sweet-Escott*[6] LAWTON J stated the general test thus:

> "Since the purpose of cross-examination as to credit is to show that the witness ought not to be believed on oath, the matters about which he is questioned must relate to his likely standing after cross-examination with the tribunal which is trying him or listening to his evidence."

In *Hobbs v Tinling & Co*[7] the court indicated how the discretion to restrict questioning should be used:

> "The court can always exercise its discretion to decide whether a question as to credit is one which the witness should be compelled to answer . . . In the exercise of its discretion the court should have regard to the following considerations: (1) Such questions are proper if they are of such a nature that the truth of the imputation conveyed by them would seriously affect the opinion of the court as to the credibility of the witness on the matter to which he testifies; (2) Such questions are improper if the imputation which they convey relates to matters so remote in time, or of such a character, that the truth of the imputation would not affect, or would affect in a slight degree, the opinion of the court as to the credibility of the witness on the matter to which he testifies; (3) Such questions are improper if there is a great disproportion between the importance of the imputation made against the witness's character and the importance of his evidence."

In addition, in cases of rape there are special limitations upon what questions may be asked of a complainant. Section 2 of the Sexual Offences (Amendment) Act 1976 provides that questions relating to the sexual experience of the complainant with a person other than the defendant shall only be asked with leave of the court. Such leave will only be granted if it would be unfair to the accused not to allow such questions. This provision has been used to prevent such questioning unless it goes to facts in issue.[8]

Even where questions relating to credit or credibility are allowed, the law needs to restrict the ambit of the trial, and prevent a multiplicity of issues arising. In relation to such matters the collateral evidence rule applies: the answers of the witness to such matters are regarded as final, and cannot be rebutted.[9] Thus in *A-G v Hitchcock*[10] the defendant was not permitted to adduce evidence to rebut a prosecution witness's denial that he had been offered a bribe. Whether questions relate to credit, and thus are within the ambit of the collateral evidence rule is not always easy to

---

3 Interception of Communications Act 1985, s 9. For interpretation of this, see *R v Preston* (1992) 95 Cr App Rep 355, CA; [1993] 4 All ER 638, HL; *R v Effick* (1992) 95 Cr App Rep 427.
4 Contempt of Court Act 1981, s 10. See p 598, *post*.
5 See p 614, *post*.
6 (1971) 55 Cr App Rep 316.
7 [1929] 2 QB 1; [1929] All ER Rep 33.
8 See *R v Viola* [1982] 3 All ER 73; [1982] 1 WLR 1138. Leave may also be granted pursuant to section 2 in respect of matters that affect the witness's credit. What is not permissible is to ask question designed to create the inference: "well, members of the jury, that's the kind of girl she is": *per* MAY J in *R v Lawrence* [1977] Crim LR 492.
9 *Harris v Tippett* (1811) 2 Camp 637.
10 (1847) 1 Exch 91.

decide. In *A-G v Hitchcock* PARKE B suggested that a matter went to issue if the party asking the question could have adduced evidence on that matter as part of his own case, a test that is unhelpful, since it raises the question as to what evidence a party can adduce as part of his case. The decision as to credit or issue should reflect what is fair in the instant case, and not be the subject of over-refined analysis.[11]

Even where a question is caught by the collateral evidence rule, there are four exceptions which can potentially apply. Firstly, if a witness denies that he has a previous conviction, that conviction may be proved.[12] Secondly, if the witness denies making a previous inconsistent statement, that statement may be put to him, to rebut his denial.[13] Thirdly, if the witness denies an allegation of bias, then that bias may be proved by other evidence.[14] Fourthly, if the witness denies having a general reputation for untruthfulness, or denies certain medical matters which affect credibility, such denials may be rebutted.[15]

Difficulties have arisen especially in cases involving allegations of police misconduct. In some situations a police officer may be cross-examined about other cases in which he has given evidence. In *R v Thorne*[16] the trial judge refused to allow defence counsel to cross-examine a police officer about verdicts of acquittal which had been returned in other cases in which a witness in the instant case, an informer, had testified. The Court of Appeal upheld this decision, because those acquittals were not evidence of bias against the defendants in the instant case, nor did they establish a general reputation for untruthfulness, nor indeed prove that the witness had lied in the earlier cases. Previous acquittal shows no more than that a jury was not satisfied beyond reasonable doubt. However, in *R v Edwards*[17] the Court of Appeal ruled that if the fact of acquittal inevitably meant that the jury had rejected as untrue the evidence of a prosecution witness, then that was a matter about which the witness could be cross-examined. In such a case any denials of the witness could not be rebutted, since they were matters affecting credit and thus caught by the collateral evidence rule unless one of the exceptions applied.

It was for a time considered that a fifth exception to the collateral evidence rule existed, namely allegations of police misconduct. However, that was rejected by the Court of Appeal in *R v Edwards*. Whilst this distinction between issue and credit is clearly drawn by the courts, it is more difficult to apply and is often blurred. This was seen in *R v Busby*[18] where questions as to alleged police fabrication went to the very heart of the case. In this case police officers were cross-examined to the effect that they had fabricated a confession, and threatened a potential defence witness to prevent him giving evidence. The decision by the trial judge to prohibit rebuttal of their denials, by virtue of the collateral evidence rule, was regarded as wrong by the Court of Appeal, which quashed the

---

11 *Per* HENRY J in *R v Funderburk* [1990] 2 All ER 482; [1990] 1 WLR 587.
12 Criminal Procedure Act 1865, s 6.
13 *Ibid*, s 4.
14 *A-G v Hitchcock* (n 10, *supra*).
15 *Toohey v Metropolitan Police Commissioner* [1965] AC 595; [1965] 1 All ER 506.
16 (1977) 66 Cr App Rep 6.
17 [1991] 2 All ER 266; [1991] 1 WLR 207.
18 (1981) 75 Cr App Rep 79.

conviction. Such matters were relevant to an issue to be tried, because such matters, if true, showed that the police would go to any lengths to secure a conviction. However, in *R v Edwards* the Court of Appeal indicated that *Busby* was to be regarded as a case falling under the bias exception to the rule.

The distinction between issue and credit is particularly difficult to draw in sexual cases, involving questions of consent, where the view of the court on the issues may be determined by the assessment of the credibility of the various parties. This was vividly demonstrated in *R v Funderburk*[19] where the charge was one of unlawful sexual intercourse. A key feature in the case was the vivid testimony of the 13-year-old complainant, which was said by the prosecution to describe the alleged offence with the accused. By contrast the defence argued that her vivid descriptions in fact related to the complainant's sexual relations with another man, and wished to call evidence in rebuttal of her denials. This was not permitted by the trial judge, and the accused was convicted. On appeal, the conviction was quashed, the court considering that these matters went to the very heart of the case, namely, whether she had sexual relations with the accused.

c   Re-examination

Following cross-examination a witness may be re-examined by the party calling him. The object of re-examination is to reinstate any part of the witness's testimony which has been shaken in cross-examination. As in examination-in-chief leading questions may not be asked. Furthermore, a party cannot use re-examination as an opportunity for raising matters which he omitted to raise in examination-in-chief unless the form of the cross-examination necessitates this.

B   DOCUMENTARY AND REAL EVIDENCE

1   Documentary evidence

It has already been seen that this is one method of proof. The best evidence rule presupposes that the document itself should be produced, though the rule is increasingly of little importance with a wide variety of exceptions. The chief objection to documentary evidence will often be the hearsay rule. This, and its exceptions, are dealt with below.[20]

Where documents are the product of a mechanical process, then often no hearsay problem arises. Even so, in relation to computer evidence there will need to be evidence to show that the computer and its programs were properly functioning.[1] There are provisions that permit this to be done by certificate,[2] but these are not the only method of proof. In *R v Shephard*[3] the question arose as to how the reliability of a computer record of the cash tills of a department store could be proved for purposes of section 69 of the Police and Criminal Evidence Act 1984. The House of Lords concluded

---

19 [1990] 2 All ER 482; [1990] 1 WLR 587.
20 See p 622, *post*.
1 Police and Criminal Evidence Act 1984, s 69; Civil Evidence Act 1968, s 5.
2 See the Police and Criminal Evidence Act 1984, Sch 3.
3 [1993] AC 380; [1993] 1 All ER 225.

that the evidence of a store detective that she was familiar with the operation of the store's computer and that it was working properly, with no evidence of malfunction, was sufficient to prove the requirements set out in section 69.

Even if evidence is otherwise admissible, the doctrine of privilege or public interest immunity may prevent such evidence being adduced. Usually it is in respect of documents that the doctrine applies, particularly when discovery is sought in civil cases. However, the doctrine applies equally to criminal proceedings, to prevent otherwise relevant and necessary documentary evidence from being adduced. It can also apply to information to be given in evidence by a witness.[4]

2   Real evidence

The nature of this has already been seen.[5]

C   OPINION EVIDENCE

It has already been noted[6] that the general rule is that a witness may testify only as to facts which he has directly perceived. He may not state a belief in facts which is based on anything but direct perception. This is the rule excluding proof by opinion. The rationale of this rule is that it is the function of the court, not of the witnesses, to draw conclusions from the facts proved.[7] The function of witnesses, and indeed of any method of proof, is simply to place those facts before the court.

However, there are exceptions to this basic rule. If a person's opinion is, in itself, a relevant fact there is no rule excluding proof of that opinion. There are also situations when the opinions of witnesses, whether "ordinary" witnesses or "expert" witnesses, are admissible.

1   The opinions of ordinary witnesses

For the reasons explained above, it is not the task of an ordinary witness to pass opinions on facts. However, where a fact to which the witness's testimony relates is incapable of precise perception by an ordinary witness, the witness may relate his belief based on impression. His impression amounts, in reality, to an opinion as to the fact in question. Thus opinion evidence is admissible on matters such as the speed of vehicles,[8] the value of common objects,[9] the identification of handwriting known by the witness,[10] the identification of a person or an object[11] or a person's age. Age is not usually proved by opinion because direct evidence such as a

---

4 See p 614, *post*.
5 See p 551, *ante*.
6 See p 552, *ante*.
7 See *North Cheshire and Manchester Brewery Co v Manchester Brewery Co* [1899] AC 83.
8 Though, as a safeguard, a person cannot be convicted of speeding on the uncorroborated opinion of one witness as to his speed: Road Traffic Regulation Act 1984, s 89.
9 *R v Beckett* (1913) 8 Cr App Rep 204.
10 *R v Silverlock* [1894] 2 QB 766.
11 *Fryer v Gathercole* (1849) 4 Exch 262.

birth certificate is generally available. Indeed where precise age is a fact in issue, as for example where infancy is raised as a defence to an action based on contract, age cannot be proved by opinion.[12]

We must, however, distinguish between impression and inference. The former is permissible, the latter not, for it is for the court to decide what inferences can, and should, be drawn from the facts found to exist. Thus whilst a witness may give evidence as to his impression of the speed of a vehicle, a witness cannot give evidence that the vehicle was being driven negligently. For the same reason questions of sanity and insanity are not matters upon which an ordinary (as opposed to an expert) witness may testify,[13] although, of course, a witness may give evidence of facts upon which a conclusion on such matters may be based. Sanity is a question of mixed law and fact and, insofar as it is a question of fact, it depends upon inferences of fact rather than upon direct perception or impression. Drunkenness, on the other hand, is solely a question of fact. It is uncertain whether it is an inference of fact or a fact in itself capable of perception. If drunkenness is an inference of fact, logic would suggest that an ordinary witness should not be permitted to testify that a person appeared to be drunk so that his testimony should be confined to his perception of direct facts such as unsteady gait, incoherent speech or alcoholic breath leaving the court to draw the inference of drunkenness from these facts. Nevertheless, in practice, there is no doubt that an ordinary witness is sometimes permitted to give his opinion to the effect that a person was drunk.

This distinction between perception and inference is one acknowledged by statute. Section 3(2) of the Civil Evidence Act 1972 states:

> "It is hereby declared that where a person is called as a witness in any civil proceedings, a statement of opinion by him on any relevant matter on which he is not qualified to give expert evidence, if made as a way of conveying relevant facts personally perceived by him, is admissible as evidence of what he perceived."

This would appear simply to restate the common law.

2   The opinions of expert witnesses

Where a court recognises a witness as an expert witness, the court may allow the witness to give evidence of his opinion within the area of his expertise. This may include opinion based upon inferences drawn from the facts, as well as the perceptions of the witness.

It is for the judge to decide both the question of whether a witness is qualified to give an expert opinion and the question of whether the fact to which his opinion relates is a matter which permits of expertise. There is no particular standard which an expert witness must satisfy. Usually he will be professionally qualified or experienced but in *R v Silverlock*[14] a solicitor was permitted to give expert evidence on the subject of handwriting comparison although his expertise was only acquired through his own private study over a period of some ten years. However the qualifications

---

12 *Haines v Guthrie* (1884) 13 QBD 818.
13 *Wright v Doe d Tatham* (1838) 4 Bing NC 489.
14 [1894] 2 QB 766.

and expertise of an expert witness may always be challenged by cross-examination. It should be remembered, however, that the fact that a large body of professional opinion disagrees with the methods or opinion of the witness does not prevent that witness being recognised as an expert, although it may affect the extent to which his opinion is accepted by the court. Thus in *R v Robb*[15] a phonetics expert was permitted to give expert opinion evidence of voice identification by comparison of two tape-recordings, despite the fact that the techniques he employed in making his comparisons were not generally accepted as complete.

The second point upon which the judge must satisfy himself is that the fact which the witness's opinion is tendered to prove is something which may be the subject of expertise. Thus expert evidence will not, at common law, be admitted to the effect that a party was negligent[16] or that a publication tends to deprave or corrupt,[17] although in *Director of Public Prosecutions v A and BC Chewing Gum Ltd*[18] the Queen's Bench divisional court stated that on a prosecution under section 1 of the Obscene Publications Act 1959 the evidence of child psychiatrists should be admitted on the question of the possible effects that a particular publication might have upon a child. This case was, however, in *R v Anderson*[19] regarded as exceptional, the principle being confirmed that expert evidence is not admissible on the issue of whether or not a publication is obscene, the question of obscenity being entirely one for the jury, though expert evidence is admissible on the issue whether, if the article is found to be obscene, its publication is justified as being for the public good "on the ground that it is in the interests of science, literature, art or learning, or of other objects of general concern."[20] The courts have indicated that because "other objects of general concern", must fall within the same field or dimension as "science, literature, art or learning", so evidence cannot be directed to the psychotherapeutic value of pornography for certain categories of persons, such as sexual deviants, with a view to demonstrating that the material published relieved their sexual tensions, thereby diverting them from anti-social and possibly criminal activities.[1]

Another area in which opinion evidence is restricted is in respect of the

---

15 (1991) 93 Cr App Rep 161.
16 *R v Davies* [1962] 3 All ER 97; [1962] 1 WLR 1111.
17 Obscene Publications Act 1959, s 1; *R v Penguin Books Ltd* [1961] Crim LR 176.
18 [1968] 1 QB 159; [1967] 2 All ER 504.
19 [1972] 1 QB 304; [1971] 3 All ER 1152 – the notorious "Oz" prosecution.
20 Obscene Publications Act 1959, s 4(1); s 4(2) expressly provides for the opinions of experts to be admitted either to establish or negative the defence under s 4(1); see also *R v Turner* [1975] QB 834; [1975] 1 All ER 70; in which the Court of Appeal upheld the trial judge's decision to exclude the evidence of a psychiatrist as to (a) how an ordinary person who was not suffering from mental illness was likely to react to the stresses and strains of life, and (b) what reliance they could place upon the evidence of someone who was not mentally disordered, both matters being within the experience and knowledge of the judge and jury.
1 *Director of Public Prosecutions v Jordan* [1977] AC 699; [1976] 3 All ER 775. This had become a standard line of defence in obscene publications cases. When the provisions of the 1959 Act were extended to cinematograph exhibitions (by the Criminal Law Act 1977, s 53) the defence under s 4, in relation to cinematograph exhibitions, was formulated rather differently, no doubt with this line of defence in mind, *viz*, "if it is proved that the publication of the film or soundtrack is justified as being for the public good on the ground that it is in the interests of drama, opera, ballet or any other art, or of literature or learning" (1959 Act, s 4(1A)).

likelihood of an accused person having committed the offence charged. In *Lowery v R*[2] two men (L and K) were charged with the murder of a young girl who had been killed at a time and in a place when L and K were present and when no one else was present. The defence of each defendant was that the other alone was the killer and that he took no part whatsoever. L gave evidence of his own good character, of his happy domestic circumstances and financial prospects and of the fact that he had neither interest nor motive to commit the offence. Furthermore he stated that he was in fear of K. In response K was permitted to adduce evidence from a psychologist who had interviewed both of the accused and had submitted them to tests commonly employed by psychologists in making assessments of personality. The psychologist concluded that K was an immature, emotionally shallow youth, who seemed likely to be led and dominated by more aggressive and dominant men. In relation to the personality of L the finding was that he showed a strong aggressive drive with weak control of his aggressive impulses, callousness and impulsiveness; furthermore, one test indicated some sadistic pleasure in observing the sufferings of others. Both L and K were convicted; L appealed, contending that the evidence of the psychologist had been wrongly admitted. His appeal was dismissed. The *ratio* of the Privy Council's decision is obscure but the speech of LORD MORRIS makes it clear that the evidence was admissible at the instance of the accused[3] not because it related to criminal tendency but on the basis that it was scientific evidence as to the respective personalities of the two accused. It was relevant for this purpose because one defendant had sought to establish that he was less likely to have committed the offence than the other: that other was, therefore, entitled to adduce scientific evidence both as to his own personality and as to that of his co-accused with a view to showing that the opposite was in fact the case. It is clear on the authorities, however, that this principle is limited to scientific evidence of disposition and would not enable one defendant to lead evidence as to the reputation or criminal convictions of the other.[4] Nor is it authority that the parties, whether prosecution or defence, can adduce expert opinion evidence to prove guilt or innocence.[5]

Expert opinion evidence may, however, be used in some circumstances to show the existence of a medical abnormality affecting intent,[6] or to show the likelihood of unreliability of a confession,[7] which will be crucial in determining its admissibility.[8] It will not be admissible to prove matters which are within the ordinary experience of the average juror. Thus,

---

2 [1974] AC 85; [1973] 3 All ER 662.

3 If this were otherwise, the prosecution would be able to lead evidence (if available) in any case to suggest guilt by showing disposition to commit crime. This would be a fundamental change, and LORD MORRIS indicated that the contested evidence would have been admissible at the instance of the prosecution.

4 Though he might be entitled to cross-examine the other on such matters. See p 612, *post*.

5 This is the "ultimate issue", to be decided by the tribunal of fact.

6 *R v Toner* (1991) 93 Cr App Rep 382; cf *R v Chard* (1971) 56 Cr App Rep 268. The key factor is whether the accused suffers from some abnormality to justify the admission of such expert evidence.

7 *R v Silcott, Braithwaite and Raghip* (1991) Times, 9 December.

8 Police and Criminal Evidence Act 1984, s 76(2)(b); see p 628, *post*.

expert evidence in relation to the defence of provocation will not, generally, be admitted.[9]

Expert opinion is limited to matters involving specialist knowledge. In some of these matters the opinion of an ordinary witness is also admissible, though possibly less cogent. Handwriting, intoxication and value are examples of subjects upon which either expert or ordinary opinion is admissible. Subjects such as sanity, banking practice, fingerprints, ballistics, shipping, trade customs and foreign law are a few of those upon which expert opinion has been received. Many of the cases on this topic have turned upon proof of foreign law. There is a presumption that foreign law is the same as English law, the effect of which is that any party who alleges that a rule of foreign law is different from the corresponding rule of English law has the specific burden of proving that fact. Proof is almost always by the opinion of an expert witness. In *Bristow v Sequeville*[10] it was suggested that only a practitioner could be an expert upon foreign law and the evidence of a jurisconsult was rejected on the basis that he was not a competent expert. This principle was almost certainly too narrow, for non-practising lawyers,[11] teachers of law[12] and even persons without legal qualification[13] have been permitted to voice an opinion upon the subject of foreign law. Any doubt which existed is now removed in relation to civil proceedings by section 4(1) of the Civil Evidence Act 1972 which declares that expert evidence as to foreign law may be given by "a person who is suitably qualified to do so on account of his knowledge or experience . . . irrespective of whether he has acted or is entitled to act as a legal practitioner". This provision is, it is submitted, no more than declaratory of the common law, so that a similar approach is appropriate in criminal proceedings.[14]   An expert witness is entitled to draw on and refer to the works of others (including unpublished work) in his field of expertise as part of the process of arriving at his conclusion. Reliance on the work of others and reference to it in evidence does not infringe the hearsay rule. The Court of Appeal so held in *R v Abadom*,[15] upholding the admissibility of evidence from a Home Office forensic scientist as to the incidence of a particular type of glass in all controlled glass samples analysed and statistically collated in the Home Office Central Research Establishment; this evidence was given in support of his opinion as to the likelihood of certain fragments of glass (found in the accused's clothing) having come from a particular window.

---

9 *R v Turner* [1975] QB 834; [1975] 1 All ER 70.
10 (1850) 5 Exch 275.
11 *Barford v Barford* [1918] P 140.
12 *Brailey v Rhodesia Consolidated Ltd* [1910] 2 Ch 95.
13 *De Beéche v South American Stores (Gath and Chaves) Ltd* [1935] AC 148. The witness, a banker, was an expert on foreign banking law.
14 Such a finding is admissible in subsequent proceedings: Civil Evidence Act 1972, s 4(2); this method of proof is subject to rules of court (s 4(3)). It will be appreciated that these provisions do not have the effect of elevating findings as to foreign law to the status of findings of law; they remain findings of fact and it will, accordingly, always be open to the other party to call expert evidence to prove that foreign law is not as found in the previously decided case.
15 [1983] 1 All ER 364; [1983] 1 WLR 126.

D   PRIVILEGE

Where privilege exists, a witness may be justified in refusing to answer a relevant question, or to produce a document, and it justifies a party in civil proceedings in refusing to produce a document on discovery. The situations in which the courts will recognise the existence of a privilege are limited, and the courts are reluctant to extend them, taking as a starting point the assumption that relevant evidence ought to be before the court. Where privilege is granted to a party or witness it is said to be a private privilege. By contrast, in some situation public policy demands that evidence otherwise relevant be excluded. These situations are dealt with below.[16]

The term "privilege" is used elsewhere in the law, in a different sense. The doctrine of absolute and qualified privilege provides defences to actions in defamation, and should not be confused with privilege as an evidential rule. Nor should this evidential rule be confused with questions of parliamentary privilege, although that doctrine may limit what the courts may consider.[17]

1   Privilege against self-incrimination

This principle states that it is for the prosecution to prove its case, and an accused in a criminal case cannot be required to incriminate himself. To the extent that statements in civil proceedings might subsequently be used in criminal proceedings it applies equally in civil cases. However, in *AT & T Istel v Tully*,[18] the House of Lords limited its operation to cases where the answers to questions could be used in criminal proceedings. In that case there was no possibility of that, in the light of an agreement by the Crown Prosecution Service not to use the answers in subsequent criminal proceedings. The privilege therefore did not apply.

No person may be compelled to answer a question the answer to which would tend to incriminate him, or (in civil cases) his spouse.[19] An answer is to be regarded as incriminating if it would expose the giver of the answer to a criminal charge or statutory penalty, whether that would be a real danger being decided by the trial judge. If there is no real and appreciable danger the claim to privilege will not be upheld. For that reason, if in civil cases the court can deal with matters so as to ensure that answers will not be usable in criminal proceedings the claim of privilege will not be upheld.[20]

In criminal cases the most obvious example of the privilege is that of an accused person when giving evidence. An accused person cannot be required to give evidence, although if the provisions of the Criminal Justice and Public Order Bill are enacted an inference may be drawn from his failure to do so. However, section 1(e) of the Criminal Evidence Act 1898 provides that a person may be asked any question notwithstanding that it would tend to criminate him as to the offence charged.[1] An important

---

16 See p 600, *post.*
17 See art 9 of the Bill of Rights 1688; *Rost v Edwards* [1990] 2 QB 460; [1990] 2 All ER 641.
18 [1993] AC 45; [1992] 3 All ER 523.
19 Civil Evidence Act 1968, s 14(1)(b).
20 *AT Istel v Tully* (n 18, *supra*).
 1 For the relationship with s 1(f) see p 609, *post.*

exception to this principle is contained in section 2 of the Criminal Justice Act 1987, which permits the Director of the Serious Fraud Office, in a case of serious fraud, to require a person to answer questions, even after charge. Numerous other statutory provisions exist.[2] In addition, the privilege extends to answers which would tend to expose the maker to forfeiture in civil proceedings.

The principle is often confused with a wider so-called "right to silence". In fact they relate to different things. The former principle regulates what a suspect or accused can be required to say. The right to silence deals with the wider question of what inferences, if any, are drawn from silence. In *R v Director of Serious Fraud Office, ex parte Smith*[3] LORD MUSTILL identified various different aspects that are often compendiously referred to together.

(1) The immunity of all persons not to be compelled, on pain of punishment, to answer the questions of other persons.[4] It should be noted that this immunity does not extend to questions being asked in court.

(2) The immunity of any person from being compelled, on pain of punishment, to answer any question the answer to which may incriminate that person. It is this which amounts to the privilege against self-incrimination.

(3) The right of a suspected person to refuse to answer questions put by the police.

(4) The immunity of an accused from being required to give evidence.

(5) The right of a person charged with an offence not to be questioned further about that offence.

(6) The right in most circumstances not to have adverse comment made by the judge about the failure to answer any questions or give evidence.

The principle against self-incrimination, summarised in the Latin maxim *nemo tenetur seipsum prodere*, does not mean that an individual cannot incriminate: by definition, all confessions are self-incriminatory.[5] Rather, individuals cannot be forced, on pain of punishment, to self-incriminate. Nor should a person be improperly induced to incriminate himself: if this occurs a court is likely, in a criminal case, to exclude the evidence obtained as a result.[6] The operation of the principle is increasingly being limited: a wide range of statutory exceptions now exists.[7] In addition, its operation in civil cases has been described as "an archaic and unjustifiable survival from the past".[8]

The question as to whether adverse inferences should be drawn from a

---

2 See, eg, Theft Act 1968, s 31; Insolvency Act 1986, s 433; Prevention of Terrorism (Temporary Provisions) Act 1989, s 12.

3 [1993] AC 1; sub nom *Smith v Director of Serious Fraud Office*; [1992] 3 All ER 456.

4 A witness who refuses, without good cause, to answer such questions asked in court is guilty of contempt of court: see p 192, *ante*.

5 Note the definition of confession in the Police and Criminal Evidence Act 1984, s 82 includes all statements whether wholly or partly adverse to the maker: see p 624, *post*.

6 See the operation of the Police and Criminal Evidence Act 1984, s 78, discussed at p 557, *ante*. The House of Lords decision in *R v Sang* [1980] AC 402; [1979] 2 All ER 1222 was based upon preserving the privilege against self-incrimination.

7 See n 2, *supra*.

8 *A T & T Istel v Tully* (n 18, *supra*).

failure to answer questions, or to give evidence, has proved controversial.[9] It has already been noted[10] that the Criminal Justice and Public Order Bill now before Parliament proposes such inferences to be drawn where it is proper to do so, and its detailed provisions mirror those introduced in Northern Ireland in 1988.[11] Whilst they do not alter the burden of proof, which will remain on the prosecution in most cases, the proposed changes are a departure from the traditional position in which an accused can, with a few exceptions, say or do nothing and require the prosecution to discharge that burden. It will not be open to a court to convict an accused solely on the basis of such an inference.[12]

2 Legal professional privilege

The legal profession is unique in at least one respect. This is that legal professional communications attract evidential privilege. This privilege does not exist in respect of communications of an apparently equal confidential nature. Thus there is no privilege for communications between doctor and patient,[13] priest and penitent[14] or banker and customer.[15] It should be noted, however, that the law does respect the confidential nature of these relationships in that it may, in appropriate circumstances, restrain a party from making public that which was divulged in confidence.[16] This is a principle which, however, may be outweighed by the need to ensure the proper adnministration of justice, which may thus mean that the confidence is not enforced by the courts. The result is that the courts might compel a person to disclose in evidence in judicial proceedings that which they would restrain him from disclosing anywhere else.[17] The privilege does not prevent a third party giving evidence by secondary means. Thus, in *Calcraft v Guest*[18] the Court of Appeal allowed copies of witnesses' proofs and notes of evidence to be proved notwithstanding that the plaintiff could claim privilege from producing the originals. In the situation, however, where a privileged document has been inadvertently disclosed the court can order the return of all copies, and that the third party refrain from use of those documents,[19]

---

9 See 11th Report, Criminal Law Revision Committee Cmnd 4991, 1972 (HMSO). For comment see Cross, 'The Evidence Report – Sense or Nonsense' [1973] Crim LR 329. Note also Royal Commission on Criminal Procedure Cmnd 8092, 1981 (HMSO); Cmnd 8092, 1981 (HMSO); Royal Commission on Criminal Justice Cmnd 2263, 1993 (HMSO).
10 See p 485, *ante.*
11 Criminal Evidence (Northern Ireland) Order 1988. For comment, see Jackson, 'Recent Developments in Criminal Evidence' (1989) 40 NILQ 105. The English position was, at the time of making of that order, under consideration by the Working Group on the Right to Silence: see Zuckerman [1989] Crim LR at 855.
12 See p 486, *ante.* Such inferences are also to be relevant in dealing with an application made to resist a notice of transfer: see p 471, *ante.*
13 *Duchess Kingston' Case* (1776) 20 State Tr 355; *Hunter v Mann* [1974] QB 767; [1974] 2 All ER 414.
14 *Wheeler v Le Marchant* (1881) 17 Ch D 675 at 681.
15 Bankers' Books Evidence Act 1879, s 7.
16 See *R v Statutory Visitors to St Lawrence's Hospital* [1953] 2 All ER 766; [1953] 1 WLR 1158; *Duchess of Argyll v Duke of Argyll* [1967] Ch 302; [1965] 1 All ER 611; *D v National Society for the Prevention of Cruelty to Children* [1978] AC 171; [1977] 1 All ER 589.
17 See eg *Jones v G D Searle & Co Ltd* [1978] 3 All ER 654; [1979] 1 WLR 101.
18 [1898] 1 QB 759.
19 *Lord Ashburton v Pape* [1913] 2 Ch 469. This principle would appear not to apply in criminal cases: *Butler v Board of Trade* [1971] Ch 680; [1970] 3 All ER 593.

even if it is not immediately clear that they are privileged. Such an order must be sought before lists of documents are exchanged, but the court has power to intervene in certain cases at a later stage.[20] Note also that the converse of *Calcraft v Guest* is not equally true. If a document is not privileged in the hands of a third party, then the fact that a copy comes into the possession of a solicitor for the purposes of litigation does not attach privilege to that copy.[1]

There are two separate heads of legal professional privilege.

(a) Communications between solicitor and client — Oral and written communications between solicitor and client are privileged provided they were made in confidence and for the purpose of obtaining or giving legal advice. The rationale of this privilege is that the client may be able to make a full and frank disclosure of his affairs to his solicitor. Provided the communication is a professional and not a merely social or business one there is no requirement that any litigation be pending or anticipated. The privilege does not depend upon a retainer and exists even if there is no retainer or if the retainer has terminated.[2] The privilege is that of the client, not of the solicitor, so that only the client can waive it. Apart from this the privilege is lost in respect of a confidential professional communication only if it was made in furtherance of a fraudulent or criminal purpose, for example seeking advice upon the commission of a crime or fraud.[3] The privilege is lost in these circumstances, even though the solicitor is an innocent party.[4]

(b) Communications made in pursuance of litigation — Communications, generally written, made in pursuance of litigation that is pending or anticipated are privileged from disclosure in that or any other litigation. This head of privilege is wider than the first head in that it is not confined to the solicitor-client relationship. It extends to communications between, for example, counsel and solicitor, an insured person and his insurance company, solicitor and prospective witness and, in proceedings under the Patents Act 1977, to communications between a party and his patent agent.[5] In one case[6] the privilege was held to justify the defendants' refusal to disclose a statement made by the plaintiff to the defendants' insurers; the statement had been made shortly after the accident in respect of which the plaintiff's action was brought. However, where a document is brought into existence for more than one purpose privilege will only be held to exist if the dominant purpose is that of submitting it to a legal adviser for advice and use in litigation. So where the British Railways Board, following a fatal

---

20 See p 349, *ante*.

1 *R v Peterborough Justices, ex parte Hicks* [1978] 1 All ER 225; [1977] 1 WLR 1371. The position is different if the copy was created for the purposes of litigation.

2 *Calcraft v Guest* (*supra*, n 18); *Minter v Priest* [1930] AC 558. The privilege extends to communications with a foreign legal adviser: *Re Duncan, Garfield v Fay* [1968] P 306; [1968] 2 All ER 395.

3 *R v Cox and Railton* (1884) 14 QBD 153. See *Butler v Board of Trade* [1971] Ch 680; [1970] 3 All ER 593 and *Crescent Farm (Sidcup) Sports Ltd v Sterling Offices Ltd* [1972] Ch 553; [1971] 2 All ER 1192, where the authorities are reviewed.

4 See *R v Central Criminal Court, ex parte Francis & Francis* [1989] AC 346; sub nom *Francis & Francis v Central Criminal Court* [1988] 1 All ER 677, in the context of the Police and Criminal Evidence Act 1984, s 10.

5 Patents Act 1977, s 104.

6 *Britten v F H Pilcher & Sons* [1969] 1 All ER 491.

accident to one of its employees, held an inquiry, the results of which were recorded in an internal inquiry report headed "or the information of the Board's solicitor", the report was held nevertheless not to be privileged in an action brought by the deceased's widow against the Board since the report was prepared for another purpose as well, namely to establish the cause of the accident so that appropriate safety measures could be taken, and the purpose for advice and use in anticipated litigation was merely one of the purposes and not the dominant purpose.[7]

The privilege is also limited in that the communication must be referable to litigation pending or anticipated. Thus in *Wheeler v Le Marchant*[8] certain reports from a surveyor to the defendant's solicitor were held not to attract privilege since, although they were prepared in respect of property which was the subject matter of the litigation, no litigation was pending or anticipated when the reports were made.

It has already been noted that the fact that a document may be protected by privilege does not prevent another party adducing secondary evidence of that document, or information contained therein, for example, by producing a copy of that document. However, if the privilege has been lost because of an error, the court has power to restrain the use of that document or information by that other party.[9] This must generally be prior to inspection of the documentary evidence listed on discovery.[10] However, the court has a wide jurisdiction to ensure fairness, and even after discovery it may restrain by the use of an injunction a party from relying on a document the disclosure of which had been procured by fraud,[11] or by an obvious mistake.[12]

3   Sources of information

The courts always resisted the extension of the doctrine of privilege to cover the sources of information obtained by journalists. However, section 10 of the Contempt of Court Act 1981 states:

> "No court may require a person to disclose, nor is any person guilty of contempt of court for refusing to disclose, the sources of information contained in a publication for which he is responsible, unless it be established to the satisfaction of the court that disclosure is necessary in the interests of justice or national security or for the prevention of disorder or crime."

For the protection to apply there must be a "publication",[13] which includes an intended publication. The presumption is one in favour of protection of the source, unless disclosure is "necessary", a term which was said by LORD DIPLOCK in *Secretary of State for Defence v Guardian Newspapers Ltd*[14] to mean "really needed". Its disclosure has to be essential, not merely helpful or expedient.

---

7 *Waugh v British Railways Board* [1980] AC 521, [1979] 2 All ER 1169.
8 (1881) 17 Ch D 675.
9 But not in a criminal case: see p 596, n 19, *supra*.
10 For discovery see p 350, *ante*.
11 *ITC Film Distributors v Video Exchange Ltd* [1982] Ch 431.
12 *Guinness Peat Properties Ltd v Fitzroy Robinson Partnership* [1987] 2 All ER 716; [1987] 1 WLR 1027.
13 As defined by the Contempt of Court Act 1981, s 1.
14 [1985] AC 339; [1984] 3 All ER 601.

The three areas of exception have been broadly interpreted,[15] making the scope of protection of sources rather limited. It should be noted, however, that even if a case falls within one of the three exceptions, the court nevertheless has a discretion as to whether disclosure should in fact be ordered.[16]

In addition, the law gives protection to other sources, on the grounds of public policy. These are part of the rules which prevent evidence being adduced on the grounds of public policy, and are dealt with below.[17]

---

15 See *X Ltd v Morgan–Grampian Publishers* [1991] 1 AC 1; [1990] 2 All ER 1; *Re an Inquiry under the Companies Securities (Insider Dealing) Act 1985* [1988] AC 660; [1988] 1 All ER 203.

16 See cases cited at n 15, *supra*.

17 See p 614, *post*.

CHAPTER 29

Matters that May Not Be Proved

The rules of evidence sometimes prohibit relevant evidence being heard. These exclusionary rules may be absolute, or, more usually, permit such evidence only in certain situations and subject to the requirements prescribed by law being satisfied. They exist to prevent evidence being considered that may be unduly prejudicial, especially in the context of jury trial, or to which may be attached more weight than the evidence in fact deserves. One such exclusionary rule is the rule which prohibits the admission of hearsay evidence: this rule, and its exceptions, are discussed separately.[1] Other rules relate to evidence of disposition, of character, and exclusion on the grounds of public policy. These are discussed in this Chapter.

A   THE SIMILAR FACT EVIDENCE RULE

1   Relevance

The fact that a person is of bad character, or has behaved in a certain way in the past, generally bears no relevance as to whether that person acted in a certain way on the occasion being considered by the court. The fact that a policeman is accused of eight offences of theft may be suspicious, but of themselves each is not relevant to the other.[2] The fact that an accused enters a house by unusual means, with consensual sexual conduct then following, has no relevance to the question as to whether, when he entered another house, he did so with intent to ravish.[3] Again, on a charge of rape the fact that it is shown on other occasions the accused offered lifts to women may heighten suspicion, but does not show what, if anything, occurred with those other women.[4] Of course, it is not always easy to decide this initial question of relevance, but the general rule must be firmly borne in mind: if evidence is not relevant it is not admitted for that reason, not because of any other exclusionary rule.

In each of these instances cited above, suspicion may be aroused, but there is no probative force logically flowing from the alleged conduct to the

---

1 See p 617, *post*.
2 *Harris v Director of Public Prosecutions* [1952] AC 694; [1952] 1 All ER 1044.
3 *R v Tricoglus* (1976) 65 Cr App Rep 16.
4 *R v Butler* (1986) 84 Cr App Rep 12.

charge being tried. The conduct does not "prove or render probable" the facts in issue. However, to ignore past conduct completely would be absurd, for in some circumstances it may have probative force and thus relevance. For example, in some situations it may assist in showing identity, or negative a defence of accident or that "nothing happened". In these circumstances where the probative value outweighs the prejudicial effect such evidence of disposition[5] creates, such evidence will be admitted. Whether or not such probative value exists is determined by an application of the similar fact evidence rule, which applies in both criminal and civil cases.

It should be remembered that the similar fact evidence rule is important in various ways. If it applies, then past conduct, whether lawful or unlawful,[6] can be used to prove guilt on the instant charge. However, it can apply equally in respect of multiple charges. Where several charges are brought together, then if the rule is satisfied the evidence of one may be admissible on the others.[7] By this means corroborative evidence can often be created where none might otherwise exist. It should also be remembered that it always has a specific purpose to serve by demonstrating who committed the offence, or by negativing some defence.

2 Formulation of the similar fact evidence rule

The first authoritative statement of the rule was by LORD HERSCHELL in *Makin v A–G for New South Wales*.[8] In this case the accused couple were charged with the murder of a child whose body was found in their garden. They had adopted the child, on receipt of a sum of money from its mother inadequate for its support. The death was consistent with death being from natural causes, although substantial other evidence existed to support a charge of murder. The Privy Council, however, held that evidence was admissible that the bodies of other children, adopted in the same way, were found buried in the gardens of homes that had been owned by the couple.

The statement of principle made by LORD HERSCHELL provided a basis for the rule, upon which the courts in subsequent cases relied. However, it did not prove entirely satisfactory, in that it was sometimes understood as creating categories into which cases had to fall in order to make past conduct, or disposition, admissible. This approach[9] was rejected by the House of Lords in the next major review of the similar fact evidence rule, in *Director of Public Prosecutions v Boardman*.[10] In this case the appellant, the headmaster of a boys boarding school, was charged with sexual

---

5 It is sometimes believed that evidence of disposition is inadmissible. This is, in fact a misstatement of the rule. Evidence of disposition is inadmissible if it has insufficient probative value. See Hoffman, 'Similar Facts after Boardman' [1975] LQR 193.
6 Lawful conduct is within the rule: see *R v Barrington* [1981] 1 All ER 1132; [1981] 1 WLR 419; *R v Butler* (*supra*, n 4).
7 For joinder of counts, see p 476, *ante*. The cases suggest that joinder is not dependent upon admissibility under the similar fact evidence rule. See *R v Tickner* [1992] Crim LR 444.
8 [1894] AC 57.
9 Described by the House of Lords in *Harris v Director of Public Prosecutions* (*supra*, n 2) as "tickets of admissibility".
10 [1975] AC 421; [1974] 3 All ER 887.

offences against two pupils. Each boy alleged features of that offence that the court considered striking and unusual, though it was accepted to be a marginal case. The House of Lords held that admissibility did not depend upon it fitting within a particular category. Nor was there a special rule to be applied in sexual cases of a homosexual nature.[11] Evidence of past conduct, or of other alleged conduct, was admissible when the probative force of the evidence justified it. LORD HAILSHAM indicated that this probative force came in this case from two boys independently coming up with the same strikingly unusual allegation. The test was whether, as a matter of logic and common sense, the "striking resemblances" or "unusual features" which the facts have in common are such that to ignore them would affront common sense. By way of example he stated:

> ". . . in a sex case . . . whilst a repeated homosexual act by itself might be insufficient to admit the evidence as confirmatory of identity or design, the fact that it was alleged to have been performed wearing the ceremonial headdress of a Red Indian chief or other eccentric garb might well in appropriate circumstances suffice."

This colourful example laid stress upon the similarities, as did LORD SALMON who used the phrase "uniquely or strikingly similar".[12] By contrast, LORD CROSS suggested that the test was "whether the similar fact evidence taken together with the other evidence . . . would point so strongly to his guilt that only an ultra-cautious jury, if they accepted it as true, would acquit in face of it."

The emphasis upon "striking similarity" as the test for determining whether probative value exists is appropriate in some cases, where, for example the court has to decide the identity of the person who committed an offence.[13] In these cases only a "striking similarity" will suffice. In *R v Straffen*[14] the accused was charged with the murder of a small girl. Evidence was admitted that the accused had previously murdered two other small girls. The evidence served to identify Straffen because of the peculiar similarity shared by the three murders; all three victims were young girls, all were strangled, there was no sexual assault or other apparent motive and no attempt to conceal the bodies. In short, the evidence showed that these three murders were all the work of one man, and did so because they were committed in what the court considered to be a strikingly similar way. Again, in *Boardman* itself, the court considered the probative force to arise from the strikingly unusual allegations, made independently by each victim.

However, probative value can arise in ways other than by showing "striking similarity". In *R v Rance and Herron*[15] LORD WIDGERY CJ stated that ". . . one must be careful not to attach too much importance to LORD SALMON's vivid phrase 'uniquely or strikingly similar'". This approach was supported by SCARMAN LJ in *R v Scarrott*[16] where he stated that "positive

---

11 Rejecting the approach illustrated by *Thompson v R* [1918] AC 221, and *R v Sims* [1946] KB 531; [1946] 1 All ER 697.
12 First used by LORD GODDARD CJ in *R v Sims, supra.*
13 Evidence that falls short of this will not have sufficient probative force.
14 [1952] 2 QB 911; [1952] 2 All ER 657.
15 (1975) 62 Cr App R 118.
16 [1978] QB 1016; [1978] 1 All ER 672.

probative value" is what the law requires. The whole situation was re-considered by the House of Lords in *Director of Public Prosecutions v P*.[17] The defendant was charged with sexual offences against his two daughters. It was held that the evidence of each was admissible on the charges relating to the other. Even though there was nothing strikingly unusual about each allegation, the probative force of the making of each allegation against the same man once collusion between the two daughters had been discounted was sufficiently strong. Probative force did not always require the existence of "striking or unusual features". Even the repetition of "stock-in-trade" features[18] could in appropriate circumstances have probative force, if, as in *P*, they go beyond coincidence.

These different approaches should not serve to obscure one important fact: that admissibility depends upon the probative value of the evidence being sufficient to justify its use, despite the prejudice it may create. Striking similarity is one means of establishing probative value, but there are others. Much depends upon the nature of the defence. It is true that in *Director of Public Prosecutions v Boardman*[19] LORD HAILSHAM indicated that admissibility did not depend upon the nature of the defence. Whilst this is true in the sense that the nature of the defence is not decisive, it does provide the context in which probative value is to be assessed, and the role the similar fact evidence has to play. This is illustrated by the case of *R v Butler*.[20] In this case the appellant denied an allegation of rape, his defence being that he was not the rapist. The issue was therefore one of identity. The prosecution was held entitled to adduce evidence from a past girlfriend that they had, consensually, engaged in the same strikingly similar sexual conduct as had occurred in the alleged rape. This conduct therefore confirmed his identity as the rapist. By contrast, if his defence had been that the complainant had consented, the evidence of the girlfriend, no matter how similar, would have had no probative value on the crucial issue of consent.

3   Applications of the rule

Various attempts have been made to classify the types of case in which similar fact evidence will be admitted. These classifications do not of themselves determine admissibility, but merely provide the context in which the probative value of the evidence can be decided, and provide some indication as to what the appropriate test might be. They are set out below as illustrations of how the law can be applied. Each case does, however, essentially turn on its own facts.

---

17 [1991] 2 AC 447; sub nom *R v P* [1991] 3 All ER 337.
18 A phrase used in *R v Inder* (1977) 67 Cr App Rep 143, where it was said that the repetition of features that amounted to the "stock-in-trade" of those who commit sexual assaults was insufficient to justify admission under the similar fact evidence rule. This was disapproved in *P*.
19 See n 10, *supra*.
20 (1986) 84 Cr App Rep 12.

a Identity

In exceptional circumstances the conduct of a person on other occasions may identify him as the perpetrator of conduct which is a fact in issue, provided that the conduct is sufficiently idiosyncratic.[1] Simple repetition of allegations which lack striking similarity sufficient to establish that each offence was the work of the same person will be insufficient.

b System

Conduct on other occasions can be relevant by showing a systematic course of conduct. What the courts will require is a probative link between different incidents. That can best be shown by demonstrating a "striking similarity", but that is not necessarily necessary, as has been seen from *Director of Public Prosecutions v P*.[2] Many of the cases link incidents together by simply showing implausibility. Thus *Makin v A-G for New South Wales*[3] was such a case. Similarly, in *R v Smith*[4] (the famous "brides in the bath" murder), the deceased, who had gone through a ceremony of marriage with the accused, was drowned in her bath having insured her life in favour of the accused. The death was claimed by the accused to have been caused by an attack of epilepsy. Evidence was admitted that two other women with whom Smith had gone through ceremonies of marriage, and who had likewise effected insurance, had also drowned in their baths.

c Rebutting defences

The past conduct may be sufficient to negative a defence of accident, lack of intent or innocent association. Again, "striking similarity" will not necessarily be needed. In *R v Armstrong*[5] the accused, a solicitor, charged with murdering his wife by arsenic poisoning, raised the defence that she had committed suicide. Evidence was admitted of a subsequent attempt by the accused to poison a rival solicitor with arsenic. Similarly in *R v Bond*[6] evidence that the accused, a doctor, had used instruments upon a woman to perform an abortion on an earlier occasion was admitted in order to rebut the defence that his use of similar instruments on the occasion in question was to carry out a *bona fide* examination. In *R v Barrington*[7] the accused was charged with indecently assaulting three young girls, the prosecution case being that he had lured them to premises on the pretext that they were required as baby-sitters and, once there, had shown them pornographic pictures, asked them to pose for photographs in the nude and indecently assaulted them. When the girls gave evidence to this effect they were cross-examined along the lines that their evidence was false and they had put their heads together to concoct a case against the accused. In those circumstances the prosecution successfully applied to call three other girls whose evidence was that they too had been lured to the premises on the

---

1 *R v McGranaghan* [1992] Crim LR 430; see also *R v Straffen* (n 14) and *R v Butler* (n 20), *supra*.
2 See n 17, *supra*.
3 See n 8, *supra*.
4 (1915) 11 Cr App Rep 229.
5 [1922] 2 KB 555.
6 [1906] 2 KB 389; [1904–7] All ER Rep 24.
7 [1981] 1 All ER 1132; [1981] 1 WLR 419.

pretext of baby-sitting and then shown pornographic pictures and asked to pose for nude photographs. The Court of Appeal upheld the admission of this evidence both on the ground advanced by the prosecution, namely as tending to rebut the defence, and on the wider ground of "striking similarity" between the surrounding circumstances of the alleged offences and those of the visits of the three other girls. The case is of particular interest because the similar fact evidence did not, as will have been observed, include evidence of the actual commission of offences similar to those with which the accused was charged.[8]

4 Statute

Certain statutes provide for the admission of evidence of conduct on the part of an accused person on other occasions. An example is section 27(3) of the Theft Act 1968 which permits certain types of evidence, including the fact that the accused has, within the preceding five years, been convicted of theft or handling stolen goods, to be given by the prosecution on a charge of handling.

B   GOOD CHARACTER AND REPUTATION

The term "character" carries different meanings. It can refer to the disposition of an individual, to general reputation, or to the previous convictions (or lack of them) of the accused. Its admissibility depends upon the purpose it serves and the effect it has. In some circumstances it is inadmissible simply because it is irrelevant. In others it has relevance but not such as to overcome the prejudice it creates. Even if character evidence has strong probative force there remains often a discretion to exclude it if admission would cause unfairness.[9] To cope with this variety of situations the law has developed specific rules regulating when, and for what purpose, evidence of character may be given.

These rules relate primarily to matters affecting the character of the parties, and are mostly of importance in criminal cases. In relation to witnesses, it has already been seen that a witness may be asked questions that affect his credit.[10] Thus the purpose of cross-examination in respect of previous convictions or discreditable action will be to show that the witness is not worthy of belief.

In most cases the term "character" is used to mean either the presence or absence of previous convictions. However, it can also refer to general reputation. This can, of course, be evidence of bad as well as good reputation.

In civil cases reputation will only rarely be relevant to issue, most commonly in defamation cases in which the reputation of the plaintiff is

---

8 Evidence of surrounding circumstances which have probative value is admissible. See, eg, *R v Barrington, supra,* n 7. *Cp* the different approach taken in *R v Novac* (1976) 65 Cr App Rep 107 with *R v Johannsen* (1977) 65 Cr App Rep 101.
9 *Selvey v Director of Public Prosecutions* [1970] AC 304; [1968] 2 All ER 497.
10 See p 585, *ante.*

at the very heart of the case.[11] It will also be relevant to the question of the quantum of damages to be awarded.[12] By contrast in criminal cases good character can go not merely to credibility, but also to the very issue as to whether the accused committed the offence in question.

Where evidence of good character is adduced the duty of the judge is to point out its primary function as relevant to the accused's credibility. If, however, the defendant does not give evidence then credibility plainly does not arise. Despite this, in *R v Vye*[13] the Court of Appeal indicated that a judge should direct the jury to have regard to the accused's good character not only where the accused had given evidence, but also where the credibility of out-of-court statements had to be considered. In addition, as noted above, good character can go to the very issue of guilt or innocence. In those circumstances the jury should be directed to consider whether they "think it likely that a person with such a character would have committed the offence".[14] Indeed, the Court of Appeal in *R v Vye* said that such a direction should be given in every case where the defendant is of good character, irrespective of whether or not he has given evidence.[15]

This approach described above lacks logic, since if an accused has bad character it goes only to credibility.[16] The distinction is, though, firmly established in English law. Strictly speaking the accused is limited to the giving or calling evidence of general reputation. Thus in *R v Redgrave*[17] the accused, charged with an offence of importuning, was not permitted to lead detailed evidence of his heterosexual relationships in order to show that he was not disposed to make homosexual approaches. The rule owes its origin to the different conditions of the nineteenth century when it could more truly be said that a person might have a general reputation.[18] Now it is a rule that depends less on logic than on practical utility, for otherwise a court might be involved in a multiplicity of matters of marginal relevance to the issues. In practice, however, trial judges will frequently allow, by way of discretion, limited evidence of specific actions or good deeds, as well as evidence that the accused has no previous convictions.[19]

Once a person adduces evidence of reputation and good character, then the whole of that reputation or character is put in issue. The effect is that

---

11 However, in prosecutions for criminal libel, evidence of the general bad character of the prosecutor is not admissible: *Gleaves v Deakin* [1980] AC 477; [1979] 2 All ER 497.

12 *Plato Films Ltd v Speidel* [1961] AC 1090; [1961] 1 All ER 876. However the fact that the plaintiff has previous convictions is admissible in defamation for the purpose of mitigating damages: *Goody v Odhams Press Ltd* [1967] 1 QB 333; [1966] 3 All ER 369. The Rehabilitation of Offenders Act 1974 has some slight effect in such cases: see s 4(1)(a) and (b). The length of the period which must elapse before the shield provided by these provisions takes effect varies according to the sentence imposed, but convictions in respect of which a sentence in excess of 30 months' imprisonment was imposed are excluded from rehabilitation (s 5).

13 [1993] 3 All ER 241; [1993] 1 WLR 471.

14 See *R v Berrada* (1989) 91 Cr App Rep 131; *R v Marr* (1989) 90 Cr App Rep 154; *R v Anderson* [1990] Crim LR 862; *R v Cohen* (1990) 91 Cr App Rep 125.

15 And, where appropriate, even where the accused has pleaded guilty to one of two or more charges: *R v Teasdale* [1993] 4 All ER 290.

16 Indeed, the jury should be directed to disregard bad character in determining matters relating to issue: see *Maxwell v Director of Public Prosecutions* [1935] AC 309; [1934] All ER Rep 168.

17 (1981) 74 Cr App Rep 10.

18 *R v Rowton* (1865) Le & Ca 520; [1861–73] All ER Rep 549.

19 See LAWTON LJ in *R v Redgrave* (*supra*, n 17).

the prosecution may then give evidence of his bad character in rebuttal. Such evidence may relate to the accused's general reputation though not to any individual witness's opinion as to the accused's character. It may also relate to the accused's previous convictions, provided the good character asserted is that of the accused himself.[20] Character is indivisible. In *R v Winfield*[1] the accused was charged with indecent assault upon a woman. He called a witness to testify as to his good behaviour with women, whereupon the prosecution was allowed to cross-examine that witness as to a previous conviction of the accused involving dishonesty.

C   BAD CHARACTER AND PREVIOUS CONVICTIONS

As a general rule, evidence of the previous convictions of a party to proceedings is not relevant to the issues, and is therefore inadmissible. To this rule there are limited exceptions, discussed below. The fact that some other person has previous convictions will also be admissible to the extent that such matters relate to issue. More usually, though, previous convictions are adduced to weaken the credit of a witness, by showing that he is of bad character and therefore less worthy of belief. Any witness may have his credit weakened in this way, but special protection is given to accused persons in criminal cases.

1   Convictions of those other than the parties

The circumstances in which these will be relevant to issue are limited. In criminal cases this will usually be where the conviction of another person for an offence is a prerequisite to conviction of the accused on the instant charge. Thus, the prosecution on a charge of handling stolen goods will need to establish that the items in question were stolen. In civil cases it may be relevant to questions of liability that another person has been convicted of, say, careless driving. At common law, the rule in *Hollington v F Hewthorn & Co Ltd*[2] prevented the use of convictions in previous criminal proceedings as evidence of guilt in subsequent proceedings, and was widely assumed to apply equally in civil cases. In civil cases the rule was reversed by section 11 of the Civil Evidence Act 1968, and, in criminal cases, by section 74 of the Police and Criminal Evidence Act 1984. Where relevant to an issue, the fact of previous conviction can be adduced, proved by certificate of conviction.[3]

In criminal proceedings, however, the passage of section 74 has had unexpected effects.[4] It allows previous convictions of a person other than the accused to be adduced where they are relevant to the issue of whether the accused committed the offence, and shall be taken as correct unless the contrary is proved. Its purpose was explained by TAYLOR J in *R v O'Connor:*[5]

> "[Its terms] were designed . . . to deal with the situation where it was necessary as a preliminary matter for it to be proved that a person other than the accused had been convicted of an offence. The object . . . is to avoid that matter having to be proved

---

20 See the Criminal Evidence Act 1898, s 1(f)(ii), p 609, *post.*
1 [1939] 4 All ER 164.
2 [1943] KB 587; [1943] 2 All ER 35.
3 See the Police and Criminal Evidence Act 1984, s 74.
4 For discussion of the problems, see Munday [1990] Crim LR 236.
5 (1986) 85 Cr App Rep 298.

twice where the other person has already pleaded guilty to the offence it was necessary to prove. In effect therefore the object of the section . . . was to deal with cases where it was necessary to prove the conviction of another as a condition precedent to the conviction of the defendant of the charge laid against him."

However, case law on section 74 has shown that the section has potentially much wider uses, which may sometimes have highly prejudicial and undesirable effects. In *O'Connor*[6] the appellant and another (B) were jointly charged with conspiracy. B pleaded guilty, and the trial judge allowed into evidence details of the charge and conviction of B. The conviction was quashed on appeal. The use of section 74 in this way meant that since it was shown that B conspired with the appellant, the jury would assume the reverse was true. This effectively reversed the burden of proof, and was unfair. The court should have used its discretion to exclude this technically admissible but nevertheless unfair evidence.

This case, and others,[7] were considered by the Court of Appeal in *R v Kempster*,[8] which identified the correct approach to be adopted. Section 74 is not confined in its operation to situations where such a conviction needs to be proved as an integral part of the offence charged. The conviction must, in combination with other evidence, show complicity: if it does not do this then, of course, it is irrelevant. However, if by itself it inevitably means that the accused is guilty of the offence charged then it is unfair and should be excluded under section 78.

2   Convictions of the parties in civil cases

The previous convictions of a party in a civil case can only be proved where the fact of conviction is a relevant fact,[9] or where the conviction is admissible under the Civil Evidence Act 1968 as proof of a relevant fact or to discredit the testimony of the party as a witness. Thus the fact of conviction would be a fact in issue in a defamation action where the defendant alleged that the plaintiff had been convicted and sought to justify the allegation, or in an action for malicious prosecution where the defendant alleged that the plaintiff had been convicted. Similarly, where the defendants in a libel action imputed dishonesty to a company which was the proprietor of a computer school, they were permitted in support of justification, to plead details of the convictions and sentences of the founder of the school.[10]

3   Convictions of accused persons in criminal cases

The extent to which an accused person, as a witness, may be cross-examined as to his previous convictions is dealt with below. However the accused's previous convictions may sometimes be proved irrespective of whether he is a witness. For example, where the accused raises a plea of

---

6 See n 5, *supra*.
7 *R v Kempster* [1989] 1 WLR 1125.
8 See n 7, *supra*.
9 *Ingram v Ingram* [1956] P 390; [1956] 1 All ER 785.
10 *London Computer Operators Training Ltd v British Broadcasting Corporation* [1973] 2 All ER 170; [1973] 1 WLR 424.

autrefois convict,[11] the conviction in question is relevant as a fact in issue. Also, there are several statutory provisions enabling the prosecution to give evidence of the accused's previous convictions. For example section 27(3) of the Theft Act 1968 allows proof of convictions as a means of proving facts in issue. Where the accused puts his character in issue by seeking to establish his good character, the prosecution may be allowed to prove his previous convictions as part of his bad character. Finally, where the similar fact evidence rule allows, an accused person's past conduct (including previous convictions) can be adduced as part of the prosecution case.[12]

Except in these circumstances, and under the provisions of the Criminal Evidence Act 1898 (*infra*) evidence of his character and of previous convictions, or lack of them, can only be adduced by the accused. The extent to which cross-examination of the accused as to character and previous convictions is allowed is limited. Unlike in the case of other witnesses, the law regards the possible prejudice that might arise as something from which the accused ought to be protected. Accordingly the law grants an accused person a "shield" in the form of the Criminal Evidence Act 1898. However, in order that a balance be maintained, the law recognises that in some circumstances this shield would create unfairness to the prosecution.

The Criminal Evidence Act 1898, section 1 (as amended) makes the accused a competent though not a compellable witness for the defence. Consequently, the accused has a choice as to whether or not to give evidence. If he does elect to give evidence the accused's position differs from that of other witnesses in that he cannot be freely cross-examined as to credit. The extent to which he can be cross-examined is governed by sections 1(e) and 1(f). These provide as follows:

> *s 1(e)*: "A person charged and being a witness in pursuance of this Act may be asked any question in cross examination notwithstanding that it would tend to criminate him as to the offence charged."
>
> *s 1(f)*: "A person charged and called as a witness in pursuance of this Act shall not be asked, and if asked shall not be required to answer, any question tending to show that he has committed or been convicted of or has been charged with any offence other than that wherewith he is then charged, or is of bad character, unless:
>
> (i) the proof that he has committed or been convicted of such other offence is admissible evidence to show that he is guilty of the offence wherewith he is then charged; or
>
> (ii) he has personally or by his advocate asked questions of the witnesses for the prosecution with a view to establish his own good character, or has given evidence of his good character, or the nature or conduct of the defence is such as to involve imputations on the character of the prosecutor or the witnesses for the prosecution; or
>
> (iii) he has given evidence against any other person charged in the same proceedings."

Section 1(e) therefore permits an accused to be asked questions the answers to which may incriminate him as to the offence of which he is accused. It must, though, be read subject to the shield created by section 1(f), which is lost in certain circumstances. Only if this occurs can questions which "tend to

---

11 See p 492, *ante*.
12 See p 600, *ante*.

show" the matters referred to be asked. This point was well demonstrated by the House of Lords in *Jones v Director of Public Prosecutions*.[13] In this case, the appellant (J) was charged with murdering a young girl, a Girl Guide. He first advanced an admittedly false alibi and later asserted an uncorroborated alibi. His explanation as to why he had not raised this alibi earlier was that he had been in trouble with the police before and was afraid that the police would not believe his uncorroborated alibi. In fact J had been previously convicted of raping another Girl Guide at which trial he had raised an alibi (similar to the one now raised) that he had been with an unnamed prostitute. He was cross-examined concerning the remarkable similarity between the two alibis. Although the fact of his previous conviction was not brought out, the cross-examination did tend to show that he was of bad character in that he had been in trouble with the police. His appeal against conviction was dismissed. The House of Lords firstly had to consider the interrelationship between sections 1(e) and 1(f), the majority concluding that section 1(e) only permitted questions that were not prohibited by section 1(f).[14] In any event, however, such questions were permissible, because the cross-examination did not "tend to show", in the sense of "tend to reveal", that Jones had been in trouble with the police. J had already revealed this himself. Consequently the shield of section 1(f) did not exist.

A strict interpretation of section 1(f) would suggest that the accused, if he loses the shield, may be asked questions to show that he has been charged with other offences. Were this interpretation adopted the section would operate to admit evidence of previous acquittals as well as of previous convictions. It is not presumed, however, that the framers of the 1898 Act intended to affect the general rule that all evidence must be relevant in order to be admissible. Consequently evidence that the accused has been "charged" with an offence is not generally admissible in spite of the wording of section 1(f). This was the basis of the decision of the House of Lords in *Maxwell v Director of Public Prosecutions*[15] which held that, although a doctor on a charge of manslaughter had put his character in issue, he ought not to have been cross-examined as to a similar charge upon which he had been acquitted. Furthermore "charged" is interpreted as meaning "charged in court" so that section 1(f) cannot operate to admit evidence that an accused person has been questioned about or suspected of a criminal offence of which he has never been formally charged unless he can be proved to have committed the offence.

Where the shield does exist it is lost only in the circumstances specified in section 1(f). It has already been noted that there are four circumstances in which the shield is lost. These are as follows:

a   Where the fact of commission or conviction of the earlier offence is relevant similar fact evidence (s 1(f)(i))

This adds nothing to the common law since relevant similar fact evidence can be admitted at common law. It does, however, permit such cross-examination in the exceptional case where similar fact evidence has not been

---

13 [1962] AC 635; [1962] 1 All ER 569. See also *R v Anderson* [1988] QB 678; [1988] 2 All ER 549.
14 Lords Simonds, Reid and Morris.
15 [1935] AC 309; [1934] All ER Rep 168.

adduced by the prosecution at the time of cross-examination of the accused.[16]

b Where the accused tries to establish his own good character (s 1(f)(ii))

This also adds nothing to the common law since the effect of the accused putting his character in issue is, as noted above, to let in evidence of his bad character including his previous convictions as part of the prosecution case. The justification for the exception is that otherwise the jury would be totally misled as to the character of the accused.[17]

c Where the conduct of the defence involves imputations on the character of the prosecutor or the prosecution witnesses (s 1(f)(ii))

The justification for allowing cross-examination in such circumstances is the overall fairness of the proceedings. As explained in *Selvey v Director of Public Prosecutions*,[18] it is based on the "tit for tat" principle: if allegations are being made against prosecution witnesses it is only fair that the character of the person making those allegations should be before the court.

In *Selvey v Director of Public Prosecutions* the House of Lords reviewed the operation of this part of section 1 (f)(ii). It considered what was an imputation: in this case it amounted to an allegation of male prostitution. The fact that an imputation was an essential part of the defence did not prevent the shield being lost, although to allege consent as a defence to rape was stated to be *sui generis* and not an imputation.[19] If what was in question was no more than a denial in emphatic terms of the charge, the shield would not be lost. However, the case law on the question of what amounts to an imputation is varied. A mere allegation of being a "liar" has been held to be an emphatic denial,[20] but, by contrast, a statement that the prosecutor was such a horrible liar that even his own brother would not speak to him has been held to amount to an imputation.[1] An allegation that the prosecutor was an habitual drunkard was held in one case not to be an imputation,[2] although, in another case, a statement that the prosecutor was drunk, driving disgracefully and shouting abuse at other drivers was.[3]

The problem often arises in the context of allegations of police misconduct. In one case criticism of the method of holding an identification parade was held not to be objectionable[4] though a suggestion that the accused's confession was dictated by one policeman to another was held to

---

16 Generally speaking such evidence should be adduced as part of the prosecution case: *Noor Mohammed v R* [1949] AC 182; [1949] 1 All ER 365.
17 See Seabrooke 'Closing the Credibility Gap'[1987] Crim LR 231.
18 [1970] AC 304; [1968] 2 All ER 497.
19 *R v Turner* [1944] KB 463; [1944] 1 All ER 599. The position is different if some allegation, such as commission of an indecent act (as was alleged in *Turner*), is made.
20 *R v Rouse* [1904] 1 KB 184; (1904) 20 Cox cc 592.
1 *R v Rappolt* (1911) 6 Cr App Rep 156.
2 *R v Westfall* (1912) 7 Cr App Rep 176.
3 *R v Brown* (1960) 124 JP 391. An allegation by a defendant that he had a homosexual relationship with a prosecution witness was held on the particular facts of the case to involve an imputation, but should not be regarded as invariably so: *R v Bishop* [1975] QB 274; [1974] 2 All ER 1206.
4 *R v Preston* [1909] 1 KB 568.

amount to an imputation.[5] Challenge to the making of an alleged confession is a particularly difficult area. If the defendant simply challenges the accuracy of the record, this will not amount to an imputation whereas if the defence is that police officers have invented admissions so as to facilitate the conviction of the accused, this will let in his character. In *R v Tanner*[6] the court made plain that it is the substance of the defence and questioning that is important, not how delicately it is put. Consequently defence counsel representing a defendant who has a bad criminal record will usually strive to go no further than he need for the purpose of "putting the case" and will suggest that the officer's evidence is "mistaken" or, simply, "challenged". However, while this is perfectly feasible when only one or two answers are disputed, it is not possible when the defendant's challenge is so fundamental that there is no room for mistake and the conflict between the officer's version and the defendant's can, as a matter of common sense, only be explained on the basis that one or other is deliberately lying.[7]

The situation referred to above is but one example of the difficulty which arises when the proper conduct of the defence necessitates imputations upon the prosecution. In such a case the accused appears to be faced with the invidious choice of being hindered in the conduct of his defence or rendering himself liable to cross-examination upon his character and convictions.

d   Where the accused has given evidence against a co-accused (s 1(f)(iii))

The question of whether evidence is given "against" a co-accused must be answered objectively. The test is whether it supports the prosecution case in a material respect or undermines the defence of the co-accused.[8] Thus there need be no intention on the part of the accused to give evidence adverse to his co-accused so long as the evidence has that effect.[9] Evidence cannot be said to have been given against a co-accused where, although it is inconsistent with that co-accused's own testimony, its effect, if believed, would be to result, not in the co-accused's conviction, but in his acquittal.[10] On the other hand where the circumstances are such that one or other of two defendants must have committed the offence charged, it seems that evidence on the part of one defendant which goes no further than a denial of the offence is evidence "against" the other.[11] Where the evidence is given against a co-accused the accused who gives the evidence renders himself liable to cross-examination under section 1(f)(iii) by both the prosecution and his co-accused.

Where an accused person loses his shield the court nevertheless has a discretion as to whether, and to what extent, to allow cross-examination by the prosecution. By contrast, this discretion does not exist to exclude

---

5 *R v Clark* [1955] 2 QB 469; [1955] 3 All ER 29. See also *R v Dunkley* [1927] 1 KB 323.
6 (1977) 66 Cr App Rep 56. *Cf R v Nelson* (1978) 68 Cr App Rep 12.
7 See the discussion of the relevant principles in *R v Britzman* [1983] 1 All ER 369; [1983] 1 WLR 350.
8 *Murdoch v Taylor* [1965] AC 574; [1965] 1 All ER 406.
9 *R v Varley* [1982] 2 All ER 519, which contains a useful summary of the relevant principles.
10 *R v Bruce* [1975] 3 All ER 277; [1975] 1 WLR 1252.
11 *R v Hatton* (1976) 64 Cr App Rep 88.

cross-examination by a co-accused, pursuant to section 1(f)(iii).[12] There is no discretion to exclude such cross-examination. The combined effect of the above rules may impede an accused in the proper conduct of his defence. If the conduct of his defence involves imputations "against" a co-accused there is no discretion to exclude cross-examination by that co-accused upon the first accused's character and convictions. The only safeguard is the power to order separate trials where the defence of one accused is likely to involve evidence against another.[13]

The principles governing the exercise of the discretion to exclude such cross-examination by the prosecution were explained by LAWTON LJ in *R v Britzman*.[14]

> "First, it should be used if there is nothing more than a denial, however emphatic or offensively made, of an act or even a short series of acts amounting to one incident or in what was said to have been a short interview. Examples are provided by the kind of evidence given in pickpocket cases and where the defendant is alleged to have said: 'Who grassed on me this time?' The position would be different however if there were a denial of evidence of a long period of detailed observation extending over hours and, just as in this case and in *R v Tanner*, where there were denials of long conversations. Second, cross-examination should only be allowed if the judge is sure that there is no possibility of mistake, misunderstanding or confusion and that the jury will inevitably have to decide whether the prosecution witnesses have fabricated evidence. Defendants sometimes make wild allegations when giving evidence. Allowance should be made for the strain of being in the witness box and the exaggerated use of language which sometimes results from such strain or lack of education or mental instability. Particular care should be used when a defendant is led into making allegations during cross-examination. The defendant who, during cross-examination, is driven to explaining away the evidence by saying it has been made up or planted on him usually convicts himself without having his previous convictions brought out. Finally, there is no need for the prosecution to rely on section 1(f)(ii) if the evidence against a defendant is overwhelming."

Where cross-examination as to previous convictions is admitted, it is important to remember that evidence of the accused's convictions (or, indeed, bad character generally) is not relevant to prove the commission of the offence charged. It is only relevant to the credibility of the defendant's evidence and the jury must be directed to this effect. Nevertheless judges are well aware of the difficulty experienced by the average juror in performing the mental gymnastics necessary to give effect to this principle and, in practice, common sense indicates that disclosure that a defendant has previous convictions for offences of a similar character to the offence charged is likely to be highly prejudicial to a fair trial. Indeed, VISCOUNT SANKEY LC in *Maxwell v Director of Public Prosecutions*.[15] stated that cross-examination "ought not to be admitted . . . if there is any risk of the jury being misled into thinking that it goes not to credibility but to the probability of his having committed the offence of which he is charged." Consequently where a defendant has previous convictions for similar

---

12 *Murdoch v Taylor* (*supra*, n 8). *R v Rowson* [1986] QB 174.
13 See p 475, *ante*.
14 [1983] 1 All ER 369; [1983] 1 WLR 350.
15 [1935] AC 309 at 321.

offences, the discretion to exclude cross-examination (or at any rate to limit it so as not to disclose the precise nature of his previous conviction) may be exercised in the defendant's favour. The extent to which this is appropriate has been the subject of conflicting views in the Court of Appeal. In *R v Watts*[16] the defence case rested on disputing a confession which was the only substantial evidence against the defendant. The result of this at trial was that a similar conviction of the accused was brought out in cross-examination. The conviction was quashed, the court emphasising the danger of the jury drawing the wrong conclusion from that conviction. Subsequently, however, the Court of Appeal in *R v Powell*[17] said that there was no rule that cross-examination about convictions similar to the offence being tried could not be allowed. Regard must be had to the fairness of the trial generally, and the "tit for tat" principle. In the end it is for the court to decide what is fair generally in each individual case.

D   PUBLIC INTEREST IMMUNITY

Relevant evidence must be excluded if its disclosure would be prejudicial to the public interest. Formerly, it was thought that the doctrine applied only to the Crown (and was known as "Crown privilege") but "public interest immunity" is available to bodies other than the Crown.[18] It is available in civil and criminal proceedings,[19] although the importance of protecting an accused person may make the establishment of such a claim in a criminal case difficult. It will apply to the production of documents, as well as the answering of questions by a witness in court. In civil cases, the objection to production of documents is usually taken at the stage of discovery of documents, although it may be taken at the trial. In criminal cases objection to production of documents may occur at the stage of pre-trial disclosure,[20] or in response to a witness summons requiring the production of documents, as well as at the trial itself.

Public interest immunity differs from claims of privilege[1] in one important respect: it cannot be waived if found to exist. Indeed, even if neither party takes the objection, the judge must exclude evidence if it appears that its reception would be injurious to the public interest.[2]

It was thought at one time that a claim of immunity made by the Crown was beyond challenge in the courts.[3] In 1968 the law was restated by the

---

16 [1983] 3 All ER 101. See also *R v John & Braithwaite* (disapproved in *R v Powell* and *R v Burke, infra*).

17 [1986] 1 All ER 193; [1985] 1 WLR 1364. See also *R v Burke* (1985) 82 Cr App Rep 156. On its facts, *Watts* was a case where the balance was correctly struck.

18 See Lord Hailsham in *D v National Society for the Prevention of Cruelty to Children* [1978] AC 171; [1977] 1 All ER 589.

19 *R v Clowes* [1992] 3 All ER 440.

20 *R v Davis* [1993] 2 All ER 643; [1993] 1 WLR 613. See further p 481, *ante*.

1 *R v Thompson* (1992) unreported: disclosure of case notes and of files relating to persons in a local authority care ordered on an application to discharge an order for production of documents. *Cf R v K* (1992) Times, 8 December: disclosure of videos of therapeutic interviews with abused children not ordered.

2 *Duncan v Cammell Laird & Co Ltd* [1942] AC 624; [1942] 1 All ER 587, *per* Viscount Simon LC.

3 This was the proposition for which *Duncan v Cammell Laird & Co Ltd* was often cited as authority, although it was strictly unnecessary for the decision on the facts. The case involved an action in negligence brought by the relatives of persons killed when a

House of Lords in *Conway v Rimmer*.[4] The House of Lords accepted that a Minister's judgment that the contents of a particular document ought not in the public interest to be disclosed would be accepted by the courts, since it was the Minister who was in the best position to judge their nature and effect of non-disclosure. In relation to claims based upon the class to which the documents belonged, a Minister's certificate was not conclusive, and a court would in appropriate case inspect the documents to assess the validity of the claim made. The final decision in such cases rested with the court. The court, however, accepted that high level government papers justified a considerable degree of protection.[5] On the facts of the case the court ordered disclosure of the documents in issue, which comprised reports concerning a probationary police constable made by a police superintendent, including a report to the Chief Constable.

It will be noted that *Conway v Rimmer* concerned claims of privilege on behalf of the Crown. Historically, the privilege was only extended beyond the Crown in respect of certain information relating to the detection of crime.[6] However, the doctrine developed away from a narrow concept of "Crown privilege" to a wider concept of "public interest immunity". In determining when protection should be granted, it is not sufficient to demonstrate that information is confidential. In *Alfred Crompton Amusement Machines Ltd v Commissioners of Customs and Excise (No 2)*,[7] LORD CROSS observed:

> "'Confidentiality' is not a separate head of privilege, but it may be a very material consideration to bear in mind when privilege is claimed on the grounds of public interest. What the court has to do is to weigh on the one hand the considerations which suggest that it is in the public interest that the documents in question should be disclosed and on the other hand those which suggest that it is in the public interest that they should not be disclosed and to balance one against the other."

An example of this process in the context of a body other than the Crown is the case of *D v National Society for the Prevention of Cruelty to Children*.[8] In that case the defendant society, recognised by statute as having a duty in respect of the protection of children, was faced with a claim for disclosure of the identity of a complainant to the Society who had falsely alleged ill-treatment. The applicant required this information for the purposes of commencing legal proceedings. The House of Lords held that the Society was entitled to withhold discovery of these documents, in the public interest. The public interest to be protected was the effective functioning of an organisation authorised by Act of Parliament to bring proceedings for the welfare of children. The House added, however, that the fact that a communication was made in confidence would not in itself be a sufficient

---

submarine was lost at sea. These events occurred in wartime, and discovery of plans and specifications of the submarine was successfully resisted on the basis of their sensitive nature. The decision on its facts was regarded as correct by the House of Lords in *Conway v Rimmer (infra)*.

4 [1968] AC 910; [1968] 1 All ER 874.
5 See LORD REID at p 952; *Air Canada v Secretary of State for Trade (No 2)* [1983] 2 AC 394; [1983] 1 All ER 910.
6 See p 616, *post*.
7 [1974] AC 405; [1973] 2 All ER 1169.
8 [1978] AC 171; [1977] 1 All ER 589.

ground to justify non-disclosure of either information communicated or the identity of an informant. It should also be noted that although the courts recognise that public interest immunity may be claimed by bodies other than the Crown, they have been reluctant to extend the application of the doctrine beyond situations where a body has a duty to investigate, or gather information, which would be hindered if immunity were not granted.

Thus claims of immunity have been upheld in respect of the activities of the Gaming Board,[9] and of investigations of police complaints.[10] Protection has also been given to records relating to the welfare of children.[11] By contrast, the courts have been unwilling to extend the doctrine of public interest immunity to journalistic sources of information.[12]

It has already been noted that one established class of case where privilege, or immunity, has been recognised is information concerning law enforcement. The right of the police to withhold information which would identify police informers was recognised in *Marks v Beyfus*,[13] although it will not be permitted to interfere with the necessity of ensuring the fair trial of an accused. This on occasion has led to prosecutions being discontinued rather than disclosure made.[14] This protection of police informants has been, more recently, extended to the identity,[15] and location,[16] of police observation posts.

In deciding whether a claim of immunity should be upheld the court is entitled to inspect the documents. It will not automatically do so. The party claiming discovery will have to show that such documents are likely to assist his case.[17] Parties will not be allowed to go on "fishing expeditions" in the hope of finding something of evidential value.

---

9 *Rogers v Secretary of State for Home Department* [1973] AC 388; [1972] 2 All ER 1057.
10 *Neilson v Laugharne* [1981] QB 736; [1981] 1 All ER 829; *Hehir v Metropolitan Police Commissioner* [1982] 2 All ER 335; [1982] 1 WLR 715; *Makanjuola v Metropolitan Police Commissioner* [1992] 3 All ER 617. Cf *Peach v Metropolitan Police Commissioner* [1986] QB 1064; [1986] 2 All ER 129.
11 *Gaskin v Liverpool City Council* [1980] 1 WLR 1549.
12 *British Steel Corporation v Granada Television Ltd* [1981] AC 1096; [1981] 1 All ER 417.
13 (1890) 25 QBD 494.
14 *R v Langford* [1990] Crim LR 653.
15 *R v Rankine* [1986] QB 861; [1986] 2 All ER 566. For the relevant principles, see *R v Johnson* [1989] 1 All ER 121; [1988] 1 WLR 1377.
16 *R v Hewitt and Davis* [1992] Crim LR 650; *Blake v Director of Public Prosecutions* [1993] Crim LR 283.
17 *Burmah Oil Co Ltd v Governor & Company of the Bank of England* [1980] AC 1090; [1979] 3 All ER 700.

CHAPTER 30

Hearsay Evidence

A INTRODUCTION

The rule against hearsay is the most important exclusionary rule of evidence. Stated simply, it amounts to this: that the court should hear evidence directly from the witness who has personal knowledge of the matters in question, and should not have to rely on what that witness was told, or what that witness said out of court. By way of precise definition, the formulation of the hearsay rule by *Cross on Evidence* has received judicial approval.[1] It states:

> "An assertion other than one made by a person while giving oral evidence in the proceedings is inadmissible as evidence of any fact asserted."

The purpose of the rule is to prevent the admission of potentially unreliable evidence. In *Teper v R*[2] VISCOUNT NORMAND explained the justification for the rule in the following way:

> "The rule against the admission of hearsay is fundamental. It is not the best evidence and it is not received on oath. The truthfulness and accuracy of the person whose words are spoken by another witness cannot be tested by cross-examination, and the light which his demeanour would throw on his testimony would be lost."

Of these reasons, the absence of an ability to cross-examine is the most crucial, since it is the testing of evidence in this way that minimises (though does not eliminate) the dangers of distortion or fabrication. Yet the utility of the rule can be questioned. First, the courts sometimes have a great deal of difficulty in determining what is within the rule and what is not.[3] Secondly, there is a multiplicity of exceptions to the rule, both common law and statutory, and in certain areas of the law the rule has largely been abandoned. Thirdly, its strict operation can exclude even reliable evidence. An extreme example of this was *Myers v Director of Public Prosecutions*.[4] In that case the House of Lords ruled that car manufacturer's records containing engine and chassis numbers, and cylinder block

---

1 *R v Sharp* [1988] 1 All ER 65; [1988] 1 WLR 7, approving statement in 6th Edn.
2 [1952] AC 480; [1952] 2 All ER 447.
3 The case of *R v Kearley* [1992] 2 AC 228; [1992] 2 All ER 345 (discussed p 555, *ante*) is a noteable example. See also *R v Rice* [1963] 1 QB 857; [1963] 1 All ER 832.
4 [1965] AC 1001; [1964] 2 All ER 881.

numbers, were inadmissible as hearsay, and could not be used in criminal proceedings relating to stolen cars. Even though the reality was that those records were likely to be highly reliable, with none of the dangers associated with hearsay evidence, no exception to the rule existed at that time under which they could be admitted.[5] Furthermore it was not for the courts to create new common law exceptions to the rule. Reform of the law must be left to Parliament. The result has been a series of legislative provisions that broaden the range of exceptions, particularly in civil cases.

B   THE RULE

From the definition given by *Cross*, and stated above, certain key features can be identified.

1   There must be an out-of-court statement

This can be oral, or documentary. It can also be by conduct.[6] For example, if in answer to a question, a person shook his head, evidence of this conduct would be inadmissible since it is equivalent to the person uttering the word "no". Conduct will usually be a fact in itself, evidence of which can be given if relevant. Only if the conduct can be described as a means of expressing a fact as an alternative to expressing it in words will a hearsay problem arise.

2   The statement must contain an assertion

In many cases this is no problem. The statement will intend to assert some fact or other, whether it is the name of an assailant, a description of negligent conduct by a defendant or some other fact or admissible opinion. It can be made orally or in a document. Thus in *Patel v Comptroller of Customs*[7] the words "Produce of Morocco" on bags of coriander were asserting the country of origin, and therefore amounted to hearsay when it was sought to use them to prove that fact.

More difficulty arises in respect of words which imply an assertion. Debate has been keen as to whether an assertion can be implied from the use of words, but authority suggests that it can. In *Wright v Doe d Tatham*[8] three letters written to a testator were held by the House of Lords to be inadmissible evidence of his sanity. They would not have been written in the way they were if the writers had not believed the testator to be sane, and thus were held to be impliedly asserting that sanity. Since it was the truth of that assertion that was in issue, they fell

---

5 As a result of this decision a statutory exception in respect of trade and business records was created by the Criminal Evidence Act 1965. This provision was repealed, and replaced by the Police and Criminal Evidence Act 1984, s 68, which was itself replaced by the Criminal Justice Act 1988, s 24.

6 An obvious example is communication by sign language: see *Chandrasekera v R* [1937] AC 220; [1937] 3 All ER 865.

7 [1966] AC 356; [1965] 3 All ER 593.

8 (1837) 7 Ad & El 313.

within the hearsay rule. More recently, in *R v Kearley*[9] the House of Lords held that the evidence of police officers that, whilst searching premises, they received telephone calls and visits from persons asking for the appellant and seeking to purchase drugs from him was inadmissible. The prosecution wished to adduce that evidence to support a charge of possession of controlled drugs with intent to supply.[10] The House held that those conversations were only relevant to that charge if reliance was placed on the assertion which was implicit in the words, ie that the appellant was a dealer in drugs. To rely on the truth of an assertion in a statement of course infringed the hearsay rule. The difficulty of this particular area is illustrated by the fact that in the whole of the proceedings, of all the judges who considered the matter six thought the evidence not hearsay,[11] and only three (the majority in the House of Lords) regarded the conversations as only relevant if there was reliance upon an implied assertion, as opposed to the fact that the statement was made, which would not infringe the hearsay rule.[12]

3 The statement must be being tendered to prove the truth of that assertion

Not every out-of-court statement infringes the rule. If the fact that a statement is made is relevant, then no hearsay problem arises. We can identify various situations.

(a) The making of a statement is, in certain cases, a fact in issue. Obvious examples occur in the torts of libel, slander and malicious falsehood where, in each case, the plaintiff must prove publication of a statement concerning himself or his property. Indeed if the plaintiff were prevented from adducing such evidence these causes of action could not exist. There are numerous types of action in which the statement is in itself a fact in issue. In actions in contract an offer, acceptance, waiver, repudiation or release may well be facts in issue and will usually consist of assertions by one of the parties.

(b) *Res gestae.* Sometimes the use of words is as much part of the events under consideration as conduct. Words which accompany and explain actions are part of those actions. This is the non-hearsay element of the *res gestae* rule, but both will be considered further below.[13]

(c) On other occasions, the use of words, though not part of the *res gestae*, will themselves be relevant to a matter in issue. The principle is illustrated by *Subramaniam v Public Prosecutor*.[14] The appellant,

---

9 [1992] 2 AC 228; [1992] 2 All ER 345. Comparison may be made with *R v Warner* (1992) 96 Cr App Rep 324, where a circumstantial inference could be drawn from *observations* made by police officers of large numbers of individuals entering and leaving premises, providing evidence to establish intent to supply.
10 Contrary to the Misuse of Drugs Act 1971, s 10.
11 The trial judge, the three judges in the Court of Appeal, and the two dissenting Law Lords in the House of Lords.
12 The case is therefore mainly an authority on the question of relevance.
13 See p 622, *post*.
14 [1956] 1 WLR 965.

on a charge of unlawful possession of firearms, set up the defence of duress. At his trial he was not allowed to testify to threats which Malayan terrorists had allegedly made to him, the trial judge regarding these threats as hearsay. The Privy Council advised that this was wrong since the threats were original evidence of the fact of duress and should have been admitted.

The difficulty is not in the stating of this principle, but in its application. For it to apply, the fact of the making of the statement must be relevant to an issue to be decided. In *R v Blastland*[15] the question was whether, on a charge of murder, third party statements were admissible. These statements showed knowledge of the murder at a time when such knowledge was not generally available. The defence naturally wished to put such statements before the court to support the defence that the wrong man was accused, an application that was refused. The House of Lords dismissed an appeal against conviction. The making of a statement itself was only relevant if it related directly to elements of the charge or to a defence raised. In *Subramaniam* they did; in this case, they did not. The knowledge, said the House of Lords, could be explained in many ways other than that the third party was the murderer.

The fact of use of words can also be relevant to an issue if circumstantial inferences can be drawn from those words. Thus evidence would undoubtedly be admissible that a person was speaking incoherently or singing if his sobriety, or even his sanity, were a fact in issue. Similarly a male person under the age of twenty-four charged with unlawful sexual intercourse with a girl under the age of sixteen[16] may testify to the fact that the girl told him she was over sixteen since this fact tends to support his belief in her age, that belief being a fact in issue. Some cases are straightforward. In *R v Lydon*[17] pieces of paper inscribed "Sean rules" and "Sean rules 85" were relevant not for the purposes of showing their truth, but to allow the circumstantial inference that the appellant (known as Sean) could be linked to the gun found adjacent to these bits of paper. Yet in other cases it is difficult to draw an inference without seeming to relying on the truth of the contents of the words. Many of the cases in this area are marginal cases, which could fall on either side of the line.[18]

(d) No hearsay question arises where out-of-court statements are used to refresh memory,[19] to show consistency or to show inconsistency affecting credit,[20] since they are not being relied upon to

---

15 [1986] AC 41; [1985] 2 All ER 1095. For comment on this case see Birch, 'Hearsay Logic and Hearsay Fiddles' in *Essays in Honour of JC Smith* (1987, Butterworths).

16 Sexual Offences Act 1956, s 6.

17 (1987) 85 Cr App Rep 221. See also: *Woodhouse v Hall* (1980) 72 Cr App Rep 39, where the *fact* that masseuses at a massage parlour offered sexual services was a fact from which a circumstantial inference could be drawn that the premises were being used as a brothel. Thus, no hearsay problem arose, and police officers were entitled to give evidence of those statements.

18 See, in particular, *R v Rice* [1963] 1 QB 857; [1963] 1 All ER 832, doubted in *Myers v Director of Public Prosecutions* [1965] AC 1001; [1964] 2 All ER 881.

19 See p 584, *ante*.

20 See p 583, *ante*.

demonstrate their truth. In reality this distinction is highly artificial, since often a witness will have little knowledge other than the document from which he is "refreshing memory". In civil cases the exception created by section 2 of the Civil Evidence Act 1968 applies: a witness's previous statement is admissible and, when admitted, constitutes evidence of any fact stated therein. However, by section 2(2) a statement from a person whom a party has called or intends to call as a witness may not be given in evidence without the leave of the court and, generally, may not be given in evidence even then before the close of the witness's examination-in-chief. Thus the main use of such statements will be in re-examination to bolster the evidence of a witness who has been cross-examined upon, for example, a previous inconsistent statement.

(e) In addition to the above, care should be taken in respect of statements produced by mechanical or technological means. This will usually in the form of a document produced by a machine, but could be, for example, a photocopy of a radar screen,[1] or a video or tape-recording.[2] Whether any hearsay problem arises depends upon the nature of the information recorded, and chiefly arises in respect of computer evidence. If a printout is the product of the computer's own processes then it is original evidence and not hearsay.[3] If, however, the computer is only a store for information fed in by an operator, then, as with any other record, the print-out is hearsay, and must be brought within one of the exceptions.[4] The words typed into a word processor by an author are as much hearsay evidence as if written in longhand. In addition, the conditions for admissibility of computer evidence (which, despite some confusions,[5] are separate from the hearsay issue) must be satisfied, unless the computer is being used in effect as a calculator.[6]

Finally, it should be noted that the hearsay rule in civil cases was radically recast by the Civil Evidence Act 1968, which governs all statements that fall within the scope of the Act. This is dealt with in more detail in due course.[7] Since the basis of admissibility in criminal and civil cases is now so different, they will be treated separately.

---

1 *The Statue of Liberty* [1968] 2 All ER 195; [1968] 1 WLR 739.
2 *R v Dodson* [1984] 1 WLR 971; *Taylor v Chief Constable of Cheshire* [1987] 1 All ER 225; [1986] 1 WLR 1479. Nor does the compilation of a photofit or videofit picture infringe the hearsay rule: *R v Cook* [1987] QB 417; [1987] 1 All ER 1049.
3 *R v Shephard* [1993] AC 380; [1993] 1 All ER 225; *R v Wood* (1982) 76 Cr App Rep 23.
4 *R v Minors* [1989] 2 All ER 208; [1989] 1 WLR 441.
5 See, for example, *R v Minors, supra.* For criticism of the approach of the courts see, JC Smith at [1987] Crim LR.
6 See, eg, *Sophocleus v Ringer* [1987] 151 JP 564. In *R v Blackburn and Wade* (1992) Times, 1 December, the court doubted whether a word processed document was within the provisions of the Police and Criminal Evidence Act 1984, s 69.
7 See p 636, *post.*

C   HEARSAY IN CRIMINAL CASES

No statutory code governing the admissibility of hearsay evidence exists, as it does (broadly speaking) in civil cases. Reference has to be made to the multiplicity of common law and statutory exceptions, bearing in mind that the first decision the court has to take is whether the hearsay rule is infringed at all.

1   Res gestae

It has already been noted that statements which form part of the *res gestae*, because they accompany and explain actions,[8] do not infringe the hearsay rule. However, that expression also describes a major exception to the hearsay rule. Both aspects of the rule were discussed by the Privy Council in *Ratten v R*.[9] In that case the evidence in question was that of a telephone operator who stated that, at about the time the deceased was shot by her husband, a woman telephoned from the deceased's premises in a hysterical state and said "Get me the police please". The defendant's version of events was that the gun had discharged by accident while he was cleaning it. Evidence of the telephone conversation was held admissible on a charge of murder. It was a fact which showed that a telephone call was made, and the mental state of the caller, thus negativing the defence of accident. It did not, therefore, infringe the hearsay rule. However, the Privy Council went on to state that even if it was hearsay evidence it was still admissible as part of the *res gestae* exception to the hearsay rule. In this second sense, evidence of words is allowed in evidence even though it is hearsay because the words are uttered in circumstances that allow the court safely to rely on them.

The conceptual question as to whether res gestae statements are original (ie non-hearsay) evidence, or hearsay evidence falling within an exception to the rule, was therefore left open. The Court of Appeal in *R v McCay*[10] similarly avoided that question, deciding that evidence could be given by a police officer as to the verbal identification of the appellant at an identification parade.[11] The words fell to be regarded as part of the *res gestae*, irrespective of which meaning the term was given. The reality is that in most cases the conceptual question is unimportant since, on either view, the admissibility of the statement depends upon its proximity, in time and place, to a fact in issue.

The traditional approach of the courts was to require proof of spontaneity and contemporaneity of such statements with the events they accompanied. Thus in *Teper v R*[12] the words of an unknown witness who exclaimed "Your place burning and you going away from the fire" were not a *res gestae* statement, even though exclaimed as a car containing a man resembling the accused drove by. The words were exclaimed some distance from where the fire began, and some 20 minutes after the event in question. In his speech LORD NORMAND indicated that the events sought to

---

8 See p 619, *ante*.
9 [1972] AC 378; [1971] 3 All ER 801.
10 [1991] 1 All ER 232; [1990] 1 WLR 645.
11 For the conduct of identification parades, see p 273, *ante*.
12 [1952] AC 480; [1952] 2 All ER 447.

be proved must be so connected in terms of time, place and circumstance to as to be part of the thing done, not simply an item of reported speech.

This approach was reconsidered in *Ratten v R.*[13] In his speech, LORD WILBERFORCE considered the different meanings of the term "res gestae", and concluded that the real test of admissibility should be whether or not there was a risk of concoction:

> "This should be recognised and applied directly as the relevant test: the test should not be the uncertain one whether the making of the statement was in some sense part of the event or transaction. This may often be difficult to establish."

Amongst the relevant factors might be the event and the speaking of the words, and the location of the speaking of the words. It is for the judge to satisfy himself that the statement was made in circumstances of spontaneity or involvement in the event so that the possibility or concoction could be disregarded. Conversely, if he considers that the statement was made by way of a detached narrative so that the speaker was so disengaged from it as to construct or adapt his account, he should exclude it.

These tests were expanded in later cases,[14] and approved in *R v Andrews.*[15] In that case the victim of murder was found some minutes after having been assaulted and robbed. He told the police that he had been attacked by two men, and named the appellant before becoming unconscious. The trial judge admitted the statement as part of the *res gestae*, a decision upheld by the House of Lords. LORD ACKNER considered and adopted the *Ratten* test. The degree of contemporaneity and spontaneity had to be such as to preclude the possibility of concoction or distortion. In order to do this, it had to be so closely associated with the event which excited the utterance that the victim's mind was still dominated by the event. If there were special features such as malice, then, again the trial judge had to be satisfied that concoction could be eliminated. In respect of the possibility of error, this went to weight, not admissibility. On the facts, this was a statement made spontaneously by a seriously injured person, and was rightly admitted.[16]

Finally, it should be noted that there is an analogous rule: statements by persons as to their present feelings or health are admissible as evidence of those feelings or state of health.[17]

2 Admissions and confessions

Evidence is admissible of the out-of-court statement of a party where that statement is adverse to the interest of the maker. The justification historically given by the law for this is that a party to proceedings is unlikely to make a statement against interest unless it were true. Since it only applies to admissions by an accused (or a party in civil

---

13 [1972] AG 378 at 389; [1971] 3 All ER 801 at 807.
14 See *R v Nye and Loan* (1977) 66 Cr App Rep 252, where LAWTON LJ added a gloss, ". . . or possibility of error".
15 [1987] AC 281; [1987] 1 All ER 513.
16 In this case the deceased was under the influence of alcohol. This does not affect admissibility, but goes to weight, creating the possibility of error; see *Edwards v Director of Public Prosecutions* [1992] Crim LR 576.
17 *R v Gloster* (1888) 16 Cox CC 471.

cases),[18] admissions and confessions by third parties are not within the exception.[19] It should also be borne in mind that the admission or confession is only evidence against its maker: thus where there are two accused the judge must direct the jury that the confession of one accused is not, generally, evidence against the other.[20]

a Definition

In a criminal case virtually all admissions (ie adverse statements by a party to proceedings) will be confessions. Section 82(1) defines a confession as:

> ". . . any statement wholly or partly adverse to the person who made it, whether made to a person in authority or not, and whether made in words or otherwise."

Some instances, though, might still be termed admissions. This is where there is deemed to be acceptance of an allegation by silence or by non-denial. The principle was established by the civil case of *Bessela v Stern*.[1] In this action for breach of promise of marriage the plaintiff was proved to have said to the defendant: "You always promised to marry me, and you don't keep your word." The defendant did not answer and it was held that his silence corroborated the plaintiff's testimony. It was stressed, however, that the defendant's silence only amounted to an admission because in the circumstances he might have been expected to deny the allegation.

The principle applies equally in criminal cases. In *Parkes v R*[2] the appellant was charged with the murder of a young woman. The woman's mother found her daughter bleeding from stab wounds whereupon she went into the yard at the premises where she saw the appellant with a knife in his hands. She twice accused him of stabbing her daughter but he made no reply and, indeed, when she threatened to detain him he attempted to stab her. The trial judge in Jamaica directed the jury that the failure of the appellant to reply to the mother's accusations coupled with his conduct immediately after those accusations were made were matters from which the jury might infer that the appellant accepted the truth of the accusation. The Privy Council dismissed the appellant's appeal against his conviction for murder. Again, silence in response to police questioning where the parties were on equal terms[3] was held in *R v Chandler*[4] to amount to acceptance of allegations put to him. Each case, though, turns on its own facts, and in many cases silence can only be equated with legitimate reliance on the right to silence and not indicative of acceptance.

---

18 Even though such statements will usually be within the Civil Evidence Act 1968, s 2 (see p 636, *post*), the common law exception is preserved by s 9(2)(a).

19 A rule which can produce seemingly indefensible results: see *R v Turner* (1975) 61 Cr App Rep 67; *R v Beckford* (1991) 94 Cr App Rep 43, distinguished in *R v Campbell and Williams* [1993] Crim LR 448.

20 *R v Gunewardene* [1951] 2 KB 600; [1951] 2 All ER 290. An exception exists where the statement is made in the presence of the co-accused, and the incriminating parts are accepted by him. In cases where the prejudicial effect of the above rules is too great the judge may order severance and separate trials. See p 476, *ante*.

1 (1877) 2 CPD 265.

2 [1976] 3 All ER 380; [1976] 1 WLR 1251.

3 See *R v Mitchell* (1892) 17 Cox CC 503

4 [1976] 3 All ER 105; [1976] 1 WLR 585.

The definition of a confession is, as has been noted, a broad one. It will include any statement which is wholly or partly adverse, and, even where it is only partially so, the whole statement is evidence of its truth. The House of Lords so held in *R v Sharp*[5] reversing the unworkable rule set out in earlier case law that only the adverse parts were to be so regarded.[6] The definition does not include statements that are not adverse on their face, but which are being used against the accused.[7] For example, a statement may be made by an accused to the police denying the offence and claiming an alibi. The prosecution may wish to adduce this statement to show its falsity.[8] This is not a confession, although the practical importance of this is slight. If such a statement was unfairly obtained, in a manner which would cause a court to exclude it if it were a confession, a court would almost certainly use its discretion under section 78 of the 1984 Act to exclude it.[9] A confession may also be made by conduct. This will include not only obvious examples such as sign language, but also police reconstructions in which the accused agrees to take part. In *Lam Chi-ming v R*[10] the appellants were charged with murder. In confessions, ruled inadmissible because of the brutal way they had been obtained, the appellants told the police where they had thrown the weapon alleged to have been used to commit the murder. The police then took them to that spot, where they indicated, on video, where they had thrown that knife. The knife was duly recovered and the Hong Kong court admitted into evidence the video showing the actions of the accused. The Privy Council allowed the appeal and quashed the conviction, because it was based essentially upon the contents of the inadmissible confession. In reality the majority of confessions will be statements made by a suspect to the police:[11] given the rules relating to police interviews these will usually be in written form either as formal statements or verified notes of interview.

b   The tests for admissibility

For a confession to be admissible for the prosecution, it has to satisfy the tests required by law. Prior to the coming into force of the 1984 Act these were based upon notions of "voluntariness", developed through the cases to protect a suspect against improper conduct by persons in authority,[12] and against improperly induced self-incrimination. The Judges' Rules[13] existed to regulate police questioning so as to ensure that only voluntary confessions were admitted. This framework was replaced by that created by the Police and Criminal Evidence Act 1984, which implemented, subject to certain modifications, the recommendations of the Royal

---

5 [1988] 1 All ER 65; [1988] 1 WLR 7.

6 See *R v Storey* (1968) 52 Cr App Rep 334.

7 *R v Sat-Bhambra* (1988) 88 Cr App Rep 55.

8 Whether this lie has evidential value in establishing guilt will depend upon the motive for lying.

9 See p 629, *post*.

10 [1991] 2 AC 212; [1991] 3 All ER 172. See also: *Li Shu-Ling v R* [1989] AC 270; [1988] 3 All ER 138, where a reconstruction of the crime was recorded on video, and held to be a confession.

11 And thus subject to the Code of Practice in the Questioning of Suspects. See p 266, *ante*.

12 *Ibrahim v R* [1914] AC 599.

13 Non-statutory guidance drawn up by the judges of the Queen's Bench Division for the guidance of the police. They have now been replaced by the Codes of Practice made under the Police and Criminal Evidence Act 1984, s 66.

Commission on Criminal Procedure.[14] The Royal Commission had recommended that the test for admissibility of a confession should be based upon the principle of reliability, but with confessions obtained by particularly serious misconduct by the police also being excluded.[15] In this context, it can be noted that many of the well-publicised cases in which convictions based upon unreliable confession evidence have had to be quashed, were cases where the pre-1984 Act rules and procedures applied.[16]

Section 76(2) of the Police and Criminal Evidence Act 1984 provides:

> "If, in any proceedings where the prosecution proposes to give in evidence a confession made by an accused person, it is represented to the court that the confession was or may have been obtained –
>
> (a) by oppression of the person who made it; or
> (b) in consequence of anything said or done which was likely, in the circumstances existing at the time, to render unreliable any confession which might be made by him in consequence thereof,
>
> the court shall not allow the confession to be given in evidence against him except in so far as the prosecution proves to the court beyond reasonable doubt that the confession (notwithstanding that it may be true) was not obtained as aforesaid."

It should be noted, however, that the discretion to exclude evidence created by section 78 of the 1984 Act is wide enough to apply to confession as well as non-confession evidence,[17] and, indeed, the exclusion of confessions has been by far the largest area of use of that discretion.[18] The consideration of admissibility of any confession is, therefore, likely to involve consideration of both sections.

c Procedure

As a preliminary to consideration of substance the procedure for dealing with questions of admissibility must be borne in mind. It was noted earlier[19] that these questions will almost always be decided on the *voir dire* or, more colloquially, within a "trial within a trial". When this happens, the accused's position is governed by the opinion of the Judicial Committee of the Privy Council in *Wong Kam-Ming v R*.[20] That case established two important principles. Firstly, that the prosecution is not entitled to cross-examine the accused as to the truth of the disputed statement, since the sole issue is whether the statement has been made voluntarily;[1] secondly, whether the statement is excluded or admitted, the prosecution is not entitled as part of its case to adduce evidence of the testimony of the defendant on the *voir dire*. However, where the accused gives evidence

---

14 Cm 8092, 1981, HMSO.
15 *Ibid*, para 4.132.
16 See eg, *R v Silcott, Braithwaite and Raghip* (1991) Times, 9 December; *R v Maguire* [1992] QB 936; [1992] 2 All ER 433.
17 *R v Mason* [1987] 3 All ER 481; [1987] 1 WLR 139.
18 See p 629, *post*.
19 See p 552, *ante*.
20 [1980] AC 247; [1979] 1 All ER 939, applied in *R v Brophy* [1982] AC 476; [1981] 2 All ER 705.
1 This terminology reflects the test of voluntariness which was applicable at that time.

and this is inconsistent with evidence which he gave on the *voir dire*, he may be cross-examined as to the latter and, if he denies that he previously gave inconsistent evidence, his testimony on the *voir dire* may be proved (generally by calling the shorthand-writer) in rebuttal under section 4 of the Criminal Procedure Act 1865. The position in magistrates' courts should also be noted. Since the magistrates are judges of both fact and law, then clearly they will hear of the confession when determining admissibility. It is nevertheless their duty to rule separately as to the admissibility of the confession, and if ruled inadmissible, to put it out of their minds.[2] This is of course easier said than done.

d General considerations

Several general points should be borne in mind. The burden of proof is upon the prosecution. The prosecution has the duty of demonstrating beyond reasonable doubt that the confession was not obtained in breach of the Act. Secondly, truth is not a determining factor: a confession can be both true and inadmissible, although the courts do not always clearly distinguish these separate matters. Logically, the admissibility of a confession might best be decided without reference to its contents; however, perusal of its contents may sometimes be important in determining the state of mind of the maker of that confession.[3] Thirdly, for a confession to be inadmissible, a causative link between the alleged conduct and the making of the confession must be shown.[4]

e Oppression

This concept had a technical meaning prior to the Act, as conduct "tending to sap the free will" of the individual.[5] Oppression has a wider meaning under the 1984 Act. Section 76(8) defines "oppression" as *including* "torture, inhuman or degrading treatment, and the use or threat of violence (whether or not amounting to torture)". This subsection is therefore illustrative, not all-embracing, and in the leading authority on oppression under the Act, *R v Fulling*,[6] the Court of Appeal ignored the statutory definition: the Act (being a codifying Act) was to be given its ordinary and natural meaning. The court relied upon the Oxford English Dictionary definition of oppression: "the exercise of authority or power in a burdensome, harsh or wrongful manner; unjust or cruel treatment of subjects, inferiors, etc; the imposition of unreasonable or unjust burdens." Accordingly the court concluded that oppression would almost always involve impropriety, and on the facts of the case there was none.

The decision whether conduct is, or may be, oppressive, has to be

---

2 *R v Liverpool Juvenile Court, ex parte R* [1985] QB 1; [1987] 2 All ER 668.

3 *R v Miller* [1986] 3 All ER 119; [1986] 1 WLR 1191: though a pre-1984 Act case, the principle remains sound.

4 See *R v Tyrer* (1989) 90 Cr App Rep 446. The wording of the statute reflects the common law rule existing prior to the passage of the 1984 Act: see *R v Rennie* [1982] 1 All ER 385; [1982] 1 WLR 64.

5 *R v Priestly* (1965) 51 Cr App Rep 1n, approved in *Callis v Gunn* [1964] 1 QB 495; [1963] 3 All ER 677.

6 [1987] QB 426; [1987] 2 All ER 65.

considered in the context of the personal characteristics of the individual suspect.[7] Plainly, violence or threats of violence constitute oppression. So too will maltreatment that amounts to torture or inhuman or degrading treatment, phrases that probably bear the same meaning as is ascribed to them by the European Court of Human Rights.[8] They all involve misconduct. The mistreatment does not, however, have to be physical. In *R v Paris, Abdullahi and Miller*,[9] the Court of Appeal categorised the tough, confrontational, repetitive and bullying approach of the police as oppressive. The interview of a mentally disabled suspect involved extended periods of questioning of this type, and the Court of Appeal quashed a conviction which was based upon such questioning, the court being of the view that "short of physical violence, it is hard to conceive of a more hostile and intimidating approach by officers to a suspect".

Significant breaches of the provisions of statutory Codes of Practice governing suspects[10] are likely to constitute oppression if they show a deliberate scheme of flouting of a suspect's rights to a significant degree. However, not every wrongdoing will amount to oppression.[11] In reality findings of oppression will be, or should be, rare, since most cases approaching the threshold of oppression will also fall to be considered under section 76(2)(b) or section 78. The advantage of showing oppression, however, is that it leads to exclusion irrespective of the likelihood of unreliability.

f   Likelihood of unreliability

It is "likelihood" of unreliability of *any* confession that determines admissibility, not whether it is in fact unreliable. That likelihood must come from "something said or done". In *R v Goldenberg*[12] it was held that there had to be something "external" to the person being questioned. Thus the fact that an accused had a motive of his own to confess will not bring the confession within section 76(2)(b). However, there may be cases where the personal characteristics of the accused make it likely that what he says cannot safely be relied upon. In such cases the very holding of the interview is likely to result in a suspect confession.[13] Despite the fact that in *R v Fulling*[14] the court ruled that no police impropriety was needed to trigger section 76(2)(b), the effect of the approach in *R v Goldenberg* suggests otherwise. The point was considered further in *R v Crampton*[15] where the Court of Appeal was prepared to assume that the holding of an

---

7 *R v Seelig* [1991] 4 All ER 429; [1992] 1 WLR 148. This reflects the pre-1984 Act law. In *R v Gowan* [1982] Crim LR 821, it was said that an "experienced professional criminal" must expect vigorous questioning from the police.
8 See *R v McCormick* [1977] NI 105, a decision on a similarly worded Northern Irish statutory provision.
9 (1992) 97 Cr App Rep 99. The fact that questioning may be rude and persistent is not of itself enough necessarily to create oppression: *R v Emmerson* (1990) 92 Cr App Rep 284.
10 See p 258, *ante*.
11 See *R v Fulling, supra*, n 6.
12 (1988) 88 Cr App Rep 285.
13 This will be the situation in cases where the suspect suffers from significant mental disability. In such cases even questioning in accordance with the Code requirements may not suffice to eliminate the likelihood of unreliability; see eg, *R v Harvey* [1988] Crim LR 241.
14 *Supra*, n 6.
15 (1990) 92 Cr App Rep 369.

interview was something "said or done". Even if this assumption was made, however, the holding of the interview was not something likely to cause unreliability. The facts of the case were that the accused was a heroin addict, who made an admission some 19 hours after arrest, at a time when he might have been suffering withdrawal symptoms. The police did not know of his addiction, and considered that he was fit to be interviewed, although they would not have done had they known of that addiction. The appeal, based on the failure of the trial judge to exclude under section 76(2)(b), was dismissed. Therefore, only where the confession is obtained as a result of something which goes beyond the very questioning, for example breach of the Codes of Practice, will the subsection operate. Some fault, albeit perhaps unintentional, is therefore required, although in "no fault" cases the facts may well be such as to justify exclusion under section 78.

Likelihood of unreliability will again have to be considered in the light of the individual characteristics of the accused. Breach of the Code requirements concerning the length and nature of questioning may create this likelihood.[16] So too, in some circumstances, might the failure to allow access to a solicitor, particularly for a vulnerable suspect.[17] The making of inducements or promises, or the playing on mental weaknesses, will all potentially give rise to the operation of this provision. Breach of the requirements for the protection of vulnerable suspects almost certainly will lead to exclusion, and, in assessing the likelihood of unreliability, the court is entitled to have regard to expert medical opinion evidence.[18] The breach of the recording provisions of the Codes may make it unsafe to rely on a confession.

Each case has to be considered individually, and precedent is of limited value, except to show the proper approach to the Act. In reality a combination of factors usually exists, including the effect and impact of earlier interviews,[19] and the court will look at the totality of the position. It should also be noted that occasionally the legal basis of exclusion of a particular confession is not made clear.[20]

g   Exclusion under s 78

Whilst section 76 of the 1984 Act requires a court as a matter of law to exclude unless the conditions for admissibility are satisfied, section 78 confers a discretion to exclude notwithstanding the fact that the conditions for admissibility are satisfied. The decision is that of the trial judge, but in many cases the Court of Appeal has ruled that if a trial judge had approached the matter in the right way then exclusion would have resulted. Section 78 applies to all types of evidence. In *R v Mason*[1] a confession was obtained after the police had represented falsely to the accused and his solicitor that they had found incriminating fingerprints. In quashing the

---

16 *R v Paris, Abdullahi and Miller, ante*, n 9.
17 *R v McGovern* (1990) 92 Cr App Rep 228. *R v Moss* (1990) 91 Cr App Rep 371.
18 *R v Silcott, Braithwaite and Raghip* (1991) Times, 9 December. *R v Ward* [1993] 2 All ER 577; [1993] 1 WLR 619. For expert evidence, see p 590, *ante*.
19 *R v McGovern* (1991) 92 Cr App Rep 228.
20 See *R v Lamont* [1989] Crim LR 813, where the court relied on all of sections 76, 77 and 78 to justify exclusion of a confession made by a mentally handicapped accused.
1 [1987] 3 All ER 481; [1988] 1 WLR 139.

conviction the Court of Appeal laid stress upon the fact that, but for the deceit, the accused would not have made a self-incriminatory statement. This protection of the right against improperly induced self-incrimination is a recurring theme in the section 78 case law. Another is the discretionary exclusion of admissions where procedural safeguards have not been complied with: proceedings can be unfair, said the Court of Appeal in *R v Quinn*,[2] if the accused is placed at a disadvantage.

It should not be assumed that any irregularity will lead to the use of the discretion to exclude a confession: the section is not a weapon with which to discipline the police. Despite this, the courts have used section 78 to protect the rights granted by the 1984 Act and the Codes of Practice. Whilst not every breach will lead to exclusion, the Court of Appeal in *R v Walsh*[3] held that "significant and substantial" breaches were likely to justify exclusion. That, of course, begs the question as to what is significant and substantial. Some examples can be given.

(a) Obtaining a confession though trickery or deceit is likely to lead to exclusion.[4] In extreme cases it may form part of conduct held to be oppressive.

(b) Refusal of the right to legal advice[5] will potentially give rise to exclusion. Whilst this is not automatic, the reasoning is that a suspect may well not have confessed if the right had been accorded. In some cases, however, the courts have held that since a suspect was fully aware of his rights, and required the presence of a solicitor as a "check" on the police, then no improperly induced self-incrimination occurred. In these cases convictions based, in whole or in part, upon confessions were upheld.[6]

(c) Significant breaches of the recording provisions[7] have been held to justify exclusion. The accused is otherwise placed at a disadvantage, if the making or content of the confession is disputed. Compliance with the Code would either have prevented the alleged fabrication, or would have confirmed it in fact occurring.

(d) Other matters; if a confession is ruled inadmissible, then any subsequent confession which can be linked to the making of that excluded is also likely to be ruled inadmissible.[8] Any evidence found as a result of the making of an inadmissible confession may be tendered, though the reason why such evidence was found may not be put to the court.[9]

3   Statements of persons since deceased

Expedience demands that certain statements which would otherwise be caught by the hearsay rule are admissible evidence when their maker is dead. This does not mean that all statements by persons since deceased are

---

2 [1990] Crim LR 581.
3 (1989) 91 Cr App Rep 161.
4 *R v Mason*, n 1, *supra*.
5 *R v Walsh*, n 3, *supra*. *R v Samuel* [1988] QB 615; [1988] 2 All ER 135. *R v Absolam* (1989) 88 Cr App Rep 332.
6 *R v Alladice* (1988) 87 Cr App Rep 380; *R v Dunford* [1990] NLJR 517.
7 *R v Canale* [1990] 2 All ER 187; *R v Keenan* [1990] 2 QB 54; [1989] 3 All ER 598.
8 *R v Ismail* (1990) 92 Cr App Rep 92.
9 Police and Criminal Evidence Act 1984, s 76(5).

admissible. Nevertheless several exceptions to the hearsay rule operate only where the maker of the statement is dead. The most important of these exceptions are set out below.

(a) Dying declarations — On a charge of murder or manslaughter an oral or written statement made by the deceased concerning the cause of his death is admissible provided that it can be proved that he was, at the time of making the statement, in settled hopeless expectation of death, and would have been a competent witness had he lived. Such a statement is termed a "dying declaration".

Dying declarations are admissible only on charges of murder or manslaughter,[10] although there is no logical reason for the courts so restricting the rule. The rationale of this exception is that dying declarations are made:

> ". . . when every motive to falsehood is silenced, and the mind is induced by the most powerful considerations to speak the truth; a situation so solemn and so awful is considered by law as creating an obligation equal to that which is imposed by a positive oath administered in a court of justice."[11]

Whether this justification still exists is debatable, but the rule is clearly established. For it to operate there must be a settled, hopeless expectation of death in the mind of the deceased. For this reason in *R v Pike*[12] the court refused to admit a statement made by a four-year-old child on the basis that the declarant would not have been capable of appreciating the awfulness of her state. Again, in *R v Bedingfield*[13] the statement of the deceased could not be admitted under this exception since, although her throat was cut from ear to ear, there was no evidence that she was conscious of her impending death. On the other hand if the declarant was in settled hopeless expectation of death a statement will be admissible even though death does not immediately occur.[14]

As a rule it is the prosecution who seek to adduce evidence of dying declarations since their value often lies in the fact that they identify the accused with the death. A dying declaration does not require corroboration; in *Nembhard v R*[15] the appellant's conviction for murder of a police officer was upheld by the Privy Council even though the dying declaration of the victim was the only evidence which implicated the appellant. It should also be borne in mind that many dying declarations may be admissible as *res gestae* statements, or under other exceptions.

(b) Declarations against interest — A statement is admissible if it is against the pecuniary or proprietary interest of the deceased. The rationale of the admission of such statements is that a person would be unlikely to make a statement against his interest unless it were true. Nevertheless such statements are only admissible if the maker can be proved to be dead. It may seem logical to suppose that a person still living would be just as unlikely to have made an untrue statement against his own interest. Such

---

10 *R v Mead* (1824) 2 B & C 605.
11 *R v Woodcock* (1789) 1 Leach 500, *per* Eyre CB.
12 (1829) 3 C & P 598.
13 (1879) 14 Cox CC 341. The court also held that the victim's statement could not be admitted as a *res gestae* statement because it was not contemporaneous with the event in question. This is no longer good law: see p 622, *ante*.
14 *R v Perry* [1909] 2 KB 697.
15 [1982] 1 All ER 183; [1981] 1 WLR 1515.

statements are not, however, admissible unless they fall within other exceptions.

Apart from the death of the declarant the principal condition for the admissibility of declarations against interest is that the declaration be against the pecuniary or proprietary interest of the deceased. It is generally accepted that the deceased must have known, at the time of making the statement, that it was against his interest,[16] and must also have had personal knowledge of the facts stated.[17] No interest other than a pecuniary or proprietary interest will suffice. Thus in *Ward v HS Pitt & Co*[18] the Court of Appeal held that an admission of paternity made by a deceased putative father was not admissible as a declaration against interest merely because it might involve possible future liability for the maintenance of the child. On the other hand a pecuniary interest is something less than a pecuniary obligation. In *Coward v Motor Insurers' Bureau*[19] the Court of Appeal admitted proof of oral declarations by the deceased to the effect that he had gratuitously promised to pay money in return for lifts to work. Despite the fact that there was no contractual or other legal obligation to pay the money the statements were against the deceased's pecuniary interest and therefore admissible.

(c) Declarations in the course of duty — Written or oral statements made by a deceased person in pursuance of a duty to record acts performed by him are admissible as an exception to the hearsay rule. However this exception is of very little importance since most instances will fall within section 24 of the Criminal Justice Act 1988.

(d) Declarations concerning pedigree — A peculiar exception to the hearsay rule operates to admit declarations of deceased persons concerning the pedigree of their relatives where this is the subject of proceedings. The rationale of this exception is somewhat obscure but appears to be based principally on the personal knowledge possessed by the declarant.

(e) Declarations as to public or general rights — A very old exception to the hearsay rule, the basis of which is simple expedience, admits declarations of deceased persons of competent knowledge as to the reputed existence of public or general rights.

(f) Evidence given in previous proceedings — Where a witness who has given evidence in previous proceedings has died, a transcript of his evidence in those proceedings may be given in evidence in subsequent proceedings.

4   Statutory exceptions under the Criminal Justice Act 1988

Statutory exceptions to the hearsay rule in criminal cases have always been limited in scope. Except for limited provisions relating to witness statements no general exception existed, and the unfortunate ruling in *Myers v Director of Public Prosecutions*[20] led to statutory intervention, in the form of the Criminal Evidence Act 1965. This was limited in scope to business documents forming part of a record.[1] The Criminal Justice Act 1988 created a more radical and broader scheme to replace the 1965 provisions, and was the

---

16 *Tucker v Oldbury Urban District Council* [1912] 2 KB 317.
17 *Lloyd v Powell Duffryn Steam Coal Co* [1914] AC 733.
18 [1913] 2 KB 130.
19 [1963] 1 QB 259; [1962] 1 All ER 531.
20 [1965] AC 1001; [1964] 2 All ER 881; see p 80, *ante*.
 1 For the meaning of "record" see *R v Tirado* (1974) 59 Cr App Rep.

subject of considerable amendment during its passage through Parliament.[2] The resulting provisions are both complex and, on occasion, obscure.

The Act does not create a broad scheme of admissibility comparable to that available in civil cases under Civil Evidence Act 1968.[3] It applies to documentary evidence only, the term "document" bearing the same meaning as in civil cases.[4] That definition is extremely wide, and includes virtually all known forms of recording of information including maps, plans, photographs, discs, tapes and films. It does not apply to oral statements,[5] though these will often be recorded in documents which may, on occasion, themselves be within the 1988 Act provisions. Whether or not a document is to be admitted under the 1988 Act has to be established by the prosecution beyond reasonable doubt: the relevant standard for the defence will be the balance of probabilities.[6]

(a) Section 23 — potentially allows admissibility for first-hand hearsay statements in a document. By "first-hand" statements we mean statements of which the maker could have given direct oral evidence if called to do so. Thus, a statement in a letter as to what the letter writer saw or did would be first-hand hearsay. Statements by the letter writer as to what was said will, generally, not be first-hand hearsay.[7] Nor will section 23 apply where the maker of the statement in the document would not have been a competent witness.

If the document *prima facie* falls within section 23, consideration has then to be given as to whether the conditions of admissibility are satisfied. There are two alternative sets of conditions:

(i) The maker of the statement is dead or by reason of bodily or mental condition unfit to attend as a witness; or, the person who made the statement is outside the United Kingdom and it is not reasonably practicable to secure his attendance; or, all reasonable steps have been taken to find the maker of the statement but he cannot be found.[8]

Whether a person is unfit to attend as a witness is presumably to be decided in the light of physical capability or mental competence. A witness who is incapable of giving meaningful evidence, because of physical or mental condition, is within this provision.[9] In terms of the availability to attend in the United Kingdom, convenience is not enough.[10] The capacity to give

---

2 See Birch, 'The Criminal Justice Act 1988 – The Evidence Provisions' [1989] Crim LR 15.

3 See p 636, *post*.

4 Criminal Justice Act 1988, Sch 2, para 5, incorporating the meaning as defined by Civil Evidence Act 1968, s 10.

5 Whether a statement is a statement made in a document depends upon the intent of the maker. In *Ventouris v Mountain (No 2)* [1992] 3 All ER 414; [1992] 1 WLR 887 SIR JOHN DONALDSON MR held that a video recording of a conversation was not a statement in a document.

6 See p 569, *ante*.

7 Unless out-of-court statements recorded in the document are themselves admissible under another exception to the hearsay rule, eg, as *res gestae* statements.

8 Criminal Justice Act 1988, s 23(2).

9 By analogy with *R v Ashford Justices, ex parte Hilden* [1993] QB 555. See also *R v Patel* [1993] Crim LR 291.

10 *R v Case* [1991] Crim LR 192.

oral testimony through a live television link[11] should also not be overlooked.

(ii) The statement was made to a police officer or some other person charged with the investigation of offences, and the person who made the statement does not give evidence through fear or because he is kept out of the way.[12] This provision may apply to those who attend court and take the oath, but who give no meaningful testimony as a result of fear.[13] The fear must be proved by admissible evidence, although the court can make a finding of fear based upon its own observation of the witness.[14]

If one of these two sets of conditions is satisfied, then the document is admissible, subject to a discretion to exclude under section 25 of the Act. This section identifies a wide variety of factors to which the court must have regard, but essentially it may exclude if the statement ought not, in the interests of justice, to be admitted. Amongst relevant factors are the authenticity of the document, the extent to which it supplies evidence not otherwise available, the relevance of the evidence, and the possibility of contravening it by other evidence and any unfairness the lack of such a possibility may cause to the defence.[15] If, however, the statement was prepared for the purposes of pending or contemplated criminal proceedings, or for the purposes of a criminal investigation, then instead of section 25 applying there is a further hurdle: such a statement will not be admissible unless the conditions in section 26 are satisfied. These are discussed below.[16]

(b) Section 24 — This section makes certain business documents admissible. Unlike section 23 it is not confined to first-hand documentary evidence. Any document created or received in the course of a trade, business or profession can be admitted, even if the maker or receiver of the document could not have given direct oral evidence of the contents of that document. It will quickly become apparent that this creates a wide scope of admissibility, for at some stage most documents are received in the course of such activities. There are complex rules to seek to ensure that if information comes via a chain of persons, each person in the chain must be acting as part of a trade, business or profession.[17]

Thus for example, if A gives information to a police officer, who passes that information to another officer who records that information, that is within section 24. If, however, that intermediary had been a friend, not receiving the information as part of such a trade, business or occupation, then the exception under section 24 would not apply. These provisions are appropriate to deal with the situation where the document was created in the course of such activities. If it is receipt of the document that brings the instant document within section 24, it not does appear to matter through whose hands the document passed before receipt within the meaning of

---

11 See p 579, *ante*.
12 Criminal Justice Act 1988, s 23(3).
13 *R v Ashford Justices, ex parte Hilden* [1993] QB 555.
14 *Neill v North Antrim Magistrates' Court* [1992] 4 All ER 846; [1992] 1 WLR 1220.
15 These are very similar to the factors relevant to the discretion under s 26 of the 1988 Act: see *R v Cole* [1990] 2 All ER 108; [1990] 1 WLR 866.
16 See p 635, *ante*.
17 1988 Act, s 24(2).

the Act, provided the maker of the document had personal knowledge of its contents.

If the terms of section 24(1) are satisfied, then the position depends upon whether the documents were created or received for the purposes of pending or contemplated criminal proceedings, or for the purposes of a criminal investigation. If they were not, then, as before, the discretion under section 25 falls to be considered. If they were, then, the same conditions as exist for the operation of section 23 apply,[18] before consideration of section 26. Alternatively, there is a possible third condition that will enable admission: that the person making the statement cannot be expected to have any recollection of the matters dealt with therein.[19] This would appear to refer to the maker of the document, not the supplier of the information.

(c) Section 26 — It has been noted that if a document has been prepared for the purposes of pending or contemplated criminal proceedings, or for a police investigation, then section 26 creates additional conditions. This will therefore apply to documents such as police statements, proofs of evidence and similar documents. The Act is designed to prevent an accused being tried on documentary evidence, as opposed to oral testimony. Under section 26 the statement shall not be adduced in evidence without the leave of the court, and this should not be granted unless the court is of the opinion that the statement ought to be admitted in the interests of justice. The court shall have regard to the contents of the statement, to the risk that the inability to controvert the statement may create unfairness to the accused, and to other relevant factors.

This provision was considered by the Court of Appeal in *R v Cole*,[20] where it was said that the possibility of controverting the statement could include contradiction by defence witnesses. The decision of an accused as to whether to give evidence is taken in the light of knowledge as to what has been admitted as part of the prosecution case. The court is entitled to assume that the accused may be a position himself to counter such evidence. Each case turns on its own facts.

5 Other exceptions

A range of other exemptions is available in particular circumstances. Various statutory provisions relating to witness statements and depositions exist.[1] The Bankers' Books Evidence Act 1879 (as amended)[2] allows secondary evidence of the content of bankers' records to be given. The provisions allowing video recordings of interviews with child witnesses in some circumstances have already been noted.[3]

---

18 See p 633, *ante*.
19 1988 Act, s 24(4).
20 [1990] 2 All ER 108; [1990] 1 WLR 866.
  1 See eg Criminal Justice Act 1925, s 13; Magistrates' Courts Act 1980, s 102; Children and Young Persons Act 1933, s 43.
  2 By the Banking Act 1987.
  3 See p 579, *ante*.

D   HEARSAY IN CIVIL CASES

In relation to civil proceedings, a very substantial inroad into the hearsay rule was made by the Civil Evidence Act 1968. It should be noted that this Act does not apply to civil proceedings in magistrates' courts.[4]

1   Admissibility of first-hand hearsay

The distinction between first-hand and second-hand hearsay drawn earlier in the context of criminal exceptions under the Criminal Justice Act 1988 is of vital importance in the context of civil cases. Section 1(1) of the Civil Evidence Act 1968 defines hearsay as:

> "a statement other than one made by a person while giving oral evidence in those proceedings . . . as evidence of any fact stated therein."

If the maker of the statement in question had personal knowledge of the facts contained in his statement, the statement is first-hand hearsay. If, on the other hand, the maker of the statement did not have personal knowledge of the facts stated, so that his evidence of those facts would be hearsay, evidence of the contents of his statement (assuming, of course, that he is not the person giving that evidence) is second-hand hearsay. Section 2(1) of the 1968 Act provides:

> ". . . in any civil proceedings a statement made, whether orally or in a document or otherwise, by any person, whether called as a witness in those proceedings or not, shall, subject to this section and to rules of court, be admissible as evidence of any fact stated therein of which direct oral evidence by him would be admissible."

This subsection has the effect of rendering first-hand hearsay admissible in civil proceedings and is, therefore, the most far-reaching provision in the 1968 Act. Where the statement was made otherwise than in a document[5] no evidence other than direct oral evidence by the maker or any person who heard or otherwise perceived it being made is admissible for the purpose of proving it, unless the statement was made by a person while giving oral evidence in some other legal proceedings (whether civil or criminal) in which event it may be proved in any manner authorised by the court.

In estimating the weight to be attached to a statement admitted under this section the court must have regard to all the circumstances from which any inference can reasonably be drawn as to the accuracy or otherwise of the statement and, in particular, to the question whether or not the statement was made contemporaneously with the occurrence or existence of the facts stated, and to the question whether or not the maker of the statement had any incentive to conceal or misrepresent the facts.[6] Furthermore where the maker is not called as a witness, any evidence which would have been admissible for the purpose of destroying or supporting his credibility, including a previous inconsistent statement (which is then

---

4 *R v Coventry Justices, ex parte Bullard* (1992) 95 Cr App Rep 175.
5 For this, see *Ventouris v Mountain (No 2)* [1992] 3 All ER 414; [1992] 1 WLR 887.
6 Civil Evidence Act 1968, s 6(1).

evidence of the facts therein stated), if he had been called as a witness, is admissible in his absence.[7]

The admissibility of statements under section 2 is expressly made subject to Rules of Court. In the Supreme Court the relevant rules are RSC, Order 38, rr 20–44. These rules contain detailed procedural requirements with which a party must comply in order to avail himself of section 2 of the Act.[8] Nevertheless there is a discretionary power to allow a party to adduce a statement in evidence notwithstanding that he has failed either to serve the requisite notice or to comply with a counter-notice.

2 Admissibility of second-hand hearsay

The Civil Evidence Act 1968 abrogated the hearsay rule in civil proceedings only in relation to first-hand hearsay. Second-hand hearsay remains, *prima facie*, inadmissible. Sections 4 and 5 of the Act do, in fact, permit second-hand hearsay evidence in certain circumstances. However, these sections are best regarded as special exceptions to the hearsay rule.

Section 4 establishes certain conditions for admissibility.

(1) The document must be, or form part of, a record[9] compiled by a person acting under a duty.
(2) It must have been compiled from information which was supplied by a person (whether acting under a duty or not) who had, or may reasonably be supposed to have had, personal knowledge of the matters dealt with in that information and which, if not supplied by that person to the compiler of the record directly, was supplied by him to the compiler of the record indirectly through one or more intermediaries each acting under a duty.

If the person having personal knowledge of the matters recorded is called as a witness, then the documentary record is unimportant. If the compiler of the document gives evidence, the document falls to be considered under section 2. Where, however, neither the supplier nor the compiler is called, the document is second-hand hearsay and admissible if at all only under section 4. In estimating the weight to be attached to such a statement, section 6(3) provides that the court must have regard to all the circumstances from which any inference can reasonably be drawn as to the accuracy or otherwise of the statement, and, in particular, to the question whether or not that person, or any person concerned with compiling or keeping the record, had any incentive to conceal or misrepresent the facts.

Any evidence which, if the person supplying the information had been called as a witness, would be admissible for the purposes of destroying or supporting his credibility, including a previous inconsistent statement

---

7 Civil Evidence Act 1968, s 7(1), (3). The admissibility of such evidence is subject to compliance with certain procedural requirements: see RSC, Ord 38, rr 30, 31.
8 See p 360, *ante*.
9 For the meaning of this term, see *H v Schering Chemicals* [1983] 1 All ER 849; [1983] 1 WLR 143, as referring to sources an historian would regard as original or primary. See also *Savings and Investment Bank Ltd v Gas Co Investments (Netherlands) Bv* [1984] 1 All ER 296; [1984] 1 WLR 271.

(which is then evidence of the truth of any fact stated therein) is inadmissible in his absence.[10]

Section 4 renders admissible a great variety of reports and records. Its extension by section 1 of the Civil Evidence Act 1972 to opinion evidence enables unchallenged expert opinions to be given without the expense of calling the expert in question. In addition, section 5 of the 1968 Act makes specific provision for the admissibility of evidence of statements contained in documents produced by computers. Such statements are admissible as evidence of any fact stated therein of which direct oral evidence would have been admissible, subject to the conditions set out in that section.[11]

3　Other exceptions

Section 9 of the Civil Evidence Act 1968 preserves certain common law exceptions. These include statements regarding pedigree, admissions, and statements in public documents. Most of these matters fall in any event within the provisions described above. The *res gestae* principle is not preserved by section 9. However, in *R v Andrews*[12] Lord Ackner assumed that the rule applied equally to criminal and civil proceedings. The provisions of the Children (Admissibility of Hearsay Evidence) Order 1991 should also be noted. Made pursuant to section 96 of the Children Act 1989 it effectively abolishes the hearsay rule in any civil proceedings relating to the custody, welfare or upbringing of children.

The Law Commission report, *The Hearsay Rule in Civil Proceedings*,[13] recommends that, in civil proceedings, evidence should not be excluded on the ground that it is hearsay. The report (to which was attached a draft Bill) contains a number of consequential recommendations relating to the giving of notices, the right to call and cross-examine the maker of any statement whose evidence has been tendered and the penalisation in costs of parties who fail to comply with the notice requirements. For the reception of records of a business or public authority, a simpler régime is recommended, allowing for such documents, if certified as such, to be received in evidence without being spoken to in court, unless the court otherwise directs.

It is to be anticipated that legislation will be passed to implement these proposals in the near future.

---

10 Civil Evidence Act 1968, s 3(1).
11 Civil Evidence Act 1972, s 1.
12 [1987] AC 281; [1987] 1 All ER 513, discussed p 623, *ante*.
13 (1994) Law Com No 216, Cm 2321.

Index